CUMBERLAND PARISH

Lunenburg County, Virginia
1746-1816

Vestry Book
1746-1816

By
LANDON C. BELL
Ph.B., M.A., LL.B.
Life Member Virginia Historical Society and of
Ohio Archaeological and Historical Society
Author of *The Old Free State*

JANAWAY PUBLISHING, INC.
Santa Maria, California

Notice

In many older books, foxing (or discoloration) occurs and, in some instances, print lightens with wear and age. Reprinted books, such as this, often duplicate these flaws, notwithstanding efforts to reduce or eliminate them. The pages of this reprint have been digitally enhanced and, where possible, the flaws eliminated in order to provide clarity of content and a pleasant reading experience.

Cumberland Parish, Lunenburg County, Virginia 1746-1816, [and] Vestry Book 1746-1816

Copyright © 1930 Landon C. Bell

Originally published
Richmond, Virginia
1930

Reprinted by:

Janaway Publishing, Inc.
732 Kelsey Ct.
Santa Maria, California 93454
(805) 925-1038
www.janawaygenealogy.com
2015

ISBN: 978-1-59641-358-0

Made in the United States of America

TO THE MEMORY OF
MY MOTHER
ETTA WILBURN (HARDY) BELL
DESCENDANT OF
COVINGTON HARDY AND WILLIAM HARDY
VESTRYMEN OF
CUMBERLAND PARISH

ILLUSTRATIONS

                                                                PAGE

MAP OF CUMBERLAND PARISH
    Showing subdivisions............................opp. 23

REVEREND JOHN CAMERON
    Minister Cumberland Parish, 1796-1815..........opp. 131

TABLE OF CONTENTS

			PAGE
CHAPTER	I.	INTRODUCTION	7
CHAPTER	II.	THE PARISH	21
CHAPTER	III.	THE VESTRY	24
CHAPTER	IV.	THE CHURCHES	32
CHAPTER	V.	THE GLEBE	46
CHAPTER	VI.	THE MINISTERS	59
CHAPTER	VII.	PROCESSIONINGS	75
CHAPTER	VIII.	THE DECLINE	80
CHAPTER	IX.	REVEREND JAMES CRAIG	98
CHAPTER	X.	REVEREND JOHN CAMERON	132
CHAPTER	XI.	GENEALOGICAL NOTES: Bacon, Ballard, Betts, Billups, Boulden, Blagrave, Brodnax, Buford, Caldwell, Cameron, Chappell, Claiborne, Clay, Cox, Cureton, Delony, Dixon, Edloe, Ellidge, Ellis, Embry, Epes, Farmer, Ferth, Fontaine	166
CHAPTER	XII.	GENEALOGICAL NOTES (Continued): Garland	214
CHAPTER	XIII.	GENEALOGICAL NOTES (Continued): Gee, Glenn, Hall, Hardy, Hawkins, Hobson, Howard, Jackson, Jefferson, Jenings, Jordan, Lamkin, Lanier, Lester, Macfarland, Marrable, Martin, Nash, Neblett, Parrish, Pettus, Phillips, Ragsdale, Read, Robertson, Smith, Speed, Stevenson, Stokes, Street, Tabb, Talbott, Taylor, Tomlinson, Tucker, Twitty, Winn	242
CHAPTER	XIV.	REVEREND JOHN CAMERON'S REGISTERS. Register of Marriages: Bristol Parish, 1784-1793 Nottoway Parish, 1794-1795 Cumberland Parish, 1796-1815 Register of Baptisms and Funerals: Cumberland Parish, 1815	299
CHAPTER	XV.	THE VESTRY BOOK, 1746-1816	321

CHAPTER I

Introduction

IN COLONIAL days and until the Statute of Religious Freedom and the "dis-establishment" of the Episcopal Church in Virginia, the Church was not only a religious institution, but it was also in a very real sense a public, official, governmental agency. The whole institution was supported from public revenue. The Church houses were built, the glebes were purchased and equipped, and the parish ministers or rectors were supported by public taxes. The repression of all forms of immorality and vice, the support and relief of the poor were matters within the jurisdiction of the vestries. The establishment and maintenance of the lines or boundaries of the lands of the various owners, through a proceeding known as "processioning" were functions of the Church acting through the vestries or their appointees. And the only records of births, marriages and death officially kept were parish or church records.

Originally, and for a very long time, marriage ceremonies could be validly performed, technically, only by duly accredited ministers of the established church; and the publication of banns was a legal substitute for a marriage bond. In other words, a marriage might be validly celebrated, under the law, pursuant to a license obtained upon execution of a "marriage bond," or pursuant to publication of banns, without a marriage bond or license. This latter fact seems to be overlooked by many learned and skillful genealogists, who evidently are under the impression that in the Colonial era every marriage would be, or at least should be evidenced by a marriage license bond, as a necessary prerequisite. This is an erroneous assumption. There has been, apparently, such real confusion of understanding respecting the subject that a brief review of it may serve a useful purpose.

In the 7th year of Charles 1st, February 1631-2, it was enacted that:

"No minister shall celebrate matrimony between any persons without a facultie or lycense graunted by the Governor, except the baynes of matrimony have been first published three several Sundays or holy days in the time of devyne service in the parish churches where the sayd persons dwell accordinge to the booke of common prayer," etc.[1] And in the same year it was enacted:

"In every parish church within this colony shall be kept by the minister a book wherein shall be written the day and year of every Christeninge, weddinge, and buriall."[2]

The provisions of the act of February 1631-2, above mentioned, respecting the celebration of marriage ceremonies pursuant to licenses or publication of banns, were, without any changes important to be noted for present purposes, repeated in the Act of 14th Charles II, 1661-2.[3]

An Act of 1696, 8th William III[4] authorized and provided for the collection of fees by ministers or "clerks," for entering births, marriages and deaths in the parish registers.

In 1705, in the 4th year of Queen Anne it was enacted[5]

"That no minister or ministers shall celebrate the rights of matrimony between any persons, or join them together as man and wife, without lawful license, or thrice publication of the banns according as the rubric in the common prayer book prescribes, which enjoins that if the persons to be married, dwell in several parishes, the banns shall be published in both parishes; and that the curate of the one parish shall not solemnize the matrimony until he have a certificate from the curate of the other parish that the banns have been thrice published, and no objection made against the parties joining together."[6]

Section IV, of this Act provides:

"That all licenses for marriage shall be issued by the clerk of the court of that county where the feme shall have her usual residence, and by him only, and in such manner, and under such

---
[1] 1 *Hening*, 156.
[2] Id., 158.
[3] 2 *Hening*, 49-50.
[4] 3 *Hening*, 151-153.
[5] 3 *Hening*, 441 et seq.
[6] Sec. 1 of Chap. XLVIII, 3 *Hening*, 441.

rules and directions as are herein mentioned and set down: (that is to say,) he shall take a bond to our sovereign lady the Queen, her heirs and successors, with good surety, the penalty of fifty pounds, current money of Virginia, under condition that there is no lawful cause to obstruct the marriage, for which the license shall be desired; and each clerk failing herein, shall forfeit and pay fifty pounds current money of Virginia; and if either of the persons intended to be married shall be under the age of one and twenty years, and not theretofore married, the consent of the parent or guardian of every such person under the age of one and twenty years shall be personally given before the said clerk, or signified under the hand and seal of the said parent or guardian, and attested by two witnesses," etc.

Section VIII of this Act provided for the fees to be paid for marriages, and among these were twenty shillings or two hundred pounds of tobacco to the governor for each license or marriage; five shillings or fifty pounds of tobacco to the clerk for issuing a license; and to the minister for publishing banns one shilling and six-pence, or fifteen pounds of tobacco; and to the minister for performing the ceremony: if by license, twenty shillings, or two hundred pounds of tobacco; if by banns five shillings, or fifty pounds of tobacco.

An Act of 11th Anne, passed in October, 1712, provided that from and after April 20th, 1713, "the minister of every parish within the colony, shall keep a fair and exact register of all the births and deaths of the persons within his parish, of which notice shall have been given to him, according to the directions of this Act." [7]

The Act, under severe penalties, required the parents of every child born free, and the owner or overseer of every child born a slave to report the births to the parish minister; and also required all masters or mistresses of every family or house, and the owners and overseers of slaves to report all deaths.

A provision of this law required the Minister annually to deliver a copy of his register "to the office of secretary of this dominion."

---

[7] 4 *Hening*, 42 et seq.

In October, 1748, the Act of 4th Queen Anne was amended and re-enacted, the old Act being repealed. The new Act[8] is very similar to the old, in its main provisions. It provided that "no minister shall celebrate the rights [rites] of matrimony between any persons . . . without lawful license, or thrice publication of banns according to the rubric in the book of common prayer," and that "if any minister shall celebrate the rites of matrimony . . . without such license, or publication of banns, as by this act required, he shall for every such offense be imprisoned one whole year, without bail or mainprise, and shall also forfeit and pay five hundred pounds current money," etc.

It thus clearly appears from this brief review of some of the laws bearing upon the subject that there were alternative methods or procedures authorizing the celebration of the marriage ceremony by parish ministers; and that marriages might take place pursuant to a publication of banns without the execution of a marriage license bond and the issuance of a license.

This procedure was authorized, so far as investigation discloses, through the whole of the Colonial era. Indeed it seems certain that in the days of the established Church, the great majority of the marriages were celebrated pursuant to publication of banns, rather than pursuant to licenses. It was the popular procedure, especially with devout churchmen; and moreover, as will be seen by the schedule of fees mentioned above, it cost less to get married that way.

Marriages by parish ministers were recorded, so far as public records were concerned, only in the Parish Registers. As to the marriages which took place pursuant to a license issued upon the execution of a "Marriage Bond," there was some evidence of them in the Clerk's office of the County, for the marriage bonds were filed and preserved there. But as to the marriages which took place pursuant to the publication of banns, there was no record of them, except that made in the Parish Register by the Minister, and the copies thereof which the ministers were directed annually, during at least a part of the era, to deliver "to the office of the secretary of this dominion."

[8] *Hening*, 81.

If any such copies were made, probably few, or none, have survived. No such copy has ever come under the observation or to the knowledge of this writer.

With the rise of the "Dissenters" in Virginia, the subject under consideration became involved in some confusion; and more and more so as the strength and numbers of the Protestant denominations, other than Episcopalians, increased.

This movement will not be here discussed; it is outside the scope of this treatment.[9] It resulted in the dis-establishment of the Episcopal Church as an institution supported by public taxes and having not only religious functions, but secular or semi-governmental functions of a civil nature as well.

One of the complaints of the dissenting ministers was against the exclusive monopoly which ministers of the established church had upon the performance or celebration of "the ordinances." Thus, for example, the Methodists claimed that their ministers were "in every essential qualification for the administration of Christian ordinances" the equal of the parish ministers, and yet "there was not a preacher from Asbury down that could administer the Holy Sacrament, celebrate the rights [rites] of matrimony, or baptize a child. These rights [rites] they were compelled to seek at the hands of the Established Clergy."[10]

Many of the converts to the churches other than the Established Church were willing and anxious to receive the ordinances at the hands of their own ministers and rebelled against being required to resort to the parish minister for such services. The dissenters claimed that they were justified in receiving the ordinances "at the hands of those whose right to administer them rested upon a call to the ministerial office, which had been put above all human questioning by the sanction of the Holy Ghost in the conversion of multitudes of souls. In their views, the great right to preach the gospel involved the lesser right to administer its appointed ordinances."[11]

---

[9]For a brief review of the Early Churches in Virginia, see *The Old Free State*, Vol. I, Chapter IX.
[10]*The Old Free State*, I, 390-91; *Memorials of Methodism in Virginia*, 105.
[11]*The Old Free State*, I, 390-91.

And so, it turned out that the dissenting ministers, without any strict warrant of civil law, began the celebration of marriage ceremonies. How widespread was the custom it is impossible now to know; nor does it appear whether they performed such ceremonies pursuant only to licenses issued upon marriage bonds or whether they published or attempted to publish banns. Either procedure would have been somewhat irregular; since the banns authorized by law were those provided in the prayer-book and according to the ritual of the Episcopal Church; and they were not of the class of ministers contemplated by the licenses issued upon the marriage bonds, prior to the Statute of 1780 mentioned below.

The parish ministers bitterly resented the interloping of the dissenters, and their presumption in administering the ordinances. And there are extant indictments of persons for illegal co-habitation, although they were, doubtless, married by dissenting ministers; the presumption being that these were extreme measures, inspired by the parish ministers, to prevent such inroads upon their prerogatives and revenues.

Reckoning with this condition the legislature passed the Act of October, 1780.[12]

It was entitled: "An Act declaring what shall be a lawful marriage," and in full is as follows:

"I. For encouraging marriages and for removing doubts concerning the validity of marriages celebrated by ministers, other than (those of) the Church of England, Be it enacted by the General Assembly, that it shall and may be lawful for any minister of any society or congregation of christians, and for the society of christians called Quakers and Menonists, to celebrate the rights (sic) of matrimony, and to join together as man and wife, those who may apply to them agreeable to the rules and usage of the respective societies to which the parties to be married respectively belong, and such marriages as well as those heretofore celebrated by dissenting ministers, shall be, and they are hereby declared good and valid in law.

"II. Provided always, and it is the true intent and meaning

---

[12] 10 *Hening*, 361-363.

of this Act that nothing herein before contained shall extend or be construed to extend to confirm any marriages heretofore celebrated, or hereafter to be celebrated between parties within the degrees of affinity or consanquinity forbidden by law. Provided also, that no persons except the people called Quakers and Menonists, shall hereafter be joined together as man and wife, without lawful license first had, or thrice publication of banns in the respective parishes, or congregations where the parties to be married may severally reside, agreeable to the directions of an act of assembly passed in the year one thousand seven hundred and forty eight, entitled, 'An Act concerning marriages.' Provided, That the license so obtained may be directed to any regular minister that the parties to be married may require. Every minister of any society or congregation, not of the Church of England, offending against the directions of the said act concerning marriages, shall be subject to the same pains and penalties in case of omission or neglect as by the said recited act are imposed upon ministers of the Church of England.

"III. And be it further enacted, That instead of the fees prescribed by the said recited act, the several ministers may demand and receive for the celebration of every marriage, twenty-five pounds of tobacco, and no more, to be paid in current money at the rate which shall be settled by the grand jury at the term of the general court next preceding such marriage.

"IV. And that a register of all marriages may be preserved, Be it enacted, That a certificate of every marriage hereafter to be solemnized signed by the minister celebrating the same, or in the case of Quakers, by the Clerk of the meeting, shall be by such minister or clerk, as the case may be transmitted to the clerk of the county wherein the marriage is solemnized, within three months thereafter, to be entered upon record by such clerk, in a book to be by him kept for that purpose, which shall be evidence of such marriage. The clerk shall be entitled to receive and demand of the party so married, ten pounds of tobacco for recording such certificate. And be it further enacted, That every minister or clerk of a Quaker's or Menonist's meeting, as the case may be, failing to transmit such certificate to the clerk of the court in due time, shall forfeit and pay the sum of five hundred pounds, to be recovered with costs of suit by the informer in any court of record. This act shall commence and be in force from and after the first day of January in the year of our Lord one thousand seven hundred and eighty one.

"V. For carrying this act into execution, Be it further enacted, That the courts of the different counties shall and are hereby authorized on recommendation from the elders of the several religious sects to grant license to dissenting ministers of the gospel, not exceeding the number of four of each sect in any one county, to join together in holy matrimony, any persons within their counties only; which license shall be signed by the judge or elder magistrate under his hand and seal."

If the provisions of this law had been carried out we would have had, from January 1, 1781, forward a very satisfactory record of the marriages which took place in any given county.

This law provided that "a register of all marriages" should be kept; and that "a certificate of every marriage" signed by the minister celebrating the same, or in the case of Quakers, by the clerk of the meeting, should be returned to the clerk of the county, within three months after the marriage, and that entry thereof should be made "by such clerk, in a book to be by him kept for that purpose, which shall be evidence of such marriage."

It is perfectly plain that it was the intention of the legislature that a separate book to be known as the Register of Marriages should be kept, and that every marriage should be entered by the Clerk in that book.

In Lunenburg County no such book was kept. Such returns as were made pursuant to this statute were recorded in haphazard fashion in Will Books and Deed Books, without any effort to assemble them in any group or order.

Some Ministers of the Episcopal Church, apparently with deliberate purpose, did not return certificates of the marriages celebrated by them. At least that clearly appears to have been the case in Lunenburg County. Reverend James Craig was the Minister of the Parish of Cumberland at the time the law was enacted, and so continued until 1795, and he was succeeded by Reverend John Cameron who served the parish until 1815. No lists of marriages returned to the Clerk by either of these ministers have been found. It is a practical certainty that neither of them ever made any such returns.

No record is known to exist of the marriages celebrated by Reverend James Craig; in other words his register or record has never been found; it presumably has been destroyed. The entire record or register kept by him from 1759 to 1795 would be of the greatest value. If this worthy minister had complied with the law, we would at least have the lists returned to the clerk by him for the period 1781 to 1795, despite the loss of his original register. As matters stand we have neither.

The register kept by the Reverend John Cameron has been preserved, and is published here for the first time.

If there were any Quakers or Menonists in Lunenburg, there is no evidence that they made any returns of marriages to the Clerk of the County pursuant to this statute.

This law was an enabling act for dissenting ministers. It was the first law in the State formally authorizing dissenting ministers to celebrate marriages. But even these ministers, who were so greatly benefitted by the enactment, made little effort to comply with its provisions. They made returns not every three months, as the law directed, but at irregular intervals, from time to time, as much as a year, and sometimes two years apart. Moreover, they were careless as to dates and names and in other particulars. Lists returned by Ministers, consolidated and arranged chronologically, for the years 1781-1851 appear in *The Old Free State*, II, 424-463.

The act authorized the appointment of four ministers of each sect in a County to celebrate marriages. This was a great inroad upon the marrying business of the parish minister, for there might be, for example, twelve ministers, four ministers from each sect, the Presbyterians, Baptists and Methodists, respectively, to compete with him in performing nuptial ceremonies.

The resentment of the Episcopal Ministers against this state of things was doubtless responsible for their refusal to comply with the provisions of the law. They argued that they could publish banns, perform marriage ceremonies and record the fact in the parish registers before this law was enacted and that as it was wholly for the benefit of the dissenting ministers, they would have nothing to do with it.

No record has been observed of any proceeding under the act to invoke the penalty for failure to make return of marriages celebrated.

It was probably not the habit of dissenting ministers, even after the Act of 1780, to publish banns for marriages; their marriages were probably all celebrated pursuant to marriage licenses, issued upon the execution of a bond. The provisions of the statute, above set out, upon this point are not entirely clear. Section II of the Act seems by its terms to authorize publication of banns "in the respective parishes, or congregations where the parties to be married may severally reside." But, inasmuch as this is coupled up with reference to the Act of 1748, it would seem that the publication of banns, even under the Act of 1780, could be lawfully made only in the Episcopal Church.

The failure of the Episcopal clergy to observe the provisions of the Act of 1780 respecting the returning of lists of marriages to the Clerks of the Counties, was particularly unfortunate, in view of the custom that prevailed of celebrating marriages pursuant to the pubication of banns; for as to such marriages, unless the ministers' register be found we are without any public or semi-public record of the fact.

The functions and prerogatives of the Colonial Church and its instrumentalities being such as have been briefly described, it follows that the records of the vestries and of the ministers were in a very high and important sense, public, official records. As already indicated, the records which were currently kept in the parish, falling into this class of public, or at least semi-official records, were the Vestry Books containing minutes of the proceedings of the Vestry and the financial statements of the Parish; and the Parish Registers containing lists of births, baptisms, marriages, deaths and funerals, and occasionally other items.

But while such records, in fact and in substance, were public records, they have not been, generally, so treated and preserved.

In one instance, and possibly in other cases the same is true, the Vestry Book of a parish found its way into the Clerk's office of the County and has been preserved as a public record of the County.[13] This was as it should be.

In a number of instances they have been gathered together from whatever source they could be obtained, and deposited in the library of the Theological Seminary, at Alexandria, Virginia. They were so gathered mainly by Bishop William Meade, for use in the preparation of his work, *Old Churches, Ministers and Families of Virginia*,[14] and left in the library, after his work was done.

For many parishes the Vestry records are entirely missing, and, in an even greater number of cases no Parish Registers have been found. There was, it seems, no definite, public depository appointed for the books containing these records, as currently made. The Vestry Books were doubtless found usually in the custody of the Church Wardens, or the Clerk of the Vestry, while the rector or minister kept the register, although the responsibility for keeping it rested by law, it seems, on the Vestry.[15]

In some instances it appears the same Parish Register was used in a parish during the incumbency of a succession of ministers, while in others, the minister who kept such a register, during his tenure, treated the volume as his private possession and took it with him when he left the parish.

The parish records of Colonial Virginia, relatively speaking, and judged by the paucity of the number known to be available, have been poorly preserved. This is much to be regretted for the records of the religious establishment in Virginia in Colonial days are interesting, in whatever aspect considered. The religious side of Colonial life was of scarcely less importance than the civil, and any picture of the period is incomplete, unless both be considered. The Church, the Vestries and the Ministers had no inconsiderable part in shaping the course of major events on many important occasions.

At one time or other in Virginia, prior to the dis-establishment

---

[13] The Vestry Book of St. Andrew's Parish is preserved in the Clerk's office of Brunswick County, at Lawrenceville, Virginia.
[14] J. B. Lippincott (Phila.), 1857.
[15] Bruce: *Institutional History of Virginia*, I, 186.

of the Episcopal Church, there were created by the General Assembly nearly a hundred parishes.[16]

During the Colonial Era not less than six hundred and eighty-five Episcopal Ministers[17] served the various parishes of Virginia.

Most of these ministers, presumably, and a very large number of them, certainly, kept registers of the character above described, and minutes of all the Vestries were of course currently kept. Considering the large numbers of parishes and of ministers, and comparing these figures with the numbers of the Vestry Books and Parish Registers known to be in existence, one is almost appalled at the thought of the vast extent and volume of the records which are missing.

While historians and genealogists have a lively enough interest in such records, one can scarcely restrain the observation that the State has shown a lack of attention to these priceless treasures which is astonishing to the highest degree. The Virginia State Library with the meagre financial resources made available to it for the purpose, has despite the limitations with which it has to reckon, made the most of its means and opportunities and has performed a service of great value by making photostat copies of all these parish records that are available. It has thus, by multiplying copies helped to assure the preservation of this material, and has made it accessible in its Department of Archives. But so far as this writer recalls, the State of Virginia has not published a single one of these records; not a Vestry Book nor a Parish Register has been published by or at the expense of the State.

Not only has the State not published any of these records, but the patriotic and historical societies of the state have done but little to remedy the remissness of the State.

The National Society of the Colonial Dames of America in the State of Virginia, in 1897, published the Register of Christ Church Parish, Middlesex County, Virginia, 1653-1812; in 1904

---

[16]The statutes have not been searched in an effort to ascertain the exact number; but it may be said with confidence that the number stated is approximately correct. One hundred and two counties were created during that period of the State's history.

[17]See the list given in *The Colonial Church in Virginia* (Goodwin).

the Register of Saint Peter's Parish, New Kent County, Virginia, 1680-1787, and in 1905 the Vestry Book of this parish, 1682-1758. No other instances are now recalled of the publication of any volumes of vestry records or Parish Registers by any historical or patriotic society.

In addition to the two volumes mentioned, published by the Colonial Dames, the few volumes of such records that have appeared in print have been the result of the patriotic impulses and the services, largely unremunerated, of a few interested scholars. The more important of such items, as they are now recalled, are:

Vestry Book and Register of Bristol Parish, 1720-1789, published by Dr. Churchill Gibson Chamberlayne, in 1898.

The Parish Register of Overwharton Parish, 1720-1760, published by William F. Boogher, in 1899.

The Vestry Book of Henrico Parish, published in the History of Henrico Parish and St. John's Church, in 1904.

Vestry Book of Christ Church Parish, Middlesex County, Virginia, 1663-1767, published by Dr. C. G. Chamberlayne, in 1927.

The Douglas Register (St. James Northam Parish, Goochland County, Virginia, King William Parish) 1750-1797, published by W. Mac. Jones, in 1928.

Considering the historical and genealogical value of the Parish Records, possibly the public at large have not been sufficiently impressed with the importance of endeavoring to locate all such records as are in existence. While many of the Vestry Books and Parish Registers, undoubtedly have been destroyed, it is difficult to believe that such loss or destruction has taken place on such an extensive scale as to embrace all the parishes for which no known records exist. It is a reasonable surmise, and an earnest hope, that many such records, especially parish or ministers' registers, are still in existence somewhere, and may eventually come to light, as the contents of old attics, trunks, chests and files of ancient documents in private hands are searched and explored.

Unexpected finds of the greatest value are from time to time made, and others, it is reasonable to expect, are in prospect. It is earnestly hoped that some of these may further illumine the early history of Cumberland Parish. What a find, for example, would be a register of the parish from 1759 to 1795, the years during which Reverend James Craig was associated with it, and embracing the Revolutionary period. It is not beyond the realm of possiblity that such a volume may be found, in possession of some descendant of that worthy man. His descendants are many; they dispersed into widely separated parts of the country, and doubtless many of his books and papers might be found, if one but knew where to look for them.

The principal purpose of this volume is to present in print the Vestry Book of Cumberland Parish, Lunenburg County, Virginia. That interesting record, save for the loss from the volume of a few leaves, which are entirely gone, is in a splendid state of preservation, considering its age and its use for so long a term of years.

It has seemed appropriate, in reproducing and publishing that volume, to take the occasion to present some chapters embodying a brief historical sketch of the early years of the parish, and to give such account of the ministers of the parish as available facts make possible. Of some of these but little is known; and of none are all the details, that might be wished, available. Possibly the sketches of Reverend James Craig and of Reverend John Cameron here presented, are the most extensive accounts of them and, it is hoped, the most accurate anywhere to be found.

As has already been indicated, no Parish Register of Cumberland Parish is, so far as is known, in existence; but Reverend John Cameron kept a register of marriages which covers the time of his residence in the parish as well as a considerable other period. He also kept in 1815 a brief register of Baptisms and Funerals.

His Register of Marriages covers the years from 1784 to 1815. It extends over that part of his career which began with his ministry to Bristol Parish and ended with his death. During this time he served, as is more particularly shown in another chapter, Bristol, Nottoway and Cumberland Parishes.

It is deemed desirable to embody in this volume the whole of his registers. His record embraces many marriages celebrated in a large number of Southside Counties, and in the City of Petersburg.

CHAPTER II

The Parish

HE history of Cumberland Parish has been so meagrely recorded, in printed sources, that it may, with substantial accuracy, be said that its history has not been written.

Bishop Meade[1] devotes a few pages to this parish and its ministers. But his work covered so broad a field that, except in few instances, no parish was treated exhaustively; and some received but scant and sketchy treatment. Cumberland Parish falls in this latter class. His whole treatment of this parish, its history, and its ministers, occupies less than six pages, and yet, so far as this writer knows, his treatment of it was the first, and has remained for nearly three-fourths of a century, the only published account of the Parish.

Attempting to cover the entire field of the whole state, in the way he did, it is not to be thought remarkable, or a subject of criticism, that his sketch is incomplete, and inaccurate in some details.

Cumberland Parish was formed at the time Lunenburg County was created, and was co-extensive with the county. The Act dividing Brunswick County, and creating Lunenburg County, was passed on March 26, 1745.[2] It is entitled: "An Act for dividing the County of Brunswick and parish of St. Andrew, and for other purposes therein mentioned."[3] By this Act Brunswick County was divided "by a line to be run from the county line, where it crosses Roanoke river, below the place called the Horse Foard, to strike Nottoway River at the fork; and that part of the said county which lies below the said line" it was provided should be a distinct county, and retain the name of Brunswick,

---
[1]In *Old Churches, Ministers and Families of Virginia.*
[2]*Journal, House of Burgesses,* 1742-47, 202; *The Old Free State,* I, 135.
[3]*Hening,* V, 310; the act is set out in *The Old Free State,* I, 135-137.

while that above the said line should be another distinct county and be "called by the name of the County of Lunenburg."

It was further provided by this Act that the parish of St. Andrew be divided, and that the part of it comprised in Brunswick County should be known as the parish of St. Andrew and that "all that part of the said parish of St. Andrew which will be in the County of Lunenburg shall be erected into one other distinct parish, and called and known by the name of Cumberland."

At the time of its creation Cumberland Parish embraced an extensive area. It then contained the territory which is now comprised in the Counties of Lunenburg, Mecklenburg, Halifax, Charlotte, Pittsylvania, Henry, Patrick, and Franklin Counties, and the greater part of Bedford and Campbell Counties, and a part of Appomattox. It was, therefore, mediately or immediately, the parent of: Antrim Parish in Halifax County, formed in 1752;[4] for most of the Parish of Russell, in Bedford County, formed in 1754;[5] of Cornwall Parish, created in 1757;[6] of St. James Parish created in 1761;[7] these parishes, Cornwall and St. James, were respectively embraced in Charlotte and Mecklenburg Counties, when those counties were created, by the Act of November 7, 1764;[8] of Camden Parish in Pittsylvania County, formed in 1767;[9] and of Patrick Parish in Henry County. Henry County was formed by an Act passed in 1776, the first year of the Commonwealth.[10] The Parish of Patrick was formed by an Act passed October, 1778,[11] which divided the parish of Camden. This Act provided:

"That from and after the first day of February next ensuing,[12] the said parish of Camden shall be divided into two distinct parishes by the line which divides the said counties of Pittsylvania and Henry, and that all that part of the said parish which lies

---

[4]*Hening*, VI, 252; *The Old Free State*, I, 139.
[5]*Hening*, VI, 381; *The Old Free State*, I, 142; the date given in *The Old Free State*, 1763, is a typographical error. The correct date is 1754.
[6]*Hening*, VII, 149-150; *The Old Free State*, I, 143.
[7]*Hening*, VII, 413-414; *The Old Free State*, I, 144.
[8]*Hening*, VIII, 41-42; *The Old Free State*, I, 148-149.
[9]*Hening*, VIII, 205; *The Old Free State*, I, 151.
[10]*Hening*, IX, 241; *The Old Free State*, I, 150-151.
[11]*Hening*, IX, 567.
[12]February 1, 1779.

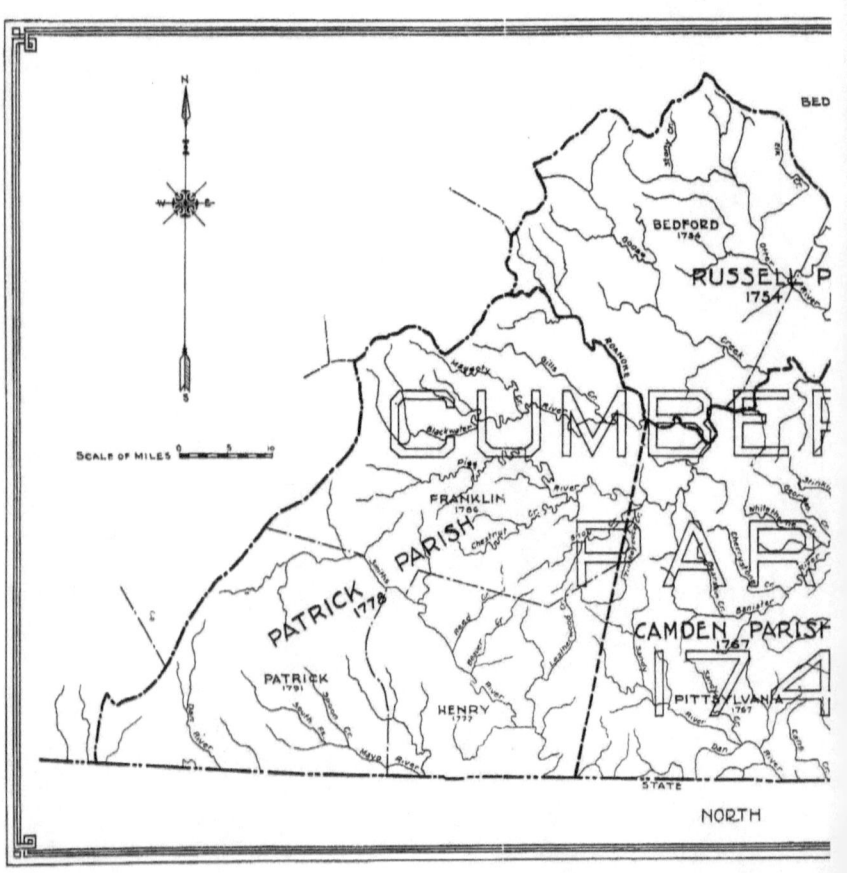

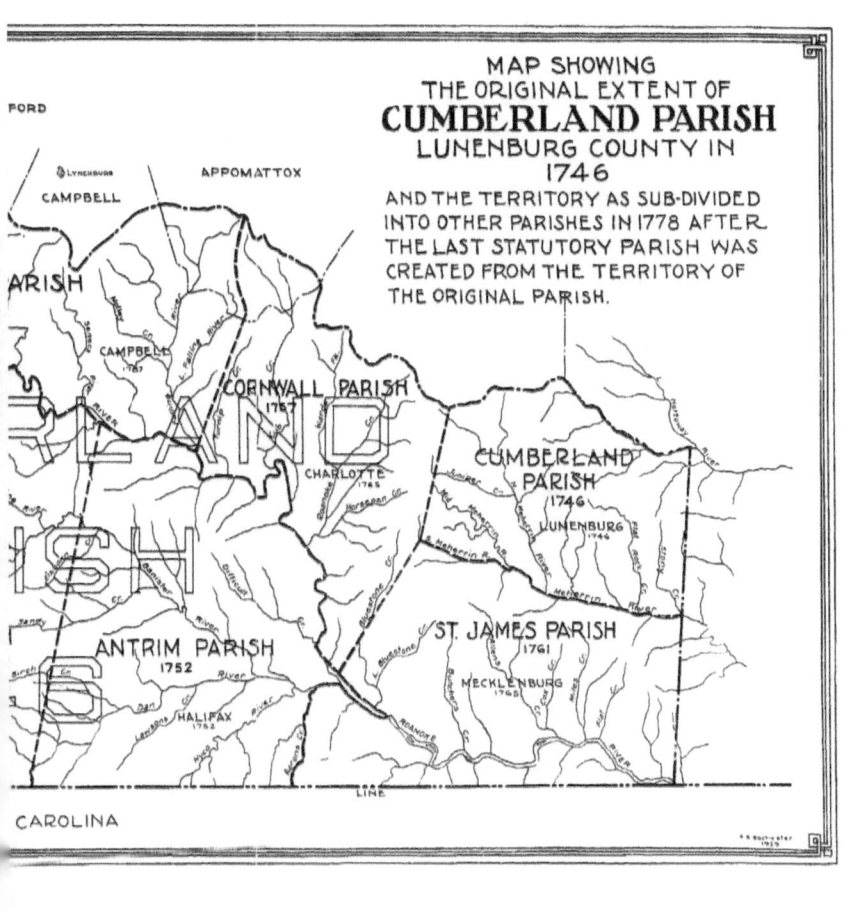

in the county of Pittsylvania shall be one distinct parish, and retain the name of Camden, and that all the other part thereof shall be one other distinct parish, and be called and known by the name of Patrick."

The parish of Patrick thus created embraced the area of the present (1929) counties of Henry, Franklin and Patrick; and the territory was Patrick Parish when Patrick County and Franklin County were formed.

Bishop Meade in speaking of Pittsylvania County and Camden Parish, says:

"Pitt and Camden are names familiar to the English and American ear. They were divided from Halifax and Antrim in the year 1767. At different times, subsequent to this, Henry, Patrick and Franklin were taken from Pittsylvania, but no new parishes established, except in Henry, the Church and State having been separated, so that the two last of them were, according to Colonial law, in the parish of Camden, until the Episcopal Convention made other arrangements." [13]

This statement is not exactly accurate, for, as we have seen above, Camden Parish was divided, by an Act of 1778, and Patrick Parish created, and it embraced the territory later erected into Franklin and Patrick Counties; so that Bishop Meade's statement should have been that they remained in the parish of Patrick until the Episcopal Convention made other arrangements.

---

[13] *Old Churches and Ministers of Virginia*, II, 14.

CHAPTER III

The Vestry

THE Vestries were, in the Colonial establishment, one of the two most important local institutions. The other was the County Courts.[1] These two bodies were the great repositories of power in Colonial Virginia; and the Vestries were second only to the County Courts in influence, if not indeed, in power. Theoretically, the Vestries represented the popular will or sentiment of the communities as they were chosen at intervals by a majority of the qualified voters, while the County Courts were a self-perpetuating body, and the members served for life. And while these facts suggest that there would be a very great difference in their points of view and wishes, such was not in fact the case; and if so at all, it was true in far less degree than might be assumed, for in the main the members of both bodies were drawn from the more prominent, influential and aristocratic element of the population.

Bishop Meade contends, not without considerable reason to support his position, that the Vestries were the real depositories of power in Colonial Virginia. Thus he says: "They not only governed the Church by the election of ministers, the levying of taxes, the enforcing of laws, but they made laws in the House of Burgesses; for the burgesses were the most intelligent and influential men of the parish, and were mostly Vestrymen." [2]

Perhaps this is a slight overstatement of the case. The county courts, it seems, were greater depositories of power than the vestries, and it was but a limited class of laws which the vestries had the duty of administering; and possibly too the county courts were as numerously, probably more numerously represented in the House of Burgesses, than the vestries. Still the

---

[1]For a sketch of the County Courts see *The Old Free State*, Vol. I, Ch. VIII.
[2]*Old Churches, Ministers and Families of Virginia*, I, 151.

Vestrymen and the Magistrates of the County Courts were often the same persons; and that the vestries were great powers in the Colonial establishment, is an undeniable fact.

The Act of 1745 which created Cumberland Parish, and cut it off from St. Andrew, provided for the election of vestries for the two parishes by "the freeholders and housekeepers" in each parish, who were to meet at the places in the respective counties, "to be appointed and publicly advertised by the respective sheriffs of the said counties of Brunswick and Lunenburg, before the first day of September next." [3]

The law directed the election of twelve of the most able and discreet persons, in each parish, to compose the Vestry, and that the vestrymen should take "the oaths appointed to be taken by law," which provided that the subscriber to the oath would be "conformable to the doctrine and the discipline of the Church of England."

It is not exactly clear who composed the first Vestry of Cumberland Parish. The first two pages of the Vestry Book of the parish are missing. This sheet probably contained a statement of those elected. John Caldwell was one of those elected, but he refused to serve. The first page (page 3), of the Vestry Book as it exists today, has as the first entry upon it the following:

"Matthew Talbot Gent. is made choice of as a vestryman to serve in this parish in the room of John Cauldwell Gent. who has refused to take the oaths of a vestryman and resigned."

His refusal was of course based upon the fact that he was not an Episcopalian, but a Presbyterian, and his coming to Virginia had been arranged in advance with Governor Gooch and the Council with the understanding that toleration would be extended him and his colony.[4]

Page 3 of the Vestry Book upon which this entry appears has entered in the top margin "A. D. 1746," indicating that the meeting of the Vestry at which the action was taken was in that year.

---

[3]This would be September, 1746, probably, as it was provided by the Act that the County should be divided and Lunenburg County and Cumberland Parish come into existence "from and immediately after the first day of May next," that is of 1746, and there was no sheriff in Lunenburg until that date.

[4]The subject is discussed in *The Old Free State*, I, 367 et seq.

The minutes are signed by Clement Read and L. Delony, Church Wardens.

The first meeting of the Vestry for which there exists a complete record of its minutes, was, doubtless, the second meeting of the vestry. It was held September 8, 1747.

The vestrymen present at this meeting were:

<table>
<tr><td>Lewis Delony,</td><td>David Stokes,</td></tr>
<tr><td>Clement Read,</td><td>Daniel Ferth,</td></tr>
<tr><td>Matthew Talbot,</td><td>Thomas Boulden,</td></tr>
<tr><td>Abraham Martin,</td><td>John Twitty.</td></tr>
<tr><td>Lyddal Bacon,</td><td></td></tr>
</table>

This body, with the exception of Matthew Talbot, who took the place of John Caldwell, was probably the first vestry, as originally elected.

An Alphabetical list of the Vestrymen, 1746-1816, showing the period of years, during which, or a part of which they served is set forth below. For some years the record is incomplete, as for example, in 1751 the pages which would have shown the date of the meeting and the vestrymen in attendance, are missing.

The list as here presented shows the year when the vestryman first appears upon the minutes, and the year when his name last appears. This does not necessarily mean that the person served continuously as a vestryman during the entire period; he may have done so, or he may have served for a time, was not a vestryman for a while, and then became a member of the vestry again. In any case where the exact facts respecting the service becomes a matter of interest they may be ascertained by examining the minutes, meeting by meeting, as printed in full in this volume.[5]

The list follows:

VESTRYMEN OF CUMBERLAND PARISH, 1746-1816

Bacon, Edmund P.,	1791-1816.
Bacon, Lyddal,	1747-1787.
Ballard, John, Jr.,	1780-1784,
Betts, Elisha,	1777-1780.

---

[5]Ch. XV.

Billups, Christopher,	1770-1780.
Billups, John,	1795-1802.
Blagrave, Henry,	1757-1768.
Boulden, Thomas,	1747-1757.
Brodnax, Stephen Edward,	1786.
Buford, James,	1786-1797.
Buford, John,	1812-1816.
Buford, Thomas,	1780-1816.
Buford, William,	1786-1815.
Buford, William, Jr.,	1812-1813.
Caldwell, John,[6]	1746.
Cameron, Thomas,	1812.
Chambers, Thomas,	1769-1780.
Chappell, Robert,	1815-1816.
Claiborne, Daniel,	1758-1763.
Claiborne, Richard,	1769-1774.
Clay, Obediah,[6]	1790.
Cox, John,	1749-1757.
Cureton, John,	1784-1786.
Delony, Lewis,	1747-1748.
Dixon, Robert,	1780-1783.
Edloe, John,	1749-1750.
Ellidge, Francis,	1749-1750.
Ellis, Ellison,	1786.
Embry, William,	1750-1758.
Epps, Peter,	1799-1806.
Farmer, Lodwick, (Lodowick)	1812-1816.
Ferth, Daniel,	1747.
Fontaine, Peter,	1750-1754.
Garland, David,	1761-1776.
Garland, Samuel,	1786.
Garland, Thomas,	1787-1794.
Gee, William,	1761-1767.
Glenn, William,	1790.
Hall, John,	1749.
Hardy, Covington,	1786-1802.

[6]Never served.

Hardy, William,	1780-1786.
Hawkins, Thomas,	1754-1758.
Hobson, John,	1761-1765.
Hobson, Nicholas,	1782-1783.
Hopson (Hobson), John,	1762.
Howard, William,	1748.
Jackson, Philip W.,	1793-1796.
Jefferson, Field,	1749-1757.
Jenings (Jennings), John,	1757-1769.
Jordan, Edward,	1780-1786.
Lamkin, Peter, Jr.,	1793-1796.
Lanier, Thomas,	1759.
Lester, Bryant (Bryan),	1786-1789.
Macfarland (Mcfarland), James,	1812-1816.
Marrable, Matthew,	1757-1759.
Martin, Abraham,	1747-1754.
Nash, Thomas,	1754-1757.
Neblett (Niblett), Sterling,	1781-1801.
Parish, John,	1757-1762.
Pettus, John,	1793.
Pettus,[7] Thomas,	1759-1779.
Phillips, George,	1761-1783.
Ragsdale, Edward,	1790-1793.
Ragsdale, John,	1757-1814.[8]
Ragsdale, William,	1812-1815.
Read, Clement,	1747-1757.
Robertson, Christopher,	1784-1802.
Robertson, Daniel,	1802.
Smith, James,	1786-1806.
Smith, Luke,	1749.
Speed, John,	1755-1760.
Stevenson, John,	1791-1793.
Stevenson, Thomas,	1786-1788.
Stokes, David,	1747-1769.

[7] This name is variously misspelled on the record: e. g., Pettis, Petties, Peaties.
[8] This may be the service of more than one person, of the same name.

The Parish

Stokes, David, Jr.,	1780-1783.
Stokes, Henry,	1781-1802.
Stokes, John,	1815-1816.
Stokes, William,	1796-1815.
Street, Anthony,	1780-1786.
Street, David,	1796-1806.
Street, John,	1793-1796.
Street, Waddy,	1815-1816.
Tabb, Thomas,	1759-1780.
Talbott, Matthew,	1746-1750.
Taylor, Edmund,	1759.
Taylor, William,	1768-1795.
Taylor, William H.,	1812-1815.
Tomlinson, Benjamin,	1772-1780.
Tucker, William,	1790-1792.
Twitty, John,	1747-1749.
Wade, Captain,	1751.
Walton, George,	1753-1756.
Winn (Wynn), Thomas,	1766-1780.

A chronological list of the Church Wardens of Cumberland Parish, as disclosed by the Vestry Book, is as follows:

    1746, Clement Read, L. Delony.
    1747, Clement Read, L. Delony.
    1748, Clement Read, L. Delony.
    1749, Thomas Boulden, John Cox.
    1750, Thomas Boulden, John Cox.
    1751, Field Jefferson, John Edloe.
    1752, Lyddal Bacon, Abram Martin.
    1753, Lyddal Bacon, Abra. Martin.
    1754, Thos. Nash, Geo. Walton.
    1755, Thomas Hawkins, John Speed.
    1756, Field Jefferson, Thos. Hawkins.
    1757, Thomas Hawkins, Wm. Embry.
    1758, John Jennings, Mattw. Marrable.
    1759, Wm. Embry, John Speed, Daniel Claiborne.
    1760, Daniel Claiborne, John Speed.

1761, Edmund Taylor, John Ragsdale.
1762, David Garland, Lyddal Bacon.
1763, David Garland, Lyddal Bacon.
1764, Geo. Phillips, Henry Blagrave.
1765, Thomas Pettus, John Ragsdale.
1766, David Stokes, Wm. Gee.
1767, Thomas Tabb, John Jenings.
1768, Thomas Winn, William Taylor.
1769, Lyddal Bacon, Thomas Chambers.
1770, Thomas Tabb, John Ragsdale.
1771, George Phillips, Richard Claiborne.
1772, David Garland, Christopher Billups.
1773, David Garland, Thomas Winn.
1774, Thomas Winn, John Ragsdale.
1775, William Taylor, Benjamin Tomlinson.
1776, Benjamin Tomlinson.
1777, John Ragsdale, Thomas Chambers.
1778, Elisha Betts, Samuel Garland.
1779, George Phillips, John Ragsdale, Benjamin Tomlinson, Christopher Billups.
1780, Thomas Chambers, Lodowick Farmer, Thomas Buford.
1781, Thomas Buford, John Ballard.
1782, John Ragsdale, Anthony Street.
1783, John Ragsdale, Anthony Street.
1784, Edward Jordan, Thomas Buford.
1785, Henry Stokes, William Hardy.
1786, Thomas Buford, Christopher Robertson, Sterling Neblett.
1787, Lyddal Bacon, Thomas Garland.
1788, Sterling Niblet, Christopher Robertson.
1789, Henry Stokes, William Beuford.
1790, Edward Ragsdale, William Tucker.
1791, James Buford, Covington Hardy.
1792, James Buford, Covington Hardy.
1793, Henry Stokes, William Buford.
1794, William Taylor, Philip W. Jackson.

1795, Philip W. Jackson, Henry Stokes.
1796, Henry Stokes, William Buford.
1797, Henry Stokes, William Buford.
1798, No meeting of Vestry.
1799, Henry Stokes.
1801, Henry Stokes, William Buford.
1802, No meeting of Vestry.
1803, No meeting of Vestry.
1804, No meeting of Vestry.
1805, No meeting of Vestry.
1806, Peter Epes, David Street.
1807, No meeting.
1808, No meeting.
1809, No meeting.
1810, No meeting.
1811, No meeting.
1812, James Mcfarland, Lodwick Farmer.
1813, Not indicated.
1814, James Macfarland, Lodowick Farmer.
1815, James Macfarland, Waddy Street.
1816, Waddy Street, James Macfarland.

CHAPTER IV

The Churches

AT THE first meeting of the Vestry of Cumberland Parish, in 1746, the exact date of which does not appear from the Vestry Book, because the first two pages of the book are missing, the vestry took action looking to the building of at least four new churches:

One near Reedy Creek,
One near Little Roanoke,
One near the fork of Roanoke, and
One near Ottar (Otter) River.

But little is known of religious activities in the territory embraced in the new parish of Cumberland prior to the creation of this parish.

The number and location of churches, if indeed there were any, are not known.

There is an expression in Bishop Meade's account of St. Andrew's Parish, which, while he did not assume to know the location of the churches, seems to indicate that he thought all the churches in St. Andrew's Parish, erected before Lunenburg was cut off, were in the area now comprised in Brunswick and Greensville Counties. Up to 1750 he was able to count seven churches, in the parish. As to their location he said, "The problem must be solved by the citizens of Brunswick and Greensville, the latter county, with one or more of the churches, having been cut off from the former at a later period."[1]

It is believed, however, that there was, at the time of the creation of Lunenburg County and Cumberland Parish, at least one church in the parish, for among the orders made at the first meeting of the vestry was one giving permission to Lewis Delony "to erect a pew for his family in a vacant place in the Church near his house."[2] This indicates, quite clearly, that the

---

[1] *Old Churches, Ministers and Families of Virginia*, I, 477.
[2] V. B. post, p. 325.

church was in existence at the time, and if so, had been built while the territory was St. Andrew's Parish, or at least before Cumberland Parish was created.

Some idea of the general location of this church may be gathered from the fact that the County Court of Lunenburg County in June, 1747, designated Lewis Delony to take the list of tithables in the precinct "from Allen's Creek to the extent of the County downwards." This territory is in what now is Mecklenburg County; in the southeastern part thereof. Delony doubtless lived within the precinct.

In addition to the church near Delony's, it is a justifiable surmise that there may have been two other churches, chapels or reading houses in existence within Cumberland parish at the time, for another order of this first meeting of the vestry was as follows:

"Robert Allen and Josias Randal are appointed Readers in their Several Precincts."

Such an order without any directions as to where they were to hold the services, seems reasonably to imply that the places of such services "in their Several Precincts" were well known.

The first church, respecting which the vestry made an order, so far as the extant record discloses, was Reedy Creek Church.

At the vestry meeting in 1746, David Stokes, John Twitty and Lyddal Bacon were ordered to "fix on some convenient place near Reedy Creek to erect a Chappel 48 by 24 and when they have so done to treat with workmen to let the building to undertakers as they think fit."[3]

The minutes of the Vestry contain no report from the persons to the Vestry as to the location or the building of the Church; they were not required by the order to make any such report, but were to fix on the place, and contract for the building. They doubtless did their work with expedition. The parish accounts at the time seem not to have been spread upon the vestry records as was customary in later years, and nothing appears as to such details as the cost of the building. But that it was built is certain.

The Vestry on February 8, 1749, ordered a payment to John

---
[3] V. B. post, p. 324.

Blaxton of ten shillings "for clearing Reedy Creek Church yard;" and while it does not appear just when John Hix began to serve this church as clerk, it does appear by an order of Vestry made the eleventh day of November, 1749, that he was "continued Clerk of Reedy C. Church [at] the usual salary."[4]

Of this Reedy Creek Church, Bishop Meade says: "In the first year after the establishment of the parish,—viz: 1746,—the vestry ordered a Chapel forty-eight feet by twenty-four to be built near Reedy Creek. This was near Lunenburg Court-House. It was consumed by fire between thirty and forty years since, during the ministry of Rev. Mr. Philips."[5]

This is not exactly a correct statement of the matter, as Bishop Meade confuses this original church building with a somewhat larger one, which was built some distance from the original building between 1771 and 1773, as we shall see. Bishop Meade overlooks the later building entirely. It was this second building which was destroyed by fire.

At the first meeting of the Vestry, in 1746, Thomas Bouldin, Abraham Martin and Clement Read were "appointed to fix on some convenient place near Little Roanoke to erect a chappel and to make report to the next Vestry."[6] They reported that "the most convenient place to erect and build a church on Little Roanoke" was "at or near a Spring on Randolphs and Talbots road near the fork."[7] The minutes fail to disclose any action taken upon the report; and an order made December 7, 1747, apparently has to do with the location of this proposed church. It was then ordered that "Mr. Talbot, Mr. Boulden, Mr. Martin, Mr. Read, Mr. Ferth and Mr. Twitty view the most convenient place for a Church near little Roanoke and make report to the next Vestry."[8]

Doubtless opposition had arisen to the location recommended by Messrs. Boulden, Martin and Read; so the committee was doubled in size, and ordered to reconsider the matter.

---

[4] V. B. post, p. 332.
[5] *Old Churches, Ministers and Families of Virginia*, I, 482.
[6] V. B. post, p. 324.
[7] Id.
[8] V. B. post, p. 329.

What the report of the new commission was does not appear; whether they adopted the location recommended, or changed to a new one is not disclosed by the vestry records. But on August 2, 1748, it was ordered that "the Church appointed to be built near Little Roanoke of 24 by 48 be lett to undertakers by L. Delony, Abraham Martin and Clement Read as soon as they conveniently can."

And on November 11, 1749, the vestry made an order allowing Henry Isbell one thousand pounds of tobacco as Clerk of "Little Roanoke Church."[9]

The Vestry at its first meeting also appointed Lewis Delony, William Howard and John Boyd to "fix on some convenient place near the fork of Roanoke to erect a Chappel, and make report to the next Vestry."[10]

The minutes of the next Vestry meeting disclose no report by these parties. For some undisclosed reason that committee did not function, and on December 7, 1747, Lewis Delony, Abraham Martin and Daniel Ferth were appointed "to fix on some convenient place near the Fork of Roanoke to erect a Chappel and make report to next Vestry."[11]

Just what they reported does not appear, but on August 2, 1748, the Vestry authorized "L. Delony, Abra. Martin and Clem. Read" to "lett the Church at the fork to Undertakers and fix on a convenient place to lett the same."[12] It is probable that nothing was done under that order, for on November 11, 1749, it was ordered that "Mr. Jefferson, Mr. Martin, and Mr. Smith treat with workmen to build a Church 40 by 24 at or near the fork and search for the most convenient place to set it."[13]

The first meeting of the vestry also took steps looking to the building of a church on Otter River. It made an order appointing Thomas Boulden, Matthew Talbot and John Phelps "to fix on some convenient place near Ottar river to build a house 20

---
[9] V. B. post, p. 333.
[10] V. B. post, p. 324.
[11] V. B. post, p. 328.
[12] Id.
[13] Id.

feet square for the reader to read in and make report to the next Vestry."[14]

These parties reported, as directed, on September 8, 1747, that the place "where the road goes from Irwins ford to Callaways mill is the most convenient place" at which "to build a Church." They also recommended "that the reader continue at the school house till the same be built."[15]

The church thus recommended was, doubtless, that referred to in the minutes of the Vestry meeting August 2, 1748, in the following order:

"Ordered that a Chappel be built at the place appointed near Mr. Phelps's 36 by 24 and that Mr. Martin, Mr. Boulden and Mr. Delony let the same to undertakers."[16]

Mr. Delony did not serve under this appointment, probably because of the distance of his place of residence from the locality of the Church, and at a Vestry meeting on February 8, 1749, it was ordered "that Matthew Talbot, John Phelps, Thos. Boulden and Clement Read or any two of them agree with workmen to build a church on Otter River pursuant to a former order of Vestry."[17]

There was another brief order entered by the Vestry on February 8, 1749, respecting the building of a church. It affords no idea of the location of the proposed building. The entry is as follows:

"Ordered that John Twitty and John Cox view the most convenient place to build a Chappel on and make report to the next Vestry."[18]

John Twitty was at about this date on the list of tithes of Cornelius Cargill, whose precinct was "In the fork and from Butchers Creek to Little Roanoke, and beyond Dan River." Doubtless the proposed chapel was somewhere in that vast area.

No report pursuant to this order appears in the minutes of the next meeting of the vestry, but at that meeting, on November

---

[14] V. B. post, p. 324.
[15] Id.
[16] Id.
[17] Id.
[18] V. B. post, p. 331.

11, 1749, the Vestry "ordered that Mr. Cox, Mr. Jefferson, Mr. Martin and Mr. Ellidge treat with workmen to undertake and build a church near the Court House of this Co[un]ty at such place as they shall think most convenient and that Mackness Good [Goode] and Julius Nichols assist them in search of a convenient Spring the Church to be fourty by twenty-four."[19]

The first courthouse of the county was located near, or within the present limits of the town of Chase City, in Mecklenburg County.[20]

The Vestry had thus in a relatively few years conducted a somewhat ambitious building program, the times and conditions considered, and, within a few years, were to begin constructing other churches; but for a time it took a respite from ordering additional churches built.

At the November, 1749, meeting of the Vestry, the petition of Wm. Hill and others for a church, the location of which is not indicated, was denied.[21]

No further such application is recorded until April 4, 1753, when the Vestry denied another request for a church, declaring:

"The Vestry do think it absurd and unreasonable there should be any Church or Chappel built between Reedy Creek Church and Little Roanoke Church."[22]

In December, 1757, the Vestry: "Ordered that a Church be built 48 by 24 on the Branches of Flatt Rock Creek in the Lower End of this Parish and that Nathll. Garland, John Jennings, John Parish and John Ragsdale do agree on the most proper place and let the same to be paid in the following manner (towit) one-half upon Raising, and the other half upon Finishing the same."[23]

In the minutes of the Vestry meeting of September 17, 1759, appears the following:

"Upon complaint made by the inhabitants of Roanoke and Butchers Creek, etc., that a great number of inhabitants in that

---

[19] V. B. post, p. 333.
[20] *The Old Free State*, I, 114.
[21] V. B. post, p. 333.
[22] Id.
[23] Id.

part are at too great a distance for any place of Divine Worship to give their attendance, it's therefore considered and ordered that John Speed, Thomas Lanier, John Hide, Wm. Harris Finniwood, Matthew Marrable, George Baskerville and John Humphreys be appointed to make enquiry into the reasonableness of the complaint and to find out the most proper place for a Church to be fixed if it's found reasonable and make report to the next Vestry."[24]

Apparently the parties reported recommending that a church be built, for while their report is not found, the vestry at a meeting held on November 12, 1759, "ordered that a Church be lett to be built at Tuslin Quarter Spring 60 foot by 30 foot and that Mr. Edmund Taylor and Mr. Thomas Lanier do lett the same to undertakers."[25]

In September, 1759, John Earl, Lewis Delony, Thomas Tabb and John Speed were by the Vestry ordered to view Mile's Creek Church and make report whether it be worth repairing or not,[26] and in the following November, the Vestry ordered "that the church at Mile's Creek be repaired and addition be made to the Broad side of the same 28 foot by 20 foot," and that John Speed and Edmund Taylor let the work.[27]

Complaints to the Vestry by "Sundry inhabitants" respecting the location of Tuslin Quarter and Miles's Creek Churches led the vestry to order:

"That that part of the Parish bounded on the North by South Meherrin, on the East by Brunswick Line; on the South by the County Line, from Brunswick Line as high as Taylors Ferry and by Roanoke from thence to the upper Parish Line and on the west by the upper Parish,[28] shall be surveyed so as to find the exact centers, in or near which the said Churches should be built." Until this was done it was ordered "that the building a Church at Tuslin Quarter Spring be suspended," and that "the

---
[24] V. B. post, p. 370.
[25] Id., p. 373.
[26] Id.
[27] V. B. post, p. 373.
[28] Probably Cornwall Parish created in 1757.

repairing the Church of Miles Creek be suspended till the laying of the next Levy."[29]

The way in which this order was executed, and the facts found do not appear.

There is no record of a vestry meeting after January 9, 1760, until November 3, 1760. On this latter date the minutes say:

"The Gentlemen who were appointed to lett Bethel Church, having reported to this Vestry that the said Church is finished in a workmanlike manner as according to the articles of agreement; we are unanimously of opinion that the said Church ought to be received, and it is by us received accordingly.[30]

The church thus received called Bethel Church was the church on Flat Rock Creek, as appears from an entry in the Vestry records of November 3, 1760, where "Mr. Burgimy" was ordered paid two thousand pounds of tobacco "for work done to Flatrock Church called Bethel more than he was obliged to do by agreement."[31]

On this same date, November 3, 1760, the vestry ordered that,

"A Chapel of Ease be built on the South Side of Roanoke River at or near Edward Goalbreaths of 40 foot by 24 foot and that Edmund Taylor, Gent., Mr. Thomas Anderson and Mr. Jacob Royster lett the same to undertakers in such manner as they think proper and that they agree to pay one half of the money at the raising and the other at finishing the same."[32]

The chapel thus located was within that part of the parish erected into St. James's Parish within the next few months, and it, of course, passed to the jurisdiction of that parish, probably before the actual construction of it was begun.

The foregoing briefly reviews the history of the erection of Churches within Cumberland Parish, as disclosed by the extant minutes of the vestry, down to the time when St. James's Parish was created and Cumberland Parish reduced in size to the area now embraced in the County of Lunenburg.

Thereafter, it seems, no additional church was built in the

---

[29] V. B. post, pp. 374-5.
[30] V. B. post, p. 377.
[31] V. B. post, p. 377.
[32] V. B. post, p. 378.

parish during the period here under review; that is to say down to the year 1816. But a new building replaced the old, and on a different site at Reedy Creek.

The Vestry at a meeting held on November 26, 1770, ordered that "there be an addition to the Reedy Creek Church twenty eight feet by twenty four, with five pews to each side, and three windows, also, with eighteen lights in each, and a gallery with two windows and eight lights to each window, and that the old Church be repaired," and at the same time directed the Church Wardens, Lyddal Bacon and John Ragsdale, together with Thomas Tabb and Thomas Winn "let the addition and the repairs to Reedy Greek Church to the lowest bidder as soon as is convenient."[33]

The persons deputed to let the addition and repairs acted but a new Vestry came into office which wanted a new church. The first action it took, at its first meeting was to revoke the order of the old vestry respecting the addition to and repair of the old Reedy Creek Church and to order the building of a new one. This action it took on May 1, 1771.

The order referred to declared that "the additions and repairs to Reedy Creek Church was not let according to the order" and "as no bonds have been executed from the undertakers to the Church Wardens, nor from the Church Wardens to the undertakers" this vestry being of opinion "that it will be more to the advantage of the Parish to set aside the old order and make a new one," it was "accordingly ordered that an entire new Church be erected at or near the old Reedy Creek Church sixty feet long, twenty eight feet wide, and Eighteen feet pitch in the clear, and agreeable to a certain plan and bill of scantling lodged in the hands of the Clerk." It was further ordered "that the said building be advertised in the Virginia Gazette, to be let at August Court next (1771), and to be finished by the last day of October, 1773, and that the payments be in manner following: the first payment of about one Hundred Pounds to be made the last day of October next, and half the balance to be paid at the end of

---

[33]V. B. post, p. 414.

October, 1772, and the other half at the time of delivering and receiving the building."[34]

George Phillips and Richard Claiborne, Church Wardens, together with Lyddal Bacon, John Ragsdale, Thomas Tabb and Thomas Winn "or a majority of them" were ordered to let the building "to the lowest bidder on August court day of Lunenburg County, or the next fair day."[35]

Some alterations were made in the plans for the church at a vestry meeting August 8, 1771,[36] and the contract to build the new Church was let to Pines Ingram.

The new church was located on three acres of land purchased from "Mr. Peter Jones of Amelia County."[37]

The history of the building of the church is not entirely clear; in fact, some parts of it are a little mystifying. It seems clear it was nothing like completed by October, 1773. In fact after the above mentioned order for building it entered in 1771, the next mention of it in the minutes of the vestry seems to be that of May 24, 1774, when the Reverend James Craig was ordered "to pay Mr. John Warran the amount of the order he shall present to him from Pines Ingram undertaker of the Church, not exceeding twenty five pounds," etc.[38]

The church was doubtless in an incomplete state, in November, 1774, when the vestry made an entry respecting a gallery in the church as follows:

"Ordered that according to an agreement with Daniel De-Gernett there be a gallory built in the new church at Reedy Creek, thirty feet by ten and a half feet to be finished in a workmanlike manner and agreeable to the plan of the other building and to be delivered with the other building, for which he is to receive £16 and the old church at the delivery of the new church."[39]

On July 8, 1775, the Vestry entered an order declaring that

---

[34]V. B. post, pp. 417-18.
[35]V. B. post, p. 418.
[36]V. B., Id.
[37]Id. post, p. 424.
[38]V. B. post, pp. 428-29.
[39]V. B. post, p. 431.

"the Gallory is not finished agreeable to the plan" and ordering that it be so finished.[40]

This church may have had two "gallories," for at this meeting of the vestry it was "ordered that the new gallory be finished agreeable to the plan of the other."[41]

Daniel DeGernett not only seems to have been the contractor or "undertaker" for the gallery, but a sub-contractor of the church itself under Pines Ingram, for the Vestry not only paid him for the construction of the "gallory," but also ordered "that at the request of Pines Ingram the collector pay Daniel DeGernett twenty pounds" part of thirty six pounds due Pines Ingram "undertaker of the church,"[42] and reserving "in their hands money enough for sufficient security for the finishing of the Church" agreed to receive it.

The church at this time was probably approaching a state where it might be used for the Vestry ordered the Church Wardens "to let to the lowest bidder the clearing of the yard around the new Church, as far as the trees are blazed, with sufficient benches, and one horse block agreeable to the plan of the other new ones."[43]

On February 26, 1776, the vestry allowed a petition of "Pines Ingram undertaker of the Church" for reimbursement for "a bad five pound bill which he received of the Collector in part pay of the Church," and ordered the amount levied in tobacco.[44]

The next mention of the new Reedy Creek Church building and of Pines Ingram was in February, 1785, when the vestry entered this order:

"This Vestry having settled with Pines Ingram for the money due for his building Reedy Creek Church, find there is due the said Ingram the sum of £ 52-ˢ18, of which sum £ 32-ˢ18 is ordered to be paid immediately; and the balance of twenty pounds is ordered to be paid on his completing his Church agreeable to bargain, except the leading the windows, which he is to finish in

---

[40] V. B. post, p. 433.
[41] Id.
[42] Id.
[43] Id.
[44] V. B. post, p. 435.

such manner that they may slip up ond down with ease, and put buttons so as to hold them up when required."⁴⁵

On May 11, 1786, the Vestry met and agreed that Pines Ingram had completed the Church "agreeable to his bargain," and ordered him paid the last installment of twenty pounds.⁴⁶

From the meagre record of the vestry book, it is a fair inference that work on the Church was suspended during the whole of the Revolutionary War, and indeed for several years thereafter. In other words, it was decided, May 1, 1771, to build a new Reedy Creek Church; it was let August court day 1771, and by the terms of the contract it was to be completed by the last day of October, 1773; it was to be an innovation in churches, in that it was to be built of "scantling"; it was let to Pines Ingram; was not completed by 1773, but was incomplete when the Revolution began, and during that war work was suspended, and was not resumed until some time after the war; and the building was not finally completed until 1785.

Although Flat Rock Church was ordered built, as we have seen, in 1757, and was doubtless built soon thereafter, yet it seems that the Vestry neglected to secure in advance title to the land upon which it was built, for on July 10, 1772, it ordered that Lydall Bacon, Thomas Winn and Thomas Tabb "treat with Mr. Richard Haies . . . for three acres of land where Flat Rock Church now stands and make him a generous offer for the land and take a deed from him for the same."⁴⁷

On July 8, 1775, the Church Wardens were ordered to repair "the horse blocks, benches and steps to the doors of Flatrock Church, and replace the banisters in the said Church."⁴⁸

During the next year, on September 12, 1776, "sundry inhabitants of the lower end of this Parish," petitioned "for liberty to erect a gallory in Flattrock Church," and the vestry unanimously agreeing "that the building the said gallory would be of great public utility" ordered "that if the said petitioners will agree that the same shall be for the use of the congregation in general that

---

[45] V. B. post, p. 458.
[46] V. B. post, p. 459.
[47] V. B. post, p. 424.
[48] V. B. post, p. 433.

leave" would be given for its erection "agreeable to a plan to be drawn up by the Revd. James Craig," and that the "Vestry will hereafter refund to them the expense of building [it]." The vestry also specified that the workmanship of the new gallery should "correspond with that of the Church. The length to be from the front door to the old gallery; and the width from the wall to the alley."[49]

But notwithstanding this provision of more space, the vestry were of opinion that the Church was too small to hold the worshippers who resorted to it under the ministry of Reverend Mr. Craig. On August 15th, 1786, the vestry "taking into consideration the smallness of Flattrock Church do resolve that Sterling Niblett, Edward Brodnax, Samuel Garland and James Buford, Gent. be appointed to raise by subscription a sum of money sufficient to build an addition to the said Church, which money so raised shall be paid by the subscribers to the Church Wardens on or before the twenty fifth day of December next, and it is further ordered that the before mentioned Gent. as soon as they shall have got a sufficient sum subscribed shall call a Vestry to consider on a proper plan for building the said addition."[50]

This order evidences the significant change that had taken place in Virginia, in the status of the Episcopal Church. This order directs that money be raised "by subscription"; that is to say, by voluntary contributions. The vestries no longer had the power to levy and collect taxes to maintain the Episcopal establishment.

The vestry book is silent upon what happened to the project to enlarge Flattrock Church. So far as the minutes disclose the parties appointed to secure subscriptions, never called the vestry together as they were directed to do when they were of opinion they had a sufficient sum subscribed.

Nor is any order found ordering the addition built. It is a safe surmise that it was never made, for the records in 1788 and 1789 show the vestry in a real struggle to collect sufficient subscriptions to pay Reverend James Craig his salary; and indeed

---

[49] V. B. post, p. 438.
[50] V. B. post, p. 464.

it seems they so far fell behind that at one time, in 1790, he was actually compelled to leave the parish, for want of support; but he was induced to return by the agreement of the vestrymen personally to pay him sixty pounds per year.

These were hard years for the Episcopal Church. The times were hard—following the Revolution. The people had been impoverished by the burdens and sacrifices of that struggle; the Church and the State had been separated, and public support of the Church by taxation withdrawn; the "dissenting" denominations, the Presbyterians, the Baptists and the Methodists, were making great inroads upon the ranks of the Church which had for so long held a monopoly, so to speak, of the religious functions of the community.

The years of decline were upon this religious institution, and so far as its church buildings were concerned, its revenues were so meagre that it was unable to secure current revenue from its adherents sufficient to maintain a minister in the parish, and to keep the church buildings in repair. Hence we find the vestry in 1796 petitioning the Convention of the Church in the Diocese for permission to sell a part of its land in order to repair the buildings on the Glebe; and in the same year it appears that the sum of fifteen dollars was the maximum the vestry even attempted to raise to be "sent by the Revrd. John Cameron to the Treasurer of the Convention to answer the general purposes of the Church."[51]

---

[51] V. B. post, p. 486.

CHAPTER V

The Glebe

Y THE Act of February, 1727, 1st George II,[1] provision was made "for the better support of the Clergy of this Dominion." From a very early time, if not from the foundation of the Colony, provision for the support of the Church and its ministers, was made by law. For the purposes of this treatment, however, the whole history of that legislation need not be reviewed. It is sufficient, for this treatment to begin with the above mentioned statute, since under it, or rather the law which took its place and repealed it, the establishment was maintained from the creation of Cumberland Parish.

The statute above mentioned provided for and fixed the amount of the ministers' salaries, required the vestries to levy and collect it; and required that glebes be provided for the ministers. By a provision of this law the ministers were required each during his incumbency to "keep and maintain the mansion-house, and all other . . . out-houses and conveniences erected . . . on his glebe, in tenantable repair;" the statute made exception of "the accidents of fire and tempests only."[2]

In case a minister failed in his duty in this regard, the Church Wardens were authorized to recover of him or his executors or administrators damages to be used in making such repairs.

A new Act was passed in 1748[3] entitled: "An Act for the support of the Clergy; and for the regular collecting and paying the parish levies." It provided an annual salary of 16000 pounds of tobacco for ministers and among other provisions of the Act were those respecting the glebes. This subject was dealt with in sections V and VI of the Act as follows:

"V. AND BE IT FURTHER ENACTED . . ., That in every parish of this dominion, where a good and convenient glebe is

---

[1]*Hening*, IV, 204-208.
[2]Id., Sec. XII, page 207.
[3]*Hening*, VI, 88-90.

not already purchased and appropriated, a good and convenient tract of land to contain two hundred acres at the least, shall be purchased by the vestry, and assigned, and set apart for a glebe, for the use of the minister of such parish, and his successors, in all times hereafter; and where mansion, and other convenient outhouses, are not already erected, for the habitation of the minister, IT IS HEREBY declared, and enacted, That the vestry of every such parish shall have power, and they are hereby authorized and required, to cause to be erected and built on such glebe, one convenient mansion house, Kitchen, barn, stable, dairy, meat house, corn house, and garden, well pailed, or inclosed with mud walls, with such conveniences as they shall think fit, and to levy the charge of the glebe land, and buildings, on the tithable persons in their respective parishes.

"VI. And to the end the buildings already erected, or hereafter to be erected, upon every glebe, may be kept in good repair, IT IS HEREBY FURTHER ENACTED, That every parish minister within this dominion shall, during the time of his being minister of the parish, keep and maintain the mansion house, and all other the out-houses and conveniences, erected, or to be erected on his glebe, in tenantable repair, and shall so leave the same at his removal from his parish, or death, accidents by fire, or tempest, only excepted; And in case any minister shall fail so to do, such minister, his executors and administrators, shall be liable to the action of the church wardens of the parish, for the time being, wherein the value of such repairs shall be recovered in damages, with cost of suit, and the damages so recovered, shall be applied and laid out in making necessary repairs upon the glebe; And every vestry of a vacant parish is hereby impowered and required, to put all the buildings upon the glebe of their parish, into such good and sufficient repair, as that the same may be fit for the reception of the succeeding minister; PROVIDED NEVERTHELESS, That any vestry, who shall judge that the minister has not wilfully committed any waste on his glebe, may make such necessary repairs, at the charge of their parish as they shall think fit; And every minister, received into any parish as aforesaid, shall be entitled to all the spiritual and temporal benefits of his parish, and may maintain an action of trespass, against any person or persons whatsoever, who shall disturb him in the possession and enjoyment thereof."

This Act repealed the Act above referred to of February, 1727.

As respects the maintenance of the buildings upon the glebes, this statute is a somewhat curious enactment. It provides in the identical words of the Act of 1727, that the ministers shall have that duty and shall keep and maintain the buildings in tenantable repair against all causes except fire and tempest. It then, in substance, by the proviso added to the language of the old law, enacts that except against damage by wilful waste of the minister the vestries "may" keep the premises in repair. This, as we shall see, at least in Cumberland Parish, seemed to have been accepted by the vestry as placing the obligation to keep the glebe property in repair upon the public and not upon the ministers.

The vestry employed the first minister of the parish, Reverend John Brunskill, at its meeting held on the second day of August, 1748. At this same meeting it ordered, "that Capt. Howard, Mr. Delony, Mr. Bacon, Mr. Stokes and Mr. Twitty are appointed to view the several lands offered to be sold for a Glebe and make report to the next Vestry."[4]

The parties thus appointed seemed in no hurry to select a Glebe, for notwithstanding they were directed to make report to the next Vestry, no further reference to the matter of the glebe is encountered in the minutes until five years later, when on April 4, 1753, the Vestry made the following entry:

"In pursuance of a former order of Vestry the persons appointed to view 302 acres of land belonging to John Cox, Gent. for a glebe do value the said land to £75-10, to which this Vestry have farther agreed for the same and under Cox's conveyance accordingly it is thereupon ordered that the parish do pay the said sum to the said Cox."[5]

---

[4] V. B. post, p. 330.
[5] V. B. post, p. 341, Cox's deed conveying the property bears date June 4, 1753. It is recorded in D. B. 3, page 251.

On November 7, 1754, there occurs an order of the vestry which may have to do with the payment to John Cox for this land, although this cannot be positively asserted. It reads: "Ordered, John Cox and Abra: Martin be first paid out of the Depositum."[6]

The lists of tithes of Lunenburg County for the year 1752 shows that John Cox was on the list taken by Cornelius Cargill. No order has been found describing the bounds or locality of his precinct for that particular year, but for an earlier year, 1749, the precinct within which Cornelius Cargill took the list was "in the fork [of Roanoke river?] and from Butchers Creek to Little Roanoke River, and beyond Dan River," and his precinct in 1752 was doubtless in this same general locality. But the proposed glebe tract seems to have been on Crupper Run Creek.

On January 15, 1766, while the buildings on the glebe of Rev. James Craig were being constructed on the Ragsdale plantation, the vestry ordered that "the Church Wardens sell the former Gleebe land and give credit as they think proper."[7]

The wardens in office at the time seem not to have made a sale, and so on November 25, 1766, the Vestry ordered that "the present Church Wardens sell the old Gleebe land and give two years credit."[8] These orders, likely, refer to the lands acquired from John Cox, though the facts do not appear clearly enough to justify that unqualified assertion.

Anthony Street seems to have had a hand in the business of selling the glebe land, if indeed he were not the chief factor in it, for in his account with the vestry in 1767 we find a charge of eight shillings and nine pence for "expences for Toddy to Anthony Street for trouble of selling the Glebe land and for trouble of selling."[9]

Very likely it was sold at public auction and Colonel Street acted as auctioneer. He was a deputy sheriff of the County at

---

[6] V. B. post, p. 436.
[7] V. B. post, p. 396.
[8] V. B. post, p. 399.
[9] V. B. post, p. 407.

the time, and later sheriff, and held several public offices for many years in the County.

Probably a little toddy was needed to tone him up to the pitch necessary to enable him to effectively and eloquently proclaim the value and desirability of the property offered for sale.

It may not be amiss to disgress a moment to add a further item about Colonel Street. Some years ago the writer in searching through the musty records of the early years of Lunenburg County, in an effort to compile a complete list of the taxable or tithable population came across the original list for one precinct taken by Anthony Street in 1783. The fading writing on crumbling paper was in his handwriting, and on the front and back covers of the document he had written and signed with his initials the following two verses of poetry:

> "How sweet to walk, my plantation through,
> And vegetations steps pursue!
> To mark how all things kindly shoot
> The leaf The Blossom, with the pride
> In the my plantation, Thus I view
> My health, my ease, and pleasure too.
>
> How soft the peach's downy skin,
> And then how sweet the juice within.
> I feel the fruit with many a smile
> And lick my dewy lips the while
> When I reflect that I must feast
> On all the Luxury of Taste."

But to recur from this digression: it seems a fair assumption that the minister in 1756 was not in the possession of a glebe, for at that time we find an allowance to the minister of twenty five pounds for his board,[10] which, doubless, would not have been made him, if he had been in the possession of a glebe. A similar order is found in 1757,[11] in 1759,[12] and in 1760.[13]

---

[10] V. B. post, p. 355.
[11] V. B. post, p. 358.
[12] V. B. post, p. 372.
[13] V. B. post, p. 376.

It may be that new parishes and counties were formed from the original territory of Cumberland Parish so rapidly that it became difficult to choose a satisfactory location of a glebe. One suitably located for a parish of a certain size and extent might be wholly unsuitable in geographical location, for a parish consisting of the territory that remained after large parts of the area were sliced away. It is possible that some such considerations led the vestry to arrange with the succession of ministers to pay them a cash amount for their subsistence, in lieu of furnishing them a glebe, as the strict letter of the law required.

The final paring off of other parishes from Cumberland occurred in 1761, when St. James's Parish was created. Reverend James Craig was then the minister of the parish, and had for several years been receiving allowance from the Vestry for his board. In this year, 1761, he seems to have become anxious to have his glebe instead of an allowance for board; he was probably already meditating matrimony, and it may be that this led him to desire to have a home, such as the law contemplated should be provided for ministers of the Established Church.

However this may be, the Vestry at its meeting July 13, 1761, appointed David Garland, John Jenings and John Ragsdale "to look out for a tract of land proper for a Glebe and make report to" the Vestry "at the next meeting."[14]

August 10, 1761, David Garland, "one of the gentlemen appointed to view a tract of land proper for a glebe, reported that they have viewed all the lands that are centrical, and he reports that they can't find any so suitable to Mr. Craig, and so much for the convenience of the Parish as Mr. John Ragsdale's Plantation, for which he asks two hundred and fifty pounds which this vestry have agreed to give and to pay him that sum at such times as will suit him after the 1st of June next, and Mr. Craig agrees to accept of the buildings that are there when properly finished with the addition of a Glebe House, and a Garden, and Yard made complete."[15]

---
[14] V. B. post, p. 379.
[15] V. B. post, p. 380.

It was at the same time ordered that a Glebe house and a Garden and a Yard be let to be built, and that David Garland and Lyddal Bacon let the same. It was specified that "the dimentions of the Mention [Mansion] House to be fifty by eighteen foot wide with inside chimneys to be four foot deep, the Hall 18 foot square, the passage 10 foot wide, the Chamber 18 foot by 14 with a Dutch Roof, and two rooms and passage above. The dimensions of the Garden and Yard to be known at the time of letting."[16]

The buildings were ordered let on Thursday the 1st of October, 1761.

In another chapter[17] some account is given of the controversy which evidently arose between Reverend James Craig and the Vestry over the fact that the Vestry released John Ragsdale from his agreement to sell his land for a glebe. That account need not be repeated here. In the end, it seems, Reverend James Craig had his way; Mr. Ragsdale decided to let the Vestry have the land, and the buildings were let, though there was some delay in the matter. Mr. Craig seems to have pressed his advantage, for now instead of being allowed twenty five pounds per annum for his board he was "allowed forty pounds per annum for his board" until "the Gleebe is compleated."[18]

On June 4, 1762, the Vestry ordered "the Gleebe Buildings be lett according to an order of Vestry made August 10, 1761,"[19] but it was decided to change somewhat the specifications for the building as the following order made August 21, 1762, shows:

"Whereas it is found by the consultation with workmen of good judgment that the former plan of 50 foot by 18 is defective, it is therefore judged more advantageous to the Parish upon the whole to adopt the following, viz: one 48 by 22, 3 rooms on a floor, with a passage 10 foot wide and 11 foot from the floor to the ceiling, etc., which said house together with the Kitchen and Landry 28 by 16 and 9 foot pitch and a Dairy 12 foot square and 9 foot pitch and garden 124 by 176 according to the plan

---
[16] V. B. post, p. 380.
[17] Chapter IX, hereof.
[18] V. B. post, p. 383.
[19] Id.

thereof lodged with the Vestry by which it is lett this day. Upon the Vestry's consent to this alteration the Revd. Mr. Craig consents to drop £15 per annum of his Board from this day and the said Buildings are accordingly lett with the necessary house 8 by 12, 8 by 10 with a sash window containing 4 pains 10 by [illegible]."[20]

Strangely enough the vestry book does not contain a record of the letting of the buildings on the glebe, with the details of that business. The transactions were, doubtless, evidenced by documents originally preserved in the hands of the Church Wardens or Clerk of the Vestry, but now no longer in existence. From scattered entries here and there in the vestry book, it is possible to gather a record of the facts. The contract for the building of the structures was let to John Powell at a price of four hundred and twenty eight pounds.[21]

While the work upon the other buildings progressed, the Vestry decided to add another to the group already let, and "ordered that there be a corn crib built on the Gleeb of Cumberland Parish of 20 foot long and 12 foot wide and that Messrs. David Garland and Jon. Jenings lett the same to undertakers."[22]

This order was made September 30th, 1763.

The slowness with which some things moved along is indicated by the fact that some four years later the crib seems to have been not entirely complete, for on February 20, 1769, the vestry ordered the Church Wardens, Lyddal Bacon and Thomas Chambers, to "give notice to David Hopkins that he meet [them] at a certain time within one month at least and settle his accounts with the Vestry for this Parish, and also that he finish the crib on the Glebe according to contract."[23]

John Powell seems not to have been without his difficulties in the erection of the buildings, for on November 23, 1764,[24] the vestry ordered him paid whatever sum was available in the hands of the Collector up to one hundred pounds, "provided his present

---

[20] V. B. post, p. 384.
[21] V. B. post, p. 398-99.
[22] V. B. post, p. 388.
[23] V. B. post, p. 412.
[24] V. B. post, p. 392.

securitys assent to the said payment."[25] Captain John Jenings, one of his sureties, gave such assent, but there is no record that the others did so.

The Kitchens at the Glebe seem not to have been embraced in the original agreement for erecting the houses thereon; the original contract was probably for the "Mansion House" only. On November 23, 1764, the Vestry ordered "that the Kitchens at the Gleeb be finished off in the following manner, viz. The walls of the Kitchen proper be lined with 3/4 plank, the floor to be layed with tile, a dresser and 4 shelves to be fixed up on each side extending from the fire place to each door, the floor of the Landry to be layed with plank, the walls to be lathed and plastered a floor to be layed up stares and the upper room lathed and plastered, 2 windows at each end of 4 paynes each, a step lather with a rail to it, and it is ordered the Church Wardens lett the same to the lowest bidder as soon as convenient some time in 3 weeks from date."[26]

A note added says that the steps are "to be eased at the bottom and risers of 7 inches."[27]

Continuing its program of improvements upon the Glebe, in order to provide the buildings and structures required by law, the vestry two years later, on November 25, 1766,

"Ordered that a stable be built for the Gleeb of sawed loggs of 20 foot by 16 with a shed of 8 foot the length of the stable, and to be shingled, to have 8 stalls with a passage between; the side of the shed to be clapboarded the whole length; but open at the ends, and be lett by the Church Wardens, and to [be] lofted with inch plank joined, but not plan'd."[28]

The building of the stable was let to Daniel Claiborne, who seemed in no hurry to do the work, and in February, 1769, the Vestry directed that the Church Wardens require him "within one month at least" to "finish the stable on the Glebe according to contract."

At the same meeting the vestry ordered "that a closett be

---

[25] V. B. post, p. 392.
[26] V. B. post, pp. 392-93.
[27] V. B. post, p. 393.
[28] V. B. post, p. 399.

made in the Gleebe house to be lett at the discretion of the Church Wardens,"[29] and on February 20, 1769, it ordered that "a glass window (with four lights, eight by ten inches) be made to the closet in the Mansion house at the Glebe and that the same be so contrived as to slip up and down."[30]

It appears that by November, 1766, the principal part of the improvements upon the Glebe were, in all probability, completed, for the minutes embody a memorandum, "That this day we settled with Mr. John Powell and he agrees that he has received £445-16-1, which is £17-16-1 more than was agreed to give him at the letting of the Glebe."[31]

On March 14, 1767, the Vestry ordered "that the Glebe buildings of this Parish be received, being viewed by this Vestry and judged to be compleated according to the contract made with John Powel, the undertaker of the same; and it is further ordered that the said John Powell be paid for additions and alterations agreed upon by this Vestry to be made to the said buildings after the first contract; the sum of Eighty Eight Pounds, Eight Shillings and Six Pence, and it is ordered that Mr. Thomas Tabb Church Warden pay Mr. Powell what he has in his hands."[32]

Although the Vestry by this order received the buildings as completed according to contract, within about a year they had come to the conclusion that some of his work was defective and called upon him to make it good. On February 20, 1769, it ordered that the Church Wardens "give notice to Jno. Powell that [by] the last day of May next, he amend the plaistering and brickwork on the Mansion House at the Glebe in this parish, according to his promise; or, if he should not, to let the said work to the lowest bidder."[33]

John Powell, however, happy no doubt in the possession of his payment in full, backed by the formal acceptance of the buildings two years before, seems to have paid no attention to

---

[29] V. B post, p. 399.
[30] V. B. post, p. 412.
[31] V. B. post, p. 398-99.
[32] V. B. post, p. 402.
[33] V. B. post, p. 412.

this demand that he "amend" his work; for on July 20, 1770, the Vestry ordered the Church Wardens to "let the repairing of the brick work and white washing on the Mansion house at the Glebe, to the lowest bidder, as soon as may be."[34]

The building program at the glebe was yet incomplete, for, on November 22, 1768, the vestry ordered the "building of a Barn (or Granary) on the Glebe 32 by 20 as per the plan."[35]

The fact that the provisions of the statute primarily placed upon the minister the obligations to keep the premises in repair, seems to have been largely overlooked. The proviso of the statute seems to have overshadowed its main provisions, and the clause which said that the Vestry may assume the cost of repairs, except those for wilful waste by the incumbent seems to have been construed into an obligation of, and not a permission to, the Vestry. At any rate Reverend James Craig seems to have been not backward in insisting that his premises be kept by the Vestry in a good state of repair.

On November 15, 1774, the Wardens were required to "view the houses on the glebe and make the repairs necessary thereto,"[36] and again on July 31, 1784, Mr. Craig seemed to be complaining again about the condition of his premises, and the vestry ordered "the necessary repairs as far as the law permits."[37]

But if Mr. Craig was strict, as he seems to have been, in insisting upon his rights, the Vestry were not always remiss in asserting theirs. Rev. Mr. Craig had purchased some land adjoining the Glebe tract and erected thereon his famous mill. The Vestry felt that in doing so he had damaged their property, the Glebe tract. The basis of this claim was the fact that as a result of the erection of his mill dam, back water encroached upon the glebe tract. At any rate, when the Wardens on July 31, 1784, were ordered to repair the glebe houses it was also "ordered that the Revd. James Craig apply the £15 due from

---

[34] V. B. post, p. 414.
[35] V. B. post, p. 410.
[36] V. B. post, p. 431.
[37] V. B. post, p. 454.

him to the Parish [for damages done the Glebe land by the building of his mill], toward making the said repairs."[38]

About two years later, on August 15, 1786, the following entry occurs in the Vestry Book:

"In consequence of a former order of Vestry which empowered the Revd. James Craig to make the necessary repairs to the Mansion house on the Glebe, this Vestry do receive the repairs made to the Chimnies, the glazeing of the windows and the plastering and white washing, and discount with him in payment for the said repairs the fifteen pounds due from him to the Parish for the damages done the Glebe by the overflowing of his mill pond."[39]

Following the decline of the Church, as a result of its ceasing to be supported by taxes, and after the lapse of some years the Convention of the Church, in the State of Virginia, endeavored to take stock of the property of the Church and requested the various vestries to report the facts to it. On April 27, 1791, the Vestry of Cumberland Parish recorded an inventry of "the property of the Protestant Episcopal Church in this Parish to be sent to the next Convention agreeable to a Resolution of the Convention," as follows:

"Consisting of a Glebe containing 825 acres of land with a mansion house and necessary out houses in need of repairs judged to be worth £412-10/.

One wooden church 60 feet by 30 in good repair.

One Do. 48 by 24 in need of repairs.

One Surplice.

A large silver flagon or tankerd, a chalice and patten which cost about twenty pounds Sterling.

Two large folio Bibles.

Four old prayer books."[40]

The last references to the Glebe, in the Vestry book, were in 1796 and 1797. On April 16, 1796, the Vestry directed the Church Wardens to "prepare a petition to be preferred to the

---
[38] V. B. post, p. 454.
[39] V. B. post, p. 463.
[40] V. B. post, p. 470.

next Convention requesting permission to sell that part of the land lying on the north side of Reedy Creek road, in order to enable the Vestry to repair the buildings on the Glebe and present the same as early as possible for subscription."[41]

And at a meeting on May 28, 1796, Henry Stokes, William Buford, John Ragsdale and William Stokes, were ordered to sell "that part of the Glebe land which lies on the North side of Reedy Creek road for the best price that can be obtained and lay out the same on the repairs of the Glebe and that they also let the said repairs as early as possible to the lowest bidder," and it was also ordered "that the same gentlemen sell the part of the glebe land which lies between Reedy Creek road and the land belonging to James Craig decd., if they think it will conduce to the interest of the Parish and lay out the proceeds as above directed."[42]

And again on May 27, 1797, the Vestry giving attention to the condition of the Glebe property ordered, "that John Billups and Edmd. P. Bacon apply to Edward Jordan and receive from him such monies as may appear to be due to the Parish of Cumberland and deliver the same to the Commissioners appointed by a former order to let the repairs to the Glebe who are hereby authorized to lay out same in such further repairs as they judge most necessary."[43]

This seems to be the final reference to the Glebe in the Vestry Book of the Parish, here under review.

---

[41] V. B. post, p. 486.
[42] V. B. post, pp. 486-87.
[43] V. B. post, p. 488.

CHAPTER VI
The Ministers

EVEREND JOHN BRUNSKILL was the first minister employed by the Vestry of Cumberland Parish. The circumstances of his employment are shown by an entry in the minutes of the Vestry, August 2, 1748, a part of the record reading:

"Letters recommendatory from Sir William Gooch Baronet, Lt. Governour and Mr. Commissary Dawson in favor of the Reverend Mr. John Brunskill Clerk, together with his Deacon's and Priest's orders being presented to this Vestry. [they] are willing to pay all due respect and deference to the Governour and Mr. Commissary's recommendation and are willing to receive the said Mr. Brunskill into this Parish as a Minister of the Gospel for one year and at the expiration thereof to cause to be paid to him the salary by law appointed. But for as much as they are not willing to be compelled to entertain and receive any Minister other than such as may answer the end of his Ministerial Function they only intend to entertain and receive him as a probationer for one year being fully minded and desirous that if they should in that time disapprove his conduct or behaviour they may have it in their power to receive another."[1]

The note of challenge or defiance in this entry is unmistakable. Virginia was now in the midst of a notable, long drawn out struggle between the Colonial governors and the Vestries. The Governors claimed to be the representative of the King in Church and State, and patron of all the parishes; and also to be the representative of the Bishop of London, having the disposal of the ministers and the exercise of discipline over the clergy.[2]

The Governor claimed the right of induction; in other words of inducting the minister into a life tenure of the parish. This

---
[1] V. B. post, p. 329.
[2] *The Old Free State*, I, 347.

the vestries stoutly opposed, for they had no desire to thus run the risk of having an unworthy minister saddled upon them, with no power to get rid of him. It was a serious matter, for the minister was supported by public taxes, which the vestry had no choice but to levy and collect.

It was true, the vestries had the right to choose a minister, but' the governors insisted that upon making their choice, they should apply to him to induct the minister into the office.

It is clear from the above order, that the Vestry of Cumberland Parish had no idea of asking or permitting the Governor to induct any minister into office in that parish.

Upon the employment of Reverend Mr. Brunskill, the Vestry directed him as to the performance of his duties, ordering "that the Reverend Mr. Brunskill preach alternately at one of the four churches in this County (viz.), at the Church near Mr. Delony's, at the Church near Mr. Bacon's, at the Church near little Roanoke, and at the Church near the fork."[3]

In addition to preaching alternately at these four churches he was directed to preach "at the Chappel near Mr. Phelps's four times in the year," and also "at or near Hogan's on the South river four times in the year," in the "months of April, October, June and December."[4]

There is nothing to indicate that Mr. Brunskill began his servives in the parish until 1749. The Vestry on February 8, 1749, entered a brief order declaring it to be their opinion that he should be received as "Minister of the parish and be paid the salary by law appointed,"[5] and made an entry of his salary at sixteen thousand pounds of tobacco.

As to the history of this minister, not a great deal is known. There were, it is said, three ministers named John Brunskill in the Colony of Virginia. John Brunskill, Sr., who came to Virginia, in 1715,[6] and who was minister of St. Margaret's Parish in Caroline County, John Brunskill, Jr., his son, who was min-

---
[3] V. B. post, pp. 329-30.
[4] V. B. post, p. 330.
[5] V. B. post, p. 330.
[6] Goodwyn: *The Colonial Church in Virginia*, 255.

ister of Hamilton Parish, in Prince William County,[7] where, upon charges brought by the Vestry he was tried before the Governor and Council and ordered dismissed.[8]

The third John Brunskill, it is thought, was the first minister of Cumberland Parish, although neither Bishop Meade nor Dr. Goodwyn seem certain as to the facts. So far as is known, this John Brunskill was not related to the other two of the name, father and son above mentioned.

This Reverend John Brunskill was admitted Sizar, at the age of nineteen, at Pembroke College, Cambridge, on October 13, 1737. He was a son of Richard Brunskill, of "Upmanhall," Westmoreland, England. He matriculated, in 1737, and received the degree of B. A. in 1741-42. He was minister of Raleigh Parish in Amelia County from 1754 to 1776. "His Congregation," says Goodwyn, "deserted him on account of his royalist sentiments, but he continued to live on the Glebe, and was reported by Bishop Madison as rector of the parish until his death in 1804."[9]

Dr. Goodwyn says he was *"Probably* Minister, Cumberland Parish, Lunenburg County, 1748."[10]

It seems reasonably clear that he was the minister of Cumberland Parish, for the John Brunskill, Sr., above mentioned, seems to have been continuously in St. Margaret's Parish from 1738 to 1758,[11] while the John Brunskill, Jr., above mentioned, was not "licensed for Virginia" until 1752.[12]

Reverend Mr. Brunskill seems to have served the parish for eighteen weeks more than one year, for in addition to his first year's salary the vestry on November 22, 1750, made an allowance of six thousand pounds of tobacco "to the Revd. Mr. John Brunskill for 18 weeks salary in this parish."[13]

---

[7]Goodwyn: *The Colonial Church in Virginia,* 255. Bishop Meade speaks of him in connection with Hamilton Parish as *Joseph* Brunskill (Vol. II, p. 217). This reference to him as *Joseph* Brunskill was an error, according to Goodwyn, *The Colonial Church in Virginia,* 255.
[8]*The Colonial Church in Virginia,* 255.
[9]*The Colonial Church in Virginia,* 255.
[10]*The Colonial Church in Virginia,* 255.
[11]Id.
[12]Id.
[13]V. B. post, 337.

The president of the Council of the Colony and Mr. Commissary Dawson recommended Reverend Mr. George Purdie to succeed Rev. John Brunskill. Mr. Purdie presented the letters recommending him to the vestry at a meeting held February 12, 1750.[14]

The Vestry employed him, but were even more cautious than in the case of the Reverend Mr. Brunskill. They entered an order that the Vestry "think fit to receive him the said Purdie as a probationer for six months, and that he be entitled to receive half the salary levied at the last vestry as an article in the said levies to the Reverend Mr. John Brunskill," etc.[15]

The order provided that if either party "hath design or inclination to part with the other that they respectively give each other six months notice," and it was further ordered "that Mr. Purdies first six months commence from the first day of January," 1750.[16]

Mr. Purdie gave the Vestry notice that he would not be able to serve the perish longer than the last day of March, 1751, "his affairs calling him abroad," and he asked leave to resign.

The vestry, at a meeting held on October 1, 1750, took notice of this request, and ordered an allowance be made in the laying of the next levy to pay Mr. Purdie as the law directs up to that date.[17]

The Vestry spoke in terms of praise of Mr. Purdie in the following order:

"This Vestry recommends the Reverend Mr. George Purdie to the Reverend and Honourable Mr. Commissary Dawson as a person who hath with diligence and industry performed his ministerial function in the discharge of every duty incumbent upon him to perform as a minister of the gospel in this parish, in consideration of which the parish hath made him an allowance of 2000 lbs. tobacco, extraordinary," etc.

---

[14]The minutes say "February 12, *1749*," obviously a clerical error, as the minutes follow in regular order those of the meeting of November 11, 1749.
[15]V. B. post, p. 335.
[16]V. B. post, p. 335.
[17]V. B. post, p. 336.

Bishop Meade throws some doubt upon the question of whether Mr. Purdie went abroad after leaving Cumberland Parish,[18] and in any event he became minister of St. Andrews Parish, Brunswick County, in 1751 and remained there until 1760,[19] although in 1757, he was by the Commissary ordered tried before the Vestry. The nature of the charge against Mr. Purdie is not disclosed either by Bishop Meade or Dr. Goodwyn, though Bishop Meade says in reference to the case that when the witnesses appeared, Mr. Purdie acknowledges his guilt and resigned his charge, whereupon the Vestry agreed "to try him for one year more,"[20] and were "not relieved from him until April, 1760."[21]

Reverend William Kay (or Key) succeeded Mr. Purdie as Minister of Cumberland Parish in 1751.

Bishop Meade says that, "In the year 1751, the Rev. William Kay . . . became the minister on a probation of two years, with the understanding that either party might be released at the end of one year."[22]

This fact is ascertained, not from the minutes of the Vestry at the time he was employed, for those minutes seem not to be in existence, but from a confirmatory order, made at a meeting of the Vestry sometime in 1751, but the exact date of which does not appear, because of the fact that a page (or more) of the volume is missing at this point. The confirmatory order states that "the said Mr. Kay should act as a minister of the gospel in this parish from the first day of April 1751 as a probationer for two years" etc.[23]

In 1753, during the ministry of Reverend Mr. Kay, the Vestry purchased from John Cox, Gentleman, three hundred and two acres of land for a Glebe for the sum of Seventy five pounds, ten shillings,[24] and in 1754, while no church was ordered there a new place of worship was designated, the vestry directing "that

---
[18] *Old Churches, Ministers and Families of Virginia*, I, 483.
[19] *The Colonial Church in Virginia*, 300-301.
[20] *Old Churches, Ministers and Families of Virginia*, I, 478.
[21] Id.
[22] *Old Churches, Ministers and Families of Virginia*, I, 484.
[23] V. B. post, p. 340.
[24] V. B. post, p. 341.

Mr. Kay preach twice a year at Rich. Palmers to the Grassy C[reek] people."[25]

The Reverend Mr. Kay continued in the parish until about the middle of the year 1755, when he died. The Vestry at a meeting held on November 4, 1755, ordered a levy of eight thousand six hundred pounds of tobacco to be paid "to the executor or administrator[26] of the Reverend Mr. William Key, Clerk, late deceased for six months salary."[27]

Reverend Mr. Kay was a son of John Kay, of Burnsall, Yorkshire, England, a farmer;[28] he was admitted Sizar, at twenty years of age, at Trinity College, Cambridge, May 18. 1741, and matriculated in 1741, and "migrated" to Emmanuel College, January 25, 1742-43.[29]

Prior to coming to Cumberland Parish, in Lunenburg County, he had been minister of Lunenburg parish in Richmond County, from 1745 to about 1750.[30] There he and a portion of the Vestry had "a most painful and protracted controversy," with another portion of the Vestry led by Colonel Landon Carter. "The dispute," says Bishop Meade, "appears to have been about the right of Mr. Kay to the parish in preference to another who was desired by some of the vestry and people."[31]

The controversy was carried before the Governor and Council, and eventually to "the higher court in England."

But the historians of the Episcopal Church do not tell us how the case was finally decided. Possibly it was never decided; it may be that with Mr. Kay's removal to Cumberland Parish the question was not of practical importance, and neither party disposed to incur the expenses of further prosecution of it.

"The sympathy of the Commissary and the Clergy," says Bishop Meade, "appears to have been with Mr. Kay."[32]

---

[25] V. B. post, p. 343.
[26] The Lunenburg County records disclose no will made by him.
[27] V. B. post, p. 351.
[28] *The Colonial Church in Virginia*, 284.
[29] Id.
[30] *The Colonial Church in Virginia*, 284, and Meade: *Old Churches, Ministers and Families of Virginia*, II, 178-9.
[31] Id.
[32] *Old Churches, Ministers and Families of Virginia*, II, 179.

If the reference to "William Key, Lunenburg, 1764," in connection with an account of the libraries of Ministers, in *Colonial Virginia*,[33] means that he died that year, as seems to be the interpretation given it in *The Colonial Church in Virginia*,[34] it is, of course, an error. The order of the Vestry of Cumberland Parish above mentioned, clearly fixes the date of his death as in the year 1755, and Bishop Meade gives that year as the date of his death.

After the death of Reverend Mr. Kay (or Key), the "Reverend Mr. Proctor" preached in the parish. He was doubtless a visiting minister, and not regularly engaged as rector of the parish. The precise arrangements under which he served the parish are not known, but, at a meeting on June 7, 1757, the vestry ordered:

"That the Collector pay to the Reverend Mr. Proctor two thousand pounds of tobacco, if he pleases to accept it, for his favors done this parish in preaching in the vacancy between the death of Mr. Key and the coming of the Reverend Mr. Barclay into this parish and that they pay the same to Mr. Lyddal Bacon for Mr. Proctor's use; and Mr. Embry and we the vestry on behalf of ourselves and the said parish take this first opportunity to return our grateful thanks to Mr. Proctor for such his favours and services to us and them done."[35]

Nowhere in the Vestry Book does "Reverend Mr. Proctor's" first name or initials appear; but since Reverend William Proctor is the only minister of that name known to have been in Virginia during the whole Colonial era,[36] he was doubtless the man.

He was a Scotsman, formerly a Presbyterian, and "was tutor and librarian at Westover, in the time of Colonel William Byrd 2d."[37] Letters to his brother written from "Westover upon James River, in Virginia," dated in 1739 and in 1740, are printed in the Virginia Historical Magazine.[38]

He was Minister of Nottoway Parish, Amelia County, in 1754,

---

[33] By Mary Newton Stanard.
[34] Page 284.
[35] V. B. post, pp. 356-57.
[36] *The Colonial Church in Virginia*, 300.
[37] Virginia Hist. Mag., X, 298.
[38] X, 298-301.

and Bishop Meade says he was in that parish in 1758,[39] and it was doubtless during his residence in that section of country that he preached in Cumberland Parish, probably in 1757.

Reverend John Barclay applied to the vestry on February 4, 1756, to fill the vacancy in the parish caused by the death of Reverend Mr. Kay.[40]

He was accepted for the position on condition "that he would be at liberty at any time when he thought fit to leave the parish" and on the further condition "that the Vestry might also when they thought fit imploy any other," in which event Mr. Barclay "should be paid in proportion to the time he stayed among us."[41]

The sum of this arrangement was that Mr. Barclay could leave without notice, and the Vestry could dismiss him without notice; its only obligation in case of dismissal being to pay him his salary up to that time.

Mr. Barclay served the parish during the remainder of 1756 and up to June, 1757, when he notified the vestry of his intention to leave the parish,[42] and at the same time requested "the favour of this vestry to give a title to Mr. James Craig a student in Divinity and to recommend him to the Reverend and Honorable Mr. Commissary Dawson as a person they are informed very well qualified to receive Holy Orders, into which he is desirous to enter."

The vestry and Mr. Barclay had a controversy over his salary, and on March 6, 1758, the vestry had before it for consideration a letter from Mr. Barclay about the matter, dated December 22nd, 1757, and came to the conclusion "that the said letter was unreasonable; but agree that in case he makes it appear that he has served the parish a longer time than he has been paid for, that then the Collector Mr. Thomas Hawkins pay him for two months salary."[43]

Mr. Barclay seemed never to have satisfied the vestry on the point, so he brought a suit to recover the amount, and was suc-

---

[39]*Old Churches, Ministers and Families of Virginia*, II, 23.
[40]V. B. post, p. 353.
[41]Id.
[42]V. B. post, p. 356.
[43]V. B. post, p. 360-61.

cessful in obtaining a judgment, for the settlement of which the vestry provided, at a meeting held November 3, 1760.[44]

Reverend John Barclay was the son of James Barclay, Canon of Windsor. He was born March 28, 1732; and entered King's College, Cambridge, as a scholar from Eton in 1752; was a fellow in 1753, a B. A. in 1755 and an M. A. in 1758.[45]

Pursuant to the recommendation made by Mr. Barclay, the Vestry, on June 7, 1757, empowered the "Church Wardens to give a title and recommendation to Mr. Jas. Craig" upon certain conditions, elsewhere mentioned herein. But some time was to elapse, as we shall see, before he took up his duties in the parish. And before he came the names of several ministers appear in the records. On December 5, 1757, the Vestry employed "Reverend Mr. Jacob Townsend to serve this parish as a minister," and it was "ordered that he be received into the parish for the space of three months.[46] And at a meeting held March 6, 1758, the Vestry ordered him paid four thousand two hundred and forty pounds of tobacco as a salary and three pounds fifteen shillings current money for board.[47]

Mr. Townsend, it seems, being uncertain of his status inquired "whether he is to be continued minister of the parish any longer," whereupon the vestry magnanimously agreed he might continue three months longer "provided he will agree to have his salary and board levyed for him at the next levy," and to this Mr. Townsend agreed.[48]

At this same meeting the vestry made orders for various payments to be made for sermons preached in the parish by "the Reverend Mr. Garden," by "the Reverend Mr. Purdie," and by "the Reverend Mr. Proctor." The payment on this occasion to Mr. Proctor of seven thousands pounds of tobacco, indicated that

---

[44] V. B. post, p. 379.
[45] *The Colonial Church in Virginia*, 248. The date and degrees are taken from this authority. It is not exactly clear how the M. A. degree was taken in 1758—unless he returned to England, which he may have done, as there seems no record of his service in Virginia after 1757.
[46] V. B. post, p. 358.
[47] V. B. post, p. 360.
[48] V. B. post, p. 361.

he must have served the parish the equivalent of some four or five months.[49]

Reverend Jacob Townsend, who served Cumberland Parish as its minister under regular and formal employment by the Vestry, for six or more months has been practically overlooked by the historians of the Episcopal Church. His name is not even mentioned by Bishop Meade, and the entire mention of him by Dr. Goodwyn is as follows: "Townsend, Jacob: In Virginia, without a cure, in 1754. (Perry)."[50]

He is one of at least two ministers who served Cumberland parish which Bishop Meade omitted to mention in his brief account of the parish. The other was the above mentioned "Reverend Mr. Garden," or Reverend James Garden, who was licensed for Virginia, September 22, 1754, received the King's Bounty three days later, and was minister of St. Patrick's Parish, Prince Edward County, Virginia.[51]

Dr. Goodwyn says he was minister there "1755-73," while Bishop Meade says: "In the year 1758 the Rev. James Garden is its minister. We find him there also in 1773,—fifteen years after."

He died there February 19, 1773.[52]

At the meeting on November 29, 1758, the vestry

"Ordered that the present Church Wardens employ the Reverend Mr. Proctor to supply the vacancy of a minister in this parish, and that they agree with him to preach at such times and places as they shall agree, and that the said Church Wardens give proper notice of the same."[53]

This arrangement with Mr. Proctor was made, and doubtless continued from November, 1758, until May or June and possibly until September, 1759, when Rev. James Craig took up his duties in the parish. The parish levy as set out in the vestry minutes November 12, 1759, contains an entry (the amount of which is illegible), for "the Reverend Mr. Proctor (for) his

---

[49] V. B. post, p. 363.
[50] *The Colonial Church in Virginia*, 313.
[51] Goodwyn: *The Colonial Church in Virginia*, 271; Meade: *Old Churches, Ministers and Families of Virginia*, II, 24.
[52] Burrell: *History of Prince Edward County*, 243.
[53] V. B. post, p. 363.

services in the Parish,"⁵⁴ and also an order for the payment to him of ten shillings for wine for the sacrament furnished by him.

At the meeting of the vestry held May 22, 1759, Matthew Marrable, Gentleman, one of the members of the Vestry represented to the Vestry that Reverend Mr. James Craig was willing to undertake the office of minister for the parish, and recommended him as in his opinion, "highly deserving the same," and referring to the order of the vestry of June 7, 1757, expressed the opinion that he was justly entitled to it, whereupon the Vestry

"Resolved that it is the unanimous opinion of this Vestry that the said Reverend James Craig, ought [to be] and is hereby chosen, elected, constituted and appointed, rector and minister of this parish, and that his time begin and commence immediately from and after the date hereof."⁵⁵

Mr. Craig entered upon the duties of his office, but within a year or two had, it seems, a disagreement with the vestry, probably about the matter of the purchase of a glebe, and some time in the latter part of 1761 or the early days of 1762 he resigned his office; and the Vestry on May 20, 1762, after reciting the fact that "our present incumbent intends to leave us," and that "Mr. Deverix Jarratte⁵⁶ a Candidate for Holy Orders" had applied to the vestry for a title to the parish, ordered "that the Church Wardens give a title and recommendation" to him, upon his giving bond and security that he would not "by virtue of the title insist upon being minister of the parish" if he "shall not be found agreeable to the Church Wardens and vestry and parishioners after trial."⁵⁷

As pointed out in the sketch of Reverend James Craig, in another chapter hereof, the difficulty seems to have been over the fact that John Ragsdale, a member of the vestry, had agreed to sell his plantation to the parish for a glebe,⁵⁸ but had changed his

---

⁵⁴V. B. post, p. 372.
⁵⁵V. B. post, p. 365.
⁵⁶Devereux Jarratt, of course.
⁵⁷V. B. post, p. 383.
⁵⁸V. B. post, p. 380.

mind and induced the vestry to release him from "the bargain."⁵⁹

Reverend James Craig, however, it seems, had his heart set on that plantation, and when the Vestry did not hold Mr. Ragsdale to "the bargain," he showed his righteous indignation and quit.

But matters were straightened out somehow. The Reverend Devereux Jarratt, though accepted by the vestry did not become minister of the parish; and on June 4, 1762 "The Reverend Mr. James Craig by his consent and the unanimous consent of this vestry is received into this parish as Rector of the same."⁶⁰

The reason for his coming back so soon into the office is doubtless to be found in the other two brief orders of that date, the only others entered at that meeting: one ordering the glebe buildings to be let according to an order of Vestry made August 10, 1761, which meant that Mr. Ragsdale had, after all, allowed the parish to have his plantation; and the other order allowed Mr. Craig forty pounds per annum for board, until the glebe should be completed.⁶¹

Thereafter Mr. Craig continued in the ministry of the parish until his death in 1795.

A separate chapter⁶² hereof, is devoted to an account of Mr. Craig and his descendants.

After the death of Reverend James Craig, the vestry met at Lunenburg Courthouse on May 15, 1795, and ordered that the Church Wardens of the parish "advertise for a minister to supply the vacancy in this parish occasioned by the death of the Reverend James Craig."⁶³

The vestry met again, at Reedy Creek Church, July 6, 1795, for the purpose of choosing a minister, but the records do not disclose that any action was taken. The next meeting of the vestry was not held until December 23, 1795, when the vestry "elected, constituted and appointed" Reverend Dr. John Cameron to be Rector and Minister of the parish.⁶⁴

---

⁵⁹V. B. post, p. 382.
⁶⁰V. B. post, p. 383.
⁶¹V. B. post, p. 383.
⁶²Chapter IX.
⁶³V. B. post, p. 482.
⁶⁴V. B. post, p. 483.

Dr. Cameron served the parish until his death in 1815. A memoir of him, with some account of his descendants is embodied in another chapter[65] of this volume.

Shortly before his death Dr. Cameron gave notice to the Vestry that because of the advanced time of his life and "increasing infirmities" he was becoming less able to discharge the duties of the clerical office, as a consequence he had resolved to resign his charge "in the course of the present year." This letter, dated April 29, 1815, suggested that they request the Bishop to take measures to provide the parish with a suitable minister in succession to Dr. Cameron.

The Vestry, at once, caused Dr. Cameron's letter to be placed before Bishop Richard Channing Moore, who after Dr. Cameron's death, under date of February 17, 1816, recommended that the Vestry of Cumberland Parish receive Mr. John S. Ravenscroft, who expected to enter into holy orders, as lay reader, until the time came, when, by the canons of the Church, he might be regularly ordained.[66]

Pursuant to this recommendation of the Bishop, the Vestry on March 14, 1816, unanimously elected Mr. Ravenscroft to the office of reader.

The Vestry held a brief meeting April 15, 1816, when the only business transacted was the election of a new Vestry.

The volume of Vestry minutes or records, from which these items have been chiefly drawn, shows no vestry meeting from April 15, 1816, until May 9, 1831, when there is the record of a meeting, at which "James Macfarland, David Street and Edward R. Chambers being all the surviving trustees," elected Wm. Bagley and Roger B. Atkinson to fill vacancies in the Vestry occasioned by the removal of Colonel Edmund L. Taylor and Edmd. P. Bacon, deceased, "leaving the other vacancy," so the record runs, "occasioned by the death of Reverend John Phillips to be filled with his successor who shall be chosen as the Minister of this parish."[67]

On the same day Roger B. Atkinson was elected lay deputy

---

[65]Chapter X.
[66]V. B. post, p. 499.
[67]V. B. post, pp. 564-65.

to represent Cumberland Parish in the General Convention to be held in the Borough of Norfolk the third Thursday in May, 1831.[68]

An alphabetical list of the clergymen who at one time or another had something to do with the ecclesiastical history of the parish is as follows:

Barclay, John	1756-1757
Brunskill, John	1748-1749
Cameron, John	1796-1815
Craig, James	1759-1795
Garden, James	1758 (?)
Jarratt, Devereux	1762
Kay (or Key), William	1751-1755
Proctor, William	1755 (?), 1758
Purdie, George	1750
Ravenscroft, John S.	1816
Townsend, Jacob	1757-1758

READERS

A part of the activities of the Church, in view of the large area of the parish, and the number of the churches and their distance from each other, was carried on by Readers, as it was quite impossible, particularly in the early days, for the minister to visit the churches very often. The information to be gleaned from the Vestry Book about the readers is incomplete and fragmentary. In most instances it does not disclose the locality where the reader was employed, though in not infrequent cases this information is given.

It is quite evident that the names of all the readers employed do not appear for often the records show appropriations to some vestryman, leading citizen or minister to employ a reader, as for example twelve hundred pounds of tobacco to "James Hunt Gent. to employ a reader,"[69] or "to the Reverend Mr. Proctor to

---

[68] V. B. post, p. 565.
[69] V. B. post, p. 351.

imploy a Reader at two of the most convenient places over Roanoke."[70]

One or two orders of this character are interesting. On November 11, 1749, the vestry "ordered that 1000 pounds of tobacco be levied annually and paid to John Caldwell Gent. toward the payment of a reader on the Cub Creek settlement."[71]

And in 1750 and in 1751 the Vestry ordered the payment of a thousand pounds of tobacco in each of those years to William Caldwell to employ a reader.[72]

When one remembers that these were staunch Presbyterians and that John Caldwell did not bring his colony to Virginia until first being assured by Governor Gooch and the Council that they might have the benefit of the Toleration Act, and might worship as Presbyterians and would not be prosecuted for not attending the Episcopal Church; and when it is further remembered that John Caldwell, though elected a member of the first vestry of Cumberland Parish, refused to take the oath of a vestryman and resigned, one is inclined to wonder about the brand of doctrine expounded by the readers employed by these men.

Not only is it clear that a good many readers were employed whose names are not shown, but the vestry records show allowances to certain named persons who were presumably readers though the fact does not appear in affirmative statement.

Many of the readers became the clerks of the churches in their respective communities, as the minutes of the vestry abundantly show.

After the final subdivision of the parish in 1761, there are very few, if any, mentions of readers employed at the churches of the parish.

It may serve a useful purpose to set down the names of the readers as shown here and there in the vestry minutes.

Readers in Cumberland Parish

Allen, Robert, 1746-1749.
Arden (Ardin), Abraham, 1747-1750.

---

[70] V. B. post, p. 362.
[71] V. B. post, p. 333.
[72] V. B. post, pp. 338-39.

Cole, Mark, 1751.
Cook, William, 1751, "Reader on Blackwater at the house of Joseph Rentfroe."
Harriss, Samuel, 1747-1751, Reader at "The Fork Church."
Hix, John, 1749.
Jones, John, 1760, Reader at Grassy Creek.
Randal, Josias, 1746.
Read, James, 1747.
Rudder, Samuel, 1760, Reader at Flatrock.
Smith, Thomas, 1756-1757, Reader at Butcher's Creek.
Tomson (Thompson), John, 1757, Reader at Settlement "near Mr. Richd. Booker's on Bush Run."
Williams, Joseph, 1759.
Wood, James, 1747-1751.

CHAPTER VII

Processioning Lands

N October, 1705, the 4th year of Queen Anne, there was passed an act[1] entitled: "An Act concerning the Granting, Seating, and Planting, and for Settling the Titles and bounds of Lands; and for preventing unlawful shooting and ranging thereupon." One of the sections of this law provided for the processioning of lands; directed how it should be done, and prescribed the effect it should have. This law, it appears was in effect when Lunenburg County and Cumberland Parish were formed.

In October, 1748, another comprehensive statute[2] was passed on the subject, and it repealed all previous acts "concerning any matter or thing within the purview of this act."

This Act by section LIV, provided for the processioning of lands, and more particular reference is made to it, as it was under its provisions, rather than under earlier laws, that the greater part of the processionings recorded in the Vestry Book of Cumberland took place.

This law "for preventing controversies concerning the bounds of lands" provided,

"That once in every four years the bounds of every person's land shall be processioned, or gone round, and the land marks renewed, in manner following, that is to say, the Court of every County, at some Court between the first day of June, and the first day of September, which shall be in the year of our Lord one thousand seven hundred and fifty one, and so between the first day of June, and the first day of September, in every fourth year thereafter, by order of the Court, shall direct the vestry of each parish within their County respectively, to divide their parishes into so many precincts, as to them shall seem most convenient for processioning every particular person's land in their

---
[1]Ch. XXI, of III *Hening*, pp. 304-329.
[2]Ch. I, of the General Assembly of 1748; V *Hening*, 408-431.

respective parishes, and to appoint the particular times, between the last day of September and the last day of March then next coming, when such processioning shall be made in every precinct; and also to appoint two or more intelligent honest freeholders of every precinct, to see such processioning performed, and to take and return to the Vestry an account of every persons land they shall procession, and of the persons present at the same, and what lands in their precincts they fail to procession, and the particular reasons of such failure."

The statute also required that notice "be given by the Church Wardens, at their parish church, at least three Sundays next before the same is to be performed, of the persons and times so appointed by the vestry, for processioning in every several precinct," and the vestry was required to "cause the accounts returned by the freeholders ... to be registered in particular books to be kept for that purpose, by the clerk of the vestry; and to prevent mistakes or omissions in any such register, the Church Wardens shall examine the same, in the presence of the vestry, and compare the register with the original returns, at the next vestry that shall be held after such return (is) made, from time to time, and shall certify the same under their hands in every register so by them examined and compared."

Severe penalties, by fines, were provided for the failure of any Court, Vestry, Church Warden or other party to perform any duty directed by the act respecting the processioning of lands. For instance, the law provided that "if any County Court shall, at any time hereafter, fail to make such order, ... every justice of the peace of such County shall forfeit and pay one thousand pounds of tobacco."

Section LVI of the act provided that processioning land three times in accordance with the act or under former laws and this act "shall be held, and is hereby declared to be, sufficient to settle such bounds, so as the same may never afterwards be altered."

Section LVIII of the act provided in case of controversy "between persons whose lands lie contiguous" if the owner or owners refused to permit their lands to be processioned, in such case the freeholders appointed to procession the lands of the precinct "shall within ten days after such refusal, certify the same . . . to the Church Wardens . . . who shall return such certificate to the court from which the order for processioning issued, at their next sitting, and such court shall thereupon order their surveyor, with a jury, to lay out the bounds in dispute, at the charge of the party against whom the right to such bounds shall be determined, and to return such survey to the next court after the same shall be made, which return shall be recorded, and a copy thereof sent by the county court clerk, within fifteen days after such return, to the Church-Wardens of the parish where the lands lie, and shall be by them caused to be registered, in the vestry book of their parish."

These enactments were of great importance in a newly settled country, where tracts of lands granted by the public authorities assumed every shape and form imaginable; in other words, at a time when governmental surveys in sectionized form, or according to a comprehensive plan to prevent interlocks and lappages were unknown.

The purpose of the law was to bring to light, and settle promptly and somewhat peremptorily, any disputes which arose over land lines; and to make the boundaries of lands so well known as to reduce to the minimum controversies over them.

Such a proceeding was held to be of such value that it survived for a long time in Virginia, though the administration of the law upon the separation of Church and State was reposed in the County Courts. The Code of Virginia of 1873[3] contains provisions for processioning lands which differ but little in substance from those of the enactment above of 1748. And in the Virginia Code of 1904 a chapter[4] is devoted to the subject of processioning lands, but its provisions apply only to counties in which "the records of deeds and wills have been lost or destroyed, either in whole or part," and to "such other counties as may deem it necessary." The proceeding came in time in most parts, if not all, of the State, to be little used, but the title "Processioning," did not disappear from the index of Virginia Codes until the revision of 1919.

[3]Chapter CXI.
[4]Chapter 106.

The great importance of the subject in the early years is evidenced by the time given to it; and by the large part of the Vestry records which the orders and returns having to do with processioning occupy in the Vestry Book printed in this volume.

No attempt will be made in this chapter to review the processioning proceedings as recorded in the Vestry Book. They appear in the minutes in such way as to be easily referred to and clearly understood by those interested.

Orders were made by the vestry appointing processioners, at a vestry meeting on September 8, 1747,[5] at a meeting, the date of which does not appear, in 1751,[6] and at a meeting on November 4, 1755.[7]

No returns by the processioners appointed for these years appear in the Vestry Book extant, and which is printed, for the first time in this work.[8]

Why these returns are missing may be a matter of speculation; they may have been recorded in a separate book which has been lost. It is possible, however, that they were recorded in the original Vestry Book of Cumberland Parish which contained the vestry records from 1746 to 1760, and not copied when the old records were copied into a new book.

At the vestry meeting November 3, 1760, there was an allowance of one shilling three pence "to Richard Witton for a quire of paper for a record book for the return of processioning."[9]

Some or all of these early processionings may have been recorded in a small book made of this quire of paper.

At the same meeting the vestry ordered "that Richard Witton do copy all the old Vestry Book into the New Record Book and bring his account for the same to this Vestry."[10]

It may be, though this seems unlikely, that the early processioning records were in the same book as the records of the proceedings of the Vestry, but were not copied when the minutes

---

[5]V. B. post, p. 325 et seq.
[6]V. B. post, p. 339 et seq.
[7]V. B. post, p. 346 et seq.
[8]Chapter XV.
[9]V. B. post, p. 377.
[10]V. V. post, p. 377.

of the Vestry were copied into the "New Record Book," which is the volume under review.

However that may be, the returns of the processioners embodied in the present volume embrace the returns, beginning with those made under the order of Vestry, September 17, 1759, and ending with those made under the order of January 8, 1784.

The processioning returns under the order of September 17, 1759, embraced the lands in the present counties of Lunenburg and Mecklenburg. Those, thereafter, were, of course, confined to the area of the present county of Lunenburg.

It is much to be regretted that the returns under the orders of 1747, 1751 and 1755 are not available, and it is hoped they may yet be discovered. They would throw much valuable light upon land owners, and neighbors in a wide expanse of country, in the early days of the County. Processioning precincts under some of these orders were expansive domains; for example, one of those described in the orders in 1751 embraced "All the lands on all the waters of Dan and Mayo rivers with their several branches as high as Augusta line."[11]

---

[11] V. B. post, p. 339.

CHAPTER VIII

The Decline

HE Anglican Church for about a century and a half from the settlement of Jamestown held undisputed, and practically exclusive sway in matters of religion in the Colony of Virginia; It not only held such sway in the realm of religion, and public worship, but, as we have seen, it performed functions of a civil and political character, or at the least semi-civil and semi-political in their nature.

This dominance was not to continue indefinitely; and it happened that the issues were being made up and the lines of conflict drawn at about the time Cumberland Parish was created, though in the early years of the parish there were probably none who would have ventured to prophesy the change that was to come within a third of a century.

It would be difficult, indeed impossible, reliably to ascertain the precise attitude of the rank and file of the populace toward the Established Church in the era in which it had an ecclesiastical monopoly in the country. Theoretically and presumptively all held to the doctrines and tenets of the Anglican Church without reservation or question. But that such was the real state of the case was, of course, not true. There were, doubtless, varying shades of opinions and widely diverse views, but these were held in private, or at least not widely expressed in public until the coming of the dissenters.

The British Government and the Anglican Church did all possible to prevent the colonies from being settled by any but those sound in the doctrine of that church. It was customary, at least for many years, for emigrants from Great Britain for Virginia before they could sail to be examined by ministers of the church who had to be satisfied concerning their "conformity to the orders and discipline of the Church of England," and moreover the emigrant had to take the oath of allegiance.

It is fair to assume that one desiring to leave England, but who was not exactly sound in the faith of the Church, of England, may have been somewhat evasive in answering the minister upon examination; and may have made some answers with reservations.

Undoubtedly it would be erroneous to assume that because there was no other church except the Established Church that it was enthusiastically supported by all the people. It would be beyond the scope of this treatment to attempt to enquire into how the Established Church came to be such. It suffices to say that at the time of which we write it was a firmly established governmental institution. It was as much a part of "the government" as the army and the navy. It was something the people, at the time, did not stop to enquire whether they liked or disliked. It was with them, and over them, whether they liked it or not.

In retrospect it is not difficult to discover facts which may have afforded reasons why some at least were not enthusiastic about the value of the function which the Colonial Church performed; that is to say, of the religious part of the function it performed.

The control of the churches in a parish was not necessarily in the hands of persons of deep religious convictions, fired with enthusiasm for the spread of religious dogmas. The control of the parishes was lodged in the vestries. The vestries were composed of men elected periodically by the freeholders and householders of the parish. About the only qualifications legally necessary for one to be eligible for election to the vestry was that he be a freeholder and be an adherent to the Church of England.

The Vestries were the taxing power, or at least a very important part of it, of the County. They supported the poor, suppressed vice, built and kept in repair the churches, bought, equipped and maintained the glebe, and employed the ministers. Such being the fact; it is but reasonable to suppose that the taxpayers selected the vestrymen quite as much for their business ability, and the soundness of their judgment in levying and expending taxes, as for their religious enthusiasm.

Doubtless these qualities united in some, but that they always did so is not to be assumed. Nor were members of the vestry always models of propriety, in their personal conduct. For example, John Hobson was for a number of years a member of the Vestry of Cumberland Parish, and yet he came under rather severe censure of a committee of the House of Burgesses, which considered a contested election case from Lunenburg County, and in its report said:

"Your committee cannot conclude this report without taking notice of the behavior of one John Hobson, which was very illegal and tumultuous, in offering to lay wagers the poll was closed when it was not; in proclaiming at the courthouse door the poll was going to be closed, and desiring the Freeholders to come in and vote, and then violently by striking and kicking of them preventing them from so doing, by which means Freeholders did not vote at the said election."[1]

Matthew Marrable, too, was a vestryman, but behaved in such manner in a canvas for the House of Burgesses that although elected he was denied his seat.[2]

It should be said, however, that when another election was ordered and held Mr. Marrable was again elected.

In considering the history of the Colonial Church, it seems to the writer that the economic side of the subject has not been adequately emphasized.

It is said that taxes are always unpopular; and if so it may happen that the cause of the taxes is likewise so. It was, in a sense, unfortunate for the Established Church that the taxes for its support bore so heavily upon the taxpayers of the community.

In the days of which we write, the Justices of the County Court served without pay. They held office for life and devoted much time and rendered invaluable service to the public. But no pecuniary benefit was attached to the office. The honor of the position and the distinction of the opportunity to serve the public were the only rewards the members of the court received.

No salary or compensation was attached to the office of Vestryman. The Clerk of the County received fees for specific

---

[1] *Journal, House of Burgesses* (March 8, 1759), 1758-61, 83-84; *The Old Free State*, I, 146.
[2] Id.

services rendered, most of these being collected from parties to litigations. The surveyor, in the early days one of the best paid officers of the Counties, was compensated by fees collected from persons to whom services were rendered. And so the record ran. There were few salaried officers; and in the counties or parishes the most expensive of these was that of the minister of the parish.

In one of the representative early years of the parish, when there were in it 2462 tithes, there were levied by the Vestry 54,164 pounds of tobacco, or twenty-two pounds per poll; and there were ordered paid out at one vestry meeting £33-11-6, and 42,785 pounds of tobacco, of which 30,293 pounds went to the church and its employees directly; to the minister, to readers, to church clerks and sextons. Eighteen thousand, five hundred and sixty pounds of the total went to the minister alone; while only 7,096 pounds of tobacco were needed for all other purposes coming within the jurisdiction of the Vestry, such as supporting paupers, burying the dead, etc., after excluding the deduction for insolvents and the fee of the collector.

When it is remembered that most all the taxpayers, at this time, were small land owners or tenant farmers, who lived largely under primitive, almost frontier conditions, and who themselves, or with little help except from members of the family, performed most of the labor in raising their crops, the burden of such taxes was by no means negligible.

While there were, here and there, plantations which boasted a residence or "mansion house" of some proportions, the vast majority of the freeholders lived in small houses, many of them constructed of logs and having but a few rooms.

The average domestic and plantation establishment made a sorry showing in contrast with such a place as, for example, the glebe plantation of the Reverend James Craig, the improvements upon which, built at public expense, are described in some detail in the vestry book, presented in this volume.

Such facts led some to feel that the material burdens of the church were disproportionately heavy compared with the spiritual benefits it conferred. The burdens were tangible and physical, —the tobacco had to be produced and delivered; the spiritual benefits were intangible,—and were not always discerned or appreciated.

And then, the Colonial Ministers were not always what they should have been.

The present historiographer of the Diocese of Virginia[3] thinks that the picture painted by Bishop Meade of the Colonial Clergy was a bit too dark; and that likewise the account of the present writer[4] who in substance accepted Bishop Meade's estimate, was too pessimistic. That is likely true. Probably a middle ground would be more nearly right, and the true view may be that the Colonial Clergy were not as bad, as a rule, as Bishop Meade represented them, nor yet as good as Mr. Brydon would like to believe they were.

But the situation in any view was bad enough. The writer has elsewhere pointed out that such parish ministers as Reverend James Craig and Reverend John Cameron were shining examples of men against whose personal character and mode of life there is not the breath of criticism. They can in no just way be included in the censure which falls upon such a large part of the Colonial Clergy.

That entirely too many of the ministers were remiss in their duties, and not greatly interested in the spiritual welfare of their parishioners does not, it seems, admit of doubt.

Bishop Meade declares: "It is a well-established fact that some who were discarded from the English Church yet obtained livings in Virginia," and the clergy themselves in seeking to have the House of Burgesses increase their salaries in their petition said: "that the small encouragement given to clergymen is a reason why so few come into this Colony from the Universities, and that so many who are a disgrace to the ministry find opportunities to fill the parishes."[5]

At one time the Colonial legislature enacted a law requiring the ministers "to preach constantly every Sabbath and administer the sacrament at least twice every year."[6] And Bishop

---
[3]Rev. G. MacLaren Brydon.
[4]In *The Old Free State*, Vol. I, Ch. IX.
[5]*Old Churches, Ministers, etc., of Virginia*, I, 16.
[6]Id., I, 15.

Meade does not hesitate, with little if any qualification, to speak of the Colonial Ministers as "the unworthy and hireling clergy of the Colony."[7] That they were such he attributed largely to the fact that there was in the colony no authority to administer "ecclesiastical discipline to correct or punish their irregularities and vices,"[8] for he declared: "The authority of a Commissary was a very insufficient substitute for the superintendence of a faithful Bishop."[9]

Not only was a law required to assure that the ministers would attend the churches and preach regularly, but a law also enjoined the attendance, at church, by the citizenry; and failure to observe this statutory provision might be punished by a fine, as a crime. In this particular matter the parishioners had the advantage of the ministers, for the law requiring church attendance gradually became a dead letter. There were few prosecutions under it, for juries would be slow to convict a person for absenting himself from a service, which only too many evaded attending; but if the minister did not attend and preach regularly, he might be disciplined for violating the law, or have his salary abated, in proportion to the sermons which he failed to preach.

As time passed, speaking of the situation as a whole, a condition gradually obtained in the Colony under which a widespread ecclesiastical establishment extended throughout the land; one maintained at great expense to the colonists, and yet it was as they believed, of little value to them spiritually. Many frankly regarded the establishment as a burden to be borne, rather than as an agency which helped them to bear their burdens.

Of the general state of things here briefly touched upon, Bishop Meade says:

"Such being the corrupt state of the Church in Virginia, it is not wonderful that here, as in England, disaffection should take place, and dissent begin."[10]

There will be no attempt here to trace the history of the rise of the dissenters. That is beyond the intended scope of this

---

[7] *Old Churches, Ministers, etc. of Virginia*, I, 16.
[8] Id.
[9] Id.
[10] *Old Churches, Ministers, etc., of Virginia*, I, 15.

work, and only such incidental reference to the broader history will be made as seems necessary to a correct understanding of the course of events in Cumberland Parish.

The Presbyterians, the Baptists, and the Methodists in the order named, made their advent in the Colony and challenged the Established Church to an accounting upon the religious condition of the people.[11]

The movement of dissent,—the history of the "dissenters" in Virginia has been recorded in greater or less detail by a large number of writers. Authors of almost every shade of religious opinion have had their say, and their accounts may be, to a degree, colored or tinted here and there according as the historian is an Episcopalian, a Presbyterian, a Baptist or a Methodist. There is an abundance of literature upon the subject.

Without attempting to review all or indeed any of these writings, the observation may be ventured, as the opinion of this writer, that they all overestimate or over-emphasize the doctrinal differences as the principal ground upon which rested the success of the movement of dissent.

Reverend Samuel Davies, who had such a highly creditable connection with the history of Presbyterianism, in Southside Virginia, especially in Prince Edward and Charlotte Counties, and contiguous areas, and who was afterwards President of Princeton College and to whom Bishop Meade accords the distinction of having "made the first serious inroads upon the unity of the [Episcopal] Church,"[12] recorded his view as follows:

"I have reason to hope that there are and have been a few names in various parts of the Colony who are sincerely seeking the Lord and groping after religion in the communion of the Church of England." And "Had the doctrines of the Gospel been solemnly and faithfully preached in the Established Church, I am persuaded there would have been few Dissenters in these parts of Virginia, for their first objections were not against the peculiar rites and ceremonies of that Church, much less against

---

[11]Some account of the history of the early churches of these denominations in the Lunenburg section is given by the author in his former work, *The Old Free State*, Vol. I, Ch. IX.

[12]*Old Churches, Ministers, etc., of Virginia*, I, 15.

her excellent Articles, but against the general strain of the doctrines delivered from the pulpit, in which these Articles were opposed, or (which was the more common case) not mentioned at all, so that at first they were not properly dissenters from the original constitution of the Church of England, but the most strict adherents to it, and only dissented from those who had forsaken it."[13]

But the dissenters who see in the particular doctrines and dogmas of their respective sects the reason why so many of the rank and file of the citizenry were ready to repudiate the Established Church overlook the economic side of the subject. The dissenters not only dissented from the doctrines of the Established Church but they "dissented" from the taxes which the maintenance of that institution made it necessary to impose.

Forms of doctrine and religious systems which dispensed with the levying of taxes made a powerful appeal to the poor and struggling denizens of a country hardly yet reclaimed, in many localities, from its primeval state. So when the early missionaries and itinerants of the Presbyterians, the Baptists and the Methodists came, with no worldly possessions, save those they could carry in a pair of saddle bags on horseback, with no assurance of support save the voluntary contributions of well wishers, with no glebes comfortably equipped as homes, but grateful for the meagre hospitality which could be afforded in the humblest cabins; and with a manner of preaching which did not assume to command or dictate, but urged and persuaded with the fiery enthusiasm of the crusader, it is scarcely a matter of wonder that many persons regarded them, rather than the parish ministers, as the successors of those of apostolic times, who at the direction of the Master went forth to preach provided with "neither gold, nor silver, nor brass in" their purses, who took no script for their journeys "neither two coats, neither shoes, nor yet staves," but who were accounted, each "worthy of his meat" and authorized to let "peace come upon" every worthy house, into which he entered.

It cannot be doubted that it was the fact that the ministrations

---

[13]*Old Churches, Ministers, etc., of Virginia*, I, 15-16.

of the dissenters were offered without the incubus of enforced taxation, rather than their respective doctrines on such subjects as predestination, fore-ordination, election, total depravity, saving by grace, close communion and trans-substantiation, that caused the colonists in such large numbers to align themselves with one or other of those groups as against the Established Church.

While that is undoubtedly true, yet it is also true, that many religious persons active in the Established Church, when there were no other religious organizations in which they might find a field for their labors, found their ideas of the Christian life, and their views of faith, doctrine and practice better interpreted by the dissenters. This fact is illustrated by the case of Reverend Samuel Harriss, who was for several years a reader in the Episcopal Church, but who with the coming of the dissenters, joined them, and became a prominent Baptist Minister.

The seeds of dissent were very definitely planted in the Lunenburg territory, when about 1738, while it was yet Brunswick, John Caldwell and his associates came to the section and located in what is now Charlotte County. From this settlement the doctrines of Presbyterianism spread into so many localities, through so many channels of influence that its extent and power would be impossible to measure or adequately appraise. A great rise in the progress of the dissenters, however, seems to have taken place beginning somewhere around the decade between 1750 and 1760, and thereafter their progress was great.

The revolt of the dissenters against the Established Church was a part, a phase, of the broader revolt that was in the making, of the Colony against the political and governmental domination of Great Britain. It was a part of the great Revolutionary movement which resulted in the war of Independence. And to that struggle Lunenburg County and Cumberland Parish lent no mean measure of support. They contributed such men as Samuel Harriss, Joseph and William Murphy, John Williams, Elijah Baker, John King, Henry Ogburn, and John Easter, to refer to but a few of the better known of the pioneers in the movement.

The rise of the dissenters measured the decline of the influence and prestige of the Established Church. And as the climax which resulted in the inauguration of the Revolutionary War approached the dissenters became strong enough and bold enough to deny the right of any Church to exist if compulsory support of it was necessary to its existence; and this demand was eventually enlarged into the proposition that the Church and the State should be wholly separated.

The Virginia General Assembly in 1776 considered the question of the dis-establishment of the English Church. The proposition, very naturally, excited great interest and precipitated much debate in the legislature. On November 19, 1776, the Assembly adopted a set of resolutions which practically settled the matter. The act as finally passed, pursuant to the decision reached in the resolutions, declared null and void all acts of Parliament "which render criminal the maintaining any opinions in matters of religion, forbearing to repair to church, or the exercising any mode of worship whatever." A part of the act recited the fact that there were in the Commonwealth great numbers of dissenters from the church established by law who have heretofore been taxed for its support; that such taxation to maintain a church which their consciences did not permit them to join is contrary to the principles of reason and justice, and exempted dissenters from all taxes and levies for the support of the Established Church, after January 1, 1777. This legislation while it exempted dissenters, continued to recognize an Established Church; but by another article of the act it suspended the levies for the Episcopal Ministers on the ground that in view of the exemption allowed dissenters it would be too burdensome, in some parishes, to levy the cost of the parish ministers upon those who were not dissenters. The Assembly enacted that "it is judged best that this should be done for the present by voluntary contributions."[14]

This act was a severe blow to the Anglican Church, for it ended the era of its history, as an establishment supported by

---

[14] *The Old Free State*, I, 349.

the public revenues. No taxes for religious purposes were ever paid in Virginia after January 1, 1777.[15]

A bitter controversy throughout the state, centering, of course, in the legislature, followed. The Episcopal Ministers and the Vestries vigorously denounced the innovation, and wherever able secured petitions to be sent to the legislature asking relief of one form or another. Some sought a return to the pre-revolutionary status. One of this character came from Mecklenburg County.[16] This was during Reverend John Cameron's ministry there, and he was doubtless instrumental in promoting the views it expressed; and very probably wrote it.

As has been stated, the act which exempted dissenters from supporting the Episcopal Church also suspended levies even against members of that church for the support of the parish ministers. This was a recognition of the fact that there were so few adherents, relatively, to that church that it would be "too burdensome" in some parishes at least to require them to pay the minister's salary. The Assembly decided that "for the present" the matter would be left to be taken care of by voluntary contributions. The enactment was phrased as it was, using the language "for the present," in recognition, doubtless, of the fact that a sentiment was growing for "a general assessment." In other words, the proposition embodied in that idea was that there should be a general and ratable assessment of all tax payers for the support of some mode of public worship; but leaving it optional with the tax payer as to what church or institution should receive his religious tax. The support of this idea was not confined to any group. Some Anglican ministers feeling that a half loaf was better than none, supported it; some dissenters supported it feeling that if the citizen had his choice as to what minister or church he would support, there was nothing oppressive or unreasonable in requiring him to pay a reasonable sum for the cause of religion.

Jefferson in his autobiography says that in the bill of 1776

---

[15]Eckenrode: *Separation of Church and State in Virginia*, 72; *The Old Free State*, I, 349.
[16]Journal: H. of D., May, 1777, 36.

there "was inserted an express reservation of the question, whether a general assessment should not be established by law, on every one, to the support of the pastor of his choice; or whether all should be left to voluntary contributions."[17]

A petition at this time, sent to the legislature from Lunenburg, and doubtless prepared and circulated under the supervision of Reverend James Craig who was minister of Cumberland Parish at the time, in caustic and bitter phrase charged the dissenters with fraud in getting up the great petition of 1776. It contained this sentence: "The undue means taken to overthrow the established church, by imposing upon the credulity of the vulgar, and engaging infants to sign petitions handed about [by] dissenters, have so far succeeded as to cause a dissolution of our usual mode of support."[18]

The question of a general assessment was not definitely settled for several years; during the interval it was debated at every session of the legislature; and was a lively topic of conversation wherever the subject of religion and the church was discussed.

One of the able papers presented to the General Assembly on the subject was a petition from Lunenburg received November 8th, 1783. It was in favor of a general assessment law,[19] and carried the signatures of many of the most prominent citizens of the county.

The legislative consideration of the subject is reviewed at some length, in the writer's former work,[20] and the way in which the members of the legislature from Lunenburg stood on the matter is mentioned. Anthony Street, though a member of the Vestry of Cumberland Parish for several years, and probably at that time, voted against the proposal.

Under the leadership of Patrick Henry in 1784 the advocates of a general assessment secured the adoption of a resolution by the House of Delegates favoring the proposition. Henry left the House, November 17, 1784, to become Governor of Virginia

---

[17] *Writings* (Memorial Asso.), I, 58.
[18] Journal: H. of D., 1777, 57; *The Old Free State*, I, 350.
[19] This petition with all the signatures to it, is printed in *The Old Free State*, I, 351-352.
[20] *The Old Free State*, I, Ch. IX.

a second time; and the matter of following up the resolution by a bill to enact a law on the subject went over until the next session. The matter being thus deferred, those opposing the assessment plan decided to direct against it a vigorous and hostile campaign of criticism. George Nicholas and George Mason persuaded Madison to undertake the leading opposition, and it thus resulted that he prepared the notable *Memorial and Remonstrance*, to which he gave the "full power of his mental strength," and produced a paper justly famous as an elaborate exposition of the relation of religion to the state.

This paper, really a petition, was widely circulated and signed throughout Virginia, and was "destined to draw forth such an expression of public opinion as the state had never seen before."[21]

Before the next Assembly met the Presbyterians formally went on record as opposing the Assessment Bill,[22] as did the Baptists.[23]

The Baptist General Association at Orange in September, 1785, adopted a remonstrance in which they took the ground that the civil power had no right to establish a religious tax, and in so doing grounded themselves upon the rock bottom of the fundamentals of the proposition.

As a result of these measures, sentiment was so clearly and overwhelmingly developed as against the assessment bill that it never was even brought up in the legislature.

Following the failure of the assessment bill to be brought up at the session of 1785, Jefferson's bill for the establishment of religious freedom was introduced on December 14th of that year. The bill as drawn by Jefferson was amended in committee and reported to the House[24] on December 16th, the House struck out the Committee substitute for the preamble by a vote of 66 to 38, and the bill passed the House 74 to 20 on December 17, 1785, Lunenburg voting for the bill. Owing to some differences as to phraseology which developed between the Senate and the House the bill was not finally passed until January 16, 1786.[25]

[21] Eckenrode: *Separation of Church and State in Virginia*, 106.
[22] Madison: *Works* II, 163.
[23] Semple: *History of Virginia Baptists*, 96.
[24] Journal: H. of D., 1785, 94.
[25] Journal: H. of D., 1785-6, 143.

This bill after a lengthy and noble preamble, enacts: "That no man shall be compelled to frequent or support any religious worship, place, or Ministry whatsoever, nor shall be enforced, restrained, molested, or burthened in his body or goods, nor shall otherwise suffer on account of his religious opinions or belief; but that all men shall be free to profess, and by argument to maintain, their opinions in matters of religion, and that the same shall in no wise diminish, enlarge, or affect their civil capacities.

"And though we well know that this Assembly elected by the people for the ordinary purposes of legislation only, have no power to restrain the Acts of succeeding Assemblies, constituted with powers equal to our own, and that therefore to declare this act to be irrevocable, would be of no effect in law; yet we are free to declare, and do declare, that the rights hereby asserted are of the natural rights of mankind, and that if any act shall be hereafter passed to repeal the present, or to narrow its operation, such Act will be an infringement of natural right."

Not only has this act never been repealed, but it has been followed in all free countries throughout the world.

During the period here under review, an act was once passed authorizing the incorporation of churches or religious bodies; but no sooner was it passed than it was justly and widely criticized "because it established an immediate, a dangerous and unwarrantable connection between the legislature and the Church"[26] and was repealed January 8, 1787.[27]

By the act exempting dissenters from supporting the Episcopal Church, and in fact withdrawing all compulsory support from it; by the defeat of the General Assessment bill; by the passage of the act for establishing religious freedom; by the repeal of the act incorporating the Episcopal Church, the complete separation of Church and State in Virginia was effected, and all denominations placed upon an equal footing respecting their legal and civil rights and privileges.

The period following the Revolution was not one in which any of the churches enjoyed a flourishing condition, but quite the contrary. Dr. William Hill said: "The demoralizing effects of

[26]Eckenrode: *Separation of Church and State in Virginia*, 124.
[27]Senate Journal, 1787, 92.

the war left religion and the church in a most deplorable condition. The Sabbath had been almost forgotten, and the public morals sadly deteriorated."[28] And another authority says: "The Anglican Church had nearly gone to wreck during the war; the few ministers who continued to serve existed precariously on the voluntary contributions of their diminished congregations. The Presbyterian ministers lived in the same way and their congregations were poor. The Baptists and the Methodists received little or no hire for preaching and eked out a living by following secular employments."[29]

Such conditions coupled with the facts above reviewed, with possibly some added factors, wrought a sad change in the fortunes of Cumberland Parish.

The statement of the parish levy embodied in the minutes of the vestry meeting held April 22, 1777, was the last to carry a levy for the minister's salary.[30]

For a time after this, the vestry seemed to be administering the poor fund; and the vestry records show that on November 21, 1782, the vestry levied for the year 9,488 pounds of tobacco, or four pounds of tobacco per tithe; which may be contrasted with 59,620 pounds or 22 pounds per tithe levied by the vestry in 1754.

In 1786 it appears that the total amount collected by the Vestry was thirteen pounds and fifteen shillings, and this was paid over to the overseers of the poor.[31]

At a meeting on August 11, 1786, the vestry acting upon a recommendation of the Convention of the Church held May 20th of that year, decided to lay off the parish into eleven districts, the vestrymen in each to "immediately apply to the inhabitants of his district to know who are members of the Protestant Episcopal Church and take a list of the same."[32]

In August, 1786, the Vestry resolved that each Vestryman would subscribe ten pounds of tobacco per tithe for the pay of

---

[28]Foote: *Sketches of Virginia* (1st Series), 412.
[29]Eckenrode: *Separation of Church and State in Virginia*, 75.
[30]V. B. post, p. 439.
[31]V. B. post, p. 459.
[32]V. B. post, p. 462.

the minister, and recommended that the other members of the Episcopal Church subscribe and pay the same.[33]

With the exception of the election on June 4, 1787, of a Vestry pursuant to an ordinance of the Convention of the "Protestant Episcopal Church held in the City of Richmond on the 16th day of May, 1787," the only business transacted by the Vestry that year was to repeat, on October 11, 1787, a request to the members in the eleven districts of the parish to subscribe and pay ten pounds of tobacco per tithe for "paying the minister, clerk and sextons of the Church in this parish," each Vestryman to "be at liberty to pursue the plan he thinks proper for collecting the said subscriptions."[34]

In 1788 two vestry meetings were held. The only business transacted at the first meeting was to ascertain the balances due on subscriptions, and to urge the vestrymen to collect them and "pay the same to . . . James Craig when collected."[35]

The record of the other meeting of that year consists of a single sentence, recording the election of Church Wardens.[36]

In 1789 the records of the vestry meetings are comprised in entries of a few lines, having to do with a suit against St. James Parish, filling vacancies in the vestry and appointing Church Wardens.

By 1790 matters had got to the point where Reverend Mr. Craig had decided to give up the parish entirely. Doubtless he would have had to do so some time before but for the fact that he was a man of affairs and of considerable property, a physician and a mill owner, in addition to being a minister.

The vestry met a single time in 1790,—on July 8th, and the whole record of the meeting is comprised in a single sentence wherein the vestry agree "to pay to the Reverend James Craig, sixty pounds for one year services provided he returns to his parish and preaches every Sunday."[37]

In 1791, the vestry seems to have determined to make an effort

---
[33] V. B. post, p. 463.
[34] V. B. post, pp. 465-66.
[35] V. B. post, p. 466.
[36] V. B. post, p. 467.
[37] V. B. post, p. 470.

to revive the fortunes of the parish. It met on July 14, 1791, and laid out the parish into eleven districts, and set forth the boundaries of each in detail on the minutes of the meeting, and assigned a vestryman to each district to take a new census of adherents to the Church and to "make the best collection he can in his district for the support of the said Church."[38]

In 1792, the minutes of the Vestry meeting held on April 23, seem to indicate that but seventeen pounds ten pence had been collected for the Reverend Mr. Craig[39] and it also appears that sixteen dollars were sent to Rev. John Buchanan for the general purposes of the church, and that the whole of it was paid by the vestrymen alone.[40]

Later on in the year the vestrymen seem to have made good the balance of the minister's salary.[41]

In 1793, several meetings were held, the whole of the proceedings being devoted to the subject of raising the minister's salary and fifteen dollars for the general purposes of the church.[42]

A single meeting of unimportant character was held in 1794,[43] and early the next year, 1795, Reverend Mr. Craig died.[44]

In December, 1795, the Vestry chose Reverend John Cameron to be the successor of Mr. Craig.[45]

In 1796 the vestry sought and obtained authority to sell a portion of the glebe, to repair the buildings on the glebe; and the sale was made.[46]

From this time forward until the record of the Vestry Book under review ends, the records of the vestry meetings are brief, and consist almost entirely of the record of elections of vestries, and of subscriptions by vestrymen "to be conformable to the doctrine, discipline and worship of the Protestant Episcopal Church."

---

[38]V. B. post, p. 472.
[39]V. B. post, p. 474.
[40]V. B. post, p. 475.
[41]V. B. post, pp. 476-77.
[42]V. B. post, pp. 478-79.
[43]V. B. post, p. 482.
[44]V. B. post, p. 482.
[45]V. B. post, p. 483.
[46]V. B. post, p. 486.

The Decline

During some years no meetings were held. This seems to have been true of the years 1798, 1803, 1804, 1805, 1808, 1809, 1810 and 1811.

The minutes of the meeting of May 11, 1815, contain the letter, mentioned elsewhere, from Dr. Cameron giving notice of his purpose to resign as minister during that year, but death instead of resignation ended the tenure of his office. He died some time between November 20th and December 14th, 1815.

On March 14, 1816, the vestry elected John S. Ravenscroft lay reader of the parish upon the recommendation of Bishop Moore[47] and on April 15, 1816, met and elected a new vestry.[48]

This was the final meeting as recorded in the Vestry Book under review, except, years later, on May 9, 1831, as appears on a page in the back of the volume, a few surviving members of an old vestry elected members to fill up the vacancies in membership of that body.[49]

---
[47] V. B. post, p. 498-99.
[48] V. B. post, p. 499-500.
[49] V. B. post, pp. 564-65.

CHAPTER IX

Reverend James Craig

EVEREND JAMES CRAIG was born in 1724. He was the son of Philip Craig, Gentleman, of Westminster, London.[1] He was a student at Westminster from 1738 to 1742, when he was elected Westminster Scholar at Christ Church, where he matriculated, June 17, 1742, at the age of eighteen. He was awarded the degree of Bachelor of Arts in 1746.[2]

On March 31, 1755, he was "Licensed for Virginia."[3]

No record of the precise date of his coming to Virginia has been found, but he doubtless came very soon after he was "Licensed for Virginia," for he received the King's Bounty[4] April 4, 1755; and yet if he did come over at that time it is somewhat strange that no record of any ministry by him prior to the year 1757 is known.

In 1757 Reverend John Barclay, the Parish Minister, decided to leave Cumberland Parish.

At a meeting of the Vestry held June 7, 1757, the following vestry-men were present: Thomas Hawkins, Lyddal Bacon, John Speed, Field Jefferson, Thomas Boulden and Clement Read. In the record of the proceedings on this occasion we find the following:

"Mr. Barclay intimating to this vestry that he intended soon to leave this parish & at the same time requesting the favour of this vestry to give a title to Mr. James Craig a student in Divinity & to recommend him to Rever^d & Honourable Mr. Com-

---

[1] Letter of October 31, 1927, from Dean H. J. White, of Christ Church, Oxford, England, to Mrs. Lillian W. Thixton, of Henderson, Kentucky, the original of which was furnished the writer by Mrs. Thixton. Dean White gave the facts ascertained from an examination of the records at Oxford.
[2] Id.
[3] Goodwin: *The Colonial Church in Virginia*, 261.
[4] The sum of twenty pounds given by successive Kings from 1690 onwards, to Ministers coming from England for service in Virginia.

missary Dawson as a person they are informed very well qualified to receive Holy Orders, into which he is desirous to enter; do unanimously agree to the above motion; and do hereby impower the Church Wardens to give a title & recommendation to Mr. Ja⁸. Craig upon his entering into Bond with proper securitys that he shall not by virtue of the Title insist upon being minister of this Parish if he shall not be found agreeable to the Gentlemen of the Vestry & Parishoners after Tryal."[5]

The record shows that Reverend John Barclay was present at this meeting of the Vestry; and the foregoing is, so far as has been observed, the first mention of Reverend James Craig, in Virginia.

What happened to Reverend Mr. Craig between that time and 1759 we do not know, nor indeed does it affirmatively appear where he was, whether in America, or not, at the time Reverend Mr. Barclay recommended him to the Vestry of Cumberland Parish.

It appears that at a meeting of the Vestry on December 5th, 1757,

"Upon a motion of the Revd. Mr. Jacob Townsend to serve this Parish as a minister it is ordered that he be received into the Parish for the space of three months."[6] And at a meeting of the Vestry on March 6, 1758, he was continued for an additional three months,[7] at the end of which time the Vestry, a new vestry, which, in the meantime had come into office, decided to follow up the action of the old vestry, respecting Reverend James Craig, and he was elected rector of the parish at a meeting of the vestry held May 22, 1759, when there were present: Daniel Claiborn, John Speed, Henry Blagrave, John Jennings, John Ragsdale, Thos. Pettis and Matt. Marrable.

A part of the record of this meeting reads as follows:

---

[5] Vestry Book post, p. 356.

[6] V. B. post, p. 358. Reverend Jacob Townsend has been practically overlooked by the historians of the Episcopal Church. Neither Bishop Meade nor Dr. Goodwin mention his services in Cumberland Parish. In fact his name does not even appear in Bishop Meade's two volumes; and the only mention of him in *The Colonial Church in Virginia* is as follows: "Townsend, Jacob: In Virginia, without a cure, in 1754. (Perry.)"

[7] V. B. post, p. 361.

"Upon a Motion made by Matt: Marrable Gent: a Member of this vestry that the Reverend Mr. James Craig now offers and is willing to undertake for this Parish, the office of a Minister, Recommending him in his opinion to be highly deserving of the same, & further that he thinks the said Reverd. James Craig from an order of the old vestry is justly Intitled to the same—whereupon the said vestry took the same into their consideration, & came to the following Resolution:

"Resolved that it is the unanimous opinion of this Vestry that the said Reverd. James Craig ought and is hereby chosen, Elected, Constituted & appointed Rector, and Minister of this Parish, and that his time shall begin and commence Immediately from and after the date hereof."[8]

It appears that his salary in 1759 was sixteen thousand pounds of tobacco, plus an allowance for cask and shrinkage of one thousand nine hundred pounds making nineteen thousand, nine hundred pounds in all.[9] And it appears, too, that he was made an allowance, by the Vestry, at the meeting at which he was elected, of twenty-five pounds, current money of Virginia, for board for one year.[10]

The records show that he attended vestry meetings with regularity from the time he was elected rector in 1759 until August 10, 1761. He was not present at the meetings held on October 30, 1761, January 23, 1762, and on May 20, 1762.[11] There may be no significance in these facts, but on this last named date the entire proceedings of the Vestry on that occasion were recorded as follows:

"Whereas Mr. Deverix Jarratte[12] a candidate for Holy Orders, applied to Vestry for a title to this Parish, and whereas our present incumbent intends to leave us, and we are of opinion, that he the said Mr. Deverix Jarratte is qualified in point of virtue and piety for that sacred office, it is therefore,

Ordered, that the Church Wardens give a title and recom-

---

[8]V. B. post, p. 364 et seq.
[9]V. B. post, p. 371.
[10]Id. post, p. 365.
[11]V. B. post, pp. 380, 382, 383.
[12]Should be Devereux Jarratt, of course.

mendation to Mr. Deverix Jarratte, upon his giving Bond and Security [that] he shall not, by virtue of the title insist upon being Minister of the Parish [if] he shall not be found agreeable to the Church Wardens & Vestry and Parishioners after trial."[13]

Doubtless a controversy of some character arose between Rev. James Craig and the Vestry, which led him to contemplate leaving the parish; and it was, as this writer believes, in all probability over the purchase of a glebe and the building of the Glebe House, that the disagreement arose.

On August 10, 1761, David Garland reported for those appointed to select a property for a glebe that the plantation of Mr. John Ragsdale was more suitable to Mr. Craig and for the purposes of the parish than any other, and the Vestry agreed to pay him two hundred and fifty pounds therefor. Mr. Craig agreed "to accept of the buildings that are there when properly finished with the addition of a gleeb house & a garden & yard made compleat."[14]

At the same time it was ordered that a "Gleeb House" and garden and yard be built and that David Garland and Lyddal Bacon let the same. The dimensions of the house, and the specifications for the building were set out, and the order provided that the letting be made on Thursday, October 1, 1761.

A meeting of the Vestry was held October 30, 1761, but the minutes contain no reference to the building of the glebe house; there was no mention of any report by David Garland or Lyddal Bacon as to the execution of the order for letting the building. Reverend James Craig did not attend this meeting of the Vestry. The next meeting of the Vestry was held January 23, 1762,[15] at which time an entry was made releasing John Ragsdale from his agreement to sell his land, and ordering that the vestry meet "as soon as convenient and fix upon another place for a Gleebe."

At the next meeting of the Vestry, May 20, 1762, as above stated, Reverend James Craig notified the vestry of his purpose

---
[13] V. B. post, p. 383.
[14] V. B. post, p. 380.
[15] V. B. post, p. 382.

to leave the parish, and Mr. Devereux Jarratt applied "for a title" to the parish.

But Mr. Jarratt did not come to the parish, nor, it seems, did Mr. Craig leave. Just what course the matter took does not appear. Pages 66 and 67 of the vestry book are missing and page 68 is blank. The lost pages might have thrown some light on the subject, but this is, of course, a surmise.

It seems Mr. Ragsdale changed his mind again, and decided to let the vestry have his land, and presumably Mr. Jarratt withdrew in favor of Mr. Craig, for at a meeting of the Vestry June 4, 1762, the record reads:

"The Rever^d. Mr. James Craig by his consent and the unanimous consent of this vestry is received into this Parish as Rector of the same.

"Ordered that the Rev^d. Mr. James Craig be allowed forty pounds per annum for his Board till the Gleebe is completed.

"Ordered the Gleebe Buildings be Lett according to an order of Vestry made August 10th, 1761."[16]

At a later meeting, August 21, 1762, some changes were made in the plans for the Glebe House, mutually satisfactory to the Vestry and to Mr. Craig.

From this time forward Reverend James Craig attended the meetings of the Vestry with great regularity up to February, 1780. In that year the records show that he was present at a meeting held February 10,[17] but at the meetings on July 13, August 10, and November 16th, it does not appear that he was present. There was but a single meeting of the vestry in 1781. It was held on December 13, and he was not mentioned as present. Considering the condition of the country, at the time, the events of the Revolutionary War then in progress, and that Virginia was becoming more and more the theatre of military operations, there is probably no significance in the circumstance of his absence from the Vestry meetings. He was probably engaged in important work which kept him away, as his mill on Flat Rock Creek was a sort of commissary depot, for provisions for the military forces.

---

[16] V. B. post, p. 383.
[17] V. B. post, p. 442.

The Vestry met twice in 1782, but he is not recorded as present at a meeting until that of May 17, 1783, when he is not only recorded as present, but along with the Church Wardens signed the minutes.[18]

Thereafter until his death Reverend Mr. Craig attended the vestry meetings with fair regularity.

It is said that he officiated for churches in Halifax County, but the circumstances under which this was done are not clear. Dr. Goodwin says briefly that he officiated "in Halifax County for several years."[19] This statement appears to be based upon a letter written by Reverend Mr. Dresser in 1830[20] wherein speaking of a certain period ending in 1787 he said: "The Rev. James Craig, of Cumberland Parish, Lunenburg, ... officiated a part of the time in this County[21] during three or four of the last years,—a gentleman highly esteemed both as a man and a preacher."

This statement taken in conjunction with the extant Vestry records of Cumberland Parish seem to make it clear that such service as he performed in Halifax County was temporary and transient, and as a guest or visiting minister.

The last meeting of the Vestry of Cumberland Parish at which he is recorded as present was that held July 27, 1793, at Reedy Creek Church, when along with Henry Stokes he signed the minutes of the meeting.[22]

There was a single meeting of the Vestry in 1794; it was held April 2nd. Reverend James Craig was not present. He was probably unable to attend, and was approaching the end of his earthly sojourn. The Vestrymen were ordered to pay the money they had collected "to James Buford for the Reverend James Craig."[23] And the next meeting of the Vestry, that of May 15th, 1795, records his death by ordering "that the Church Wardens of this Parish do advertise for a minister to supply the

---

[18] V. B. post, p. 449.
[19] *The Colonial Church in Virginia*, 261.
[20] Meade: *Old Churches and Families of Virginia*, II, 10.
[21] Halifax.
[22] V. B. post, p. 481.
[23] V. B. post, p. 482.

vacancy in this parish occasioned by the death of the Reverend James Craig."[24]

His successor was not chosen until December 23, 1795, when Reverend Dr. John Cameron was elected "Rector and Minister" of the parish.

Reverend James Craig was not only a parish minister, he was a substantial man of affairs of his community. In 1764 the list of tithes taken by Thomas Tabb listed him for six tithes and as the owner of three hundred and eighty acres of land. Two of these tithes were John Byng and Edward Bullock, probably indentured servants, and at least three of his tithes were slaves. In 1772 he was listed with fifteen tithes, and "a Riding Chair," the ownership of which indicated, in those days, a measure of affluence. Apparently at this time he owned thirteen slaves. In 1775 he was listed with nineteen tithes, while in 1783 the tax records show that he owned forty slaves and was listed with eleven white tithes and a riding chair besides.[25]

He owned a mill on Flat Rock Creek, near the present town of Kenbridge, known in the decades after the Civil War as Bagley's Mill. There is a tradition among his descendants that his mill was a cloth manufacturing establishment as well as a grist mill, but upon what authority the statement rests is not known.

Reverend James Craig's experience with Tarleton, is a well known incident of the Revolution.

On July 9, 1781, Colonel Banestre Tarleton left Cobham on one of his destructive raids "with orders to ravage the country as far as New London, in Bedford County; to destroy a depot of supplies supposed to be at Prince Edward Court House, to intercept any British prisoners or American light troops, returning to the northward from Greene's army; and then to retire at his leisure to Suffolk."[26] In making this raid Tarleton's expedition travelled four hundred miles, and was engaged in it fifteen days.[27]

One of Tarleton's acts as he passed through Lunenburg on his

---

[24] V. B. post, p. 482.
[25] The records subsequent to 1783 have not been examined for such data.
[26] *The Old Free State*, I, 252; Carrington: *Battles of the Revolution*, 610.
[27] Id.

westward[28] march was to destroy Reverend James Craig's mill and the provisions depot there maintained.

Bishop Meade gives an account of the happening[29] and Howe[30] also has an account of it. The accounts do not agree in all particulars; the discrepancies, which are not important, are noticed by the author in his former work.[31] Tarleton, it seems, required the old parson to "off with his coat and assist in slaughtering his pigs for their use." He carried off too, all of the parson's slaves, but all except one, as soon as they could give Tarleton the slip returned home.

Reverend James Craig was one of the citizens of the County required by Tarleton to take a parole "not to take arms, be of counsel, or commit any other act that might militate against the success of the British Arms."

This parole of Reverend James Craig was the subject of the following communication to the Governor of the State:

"To his Excellency Thomas Nelson Esquire, Governor, or Chief Magistrate of the State of Virginia, and the Honorable the members of the Privy Council of the same:"

"The petition of the inhabitents of Lunenburg County humbly sheweth, That in a late excursion of Col. Tarleton's Legion through this county, many citizens were greatly injured in their property; and compelled (in order to obtain their personal liberty) to sign such paroles as their captors thought proper to dictate. We know these paroles, by Law, are not binding on peaceable citizens, thus taken from their own homes: But your Petitioners beg leave to represent to your Excellency and your Honors, the peculiar case of the Reverend James Craig, rector of Cumberland Parish in this county; a person eminently distinguished for his zeal & attachment to the cause of American Liberty; a rule of conduct adopted in the very earliest period and pertinaciously persisted in, through every vicissitude of the present contest; no less esteemed for his charity, devotion and exemplary piety in his public character, than respectable for his

---

[28]David Garland to Governor Nelson, *The Old Free State*, I, 253; *Calendar of Virginia State Papers*, II, 240-41.
[29]*Old Churches and Families of Virginia*, I, 484-5.
[30]*Virginia, Its History and Antiquities*, 359.
[31]*The Old Free State*, I, 254-55.

virtues in private life, equally alert in engaging in every scheme for the welfare of his country and the success of its arms; and successful in removing dangerous prejudices from the minds of the people, by drawing the proper line, and pointing out the true distinctions between resistance of Lawless power and Rebellion. This Gentleman, after seeing the cruel vengeance of the enemy, in the destruction of a very great part of his property, and himself treated with indignity and insult, tho' in a very low and precarious state of health; was detained as a prisoner until he subscribed an engagement not to take arms, be of council, or commit any other act that might militate against the success of the British Arms,' and all this under a pretence, that in addition to his other crimes, he had at that time a Public Magazine at his house.

Your Petitioners consider it as a public misfortune to be deprived of the ministerial office which has been exercised by Mr. Craig, since the declaration of independency, for a very small and precarious reward, no way adequate to the trouble & fatigue attending it, but which he can now no longer execute in the manner directed by Congress, without exposing himself to dangers, from which his country, in its present vulnerable state, cannot protect him.

Your petitioners therefore pray that the Executive will consider how far Mr. Craig is bound by these engagements; and as far as may be consistent with the Constitution and the Articles of War, endeavor to have him exchanged — And your Petitioners, as in duty bound will ever pray &c.

12th Aug. 1781.

D. Stokes, Jnr. Colo.,
J. Garland, Magistrate,
James Johnson, Magistrate,
John Cureton,
   Commissioner, Tax,
John Bowers,
W. Hayes [?], Capt.U.S. S.[?]
Ellick Moore,
Moses Hurt,

Danl. Dejarnott,
W. Glenn, 2d Lieut. [?]
Benj. Edmundson,
R. Hayes,
John Hammock,
Robert Chappell,
Ed'd Brodnax, L. Collo.
Joshua Ragsdale, Capt.
Wm. Taylor,

Reverend James Craig   107

John Ballard, Jr., Magistrate,
John Robunson [Robinson?]
Thos. Williams,
Alexander Rudder, Junr.,
John Ragsdal,
Chas. Cross,
John Hardie, Senr.,
David Moor,
Thos. Lewis,
George Hightower,
Jno. Mallory,
John Cross,
Thos. Jones,
Benj. Tomlinson,
Jo. Knight,
John Booker,
Peter Andrus,
Thos. Hayse,
William Coopper,
John Lucas,
Fred. Andrus,
Henry Gill,
Robt. Floyd,
John Allen,
Daniel Williams,
Jas. Beuford, Senr.,
James Buford,
Abraham Cocke,
John Hix,
Will. Stone,
William Gordan,
Stephen Wood,
Elisha Estes,
Jas. Murrell,
Thos. Dozier,
Baxter Poole,
John Pool,
Curtis Cates,
John Ussery,
Jeremiah Burnett,
David Walker,
Jeremiah Morgn [Morgan?]
Henry Gee,
Saml. Rudder,
John Connell,
Sakamus [?] Morgan,
James Amoss,
Abraham Anders,
Jno. Moody,
John Bailey,
David Vandyke,
Young Bowers,
Thos. Andrus,
Harris Tomlinson,
Sanford Bowers,
Henry VanDyck,
Lowry Baker [Baxter?],
Henry Young,
William Gill,
Wm. Tisdale,
Sam. Harris,
LeRoy Buford,
Thomas Leveritt,
Will. Love,
J. Buzendine,
William Tucker, Jr.,
Jas. Cates,
William Tucker,
William Dozier,
David Abernathy,
Martin Elliott,
Michail Johnson,
David Garland, late Colo.,
William Johnson,
Henery Hayes,
Rob. Brown,

Covington Hardy, David Thomson,
John Calnel [?], Wm. Ragsdale,
Nathaniel Laffoon, Jon. Ruddy.

This paper is printed in the *Calendar of Virginia State Papers*[32] and as it there appears was reproduced in *The Old Free State*,[33] but the names of only seven or eight of the signers of the petition are given in the *Calendar*. The list in full of the signers of the petition, so far as is known, appears here, in print, for the first time.

Rev. James Craig's experiences with Tarleton, and this petition addressed to the Governor of Virginia in his behalf, and so numerously signed by citizens of the County fully attest his devotion, and the value of his services to the cause of the Colonies in the Revolutionary War.

One of his sons was a soldier of the war of 1812. This was George Craig who served as a First Lieutenant in the 1st Battalion and 73rd Regiment, in which Captain Lewis L. Taylor was a Captain, and of which Lieutenant Colonel Waddy Street was the Commanding Officer.[34]

A grandson, Major Edward Chambers Craig, and a great-grandson, Captain George C. Orgain,[35] and several other descendants served in the armies of the Confederate States of America.

A muster roll of Captain Orgain's Company, and mention of the date of its enlistment are given in *The Old Free State*.[36] But, so far as is known to this writer, no account of Major Edward Chambers Craig has ever been printed. He was born in Lunenburg County, Virginia, and, as is shown in the genealogy herewith presented, was the son of George Craig (1774-1828), and Ann Walthall Chambers, daughter of Edward Chambers and Martha Cousins. He married Ann Park Jones, daughter of Edward Montfort Jones and his wife Mary Ann Street of Lunenburg County.

---

[32]Vol. II, 323-4.
[33]I, 255-256.
[34]Lt. George Craig qualified June 11, 1812—*The Old Free State*, I, 282. He was a Justice of the County Court, 1816-1821—*The Old Free State*, 328.
[35]Otherwise Judge George C. Orgain, for many years Judge of the County Court of Lunenburg County. See *The Old Free State*, I, 342.
[36]Vol. I, Chapter XIII.

After his marriage he settled in Chesterfield County, Virginia, not far from Petersburg. His home was known as *Rosewood*. The house stood not very far from the railroad, and faced the little station, Walthall Junction.

Major Craig, as he was known, was a brother-in-law of John James Jones, who at the outbreak of the war resigned from the United States Navy. He and Mr. Jones and Captain Archer Dunn, who lived on a place adjoining *Rosewood*, served the Confederacy in the Quartermaster Department and were stationed at Petersburg. Major Craig had a son Waddy Street Craig, who, at the outbreak of the war was attending school in Lunenburg County. He too joined the Confederate forces and is said to have enlisted as a "sergeant with pay and rations under his father," although only fifteen at the time.

Two other sons of Major Craig were Confederate soldiers. These were John Anthony Craig and George Edward Craig.

George Edward Craig was a member of Company "D" of Virginia Volunteers, was wounded and captured at Drury's Bluff, and was confined, as a prisoner of war, in Fortress Monroe, where he remained for three months after the end of the war, before he would swear allegiance to what he termed a "Yankee lie."

John Anthony Craig was a member of Company "F" of Virginia Volunteers. He served under "Stonewall" Jackson, and ministered to him in his last moments, by providing his overcoat upon which Jackson reposed after he was fatally wounded. At a later time, after being transferred to another Company, John Anthony Craig served under General John B. Gordon, and became his secretary, serving in that capacity until the end of the war.[37]

The Craig home *Rosewood* saw some of the horrors of war, during General Benjamin F. Butler's attempt to take Petersburg. When it became apparent that the place was in the area where active military operations would soon be in progress, Major Craig, who was then in Petersburg, barely had time to reach his home and bring his family to safety. They were sent to Lunen-

---

[37]This information is furnished by Mrs. Harry E. Thixton, of Henderson, Kentucky.

burg, where they remained as refugees until the end of the war. A faithful old slave "Mammy Tina," insisted upon staying and trying to take care of things, and because of this and the difficulty, if not impossibility of removing her on account of her age and infirmities, she remained at *Rosewood,* when the others left.

The Confederates were entirely unprepared to oppose Butler's advance. The story of that military episode is beyond the scope of this sketch.[38]

Butler had a force in excess of thirty thousand men, the Confederates but nine hundred, in the beginning, and never more than a tithe of Butler's numbers, and why under the circumstances Petersburg was not instantly captured is really inexplicable, except upon the theory that Butler was ignorant of the forces opposed to him, and was afraid to attack.

When Butler landed his forces at City Point and along the neighboring shores of the Appomattox and the James, *Rosewood* was in the line of his approach, and the residence suffered from cannon fire, a ball having rent the roof and ceiling.

As Butler prepared to advance upon Petersburg, the only course open to the Confederates was to endeavor to delay the progress of the enemy until re-enforcements could arrive. It was imperative that the pitiful meagreness of numbers be concealed. The defensive operations, therefore, began by running trains up and down the railroad through the cut in front of the Craig home, "puffing and whistling and screaming and camouflaging with fine effect." A breast work hastily improvised from a division rail fence helped to make difficult an accurate estimate of the Confederate strength.[39]

Young Waddy Street Craig, in his curiosity to see what was going on, with others ventured so close to the active theatre of operations, near the Craig home, that he was knocked down by an exploding shell, and so covered with dirt that he was almost unrecognizable. Sacred almost to death, he was glad to mount

---

[38]It is well told in several sources, for example, in *War Talks of Confederate Veterans* (Bernard), 107 et seq.

[39]This account is condensed from one furnished by Mrs. Harry E. Thixton, based largely upon the personal observations of young Waddy Street Craig, who saw much of the operations, and who personally related them to Mrs. Thixton.

a horse, behind his uncle, John James Jones, and be taken back to Petersburg for the night.

The Confederates eventually gave ground and fell back to Swift's Creek, but like that "little band that stood in the Thermopylae, at Rives' farm" they stubbornly resisted Butler, and delayed his progress for a day. When a few re-enforcements arrived, although in no way comparable to Butler's numbers, he decided to retreat.

In these operations the Craig place was alternately in possession of the Northern and the Confederate forces, respectively. All the buildings on the place were destroyed except the residence; it doubtless would have been burned, also, but for its utility as headquarters. The family hurriedly left in a panic as they were completing breakfast. With the exception of a few pieces of tableware picked up as they left, the contents of the house remained to the tender mercies of as reprehensible a character as ever sullied a uniform.

The family portraits on the walls were slashed with swords and ruined; and "Mammy" Tina bore testimony that Butler had the silver, and even some of the valuable china packed in barrels and sent away. It is a possibility that the invaluable parish records kept by Reverend James Craig were here destroyed or stolen.

It is an interesting speculation that Butler's greed to secure such loot, and the delay incident to so doing, may have saved Petersburg; for all authorities seem to indicate that if he had pressed his advance, or rather if he had not, apparently, delayed his advance, Petersburg would inevitably have fallen into his hands.

The Craig house was used as a field hospital, and as Butler found it inconvenient to ship away the piano, it was used as an operating table. After the repulse of Butler's forces young Waddy Street Craig went back to the home with a horse cart to salvage such things as might remain. In addition to a few household articles of little value, which were left by the soldiers, he secured a number of pairs of good boots from the legs of Northern soldiers, which had been cut off on the piano as an operating table and tossed through the window, out into the rose garden.

At the end of the war the father, the three soldier sons, and the others of the refugee family foregathered around a shattered home. The ravages of war had done their worst. The plantation was stripped, all the buildings save one burned down; and that one dismantled and well-nigh wrecked. Fences and improvements had been destroyed, stock and cattle were gone; all movable property was missing.

A struggle against odds during a period of four years of the "Reconstruction" era which followed the war, coupled with the burden entailed by the payment of security debts, led to the conclusion that the wise thing to do was to wind up affairs in war scarred Virginia and go to a less oppressed and more promising section.

Major Craig removed with his family to Henderson, Kentucky, and resided there the remainder of his life. He died February 19, 1894; and his wife followed him August 25, 1897. They and their son John Anthony Craig are buried in Fernwood Cemetery at Henderson.

This sketch of Reverend James Craig seems an appropriate place in which to mention some of the family connections of the Craigs and to set down such a genealogy of his descendants as available information makes possible.

Reverend James Craig married (M. B. Mecklenburg Co., Va., dated, Feb. 19, 1766), Mary Booker Tarry (b. circa 1744, d. 1798), daughter of Samuel Tarry and his wife Mary Booker.

The earliest of the Booker line of Reverend James Craig's wife, in the present state of investigation, definitely known in Virginia, was:

Richard[1] Booker of Gloucester County, Virginia, whose first wife was named Rebecca. Doubtless her name was Rebecca Leake.[40]

They had issue:
    Edmund[2] Booker,
    Judith[2] Booker,

---

[40]In the York County records, in 1672, there is mention of John Leake, innkeeper, "father-in-law" of Richard Booker, of Gloucester County.

Edward² Booker, baptized June 2, 1680,
Richard² Booker (probably died young),
Ann² Booker,
Richard² Booker, baptized Oct. 29, 1688,
John² Booker, baptized August 3, 1690.

Richard¹ Booker married, a second time, Hannah Hand, (widow of Captain William Marshall, who was killed in 1692), and had:

Frances² Booker, who married a Mr. Stokes, and moved to Amelia County, Virginia, where her will, dated Nov. 1, 1751, was recorded December 28, 1752.

George² Booker.

Edward² Booker (bap. June 2, 1680, d. circa 1750), son of Richard¹ Booker and his wife Rebecca, married 1st, Mary (last name not known), and 2nd, Judith Archer, widow of John Worsham. He was Colonel Edward Booker, and was a member of the House of Burgesses,[41] from Amelia County from 1736 to 1747.

Samuel Tarry and Richard Clark are mentioned as his executors—"executors of Edw. Booker deceased" 1750.[42]

Edward² Booker and Mary his first wife had:

1. Richard³ Booker (d. 1760), married Morot, and had:
   (1) Edward⁴ Booker, (will in Halifax County, Va.) m. Henrica (last name not known), and had:
      (a) Elizabeth⁵ Booker,
      (b) Rebecca⁵ Booker,
      (c) Richard⁵ Booker, who married, October 6, 1788, Anne Moore.
   (2) Richard Morot⁴ Booker who married, 1770, Elizabeth Palmer, daughter of John Palmer.
   (3) Parham⁴ Booker (will in Halifax County, Va. 1786), married Frances Martin, and had:
      (a) Susannah⁵ Booker,

---

[41]*Colonial Virginia Register,* 108 (1736-1740); 110; 1744, p. 116; 1745, p. 117; 1747, p. 120.
[42]William and Mary College Quarterly, Hist. Mag. VII, p. 49.

(b) Richard[5] Booker,
(c) James[5] Booker.
   (4) John[4] Booker,
   (5) Wm. Marshall[4] Booker.
2. Rebecca[3] Booker, who married (Amelia Co. M. B. Sept. 27, 1735), Thomas Tabb of Amelia County, Virginia.
3. Mary[3] Booker (b. Nov. 3, 1711, d. 1756), married Samuel Tarry (d. Sept. 30, 1761), who, it is said, immigrated from the Isle of Man in 1720. He was one of the "Gentlemen Justices" of the County Court of Amelia County; and in 1735 was Sheriff of the County.

After the death of Mary Booker, Samuel Tarry is said to have married a Miss Crawley, or Cralle.

By his first marriage Samuel Tarry had:
   (1) George[4] Tarry (b. June 12, 1740, d. 1814), of "Ivy Hill," Mecklenburg County, Virginia, who married (M. B. Mecklenburg Co., Va., Dec. 7, 1790), Sarah Taylor, and had:
      (a) Edward[5] Tarry (b. Dec. 2, 1791, d. April 29, 1862), who married in 1821, Lucy Davis Little.
      (b) William Taylor[5] Tarry (b. April 10, 1794, d. 1807—drowned at Lewisburg, N. C.)
      (c) Samuel[5] Tarry (b. Nov. 19, 1795), of "Wildwood," Mecklenburg County, Virginia. Never married.
      (d) George[5] Tarry (b. Jan. 26, 1801, d. Feb. 16, 1884), married May 3, 1832, Mary E. Hamilton, daughter of Patrick Hamilton, of "Burnside," Granville County, N. C.
   (2) Edward[4] Tarry (never married).
   (3) Mary Booker[4] Tarry (b. 1744, d. 1797, inventory of estate in Lunenburg County, 1798), married (M. B. Feb. 19, 1766), Reverend James Craig, Rector of Cumberland Parish, Lunenburg County, Virginia.
   (4) Rebecca[4] Tarry, married Chilton Masters. They had no children.

By his second wife Samuel Tarry had:

(5) Gracy[4] Tarry, who married Gideon Flournoy of Chesterfield County, Virginia,
(6) Virginia[4] Tarry and
(7) Thomas[4] Tarry.

Edward[2] Booker and his 2nd wife Judith Archer, had:

4. Edward[3] Booker (d. 1760), who married (M. B. in Amelia County, Feb. 21, 1739), Anne Cobbs, and had:

   (1) Edward[4] Booker, Captain Amelia Militia, 1776; Lt. Col., 1780.
   (2) Kitty[4] Booker.
   (3) Statira[4] Booker, who married, M. B. in Amelia County, Oct. 27, 1782 (?), Samuel Baskerville.
   (4) Mary Marshall Parham[4] Booker, who married (M. B. in Amelia County, Apr. 18, 1767), James Henderson.

5. Judith[3] Booker.

It should be noted, in order to avoid any misunderstanding, that no effort is here made to trace the descendants of the children of Richard[1] Booker and his wife Rebecca, except those of their son Edward[2] Booker.

The foregoing, while not confined entirely to that point, has been presented mainly to give the ancestry of Mary Booker[4] Tarry (b. 1744, d. 1797), who married (M. B. Mecklenburg Co. dated Feb. 19, 1766) Reverend James Craig, and for convenience the numbering foregoing of the generations is continued.

It is much to be regretted that a fuller genealogy of their descendants cannot be incorporated herein. As to some of the children, the writer has been unable, although considerable inquiry has been made, to learn anything of their descendants, if any there be at the present time. What information it has been possible to assemble is here given. It is hoped it may be enlarged and supplemented from sources unknown to the writer, when his inquiries were made.

Reverend James Craig and his wife Mary Booker[4] Tarry had:
1. James[5] Craig. Nothing is known of his history. He is men-

tioned in his father's will which was dated November 3, 1789, and probated September 10, 1795.[43]

2. George[5] Craig (b. 1774, d. 1828). He was a member of the House of Delegates from Lunenburg County, 1811-1812;[44] was a Lieutenant in the war of 1812, and was a Justice of the County Court of Lunenburg County, from 1816 to 1821.[45] He married July 11, 1805, Ann Walthall Chambers (b. Dec. 18, 1786, d. 1874). She was a daughter of Edward Chambers (b. March 20, 1754, d. Feb. 16, 1828), and his wife Martha Cousins (b. October 15, 1764, d. Oct. 27, 1810).[46]

George[5] Craig and Ann Walthall Chambers had:

(1) Mary Tarry[6] Craig (b. Oct. 3, 1806, d. Apr. 7, 1816).
(2) Martha Cousins[6] Craig (b. Dec. 8, 1808).
(3) Edward Chambers[6] Craig (b. Oct. 20, 1817, in Lunenburg County, Virginia, d. Feb. 19, 1894, in Henderson, Kentucky). Married, January 4, 1837, Ann Parke Jones (b. Oct. 27, 1821, d. Aug. 25, 1897), daughter of Edward Montfort Jones and Mary Ann Street,[47] and had:

(a) John Anthony[7] Craig (b. 1843, d. unmarried 1901). He joined the Confederate Army at eighteen, and among other of his services was secretary to General John B. Gordon.
(b) George Edward[7] Craig (b. 1845), entered the Confederate Army at 16; wounded at Gettysburg; taken prisoner, and remained in prison until about three

---

[43]And is of record in Lunenburg County, Virginia, in Will Book 4, pages 98-100.
[44]*The Old Free State*, II, 72.
[45]Id., I, 328.
[46]The other children of Edward Chambers and Martha Cousins were: Eliza Chambers (b. Aug. 18, 1784), who married November 29, 1803, Robert Scott; Robert Chambers (b. Feb. 5, 1789, d. unmarried, Nov. 7, 1810); Thomas Chambers (b. Oct. 19, 1792), who married Oct. 15, 1815, Petronella Logan; Henry Chambers (b. Oct. 1, 1790, d. Jan. 6, 1826), United States Senator from Alabama, died while en route from Alabama to Washington, at his old home, and is buried in the yard of the old Chambers place—the Dr. Robert S. Bagley place—where a monument to him stands; Edward R. Chambers (b. May 23, 1795, d. March 20, 1872), who married Lucy Goode Tucker, of Brunswick County, Virginia; and Martha Chambers (b. October 10, 1797).
[47]For the Branch-Tanner-Stokes-Street-Jones ancestry of Anne Parke Jones, see *The Old Free State*, II, 328 et seq.

months after the end of the war. Subsequently studied medicine in Louisville, Kentucky; married Addie Bacon, of Lunenburg County, Virginia; removed to Evening Shade, Arkansas.
Issue:
- I. Edward Orgain[8] Craig,
- II. Virginia[8] Craig,
- III. Ella Archer[8] Craig,
- IV. Samuel Bacon[8] Craig,
- V. Minnie[8] Craig,
- VI. Sue[8] Craig,
- VII. Thomas[8] Craig,
- VIII. Hal Chambers[8] Craig,
- IX. Catherine[8] Craig.

(c) Mary Ann[7] Craig (b. Dec. 25, 1849), married September 25, 1875, James Hatchett Farmer.
Issue:
- I. Judge Henry Hughs[8] Farmer.
- II. Edward Chambers[8] Farmer, who married Julia Frances Lambert, and had:
    - (aa) Edward Lambert[9] Farmer.

(d) Waddy Street[7] Craig (b. Feb. 9, 1851), married December 26, 1883, Martha Ermin Baskett. They had one son:
- I. James White[8] Craig, who married Odessa Baskett May. They have one son: James W.[9] Craig, Jr., who is married and has the following children:
    Ann Mary[10] Craig,
    Katherine Daisy[10] Craig,
    John Tyre[10] Craig (who died an infant),
    Jesse Basket[10] Craig (b. 1897) and served in World War,
    William Stone[10] Craig, who also served in World War.

(e) Elizabeth Montfort[7] Craig (b. Apr. 7, 1853), married Lee Norman.

(f) Jayne Stokes[7] Craig (b. June 4, 1855, in Hanover County, Va.), married in Shawneetown, Ill., Oct. 24, 1872, Richard Mathew Walker (b. Oct. 27, 1847, d. Sept. 11, 1920), son of William Alonzo Walker and Sally Ann (Ligon) Walker.
They had issue:
- I. William Herbert[8] Walker, M. D., Capt. World War; married Minnie Kershaw,—live in Kansas City, Mo.
- II. Edward Craig[8] Walker (b. Apr. 19, 1877), married Mary Clifton Penick, dau. Bishop Clifton and Mary (Hoge) Penick. One child, Mary Hoge Walker.
- III. Lillian[8] Walker, married Harry Ellyn Thixton, Henderson, Ky.
- IV. Frank Hart Kitchell[8] Walker (b. March 14, 1881), married Mary Louise Norwood, daughter of Prof. Charles Norwood, of Lexington, Ky. Children:
  Sarah Norwood[9] Walker,
  Jane Craig[9] Walker,
  Louise Norwood[9] Walker.
- V. Sarah Clarence[8] Walker, married Claude Ambrose Morton, of Madisonville, Ky. Children:
  Jayne Stokes[9] Morton,
  Harry E. Thixton[9] Morton.
- VI. Florence Georgia[8] Walker, married Ralph Mitchell Overstreet, C. E.; World War. Children:
  Ralph Mitchell[9] Overstreet, Jr.,
  Ann Parke[9] Overstreet.

(g) St. George Tucker[7] Craig (b. Sept. 17, 1857, at Ashland, Hanover Co., Va.), D. D. S. Univ. Maryland, Henderson, Ky., unmarried.

(h) Florence Overton[7] Craig (b. Dec. 31, 1861, in Ches-

terfield Co., Va.), married July 24, 1890, in Henderson, Ky., Abraham Glenn Scott, of Nottoway Co., Va. They had issue:
  I. Robert Craig[8] Scott, who married Mary Cornett, of Harlan, Ky.
  II. Annie Douglas[8] Scott,
  III. Edward Glenn[8] Scott,
  IV. Frances Epes[8] Scott.
(i) Robert Lee[7] Craig, Minister (b. in Lunenburg Co., Va., while the family were refugees there during the war 1861-65). Died in Houston, Texas. Married Beatrice McWillie, of Jackson, Miss.
One child:
  Elizabeth[8] Craig.
(j) Henrietta Chambers[7] Craig,
(k) Thomas[7] Craig.

(4) James[6] Craig, M. D., married Lucy Prior. It is said they had no children. The information received was meagre and not positive.

(5) Ann Walthall[6] Craig, married (M. B. dated Dec. 30, 1834), John Orgain, Jr., son of John Orgain, Sr., and grandson of Major William Orgain.

John Orgain, Jr., who married Ann Walthall[6] Craig, was educated at Amherst College, where, it is said, he received M. A. and Ph. D. degrees. He was a professor, a lawyer and represented Lunenburg County in the Legislature in 1859, 1860, 1861 and in 1863.[48]
They had:
(a) Edward C.[7] Orgain, C. S. A. He died unmarried. There is a discrepancy in information received as to whether his middle initial was "B" or "C." His name appears as "E. C. Orgain" on the roster of Captain Reps Connolly's Company, the *Nottoway Grays*.[49]

His sister-in-law, Mrs. Theodore Orgain, gives his name merely as "Edward Orgain," while another

---
[48]*The Old Free State*, II, 74.
[49]Roster 2, page 352, et seq. Va. State Library; *The Old Free State*, I, 620.

relative refers to him in correspondence as "Edward B. Orgain."

This correspondent says he was a member of the Company of his brother, "Captain George C. Orgain, the Nottoway Blues," and was killed the same day as his brother, Thomas Adams Orgain, at Gaines Mill.

There seems some little confusion here. Captain George C. Orgain's Company was a Lunenburg, not a Nottoway County Company, and the muster roll of the Company[50] does not show him a member; while the roll of Captain Reps Connolly's[51] Company does show him; and indicates that he was killed at Gaines Mill,—the second man of the Company to be killed, his brother Thomas Adams Orgain being the first.

(b) Thomas Adams[7] Orgain, C. S. A., second Lieut. in the Company of his brother, Captain George C. Orgain,[52] killed at Gaines Mill, while a member of Capt. Reps Connolly's Company; first member of the Company killed.[53] Died unmarried.

(c) James R.[7] Orgain, C. S. A., Second Sergeant in the Company of his brother, Captain George C. Orgain,[54] later a member of Captain Bolling's Company in J. E. B. Stuart's Cavalry. Killed at Brandy Station. Died unmarried.

(d) Lucy Marshall[7] Orgain, married Dr. John Randolph May,[55] and had:
    I. John Orgain[8] May,
    II. Henry Clay[8] May,
    III. Anne[8] May, who married a Mr. Moore, of Texas,
    IV. Emma[8] May,
    V. David[8] May,
    VI. Richard[8] May.

---

[50] *The Old Free State*, I, 590.
[51] *The Old Free State*, I, 620.
[52] *The Old Free State*, I, 590.
[53] Id., 620.
[54] Id., 590.
[55] For his ancestry see: Slaughter's *Bristol Parish*, 193; *The Old Free State*, II, 316.

(e) Mary Jackson[7] Orgain, who married Mason Cabell Morris, and had:
  I. John[8] Morris,
  II. Annie[8] Morris,
  III. Henrietta[8] Morris.
(f) George Craig[7] Orgain, Captain C. S. A. See roster of his company in *The Old Free State*,[56] Lawyer, Commonwealth's Attorney, Judge of the County Court of Lunenburg County, Virginia, 1892-1904.[57] He married Rebecca Lucas Orgain, and had:
  I. Edward Thomas[8] Orgain, who married Mrs. Elizabeth Field Yancey.
  II. George C.[8] Orgain, who married, first Josephine Stewart; and secondly, a Miss Anderson, of South Carolina.
  III. John Barbour[8] Orgain, who married Sallie Yancey, and had:
    (aa) John Barbour[9] Orgain, Jr.,
    (bb) Dr. Edward Stewart[9] Orgain,
    (cc) Elizabeth Field[9] Orgain.
  IV. Rebecca[8] Orgain, who married R. Walter Blanton, and had:
    (aa) M. Linwood[9] Blanton, who married Frances Terry.
    (bb) John Ellyson[9] Blanton,
    (cc) Elizabeth[9] Blanton, who married L. Ashton Coleman, and had:
      (A) Walter Emerson[10] Coleman,
      (B) Frances Rebecca[10] Coleman.
    (dd) Lucy[9] Blanton,
    (ee) Rebecca[9] Blanton, who married Edward Waddell.
  V. Sallie Lucas[8] Orgain, who married Llewellyn C. Jones, and had:
    (aa) Stanhope[9] Jones, who married Gladys (?) Craig.

---

[56]Vol. I, page 590.
[57]*The Old Free State*, I, 342.

- (bb) Richard[9] Jones,
- (cc) Claiborne[9] Jones,
- (dd) Hunter[9] Jones,
- (ee) Joseph[9] Jones,
- (ff) Marjorie[9] Jones.

VI. Virginia[8] Orgain, who married, first, Stanhope R. Gregory, and had:
- (aa) Henry Chamberlain[9] Gregory, who married Zelle Brown, and married second, N. Macfarland Neblett,[58] and had:
- (bb) Virginia Macfarland[9] Neblett,
- (cc) Frances Rebecca[9] Neblett.

VII. Henrietta Craig[8] Orgain, who married Richard H. Mann, and had:
- (aa) Mary Orgain[9] Mann, who married Richard Hillsdon Ryan, who had:
  - (A) Donald Hillsdon[10] Ryan.
- (bb) Frances Harrison[9] Mann, who married Robert Baskerville Patteson,
- (cc) Charles Benjamin[9] Mann,
- (dd) Margaret Gordon[9] Mann.

VIII. Sue E.[8] Orgain, who married Charles H. Bridges.

IX. Josephine Addison[8] Orgain, who married Richard M. Harrison, and had:
- (aa) Richard[9] Harrison.

X. Rosa Chambers[8] Orgain, who married Edmund W. Townes, and had:
- (aa) Edward Taylor[9] Townes,
- (bb) Stuart[9] Townes,
- (cc) Rosa Orgain[9] Townes.

(g) Theodore[7] Orgain (b. 1854, living 1929), married February 14, 1882, Mary Collier Bridgforth (b. July 8, 1855, living 1929), daughter of George Baskerville Bridgforth and his wife Sallie Seay, and had:

I. Lucie Lee[8] Orgain, who married, August 21,

---

[58]For the Neblett family see: *The Old Free State*, II, 319 et seq.

1912, A. G. Fray, of Advance Mills, Va., and have:
- (aa) Audrey Lee[9] Fray,
- (bb) Gaines[9] Fray, Jr.

II. Ann Craig[8] Orgain (1929 unm.)

III. Eva Chambers[8] Orgain, who married February 24, 1914, J. R. Adams, and had:
- (aa) Mary Jacqueline[9] Adams.

IV. Mary Collier[8] Orgain, who married November 18, 1919, Robert Baylor, of Dante, Virginia, and had:
- (aa) Ann George[9] Baylor (b. Oct. 25, 1920),
- (bb) Julia[9] Baylor (b. March 31, 1925).

V. James Robert[8] Orgain (b. June 13, 1890), of Alberta, Virginia, who married Alice Clark, and had:
- (aa) James Robert[9] Orgain, Jr.,
- (bb) Clarence[9] Orgain,
- (cc) Anne Collier[9] Orgain.

(h) J. Tarry[7] Orgain, married Mary Boisseau, and had:
I. William[8] Orgain, of Danville, Virginia.
II. Robert[8] Orgain, of Danville, Virginia.
III. Dean[8] Orgain, a Presbyterian Minister, who died in training during the World War.
IV. Mary[8] Orgain,
V. Virginia[8] Orgain.

(i) Sterling[7] Orgain (b. March 15, 1852, d. March 10, 1911), married January 29, 1879, Eva Marshall Puryear (b. June 21, 1854, living 1929), daughter of John Puryear, of Brunswick County, Virginia, and his wife Ann Sturdivant.
They had:
I. Robert Sturdivant[8] Orgain (d. in early childhood),
II. Jessamine[8] Orgain, now (1929), residing in Tallapoosa, Georgia.

(j) Henrietta Chambers[7] Orgain, married John E. Eanes, and had:

>
> I. John Orgain⁸ Eanes (d. at the age of 21).
> II. Marie Harrison⁸ Eanes,
> III. Virginia Craig⁸ Eanes, who married Harris Jones of Lunenburg County, Virginia.
> IV. E. Chambers⁸ Eanes.

3. Martha Anderson⁵ Craig who married Thomas Stevenson. The date of their marriage is not known; but it evidently occurred before November 3, 1789, for Rev. James Craig in his will, which bears that date, mentions his daughter "Martha Anderson Stevenson."

    Her husband Thomas Stevenson died in 1795; his will is dated July 14, 1795, and was probated in Lunenburg County, Virginia, October 8, 1795.

    This couple probably had no children; this surmise is based upon the fact that the will mentions none, the only person named in it being the wife Martha Anderson Stevenson, who was the beneficiary and the executrix.

4. Mary Booker⁵ Craig, who married July 17, 1796,⁵⁹ John Stevenson.

    The writer has been unable to trace any descendants, if descendants there were, of this couple. An unverified report that they had descendants in the State of Kentucky, was his nearest approach to any information on the subject. Considerable inquiry and correspondence have been unavailing. None have been found.

5. Frances⁵ Craig, who married October 17, 1805,⁶⁰ Richard Claiborne Gregory, and had:

    (1) Richard C.⁶ Gregory, who married (M. B. in Lunenburg County, Va., dated Nov. 9, 1835), Martha A. Hamlin.

    (2) James Craig⁶ Gregory (b. Oct. 21, 1813, d. Sept. 17, 1880), who married first in 1843, a Miss Coleman, of Mecklenburg County, Virginia, and second in 1851 (license dated Jan. 11, 1851), Elizabeth Ann Walker (b. Dec. 25, 1820,

---

⁵⁹Married by Rev. John Cameron, see his Register printed in this volume, Chapter XIV.
⁶⁰Married by Rev. John Cameron; see his Register, printed in this volume, Chapter XIV.

d. July, 1887), daughter of Allen Walker and his wife Elizabeth Parish of Mecklenburg County, Virginia.

Issue by the first marriage:

(a) William H.[7] Gregory (b. 1844), a Confederate soldier (died "in the nineties").

(b) James F.[7] Gregory (who also died "in the nineties").

Issue by the second marriage:

(c) Susan Ann[7] Gregory, who married James W. Simmons.

(d) Mamie Agnes[7] Gregory, who married Richard T. Tisdale, who was a Lieutenant in the Confederate Army.

(e) Pattie W.[7] Gregory, who married N. Derick Potts, of Loudon County, Virginia.

(f) Sallie E.[7] Gregory, who married Eppa Hunton Potts of Loudon County, Virginia.

(g) Charles Allen[7] Gregory, who married a Miss Womack of Halifax County, Virginia.

(h) Richard C.[7] Gregory, who married Mary Belle Bowman of Halifax County, Virginia.

(i) Edward W.[7] Gregory, who married, first Mrs. Ferrell, of Danville, Virginia, and second Kate Cleveland, of Charlottesville, Virginia.

(j) Walter V.[7] Gregory, who married Etta Simcoe, and had:

> I. Sue A.[8] Gregory.
> II. Hunter Lee[8] Gregory, of Stockton, California, M. D., Medical College of Virginia. Soldier of the World War. In France 1918-1919.
> III. Sarena[8] Gregory, teacher.
> IV. James Edward[8] Gregory, m. Marjorie Grantham of Wilson, N. C.

(k) Lucius[7] Gregory, who married first, Berta M. Hutcheson, daughter of Robert M. Hutcheson, of Mecklenburg County, Virginia, and second, Rosa Lee Gregory, daughter of Dr. Flavius J. Gregory of Charlotte

County, Virginia, who was Surgeon in Stonewall Jackson's Brigade, C. S. A.

No children of the first marriage.

Issue of second marriage:

  I. Myrtis Lestelle[8] Gregory, who married William Kirkham Taylor, tobacconist, Clarksville, Va., and had:
    (I) James Preston[9] Taylor.
  II. Marjorie[8] Gregory, who married R. Dan Jones, of Richmond, Va.
  III. Richard Flavius[8] Gregory, banker, Chase City, Virginia.
  IV. Esther Ellen[8] Gregory, who married Robert Lucius Wallace, of Chase City, Virginia, and had:
    (I) Rose Ellen[9] Wallace.
  V. Agnes Lee[8] Gregory, Teacher, Chase City, Virginia.

Walter V.[7] and Lucius[7] Gregory were for many years leading merchants and manufacturers of Chase City, Virginia, conducting the general merchandise concern of W. V. & L. Gregory, and were largely interested in a woodworking plant at that place.

Lucius[7] Gregory is Colonel Lucius Gregory, having held that rank upon the Staff of Governor William Hodges Mann. He has been for twenty years a member of the Board of Supervisors of Chase City District, Mecklenburg County, Virginia.

The experience of his father, James Craig Gregory, with the vandals of the North, as detailed by Colonel Lucius Gregory, illustrates the treatment received by hundreds and thousands of non-combatants, at the South, experiences so shameful that the descendants of the perpetrators of such deeds are only too ready to deny that such vandalism was practiced.

In the morning of the day when Wilson's Raid passed our home, says Colonel Gregory, my father, James Craig Gregory, was a man of affluence; he had everything needed in the line of crops, he had a store well filled. When the raiders passed the family was left so poor and utterly destitute that the negro families on the plantation had to bring food to the Gregory family. The raiders took away everything they could, and destroyed the rest. The heads of barrels of molasses were knocked out with fence rails and the molasses allowed to run out on the ground.

With a family of twelve left in such destitution "my father," adds Colonel Gregory, "was unable to educate any of us except to send us to the one room schools which were established some years later."

The picture of this family thus presented was typical of most who likewise suffered throughout the South.

Lincoln's war upon the South was a diabolical war made upon women, and children, and upon the non-combatant population in a manner and upon a scale hitherto unknown to civilized people.

(3) Martha Anderson Craig[6] Gregory, who married July 24, 1832, Sharpe Carter (son of William Carter, and grandson of Raleigh Carter), a graduate of Hampden-Sidney College, of "Hickory Hill," Nottoway County, Virginia,[61] and had:

(a) William R.[7] Carter (b. April 22, 1833, d. July 8, 1864, of wounds received at Trevillians). "He was graduated from Hampden-Sidney in 1852, with the highest honors of his class. He later studied law, and at the beginning of the war was a member of the law firm of Howard & Sands, Richmond. He entered the Nottoway Cavalry as a private and was soon made Colonel of the Third Virginia and shortly before he was wounded was commissioned a brigadier-general."[62]

(b) Isabella[7] Carter (b. July 29, 1835), who married May 26, 1860, Joseph B. Friend, of Charlotte County, Virginia.

(c) Josephine[7] Carter (b. Nov. 29, 1837), who married 1st, September 27, 1858, Captain David R. Stokes,

---

[61] *William and Mary Quarterly*, XIX, 191.
[62] Id.

C. S. A., of *Mt. Holly*, Lunenburg County, Virginia,[63] and married 2nd, November 26, 1890, William J. Neblett[64] of *Brickland*, Lunenburg County, Virginia. Issue by the first marriage:

    I. Terry[8] Stokes, who married Annie Bond, daughter of Major Thomas Bond of Petersburg, and had:

    (aa) Anne Bond[9] Stokes.

    II. Martha Craig[8] Stokes, who married Peyton G. McCabe. (No issue.)

    III. Richard Carter[8] Stokes, of Lynchburg, Virginia, who married Lillie A. Lee, daughter of John A. Lee, of Lynchburg, and had:

    (aa) Richard Carter[9] Stokes, Jr.

    IV. David R.[8] Stokes, Jr. (d. 1902, unmarried).

    V. Isabella Overton[8] Stokes, who married E. H. Conquest, of Accomac County.

    VI. Irby[8] Stokes.

    VII. Susan Jones[8] Stokes, who married John A. Suiter, of Garysburg, N. C., and had:

    (aa) John A.[9] Suiter,

    (bb) Florence Carter[9] Suiter,

    (cc) Overton Stokes[9] Suiter.

No issue by the second marriage, to William J. Neblett.

NOTE: Richard Claiborne[6] Gregory, married second, Eliza Twitty Bailey, of Mecklenburg County, Virginia.

Issue by second marriage:

    (a) John[7] Gregory,

---

[63]For a genealogy of the Stokes family see *The Old Free State*, II, 328-362.

[64]William J. Neblett represented Lunenburg County in the "Secession Convention," and at one time in the legislature. He was a nephew of the celebrated lawyer of Lunenburg County, later of Richmond, William J. Macfarland, who had the honor of entertaining in his home, the Prince of Wales (King Edward), when he toured this country, who was one of the counsel of President Jefferson Davis, upon the charge of treason, which despite the repeated demands of Mr. Davis and his counsel was never brought to trial.

(b) Roger⁷ Gregory (d. without issue),
(c) West⁷ Gregory,
(d) Werter⁷ Gregory,
(e) Lucy⁷ Gregory (b. 1840, d. 1912),
(f) Annie⁷ Gregory.

Of these:

Werter⁷ Gregory (b. Aug. 31, 1846, 1. 1929), married twice: first, Sallie J. Payne of Pittsylvania County, Virginia, and second, Lillie Beatrice Thomas of Salem, Va., (1. 1929). No children by second marriage.

Issue by first marriage:
  I. Rev. Henry Claiborne⁸ Gregory, of Amherst, Va.
  II. Frank Hancock⁸ Gregory, of Roanoke, Va.
  III. Edgar Price⁸ Gregory, of Roanoke, Virginia.
  IV. Herbert Bailey⁸ Gregory, Judge Law and Chancery Court, Roanoke, Virginia.
  V. William Payne⁸ Gregory, Oak Hill, West Virginia.
  VI. Hugh Wingfield⁸ Gregory, San Francisco, Cal.
  VII. Paul Whitehead⁸ Gregory, Wheeling, W. Va.

Lucy⁷ Gregory (b. 1840 in Mecklenburg County, Va., d. in 1912; buried in Blandford Cemetery),[65] married John H. Hatcher (b. 1840 in Cumberland County, Va., d. in 1911), son of Samuel and M. L. Hatcher of Cumberland County, Va. They were married August 27, 1861.[66]

They had:
  (a) Viola⁸ Hatcher (d. unm. early in life).
  (b) Elizabeth⁸ Hatcher, who resides in California.
  (c) Louise⁸ Hatcher, who married a Mr. Blackwell, of Roanoke, Va.
  (d) Dr. Samuel C.⁸ Hatcher, Vice-President and Secretary-Treasurer of Randolph-Macon College.

---

[65] Information as to Lucy Gregory, her marriage and descendants was furnished the writer by Dr. Samuel C. Hatcher, her grandson, of Randolph-Macon College, Ashland, Va.
[66] By Rev. Henderson Lee, as shown by the marriage records of Mecklenburg County, Va.

(e) Lucy[8] Hatcher, who married Oliver Mowat, and resides in California.
(f) John[8] Hatcher (d. in early manhood).
(g) W. Gregory[8] Hatcher, Treasurer of the State of Texas, Austin, Texas.

Annie[7] Gregory married Joseph B. Friend, of Charlotte County, Virginia.

REVEREND JOHN CAMERON
MINISTER OF CUMBERLAND PARISH, 1796-1815.

From photograph of a miniature, now in possession of a descendant, in Pensacola, Florida.

THE MINIATURE

The miniature, from which the likeness on the opposite page was taken, was undoubtedly painted from life, though the name of the artist and the date of painting are no longer known.

Reverend John Cameron gave the miniature to his daughter, Mary Read Cameron, who married James Anderson. She gave it to her son, Walker Anderson, and he in turn to his son, William Edward Anderson, grandfather of Mrs. Melvin D. Chase, of Greenville, South Carolina, who has supplied the facts of its history.

The photograph from which the cut was made was furnished by Mrs. Bennehan Cameron, of Boyce, Virginia.

Both the photograph and the facts of the history of the miniature were secured for the writer through the interest and aid of Miss Katherine Cameron Shipp, of Fayetteville, North Carolina.

CHAPTER X
Reverend John Cameron

HE Reverend John Cameron was a native of Scotland, and sprung from a family "ancient and highly respectable."[1] He was educated at King's College, Aberdeen, and was ordained by the Bishop of Chester, according to Bishop Meade, in 1770.[2] The memorial tablet at Old Blandford Church, hereinafter mentioned, gives the date of his ordination as 1768.[3] He was one of four brothers who came to Virginia.[4] His three brothers were Donald, Ewen and William.[5] Donald is said to have returned to Scotland.[6] There is a single mention of Donald Cameron in the Vestry Book of Bristol Parish. On December 31, 1788, he was appointed to collect the subscriptions for the year 1788, and was to be allowed five per cent. for so doing.[7] This, it seems probable, was Donald, the brother of Reverend John Cameron.

William Cameron, like his brother John was a Minister, and served Manchester Parish, Chesterfield County, Virginia, from 1790 to 1794.[8] A descendant of Reverend John Cameron says of the brother William that he "was chaplain to Bishop Madison, and was killed by being thrown from a carriage, as he was driving with Bishop Madison, down Warm Springs Mountain, Bath County, Virginia."[9]

The other brother, Ewen Cameron, is said to have settled in Tennessee.[10]

---

[1]Meade: *Old Churches and Families of Virginia*, I, 485.
[2]Id.
[3]Dr. Goodwyn, follows Bishop Meade and gives the date as 1770. *The Colonial Church in Virginia*, 257.
[4]Meade: *Old Churches and Families of Virginia*, I, 485.
[5]Miss Katherine Cameron Shipp to the writer, quoting Miss Rebecca Cameron.
[6]Id.
[7]*Bristol Parish Vestry Book*, 273.
[8]Meade: *Old Churches and Families of Virginia*, I, 453.
[9]Statement of Miss Rebecca Cameron, already referred to.
[10]Id.

From the marriage bonds of Lunenburg County, it appears that Ewen Cameron married Frances Buford in 1797.[11] Frances Buford was the daughter of Joseph Buford[12] and Reverend John Cameron's marriage register shows that he performed the marriage ceremony Deecmber 21, 1797.

The history of Rev. John Cameron's early years, those immediately following his arrival in America, is very meagre. Bishop Meade says: "It is probable that he was Minister in Mecklenburg from his first coming into this country, in the year 1770, until 1784, when he moved to Petersburg; though one of his descendants informs me that he was living in Charlotte in 1771, where he married a Miss Nash. He may have settled there first and after a year or two removed to Mecklenburg."[13]

Dr. Goodwin says he was "Minister, St. James' Parish, Mecklenburg County, 1770-84."[14] In making this statement Dr. Goodwin was probably following Bishop Meade, although his statement is more positive than the Bishop's. It is clear from Bishop Meade's account that he was not certain of the facts regarding Rev. John Cameron's early years. He does not give the full name of the "Miss Nash" who became his wife; and the information given him by a descendant that Rev. Cameron was married in 1771 was erroneous. Dr. Goodwin does not attempt to fix the date of his marriage.[15]

The discovery of Dr. Cameron's marriage bond in the Charlotte County records clears up several details. The bond is dated September 1, 1773, and is for his marriage to Ann Owen Nash. This establishes not only the Christian name of his wife, which is given neither by Bishop Meade nor by Dr. Goodwin, but fixes with approximate certainty the date of the marriage.

The marriage bond, too, affords some evidence, slight though it be, that John Cameron was at the date of the marriage bond residing in Charlotte County, for he is not described as from any

---

[11]*The Old Free State*, II, 389. The bond is dated December 16, 1797.
[12]Letter of consent to the marriage in Lunenburg County, Clerk's Office.
[13]Meade: *Old Churches and Families of Virginia*, I, 488.
[14]*The Colonial Church in Virginia*, 257.
[15]*The Colonial Church in Virginia*, 258; and the memorial tablet gives it incorrectly.

other county, and such description was customary, where a prospective bridegroom came from another county into Charlotte County to execute such a bond, for a marriage with a resident of that county.

While Bishop Meade, as above shown, seems to think it probable that Rev. John Cameron was the Minister of the Parish in Mecklenburg County from 1770 when he first came over until his removal to Petersburg in 1784, still the Bishop recognizes the possibility that he resided a few years in Charlotte County before taking up his residence in Mecklenburg County. That the latter was the fact, this author believes to have been the case. The meagre evidences at hand point to that conclusion.

As we have seen, one of his descendants informed Bishop Meade that "he was living in Charlotte in 1771."[16] He married there in 1773, and in his marriage bond did not indicate that he was a resident of another county; and Bishop Meade, in speaking of St. James' Parish, Mecklenburg County, says: "He is on our list of clergy from this parish in 1774-76 . . ."[17]

These circumstances tend to show that soon after his coming over he found his way to Charlotte County, was there in 1771 and probably was resident there from that time until after his marriage in 1773, and that he began his connection with St. James' Parish in Mecklenburg County in 1774 and continued to serve that parish until 1784. These circumstances also suggest the possibility that he may have served Cornwall Parish in Charlotte County for a year or two before beginning his labors in St. James' Parish. If this be true, both Bishop Meade[18] and Dr. Goodwin[19] are in error in saying that his first charge was that of St. James' Parish.

Whether his charge in St. James' Parish began in 1774 or in the earlier year, the period during which he served that parish embraced eventful years, and his lot was cast with an interesting people. It is highly to be regretted that the records of the parish for that period are not extant. The vestry book covering the

---

[16]*Old Churches and Families of Virginia*, I, 488.
[17]Id.
[18]*Old Churches and Families of Virginia*, I, 485.
[19]*The Colonial Church in Virginia*, 258.

period of his ministry would furnish many facts of interest while a register, if one was at that time kept by him, similar to that here presented for later years, would be of a value and importance scarcely to be exaggerated.

In 1784 he was invited to become Minister to Bristol Parish; he accepted and removed to Petersburg, and served that parish until 1793.[20]

The minutes of the Vestry of Bristol Parish, of February 4, 1780, contains this entry:

"This day the late Recter, the Revd. Mr. Harrison, wrote in his Resignation of his Cure of this Parish, which is accepted."[21] The "Revd. Mr. Harrison" here mentioned was Reverend William Harrison, who had been rector of the Parish since 1762.[22] He was elected Nov. 22, 1762, to succeed the "Rev. Mr. Thomas Wilkerson."

The circumstances of the resignation of Rev. Mr. Harrison are not known; but it does appear that no meeting of the Vestry was held from May 1, 1779, when he was present, until February 4, 1780, when he was not present, at which meeting his resignation was presented.[23] Possibly he had become incapacitated because of ill health; this speculation is merely a surmise however. This seems to have been the only Parish he served. He did not die until 1814, at the age of eighty-four.[24]

After the resignation of Rev. William Harrison, the Vestry seemed in no hurry to fill the office of Rector. It was not until October 16, 1783, that they ordered "That the Church Wardens Advertise in the publick Gazette, That the Parish of Bristol, is vacant for want of a Minister."[25]

There were two applicants for the position, Rev. John Cameron and Rev. Thomas Kenedy. The record of the March 17, 1784, meeting of the Vestry contains, among others, the following entry:

---

[20]Meade: *Old Churches and Families of Virginia*, I, 485; Goodwin: *The Colonial Church in Virginia*, 258.
[21]Chamberlayne: *Bristol Parish Vestry Book and Register*, 261.
[22]Id., 184; Goodwin: *The Colonial Church in Virginia*, 277.
[23]Chamberlayne: *Bristol Parish Vestry Book and Register*, 260, 261.
[24]Goodwin: *The Colonial Church in Virginia*, 277.
[25]Chamberlayne: *Bristol Parish Vestry Book and Register*, 267.

"Agreeable to an order of Vestry, Bearing Date October 16, 1783.

"That the Church Wardens Advertise for a Minister, which Advertisement was Duly Complyed with; Agreeable to the said order, The Revd. Mr. John Cammeron and the Revd. Mr. Thomas Kenedy, Appeared, and were both Nominated.—The Revd. Mr. John Cammeron was Elected for one year,—And that the Glebe, is now Rented, he is to have the profits of, from this Date for Twelve Months."[26]

This is one of the few mentions made of Rev. Thomas Kennedy in the annals of the Episcopal Church. He is not mentioned in Dr. Goodwin's work, *The Colonial Church in Virginia,* because presumably he was of a date later than the period with which that book deals. The sole reference to him by Bishop Meade, is the mere mention of his name where speaking of the vacancy in Bristol Parish above mentioned, he says:

"The parish being advertised as vacant, the Rev. Mr. Kennedy and the Rev. Dr. Cameron were candidates in 1784."[27]

Dr. Cameron evidently made a very favorable impression in his new field of work, for at the end of his first year in the parish, on November 1, 1784, he was again elected without restriction as to time, the record reading:

"The Revd. Mr. John Cammeron, came this day in Vestry when the Vestry Unanimously, Elected him Rector of this Parish."[28]

The Vestry Book seems to be silent upon the salary to be paid the rector at this time, but Dr. Slaughter states that in 1790 it was one hundred and sixteen pounds per year.[29]

"In 1789 the diocese was laid off into districts, and the clergy of adjoining parishes were instructed to assemble annually in presbytery and choose one of their number to preside, with the title of visitor, whose duty it was to visit each Parish in his district to see that the canons of the Church were observed, to inspect the morals of the clergy, and report the state of each Parish

---

[26]Chamberlayne: *Bristol Parish Vestry Book and Register,* 268.
[27]*Old Churches and Families of Virginia,* I, 443.
[28]Chamberlayne: *Bristol Parish Vestry Book and Register,* 269.
[29]Slaughter: *History of Bristol Parish,* 30.

to the Convention. There was no Bishop then. Under this canon, Dr. Cameron was made visitor of the parishes of Martin's-Brandon, Albemarle, Bristol, Bath and Manchester. It was in this presbytery, that the first motion was made towards the formation of a society for the relief of widows and orphans of deceased clergymen, along with a proposition for the instruction of students in divinity."[80]

It was during Dr. Cameron's ministry, in 1790, that a new Church was built in the Parish upon the site where the courthouse stands, in the City of Petersburg,[81] and it was in connection with the building of this Church that a committee was appointed to petition the General Assembly of Virginia for authority to conduct a lottery in order to raise seven hundred and fifty six pounds to be expended for that purpose.[82]

During the same year, 1790, Dr. Cameron preached the Convention sermon, and "the Convention thanked him for his judicious, affectionate and seasonable discourse, and asked a copy for publication."[83] At this Convention he was chairman of a committee charged with the duty of preparing a memorial to the legislature, asserting the right of the churches to the glebes.[84]

In 1792, Bishop Madison, who had been made a bishop in 1790, visited the parish. It was a notable occasion, for "It was the first Episcopal visit with which this Parish had been favored since its establishment in 1642."[85]

A committee of the Vestry was appointed to draw up a suitable address to be presented to the Bishop. Dr. Cameron was authorized to secure a singing master for the occasion, and eight dollars were appropriated to pay expenses! The meeting on the occasion of the Bishop's visit was held "At Armstead's in Blandford."[86]

In 1793 Dr. Cameron resigned his charge in Bristol Parish. In December of that year, following his resignation, the Vestry

---
[80]Slaughter: *History of Bristol Parish*, 33.
[81]Id., 30.
[82]Slaughter: *History of Bristol Parish*, 30.
[83]Id., 32.
[84]Id., 32, 33.
[85]Id., 30.
[86]Slaughter: *History of Bristol Parish*, 31.

"RESOLVED unanimously, that the church wardens be requested to furnish the Rev. Dr. Cameron with a certificate of the thanks of the vestry for the fidelity with which he discharged the duties of his office as rector of this Parish, and that his conduct and conversation during that time has been, in the highest degree, pious and exemplary."[87]

The *Virginia Gazette* and *Petersburg Intelligencer* carried a notice dated October 28, 1793, by the church wardens, advertising the fact that a minister was wanted due to the fact that "The Rev. Mr. John Cameron present minister of the Protestant Episcopal Church in this Parish, being about to remove from the Parish" had "notified the vestry of his intention to vacate it." The notice further stated that the emoluments of the office amounted to about one hundred and twenty pounds, "besides the use of the glebe lands," etc.[38]

Beginning in 1794, or possibly in 1793, he was minister, for a time, of Nottoway Parish, Nottoway County, Virginia.[39]

The entry upon the fly leaf of the Register here presented would seem to fix the date of his connection with the parish in Nottoway. It is as follows: "John Cameron, Nottoway County, January 28, 1794."

The statement by Dr. Goodwin, in *The Colonial Church in Virginia*,[40] that he was "Rector, Nottoway Parish, Southampton County, 1793——," seems to be an error. Dr. Goodwin was no doubt confused by the fact that there were two parishes, in different counties, named Nottoway. In his account of Nottoway Parish, Nottoway County, Bishop Meade says: "The Rev. Mr. Jarratt informs us that Dr. Cameron was its minister for about two years after leaving Petersburg in 1793, but was obliged to resign for want of support."[41] No mention is made by Bishop Meade, of Rev. John Cameron in his account of Nottoway Parish, Southampton County, nor has his name been found associated with that parish in any source, except Dr. Goodwin's

---
[87]Slaughter: *History of Bristol Parish*, 31.
[38]Id., 31, 32.
[39]Meade: *Old Churches and Families of Virginia*, II, 23.
[40]Page 258.
[41]Meade: *Old Churches and Families in Virginia*, II, 23.

work mentioned. The Register here presented in print for the first time, affords internal evidence that his association was with the parish in Nottoway County, rather than with that in Southampton.

Reverend James Craig, who had been the rector of Cumberland Parish, Lunenburg County, since 1759, died in 1795. He was succeeded, beginning January 1, 1796, by Reverend John Cameron.[42]

As a meeting of the Vestry of Cumberland Parish, Lunenburg County, Virginia, held at Lunenburg Courthouse on Wednesday the 23rd of December, 1795, on the motion of Philip W. Jackson, a member of the Vestry, the Reverend Dr. John Cameron was chosen rector of the parish. The resolution reads as follows:

"Resolved that it is the unanimous opinion of this vestry that the said Reverend Dr. John Cameron is Hereby Chosen Elected Constituted and appointed Rector and Minister of this parish and that his time shall commence from the first day of January one thousand seven hundred and ninety six."[43]

The first meeting of the vestry which he attended, in Cumberland Parish was that held on March 11, 1796.[44]

The minutes of the vestry through the succeeding years to the end of his ministry, throw little light upon the status of the church in the parish, either with respect to membership or its financial condition. After the church ceased to be a state institution, the financial statements of funds received and disbursed were no longer regularly spread upon the vestry minutes, nor does it affirmatively appear anywhere what was the number of adherents to the church in the parish, though it does appear that steps were at least once taken, after the dis-establishment, to ascertain that fact.

But it does appear that Dr. Cameron was a very regular at-

---

[42]V. B. post, p. 483. Meade: *Old Churches and Families of Virginia*, I, 485-486. In *The Colonial Church in Virginia* (Goodwin), at page 258, it is said that Dr. Cameron was in 1806 rector of Cumberland Parish, Lunenburg County, and "till his death in 1815." The implication of this language is that he was not rector of Cumberland Parish prior to 1806. That is erroneous.
[43]V. B. post, p. 483.
[44]Id. post, p. 484.

tendant upon the Vestry meetings, and he doubtless officiated in the pulpit with similar regularity and faithfulness.

On April 29, 1815, Dr. Cameron addressed the following letter to the Vestry of Cumberland Parish:

"Gentlemen:

Finding, from my advanced time of life and increasing infirmities that I am becoming daily less able to discharge the duties of my clerical office, I take this method of notifying to you my intention of resigning the charge of this parish, in the course of the present year. My design in giving you this early notice is, that you may take the necessary steps to provide a successor, who may be ready to take upon him the care of the parish, as soon as I shall relinquish it. And as the Church in this Diocese is now blessed with an able, vigilant, zealous & pious Bishop at its head, I would recommend as early an application as possible to him requesting him to look out and provide a suitable pastor for this parish. That the Supreme head of the Church may direct you and grant you success in this important business & in all other measures that you may undertake for the Welfare of our zion, is the fervent prayer of Gentlemen,

Your truly sincere friend & very humble servant,

Cumberland Glebe,
April 29th, 1815."

John Cameron.

The Church Wardens, James Macfarland and Waddy Street, pursuant to direction of the Vestry, on May 13, 1815, addressed a letter to The Right Reverend Richard Channing Moore, D. D., enclosing a copy of Dr. Cameron's letter, and asking his best endeavors to procure for the parish a "learned, virtuous, exemplary, and pious pastor."

"The salary," said the letter, "may be considered as equal to an hundred pounds per annum, which arises from a small estate consisting of *Land* and *Negroes*, left, about twenty years ago, to the Protestant Episcopal Church in this parish, by a very pious and zealous member of the Church, whose name was Thomas Buford."[45]

---

[45] V. B. post, p. 498.

The letter concluded with an invitation to the Bishop to visit the parish "in the course of this Summer or Fall."

February 17, 1816, Bishop Moore responded, recommending Mr. John S. Ravenscroft as lay reader "until the period marked out by the canons of the Church shall arrive in which he may be regularly ordained," and the Vestry at a meeting March 14, 1816, elected him to the office of Reader.[46]

Dr. Cameron's death occurred between November 20, 1815, and December 14th, of that year, as his will was dated and probated respectively on those dates.[47] In his will he mentions his wife, Anne Owen Cameron, his sons Thomas N. and William Cameron, a daughter Anne M. Cameron, and another daughter Jean M. Syme, wife of Rev. Andrew Syme.

While the records of the parish which he served in his earlier years are not now extant, it is a justifiable surmise that these years were the better days of his ministry, from the standpoint of worldly success and material well being. That this was so is argued not only by the length of time he remained in his early charge, St. James' Parish, but also by the trend of events, religious, political and otherwise.

The rise of the dissenters, the growth of the Presbyterians, Baptists and Methodists; the association, in a way, in the popular mind of the "Established" Church with the regime and the policies of the British; the "dis-establishment" of the Episcopal Church as an institution supported by public taxes; the passage of the statute of religious freedom; and the general growth of the democratic spirit as opposed to that of a period regarded as more aristocratic; all these, and other circumstances tended to make the lot of a parish minister, during the days of Rev. John Cameron, a hard one indeed.[48]

This was especially true after the Revolution. The clergy were quite naturally divided on the issues between the Colonists and Great Britain, which resulted in the Declaration of Independence,

---

[46] V. B. post, p. 498.
[47] It is of record in Lunenburg County, Virginia, in Will Book No. 7, at page 211.
[48] See the subject reviewed at some length in *The Old Free State*, Vol. I, Ch. IX.

and in the final achievement of it. Rev. John Cameron, we are told,[49] was "Loyal to the American cause in the Revolution." While Dr. Goodwin cites no authority for his statement, and the subject has been nowhere else mentioned, so far as this writer's observations have gone, the statement is doubtless correct. The circumstances argue it to be so; for Dr. Cameron seems to have continued in his charge in Mecklenburg County through the war; and in later years, when the stirring events of the period were, however, well remembered, he was accepted in Cumberland Parish, Lunenburg County, as the successor of Rev. James Craig, who was conspicuous for his championing of, and substantial aid to the American cause. But loyalty to the American cause during the Revolution was not sufficient to guarantee him any considerable following as a parish minister after that event.

After compulsory support of the parish ministers was discontinued in Virginia, Dr. Cameron was supported so meagerly by his congregations that he had to resort to other labors to support his family; his lot in this respect was that of many, if not most such ministers.

Reverend Devereux Jarratt, in a letter quoted by Bishop Meade, throws some light upon the general subject of the migratory course to which the clergy had to resort, for want of support after the Revolution, and also makes interesting mention of Dr. Cameron. Says Mr. Jarratt:

"Among others, we have a recent instance of this [migratory course], in the case of Dr. Cameron, whom you saw at my house as a visitor. He then lived at Petersburg. But, induced by necessity, having a large and increasing family, he removed into a parish above me, called Nottoway,[50] where the vestry obligated themselves to pay him a hundred pounds annually for three years successively. But, meeting with no assistance from any one of the people, the whole fell upon themselves alone. This burden they found too weighty, and it caused them to wish to get rid of the incumbent, which I am told they have effected, and Dr. Cameron is now the minister of a parish in Lunenburg County.

---

[49]Goodwin: *The Colonial Church*, 258.
[50]This indicates the point already made, that Dr. Goodwin was in error in supposing it was Nottoway Parish, Southampton County.

Few or none of the people would go to hear him (at least very seldom), and very few of the vestry made a constant practice of going to church, as I have been informed, so that frequently his congregation would not exceed five or six hearers. Surely this was enough to weary him out and make him think of new quarters."[51]

Under these circumstances, Cumberland Parish offered a more remunerative field, pecuniarily considered, than Nottoway Parish, for one reason, because of the "Land and Negroes" left for the support of the Church by Thomas Buford, mentioned in the letter of the Church Wardens to Bishop Moore on the occasion of seeking a successor to Dr. Cameron.[52]

But his change to Cumberland Parish, even with the income from the Buford trust, did not result in sufficient support from his ministerial office to meet his needs. He had been made a Doctor of Divinity by William and Mary College, and his excellent education and classical training now stood him in good stead. "He was obliged," says Bishop Meade, "to resort to school-keeping, and had a select classical school, for which, by his scholarship, he was eminently fitted."[53]

Of his temperament and discipline, Bishop Meade gives us a glimpse.

"If," says Bishop Meade, "for his strictness he was even then complained of, how would such a school as his be now endured, by either parents or children? By nature stern and authoritative, he was born and educated where the discipline of schools and families was more than Anglican. It was Caledonian. But he made fine scholars. There is one at least now[54] alive, who is an instance of this, and bears testimony to it. His sincere piety and great uprightness commanded the respect of all, if his stern appearance and uncompromising strictness prevented a kindlier feeling. I never saw him but once, and then only for a few hours around a committee-table at our second convention in

---
[51]Meade: *Old Churches and Families of Virginia*, I, 485.
[52]Thomas Buford's will devising the property for the purpose was dated November 4, 1788, was probated July 11, 1793, and is of record in the Clerk's Office of Lunenburg County, in Will Book 4, pages 38-40.
[53]Meade: *Old Churches and Families of Virginia*, I, 485.
[54]Bishop Meade was writing between 1854 and 1857.

Richmond, and then received a rebuke from him; and, though it was not for an unpardonable sin, yet I sincerely thanked him, and have esteemed him the more for it ever since."[55]

In 1816, Bishop Moore, in his address to the Convention, spoke of the death of Dr. Cameron in these words:

"The venerable Dr. Cameron, a clergyman of dignity and deportment, becoming his standing and years, has been taken from our embrace. His little flock has been called to part with their beloved pastor and his widow and children with a husband and father endeared to them not only by the ties of nature, but by the faithful and honorable discharge of all the duties of life. He died resigned to the will of Heaven, and has entered into the joy of his Lord."[56]

Nearly a century after his death, and a little over a century after he had served Bristol Parish, his descendants, holding a proper reverence for his memory, foregathered at Old Blandford Church to witness the unveiling of a bronze memorial tablet provided by Bennehan Cameron, a descendant, of Raleigh, North Carolina. The dedicatory oration was pronounced by another descendant, Governor William E. Cameron, of Virginia. This interesting ceremony took place October 11, 1908.

The following is the invitation issued to the unveiling of the tablet:

"Mr. Bennehan Cameron
requests the honour of your presence at the
ceremonies incident upon the unveiling of a
Bronze Tablet
in the Old Colonial Church
of Blandford at Petersburg, Virginia,
which is placed there by reason of the request
of the
Ladies' Memorial Association of Petersburg
to commemorate the services and virtues
of its former Rector, our ancestor,
Rev. John Cameron, D. D.

---

[55] *Old Churches and Families of Virginia*, 485-6.
[56] Slaughter: *History of Bristol Parish*, 33.

at three o'clock Sunday afternoon,
October eleventh, nineteen hundred and eight
Governor William E. Cameron
will make the presentation.
Misses Belle Mayo and Sallie Talliaferro Cameron
the great-great-grandchildren will unveil it.
Rev. Carter Braxton Bryan, D. D.,
will receive it for the Ladies Memorial Association.

The size of the tablet is about three feet long by two high. The frame is the oak leaves and acorns, the emblem of the clan Cameron. The corners of the same are the emblems of the Church."[57]

The following is the inscription upon the tablet:

"In Memory of
Rev. John Cameron, D. D.,
son of Duncan and Margaret Bain Cameron,
of Ferintosh, Scotland.
Rector of this Church 1784-1794.
Graduate of King's College, Aberdeen, M. A., 1767.
Admitted to orders May 23, 1768,
by the Bishop of Chester, England.
Settled in Virginia 1770
Married Anne Owen Nash 1771[58]
Doctor of Divinity of the College of William and Mary, 1793.
Rector of the Parishes of St. James, Bristol,
Nottoway and Cumberland.
Rector of the Diocesan School in Lunenburg County.

Elected by the Church Convention as supervising Clergyman or "Visitor" after the Revolution and before the Consecration of Bishop Madison.

Selected by the Church as Chairman of its Committee to cope with Mr. Thomas Jefferson against his Act for the Despoliation of the Church, with the final result that, the Court of Appeals,

---

[57]For this interesting souvenir of the occasion the author is indebted to Miss Kate Cameron Shipp, of Lincolnton, North Carolina.
[58]This is an error. The Marriage Bond mentioned above is dated September 1, 1773.

being equally divided, the statute stood without being declared constitutional.

He died in Lunenburg County 1815.

Erected by his great-grandson, Bennehan Cameron, on September twenty-fifth, Nineteen hundred and eight, the one hundredth anniversary of the birth of his grandson, Paul Carrington Cameron, who was the son of Judge Duncan Cameron, of North Carolina, Chairman of the Committee of the General Convention of the Episcopal Church which established the General Episcopal Seminary in New York City, and founder of St. Mary's School, of Raleigh, North Carolina."

One can but admire the impulse which prompted such a fine memorial to one's ancestor. It is altogether fitting to hold in reverence the memories of our worthy progenitors. But this is not to say, that all of the inscription on the memorial is accurate, nor that a part of it does any great credit to its author.

The reference to Thomas Jefferson and to an Act of the General Assembly of Virginia, as an "Act for the Despoliation of the Church," and the statement that the "Statute stood without being declared constitutional," constitute blemishes which ought not to have marred what is otherwise so fitting a memorial.

This part of the inscription is, implicitly, a criticism of the Virginia Statute of Religious Freedom, which has been everywhere followed, by all free peoples throughout the civilized world. It is an historical fact, moreover, that the Episcopal Church, as a state church, so recognized by law, and supported by public taxes, had lost most of its strength and power, through loss of popular support and approval, before the Virginia Statute of Religious Freedom was enacted.

The specific law, however, to which this paragraph of the inscription was directed, was a law enacted in relation to the glebes. It was a logical if not necessary consequence of the policy embodied in the Statute of Religious Freedom, and in the enactment "dis-establishing" the Episcopal Church as a state supported institution, and the act repealing the law providing for the incorporation of the religious bodies.

The case referred to in the inscription was *Turpin et al.* v.

Locket et al.[59] and was a controversy over the glebes, decided in the lower court by Chancellor Wythe. The glebes were plantations or tracts of lands designed for the use of parish ministers. They were often farms with residences upon them, intended for homes for the ministers. While incumbents of the office of rector of a parish, the ministers were entitled to the revenues from the glebes, whether they resided upon them or not. The glebes were purchased with public funds, that is, from taxes collected from the inhabitants of the parishes.

On January 24, 1799, the General Assembly of Virginia passed a law which after reciting that certain laws enacted in 1776, 1779, 1784, 1785, 1786 and 1788, "admit the church established under the regal government, to have continued so, subsequently to the constitution; have bestowed property upon that church; have asserted a legislative right to establish any religious sect, and have incorporated religious sects, all of which is inconsistent with the principles of the constitution and of religious freedom and manifestly tends to the establishment of a national church," repealed those laws.[60]

The law provided that glebes which were vacant, as many of them were,, should be sold; and that those that thereafter became vacant be sold, and the proceeds applied to the use of the poor. The law did not affect any glebes in possession of ministers, or in possession of anyone else, under lease made prior to the enactment of the law. But the law appropriated the vacant glebes as property of the public, and used the proceeds for the poor; whereas, the Episcopal Church contended that the glebes were the property of that religious body.

It seems safe to say that the great leaders of the Episcopal Church, in later years, such as Bishop Meade, one of its chief historians, held the opinion that the withdrawal of official, compulsory support from that church, was a measure of wisdom. In other words, that the "dis-establishment" of the Church was beneficial, not only to the public, but to that church as well.

But there were few Episcopalians who at the time entertained

---
[59]VI Call., 113.
[60]1 Rev. Code, p. 79, ch. 32; Code of 1849, 360 et seq.

that view. They bitterly opposed putting the Episcopal Church upon a common footing with the denominations of dissenters, such as the Presbyterians, Baptists and Methodists.

It may be remarked, in passing, that Thomas Jefferson has chiefly to thank the Episcopalians for his reputation, in history, as an infidel. The ardent churchmen, of the Established Church, could not look upon the Statute of Religious Freedom, and the laws withdrawing public, official support, by taxation from their church, as works of any influence, except that of the devil. As Jefferson was the leader in all this great movement, they hated him with the bitterest hatred. Anyone who held Jefferson's views, they contended, could be neither a Christian nor a believer in the Bible.

And their repeated charges in sermons, letters and otherwise were responsible for the widespread belief that he was an infidel. The claim seems wholly unfounded, but it was so widely and vehemently made, that, to a degree, the belief still persists, in some quarters.

The law thus briefly referred to, was claimed by the Episcopal authorities to be unconstitutional, and, as stated, that question was before the Supreme Court for consideration, in the case above mentioned.[61]

The court, when the case came to be decided, due to the death of Judge Pendleton, consisted of an even number of Judges—four. The court as thus constituted, divided, there being two on each side of the question. The law, therefore, stood. Laws are presumptively constitutional, and when attacked for unconstitutionality, that must be established, and so voted by at least a majority of the court.

It seems fair, therefore, to say that Mr. Bennehan Cameron, in honoring his worthy ancestor, the Rev. John Cameron, reflected no great credit upon himself by the sentence of his inscription, intended to belittle Thomas Jefferson, and the policy of the State of Virginia toward the great subject of the relations of Church and State.

The Statute which he attempted to ridicule was a Statute of

---

[61] *Turpin et al.* v. *Locket et al.*, VI Call., 113.

the Commonwealth of Virginia, and not of Thomas Jefferson, as the inscription inaccurately declares; it was in no true or proper sense an "Act for the despoliation of the Church"; and moreover it is highly inaccurate to say that "the statute stood without being declared constitutional"; for the truth is that it stood, a wise constitutional enactment; and thus stood because those who assaulted it as unconstitutional did not succeed in getting it so declared by the court.

Moreover, it may be added, that while the case of *Turpin* v. *Locket* was decided by an equally divided court, the question of the constitutionality of the law was again tested in the case of *Selden* v. *Overseers of the Poor*,[62] and its constitutionality sustained by a unanimous court.

It seems appropriate here to set down some account of the descendants of the Reverend John Cameron.

Rev. John Cameron is said to be a descendant of Sir Edward Cameron of Lochiel, Chief of the Cameron Clan,[63] but upon what authority that statement is made does not appear. It is entirely possible that it is true; but seems to lack authentication.

The genealogy, so far as this writer has been able to satisfy himself, seems to be as follows:

Duncan[1] Cameron, of Fertintosh, Scotland, married Margaret Bain and had:

1. Rev. John[2] Cameron, D. D., the subject of this sketch.

2. Rev. William[2] Cameron, and two other sons who came to Virginia, whose names have not been ascertained. Rev. William Cameron in some manner was accidentally killed.

Rev. John[2] Cameron married Ann Owen Nash,[64] daughter of Colonel Thomas Nash, of Charlotte County, Virginia, who was an elder brother of Governor Abner Nash of North Carolina, and of General Francis Nash.

The ancestry of Ann Owen Nash, through her mother, Mary Read, is a notable one. It may be very briefly here noticed.

---

[62]XI *Leigh*, 127.
[63]*Abridged Compendium of American Genealogy*, III, 211. Doubtless what was meant is, Sir Ewan Lochiel, Chieftain of the Clan Cameron.
[64]The Marriage Bond, in Charlotte County, Va., is dated September 1, 1773. The statement on the memorial tablet in Old Blandford Church, at Petersburg, Virginia, that they were married in 1771 is incorrect.

George Reade (1600-1671) of York and Gloucester Counties, Virginia, who was born in England and died in Virginia, was a member of the Council 1657-8,[65] was Lieutenant Colonel of York County, and a Burgess from that County, in 1655-56.[66] He married Elizabeth Martin and had twelve children, among whom was Thomas Reade, who married Lucy Gwynne, daughter of Edward Gwynne, of Gloucester County. They are said to have had eleven children; the sixth of which was Colonel Clement Read (b. Jan. 1, 1707), educated at William and Mary College; first clerk of Lunenburg County, Virginia; Burgess in 1748-1749. His home was at Bushy Forest, Lunenburg County, which was in that part of the county later cut off into Charlotte County. Upon the creation of that County he became a resident of it, and so continued until his death. He married in 1730 Mary Hill who is said to have been "the only daughter of William Hill, an officer of the British Navy of the same family as the Marquis of Downshire, by his wife Priscilla Jenings, daughter of Governor Edmund Jenings of Virginia."[67]

Mary Hill's mother was, thus, a sister of Frances Jenings, great-grandmother of General Robert E. Lee.

Colonel Clement Read and Mary Hill had:

Colonel Clement Read, Jr., who married Mary Nash;

Isaac Read, who married Sarah Embry;

Thomas Read, who married Elizabeth Nash;

Major Edmund Read who married, first, a Miss Lewis, and secondly, Pauline Cabell, daughter of Colonel William Cabell.

Captain Jonathan Read, who married Jane Lewis; and

Mary Read, who married Thomas Nash, who were the parents of Anne Owen Nash, wife of Reverend John Cameron. Ann

---

[65]*Colonial Virginia Register*, 38.

[66]Id., 72.

[67]Brown: *The Cabells and Their Kin*, 208; this language is quoted by Alexander Brown, without citation of the source of it. Miss Katherine Cameron Shipp, a descendant, of Lincolnton, North Carolina, writes that Mary Hill was the only daughter of Colonel Isaac Hill, private secretary of Governor Jenings, who married his daughter Margaret Jenings. But she has probably confused some of the names as she speaks of the Governor's wife as named Priscilla. The governor's wife was Frances Corbin. *Lee of Virginia*, 301.

Owen Nash had a brother, Major Clement Read Nash, who was killed at the siege of Yorktown.

Dr. Cameron's wife, Ann Owen Nash Cameron, survived him several years "living with her son, Judge Duncan Cameron, at his home, Farintosh, Orange (now Durham) County, North Carolina. She is buried in the family burying ground at Farintosh."[68]

As to the number of the children born to Rev. John Cameron and his wife Ann Owen Nash, there seems to be some doubt. They had at least seven, possibly more.

The Census Records, State enumeration for 1782, show Rev. John Cameron of Mecklenburg County, Virginia, as having a family of ten white persons. If these were not himself, his wife and children, it is difficult to surmise who they were. They had at least one child born after that date, while they resided at Petersburg, for Bristol Parish Register contains the entry[69] of the birth of their son Thomas Cameron on January 16, 1793.

In 1894 the University of North Carolina Magazine contained a sketch of Paul Cameron, written by a kinsman, Colonel John D. Cameron. In this article it is said:

"Rev. John Cameron emigrated to Virginia during Colonial times, and married Anne Owen, daughter of Col. Thomas Nash, (of Charlotte County, Virginia), the elder brother of Gov. Abner Nash and Gen. Francis Nash, both distinguished in North Carolina Revolutionary annals. Gen. Francis Nash was killed at the battle of Germantown.

"There were born of this union four sons and three daughters. All the sons and one daughter removed to North Carolina and became prominent in social, professional and political life."

The seven children here referred to were as follows:

1. Mary Read[3] Cameron who married August 19, 1797,[70] Daniel Anderson, a Scotsman, who according to his grandson, William E. Anderson, settled in Petersburg "at the close of the Revolu-

---

[68]Miss Katherine Cameron Shipp to the author, April 22, 1929.
[69]On page 303, as printed by Chamberlayne.
[70]This date is obtained from the Register of Rev. John Cameron father of Mary Read Cameron who performed the marriage ceremony, in Lunenburg County, Virginia. See the entry in the Register printed in this volume, *post* p. 315. William E. Anderson in *Tales of a Grandfather* says they were married "in 1798." That of course is an error.

tion." He was a merchant and ship owner, and was engaged in business with Robert Walker, for whom he named a son Walker, thus introducing into the family a name which has been persistent and popular among his descendants.

They had:

(a) Walker[4] Anderson, who studied law; was Professor in the University of North Carolina; Principal of a Girls' School at Hillsboro, North Carolina; and who in 1835 emigrated to Florida, settling at Pensacola, where he entered the lumber business. This proving unsuccessful he resumed the practice of the law, with success and became the first Chief Justice of Florida. He married, in North Carolina, Phebe Rice Hawks, grand-daughter of Major John Hawks (and his wife Sarah Rice, of Newberne, N. C.), an English engineer officer who came over with Governor William Tryon of N. C. Major Hawks is said to have been a paymaster in the Revolution.

They had:

  I. William Edward[5] Anderson (b. 1833), who married Anna Hawks, and had:
    (aa) Malcolm Cameron[6] Anderson, who married Kathleen Sullivan and had:
      A. Kathleen[7] Anderson,
      B. Malcolm[7] Anderson,
      C. Emily[7] Anderson.
    (bb) Walker[6] Anderson who married Elizabeth ("Lillie") Maury, and had:
      A. Grace Fontaine[7] Anderson, who married Melvin Dietz Chase.
      B. Walker[7] Anderson, who married Katherine Gertrude McQuiston, who had:
        (1) Jane Maury[8] Anderson.
        (2) Walker[8] Anderson.
      C. Elizabeth Maury[7] Anderson (died 1919).
      D. Edith Harvey[7] Anderson.
    (cc) Rosa[6] Anderson (d. unm.)

(dd) May⁶ Anderson, who married Arthur Aylett Brown, and had:
- A. Mildred Cameron⁷ Brown, who married Enoch Broyles McIntosh, and had:
  - (1) Mildred⁸ McIntosh.
- B. Matilda Gault⁷ Brown.
- C. William Edward⁷ Brown, who married (unknown), and has one son.
- D. Margaret⁷ Brown who married Hobart Whitney, and had:
  - (1) Betty⁸ Whitney,
  - (2) Claire⁸ Whitney,
  - (3) Hobart⁸ Whitney.
- E. Lawrence⁷ Brown.
- F. Malcolm Cameron⁷ Brown.
- G. Norborne⁷ Brown.
- H. Halcott Cameron⁷ Brown.

(ee) Mildred Devereux⁶ Anderson.

(ff) Edward Cameron⁶ Anderson, who married Helen Cameron, and had:
- A. Edward⁷ Anderson.
- B. Helen Cameron⁷ Anderson, who married Walter Anderson.
- C. Elizabeth Cameron⁷ Anderson, who married Bernard J. Sullivan, and had:
  - (1) Bernard J.⁸ Sullivan.

(gg) Halcott Cameron⁶ Anderson, who married Elizabeth Higgins and had:
- A. Halcott Cameron⁷ Anderson.

(hh) Duncan Cameron⁶ Anderson (d. in infancy).

(ii) Ravenscroft⁶ Anderson (d. in infancy).

II. Walker⁵ Anderson (b. 1835), married Kate Cameron of Raleigh, N. C.

III. Julia⁵ Anderson, who married Judge Maxwell and had:
(aa) Evelyn Croom⁶ Maxwell who married Willie Thornton and had:

A. Evelyn[7] Thornton (d. 1926), who married Edward (?) Biggers, and had several children.
B. Judith[7] Thornton.
(bb) John[6] Maxwell, who married Clara Chipley and and had several children.
(cc) Walker[6] Maxwell (dead), who married Julia (last name not ascertained).
IV. Phebe[5] Anderson, who married a Mr. George.
V. Mildred[5] Anderson.

(b) William E.[4] Anderson, who married Eliza Burgwyn, and had:
I. William[5] Anderson, a banker of Raleigh, N. C., who married his cousin Mary Syme. (They left no children).
II. General George Burgwyn[5] Anderson (b. April 30, 1830, near Hillsboro, N. C.). Attended University of North Carolina; when seventeen years of age entered West Point; in 1852 graduated with highest honors in a class of forty three, and was commissioned Second Lieutenant in the Second Regiment of Dragoons; in 1855 was promoted to First Lieutenant. He was the first United States officer from North Carolina to join the Confederacy; he wore the sword of his uncle John H. Anderson, who was killed in 1847, in the Mexican War; he was made Colonel of the 4th Regiment of North Carolina State Troops by Governor Ellis; he reached Manassas, Virginia, July 21, 1861, and on the day after the battle was made Commandant of that army post; he was recommended by General D. H. Hill and by General Joseph E. Johnson for a Brigadiership; later his conspicuous bravery was witnessed by President Davis, and he was made a Brigadier General; in the Battle of Manassas his regiment took in 520 officers and men in killed and wounded, and lost 26 out of 27 officers and a total of 462 officers and men; at Sharpsburg (or Antietam as

the Northerners call the battle) he was wounded in the foot and died of blood poisoning, October 16, 1862.

He married in November, 1859, Miss Mildred Ewing of Louisville, Kentucky.

III. Walker[5] Anderson[71] (b. June, 1835); Capt. C. S. A. Crippled by a fall in childhood; enlisted in the C. S. A., and was in the battle of Santa Rosa Island, his first battle, and afterwards in all the great battles of the Army of Tennessee; he was killed in the battle of Resaca, Georgia, while carrying orders on horseback. He was a Captain and Staff Officer at the time. He was buried first at Columbus, Georgia, and after the war his remains were removed to St. John's Cemetery, Pensacola, Florida.

He married Rebecca Cameron, daughter of Paul Cameron, of Hillsboro, N. C.

IV. Bettie[5] Anderson, who married a Mr. Thompson.

V. Mary[5] Anderson, unmarried.

2. Duncan[3] Cameron (b. 1777),[72] who studied law in the office of Paul Carrington, of Charlotte County, Virginia, a distinguished lawyer, and settled in Hillsboro, North Carolina; and was during his career Judge of the Superior Court, President

---

[71] William E. Anderson, writing in 1903, *Tales of a Grandfather* (unpublished), for his grandson, Walker Anderson, said: "Your uncle [he meant great-uncle] Walker was married during the war to Kate Cameron of Raleigh, North Carolina. There was a very singular chain of coincidences in connection with his marriage. His cousin, Walker Anderson, of North Carolina, of the same age as himself, was also a captain in the Army of Northern Virginia. They were engaged to two young ladies, Kate and Rebecca Cameron, who also were cousins. They obtained furloughs from their respective commands and met in Raleigh for the first time. They were married on the same day, and were killed in the same week, about ten months after, one in Virginia and one in Georgia. Thus two cousins, of the same name and age, and both captains of artillery, were engaged to two cousins of the same family name. They were married on the same day, and were afterwards killed in the same week."

[72] A memorandum courteously furnished the author by Miss Kate C. Shipp, of Lincolnton, N. C., says he was born in Prince Edward County, Virginia. This is possible, but should be verified. We have found no evidence of Rev. John Cameron's residence in Prince Edward County. He seems, as shown above, to have removed from Charlotte County, Virginia, to Mecklenburg County, Virginia.

of the Old State Bank of North Carolina, and Clerk of the Supreme Court of the State. A great friend of the State University, he was instrumental in reopening it after the dark days of the "Reconstruction."

He married Rebecca Bennehan, daughter of Richard Bennehan, a planter of Orange County, N. C., of which Hillsboro is the county seat.

They had two sons and six daughters. The older son died unmarried; all of the daughters, except Margaret, died unmarried. Margaret married George Mordecai, of Raleigh, North Carolina. But they left no children.

The other child:

(a) Paul Carrington[4] Cameron, married Anne Ruffin, daughter of Thomas Ruffin, Chief Justice of the Supreme Court of North Carolina, and they had:

    I. Rebecca[5] Cameron, who married, first, Walker[5] Anderson, and, second, Major John Washington Graham. Issue by first marriage:

    (1) An only child, who died in infancy.

    Issue by the second marriage:

      There were four children who died in infancy. Besides these there were:

      (1) Paul Cameron[6] Graham, who married Mary Courtney Chestney.

      (2) George Mordecai[6] Graham (unmarried).

      (3) Isabella Davidson[6] Graham, who married Thomas Webb.

      (4) William Alexander[6] Graham, who married Anne Cameron Shepard.

      (5) Joseph[6] Graham, who married Henrietta Heartt.

      (6) Anne Cameron[6] Graham, who married Robert F. Smallwood.

    II. Anne Ruffin[5] Cameron, who married Major George Pumpelly Collins, and had:

      (1) Annie Cameron[6] Collins, who married William Lewis Wall.

(2) Rebecca Anderson[6] Collins, who married Frank Wood.
(3) Mary Arthur[6] Collins (who died at the age of five).
(4) George William Kent[6] Collins (unm.).
(5) Henrietta Page[6] Collins (unm.).
(6) **Mary Arthur[6] Collins, who married (as his 2nd wife), Frank Wood.**
(7) Alice Ruffin[6] Collins, who married Frank Carter Mebane.
(8) Paul Cameron[6] Collins, who married Mary Hyman McNeill.

III. Margaret[5] Cameron, who married Judge Robert B. Peebles, and had:
(1) Annie Ruffin[6] Peebles, who married Thomas Norfleet Webb.

IV. Duncan[5] Cameron, who married Mary Bagby Short, and had:
(1) Mary Warren[6] Cameron, who married Joseph Russell Ross.
(2) Pauline Carrington[6] Cameron, who married Roy McDuffy.
(3) Rebecca Bennehan[6] Cameron (who died in childhood).

V. Pauline Carrington[5] Cameron, who married William Blount Shepard, and had:
(1) Anne Cameron[6] Shepard, who married William Alexander Graham.

VI. Bennehan[5] Cameron, who married Sallie Taliaferro Mayo, and had:
(1) Paul Carrington[6] Cameron (who died at the age of two years).
(2) Isabella Mayo[6] Cameron.
(3) Anne[6] Cameron (d. in infancy).
(4) Sallie Taliaferro[6] Cameron, who married John Witherspoon Labonisse.

VII. Mildred Coles[5] Cameron, who married (2nd wife), William Blount Shepard.

3. Jean³ Cameron, who married July 27, 1806, the Reverend Andrew Syme (b. Sept. 2, 1755, in Lanockshire, Scotland, d. Oct. 26, 1845), who came to Virginia in 1792[73] as a tutor in the family of Dr. John Brockenbrough, of Tappahannock. He served several churches, in Hungars Parish and elsewhere; and at one time was rector of "Old Blandford" Church in Petersburg.
They had:
  (a) John W.⁴ Syme (b. Jan. 16, 1811, d. Nov., 1865), married April 10, 1833, Mary Cowan Maddin, daughter of M. Maddin, of Petersburg, Virginia, and had:
    I. Jean Cameron⁵ Syme (b. Jan. 14, 1834, d. March 19, 1834).
    II. Elizabeth Batte⁵ Syme (b. March 14, 1836), married November 17, 1853, Buckner Davis Williams, and had:
      (aa) Rebecca Davis⁶ Williams (b. July 24, 1858, d. 1903, unm.).
      (bb) Mary Louisa⁶ Williams.
      (cc) John Syme⁶ Williams, who married Betty Council.
      (They have a number of children.)
      (dd) Hugh Davis⁶ Williams, who married Mary Ingram. (No children.)
      (ee) Walker Anderson⁶ Williams, who married, Feb. 21, 1914, Isabella Willis Pescud, and had:
        (1) Peter Pescud⁷ Williams (b. Dec. 15, 1914).
        (2) Rebecca Davis⁷ Williams (b. Aug. 29, 1919).
      (ff) Ewan Cameron⁶ Williams (unm.).
      (gg) Elizabeth Winthrow⁶ Williams, who married John W. Brown, and had:
        (1) Elizabeth⁷ Brown, who married William Yoder, and had:
          I. William⁸ Yoder, Jr.
        (2) John W.⁷ Brown.

---

[73] Meade: *Old Churches and Families of Virginia*, I, 390.

(hh) Emma Buckner[6] Williams, who married Ovid Porter. (No children.)
III. Mary Louisa[5] Syme (b. Dec. 16, 1838, d. 1917), married April 26, 1860, William E. Anderson. No issue.
IV. Andrew[5] Syme (b. June 24, 1841, d. July 5, 1894), married first, April 28, 1869, Blanche Bragg (d. Feb. 1, 1870), daughter of Thomas Bragg, and had:
- (aa) Blanche Bragg[6] Syme (b. Jan. 31, 1870), who married Charles M. Gilliam, of Petersburg, Virginia, and had:
  - (1) Charles M.[7] Gilliam, Jr., who married June 18, 1929, Virginia Randolph Goodwin, of Louisa, Va.
  - (2) Mary Anderson[7] Gilliam,
  - (3) Charlotte[7] Gilliam.

Andrew[5] Syme, married, second, Jan. 29, 1874, Annie S. Bryan (d. July 5, 1926), and had:
- (bb) Andrew[6] Syme (b. Dec. 29, 1874), who married May Bryan, of Pittsboro, North Carolina. (No children.)
- (cc) George Frederick[6] Syme (b. April 6, 1878), married January 15, 1908, Harriet Haywood, of Raleigh, North Carolina. (No children.)
- (dd) William Anderson[6] Syme (b. July 11, 1879, d. Dec. 15, 1909, unm.).
- (ee) John Bryan[6] Syme (b. Jan. 21, 1881, d. Sept. 7, 1881).

V. John Cameron[5] Syme (b. Dec. 20, 1843, d. unm.).
VI. Mildred Cameron[5] Syme (b. June 26, 1849, d. unm.).
VII. Duncan Cameron[5] Syme (b. Feb. 16, 1852, d. 1928, unm.).

4. John Adams[3] Cameron (b. in Mecklenburg County, Virginia, in 1788, d. June 14, 1839).[74]

---

[74]Memorial tablet in Christ's Church, Pensacola, Florida. The account on this tablet continues, "Judge of the Federal District Court of Florida, 1831 to 1839, one of the founders of the Diocese of Florida and a member of the first Diocesan Convention. He drafted the Constitution and Canons of the Diocese. He was author of the first missionary address to the Diocese and vestryman of the Parish which he served with faithful and intelligent devotion."

He graduated from the University of North Carolina in 1806, at which institution he was registered from Virginia. At the time, his brother Duncan Cameron lived only a few miles from the College. He established himself at Fayetteville, North Carolina; was a member of the State Legislature; a Major in the War of 1812; Consul to Vera Cruz, and as stated, United States District Judge in Florida. He was lost at sea in the wreck of the ship *Pulaski* while going from Savannah to New York, to bring home his daughters, who were attending a school there.

He was twice married: first to Miss Eliza Adam, and second, to Mrs. Catherine McQueen Halliday, a widow, whose maiden name was McQueen.

Issue by the first marriage:

(a) Mary[4] Cameron, who married Dr. Pride Jones, of Hillsboro, North Carolina, and had:
  I. Eliza[5] Jones (never married).
  II. Mary[5] Jones (never married).
  III. Halcott[5] Jones, who married Olive Eccles of Alabama and had several children, one of them Mrs. Ernest Cruikshank, is Principal of Columbia Institute, a church school, in Tennessee.

Issue by the second marriage:

(a) John Donald[4] Cameron, who married Rebecca Waddell, of Hillsboro, N. C., and had:
  (Children surviving childhood):
    I. Katherine[5] Cameron, who married Walter Cushman, and had:
      (aa) Rebecca[6] Cushman.
    II. Mary[5] Cameron (unmarried).

(b) Anna Nash[4] Cameron, who married, Jan. 6, 1848, Reverend Jarvis Buxton, of Fayetteville, N. C., who, for about forty years, was Rector of Trinity Church, Asheville, N. C., and had:
  I. Katherine Cameron[5] Buxton, who married Joseph McRee, and had:

(aa) Anna C.[6] McRee, who married Herbert Luterloh, of Fayetteville, N. C., and has three sons.
II. Jarvis Barry[5] Buxton, who married Eva Peebles. (No children.)
III. John Cameron[5] Buxton, who married Agnes Belo, and had:
   (aa) Cameron[6] Buxton (d. unm.).
   (bb) Caro[6] Buxton, who married a Mr. Edwards, of England.
   (cc) Jarvis[6] Buxton (d. in childhood).
   (dd) Anna[6] Buxton, who married a Mr. Beck.
IV. Frances Ellen[5] Buxton (d. unm.).
V. Eliza McQueen[5] Buxton.
VI. Anna Nash[5] Buxton (d. in childhood).
VII. Margaret Halliday[5] Buxton, who married Charles Kain, of Philadelphia, Pa.
VIII. Mary R.[5] Buxton, who married Moses E. Banks.

(c) Catherine[4] Cameron, who married Judge William M. Shipp, and had:
   I. Anna[5] Shipp, who married Dr. Sumner McBee, of Lincolnton.
   II. William Ewen[5] Shipp, Lt. U. S. A. (killed on San Juan Hill, in 1898), who married Margaret Busbee, and had:
       (aa) Major William Ewen Shipp, now Assistant Military Attache, at the American Embassy, at Rome.
   III. Bartlett[5] Shipp (attorney), who married Prue Crouse.
   IV. Katherine Cameron[5] Shipp, who has been very helpful to the writer in connection with this genealogy.

(d) William[4] Cameron (d. in early manhood unmarried).

5. Anne[3] Cameron (died young).
6. William[3] Cameron, attorney, of Hillsboro, North Carolina, married Anna Call, daughter of Daniel Call, an eminent lawyer, Reporter of the Virginia Supreme Court, and brother-in-law of Chief Justice John Marshall. They had:

(a) Walker Anderson[4] Cameron, who in 1841 married Elizabeth Harrison Walker,[75] who was a granddaughter of Benjamin Harrison, of "Berkeley," and a great-granddaughter of William Byrd, of "Westover," and they had:
  I. William Evelyn[5] Cameron[76] (b. November 29, 1842), who at the outbreak of the war between the states was in St. Louis, Missouri. He at once returned to Virginia, and enlisted as a private in Company A, 12th Regiment of Virginia Volunteers. He rose through the non-commissioned grades to the rank of Lieutenant of his Company, and subsequently to the post of Regimental Adjutant and Brigade Inspector. "He served with uniform gallantly throughout the war, was several times severely wounded, and surrendered finally at Appomattox Court House with the rank of Captain."[77]

  After the war he entered the field of journalism, beginning as a protege of Honorable Anthony M. Keiley, who was then conducting the *Daily News* of Petersburg. His first contributions were a series of sketches of the war. This paper was suppressed by the Carpet-bag authorities; but was renewed as the *Index*, and later became the *Index and Appeal*. He later edited the *Norfolk Virginian*, but returned to Petersburg to take editorial charge of the *Index*, which he conducted until 1870, when he became the editor of the Richmond *Whig*. In 1872 he assumed control of the Richmond *Enquirer*, but in October, 1873, returned again to Petersburg and was con-

---

[75] *Virginia and Virginians* (Brock), I, 252.

[76] There is some confusion about the middle name of Governor Cameron. In *Virginia and Virginians* (Vol. I, p. 251), his name is given—and repeated as "William Ewan Cameron." That such was his middle name might easily be supposed as he was of the Clan Cameron of which Sir Ewan Lochiel was, at one time, the head. But on the other hand his mother was a descendant of William Byrd, of *Westover*, and the name Evelyn is a favorite one in that family. Several sources, including descendants, give his middle name as "Evelyn," as does a Petersburg, Va., newspaper with which he was connected.

[77] *Virginia and Virginians*, I, 252.

nected with the editorial staff of the *Index*. In 1877 he was again with the *Whig* and continued in editorial control thereof until December, 1879.

In 1868 he fought a duel, growing out of political differences with Robert W. Hughes, at one time United States Judge for the Eastern District of Virginia, and was severely wounded.

In 1876 he was elected Mayor of Petersburg, Virginia, and thus served continuously as the result of four successive elections, until he was nominated for the Governorship of Virginia. In 1881 Captain Cameron was elected Governor of Virginia over the Conservative Candidate Major, later United States Senator, John Warwick Daniel. He assumed his duties of the Governorship January 1, 1882, and served for the term of four years. He was of medium stature, prepossessing in appearance, a vigorous writer and an effective public speaker.

He married Louisa C. Egerton, of Petersburg, Virginia, and had:

(1) Robert Walker[6] Cameron, who married Ellen Sims, of Chicago, Illinois, and had:
    (aa) William Walker[7] Cameron.

(2) Susie C.[6] Cameron, who married Byron C. Whitfield, of Florida, and had:
    (aa) Evelyn Cameron[7] Whitfield,
    (bb) Lou Egerton[7] Whitfield.

(3) George W.[6] Cameron, who married Anne C. Smith, of Louisa, Virginia, and had:
    (aa) Evelyn Byrd[7] Cameron, who married William H. Pond.
    (bb) George Egerton[7] Cameron.

II. Evelyn[5] Cameron, who married Judge Raney of Florida.

(b) John[4] Cameron, who married Frances Hawks, and had:
  I. Francis[5] Cameron, who married 1st, Margaret Haywood, and 2nd, Jeannie Weaver.

Issue by first marriage:
- (aa) Captain Frank[6] Cameron, U. S. A.
- (bb) Duncan[6] Cameron, who married Theodora Marshall.

Issue by second marriage:
- (cc) Jeannie[6] Cameron.
- (dd) Fanny[6] Cameron (and two other daughters—names not ascertained).

  II. John[5] Cameron, who married Eliz. Fitzpatrick, and had:
- (aa) Helen[6] Cameron, who married Edward Anderson.
- (bb) Frank[6] Cameron, a Professor in the University of North Carolina.

(c) Dr. William[4] Cameron, C. S. A., who married Emma Moore, and had:
  I. Anna[5] Cameron,
  II. Emma[5] Cameron,
  III. Rebecca[5] Cameron,
  IV. Donald[5] Cameron,
  V. Marshall[5] Cameron,
  VI. Alan[5] Cameron, who married Emily Sutton.

(d) Anna[4] Cameron, who married Alex. Kirkland, and had:
  I. William[5] Kirkland,
  II. Robert[5] Kirkland.

(e) Rebecca[4] Cameron, who married Benj. Edmunds, and had:
  I. Mary[5] Edmunds, who married W. H. Day.

(f) Mary[4] Cameron, who married William Edwards, and had:
  I. Walter[5] Edwards, who married Sarah Hardison.

(g) Elizabeth[4] Cameron, who married Henry Witherspoon.

7. Thomas[3] Cameron, a physician of Fayetteville, North Carolina, married twice: First, Jane Wilder, of Petersburg, Virginia, sister of Josepha Wilder, who married Bishop Thomas Atkinson, third Bishop of the Diocese of North Carolina; second, Miss Isabella Wilkins.

Issue by the first marriage:
(a) John[4] Cameron, of Wilmington, N. C.

(b) Mary[4] Cameron, who married Major Seaton Gales, of Raleigh, North Carolina.

Issue by the second marriage:

(a) Kate[4] Cameron, married her cousin, Walker Anderson, who was killed in the Civil War. They had no children, and both died young. Kate Cameron married a second time, Major John Graham, of Hillsboro, N. C., and had several children by this second marriage.

CHAPTER XI

Genealogical Notes

BACON, BALLARD, BETTS, BILLUPS, BOULDEN, BLAGRAVE, BRODNAX, BUFORD, CALDWELL, CAMERON, CHAPPELL, CLAIBORNE, CLAY, COX, CURETON, DELONY, DIXON, EDLOE, ELLIDGE, ELLIS, EMBRY, EPES, FARMER, FERTH, FONTAINE.

THESE notes, relating in the main to families which furnished Vestrymen to Cumberland Parish, will, doubtless, in their brevity and fragmentary character, be disappointing. Possibly much of the material in the three chapters devoted to these notes might well have been wholly omitted from this volume. In considering whether to incorporate it, the choice was between presenting the material as it here appears, if it were to be presented at all, or omitting it altogether.

Obviously in a work primarily devoted to another purpose, extended genealogies of the many families mentioned could not be embodied, for want of space, even if material for them were at hand. But material for anything approaching an adequate genealogy of these families was not at hand. Such material, in a majority of the cases, is doubtless in existence, but could be assembled only by travel, research and correspondence of a character and extent which the writer has not been able to indulge.

The material from which these notes, such as they are, have been drawn, is the by-product, in the main, of investigations and observations and jottings, preserved through a number of years in the hope that parts of it might be useful at some time.

Upon the whole, it has seemed appropriate to set down these items here, for what they may be worth, with the explanation that in no instance do they assume to be even approximately adequate sketches of any of the families mentioned.

The highest hope that can be indulged respecting them is that they may be helpful, in some degree, to those engaged in genealogical research respecting the families mentioned.

BACON.

There is a tradition that the Bacons of Lunenburg and elsewhere are *descended from* Nathaniel Bacon, "the Rebel." If so it would be an honorable and highly prized descent. They were doubtless related to, but not descended from him, as he left no male descendant.

This family seems from an early date, allied with the Lyddall Family, as that name is persistent in the Bacon family. The Lunenburg Bacons seem descended from

Edmund[1] Bacon, of New Kent County, "who in 1687, as 'Capt. Edmund Bacon,' patented lands in that County on the Pamunkey River."[1] On this patent, among the headrights or immigrants mentioned are Ann Lyddall and Thomas Bacon. The author[2] of the article in *William and Mary Quarterly* says: "It is very probable that Capt. Bacon married Ann Lyddall, and that Thomas was his son. Ann Lyddall was a daughter doubtless of Capt. George Lyddall, a prominent character in our early annals."[3]

"Captain Edmund Bacon was doubtless a relation, but could not have been a son of Nathaniel Bacon, the Rebel, as he was a grown man and a 'Captain' ten years after Nathaniel Bacon's death."[4]

Captain Edmund[1] Bacon is believed to have had a son John[2] Bacon[5] who in 1701 patented a tract of land "formerly patented" by Captain Edmund Bacon. He was Sheriff of New Kent County, Va., and a Vestryman of St. Peter's Parish.

He married twice: first, Sarah (Langston?) (d. Jan. 4, 1709-10), and second, July 4, 1710, Susannah Parke, daughter of John Parke.

By the first marriage he had children, whose names are lost from the parish register, which at this point is mutilated. They were born, one on August 14, 1708, and the other on December

---
[1] *William and Mary Quarterly*, X, 267.
[2] Presumably Dr. Lyon G. Tyler.
[3] *William and Mary Quarterly*, X, 268.
[4] *William and Mary Quarterly*, X, 268.
[5] Id.

30, 1709. Their names, as other records indicate, were doubtless:
Nathaniel[3] Bacon and
William[3] Bacon.[6]

By the second marriage he had:
John[3] Bacon (b. May 4, 1711),
Sarah[3] Bacon (b. December 28, 1712),
Lyddall[3] Bacon (b. 1717),
Edmund[3] Bacon (b. April 8, 1722),
Anne[3] Bacon (b. October 29, 1727),
Fanny[3] Bacon (b. February 5, 1734).

John[3] Bacon (b. May 4, 1711), moved to Lunenburg County, and died there, presumably in 1759, as his will, dated October 20, 1758, was probated in Lunenburg County, July 3, 1759.[7] He was married twice: 1st wife, Ann (last name not known). His second wife's name was Frances (last name not known), and his children as disclosed by the will were:

1. John[4] Bacon,
2. William[4] Bacon,
3. Edmund[4] Bacon,
4. Nathaniel[4] Bacon,
5. Francis[4] Bacon [abstract says Frances—a son],
6. Elizabeth[4] Bacon,
7. Sarah[4] Bacon,
8. Susannah[4] Bacon,
9. Mary[4] Bacon.

In addition to this information from the will, the writer in *William and Mary Quarterly*[8] gives the added items that:

John[4] Bacon was born November 20, 1733, and was a child of the first wife, and gives the names of the children of the second marriage as follows:

1. Alice[4] Bacon (b. Nov. 22, 1736),
2. Frances[4] Bacon (b. April 24, 1738), who married Benjamin Estes.
3. William[4] Bacon,
4. Edmund Parkes[4] Bacon,

---

[6]*William and Mary Quarterly*, X, 268.
[7]It is of record in Will Book 1, at page 258.
[8]X, 269.

5. Nathaniel⁴ Bacon,
6. Elizabeth⁴ Bacon,
7. Sarah⁴ Bacon,
8. Susanna⁴ Bacon,
9. Mary⁴ Bacon.

Lyddall³ Bacon (John,² Edmund¹) (b. 1717), married Mary (Allen?), and had:
1. Elizabeth⁴ Bacon (b. Dec. 14, 1741),
2. Lucy⁴ Bacon (b. April 11, 1744),
3. Langston⁴ Bacon (b. May 26, 1746),
4. Anne⁴ Bacon (b. October 11, 1748),
5. Susannah⁴ Bacon, (b. Jan. 6, 1750),
6. Sarah⁴ Bacon (b. Aug. 19, 1753, d. Nov. 2, 17—),
7. Lyddall⁴ Bacon (b. Nov. 27, 175—),
8. Mary⁴ Bacon (b. March 14, 1758, d. Dec. 16, 1760),
9. Edmund Parkes⁴ Bacon (b. Nov. 13, 1762),
10. Richard⁴ Bacon (b. Nov. 20, 1760),
11. Drury Allen⁴ Bacon (b. Dec. 14, 1765, d. in Mecklenburg Co., Va., Sept. 3, 1845).

The will of Lyddall³ Bacon was dated July 21, 1775, and probated October 12, 1775.[9] It shows that his daughter Elizabeth Bacon married William Gordon; that his daughter Ann Bacon married Robert Dixon and that his daughter Sarah Bacon married John Glenn.

William Gordon was a Sergeant in the company of Captain John Stokes, from Lunenburg, in the Revolution.[10]

Robert Dixon and John Glenn were two of the Justices of the County Court of Lunenburg County, to whom the land for the Court House was conveyed,[11] and John Glenn was successively a Captain and a Colonel in the Revolution.[12]

Another of his daughters married Charles Allen,[13] who was doubtless, the same Charles Allen who was a member of the County Court of Lunenburg County in 1763-1764, and who prob-

---

[9] It is recorded in Lunenburg County, Va., in W. B. 2, p. 428.
[10] *The Old Free State*, I, 234.
[11] Id., 119-121.
[12] *The Old Free State*, I, 266-267.
[13] The will mentions Charles Allen as a son-in-law.

ably became a resident of Mecklenburg County, when that County was cut off from Lunenburg County.

Edmund[3] Bacon (John,[2] Edmund[1]) (b. April 8, 1722)[14], was married twice. The first wife was Elizabeth (last name not known); name of second wife not known. By the first wife he had:

1. Lyddall[4] Bacon (b. January 10, 1756), and (probably) also,
2. Sarah[4] Bacon, who married Honorable John Clopton, member of Congress (b. Feb. 7, 1756, d. Sept. 11, 1816),[15]

John[4] Bacon (John,[3] John,[2] Edmund[1]), married Agnes Hobson, daughter of Nicholas Hobson, of Lunenburg County, Virginia, son of Mathew Hobson, of Henrico County.[16]

Edmund Parkes[4] Bacon (John,[3] John,[2] Edmund[1]), married November 21, 1781, Martha Pettypool.[17] His will is dated November 1, 1825, and was probated in Lunenburg County, November 14, 1825.[18]

They had:

1. Richard C.[5] Bacon, married Jan. 21, 1817, Mary E. Jordan.
2. Gillie M.[5] Bacon,
3. Lyddall[5] Bacon,
4. Mary A. G.[5] Bacon (called "Polly"), who married May 9, 1804, Isaac Oliver.
5. Sally[5] Bacon, married June 2, 1807, Peter Jones.

William and Mary Quarterly (X, 270), says one of the daughters was "Sally Glenn." The will mentions one of the daughters as "Sallie G. Jones." She married June 2, 1807, Peter Jones, Jr.,[19] who was "Major" Peter Jones, by whom she had:

Julia[6] Jones, who married Dr. Henry May.[20]

6. Susanna R.[5] Bacon, who married Nov. 20, 1807, Peter R. Bland.
7. Narcissa[5] Bacon, who married November 30, 1812, Wil-

---

[14]*William and Mary Quarterly*, X, 269
[15]Id., 270.
[16]Id.
[17]Id.
[18]It is recorded in W. B. 8, p. 523.
[19]*The Old Free State*, II, 403, and Rev. John Cameron's Register.
[20]For the May Family see: *The Old Free State*, II, 311-319.

liam Henry Taylor,[21] Clerk of Lunenburg County 1814-1846.
8. Montfort S.[5] Bacon.[22]
9. Young H.[5] Bacon.

Gillie Marion[5] Bacon (Edmund Parkes,[4] John,[3] John,[2] Edmund[1]) (b. Aug. 4, 1795, d. July 27, 1865). Married twice: First a Miss Rose (or Rhodes). The record of this marriage has not been found. The date is not known, nor is the name of his first wife positively established. Three children by this marriage were:

(1) Maria Stokes[6] Bacon.
(2) Edmund Parke[6] Bacon.
(3) William[6] Bacon.

He married second (M. B. July 13, 1825), Mary Ann Street Jones (b. March 5, 1800, d. July 15, 1873), dau. Waddy and Elizabeth (Smith) Street, and widow of Edward Montfort Jones, and had:

(4) Indiana Marian[6] Bacon.
(5) Waddy Street[6] Bacon, Confederate soldier. Emigrated from Lunenburg Co., Va., to California in 1849. M. Inez Street, no children. He died in 1905 in Dinwiddie Co., Va.
(6) Gillie Marion[6] Bacon, Jr. (b. March 25, 1831, at Lunenburg C. H., Va., d. in Waco, Texas, March 24, 1897). Married, January 24, 1867, Cora A. West, at the home of James S. Parrish, in Christian County, Kentucky, and moved to Texas in March, 1881.

They had:
(a) James Parish[7] Bacon (b. April 9, 1868, d. Dec. 2, 1884).
(b) Mary Gillie[7] Bacon (b. Feb. 14, 1871, living 1929, at Ada, Okla.) Married ———— Reeves, and has one daughter,

---
[21]*The Old Free State*, II, 445, 366.
[22]The name is spelled in the will "Muntford," and in William and Mary Quarterly (X, 270), "Mountford." It should be Montfort. The name originated with the Montfort ancestor of a part of the family.

I. Mrs. James[8] Wesson, of Waco, Texas (b. Jan. 28, 1898).
  (c) Parke Street[7] Bacon (b. July 29, 1873, living 1929), in Waco, Texas.
  (d) John Barrett[7] Bacon (b. March 24, 1878, living 1929, in San Francisco, California.
  (e) Waddy Lee[7] Bacon (b. July 9, 1881, living 1929, in Waco, Texas).
(7) Mary Jane[6] Bacon (d. at the age of 96, at Sulphur, Okla.), married a Mr. Lester.
(8) Martha[6] Bacon, married Thomas Bacon (a first cousin), died at Henderson, Kentucky.
(9) George[6] Bacon, a Confederate soldier, lost his life by drowning, in the War Between the States. Unm.
(10) Alex[6] Bacon, a Confederate soldier, killed in action in the War. Unm.
(11) Sydney Montfort[6] Bacon, died unm. in Henderson, Kentucky.

Four members of the Bacon family of Lunenburg County, Virginia, emigrated to Caldwell County, Kentucky. One of these was Lyddall Bacon, doubtless Lyddall[5] Bacon, brother of Gillie Marion[5] Bacon, Sr.

Parke Bacon, M. D., married a Miss Maize and lived in Evansville, Indiana.

Thomas Bacon, M. D., married (as above mentioned) Martha[6] Bacon, daughter of Gillie M.[5] Bacon.

It seems that Lyddall[3] Bacon (whose will was probated in 1775), was the first vestryman of that name in Cumberland Parish, while his son Lyddall[4] Bacon also was a vestryman from 1784 to 1787.

It seems that Edmund Parkes[4] Bacon was the vestryman of Cumberland Parish, spoken of in those records as Edmund P. Bacon.

BALLARD.

Thomas[1] Ballard (b. 1630, buried March 24, 1689), was clerk of York County from 1652 to 1690.[23] He was a burgess from

---

[23] Johnson: *Memorials of Virginia Clerks*, 405.

James City in 1666, and a member of the Council in 1675, and was speaker of the House of Burgesses in 1680.

His case as a creditor of "Bacon the rebel" was in 1686 submitted to the King by the Council.[24] He married Anne Thomas, who died September 26, 1678.[25] He was known as Major Thomas Ballard,[26] and his wife "was captured by Bacon and placed, with other ladies of the Council, upon his breastworks before Jamestown, where their white aprons warned Berkeley from attack."[27]

He [probably] had three sons:

Captain Thomas[2] Ballard, sheriff of York County, and
Francis[2] Ballard (probably born in 1675), sub-sheriff, and
John[2] Ballard, who, likely, died without issue before 1694.[28]

"The Ballards resided for generations at a spot [in York County] known as 'Pryor's Plantation'."[29]

Captain Thomas[2] Ballard (Thomas[1]), "was burgess, justice of the peace, and Colonel of York County."[30] His will was proved June 18, 1711. He married Katharine Huberd, daughter of John Huberd,[31] and had:

1. Anne[3] Ballard, who married John Major,
2. Matthew[3] Ballard,
3. Elizabeth[3] Ballard,
4. Katharine[3] Ballard,
5. Thomas[3] Ballard,
6. Robert[3] Ballard,
7. John[3] Ballard,
8. William[3] Ballard,
9. Mary[3] Ballard.

The last five of these may have been "by a second wife, being under age."[32]

The son,

---

[24] *William and Mary Quarterly*, II, 274.
[25] Id.
[26] Id., I, 82.
[27] Id., II, 274.
[28] *William and Mary Quarterly*, II, 274.
[29] Id., I, 82.
[30] Id., III, 208.
[31] Id.
[32] *William and Mary Quarterly*, III, 208.

Captain John³ Ballard, of Yorktown (will proved in 1745),³³ had:
1. Thomas⁴ Ballard,
2. John⁴ Ballard,
3. Robert⁴ Ballard, Clerk of Princess Anne County, Va.,
4. William⁴ Ballard,
5. Catherine⁴ Ballard,
6. Elizabeth⁴ Ballard,
7. Anne⁴ Ballard.

Francis² Ballard (Thomas¹) (d. March 12, 1719), married Mary Servant, daughter of Bertrand Servant, "a natural born subject of ye kingdom of France," who at the age of sixty six was naturalized by the Virginia Council and Assembly in 1698,³⁴ and had:
1. Francis³ Ballard,
2. Servant³ Ballard,
3. Frances³ Ballard,
4. Mary³ Ballard,
5. Lucy³ Ballard,
6. Anne³ Ballard.

Thomas Ballard, of Charles City County (who died circa. 1794), had children, of whom mention is made as follows:
John Ballard,
Thomas Ballard,
William Talbot Ballard,
Francis Dancy Ballard,
Elizabeth Ballard, who married Moses Fontaine,
Sarah Ballard, who married Abraham Fontaine,
Lucy Ballard, who married Peter Eppes,
Ann Eliza Ballard (who married Henry Talman before 1733), is mentioned as a daughter of Thomas Ballard.

"The Ballard Family," says the writer (presumably Dr. Lyon G. Tyler), in *William and Mary Quarterly* (Vol. III, 208), "is a numerous one, and difficult to trace in later generations."

In *William and Mary Quarterly*, V, pages 272-273, is preserved

---
³³*William and Mary Quarterly*, XXIII, 219.
³⁴*William and Mary Quarterly*, IX, 123.

a record of some of the descendants of Lucy Ballard and Peter Eppes.

John Ballard came to Lunenburg County certainly as early as 1751, for that year we find him listed for one tithe on the list of Field Jefferson, which indicates that he was then in that part of Lunenburg afterwards cut off into Mecklenburg.

He was probably (though the writer cannot assert it positively) the son of Captain John[3] Ballard (of Yorktown), whose will was proved as above noted in 1745.

If this assumption be correct he was

John[4] Ballard of this line. There is some slight support of the correctness of this surmise found in the Mecklenburg County records, for on March 2, 1765, "John Ballard, Jr.," probably this John, was appointed an "under" or deputy sheriff under Richard Witton, Sheriff.[85]

This would indicate that his father was also named John Ballard.

It may be however that the "John Ballard, Jr.," appointed deputy sheriff was the son of the first John Ballard in Lunenburg County.

Captain John Ballard of Mecklenburg County, in the Revolution[36] was presumably John[5] Ballard. But there is a possibility that this "Captain Ballard" was the Major Francis Ballard, who died Aug. 4, 1808, and whose nuncupative will was probated in Mecklenburg County, August 9, 1808.[87]

If the surmise indulged be correct, the John Ballard who appeared in Lunenburg about 1751,

John[4] Ballard was the same John Ballard whose will, dated August 26, 1783, was probated in Mecklenburg County, Virginia, July 9, 1787.[88]

His wife, mentioned in the will, was named Faitha (last name not known). They had:

---

[85]Mecklenburg County O. B. 1, pages 1-2.
[36]*Eighth Annual Report of Library Board and State Librarian* (Va.), 1910-11, page 30.
[87]It is recorded in W. B. 6, page 133.
[88]It is of record in W. B. 2, page 214.

1. Lucy[5] Ballard, who married a man named Holmes. She is spoken of in the will as "my daughter Lucy Holmes."
2. Becky[5] Ballard, who married a man named Holloway. She is mentioned in the will as "my daughter Becky Holloway."
3. Martha[5] Ballard, who also married a man named Holloway. She is mentioned in the will as "my daughter Martha Holloway."
4. Betty[5] Ballard, who married a man named Cook. She is spoken of in the will as "my daughter Betty Cook."
5. John[5] Ballard, who married Mary Garland, daughter of David Garland of Lunenburg County, Virginia.[39]
6. William[5] Ballard,
7. Robert[5] Ballard,
8. Francis[5] Ballard.[40]

Of these children,

William[5] Ballard (d. circa. 1817), whose will was dated January 9, 1811, and probated in Mecklenburg County, Virginia,[41] June 15, 1817, had (as shown by the will):

1. Faitha[6] Ballard,
2. Mary[6] Ballard,
3. Elizabeth[6] Ballard, who married (M. B. in Mecklenburg Co., Va., dated Jan. 5, 1803), Caleb Wilson of Orange County, North Carolina.
4. Rebecca[6] Ballard, who married (M. B. in Mecklenburg Co., Va., dated Dec. 10, 1804), John Davis, Jr.

The will speaks of "my son in law John Overton" and "my grand-children Faitha Gray and William B. Overton, children of John Overton."

---

[39] This was "Colonel" David Garland, of Lunenburg County, whose will dated March 18, 1780, was probated May 8, 1782, and is of record in W. B. 3, page 108. In it he mentions one of his daughters as "Mary Ballard, wife of John Ballard."

[40] This was "Major Francis Ballard," whose nuncupative will was probated in Mecklenburg County, Va., August 9, 1808. He is not mentioned in the will above mentioned of John[4] Ballard. All the others mentioned as children are mentioned in the will. But that he was a child is proved by the fact that he left his niece Fathy Ballard Overton, daughter of John Overton, a tract of land in Lunenburg County, Va., and William Ballard in his will mentions this granddaughter, and speaks of his son-in-law John Overton.

[41] It is recorded in W. B. 7, page 245.

It does not affirmatively appear which one of his daughters married John Overton. Probably it was "Faitha."

There is in Mecklenburg County, Va., a marriage bond dated November 10, 1806, for the marriage of John Overton and *Elizabeth* Ballard, on which Francis Ballard is surety. This is a little confusing, except on the supposition that the name "Elizabeth" is an error. The daughter Elizabeth Ballard married Caleb Wilson.

John[5] Ballard (John Ballard, Jr.), who married Mary Garland resided in Lunenburg County, Va., and was prominent in the affairs of the county. He was a Justice of the County Court from 1780 to 1784, and during the same period was a vestryman of Cumberland Parish. He is thought to have emigrated from the section about this time.

The lists of Revolutionary soldiers as published by the Virginia State Library contains the names of many Ballards, including those named John, Robert, Thomas, William, and Francis.

John Ballard and Francis Ballard of Mecklenburg, both almost certainly sons of John[4] Ballard were officers of the Revolution.

It is highly probable that John, William, Robert and Francis Ballard, all sons of John[4] Ballard, were soldiers of the Revolution from Mecklenburg or Lunenburg Counties. The son John Ballard, it seems was residing in Lunenburg at that time.[42]

BETTS.

There is a brief genealogy of the Betts Family in *The Old Free State*.[43]

Elisha Betts, who was the Vestryman of Cumberland Parish, 1777-1780, was born Aug. 21, 1720, and his will was recorded in Lunenburg County, Virginia, May 13, 1784.[44]

He was a Justice of the County Court of Lunenburg County, Virginia, 1770-1779.[45]

---

[42]He signed the petition to the Governor respecting Rev. James Craig's parole, mentioned in Chapter IX.
[43]Vol. II, 149-154.
[44]It is recorded in W. B. 3, page 159.
[45]*The Old Free State*, I, 327.

Some of his descendants through several generations, are traced in the genealogy above referred to.

BILLUPS.

According to a statement of Mrs. Edwin L. Wood, a Billups descendant, preserved in the family[46] Joseph[1] Billups and his wife Ann, after they were married in England, came to Virginia and settled in Lunenburg County.

The earliest mention of him upon the lists of tithes of the county was in 1751 when he appeared on the list of Lyddall Bacon charged with four tithes.

In 1772 he was on the list taken by Christopher Billups charged with eight tithes.

He was a Captain in the Revolution.[47]

In 1783 he appears upon the lists of tithes, and the name of Richard Billups appears in conjunction with his name in such way as to indicate, most likely, that Richard Billups was over sixteen but under twenty-one years of age at the time. On the same list John Billups and Christopher Billups are listed in their own right, which indicates they were over twenty-one years of age at the time.

He had, according to Mrs. Wood's statement, which seems to be confirmed at least in part by the lists of tithes:

1. John[2] Billups,
2. Christopher[2] Billups,
3. Richard[2] Billups.

Richard[2] Billups removed to Mathews County, Virginia, and settled at a place called Milford Haven. John and Christopher remained in Lunenburg County.

While Mrs. Wood's memorandum does not mention this son, doubtless there was another,

4. Robert[2] Billups (will in Mecklenburg County, Va., dated October 17, 1797, probated April 9, 1798.

John[2] Billups (b. Sept. 25, 1752, d. 1825), married (M. B.

---

[46] And lent to the writer by Miss Christie May Harris, of South Hill, Virginia.
[47] *The Old Free State*, I, 266.

dated April 2, 1783, in Charlotte County), Frances Bedford (b. Nov. 3, 1767), daughter of Robert Bedford, of Charlotte County, Virginia. He was a Justice of the County Court from 1785 to 1800, and a Vestryman of Cumberland Parish from 1795 to 1802, or at least for most of that period. He was sheriff of the County in 1802. His principal occupation was that of merchant, in which business he is said to have been notably successful.

He had:
1. Robert Bedford[3] Billups (b. Jan. 28, 1784).
2. Jane Flippen[3] Billups (b. Nov. 7, 1786), who married April 3, 1805, Charles Brydie (b. Nov. 27, 1777), who came from St. Andrews, Scotland, and who sailed from Great Britain in August, 1792, and landed in Virginia in October, 1792.
3. John[3] Billups (b. April 30, 1791), who married January 3, 1822, Susannah J. (or I.), (last name not known),[48] (b. Feb. 17, 1802).

Of this John[3] Billups, Mrs. Edwin L. Woods' statement says he "moved south," and she does not "know what became of him."

Christopher[2] Billups (will dated January 18, 1782, probated in Lunenburg County, Virginia, July 19, 1789).[49] His wife was named Ruth (last name not known). He was a Captain of Militia in 1760; Sheriff of the County of Lunenburg in 1777; Lieutenant Colonel in 1778 (during the Revolution); a Justice of the County Court from 1764 to 1789; and a Vestryman of Cumberland Parish from 1770 to 1780.

He had:
1. Mary[3] Billups, who married (M. B. in Lunenburg County dated December 9, 1773), William Cowan (who according to Mrs. Wood's statement was a Captain in the Revolution), who was a Justice of the County Court from 1800 to 1803.

William Cowan's will was dated December 12, 1806, and was probated in Lunenburg County, June 11, 1807.[50]

---
[48]The entry in the Billups Family Bible, now in the possession of Miss Christie Harris says "John & Susannah J. (or I.) Billups were married Jan. 3rd, 1822."
[49]Recorded in W. B. 4, pages 62-63.
[50]It is recorded in W. B. 6, pages 183-185.

By this will it appears he had:

(1) William Bowie⁴ Cowan, who was a Justice of the County Court 1822-1823.⁵¹
(2) Grizel Bowie⁴ Cowan.⁵²

2. Nancy³ Billups.

Robert² Billups, of Mecklenburg County, Virginia (will dated October 17, 1797, probated in Mecklenburg County, April 9, 1798),⁵³ married Lucy (last name not known), and had:

1. Virginia³ Billups,
2. Robert³ Billups,
3. Mariah³ Billups.

The will in addition to mentioning these children also mentions the testator's brother John Billups, naming him executor.

A writer in *Joseph Habersham Historical Collection*⁵⁴ says: "... Virginia Billups was the niece and ward of the father of Colonel John Billups (late of Athens, Georgia). She and her sister Maria, and brother, Robert, lost both parents when quite young, in Mecklenburg County, Virginia, where they had a large estate. They were brought by their uncle and guardian to Georgia and settled near Lexington. Virginia married Walton Harris, a lawyer, who was the son of Walton Harris and Rebecca Lanier."

Another writer referred to in the last quoted article says that "Virginia Billups was the sister of the father of Colonel John Billups (late of Athens), etc."

It thus seems that while all agree that the children of Robert² Billups went to Georgia, there is some uncertainty about the identity of the kinsman who went with them. In this state of the case, it is suggested (as a possibility merely), that it may have been the John³ Billups (who married "Susannah J." and "moved South," according to the statement of Mrs. Edwin L. Wood), who went with them.

---

⁵¹*The Old Free State*, I, 328.
⁵²Her grandfather Christopher Billups in his will mentions a granddaughter, "Peggy Cowan."
⁵³And recorded in W. B. 4, page 19.
⁵⁴Vol. II, 354.

Virginia³ Billups (Robert² of Mecklenburg Co., Va.), married Walton Harris, of Georgia,⁵⁵ and had:
1. Walton⁴ Harris, a lawyer.
2. Eliza⁴ Harris, who married a Mr. Boothe.
3. Caroline⁴ Harris, who married Dr. Gibbs.
4. Augustine⁴ Harris, who removed to Alabama.
5. Milton⁴ Harris (d. in infancy).
6. Catherine⁴ Harris (d. in infancy).
7. Robert⁴ Harris, married twice (lived in Clarke County, Georgia).
8. Mary Ann⁴ Harris, who married Dr. Swift.
9. Young L. G.⁴ Harris, of Athens, Georgia.
10. Jeptha⁴ Harris, of Columbus, Georgia.
11. Willis⁴ Harris, "who lived in lower Georgia."

Jane Flippen³ Billups (John,² Joseph¹) (b. Nov. 7, 1786), married, April 3, 1805, Charles Brydie (b. Nov. 27, 1777, d. July 26, 1858 (?)), from St. Andrews, Scotland, and had:
1. Frances Ann⁴ Brydie (b. Jan. 27, 1807), married June 3, 1825, John Taylor Wootton.
2. Alexander Falconer⁴ Brydie (b. Nov. 7, 1808).
3. James Lawrence⁴ Brydie (b. May 16, 1815, d. Oct. 26, 1815).
4. Mary Emily⁴ Brydie (b. Dec. 29, 1816), married (M. B. in Lunenburg County, dated May 4, 1835), Samuel T. Morgan.
5. Martha Jane⁴ Brydie (b. Jan. 17, 1820), married November 10, 1842, William Y. Neal.
6. Robert Bedford⁴ Brydie (b. July 19, 1824).
7. George Canning⁴ Brydie (b. Oct. 2, 1827).

Martha Jane⁴ Brydie (b. Jan. 17, 1820, d. May 9, 1873), married November 10, 1842, William Y. Neal (b. March 23, 1821, d. Nov. 22, 1887), son of James and Mary E. Neal, and had:
1. William Y.⁵ Neal (b. August 18, 1843), married October 30, 1877, Martha J. Wray (b. Oct. 4, 1847), and had:
   (1) William H.⁶ Neal (b. June 9, 1880),
   (2) Louisa Stokes ⁶ Neal (b. July 18, 1882).
Mary Emily⁴ Brydie (b. Dec. 29, 1816, d. April 10, 1895), mar-

---
⁵⁵*Joseph Habersham Historical Collection*, II, 354.

ried (M. B. in Lunenburg Co., Va., dated May 4, 1835), Samuel T. Morgan, and had:

Jennie F.[5] Morgan (b. Nov. 20, 1841, d. Feb. 12, 1927), who married December 8, 1869, Edwin LaFayette Wood (b. September 24, 1842, d. Aug. 9, 1895), and had:

1. Samuel C.[6] Wood (b. April 1st, 1873, d. Aug. 8, 1900).
2. Pattie May[6] Wood (b. Nov. 1, 1879, d. May 13, 1928), married November 10, 1897, Charles H. Harris, of Lunenburg County, son Junius Harris and Laura Green Wall[56] and had:
    (1) Edwin Haskins[7] Harris (b. March 23, 1900),
    (2) Christie May[7] Harris (b. May 26, 1902),
    (3) Laura Frances[7] Harris (b. March, 1904),
    (4) Robert Hiram[7] Harris (b. May 11, 1907, d. Sept. 25, 1926).

BOULDEN.

Thomas Bouldin, the vestryman of Cumberland Parish from 1747 to 1757, was the first sheriff of Lunenburg County, Virginia.[57] It was possibly at his house that the first term of Court to organize Lunenburg County, was held,—and it is certain that the second term of the court was held at his house.[58] He was a Justice of the Court from 1749 to 1759[59] and was one of the vestrymen who at the very beginning of the functioning of the parish machinery made it clear that the vestry of Cumberland Parish would permit the incumbency of a minister only so long as they were of opinion he answered "the end of ministerial function."

His father came from England, and he was born in Pennsylvania; he removed first to Maryland where he married Nancy Clarke, and with his young wife emigrated to Virginia, settling in 1744 in what was then Brunswick County, but in a part of it which later became Lunenburg County, and still later Charlotte County.

---

[56]For her ancestry through the Hardy line see *The Old Free State*, II, 258 and ante.
[57]*The Old Free State*, I, 109.
[58]Id., 113.
[59]Id., 327.

He was in addition to being sheriff, magistrate and vestryman, also a Colonel of Militia and a merchant of considerable prominence.

He was the founder of the Charlotte County family of the name; a family which has had a worthy part in many fields of endeavor.

BLAGRAVE.

This name in some of the early records is occasionally spelled Blackgrove; and is very often spelled Blagrove. The correct spelling, however, at least so far as its use by the family in Lunenburg is concerned, was Blagrave.

The name is, relatively speaking, a rare one, but it is encountered in the records as early as 1654, when Henry Blagrave was witness to a paper in York County.[60] And even the few of the name found in the early years were of several different families, at least that is the opinion of the editor of the *Virginia Historical Magazine.*[61]

One of the Colonial Clergy was Reverend Benjamin Blagrove,[62] the son of John Blagrove of Oxford. He was licensed for Virginia March 5, 1772, and received the King's bounty March 10, 1772. He served at different times Elizabeth City Parish, Southwark Parish, Martins-Brandon, Westover, and St. Peter's Parish between 1772 and 1789. He was a member of the Committee of Safety of Surry County in 1776,[63] and was Chaplain of the General Assembly in 1783.

If he was in any way connected with the Lunenburg County family of the name, the connection is not known.

The name Blagrave seems to first appear on the lists of tithes in Lunenburg County in the year 1752. For that year Henry Blagrave, Senr. and Henry Blagrave, Jun. are on the list of Lyddal Bacon for seven tithes; five of these were slaves.

In 1764 Henry Blagrave was listed with eleven tithes and 1870

---

[60]*William and Mary Quarterly*, XXIV, 41.
[61]XIII, 204.
[62]Goodwyn: *The Colonial Church in Virginia*, 251.
[63]*William and Mary Quarterly*, V, 249.

acres of land, and Henry Blagrave, Jun., with one tithe and 200 acres of land.

In 1758 Henry Blagrave was a candidate for the House of Burgesses from Lunenburg,[64] Clement Read and Mathew Marrable being the other candidates. Read and Marrable were returned elected, but Blagrave contested the election, and Marrable was unseated, and a new election ordered, in which he was again a candidate and again elected. But in 1761 Blagrave was elected a burgess and thereafter was continuously a member of the House of Burgesses until, and including 1769. He was a member of the County Court of Lunenburg County from 1764 to 1776.[65]

He was Sheriff of the County from 1775 to 1777; and was a Vestryman of Cumberland Parish from 1757 to 1768.

He had:

1. Henry Blagrave, Jun.
   Either the father or the son Henry Blagrave married Elizabeth Stokes, daughter of Young Stokes. This was, however, probably Henry Blagrave, Senr.
2. Anne Blagrave, who married (M. B. in Lunenburg County, dated January 28, 1765), Jeremiah Glenn.[66]
3. Mary Newsteys Blagrave, who married, Dec. 18, 1781, Edward Hatchett.[67]
4. Nancy Blagrave, who married, Dec. 27, 1781, Aaron Hutcheson.

BRODNAX.

In *William and Mary College Quarterly*[68] there is an account of the Brodnax family, tracing it from about the time of Henry V, the English part of the pedigree being taken from Berry's *Kentish Genealogies*.

---

[64] *The Old Free State*, I, 144.
[65] Id., 327.
[66] *The Old Free State*, II, 390; *William and Mary Quarterly*, IX, 177, where mention is made of the letter of consent from "Henry Blagrave, father of Anne."
[67] Presumably Mary Newsteys Blagrave was the daughter of Henry Blagrave, but this writer cannot positively affirm it. *The Old Free State*, II, 429.
[68] Vol. XIV, 52-58, 135-138.

The account says that: "Towards the end of the seventeenth century there appeared in Virginia two brothers, William and John Brodnax, sons of Robert Brodnax, a goldsmith of London and a native of Godmersham, County Kent, England. They must have been great-nephews of Major John[7] Brodnax, and sons of 29 Robert[8] Brodnax, who married . . . Gibbon. William Brodnax, the younger son, settled at Jamestown Island, and John Brodnax, his elder brother, settled first in Henrico County, and afterwards in Williamsburg, where he carried on his father's trade as a goldsmith, and died in 1719."[69]

That part of the pedigree printed in pages 135 to 138 of Volume XIV of the *William and Mary College Quarterly* is corrected and as corrected reprinted in Volume XXI, pages 265 to 269.

In none of the accounts of the family (and there are several), so far observed there is no definite identification of Stephen Edward Brodnax, of Lunenburg County, Virginia. Indeed so far as has been observed, his name is not mentioned in any of these articles, or if so his first name Stephen is not used.

The association of the name Brodnax, or Broadnax, as it is often spelled, with the history of Lunenburg County, dates from the creation of the County.

In 1745 William Broadnax secured a grant for 521 acres of land on the branches of Reedy Creek.

Even before Lunenburg County was formed, Edward Brodnax, of Charles City County, purchased in 1738, a tract of land on Flat Rock Creek, in Brunswick County (in that part later to be Lunenburg County), from Thomas Moody.[70]

And in 1756, Stephen Edward Broadnax acquired a grant for 413 acres of land on Miles Creek.[71]

The name Brodnax is met with in many counties, including Prince George, Brunswick, Dinwiddie and Lunenburg.

Stephen Edward Brodnax, the vestryman of Cumberland Parish in 1786, was a Captain in the Revolutionary War from

---

[69]Id., 53-54.
[70]*William and Mary College Quarterly*, XIV, 57.
[71]*The Old Free State*, I, 107.

Lunenburg County, Virginia;[72] was sheriff of the County from 1792 to 1794, and was a Justice of the County Court from 1781-1787.

There is some confusion about the use of his name, as it seems that while his name was Stephen Edward Broadnax, he was often called merely Edward Brodnax. This fact is indicated by a number of circumstances: thus while he is referred to as Stephen Edward Brodnax, on the records as a Captain in the Revolution, he is referred to in a pension paper as "Captain Edward Broadnax," from Lunenburg County,—and there is no evidence that there was a Captain Stephen Edward Brodnax, and a Captain Edward Brodnax also from Lunenburg in the Revolution.

Again while the Clerk of the Court at various terms from 1781 to 1787 noted his presence as "Edward Broadnax," one of the Gentlemen Justices,[73] yet the deed dated March 14, 1783, from Michael Johnson and wife to the Justices of the County Court, for the land upon which the court house was erected[74] shows that his full name was "Stephen Edward Broadnax."

It is probable that he was a son of the Edward Brodnax of Charles City County, who purchased the land, as above noted, in 1738, on Flat Rock Creek. Of that Edward Brodnax it is said, "In 1748 he was elected as a burgess to the General Assembly from Charles City County, but died before taking his seat."[75]

The list of tithes of Lunenburg County, for 1748, taken by Hugh Lawson has a charge of four tithes "at Edward Broadanack's Quarter," which seemed to be under the superintendence of "Phillamon Russel." In 1749 the charge is against "ye estate of Edward Broadnax, decd."

In 1772 the list of tithes taken by John Ragsdale has a charge of nine tithes, seven of them, presumably, slaves, to "S. Edward Broadnax."

---

[72]*The Old Free State*, I, 267.
[73]*The Old Free State*, I, 327.
[74]Id., 119-121.
[75]*Colonial Virginia Register*, 122, 124; *William and Mary College Quarterly*, XIV, 57.

BUFORD.

The genealogy of the Buford Family has been very well worked out in a volume entitled *The Buford Family in America*, by Marcus B. Buford. The work has passed into a second or revised and enlarged edition, this being edited by George Washington Buford and Mildred Buford Minter.

There is a short sketch of the Buford Family in *The Old Free State*.[76]

There were five members of the family who were at one time or other vestrymen of Cumberland Parish. Of these William Buford and James Buford were sons of Henry Buford or Beuford who was born in Lancaster County, Virginia, and who settled in Nottoway Parish (afterwards Nottoway County), and his wife Frances.

The John Buford, Vestryman 1812 to 1816, and William Buford, Jr., vestryman in 1812 and 1813, were sons of the earlier vestryman William Buford, and his wife Mary Ragsdale, daughter of Captain John Ragsdale, who was a corporal in Captain James Johnson's Company in the Revolution.[77]

CALDWELL.

John Caldwell was elected a Vestryman of Cumberland Parish in 1746, but resigned, or rather refused to take the oath of a vestryman, to be conformable to the doctrine and discipline of the English Church. He was a prominent, leading Presbyterian. He was one of the first Justices of the County, being named in the Commission for organizing the County, and was in attendance upon the first session of the Court when the County was organized.

He was a soldier in the French and Indian, or Colonial Wars.[78]

There is a partial genealogy of the family in *The Old Free State*.[79]

---
[76]Vol. II, pp. 176-182.
[77]*The Old Free State*, I, 219.
[78]*The Old Free State*, I, 193.
[79]Vol. II, 182-191.

CAMERON.

Thomas Cameron, the vestryman of Cumberland Parish in 1812, was doubtless a son of the Rector of the parish at the time, Dr. John Cameron.

As complete a genealogy of the descendants of the Rector as the writer has been able to compile is given in this volume.[80]

CHAMBERS.

Thomas Chambers, the vestryman of Cumberland Parish from 1769 to 1780, was a Justice of the County Court of Lunenburg County from 1764 to 1783.[81]

He was one of the Justices to whom the deed was made March 14, 1783, for the property upon which the Court House was built[82] and he was sheriff of the County from 1780 to 1785.

Possibly his earliest appearance upon the lists of tithes in Lunenburg County, Virginia, was in 1764 when he appeared on the list taken by Thomas Tabb. He was charged with eleven tithes and four hundred acres of land. That may give some idea of the approximate time when he came to the county.

There were a number of persons by the name of Chambers who came into the Colony of Virginia between 1637 and 1656 and the name is met with in the early records of several counties, but this writer has not discovered the earlier links in the chain of ancestry of Thomas Chambers.

As he had a son Thomas Chambers, he was known as

Thomas[1] Chambers, Sr. (will dated July 11, 1798, and recorded in Lunenburg County, Virginia).[83]

He had:

1. Edward[2] Chambers,
2. John[2] Chambers,
3. Thomas[2] Chambers,
4. Moses[2] Chambers,
5. William[2] Chambers,

---

[80]In Chapter X.
[81]*The Old Free State*, I, 327.
[82]Id., 120.
[83]In W. B. 4, pages 222-223.

6. Polly[2] Chambers,
7. Nancy[2] Chambers,
8. Lucy[2] Chambers,
9. Jennie[2] Chambers,
10. Elizabeth[2] Chambers,
11. Sally[2] Chambers,
12. Tempie[2] Chambers,
13. Cincy[2] Chambers, who married (M. B. in Lunenburg Co., dated Dec. 17, 1787), Edward Rudder, and had:
    (1) Polly[3] Rudder.[84]
14. A daughter who married a Mr. Cole, and had:
    (1) Johanna[3] Cole.[85]

None of the descendants of any of these children are herein traced, except those of the son,

Edward[2] Chambers, who is said to have married Martha Cousins (b. October 15, 1764, d. Oct. 27, 1810). His will was dated Jan. 8, 1828, and was probated in Lunenburg County, Virginia, March 10, 1828.[86]

They had:

1. Eliza[3] Chambers (b. August 18, 1785, d. March 23, 1838), who married November 19, 1803, Robert Scott (b. Nov. 26, 1783, d. Aug. 9, 1850), and had:
    (1) Martha Ann[4] Scott (b. May 28, 1806).
    (2) James Archer[4] Scott.
    (3) Michael Branch[4] Scott.
    (4) Robert[4] Scott, Jr. (b. Jan. 28, 1812, d. Dec. 8, 1887), who married, 1st, Sept., 1835, Mary A. Hamlin (d. Oct. 20, 1850), and 2nd, Nov. 10, 1852, Mary Elizabeth Marshall.
    (5) Milicent Chambers[4] Scott (b. Jan. 23, 1810, d. March 10, 1816).
    (6) William Henry[4] Scott (b. Nov. 1, 1813).
    (7) Edward Chambers[4] Scott (b. July 27, 1815, d. Aug. 30, 1881).
    (8) Eliza Jane[4] Scott (b. June 10, 1817, d. Sept. 18, 1881).

---
[84]Mentioned as a granddaughter in the will.
[85]Id.
[86]It is recorded in W. B. 9, page 241.

(9) George Anna[4] Scott (b. Apr. 21, 1819, d. July 25, 1822).

(10) Mary Elizabeth[4] Scott (b. Sept. 12, 1819, d. July 25, 1822).

(11) Thomas Chambers[4] Scott (b. May 15, 1823, d. Aug. 4, 1824).

2. Ann W.[3] Chambers (b. Dec. 18, 1786, d. 1874), who married George Craig (1774-1828), son of Reverend James Craig, Minister of Cumberland Parish. An account of their descendants appears in this volume.[87]

3. Henry[3] Chambers (b. Oct. 1, 1790, d. Jan. 6, 1826), United States Senator from Alabama, died while en route from Alabama to Washington, at his old home, and is buried in the yard of the old Chambers place—the place in later years known as the Dr. Robert S. Bagley place—where a monument to him stands.

4. Edward R.[3] Chambers (b. May 23, 1795, d. March 20, 1872), "Judge Chambers," a prominent lawyer of his day. He married (M. B. in Brunswick County, Virginia, dated Feb. 3, 1824), Lucy Goode Tucker, daughter of John Tucker, of Brunswick County, Virginia.

5. Martha[3] Chambers (b. October 10, 1797), who married Charles Betts (M. B. Lunenburg Co., dated Dec. 30, 1814).[88]

CHAPPELL.

Robert Chappell was a vestryman of Cumberland Parish in 1816 and in 1817. A Robert Chappell, doubtless the same person, was a Justice of the County Court of Lunenburg County, Virginia, from 1804 to 1822, in which last named year he is mentioned as "Robert Chappell, Sr.," if the several references were, as is believed the case, to one person.[89] He was a member of the Legislature from Lunenburg from 1804 to 1815, though not continuously for the entire period.[90]

---

[87] In Chapter IX.
[88] *The Old Free State*, II, 401.
[89] *The Old Free State*, I, 327.
[90] Id., II, 71-72.

There is a genealogy of the Chappell Family in a book entitled *A Genealogical History of the Chappell, Dickie and Other Kindred Families of Virginia*,[91] but it throws little light upon the Lunenburg branch of the family. The book has no index, and the material is not well organized.

The earliest will of a Chappell of record in Lunenburg County, Virginia, is that of Thomas Chappell. It is dated February 19, 1788, and was probated October 14, 1790.[92] This Thomas Chappell may have been a son of James Chappell of Sussex County, Virginia. This James Chappell made his will October 31, 1768, and mentions a son Thomas, who had a daughter Mary. The date and the names all harmonize with, but do not prove, the supposition that Thomas Chappell of Lunenburg, was the son of James Chappell, of Sussex County, Virginia.

On this surmise,

James[1] Chappell, of Sussex Co., Va. (will dated October 31, 1768) (d. Feb. 12, 1769), married twice: 1st wife probably a daughter of Thomas Howell; 2nd wife name unknown. He had a large number of children, among them,

Thomas[2] Chappell (will dated Feb. 19, 1788, probated in Lunenburg County, Va., October 14, 1790),[93] who married Mary (last name not known), and had:

1. James[3] Chappell,
2. Thomas[3] Chappell,
3. William[3] Chappell,
4. John[3] Chappell,
5. Mary[3] Chappell, who married . . . Clay, and had:
   (1) Thomas Chappell[4] Clay.
6. Anna[3] Chappell, who married, 1st, Daniel Malone, 2nd, ... Robertson, who had by the 1st marriage:
   (1) William[4] Malone,
   (2) Thomas[4] Malone,
   (3) Mary[4] Malone,
   (4) Rebecka[4] Malone.

---

[91]By Phil E. Chappell—Hudson-Kimberly Publishing Company (1900), Kansas City, Mo.
[92]It is of record in W. B. 3, page 370.
[93]It is of record in W. B. 3, page 370.

7. A daughter, who married . . . Fowler, and had:
   (1) Sarah[4] Fowler,
   (2) Wilmouth[4] Fowler,
   (3) Mary Briggs[4] Fowler.

Robert Chappell, the vestryman of Cumberland Parish in 1815 and 1816, was doubtless the son of Robert Chappell, whose will was dated September 5, 1794, and was probated in Lunenburg County, Virginia, December 11, 1794,[94] and whose wife Martha, probably married, a second time, a Mr. Rogers.[95]

He had:
1. John Chappell,
2. Robert Chappell,
3. Molly Chappell, who married Anderson Bagley, and had:
   (1) Polly Chappell Bagley.
4. Betsy Chappell, who married Samuel Watkins.

The son, Robert Chappell, the Vestryman, who in his will calls himself "Robert Chappell, Jr.," died in 1824. His will is dated January 14, 1824, and was probated April 12, 1824.[96]

He seems to have married twice, first in July, 1808, Salley Garland.[97] And second, in April, 1817, Julia A. Jefferson,[98] daughter of Samuel Jefferson.

The marriage bond was dated April 23, 1817.[99]

CLAIBORNE.

There is an extended genealogy of the Claiborne family in the *Virginia Historical Magazine.*[100]

Daniel Claiborne, the vestryman 1758 to 1763, was doubtless of the family whose genealogy is traced in the account referred to; but his place on the family tree is not clear, to this writer.

Richard Claiborne, vestryman 1769 to 1774, was a Justice of

---

[94] It is recorded in W. B. 4, p. 73.
[95] Robert Chappell, Jr., in his will dated in 1824, mentions his mother "Martha Rogers."
[96] It is recorded in W. B. 8, page 335, in Lunenburg Co., Va.
[97] *The Old Free State*, II, 445, married by Rev. Thomas Adams.
[98] *The Old Free State*, II, 446, married by Rev. Thomas Adams.
[99] *The Old Free State*, II, 403.
[100] I, 313-324.

the County Court from 1766 to 1774,[101] and was a member of the Conventions of 1774 and of 1775 from Lunenburg County, Virginia.

There seems to be a discrepancy between the account of his children as given in the *Virginia Historical Magazine*, and in his will.

The *Virginia Historical Magazine* gives them as follows:

John Claiborne of Lunenburg County.
Richard Henry Claiborne, and
Mary Claiborne, who married William Warwick.

The will mentions children as follows:

John Claiborne.
It is not clear from the record of the will whether there were sons named Richard Claiborne and Henry Claiborne, or a son whose name was Richard Henry Claiborne.
Leonard Claiborne,
Mollie Warwick, and
Ann Dudley.

Edward Dudley of Amelia County and William Warwick of North Carolina were mentioned as executors.

The account in *Virginia Historical Magazine* says he married first a Miss Dudley and second, Mary Glenn.

This is thought (by this writer), to be an error; it is believed he probably was the Richard Claiborne who married in Amelia County (M. B. Apr. 17, 1755), Mary Hamlin, daughter of Charles Hamlin.

Daniel Claiborne, the vestryman from 1758 to 1763, was sheriff of Lunenburg County from 1767 to 1769, and was a Justice of the County Court from 1757 to 1767.[102]

There is a brief sketch of the Claiborne family in Dr. Slaughter's *History of Bristol Parish*.

Dr. John Herbert Claiborne, prominent physician and citizen of Petersburg, Virginia, Confederate soldier, and author of *Seventy-five Years in Old Virginia*, was of this family.

---
[101] *The Old Free State*, I, 328.
[102] *The Old Free State*, I, 328.

CLAY.

Obediah Clay was elected a vestryman of Cumberland Parish in 1790, but declined to serve.

The will of Obed Clay (doubtless the same as Obediah Clay), was dated March 31, 1814, and was probated in Lunenburg County, Virginia, November 9, 1815.[103]

In it he mentions the following children:

1. Levi Clay
2. Olin Clay[104]
3. Thomas Clay,
4. Betsy Clay,
5. Polly Rutledge.

The will also mentions a grandson Mitchell Clay, a son of Levi Clay.

Levi Clay and Charles Brydie were named executors.

Levi Clay was a Justice of the County Court of Lunenburg County from 1816 to 1824.[105]

His daughter, Polly Rutledge, was the wife of Blanks Rutledge. They were married October 17, 1805.[106]

Olin Clay died in 1825; his will is dated December 28, 1819, and probated in Lunenburg County, Virginia, November 14, 1825.[107] In it he refers to his wife whose name is not given, and he mentions the following who presumably were his children, though the will does not explicitly so state:

1. Mitchell Clay,
2. Woodson Clay,
3. John Clay,
4. Charles Carlus Clay,
5. Polly W. Clay,
6. Eliza Clay, and
7. Martha Clay.

---

[103] And is recorded in W. B. 7, page 206.
[104] It is difficult to read the first name as it appears on the record. It seems to be Olin. It may be "Orbin."
[105] *The Old Free State*, I, 328.
[106] Id., II, 434.
[107] It is recorded in W. B. 8, page 524.

He speaks of his brother "Levi Clay's children," thus identifying himself as a son of Obed or Obediah Clay.

The daughter Eliza Clay married (M. B. November 2, 1835), William B. Rowlett.[108]

COX.

In 1749 John[1] Cox appears on the list of tithes taken by "L. Bacon." The Vestry Book of Cumberland Parish seems to indicate that he was elected a Vestryman of the parish that year; and he was certainly a member of the vestry as early as October, 1749. The period of service as vestryman is shown in the tabulation at the end of the chapter hereof entitled "The Vestry."

In 1753 he conveyed to the Church Wardens of Cumberland Parish three hundred and two acres of land on Crupper Run Creek. While the purpose of this conveyance is not stated, the fact that it was intended for a glebe seems fairly well established, both by the vestry minutes respecting its purchase, as well as proceedings, elsewhere noted in this volume respecting its sale, after the purchase by the vestry of the Ragsdale plantation, which seems to have been the selection of the Reverend James Craig.

John[1] Cox is thought to have been born about 1700. He was an early settler of Lunenburg County, and is thought to have come to the county about middle age. In 1748 he secured a patent for 404 acres of land to the south fork of Meherrin River and Finneywood Creek. This seems to have been the family seat. His son

John[2] Cox is referred to in early records as John Cox of Finneywood to distinguish him from other John Coxes, in the Lunenburg and Mecklenburg section. The location of the family seat was near the present village of Finneywood, in Mecklenburg County.

John[1] Cox owned considerably more land in that section than the area of the patent mentioned, for just before his death he conveyed 550 acres on Finneywood Creek to his son John[2] Cox, and in his will he left his "plantation" to his son Bartley[2] Cox.

---

[108]*The Old Free State*, II, 410, 441.

John[1] Cox was a Justice of the County Court of Lunenburg County from 1748 to 1757. At least he was recommended in March, 1748, and received his commission in December, 1748. He was an active participant in the deliberations of the court from 1754 to 1757.[109]

In 1755 the records show that there was a petition presented requesting the removal of "this Court House to Mr. John Cox's."

John[2] Cox was recommended as a member of the bench of Gentlemen Justices, in 1759; was a Captain of Militia as early as that year, and apparently continued to hold that office until his death. The Journal of the House of Burgesses contains an order that the estate of John Cox deceased be taxed with the cost of a gun and bayonet impressed for the use of Captain John Cox of the Lunenburg Militia.

John[1] Cox was known as "John Cox, the elder," and so describes himself in his will, which was dated July 15, 1764, and probated in Lunenburg County, Virginia, September 13, 1764.[110]

The indications are that John[1] Cox was married only once; his wife's name was Mary (last name not known).

In his will he mentions his wife Mary Cox, and his son John Cox as co-executors, and John Cox was his residuary legatee. He was probably the eldest son.

John Cox, in extant records, refers to "My mother Mary Cox," who was still living in 1793.

The will of John[1] Cox mentions eight children, in the order given below, as follows:

1. John Cox
2. Anne Ship
3. Delitia Chandler
4. Mary Smithson
5. Edith Minor
6. Talitha Cox
7. Frederick Cox
8. Bartley Cox

---

[109] *The Old Free State*, I, 328.
[110] It is recorded in W. B. 2, page 232.

Of these:
1. John[2] Cox married (M. B. in Lunenburg County, dated July 15, 1758), Francinia Bouldin. Inasmuch as the marriage bond was co-signed by Thomas Bouldin, there is some basis for the assumption that he was her father.[111]

They had:

(1) Mary[3] Cox.[112]

John[2] Cox lived in that part of Lunenburg County which became Mecklenburg County, when that county was created in 1765. He was a member of the Commission of the Peace for organizing that county and he died in 1793 or 1794. He made a will which is of record in Mecklenburg County, but in it he mentions only his wife Francinia and his brothers and sisters. His widow, Francinia Cox, was still living in 1799.

It is certain that he had at least one child,

Mary[3] Cox, mentioned as a granddaughter in the will of John Cox.

It is thought (though not positively established) that there were other children as follows:

John[3] Cox,
Richard[3] Cox,
Nancy[3] Cox.

2. Anne[2] Cox (b. 1724, d. July 3, 1828—age 104 years); she married about 1750, Josiah Shipp, of Lunenburg County, Virginia, who died in December, 1800. They removed about 1774 to Surry County, North Carolina. There were, very probably, more than the two children mentioned below. These two were born in Lunenburg County, Virginia.[113]

They had:

(1) Thomas[3] Shipp (b. October 26, 1757, d. April 26, 1853), married Hannah Joyce (b. June 20, 1754, d. Sept. 26, 1816), and had:

---

[111]The Bouldin family was a very prominent one in early Lunenburg and later in Charlotte County, Virginia. Thomas Bouldin was the first sheriff of the County, etc. See *The Old Free State*, passim.

[112]Whether there were other children, as there probably were, does not appear. This one is named in the will of the grandfather.

[113]According to information furnished by Mr. Curtis Bynum.

(a) Bartlett[4] Shipp (b. March 8, 1786, d. May 26, 1869).
(b) Nancy[4] Shipp (b. Dec. 8, 1789), who married Henry P. Gaines.
(c) John[4] Shipp (b. Oct. 18, 1791, d. Aug. 25, 1820).
(d) William[4] Shipp (b. Sept. 8, 1794, d. Sept. 3, 1815).
(e) Thomas[4] Shipp (b. May 3, 1798, d. April 17, 1805).

(2) Nancy[3] Shipp (b. 1763, d. Jan. 25, 1841), who married in June, 1784, John Martin of Rockhouse, Surry County, N. C. (b. 1756, d. April 5, 1822).

They had: (Ten children.)

The descendants of Thomas[3] Shipp and of Nancy[3] Shipp, who married John Martin, are many, in North Carolina and elsewhere. They include Mr. Curtis Bynum, of Asheville, N. C., who has placed at the writer's disposal the results of his researches respecting the Cox and Cox-Shipp pedigrees. Mr. Bynum is not responsible for the arrangement of the material, but is due credit for the greater part of the data herein incorporated. In this brief sketch the writer has combined his own material with that supplied by Mr. Bynum, in an effort to present it all as clearly, and with as much condensation as possible, the major portion as stated being supplied by Mr. Bynum.

These descendants also embrace Miss Katherine Cameron Shipp ("Kate C. Shipp"), of Fayetteville, N. C., who is not only a descendant of these Lunenburg families, but of Reverend Doctor John Cameron, of Cumberland Parish, Lunenburg County, to whom a chapter of this work is devoted.

Miss Shipp has been most helpful to the writer, respecting the Cameron pedigree.

The investigation of the Cox-Shipp pedigree has not been completed, and Mr. Bynum and Miss Shipp (as well as the writer), would be interested in receiving additional data respecting these lines.

3. Delitia[2] Cox married William Chandler and had:
   (1) Rebecca[3] Chandler,
   (2) Keziah[3] Chandler.

These two grandchildren are mentioned in the will of John¹ Cox.

4. Mary² Cox married Micajah Smithson, and had:
    (1) Mary³ Smithson,
    (2) Keziah³ Smithson.

   These are mentioned in the will of John¹ Cox.

5. Edith² Cox, who married Joseph Minor (M. B. dated Oct. 11, 1750), and had:
    (1) Letitia³ Minor.

   This grandchild is mentioned in the will of John¹ Cox.

6. Tallitha (or Tabitha)² Cox,[114] who married (M. B. in Lunenburg County, Virginia, dated Feb. 3, 1767), Isham Browder, of Halifax County, Virginia.

   (They had children)

7. Frederick² Cox married Milly Estes, daughter of Robert Estes, and removed to Pittsylvania County, Virginia, before 1768. Later he removed to Surry County, North Carolina, where he is listed as early as 1774. "Milley Cox" administered on her husband's estate in 1781. They had at least one child,
    (1) Franky Coleman³ Cox.

8. Bartley² Cox, removed to Georgia. He died before 1793. He was married and left children. It is thought that the Bartley Cox who married Susannah Carleton (M. B. dated Nov. 12, 1781), was Bartley³ Cox, his son.

   It is thought that this Bartley³ Cox[115] is the same as the Bartlett Cox or Coxe who in 1788 was granted a pension for the loss of a leg in the Revolution. This Bartley Cox was born in 1762 and died December 25, 1845.

---

[114] The name is spelled "Tabitha" in the marriage bond; it is spelled "Tallitha" in the will of John Cox.

[115] This name in some of the records of the Revolutionary period also seems to be spelled "Barclay" Cox.

CURETON.

John Cureton, the vestryman of Cumberland Parish 1784 to 1786, was a soldier of the Revolution. He was an Ensign, in the Company of Captain Edward Jordan, from Lunenburg County, Virginia.[116] He married (M. B. in Lunenburg Co., Va., dated March 14, 1783), Hannah Davis.[117]

The records of Bristol Parish contain a number of items respecting the Cureton family and those of Lunenburg are thought to have been from that section—from Prince George County. From the Parish Register of Bristol Parish, it appears that John[1] Cureton and his wife Frances had:

1. Susanna[2] Cureton (b. Jan. 19, 17( ), probably 1724).
2. Eliza.[2] Cureton (b. Jan. 20, 1796).
3. John[2] Cureton (b. Sept. 27, 1731).

John[2] Cureton, it seems married Winifred (last name unknown), and had:

1. John[3] Cureton (b. Nov. 13, 1757).
2. Louisey[3] Cureton (b. Jan. 28, 1760).
3. Frances[3] Cureton (b. Dec. 13, 1762).
4. Charles[3] Cureton (b. Sept. 20, 1765).

It was doubtless this John[3] Cureton who was the Revolutionary soldier from Lunenburg County, Virginia, and a Vestryman of Cumberland Parish.

Certificates of consent filed in connection with the issuance of marriage license bonds in Lunenburg County, Virginia, indicate the following marriages:

John Cureton to Sarah Moon, daughter of Gideon Moon, certificate dated December 17, 1778.

Nathaniel Cureton to Elizabeth Esthem, certificate dated May 4, 1795.

---

[116] *The Old Free State*, I, 267.
[117] *The Old Free State*, II, 395. The name is there given as "John Curlton," instead of "John Cureton." As there given the writer followed a certified abstract of the marriage bonds, made by the Clerk of the County, but investigation convinces him that the name was incorrectly deciphered. Some of these old documents are very difficult to read with certainty.

DELONY.

Lewis Delony, the Vestryman in 1747 and 1748, was one of the members of the first bench of Justices of the County of Lunenburg. He was present at the first meeting, May 5, 1746, when the County was organized,[118] and he was one of the two Justices authorized to administer on that occasion the oath of office to the other Justices.[119]

He and Thomas Lanier (Lanear), were appointed commissioners, on the part of Lunenburg County, to run the dividing line between Lunenburg and Brunswick Counties.[120]

At that time he resided in the part of the county afterwards to be cut off into Mecklenburg County, in the neighborhood of Roanoke River and Allen Creek.

He drew the plans for the first Courthouse of Lunenburg County; built the first prison or jail of the County, and built an "office in the Courthouse and a press for the safe keeping and preservation of the Law Books, Papers and Records" to be preserved there.[121]

Henry Delony, Justice of the County Court of Lunenburg County, Virginia, from 1757 to 1763,[122] was one of the first Justices of Mecklenburg County, and attended the first court held in the County, on March 11, 1765,[123] and helped to organize that county.

On September 8, 1777, he was recommended to the Governor to be Colonel in the "Second Battalion,"[124] though he probably did not serve in that capacity, at that time, for on October 13, 1777, the order of September 8, 1777, was set aside, and new recommendations made, and on this occasion Bennett Goode was recommended to be Colonel in the Second Battalion.[125] He however served in the Revolution in some capacity.[126]

---

[118]*The Old Free State*, I, 108.
[119]Id.
[120]Id., 111.
[121]Id., 115.
[122]*The Old Free State*, I, 328.
[123]Mecklenburg County Court O. B. 1, page 1, opening order.
[124]O. B. 4, page 371.
[125]O. B. 4, 374.
[126]*Report of the State Librarian* (Va.), 1910-1911, 135.

This Henry Delony was, doubtless, the son of Lewis Delony, the Vestryman of Cumberland Parish, and Justice of the County Court in Lunenburg County.

The will of Henry Delony was dated April 29, 1785, and was probated in Mecklenburg County, Virginia, June 13, 1785.[127]

He married Rebecca Walker[128] of Brunswick County. They had the following children:

1. Edward Delony, who married (M. B. in Mecklenburg County, dated Nov. 23, 1796), Elizabeth Lucas, daughter of William Lucas.
2. Mary Delony, who married (M. B. in Mecklenburg County, dated Sept. 19, 1768), Thomas Pearson.[129]
2. Henry Delony, who was mentioned in connection with some lands in Brunswick County.
4. Lucy Delony, who married (M. B. in Mecklenburg County, dated May 9, 1779), Robert Edward Brooking, whose father was Vivian Brooking.
5. William Delony.
6. Fanny Delony, who married (M. B. in Mecklenburg County, dated Sept. 18, 1788), Daniel Hicks.

DIXON.

Robert Dixon, the Vestryman 1780-1783, was a Justice of the County Court of Lunenburg County in 1781 and 1782.[130] He was very probably the "Captain Dixon," from Lunenburg County, Virginia, in the Revolutionary War,[131] but unfortunately the full name of Captain Dixon has not been preserved, or at least so far has not been discovered.

---

[127]It is there recorded in W. B. 2, page 103.

[128]The deduction that he married Rebecca Walker is arrived at in this way: In Brunswick County is the marriage bond dated May 11, 1753, for the marriage of Henry Delony of Lunenburg County [this was before Mecklenburg was created] to . . . . Walker." The first name of the bride is lost from the bond which is torn. Henry Delony's will, however, mentions his "wife Rebecca Delony." As there seems no suggestion that he was twice married, the inference is that his wife was Rebecca Walker.

[129]In the will she is spoken of as "Mary Persons."

[130]*The Old Free State*, I, 328.

[131]*Report of the State Librarian* (Va.), 1910-1911, 139; *The Old Free State*, I, 267.

Robert Dixon married about Sept. 24, 1764,[132] Anne Bacon, daughter of Lyddall Bacon, but information of their children and descendants is not at hand.

There is no will of any person named Dixon recorded in Lunenburg County, from the formation of the county up to 1825.

EDLOE.

The Edloes were in the Lunenburg section, or at least secured grants for land there a number of years before the county was cut off from Brunswick.

In 1731 Henry L. Edloe secured a grant for a tract of land on Great Creek, and in 1739 John Edloe secured a grant for lands on the south side of Flat Rock Creek, and on both sides of the Beaverpond Branches.[133]

Soon after the County was organized, John Edloe on July 5, 1751, secured a grant for 2000 acres of land on Crooked Creek and 2700 acres on Flat Rock Creek.[134]

John Edloe, the vestryman in 1749 and 1750, probably did not remain in Lunenburg very long.

A John Edloe (possibly the vestryman, who was probably a son of Henry Edloe), sold 1222 acres of land to David Garland of Hanover County,[135] about 1751. That probably marks the time of his ceasing to be associated with the history of the county.

The progenitor of the Edloe family in Virginia, was it seems Matthew Edloe, who was a burgess for the College Plantation in 1629, and who died prior to 1637.

There is a brief genealogy of some of the members of early generations of the family in *William and Mary Quarterly*.[136]

ELLIDGE.

The will of Francis Ellidge, the vestryman in 1749 and 1750, bears date October 20, 1750, and was probated in Lunenburg County, Virginia, October 3, 1751.[137]

---

[132]That is the date of the note from Lyddall Bacon consenting to the marriage.
[133]*The Old Free State*, I, 100-101.
[134]Id., 105.
[135]*Hening's Statutes*, VI, 312.
[136]XV, 282-3.
[137]It is recorded in W. B. 1, pages 51-52.

In it he mentions his wife, Mary Ellidge, and the following children:
1. William Ellidge.
2. Mary Ellidge.
3. Elizabeth Ellidge, then married to a Mr. Land, and who had a son Ellidge Land.

ELLIS.

The name Ellis is met with almost innumerable times in the early records of Lunenburg County, Virginia; but to weave all the names into a connected genealogy would be a stupendous undertaking.

Captain Ellison Ellis was the first Captain recommended by the County Court in 1776; and he was doubtless active in the Revolution, where and under what circumstances he served is not now known. His name in fact is not preserved in the lists of Revolutionary soldiers published by the Virginia State Library, and but for the record in the County Court order book of Lunenburg County, his connection with the Revolution, would, presumably, be lost to history.

He married Mary Zachary of Amelia County, Virginia, his marriage bond being dated November 9, 1763. In it his name is spelled "Ellyson Ellis," which is probably the correct spelling.

The earliest will of a person by the name of Ellis upon the records of Lunenburg County is that of

Jeremiah Ellis, dated November 13, 1756, and probated May 3, 1757.[138] In it he mentions his wife, Priscilla Ellis, and the following children:
1. Abraham Ellis,
2. Daniel Ellis,
3. James Ellis,
4. Nathaniel Ellis,
5. Priscilla Ellis, at that time the wife of a man named Nipper.
6. Lydia Ellis, at that time the wife of a man named Nipper.

---

[138] W. B. 1, page 178.

7. Ann Ellis, at that time the wife of a man named Mulkey.
8. Joanna Ellis,
9. Mary Ellis, at that time the wife of a man named Murfrey.

EMBRY.

The Embry family were associated with the history of Lunenburg County from the beginning of the settlement of the section. In 1738 Henry Embry secured a grant for a tract of land on Banister River,[139] and in the next year, 1739, he, described as "Colonel Henry Embry" secured another grant for four hundred acres of land on the ridge "between the nap of Reeds Creek and Couche's Creek."[140]

In 1755 Henry Embry, Jr., secured a grant for 400 acres of land on Great Toby's Creek.[141]

William Embry in 1751, acquired a patent for 119 acres of land on Reedy Creek.[142]

Henry[1] Embry, Sr., of Brunswick County, Virginia (d. 1763), was Colonel of Militia, and a member of the House of Burgesses from Brunswick County, 1736-1740.[143]

His wife was named Martha.

His son,

Henry[2] Embry, Jr. (d. 1753), was a member of the House of Burgesses from Lunenburg County, 1748-1749,[144] and a Justice of the County Court 1749-1750.

He married Priscilla Wilkinson, and had:
  1. Mary[3] Embry who married John Coleman.
  2. Sarah[3] Embry, who married, first, Isaac Read, and second, Thomas Scott.

William Embry, the Vestryman 1750-1758, and Justice of the

---
[139] *The Old Free State*, I, 101.
[140] Id.
[141] Id., 106.
[142] Id., 105.
[143] *Colonial Virginia Register, William and Mary Quarterly*, XXV, 116.
[144] *The Old Free State*, II, 68; *William and Mary Quarterly*, XXV, 116; *Colonial Virginia Register*.

County Court 1754-1757, was probably a brother of Henry² Embry, Jr. His identity has not been fixed, as to his relationship to the others mentioned, so far as this writer's observations have gone. His will is dated May 6, 1759, and was probated in Lunenburg County, Virginia,[145] February 5, 1760. In it he mentions his wife, Elizabeth Embry, and the following children:

1. William Embry,
2. Henry Embry,
3. Eliza Embry, married to a Mr. Brooks.
4. Ermine Embry.

David Garland, John Ragsdale and Thomas Edmonds were named as his executors.

EPPS.

The Epps (the name is variously spelled, Eppes, Epes, Epps) family is a prominent and numerous one of Virginia, particularly of the Southside.

In Lunenburg County, Virginia, the following members of the family were members of the County Court during the periods indicated:

Francis Epes,	1797-1799,
Peter Epes,	1799-1808,
John C. Epes,	1832-1851,
William P. Epes,	1837-1851.[146]

Francis Epes, or Eppes, was a member of the General Assembly of Virginia from 1797 to 1799 or 1800.[147]

It may be stated upon the authority of Dr. Philip Slaughter[148] that "the several families of Eppes, Epes, and Epps, of the Counties of Prince George, Nottoway and Chesterfield" are descended from Francis¹ Eppes, who settled at City Point, Prince George County, while it was a part of Charles City County, during or prior to the year 1635. "He was County Lieutenant, and thus by designation, Colonel; and a member of the Council of Virginia."

---

[145] And is of record in W. B. 1, page 290.
[146] *The Old Free State*, I, 328-329.
[147] Id., II, 71.
[148] *History of Bristol Parish*, 172.

The emigrant Lieut. Col. Francis[1] Eppes, was the father of Lieut. Col. Francis[2] Eppes (1628-1678),[149] who married Elizabeth (Littleberry?), and had:

Col. Littleberry[3] Eppes (d. 1746), of Charles City County, Justice in 1699, Burgess 1710, 1714. He had:

1. Lewellin[4] Eppes (or Epes), Clerk of Charles City County, who had:
   (1) Peter[5] Epes, whose will was proved July 7, 1773, who had:
      (a) Peter[6] Epes.

It is probable, though not certain, that this last named Peter Epes was the vestryman of Cumberland Parish, 1799-1806.

The vestryman, Peter Eppes, may have been the one who married (M. B. in Lunenburg County, 1793), Peggy Baker Cowan.[150]

There is in the clerk's office of Lunenburg County a letter of consent to the marriage, dated May 9, 1793, from William Cowan, father of Peggy Baker Cowan. In this the groom is spoken of as "Peter Epes, Sr."

William Cowan was a Justice of the County Court of Lunenburg County, from 1800 to 1803.[151]

FARMER.

Lodowick[1] Farmer, along with Thomas Pettus, represented Lunenburg County, Virginia, in the House of Burgesses in 1769.[152]

He was a member from Lunenburg of the Virginia Convention of May 6, 1776, one of the most notable assemblages of men in the history of the world, for it "framed the first written constitution of a free state in the annals of the world,"[153] and he was a member of the County Court of Lunenburg County, from 1770 to 1778.[154]

---

[149]*William and Mary Quarterly*, VIII, 238.
[150]*The Old Free State*, II, 390.
[151]Id., I, 328.
[152]*Colonial Virginia Register*, 184.
[153]*The Old Free State*, I, 210-211.
[154]Id., 329.

His will is dated May 8, 1780, and was probated in **Lunenburg County, Virginia**, June 8, 1780.[155]

From the will, it appears he had:

1. Lodowick[2] Farmer. He was quite certainly the second lieutenant in the Company of Captain Billups, in the Revolutionary War.[156]

He was probably married three times. There is the record of a marriage bond in Lunenburg County, Virginia, dated October 27, 1779, for the marriage of "Lod." Farmer, Jr., to Elizabeth Herring.[157]

There is in Amelia County, Virginia, a marriage bond dated June 14, 1784, for the marriage of "Ludowick" (Lodowick?) Farmer to Frances Brooks.

And there is in Lunenburg County, Virginia, another marriage bond dated October 11, 1787, for the marriage of Lodowick Farmer to "Betsy" Knight.[158] This is evidently the wife mentioned in his will as "Elizabeth."

The first and third of these marriages were almost certainly, and the other most probably of the Lodowick[2] Farmer under discussion.

2. Benjamin[2] Farmer,
3. Henry[2] Farmer,
4. Jeremiah[2] Farmer, who married (M. B. in Lunenburg Co., dated Aug. 16, 1788), Polly Knight.
5. Thomas[2] Farmer,
6. Elijah[2] Farmer,
7. James[2] Farmer, who married (M. B. in Lunenburg Co., Va., dated April 15, 1794), Elizabeth Harding.
8. John[2] Farmer, who married (M. B. in Lunenburg Co., Va., dated Sept. 14, 1797), Nancey Crymes.
9. Sally Cheatham[2] Farmer,
10. Julany Ann[2] Farmer, who married a Mr. "Eastmen" (Eastham?),
11. Dycie[2] Farmer, who married (William?) Thweatt.

---

[155]It is of record in W. B. 3, page 43.
[156]*The Old Free State*, I, 267.
[157]*The Old Free State*, II, 391.
[158]Id., 390.

Lodowick[1] Farmer does not mention his wife in his will, but it seems certain her name was Sarah, and that she survived him. Sarah Farmer's will was dated May 2, 1788, and probated in Lunenburg County, Virginia, February 12, 1789.[159]

Her identity as the wife of Lodowick[1] Farmer is established by the number of identical children mentioned in the respective wills; and yet a few added details are to be gathered from the will of Sarah, so the children as she gives them are here set out, as follows:

1. Lodowick Farmer, son,
2. Benjamin Farmer, son,
3. Elijah Farmer, son,
4. James Farmer, son,
5. John Farmer, son,
6. Jeremiah Farmer, son,
7. Ann Eastham, daughter,
8. Sarah C. Pittman, daughter,[160]
9. Julaney Moon.

Lodowick[1] Farmer, it seems had at least one other child,
William A.[2] Farmer,
not mentioned in his will or that of his wife Sarah. This seems to be established by the following facts:

William A. Farmer made his will on December 31, 1823, it was probated in Lunenburg County, January 12, 1824.[161] In it he speaks of a brother Lodowick Farmer,—seemingly Lodowick[2] Farmer. He also speaks of a niece Elizabeth E. Hatchett.

William H. Hatchett married Elizabeth Farmer, daughter of Benjamin Farmer, as appears from a letter of consent from Benjamin Farmer, dated December 18, 1804, preserved in Lunenburg County, Clerk's Office. Their marriage bond is also preserved dated Dec. 10(?), 1804,[162] but it is the letter of consent which discloses the parentage of Elizabeth Farmer.

Lodowick[1] Farmer had sons Lodowick[2] Farmer and Benjamin[2]

---

[159]And is of record in W. B. 3, page 333.
[160]Married John Pittman, M. B. dated March 9, 1787—*The Old Free State*, II, 392.
[161]And is recorded in W. B. 8, page 318.
[162]*The Old Free State*, II, 396.

Farmer; so the fair assumption is that they were brothers of William A. Farmer.

Lodwick[2] Farmer died in Lunenburg County in 1816. His will is dated August 6, 1816, and was probated October 10, 1816.[163]

It is pointed out above that he was almost certainly married twice, and probably three times. His will mentions a number of children (listed below); but this writer has not knowledge as to which children were by the different wives.

The children mentioned in the will were:

1. John[3] Farmer. A John Farmer, probably this John, married Elizabeth Shelburn, July 18, 1799.[164]
2. Henry[3] Farmer.
3. Joseph[3] Farmer.
4. Polly[3] Farmer, who married Sept. 30, 1802, Isaiah Hawkins.[165]
5. Bettie[3] Farmer, who married in Lunenburg County, Virginia, Nov. 24, 1806, Tarlton W. Knight. She is called "Betsy W. Farmer," daughter of Lodowick Farmer, in the certificate of consent to the marriage.

   The date of the marriage—Nov. 24, 1806—is that given in the return of marriages by James Shelburne, the minister who performed the ceremony.[166]

That date is probably incorrect, and should be December 24, 1806. In the clerk's office of Lunenburg County, Virginia, is preserved the letter of consent from Lodowick Farmer, for the issuance of the license for this marriage. It is dated December 12, 1806. The early ministers were sometimes careless in making returns of marriages, apparently sometimes making up the lists from memory a considerable time after the event.

---

[163] It is recorded in W. B. 7, page 278.
[164] *The Old Free State*, II, 427.
[165] The will does not give the name of this daughter, but does indicate that the testator had a daughter married to a man named Hawkins. Among the marriages celebrated in Lunenburg County, Virginia, by Rev. W. M. Ellis, is that of Isaiah Hawkins to Polly Farmer, Sept. 30, 1802. It is a tenable assumption that Polly Farmer is the daughter of Lodwick Farmer, married to a Hawkins, mentioned in the will—*The Old Free State*, II, 435.
[166] *The Old Free State*, II, 428.

6. Sarah C.³ Farmer, who married Bagley.¹⁶⁷
7. Dicey³ Farmer, who married (M. B. in Lunenburg County, Va., dated Feb. 14, 1811), John Scott.¹⁶⁸
8. Martha³ Farmer, who married Jan. 9, 1818, Francis Carter.¹⁶⁹
9. Lucinda³ Farmer, who married Jan. 13, 1818,¹⁷⁰ Richard H. Stokes.

Benjamin² Farmer (Lodowick¹). But little is known at present (by this writer), of the history of Benjamin² Farmer. His brother, William A. Farmer, who seems to have died unmarried, mentions the children of Benjamin Farmer, as follows:

1. America³ Farmer,
2. Henry³ Farmer,
3. Grief³ Farmer,
4. Mary Anne³ Farmer,
5. John Herrin³ Farmer,
6. Elizabeth E.³ Hatchett.

Of these:

Henry³ Farmer seems to have married Martha A. Walton, ward of Merriweather Hurt (M. B. in Lunenburg Co., June 5, 1824.)¹⁷¹

Mary³ Farmer married John F. Day (M. B. in Lunenburg Co., Va., dated Dec. 18, 1836)¹⁷² and a letter of consent to the marriage discloses that "Mary Farmer" was the daughter of Benjamin Farmer.

The will of Benjamin Farmer, dated June 2, 1757, and probated August 2, 1757,¹⁷³ is the earliest will by one of the name discovered in Lunenburg County.

---

¹⁶⁷William Ellis, a minister, has the return of a marriage Sept. 18, 1805, *Asa Fowlkes* to Sarah C. Farmer. The will speaks of the daughter as "Sarah C. Bagley."
¹⁶⁸*The Old Free State*, II, 400.
¹⁶⁹Id., 444.
¹⁷⁰Id., 443.
¹⁷¹*The Old Free State*, II, 405.
¹⁷²Id., 413.
¹⁷³Of record in W. B. 1, page 193.

In it, Benjamin Farmer mentions his wife, Sarah Farmer, and the following children:
1. Benjamin Farmer,
2. John Farmer,
3. Stephen Farmer,
4. Isham Farmer,
5. Sarah Farmer.

He names Thomas Boldin, Thomas Bedford, John Farmer and Mark Farmer as his executors.

The kinship, and there was doubtless a kinship, between this Benjamin Farmer and the Lodowick[1] Farmer above mentioned and his descendants, has not been discovered by this writer.

The name Farmer is encountered early in the Amelia County records and the Lunenburg family probably came from that section.

FERTH.

Daniel Ferth, the Vestryman of Cumberland Parish in 1747, was on the list of tithes taken by Matthew Talbot in 1748. That year the precinct within which Talbot was directed to take the list of tithes was briefly described as "from the fork to Cubb Creek." His name was there spelled "Danl. Firth," which was probably the correct spelling. He was listed for one tithe.

He was not on Talbot's list for 1749; nor indeed on any other available list for that year or several succeeding years, so far as a somewhat critical examination discloses.

He probably had died or moved away.

On February 8, 1757, there was executed in Lunenburg County, Virginia, a marriage license bond for the marriage of Betty Firth, widow, to Charles Allen. She may have been his widow.

These three places, the vestry record for 1747, the tithe record for 1748, and the marriage license bond in 1757 are the only places items throwing any light upon the name are encountered.

FONTAINE.

Peter Fontaine, the Vestryman of Cumberland Parish 1750 to 1754, was present at the organization of the County of Lunenburg and presented his commission "from the Masters and

Professors of William and Mary College at Williamsburg" authorizing "Peter Fontaine Jr. Gent., to be the surveyor of the South District" of the County.[174]

The office of surveyor was at the time regarded as the most lucrative position in the county.

The Peter Fontaine, the Vestryman and surveyor was a son of Reverend Peter Fontaine, Minister of Westover Parish (Colonel William Byrd's parish), and a nephew of John Fontaine the friend and intimate of Governor Alexander Spotswood, his companion on his trip to Fort Christanna, and on the Expedition of the Knights of the Golden Horse Shoe. There is an account of both in *The Old Free State*,[175] and in *Memoirs of a Huguenot Family*.[176]

Peter Fontaine helped to organize Halifax County, and had a prominent part in the public affairs of the section for a long time. He was one of the first Justices of Halifax County, Virginia.

He made the first map of the Southside section of Virginia, embracing the section from "Currytuck" inlet to the "Mississippi or Allegany Ridge of Mts.," and from the North Carolina line northward to the Falls of the Appomattox—Petersburg. This map was made July 9, 1752.[177]

---

[174]*The Old Free State*, I, 110.
[175]Vol. I, 58 et seq.
[176]By Ann Maury, G. P. Putnam & Co., 1853, page 270 et seq.
[177]It is reproduced in *The Old Free State*, I, 141.

CHAPTER XII

Genealogical Notes—Continued

GARLAND.

THE Lunenburg County branch of the family has received scant notice, at the hands of those who have written of the Garlands, so far, at least, as appears from such printed accounts as have come to the notice of this writer.

That such is the case is altogether regrettable, since in some aspects, at least, it is not excelled in interest and importance by any branch of the family. A part of the Lunenburg family have the distinction of being lineal descendants of Governor Alexander Spotswood "the noblest figure of his day in America, and the greatest of all the Colonial Governors of Virginia." This same branch of the family are blood relatives of General Robert E. Lee; and were closely allied by marriage with the Jefferson family. Several members were prominent in the Southside, being members of th County Courts and Vestrymen, and holding other civil offices, while a number had important parts in the Revolutionary War.

The places of distinction and honor filled by members of the family in various localities will be noted as the sketch progresses.

A leading article on the Garland Family, in *The Times-Dispatch* says:

"There were in England three Garland families entitled to bear a coat of arms—one in York, one in Lincolnshire, and one in Sussex. Family tradition says that the Sussex branch moved into Wales. Their common ancestor was a warden of the Cinque Ports, and as such was a lord, entitled to a seat in Parliament, had entire jurisdiction, civil, military and naval, over the five ports, and lived in Dover Castle. The history of this distinguished family in America dates far back to Colonial times, beginning about the year 1650. Their descendants have wrought well, filling positions of honor and trust in the history of both

Church and State. They have intermarried with the old families of the Commonwealth."[1]

This account then proceeds to mention the parish record of New Kent which, as will be more particularly detailed below, shows the "record of Edward, son of Edward Garland, born May 20th, baptized July 8, 1700," and, continues the account, **"This baby Edward was most probably the father of John Garland**[3] who lived at Garland's Neck, Hanover County, Va., more recently called Blackwell's Neck."[2]

Proceeding, the article gives the children of this John Garland and some of his descendants.

Neither this article nor any other account that has ever come to this writer's attention attempts to give any genealogy of the Lunenburg County, Virginia, branch of the Garland family.

According to an article in *The Times-Dispatch*[3] by Professor William Elmore Dickinson, of the University of West Virginia, the Garlands of Virginia are of the Sussex branch of the Garland family of England, and he says:

"Edward Garland, Sr., from whom the Hanover branch of the Virginia family descends, was a son of Peter Garland, the immigrant of about 1650."[4]

As there were three immigrants named Peter Garland, who came in "about 1650," the description "Peter Garland, the immigrant," leaves the matter somewhat indefinite. One Peter Garland arrived in 1650, another Peter Garland came in 1655, and still another Peter Garland in 1656.[5]

Unfortunately Prof. Dickinson does not state the evidence or the authority upon which he bases the statement that Edward Garland, Sr., was the son of Peter Garland.

The Peter Garland who came in 1650 came to York County. New Kent County was formed from York in 1654. Robert Garland who came over in 1655 came to New Kent. So both Peter

---
[1] Sunday, July 26, 1908.
[2] Id.
[3] Dec. 28, 1913.
[4] Id.
[5] Greer: *Early Virginia Immigrants*, 123-4. There were at least two other Garland immigrants: Francis Garland, who came in 1653, and Robert Garland, who came in 1655.

and Robert were in the same county or locality where we later find Edward Garland.

Prof. Dickinson describes Edward Garland, Sr., as a wealthy and influential planter of St. Paul's Parish, Hanover County. But we are on firm ground respecting the family a little before this.

Edward Garland was in New Kent County before Hanover was created, in 1720.

St. Peter's Parish Register, on page 13, has this entry:

"Edwd son of Edward Garland was born the 20th May, Bapt. 8 July, 1700."

Prof. Dickinson states that Edward Garland, Sr., owned "more than 5,000 acres of land" in Hanover County, and that the "Virginia land records show that much of this land was granted from 1714 to 1717, for bearing the expenses of bringing into Virginia ninety-five settlers."[6]

According to Prof. Dickinson, Edward Garland, Sr., "married about 1680, and had at least the following children: Margaret, Peter, John, Martha, Mary, Edward, Jr., and James."[7]

It is much to be regretted that Prof. Dickinson does not state the evidence, or cite his authority for the facts given regarding the date of the marriage and the children of Edward Garland, Sr.

The present writer, not long since, discovered an act passed by the Virginia Assembly, of the greatest importance to students of the Garland pedigree. This act, so far as he has observed, has not been heretofore known to or noticed by any writer on any branch of the Garland family.

The act passed in February, 1752,[8] recites that Edward Garland, the elder, "late of the County of New Kent," owned certain land, 600 acres more or less in the Parish of St. Paul, "then in the County of New Kent, but now in the County of Hanover," by will dated March 14, 1719, devised the same unto his son Edward Garland, and the heirs of his body lawfully begotten,

---

[6] *The Times-Dispatch,* Dec. 28, 1913.
[7] Id.
[8] 6 *Hening,* 311 et seq. (Chap. XLIX).

etc., excepting a life estate to his wife Jane Garland, but "failing of such heirs to the other brother in the manner before directed by the said will as in the said will proved and recorded in the Court of the said County of New Kent more fully is contained."

That the said Edward died, and after his death the said Jane Garland died and "the said Edward Garland the son, entered into the said land, with the appurtenances," and died so seised, "after whose death David Garland, the eldest son and heir of the said Edward Garland the son, entered into the said land," etc.

The act then recites that the said David Garland is seised in fee simple of 1220 acres of land in the County of Lunenburg, lately purchased by him of John Edloe and Ann his wife, and another tract of 826 acres in said County of Lunenburg purchased of William Edloe and Anne his wife, and also was possessed of certain slaves, eight in number.

David Garland therefore petitioned the assembly to dock the entail of the said tract of land in Hanover County "whereby the said David Garland may be enabled to make a better provision for his younger children, and to settle his said lands, in the County of Lunenburg, with the slaves aforesaid to be annexed thereto, being of greater value, to the same uses."

Accordingly the Assembly docked the entail of the Hanover lands and transferred the same to the Lunenburg lands.

From this act we learn the date of Edward Garland, Sr.'s will; the name of his wife and the name of his oldest son; furthermore it definitely establishes the precise relationship of the Lunenburg Garlands, descendants of David Garland, to the Hanover and New Kent Garlands, and fixes the approximate period when the family came to Lunenburg County.

David Garland first appears on the Bench as one of the Gentlemen Justices of Lunenburg County in 1754.[9]

From the foregoing we may condense, for conciseness, the line as follows:

Peter[1] Garland, the immigrant, of the Sussex branch of the Garlands in England, came to Virginia, in 1650, and settled in York County, and had:

---

[9] I *The Old Free State*, 329.

Edward[2] Garland, of New Kent County (d. circa. 1719), married about 1680, Jane (last name unknown), and had:
1. Edward[3] Garland, Junior, of Hanover, who married, unknown, and had:
   (a) David[4] Garland, of Hanover and Lunenburg, founder of the Lunenburg branch of the family (living in 1752, will in Lunenburg County, dated March 18, 1780, probated, May 9, 1782), Justice of the County Court, 1754 to 1777, married Mary (last name unknown).
   (b) John[4] Garland (dates unknown), lived at "Garland's Neck, Hanover County."
2. Margaret[3] Garland (called "Peggy"), married William Overton, Jr. (b. Aug. 14, 1675), son of the immigrant William Overton and his wife, Elizabeth Waters.
3. Peter[3] Garland (Sheriff of Hanover County, 1735).
4. John[3] Garland, of Hanover, patented land in that County in 1719, will in Hanover County, dated July 27, 1731, probated April 15, 1734. The will mentions his wife, Ann; and sons, Peter, Robert, John, James and Nathaniel.
5. Martha[3] Garland, who married about 1710, John Cosby.
6. Mary[3] Garland (b. 1698), married in 1719, Edward Nelson (b. 1690), son of James Nelson, of Essex County, England, who emigrated to Virginia in the year 1718.[10]
7. James[3] Garland, acquired (by patent), June 22, 1727, 315 acres of land adjacent to Edward Garland's tract, called St. James, on the south side of North Anna River, in Hanover County.

David[4] Garland, of Hanover County, and Lunenburg County, and founder of the Lunenburg branch of the family, was Vestryman of Cumberland Parish from 1761 to 1776; was a Justice of the County Court of Lunenburg County, Virginia, from 1754 to 1777.[11] His will dated March 18, 1780, was probated in Lunenburg County, Virginia, May 9, 1782.[12]

David Garland was deputy sheriff in Lunenburg County in

---

[10]*History of Henrico Parish and St. Johns Church* (Moore), note by Brock, p. 188; see also *The Times-Dispatch*, Dec. 28, 1913, article by Prof. William Elmore Dickinson.
[11]*The Old Free State*, I, 329.
[12]It is recorded in W. B. 3, page 108.

1759, was sheriff from 1771 to 1773; was a Captain of Militia in 1757, and was a Colonel in 1767. He had:

1. Elizabeth[5] Garland, who married about July 2, 1764,[13] George Jefferson, son of Field Jefferson, and first cousin of Thomas Jefferson, the President.
   They had:
   (1) George[6] Jefferson,
   (2) John Garland[6] Jefferson, and very probably,
   (3) Peter[6] Jefferson, whose marriage bond dated May 5, 1804, for his marriage to Martha Russell, is in Lunenburg County, Virginia.[14]
2. Patty[5] Garland.
   In Lunenburg County, Virginia, Clerk's Office, is preserved a letter of consent dated March 12, 1765, from David Garland, for the marriage of his daughter Martha Garland to Peter Garland.
   It seems that "Martha Garland" mentioned in this letter was the "Patty Garland" of the will.
   The Peter Garland who married her has not been definitely identified, but he was probably a cousin.
3. Mary[5] Garland, who married John Ballard, son of John Ballard, Justice of the County Court of Lunenburg County, Virginia, 1780-1784, and Vestryman of Cumberland Parish, 1780-1784.
   He was John[5] Ballard, of the Ballard sketch foregoing.
4. Samuel[5] Garland, Captain in the Revolution,[15] Justice of the County Court of Lunenburg County, in 1770, married (M. B. in Brunswick County, Virginia, dated May 27, 1775 (1771?), Elizabeth Edmunds, daughter of Nicholas Edmunds,[16] and sister of Sterling Edmunds of Brunswick County. The date of Samuel Garland's death has not been learned, but his wife died in 1806.

---

[13]Letter of consent in Lunenburg County, dated July 2, 1764, from her father David Garland.
[14]*The Old Free State*, II, 396.
[15]*The Old Free State*, I, 267.
[16]The record of marriage bonds seems to show the date of the marriage bond to be 1775, while the note from Nicholas Edmunds giving his consent to the marriage is dated May 27, 1771.

The will of Elizabeth Garland bears date May 9, 1806, and was probated June 12, 1806.[17]

From it we learn they had the following children:

(1) Edward[6] Garland,
(2) Sarah[6] Garland,
(3) Lucy[6] Garland,
(4) Mary[6] Garland, who married Copeland Davis. She is mentioned in the will as "Mary Davis." There is in the Lunenburg County, Virginia, Clerk's Office, a letter of consent, dated November 28(?), 1791, from Sam. Garland, consenting to the marriage of his daughter "Polly Garland" to Copeland Davis; and the marriage bond for the marriage of Copeland Davis and Polly Garland is dated November 21, 1791.[18]

They had three children:

   I. Nicholas Edmunds[7] Davis (b. Oct. 16, 1772).
   II. Maria[7] Davis, and
   III. Eliza[7] Davis.

Maria[7] Davis married John Flood Lewis, son of Benjamin Lewis and Lucy Gray Edmunds, and had one son only, Nicholas Edmunds[8] Lewis, who died unmarried.

   I. Nicholas Edmunds[7] Davis (b. Oct. 16, 1772), married twice. The first wife was Amanda Lewis, daughter of Benjamin Lewis, who married March, 1787, Lucy Gray Edmunds. He married, secondly, Eliza Lewis P. Lampkin (b. Dec. 23, 1807, d. Jan. 11, 1867), and by this second marriage had:

(aa) Mary Jane[8] Davis (b. April 30, 1830, d. June, 1900), married Nov. 10, 1853, Dr. Edmund W. Wilkins, son of Dr. William Webb Wilkins (whose wife was Mary F. Beasley), and had:

(I) Ashley[9] Wilkins, who married Mary T. Pugh. (No issue.)

---

[17]It is of record in Lunenburg County, Virginia, in W. B. 6, pages 151-152.
[18]*The Old Free State*, II, 394.

  (II) Nicholas Davis[9] Wilkins (d. 1912 unmarried).
  (III) Elizabeth Garland[9] Wilkins (l. unm.).
  (IV) Edmonia Cabell[9] Wilkins (unm. 1929).[19]
  (V) Mary[9] Wilkins, married July 15, 1895, Copeland Davis[9] Miller, son of Lucy Garland Davis and William H. Miller.

(bb) Ashley L.[8] Davis (b. April, 1835, d. 1904), married July 20, 1864, Sallie Cabell, sister of George C. Cabell and widow of Junius Epes, and had:

  (I) Mary Pocahontas[9] Davis (dead), who married George Muncaster, of Kentucky (dead), and had:

    (1) Charles Ashley[10] Muncaster, who married August 13, 1926, Vera Denning, of Cleveland, Ohio.
    (2) Maggie D.[10] Muncaster, who married September 28, 1917, Alexander B. Venable, and had:
     (a) A. B.[11] Venable, and
     (b) Charles M.[11] Venable.

  (II) Joseph Cabell[9] Davis, married Lucy (last name not ascertained). No issue.

(cc) Lucy Garland[8] Davis (b. April 8, 1838, d. Aug. 17, 1917), who married June 2, 1859, William H. Miller (d. 1922), and had:

  (I) Nicholas E.[9] Miller, who married Roberta L. Epes, and had three children, two of whom died unmarried. The surviving child was
    (1) Lucy Garland[10] Miller.
  (II) Mary Shepard[9] Miller, who married Fletcher W. Ammons, and had:

---

[19]For information concerning the descendants of Nicholas Edmunds[7] Davis and Eliza[7] Davis, the writer is principally indebted to Miss Wilkins.

    (1) Emery[10] Ammons,
    (2) Ashley D.[10] Ammons.
  (III) Eliza Lewis[9] Miller.
  (IV) E. W.[9] Miller.
  (V) Copeland Davis[9] Miller, who married July 15, 1895, Mary Wilkins. (No issue).
  (VI) Ashley[9] Miller.
  (VII) Julia[9] Miller, who married J. E. Ogler, and had:
    (1) William[10] Ogler.
    (2) Mabel[10] Ogler.
    (3) Lucy[10] Ogler.
(dd) Nicholas E.[8] Davis (b. Aug. 1840, killed in the war, October, 1863).
(ee) Amanda Eliza[8] Davis (b. 1842, d. Nov. 1854).

II. Eliza[7] Davis, who married (M. B. Jan. 1, 1812),[20] Gray Dunn, and had:

(aa) Fannie Gray[8] Dunn, who married Richard J. Epes, and had:
  (I) Thomas[9] Epes, who married Isabella Neblett (b. Dec. 23, 1856),[21] daughter of Colin Neblett and Victoria Garland, and had:
    (1) Victor[9] Epes,
  (II) Richard[9] Epes (d. unm.),
  (III) Bettie Garland[9] Epes (d. unm.),
  (IV) Copeland Davis[9] Epes, who married Mary Harrison, daughter of Matthew Myrick Harrison, and Martha Cunningham, and had:
    (1) Martha C.[10] Epes (living 1929), married a Mr. Adams.
    (2) Mary H.[10] Epes, married a Mr. Taylor.
    (3) Fannie[10] Epes (d. unm.).

---

[20] *The Old Free State*, II, 399.
[21] *The Old Free State*, II, 325.

(4) Richard[10] Epes (d. unm.).
(5) Edward Dromgoode[10] Epes (l. unm.).
(6) Fletcher[10] Epes (d. unm.).
(7) Annie[10] Epes (l. married).
(V) Dudley Dunn[9] Epes.
(VI) Archer Jones[9] Epes (living 1929, unm.).
(VII) Fannie Ashley[9] Epes (living 1929, unm.).
(VIII) Roberta L.[9] Epes (dead), married Nicholas Edmunds Miller, son of Lucy Garland[8] Davis and William H. Miller.

DAVIS EXCURSUS.

The destruction of the Prince George County and Dinwiddie County records probably makes impossible an adequate account of the Davis family which was closely allied with the Garland family.

Copeland[1] Davis, the elder, died before November, 1768, for in the chancery suit in Lunenburg County, Virginia, of *Peter Stainback and Mary C., his wife, Thomas Hamlin, guardian of Ashley Davis, decd., v. Jane Scott, widow and executrix of James Scott, decd.*, it appears that the inventory of the personal estate of Copeland Davis was made in November, 1768.

In this case there is an allegation that Copeland Davis died *intestate,* and another allegation that Jane Davis, his widow, became *executrix* of his estate. This latter allegation is probably an error; for no will is otherwise referred to,—and the fact is she probably qualified as his administratrix, instead of his executrix.

Copeland[1] Davis left only two children:
(1) Ashley[2] Davis, his eldest son, who was doubtless the Ashley Davis who married Mary Cross, daughter of John Cross,[22] and had:

---

[22]There is in Lunenburg County, the M. B. dated Dec. 17, 1785, for the marriage of Ashley Davis and Mary Cross—*The Old Free State*, II, 389; and there is a certificate of consent from John Cross for the marriage of his daughter Mary Cross to Ashley Davis. This seems to be dated Dec. 16, *1781.* The clerk has evidently misread, either the date of the M. B. or of the certificate. 1785, in both cases is probably correct.

(a) Mary C.[3] Davis who married Peter Stainback.
(b) Ashley[3] Davis,
(c) Elizabeth[3] Davis.

(2) Copeland[2] Davis, who, as shown above, married Mary Garland.

It appears that after the death of Copeland Davis, the elder, his widow Jane Davis, married James Scott; that James Scott became the guardian of the children Ashley Davis and Copeland Davis, by appointment of the Court in the County of Dinwiddie.

The estate which thus passed into his hands was relatively large; and the suit above mentioned was brought, undertaking to establish that he had squandered and appropriated to his own use the proceeds and income of the estate which belonged to the wards. The final result of the suit is not clear due to the loss of the files, or a part of the files of the papers.

Ashley Davis seems to have died intestate and his widow, Mary Davis, qualified as his administratrix; and in an answer which she filed March 14, 1794, in a suit brought against her by Dyer Phillips, she states that Ashley Davis died November 3, 1790.

At July Court, 1804, Edward Garland qualified as the Administrator of Copeland Davis, decd. (Lunenburg Co., Va., O. B. 19, page 150).

Captain Samuel Garland died intestate, and he left at least the following children:

1. Mary Garland who married Copeland Davis.
2. Sarah Garland,
3. Lucy Garland,
4. Elizabeth Garland, who married David Dunn.

Some light is shed upon the family relationship by a suit in Lunenburg County, Virginia, in which an order was entered August 15, 1806 (O. B. 20, page 81), of Mary Davis (who married Copeland Davis), Sarah Garland and Lucy Garland against Eliza Dunn, infant of Elizabeth Dunn, decd.

In this suit, commissioners to divide land filed a report Jan. 8, 1807 (O. B. 20, p. 121), assigned certain parcels to Eliza Dunn, Lucy Garland, Mary Garland and Mary Davis.

On June 8, 1809 (O. B. 20, p. 378-9), there was an order entered in a suit brought by Mary Davis against John Taylor, admr. of Copeland Davis, Nicholas Davis, Eliza Davis, Jane Davis and Maria Davis, confirming an award made January 13, 1807, assigning Mary Davis widow of Copeland Davis 429 acres, part of 925 acres of land on both sides of Flat Rock Creek, as her dower in all the lands of Copeland Davis.

5. Edward[5] Garland, Captain in the Revolution.[23] A roll of his Company as it existed July 3, 1777, is printed in *The Old Free State*.[24] He represented Lunenburg County in the General Assembly in 1787 and 1788.[25] His will was dated Nov. 17, 1788, and was probated June 9, 1791.[26] He seems to have died unmarried, as his will mentions only his brothers Samuel Garland and John Garland and names them executors.
6. John[5] Garland. (Descendants not traced.)
7. William Terrell[5] Garland, who married (M. B. in Lunenburg County, Va., dated Dec. 29, 1786),[27] Martha Broadnax (Brodnax).
8. Peter[5] Garland, Captain in the Revolution.[28] Representative of Lunenburg County in the Legislature, 1794.[29]

There is a record of the children of Peter Garland, Captain in the Revolutionary War,[30] doubtless the above Peter[5] Garland, as follows:

David[6] Garland,
John[6] Garland,
Mary[6] Garland,
Susanna T.[6] Garland,
Garland[6] Garland,

---

[23] *The Old Free State*, I, 267.
[24] Vol. I, 215-216.
[25] *The Old Free State*, II, 70.
[26] It is recorded in Lunenburg County, Virginia, in W. B. 4, page 10.
[27] *The Old Free State*, I, 391.
[28] *The Old Free State*, I, 217, 219, 220.
[29] Id., II, 71.
[30] *Virginia Soldiers of 1776*, 140; *The Old Free State*, I, 213, 217, 225, 233, 267.

Nancy[6] Garland, who married Joshua Whorley,
Martha Elizabeth[6] Garland, who married Elijah Jourdan.[31]
9. David[5] Garland, Second Lieutenant in the Revolution,[32] Justice of the County Court of Lunenburg County.[33]
10. Robert[5] Garland.
11. Thomas[5] Garland, Captain of Militia of Lunenburg County, Virginia, married "Polley" (Mary) Lowry of Mecklenburg County, Virginia. The marriage bond, in Mecklenburg County, Virginia, is dated July 8, 1783, for the marriage of Captain Thomas Garland of Lunenburg County, Virginia, to "Polley Lowry." Consent was given by John Ragsdale, Guardian of "Polley."

Thomas Garland died intestate; but his wife made a will.

Thomas Garland died, doubtless, late in the year 1805. An inventory and appraisement of his estate, the estate of "Capt. Thomas Garland" bears date January 10, 1806. It was made by Anderson Bagley, Waller Taylor, and Samuel Jefferson.[34]

He left a number of infant children; but his son Thomas Lowry Garland seems to have been of age, for he qualified as the Administrator of his father's estate. To settle the estate he brought a suit: *Thomas Lowry Garland, admr. of Thomas Garland, v. Reuben Vaughan, Junr., Guardian of Fanny Garland, David Garland, Samuel Garland and John Garland, infant children of Thomas Garland.* As these five children exactly correspond in names and numbers to those mentioned in the will of their mother, it may be safely assumed that they were all the children of this pair.

Mary Garland, the widow of Captain Thomas Garland, did not

---

[31]These children of Captain Peter Garland proved in Court in Charlotte County, Va., Nov. 6, 1809, that they "are the children and legal representatives of Peter Garland, dec'd, who was an officer in the army of the United States in the Rev. war, and are the only persons entitled to the estate of the said Peter Garland."

On November 9, 1809, they sold their right to any land due for his services to Thomas D. Harris of Richmond, Virginia—*Virginia Soldiers of 1776*, 140.

[32]*The Old Free State*, I, 267.

[33]Id., I, 329.

[34]It is of record in Lunenburg County, Va., in W. B. 6, p. 154.

GENEALOGICAL NOTES—CONTINUED 227

long survive him, for her will, dated September 1, 1800, was probated in Lunenburg County, on June 12, 1806.[35]

From the extant proceedings in this case it appears that the parents of Mary Lowry (who married Capt. Thomas Garland), were Thomas and Frances Lowry, and that Captain Thomas Garland left the following children:

(1) Thomas Lowry[6] Garland,
(2) David[6] Garland,
(3) Samuel[6] Garland,
(4) Fanny[6] Garland,
(5) John[6] Garland.

The will of Mary (Lowry) Garland, names her brother Thomas Lowry, her executor.

Thomas Lowry[6] Garland did not live very long after his parents, for on November 12, 1808, Reuben Vaughan was appointed his administrator,[36] and the "John Garland" of the will of Mary Garland was doubtless "John T. Garland," for on December 14, 1809:

"David Garland with the approbation of the Court is appointed guardian of John T. Garland." This was, it seems, the "John Garland" for whom Reuben Vaughan, Junr. had previously been guardian. It indicates, also, that David Garland had by this date (1809), attained his majority.

A suit brought in 1809 by David Garland, against Thomas L. Garland's administrator shows that Thomas L. Garland died, intestate in 1807;

That Fanny Garland had married "Bozwell" [Boswell] B. Degraffenreid, and that Samuel Garland and John Garland were still infants.

It seems quite certain that the children above mentioned of Captain Thomas Garland, as David Garland and John Garland were in fact David *S.* Garland and John *T.* Garland.

There is in Lunenburg County, Va., the record of a suit of *David Garland, v. Reuben Vaughan, Admr. of Thomas L. Garland, decd., Boswell B. DeGraffenreid and Frances his wife,*

---

[35]It is recorded in W. B. 6, page 151.
[36]Lunenburg Co. Court O. B. 20, p. 328.

Samuel Garland and John T. Garland, by their guardian and next friend.

Thomas L. Garland died unmarried and intestate. The parties to this suit, David Garland, Frances DeGraffenreid, Samuel Garland and John T. Garalnd, were his surviving brothers and sister.

The *John T. Garland,* therefore, of this suit was the *John Garland* of Mary Garland's will; and *David S. Garland* who died, it seems, unmarried, and whose will is dated September 25, 1865,[87] mentions John T. Garland was his brother. It seems quite clear from this analysis that the children of Captain Thomas Garland were:

(1) Thomas Lowry[6] Garland,
(2) David S.[6] Garland,
(3) Samuel[6] Garland,
(4) Fanny (Frances)[6] Garland,
(5) John T.[6] Garland.

The evidence seems satisfactory that it was:

John T.[6] Garland (son of Captain Thomas Garland), who married Christian Blair Boyd, daughter of Richard Boyd and Panthea Burwell.[38]

The descendants of John[6] Garland and Christian Blair Boyd, were descendants of Governor Alexander Spotswood by the following line:

Governor Alexander[1] Spotswood had a son:

John[2] Spotswood who married Mary Dandridge, and they had a daughter:

Ann[3] Spotswood, who married Colonel Lewis Burwell (1745-1800), of "Stoneland," Colonel in the Revolution, from Mecklenburg County, and they had:

Panthea[4] Burwell, who married Nov. 19, 1799, Richard Boyd, and they had:

Christian Blair[5] Boyd, who married John Garland.

The relationship of this family to General Robert E. Lee results

---

[87]Lunenburg Co., Va., W. B. 14, p. 185-6.
[88]Letter of Mrs. Sallie Garland Pippen, of Hanover and Cumberland Counties, to the writer, August 30, 1928. Mrs. Pippin is a great-granddaughter of John Garland and Christian Blair Boyd.

from the fact that he too was a descendant of Governor Alexander Spotswood, being descended from Ann Catherine Spotswood his daughter who married Colonel Bernard Moore of King William County, Virginia.

They had Ann Butler Moore, who married Charles Carter, of Shirley, and they had

Ann Hill Carter, who married General Henry Lee—"Light Horse Harry" of the Revolution.

They were the parents of General Robert E. Lee.

The names and number of the children of this couple—John[6] Garland and Christian Blair Boyd—have not been ascertained, but they had:

(1) John Richard[7] Garland, who married a widow Mrs. Warwick, whose maiden name was Lucie Norvell of Lynchburg, Virginia.

John Richard Garland was a Justice of the County Court of Lunenburg County, Virginia, from 1844 to 1850; he owned the mill just below the junction of Mason's and Little Bears Element Creeks, and his name and the date 1855 is carved in deep bold letters in the large rock or ledge near the end of the mill dam.

He was chairman of the famous public meeting in Lunenburg County held at the Court House, January 14, 1861, which adopted the resolutions upon the pending crisis, set forth in *The Old Free State*.[39] His home was the old Garland Homestead, later known as *Wilburn*, the home of Isaac Bonaparte Bell.

His plantation was a particular object of raiding and pillaging operations in the War Between the States, such as those of Wilson's raid, presumably because of the vigorous views he held and the course he pursued respecting the issues of the period. He had:

  (a) Panthea[8] Garland, who married William W. Boswell[40] (b. 1845), and had:

    I. Garland[9] Boswell,

    II. Claire[9] Boswell, who married Dr. Hugh B. Mahood of Emporia, Virginia.

    III. Emund[9] Boswell.

---

[39]Vol. I, 563-564; originally published in the *Richmond Enquirer*, January 28, 1861.

[40]See Boswell Genealogy, *The Old Free State*, II, 171-176.

(b) David[8] Garland, who married April 11, 1881, Rosa Hubbard of "Guinea Farm,"[41] and had:
   I. Sallie Macon[9] Garland (b. 1883), who married 1921, Reverend Walter Woodfin Pippin, of Alabama, and had:
      (aa) Woodfin Garland[10] Pippin (b. and d. Dec. 5, 1921).
      (bb) Lucie Garland[10] Pippin (b. Jan. 8, 1923, d. in infancy).
   II. Lucie Edley[9] Garland (b. 1885, d. 1907).
(c) John[8] Garland, who married Semmie Jones of **Lunenburg** County, Virginia, and had:
   I. Marion[9] Garland,
   II. Lucie[9] Garland,
   III. Robert[9] Garland (and possibly others).
(d) Sallie[8] Garland (d. unmarried).
(e) Rosa[8] Garland, who married Leslie Revely, of Lynchburg, Virginia, and had:
   I. Nowlin[9] Revely,
   II. Panthea ("Thea")[9] Revely, (and possibly others).
(f) Lula[8] Garland, who married Ad Allen. (The writer has been unable to ascertain whether they had any children.)
(g) Richard[8] Garland,[42] who married Annie Stovall, of Danville, Virginia, and had:
   I. May[9] Garland,
   II. Richard[9] Garland (d. at the age of seventeen).

Samuel Garland, Vestryman of Cumberland Parish in 1786, and Thomas Garland, Vestryman from 1787 to 1793, were evidently sons of Colonel David Garland, the earlier Vestryman from 1761 to 1776.

2. John[4] Garland (dates unknown—Edward,[3] Edward,[2] Peter[1]), lived at "Garlands Neck," Hanover County, Virginia, M. unknown, and had:

---

[41]The ancestral home of the Macons and the Swanns, maternal ancestors of Rosa Hubbard. So named because of the finding of a golden coin, an English Guinea on the place, after English money ceased to be current in the United States.

[42]One of the principals in the Garland-Addison duel, in Lunenburg County, doubtless the last duel fought in the County.

(1) Thomas⁵ Garland, "who inherited the neck and founded the Goochland branch of the family."[43]
(2) Edward⁵ Garland.
(3) Robert⁵ Garland (the reputed founder of the Louisa branch of the family),[44] who married, unknown, and had:
  (a) Mary⁶ Garland (b. March 20, 1755, in Louisa County, Virginia), who married John Nuckolls (b. July 12, 1755),[45] and had:
    I. David⁷ Nuckolls (b. Oct. 26, 1778).
    II. Rhodes⁷ Nuckolls (b. June 11, 1780).
    III. Robert G.⁷ Nuckolls (b. Aug. 7, 1782).
    IV. Peter⁷ Nuckolls (b. June 18, 1784).
    V. Elisha⁷ Nuckolls (b. Sept. 4, 1786).
    VI. Nathaniel⁷ Nuckolls (b. Jan. 12, 1789).
    VII. Samuel⁷ Nuckolls (b. Dec. 26, 1790).
    VIII. Patsy⁷ Nuckolls (b. Nov. 27, 1792).
    IX. Asa⁷ Nuckolls (b. Feb. 11, 1795).
    X. Ezra⁷ Nuckolls (b. March 28, 1798).[46]
  (b) Charles⁶ Garland (d. unmarried).
(4) James⁵ Garland (b. 1722, d. 1812), married, in Hanover County, Virginia, in 1749, Mary Rice, daughter of David Rice, and his wife, Mary Howlett; moved from Hanover County, to Albemarle County, in 1761; Acting Magistrate of Albemarle County in 1783; sheriff in 1812,[47] and had:
  (a) Elizabeth⁶ Garland, who married Thomas Garland.
  (b) Edward⁶ Garland (d. 1817), Commissioner of the

---

[43]Nuckolls: *Pioneer Settlers of Grayson County, Virginia*, 141.

[44]Id. In giving the children of John⁴ Garland, we are endeavoring to utilize the data found in Nuckoll's *Pioneer Settlers of Grayson Co., Va.*, as we know of no other place where that information is attempted to be given. However, we are not certain that the information here recorded is accurate, or that it, in all instances, conveys the meaning intended by Mr. Nuckolls. No more confused and jumbled genealogical writing has ever been encountered, in all our experience, than that embraced in this writer's chapter on *The Garland Family*. He follows no system, mechanical, numerical or otherwise to preserve the clarity of what he presents, and his pronouns could not be more annoying if deliberately planned to confuse.

[45]Nuckolls: *Pioneer Settlers of Grayson Co., Va.*, 65.

[46]The descendants of some of these children of John Nuckolls and Mary Garland are given in *Pioneer Settlers of Grayson County, Va.* (Nuckolls), pp. 67 et seq.

[47]Woods: *History of Albemarle*, 199.

Revenue, married Sarah Old, daughter of Colonel John Old, and had:
(1) Nathaniel[7] Garland.
(2) Mary[7] Garland, who married Nicholas Hamner.
(3) Fleming[7] Garland.
(4) James[7] Garland.
(5) Elizabeth[7] Garland, who married Joseph Sutherland.
(6) Sarah[7] Garland, who married Pleasant Sowell, and
(7) Maria[7] Garland, who married Thomas Hamner, and removed to Lewis County, Virginia (now West Virginia).

(c) Rice[6] Garland (d. 1818), resided near Ivy Depot, Magistrate 1791; member of Legislature 1808; Sheriff 1811. Married Elizabeth Hamner, daughter of Samuel Hamner.
They had:
I. William[7] Garland (d. 1841).
II. James[7] Garland.
III. Rice[7] Garland, attorney, lived in Leakesville, N. C.
IV. Samuel[7] Garland, resided in Lynchburg, Va., m. Mary Lightfoot Anderson.
V. Elizabeth[7] Garland, who married Henry White, and had:
(aa) Elizabeth[8] White, who married Edward C. Hamner, Sr.
They had:
(I) Samuel Garland[9] Hamner, attorney at law, Lynchburg, Va., who married Mary Winchester, dau. of Dr. W. R. Winchester and his wife Sarah Harrison.
(II) Edward C.[9] Hamner, Jr., Commander, U. S. N. m. Dorothy Lisk, of Beverly, New Jersey.
(III) Sallie Cole[9] Hamner, Assistant Librarian, Jones Memorial Library, Lynchburg, Va.
(IV) Bessie[9] Hamner (deceased).
(V) Henry Rawlings[9] Hamner.

VI. Mary Rice⁷ Garland, who married Robert H. Slaughter.
VII. Burr⁷ Garland.
VIII. Maurice⁷ Garland, and
IX. Nicholas⁷ Garland.

(d) James[6] Garland, Jr. (b. 1753), was an officer in the Revolution in 1781, at Albemarle Barracks. He married Anne Wingfield, daughter of John Wingfield and his wife Mary Hudson. They had:

I. Hudson Martin[7] Garland, attorney; represented Amherst in the legislature; Captain war of 1812; intimate friend of General Andrew Jackson. Married Elizabeth Penn Phillips (grand-niece of William Penn), and had:

(aa) Henrietta[8] Garland. m. Rev. Mr. Boyd of the Methodist Episcopal Church.

(bb) Betsy Ann[8] Garland.

(cc) Maria[8] Garland, m. a Mr. Wolfe.

(dd) James[8] Garland, of Lynchburg. Member of Congress 1835-1841; Commonwealth's Atty. 1852-1870; Corporation Judge 1870-1883; blind for many years; died 1883, age 93 years. He had two daughters:

(I) Mrs. Cole.[9]

(II) Mrs. Aurelius[9] Christian.

(ee) Hudson Martin[8] Garland, Jr.,[48] married Letitia B. Pendleton, daughter of Micajah Pendleton and his wife Mary Cabell Horsley. Micajah Pendleton was a son of Philip Pendleton, and nephew of the famous jurist Edmund Pendleton.

(ff) General John[8] Garland, distinguished in the Mexican war. His daughter married General Longstreet.

---

[48]The record of the children and grandchildren of James[6] Garland is taken from R. H. Early's *Campbell Chronicles*, page 414. As there set down it is unclear whether Hugh Martin Garland, Jr., is the son or grandson of Hugh Martin[6] Garland. If he was not the son, then he was (by that account) the son of Judge James[7] Garland.

II. James Parker⁷ Garland, married Katura Stone and had:
  (aa) Bettie⁸ Garland.
  (bb) Henrietta⁸ Garland, married a Mr. Watts and moved to Alabama.
  (cc) Addison⁸ Garland, U. S. Navy. He endeavored to land and join the Southern Army, but was prevented; he died at sea.
  (dd) Benami Stone⁸ Garland.
  (ee) Alexander⁸ Garland.
  (ff) Catherine Malvina⁸ Garland, married in 1846, Charles Rice Slaughter, of Lynchburg, Va., son of Dr. Robert Slaughter, of Campbell Co., Va.
  (gg) Althea C.⁸ Garland, m. a Mr. Brown of Alabama.
  (hh) Colonel Robert⁸ Garland, m. Elizabeth Wolfe. He contracted tuberculosis in a Northern prison and died soon after the war.

III. Alexander Spotswood⁷ Garland, married Lucinda Rose, daughter of Colonel Hugh Rose and his wife Caroline Jordon. They had:
  (aa) Landon Cabell⁸ Garland, Pres. Randolph-Macon College, Chancellor of Vanderbilt University, Nashville, Tenn., who married Louise Garland, and had:
    (I) Rose⁹ Garland, who married Prof. Burwell B. Lewis, of the University of Alabama.
    (II) Louise Frances⁹ Garland (1843-1901), married May 3, 1877, Milton Wylie Humphreys (b. Sept. 15, 1844, in Greenbrier Co., Va.), C. S. A., A. M., Ph. D., LL. D., Prof. Greek U. Va., 1887-1912.⁴⁹

    They had:
      (aa) Louise Garland¹⁰ Humphreys (b. June 2, 1878).

---

⁴⁹See: *Abridged Comp. Am. Genealogy*, II, 136, and *Who's Who in America*.

- (bb) Annie Fulton[10] Humphreys (b. Dec. 21, 1881), m. Edward Ryan Dyer.
- (cc) Mary Meredith[10] Humphreys (b. Nov. 29, 1882), m. Dean W. Hendrickson.
- (dd) Jeannette Rose[10] Humphreys (b. June 4, 1885), m. John Sebastain Derr.
- (III) Maurice[9] Garland, m. Lucy Galt.
- (IV) Jennie[9] Garland, m. Prof. Smith, of Tuscaloosa Univ.
- (V) Annie[9] Garland, m. Prof. Robert Fulton of Mississippi.

- (bb) Hugh A.[8] Garland, Member of Virginia Legislature, Clerk of the United States House of Representatives, a man of vast and varied learning, and a writer of distinction; author of the Life of John Randolph of Roanoke. m. Ann Powell Burwell, and had:
    - (I) Nannie R.[9] Garland, m. General Gilbert Meem.
    - (II) Minnie[9] Garland, m. a Mr. Papan.
    - (III) Spottswood[9] Garland, m. Mary Jenkins.
    - (IV) Maggie[9] Garland, m. Robert Hoskins.

- (cc) Caroline[8] Garland, married Maurice[7] Garland, son of Rice[6] Garland and his wife Elizabeth Hamner, and had:
    - (I) General Samuel[9] Garland, m. Eliza Meem, daughter of John Meem of Lynchburg, Va.

(e) Robert[6] Garland (b. 1768), attorney, in Albemarle County, Virginia, and about 1822, removed to Nelson County, Virginia.

(f) Clifton[6] Garland (b. 1769, d. unmarried in 1815), Magistrate in 1806.

(g) Mary[6] Garland, who married James Woods, and in 1797 emigrated to Garrard County, Kentucky.

(h) Nathaniel[6] Garland (James,[5] John,[4] Edward,[3] Edward,[2] Peter[1]) (d. 1793), wife named Jane.
Children:
  I. Frances[7] Garland, who married John Woodson.
  II. Nelson[7] Garland.
  III. Mary[7] Garland, who married Isham Ready.
  IV. Anderson[7] Garland, whose widow married Richard Bruce, and whose children removed to Lewis County, Kentucky.
  V. Elizabeth[7] Garland.
  VI. Peter[7] Garland, who married Elizabeth Martin, daughter of Benjamin Martin, who after her husband's death married Daniel White, son of Thomas Martin and Mary Ann White.
  Issue:
    (a) James[8] Garland.
    (b) Goodrich[8] Garland.

(5) John[6] Garland.
(6) Lucy[5] Garland.
(7) Peter[5] Garland.
(8) William[5] Garland (b. 1746), married Ann Shepherd of Amherst County, Virginia, daughter of Christopher Shepherd, and died "comparatively young in 1777."[50]
They had:
  (a) Frances[6] Garland, who married Reuben Pendleton.
  (b) Mary[6] Garland, m. one Camden.
  (c) James[6] Garland (never married).
  (d) David Shepherd[6] Garland (b. Sept. 27, 1769, d. 1841), Congressman 1807, m. Jane Meredith, daughter of Colonel Samuel Meredith, and his wife Jane Henry, who was the sister of Patrick Henry the "renowned orator."
  They had:
    I. Samuel Meredith[7] Garland (b. Nov. 15, 1802, d. 1880), buried at Kenmore. Married July 8, 1830, Mildred Jordan Powell, dau. of Dr. James Powell.

---

[50]Woods: *History of Albemarle*, 200.

Represented Amherst in the legislature; member Constitutional Convention of 1850-51; and of the "Secession Convention," of 1861; advocated the sovereignty of the states, and voted "for secession." They had:
- (aa) Mildred Irving^8 Garland, who married Col. John T. Ellis.
- (bb) Moritia Henry^8 Garland, who married Colonel Thomas Whitehead, M. C.
- (cc) Ella Rose^8 Garland, who married N. W. Wills.
- (dd) Jane Meredith^8 Garland, who married Willis H. Wills.
- (ee) Sally^8 Garland (d. in infancy).
- (ff) David Shepherd^8 Garland, Confederate soldier at 18; died during the war.
- (gg) Samuel Meredith^8 Garland, Confederate soldier at 16; died during the war.
- (hh) Waller^8 Garland (d. in youth).
- (ii) Paulus Powell^8 Garland, who married Lucy Ellis.
- (jj) Betty Powell^8 Garland (b. Jan. 28, 1851), married 1880, Rev. Richard T. Wilson, D. D. (d. 1907), and had:
    - (1) Richard Taylor^9 Wilson, lawyer, who married Julia Meade Patteson, and had:
        - (a) Julia Meade^{10} Wilson.
        - (b) Helen Garland^{10} Wilson.
        - (c) Richard T.^{10} Wilson, III.
    - (2) Charles Garland^9 Wilson, who married Ellen Taylor Baxter.
    - (3) Samuel Meredith Garland^9 Wilson, who married Louise Ellis Garland, and had:
        - (a) Samuel Meredith^{10} Wilson, Jr. (d. in infancy).
        - (b) Louise Ellis^{10} Wilson.
    - (4) Bessie Garland^9 Wilson, who married Richard Fox.

(5) Daisy Powell⁹ Wilson.
(6) Mildred Leigh⁹ Wilson.
(7) Landon Pierce⁹ Wilson (d. in infancy).
(8) Helen Irving⁹ Wilson (d. Jan. 6, 1924), m. Dr. Meade S. Brent. (No children.)

  II. Annie Shepherd[7] Garland, who married Dr. C. A. Rose.
 III. Sally Armistead[7] Garland, who married William Wallis (?).
 IV. Jane Henry[7] Garland, who married Dr. John P. Cobbs.
  V. Mary Rice[7] Garland, who married Col. Ed. A. Cabell
 VI. Wm. Henry[7] Garland, who married 1st a Miss Eubank, and 2nd, a daughter of Judge Baldwin of Mississippi.
VII. Patrick Henry[7] Garland, who married a Miss Floyd.
VIII. Eliza Virginia[7] Garland, who married George K. Cabell.
 IX. Louise Frances[7] Garland, who married Landon C. Garland, Chancellor of Vanderbilt University.
  X. Caroline A.[7] Garland, who died single.
 XI. Martha Henry[7] Garland, who died single.

4. John[3] Garland (Edward,[2] Peter[1]), of Hanover County; patented land in that county in 1719; will in Hanover County, dated July 27, 1731, probated April 15, 1734. Wife named Ann (last name not known). The will shows he had the following sons:

(a) Peter[4] Garland,
(b) Robert[4] Garland,
(c) John[4] Garland,
(d) James[4] Garland,
(e) Nathaniel Garland, who married Elizabeth (last name not known).[51]

The confusing and misleading character of much that has been printed about the Garland family is readily apparent when one considers the facts.

---

[51] *Times-Dispatch* (Richmond), April 23, 1908(?).

There have in years past been several articles on the family in *The Times-Dispatch*.[52]

There is a sketch of the family in *Pioneer Settlers of Grayson County*,[53] and one in the *History of Albemarle*,[54] an unusually valuable volume, as a whole, and another in *Campbell Chronicles and Family Sketches*,[55] and there are many mentions of the family in the genealogical and historical magazines.

In none of them, so far as this writer's investigations have gone, is there any mention of David Garland as a son of Edward Garland; not only is there no mention of him but the implication at least of one of the articles above referred to is that John Garland, of Garland's Neck, was the eldest son of Edward Garland. Yet, the act above cited from *Hening's Statutes at Large* for docking the entail of the Hanover land and transferring it to the Lunenburg lands abundantly establishes the fact that David Garland of Hanover and Lunenburg Counties was not only a son, but the eldest son of Edward Garland.

In fact the Lunenburg branch of the Garland family has not even been referred to in some of the accounts, and in others a mere reference is made to the fact that there was a Lunenburg branch of the family, without mentioning any facts respecting it, as to who founded it, or who composed it. This present account is thought to be the first to give David Garland of Hanover and Lunenburg and his descendants their places upon the family tree.

It is said that Augustus H. Garland, United States Senator from Arkansas, and Attorney General of the United States under President Cleveland, was of the Lunenburg County, Virginia, branch of the family. This writer has not been able to trace his lineage. Several inquiries in quarters in Tennessee and Arkansas which should have yielded information, met with no response.

A brief note of the career of General Garland follows:

Augustus Hill Garland, a senator from Arkansas, b. in Tipton

---
[52]Issues of July 26, 1908; of Aug. 16, 1908; of Dec. 28, 1913, and in two other issues, copies (photostats) of which are before us, but the dates are not reproduced.
[53]By Nuckolls.
[54]By Rev. Edgar Woods.
[55]By R. H. Early.

Co., Tenn., June 11, 1832; his parents moved to Hempstead Co., Ark., in 1833; attended St. Mary's College and St. Joseph College in Kentucky, and was graduated from the latter in 1849; studied law and was admitted to practice in 1853, in Washington, Ark., moved to Little Rock in 1856; elector on the Bell and Everett ticket in 1860; union delegate in the State Convention that passed the ordinance of secession in 1861; member of the provisional congress that met in Montgomery, Ala., in May, 1861, and subsequently of the Confederate Congress and served in both houses; elected to the United States Senate for the term beginning March 4, 1867, but not admitted to his seat, as Arkansas had not been readmitted to representation; argued the test-oath case as to lawyers in the Supreme Court of the United States and won it (see Garland, ex parte, 4 Wallace); followed the practice of law until the fall of 1874, when elected governor; elected as a Democrat in January, 1876, to the United States Senate; re-elected in 1883, and served from March 4, 1877, until March 6, 1885, when he resigned to accept the position of Attorney General in President Cleveland's Cabinet, and served from March 9, 1885, to March 5, 1899; died in Washington, D. C., January 26, 1899.

In addition to David[4] Garland of Hanover and Lunenburg Counties, it seems that other Garlands came into Lunenburg County, some years subsequent to his coming. It seems certain one other so came. This was Nathaniel Garland. There is an entry in the Vestry Book of Cumberland Parish, which indicates that Nathaniel Garland was elected a vestryman of the parish. A somewhat critical examination of the minutes fails to disclose his attendance upon a vestry meeting; but on November 29, 1758, the vestry entered an order declaring that,

"Mr. Thomas Pettis [Pettus] is chose a Vestry man in the room of Mr. Nath'll Garland who is removed out of the parish."

This Nathaniel Garland, it will be observed, apparently came into the parish at about the same time as David[4] Garland, and held office as a vestryman about the same time as did David, in fact, the above order was entered a few years before David[4] Garland was elected as vestryman.

This Nathaniel Garland who resided for a time in Lunenburg

GENEALOGICAL NOTES—CONTINUED 241

County, was vestryman of Cumberland Parish, and in 1758 "is removed out of the Parish," is believed to have been a son of John³ Garland of Hanover, and Ann his wife, and is believed to have been the Nathaniel⁴ Garland who married Elizabeth (last name not known).

That Nathaniel Garland, who was the Vestryman of Cumberland Parish, and who removed therefrom in 1758, or before that date, removed to Louisa County, Virginia, is indicated by certain deed of record in Lunenburg County, Virginia.

For example, on May 3, 1762, Nathaniel Garland of Trinity Parish, Louisa County, made a deed to William Hardy conveying him 225 acres of land on Great Hounds Creek,[56] and on December 11, 1762, Nathaniel Garland of Louisa County, conveyed to Joseph Winn, 115 acres of land in Lunenburg County, Virginia.[57]

There was also in Lunenburg County, Virginia, in 1774, 1776 and other years, a Peter Garland, on the list of tithes, for ten tithes.

This may have been David⁴ Garland's son Peter; it may, however, have been, and probably was Peter⁴ Garland, son of John³ Garland and Ann his wife, and brother of Nathaniel⁴ Garland who moved to Louisa County, Virginia.

There is in Lunenburg County, the certificate of consent, dated March 12, 1767, from David Garland, for the marriage of his daughter Martha to Peter Garland. It is thought this was her first cousin, Peter⁴ Garland, son of John and Ann Garland, and they possibly (rather than Peter, son of David Garland), may have been the parents of the David, John, Mary, Susanna, Garland, Nancy and Martha Elizabeth Garland mentioned as children of a Peter Garland of the Revolution.[58]

---

[56] D. B. 8, p. 43.
[57] D. B. 9, p. 201.
[58] *Virginia Soldiers of 1776*, 140.

CHAPTER XIII

Genealogical Notes—Continued

GEE, GLENN, HALL, HARDY, HAWKINS, HOBSON, HOWARD, JACKSON, JEFFERSON, JENINGS, JORDAN, LAMKIN, LANIER, LESTER, MACFARLAND, MARRABLE, MARTIN, NASH, NEBLETT, PARRISH, PETTUS, PHILLIPS, RAGSDALE, READ, ROBERTSON, SMITH, SPEED, STEVENSON, STOKES, STREET, TABB, TALBOTT, TAYLOR, TOMLINSON, TUCKER, TWITTY, WINN.

GEE.

JAMES GEE appears on the list of tithes taken in 1748 by Lyddal Bacon, for two tithes. The precinct of Lyddal Bacon for that year was "from Hounds Creek to the head of Nottoway and Meherrin Rivers."

He is on Hugh Lawson's list in 1749, who had substantially the same precinct.

William Gee appears on this list also.

Both James Gee and William Gee are on the list for a single tithe each in 1750.

In 1752 William Gee for three tithes and James Gee for one tithe were on the list of Richard Witton.

In 1764 on the list of Thomas Tabb, for Cumberland Parish, appears:

Henry Gee for one tithe and 500 acres of land,
Nevil Gee for one tithe and 300 acres of land,
Benjamin Gee for one tithe,
James Gee for one tithe and 624 acres of land,
Charles Gee for 200 acres of land, and
William Gee for three tithes and 243 acres of land.

It would take more collateral research than opportunity has afforded to determine definitely where they came from and their exact relationships to each other.

The list of John Ragsdale in 1772 affords some indication that

James Gee, at that time had two sons who were between sixteen and twenty-one years of age, named David Gee and James Gee, Jr.

In 1783 on the list taken by Edward Brodnax appears
> Henry Gee,
> Jessey Gee,
> Benjamin Gee,
> Nevil Gee,

and on the list of Nicholas Hobson for the same year appear
> James Gee and James Gee, Jr.,
> Charles Gee,
> David Gee and
> Jessie [Jesse] Gee.

There are a number of wills made by various members of the family in Lunenburg County between 1746 and 1825, from which data may be briefly noted.

The earliest of these is that of

James Gee, dated May 3, 1788, and probated February 11, 1802.[1] It mentions the following children:

1. David Gee,
2. James Gee,
3. Charles Gee,
4. Sarah Barry.

The next is that of

Neavil Gee, dated June 19, 1804, and probated July 12, 1804.[2] It mentions the following children and grandchildren:

1. Jones Gee, son,
2. Jesse Gee, son,
3. George Gee, son,
4. Lucas Gee, son,
5. Neavil Gee, son,
6. James Gee, son,
7. Nanny Bowers, daughter,
8. Amey Andrews, daughter,
9. Patsey Jefferson, granddaughter,
10. Letty Gee, granddaughter.

---
[1] Recorded in W. B. 5, p. 81.
[2] Recorded in W. B. 6, pages 88-89.

11. Elizabeth Gee, granddaughter,
12. Nancy Gee, granddaughter,
13. Dolly Gee, granddaughter,
14. Elizabeth Andrews, granddaughter, and
15. Catherine Gee, daughter-in-law.

Chappell Gee married in Brunswick County, Virginia, Rebecca Lucas, daughter of William Lucas. The marriage bond was dated March 18, 1773.[3]

The name of this testator and of some of his children suggest that he may have been a son of this pair.

There is in Mecklenburg County, Va., the record[4] of the nuncupative will of Jones Gee made in Claiborne County, Mississippi, and proved there September 27, 1824, and probated in Mecklenburg County, Virginia, September 19, 1825.

It mentions a brother, whose name on the record is almost undecipherable, but is presumed to be Lucas (or Luke) Gee.

Jones Gee had a daughter Lucy Gee who married (M. B. in Mecklenburg County, Va., dated Feb. 28, 1803), William Drumright, Jr.

Jesse Gee married Jincy Moore M. B. in Lunenburg Co., Va., dated Dec. 15, 1806.[5]

Neavil Gee, son of Neavil Gee, married in Mecklenburg County, Virginia, Elizabeth Andrews, daughter of George Andrews. The marriage bond is dated July 19, 1797.

James Gee of Lunenburg County, Virginia, son of Neavil Gee, married Lucy Bugg of Mecklenburg County, Virginia; the marriage bond was dated February 6, 1797.

William Gee, son of Jesse Gee, made his will October 24, 1807; it was probated January 14, 1808.[6] In it he mentions his wife Salley Gee, and his sister-in-law Martha Moody. He names his father Jesse Gee, William Ragsdale and Sally Gee, as executors.

Henry Gee's will is dated April 22, 1810, and was probated March 9, 1815.[7]

---

[3] *William and Mary Quarterly*, XII, 16.
[4] In W. B. 10, p. 323.
[5] *The Old Free State*, II, 402.
[6] And is recorded in W. B. 6, page 203-4.
[7] And is recorded in W. B. 7, page 157.

He mentions his wife Elizabeth Gee and the following children and grandchildren:

1. George Gee,
2. Henry Gee,
3. Benjamin Gee,
4. Thomas Gee,
5. Matthew Gee,
6. Drury Gee,
7. Nancy Gee,
8. Beckey Gee,
9. Martha Ragsdale, granddaughter,
10. Betsy Jennings Moore, granddaughter.

Benjamin Gee made his will in 1815. It is dated March 13, and was probated June 8, 1815.[8] In it he mentions his brother Henry Gee, and sons:

Jeremiah Gee,
Jesse Gee and
Francis Gee, and

Daughters:

Fanny Gee, and
Amy Gee,

Grandsons:

Joel M. Ragsdale and
Benjamin Ragsdale, and

Granddaughters:

Frances Ragsdale,
Elizabeth Ragsdale,
Mary Ragsdale, and
Jane Ragsdale, and

A nephew:

Charles Gee, son of his brother Jesse Gee.

He named his sons Jeremiah Gee and Jesse Gee, and his son-in-law William Ragsdale, Executors.

---

[8]It is recorded in W. B. 7, page 155.

Jeremiah Gee married Patsey Andrews of Mecklenburg County, Virginia. The marriage bond is dated November 19, 1804.

Jesse Gee married Jincy Moore, of Lunenburg County, Va. The marriage bond is dated December 15, 1806. It is not clear whether the Jesse Gee who married Jincy Moore was the son of Benjamin Gee, or the son of Neavil Gee.

The daughter of Benjamin Gee who married William Ragsdale, was doubtless, Milley Gee. The marriage bond for their marriage in Lunenburg County, Virginia, is dated Jan. 29, 1794.[9]

The will of Jesse Gee is dated August 7, 1817, and was probated November 10, 1823.[10] In it he mentions his wife Elizabeth Gee, and sons:

1. James S. (or I.) Gee, who married Martha J. Crowder, daughter of Bartholomew Crowder. The marriage bond is dated Jan. 18, 1836,[11] and a letter of consent discloses the name of the bride's father.

2. Benjamin Gee,
3. Charles Gee,
and daughters:
4. Bridgett N. Gee,
5. Jane Gee.

The will of Lucas Gee is dated October 23, 1817, and was probated February 20, 1820.[12]

He refers to his wife, but does not mention her name.

He mentions his brother Jones Gee, which identifies him as a son of Neavil Gee (the elder), whose will was dated June 19, 1804, as above noted.

Two sons:
    Sack Gee and
    William L. Gee, along with his brother Jones Gee, are named executors.

Lucas Gee was a member of the County Court of Lunenburg County in 1811, 1813 and in 1817.[13]

---

[9] *The Old Free State*, II, 394.
[10] It is of record in W. B. 8, page 312.
[11] *The Old Free State*, II, 413.
[12] It is recorded in W. B. 8, p. 75.
[13] *The Old Free State*, I, 329.

Matthews Gee made his will January 27, 1819, and it was probated December 7, 1819.[14] He evidently never married as he mentions no wife or child in his will. He does mention Mrs. Martha Estes, wife of Edmund Estes. She was Martha Gee Ragsdale, and married Edmund Estes in 1814.[15] He mentions also his sister, Rebecca Gee, wife of Charles Gee; and names his cousins Jesse Gee and Charles Gee, his executors.

The will of Nevel (Neavil) Gee is dated January 16, 1819, and was probated March 12, 1819.[16] He mentions his wife, Elizabeth Gee, who as above noted, was Elizabeth Andrews, daughter of George Andrews of Mecklenburg County, Virginia, and also the following sons: (No daughters.)

1. George L. Gee,
2. William B. Gee,
3. Alfred Gee,
4. Claiborne Gee,
5. Nevil A. Gee.

He names his brother Lucas Gee, and George L. Gee, executors.

There is in Mecklenburg County, Virginia, the marriage bond, dated December 12, 1787, of William Gee of Lunenburg County, to Caty Jones.

He seems about of the right date for the generation of the children of the Vestryman, William Gee, who served in that capacity from 1761 to 1767; but this writer has not ascertained who (if any be had), were his children.

GLENN.

The Tyree family and the Glenn family are both found in New Kent County, Virginia, as the Parish Register of St. Peter's Parish attests. It is a reasonable surmise that Tyree Glenn received his name as a result, some time, of a union between the two families.

Tyree[1] Glenn was probably the first of the name in Lunenburg County. He was certainly there as early as 1750 for he is on

---

[14] And is recorded in W. B. 8, p. 65.
[15] *The Old Free State*, II, 401.
[16] It is of record in W. B. 8, p. 37.

Lyddall Bacon's list of tithes for that year charged with four tithes. The spelling of his name on this list is Tyra Glen.

Tyree[1] Glenn died in 1763. His will was dated July 2, and probated on September 8, of that year.[17] He married Mary Roe (M. B. in Lunenburg County, Va., dated April 5, 1751). He mentions his wife, Mary Glenn, and children as follows:

1. Jeremiah[2] Glenn,
2. John[2] Glenn,
3. William[2] Glenn,
4. Anne[2] Glenn,
5. Sarah[2] Glenn.

Jeremiah[2] Glenn married Anne Blagrave, daughter of Henry Blagrave.[18] The marriage bond in Lunenburg County is dated Jan. 28, 1765.[19]

John[2] Glenn married Sarah Bacon. The marriage bond is in Lunenburg County, dated July 12, 1770. He was a Captain in the Revolution, and attained the rank of Colonel.[20] He was a Justice of the County Court from 1782 to 1790,[21] a member of the General Assembly from 1778 to 1781,[22] and again in 1784,[23] when he voted in the negative on the proposition to incorporate "all societies of the Christian religion which may apply for the same."[24]

William[2] Glenn, the Vestryman of Cumberland Parish in 1790, was one of the sureties upon the bond guaranteeing the proper construction of the Court House of the County.[25]

Sarah[2] Glenn married Nat. Nesbett. The marriage bond for this marriage has not been found, but there is in the clerk's office of Lunenburg County a letter of consent (undated) from John Glenn, for the marriage of his daughter "Sary Glenn" to Nat. Nesbett.

---

[17] It is recorded in W. B. 2, page 179.
[18] See mention of him foregoing in these notes.
[19] *The Old Free State*, II, 390.
[20] Id., I, 266-267.
[21] Id., I, 329.
[22] Id., II, 70.
[23] Id.
[24] Journal: H. of D. 1784, 92.
[25] *The Old Free State*, I, 118.

Probably all of Tyree[1] Glenn's children were not mentioned in the will.

There is in Lunenburg County, Va., a marriage bond for the marriage of Tyree Glenn to Rachel Moon, daughter of Gideon Moon. It was dated May 12, 1785.[26] He was probably a son of Tyree[1] Glenn.

There was also a James Glenn who married Mourning Winn (M. B. Dec. 4, 1789), who is not definitely identified.

HALL.

Moses Hall and Thomas Hall were on Matthew Talbot's list of tithes for 1748, for one tithe each. William Hall was on the same list for the same years for two tithes.

On John Phelps list for 1748 there appeared Thomas Hall and John Hall, apparently charged jointly with two tithes. John Phelps' precinct was "from the mouth of Falling River upwards," for this year. John Hall therefore lived, it seems, in the section which a few years later was formed into Bedford County.

John Hall was one of the first Justices of Lunenburg County. In fact he was the first or senior Justice mentioned in the commission of the peace, for organizing the county, and signed the minutes of the first term of Court of the County.[27]

He was the surveyor for the North District of the County, and Peter Fontaine for the South District.

He was a member of the County Court from 1746 to 1748,[28] was Sheriff of the County from 1748 to 1750, and was a soldier of the French and Indian wars.[29]

John Hall ceased to be a vestryman of Cumberland Parish, and a member of the County Court of Lunenburg County at about the same time. It is probable that soon thereafter he became identified with Bedford, the newly created county. There is in Bedford the will of a John Hall, probated September 22, 1794. It is probable that was John Hall the vestryman of Cumberland Parish.

---

[26] *The Old Free State*, II, 389.
[27] *The Old Free State*, I, 108, 113.
[28] Id., 329.
[29] Id., 194, 196.

From the beginning of the county up to 1825 the records of Lunenburg County, Virginia, show only one will made by a person of the name. That was the will of William Hall, dated January 12, 1753, and probated August 8, 1753.[80]

It mentions sons:
> Thomas Hall and
> Moses Hall,

and a granddaughter,
> Elliball Hall.

HARDY.

William Hardy was a Vestryman of Cumberland Parish from 1780 to 1786. He was a Revolutionary soldier.

There were two Covington Hardys in Lunenburg County, one a brother and the other a son of William Hardy. The Covington Hardy who was Vestryman of Cumberland Parish from 1786 to 1802, is thought to have been a son of William Hardy, the Vestryman.

There is an extensive genealogy of the Hardy family in *The Old Free State*.[31]

HAWKINS.

Thomas Hawkins was a Vestryman of Cumberland Parish from 1754 to 1758.

He was a deputy sheriff under Lyddall Bacon, from 1757 to 1759, in which year he died. His will dated November 14, 1758, was probated in Lunenburg County, May 1, 1759.[32]

In it he mentions his wife Mary Hawkins, and the following children:
1. Matthew Hawkins,
2. John Hawkins,
3. Sarah Hawkins,
4. An unborn child.

He named his brother Pinkethman Hawkins one of his executors; his wife was the other.

---

[30]It is recorded in W. B. 1, page 125.
[31]Vol. II, Chapter VI, comprising pages 216 to 280.
[32]It is recorded in W. B. 1, page 251.

HOBSON.

Nicholas[1] Hobson died in Lunenburg County, Virginia, in 1758. His will was dated May 25, and probated December 5, of that year.[33] In it he mentions his wife Agnes Hobson[34] and the following children:

1. John[2] Hobson. This was John Hobson the vestryman of Cumberland Parish, 1761 to 1765.
2. Matthew[2] Hobson, removed to Georgia, and "was one of the most conspicuous of the Colonial patriots in Georgia."[35] "His descendants are numerous."[36]
3. Nicholas[2] Hobson, Captain in the Revolutionary War, from Lunenburg County, Virginia. Served under General Washington in the northern campaigns; resigned September 23, 1777.[37] A list or roll of the Company of Captain Nicholas Hobson, as it stood May 31, 1777, is printed in *The Old Free State*.[38] He was a member of the County Court of Lunenburg County, Virginia, in 1782 and 1783,[39] and was a member of the General Assembly of Virginia in 1781 and 1782.[40] He was Vestryman of Cumberland Parish from 1761 to 1765. He removed to Georgia where he died. His will was probated in Jackson County, Georgia, on May 1, 1809.[41] The will mentions the following children:

   1. William[3] Hobson,
   2. Jenny[3] Smith,
   3. John[3] Hobson,
   4. Matthew[3] Hobson,
   5. Baker[3] Hobson,
   6. Christopher[3] Hobson,
   7. Francis[3] Hobson,

---

[33] It is recorded in W. B. 1, page 216.
[34] Who after his death married Richard Guilliam of Halifax Co., Va.—*Hist. Collections, Joseph Habersham Chap. D. A. R.*, II, 318.
[35] *Historical Collections, Joseph Habersham Chap. D. A. R.*, II, 88.
[36] Id.
[37] *The Old Free State*, I, 223.
[38] I, 220-221.
[39] Id., 329.
[40] Id., II, 70.
[41] Burgess: *Virginia Soldiers of 1776*, 910.

8. Allen³ Hobson,
9. Polly B.³ Hobson,
10. Agnes G.³ Hobson,
11. Patsy³ Hobson.

4. William² Hobson was a soldier of the Revolution; he was a Sergeant in the Company of Captain James Johnson,[42] which was one of the first companies from Lunenburg County, Virginia, to participate in the Revolution.

5. Obedience² Hobson, who married a man named Bacon.
6. Agnes² Hobson, who also married a man named Bacon.
7. Sarah² Hobson,
9. Margrata² Hobson,
9. Elizabeth² Hobson, married to a man named Bugg.

The will also mentions a grandson, Nicholas Bilbo.

The testator named his wife Agnes Hobson, his son John Hobson and Edward Goode, executors.

Undoubtedly in some sections the spelling of this name has become Hopson.

HOWARD.

William Howard, the Vestryman of Cumberland Parish in 1748, was one of the first Justices of the County Court of Lunenburg County, Virginia, and helped to organize the County. He was the second named in the Commission of the Peace for that purpose.[43] He evidently resided in that part of the County, now comprised in Mecklenburg County, for he was at the first term of the Court appointed surveyor of the road from Allen Creek to Butchers Creek.[44] He was a soldier of the Colonial or French and Indian Wars.[45]

The father of William Howard was Francis Howard, whose will was dated February 6, 1648, and probated in Lunenburg County, Virginia, June 5, 1749.[46]

---

[42] *The Old Free State*, I, 217.
[43] *The Old Free State*, I, 108.
[44] Id., 112.
[45] Id., 195.
[46] And recorded in W. B. 1, pages 479-480.

In it he mentions his wife Dianna Howard, and also the following:
1. William Howard, a son,
2. Francis Howard, a son,
3. Elizabeth Howard, eldest daughter,
4. Eleanor Howard, a daughter,
5. Hannah Howard, a daughter,
6. Dianna Howard, a daughter,
7. Mary Howard, a cousin,
8. William Howard, a brother.

JACKSON.

The name Jackson is numerously represented in many counties. From an early period the members of the family were plentiful in Amelia and Charlotte, and Mecklenburg Counties, to say nothing of those of the earlier counties, such as New Kent and Prince George.

Although the writer has not been able to exactly place in the family connection, Philip W. Jackson, the Vestryman of Cumberland Parish, 1793-1796, yet he was undoubtedly of the family of that name in Lunenburg County, several of whom left wills that will be referred to below. The writer, it should be stated, has not had opportunity to make any particular investigation respecting Philip W. Jackson.

The will of Josiah Jackson is the earliest noted in Lunenburg County in the period between 1746 and 1825. His will is dated September 3, 1786, and was probated July 12, 1787.[47]

In it he mentions his wife Elizabeth Jackson, a son Carter Jackson, a daughter Martha Jackson, and a brother Benjamin Jackson.

The will of Benjamin Jackson (doubtless the brother of Josiah Jackson, mentioned in the latter's will), was dated July 6, 1791, and probated February 9, 1792.[48]

In it the testator mentions his wife, Elizabeth Jackson, and the following children:

---
[47]It is recorded in W. B. 3, page 282.
[48]It is recorded in W. B. 4, page 17.

1. Steward Jackson,
2. Benjamin Jackson,
3. Sally Jackson,
4. Polly Noden Jackson,
5. Betsey Levington Jackson,
6. Patsy Noden Jackson,
7. Katy Jackson.

The wife, Elizabeth Jackson, Joel and Frances (Francis?) Jackson, were executors.

The will of Amy Jackson bears date June 30, 1803, and was probated May 16, 1821.[49]

It mentions the following children:

1. Peter Jackson,
2. Willis Jackson,
3. John Jackson,
4. Lucy Jackson,
5. Susannah Johnson,
6. Zatha Jackson.

The will of Elizabeth Jackson, doubtless the widow of Benjamin Jackson (whose will is referred to above, as dated July 6, 1791), bears date June 27, 1823, and was probated November 8, 1824.[50]

It mentions:

1. Stewart Jackson, a son,
2. Benjamin Jackson, a son,
3. Sally Buford, a daughter,
4. Polly White, a daughter,
5. Francis Thompson Jackson, a grandson.

Joel Blackwell was named executor.

---

[49] It is recorded in W. B. 8, page 161.
[50] It is recorded in W. B. 8, page 405.

JEFFERSON.

Field Jefferson was a Vestryman of Cumberland Parish from 1749 until 1757. He was a member of the County Court of Lunenburg County, Virginia, from 1749 to 1752.[51] He lived in that part of Lunenburg County, cut off into Mecklenburg and his later history is identified with that county.

There is a brief sketch of the Jefferson family in *The Old Free State*.[52]

A few items may be added to what there appears. Some time after the publication of his former work, the writer discovered the marriage settlement agreement, never theretofore noticed by any genealogist, of Field Jefferson with his second wife Mary Allen. It is of record in Lunenburg County, Virginia, in Deed Book 3, at page 412, and is as follows:

Articles Between Jefferson and Allen.

The following articles was this day made and *muterly* agreed upon and confirmed between Field Jefferson of Lunenburg County and Mary Allen of Albemarle Co^{ty}. (to wit)

Whereas there is a marriage suddenly intended between the s^d. Field Jefferson & Mary Allen it is agreed that the s^d. Field will give the s^d. Mary Lieve to give and dispose of one negro man when and to whom she shall think proper immediately after her marriage, and the Residue of her Estate at the day of her Death in case he should be the longest liver so that the s^d. Field his heirs &c shall not Injoy nor be Persest with any Part of it after her Death, and the s^d. Mary for her part doth by these Presents agree and oblige herself to give up Deliver and Relinquish all her Rite and Dower to His heirs Executors &c Emediately after the s^d. Field Jefferson's Death. In Penlty thereof we do bind ourselves Each to Either our heirs &c in the just and full sum of five hundred Pounds Current money of Virginia. In witness

---
[51]*The Old Free State*, I, 330.
[52]Vol. II, 289-297.

whereof we hereunto set our hands and seals this first day of November one thousand seven hundred and fifty three.

Interline our heirs &c Before sign'd.

      Field Jefferson L. S.
      Mary Allen   L. S.

Signed seal'd & delivered
 In Presence of
 George Baskerville
 Hutchins Burton
   his
 Rubin X Morgin
   mark

At a court held for Lunenburg County the 1st day of January 1754.

The within written articles was proved by the oaths of two of the witness's thereto subscribed to be the act & deed of the within Field Jefferson & Mary Allen and the same was ordered to be Recorded.

      Test Clement Read C. L. C.
      Truly Recorded
      Test Clem^t Read C. L. C.

The writer furnished a copy to the editor of *Tyler's Quarterly*, and the instrument was printed in that publication.

This instrument left open the question of the status of Mary Allen at the time of the marriage, whether widow or single. It was the good fortune of Mr. Curtis Bynum of Asheville, North Carolina, to clear up that matter, by the discovery of the marriage bond. It is dated October 31, 1753, and shows the contracting parties were Field Jefferson and Mary Allen, widow. The sureties were Robert Wooding and Paul Carrington.

JENINGS.

This name is also frequently spelled Jennings. The Lunenburg family of this name are, by tradition, of the family interested in the "Jenings fortune," said to be awaiting in England, proof of parties in America entitled thereto.

Captain John Jenings was a Vestryman of Cumberland Parish from 1757 until it seems 1772, although for several years prior to 1772 there is no record of his attendance upon a meeting of the vestry.

He removed from Lunenburg County to "Carolina,"—presumably North Carolina—about 1772, as the minutes of the vestry held on July 10, 1772, contains this entry: "On the removall of Capt. John Jenings to Carolina this vestry has chose Capt. Benjamin Tomlinson to act in his stead."

There is of record in Lunenburg County during the period 1746-1825, a single will by a person of the name, that of Lemuel Jennings. It is dated February 8, 1801, and was probated July 9, 1801.[53]

It mentions a brother James Jennings, and the following persons without indicating any relationship: Sterling Fowlkes, Daniel Crenshaw, and David Thompson.

The Amelia County, Virginia, records show a marriage bond dated February 22, 1788, for the marriage of Sterling Fowlkes to Elizabeth Jennings, daughter of James Jennings.

There is in Lunenburg County, Virginia, a marriage bond dated June 11, 1789, for the marriage of Daniel Crenshaw and Nancy Jennings.

JORDAN.

Edward[1] Jordan was a Captain in the Revolution from Lunenburg County, Virginia;[54] he was a Justice of the County Court of Lunenburg County from 1780 to 1797;[55] and was a vestryman of Cumberland Parish from 1780 to 1785.

His father was doubtless named Edward Jordan, and was likely the Edward Jordan who in 1748 secured a grant for 654 acres of land on Couches Creek.[56]

The Lunenburg County records show that Edward Jordan, Jr., was deputy sheriff under Daniel Claiborn, sheriff from 1767 to

---
[53]It is recorded in W. B. 5, page 65.
[54]*The Old Free State*, I, 267.
[55]Id., 330.
[56]Id., 103.

1769. This is thought to be the Edward Jordan, the Vestryman and Captain in the Revolution.

There is a record in Bristol Parish Register[57] of the birth March 27, 1742-3, of Edward Jordans, son of Samuel and Milson Jordans.

Edward[1] Jordan, of Lunenburg County, made his will July 21, 1820, it was probated August 16, 182—.[58]

In it he mentions his wife, Susannah Jordan, and the following children and grandchildren:

1. Baxter[2] Jordan,
2. Miles[2] Jordan,
3. Labon[2] Jordan,
4. John[2] Jordan,
5. James[2] Jordan,
6. Susannah[2] Pettus,
7. Mary[2] Jeffress,
8. Polly[2] Jordan,
9. Francis[2] Jordan (a deceased son), who had:

   (1) Nancy[3] Jordan,
   (2) Martha Francis[3] Jordan,
   (3) William[3] Jordan.

Baxter[2] Jordan married Polly Lipscomb Pettus,[59] daughter of John Pettus.[60]

Miles[2] Jordan married Harriott Pettus, of Mecklenburg County, Virginia. The marriage bond is dated Nov. 12, 1804. In connection with it there is on file a note from W. Pettus, brother of Harroitt.

John Jordan, probably John[2] Jordan above, married Elizabeth Jordan, daughter of Benjamin Jordan of Charlotte County, Virginia. The marriage bond, in Charlotte County, is dated Aug. 3, 1799.

---

[57]P. 326.
[58]It is of record in W. B. 8, page 112.
[59]M. B. in Lunenburg County dated Dec. 29, 1803—*The Old Free State*, II, 397.
[60]Letter of consent on file in Lunenburg County Clerk's Office.

James Jordan, possibly James[2] Jordan, was a member of the County Court in Lunenburg County, Virginia, in 1781.[61]

Susanna[2] Jordan married, Feb. 11, 1796, Robert Winn.[62]

Polly[2] Jordan married Thomas Cheatham. The marriage bond in Lunenburg County, Virginia, is dated Jan. 31, 1825.[63]

Susannah Jordan, the wife of Edward[1] Jordan, made her will May 4, 1823, and it was probated in Lunenburg County, Virginia, June 13, 1825.[64] In it she mentions her sons Laban Jordan and Miles Jordan and her daughters Mary Jeffress and Susannah Pettus.

The will of Thomas Jordan of Lunenburg County, Virginia, bears date March 13, 1815, and it was probated May 11, 1815.[65] He mentions his wife Elizabeth Jordan and the following children:

1. Freeman Jordan, Jr.,
2. Thos. Jordan, Jr.,
3. James Jordan,
4. Edward Jordan, Jr.,
5. Polly E. Jordan,
6. Elizabeth B. Tucker,
7. Elizabeth T. Jordan,
8. Mary Anne Jordan.

He mentions Thos. W. J. Jordan and Thomas E. Jordan, sons of Freeman Jordan. But it is not clear whether or not they are sons of his son Freeman Jordan, Jr.

He named as his executors Thomas Jordan, Jr., and John Wilson.

In Lunenburg County, Virginia, there is the record of a marriage of Thomas Jordan to Rosary Wilson, Aug. 2, 1831,[66] and of that of Elizabeth B. Jordan, daughter of Thomas Jordan, to Charles S. Tucker, son of Joseph Tucker (M. B. dated Feb. 23, 1811).[67]

---

[61] *The Old Free State*, I, 330.
[62] *The Old Free State*, II, 437—marriage return of Rev. John Neblett.
[63] *The Old Free State*, II, 407.
[64] It is recorded in W. B. 8, p. 478.
[65] It is recorded in W. B. 7, page 176.
[66] *The Old Free State*, II, 457.
[67] Id., 399.

There is in Lunenburg County, Virginia, the will of Elizabeth Jordan, dated October 4, 1794, and probated January 8, 1795,[68] in which the testatrix mentions the following children and grandchildren:

1. Benjamin Jordan, son,
2. Samuel Jordan, son,
3. William Jordan, son,
4. Edward Jordan, grandson,
5. Presley Hightower, grandson,
6. Frances Hightower, granddaughter.

The will of Elizabeth Jordan, wife of Thomas Jordan, was dated July 14, 1822, and probated October 14, 1822;[69] in it the testatrix mentions her daughter Elizabeth Tucker and her son Edward Jordan.

The will of Baxter Jordan, son of Edward Jordan, bears date April 11, 1823, and was probated August 11, 1823.[70] It mentions no children, but mentions his wife Mary L. Jordan, and names her and Dr. Edward H. Birchett executors.

There is in Lunenburg County a marriage bond dated Dec. 29, 1803,[71] for the marriage of Baxter Jordan to Polly Lipscomb Pettus. "Polly" was doubtless a nickname.

LAMKIN

Peter Lamkin (or Lampkin) was a member of the County Court of Lunenburg County, Virginia, from 1789 to 1806.[72] From 1790 to 1795, the name is met with in the record of Justices with "Jr." added; probably, however, the entire service is that of one man.

Peter Lamkin, Jr., was a vestryman of Cumberland Parish from 1793 to 1796.

The "Peter Lamkin, Jr.," of the Vestry records was probably the "Peter Lamkin, Sr.," of Sharp Lamkin's will.

The will of Sharp Lamkin was dated January 1, 1801, and

---

[68]W. B. 4, pages 79-80.
[69]It is recorded in W. B. 8, page 240.
[70]It is recorded in W. B. 8, page 296.
[71]*The Old Free State*, II, p. 397.
[72]*The Old Free State*, I, 330.

probated July 9, 1801.[73] From this will it can be deduced that there was a
   Peter[1] Lamkin, who had
   Peter[2] Lamkin,[74] who had:
      1. Peter[3] Lamkin,
      2. Sharp[3] Lamkin.

Sharp[3] Lamkin (b. Nov. 18, 1766), married Dec. 22, 1791, Mary Epes Jones, daughter of Richard Jones.[75] She is spoken of in the will as "Polly Lamkin." They had:

1. Mary Epes Jones[4] Lamkin (b. March 18, 1793, d. March 2, 1853). She was the adopted daughter of Major George Craghead, a distinguished lawyer of Lunenburg County, who married her Aunt Petronella Lamkin, but had no children. She married Dr. Archibald[4] Hatchett (b. 1785, d. 1820). For their children and descendants, see the Hatchett Genealogy in *The Old Free State*.[76]

2. Susanna Lewis[4] Lamkin,

3. Petronella Sharp[4] Lamkin, who married (M. B. in Lunenburg County, dated Feb. 13, 1809),[77] Edmund F. Taylor.

The will of Sharp Lamkin mentions a brother-in-law John Wimbish, and designates him as guardian for Susanna L. Lamkin and Petronella S. Lamkin.

LANIER.

The Laniers were in Brunswick County, when Lunenburg County was formed. In 1750 Lemuel Lanier and James Lanier secured grants for lands on Three Creek.[78]

On January 12, 1747, Thomas Lanier secured a patent for 380 acres of land on Mitchell's Creek; on April 5, 1748, Benjamin Lanier was granted 368 acres of land on Allen's Creek, and on January 12, 1748, Byrd Thomas Lanier secured 374 acres of

---

[73]It is recorded in Lunenburg County, Virginia, in W. B. 5, pages 60-63.
[74]Will in Nottoway County, dated Aug. 20, 1796, proved Feb. 2, 1797— *The Old Free State*, II, 284.
[75]*The Old Free State*, II, 284.
[76]Vol. II, 285 et seq.
[77]*The Old Free State*, II, 403.
[78]*The Old Free State*, I, 101.

land also on Allen's Creek, and October 1, 1747, Nicholas S. Lanier acquired a grant for 415 acres on Mitchell's Creek.[79]

Thomas Lanier[80] was one of the first Justices of Lunenburg County,[81] and was in attendance upon the first term of court and helped to set the county machinery in motion.

He was by the court, at that term, appointed a commissioner, the other being Lewis Deloney, to attend the surveyor in running the dividing line between Brunswick and Lunenburg Counties.[82]

In 1751 he increased his land holdings by securing another grant of land, this time for 318 acres on the lower side of Butcher's Creek.[83]

He was a Justice of the County Court from 1746 to 1761,[84] and was a Vestryman of Cumberland Parish in 1759.

He was the son of Sampson Lanier, of Brunswick County, Virginia, whose will was dated Jan. 8, 1742/3 and was probated May 5, 1743.[85]

In this will are mentioned the following children:

1. Thomas Lanier,
2. Sampson Lanier,
3. Richard Lanier,
4. Eliza. Burch,
5. Samuel Lanier,
6. James Lanier.

Sidney Lanier, the poet, was a descendant of Sampson Lanier, being descended from a brother of Thomas Lanier, the Vestryman.

There are a vast number of Lanier items to be found in the Brunswick records; far too many to attempt to abstract or to epitomize them here. There are many also in Mecklenburg County.

---

[79]Id., 103.
[80]The name is spelled "Lanear" on the Order Book, but that is a mere clerical error.
[81]*The Old Free State*, I, 108.
[82]*The Old Free State*, I, 111.
[83]Id., 105.
[84]Id., 330.
[85]And is of record in Brunswick County, Virginia, in W. B. 2, pages 52-53.

In a work on the Lanier family, entitled *Sketch of the Life of J. F. D. Lanier* (1877),[86] the statement is made that the immigrant progenitor of the family was Thomas Lanier, and that he had the following children:

1. Richard Lanier,
2. Thomas Lanier,
3. James Lanier,
4. Elizabeth Lanier, and
5. Sampson Lanier.

This last named was, doubtless, the Sampson Lanier, of Brunswick County, father of Thomas Lanier, the Justice of Lunenburg County, Virginia, and Vestryman of Cumberland Parish.

The sketch cited is not of very much value as a genealogical source, as no records or authorities are cited for many statements of the most important kind, and which could not possibly have been a matter of personal knowledge of the writer.

There is a very good account of the Lanier family in *Tyler's Quarterly Magazine*.[87] In this article reference is made to the sketch of J. F. D. Lanier, above mentioned, in the light of facts developed from the records, as follows: "Interest attaches to them, however, because of the fact that J. F. D. Lanier, who was a prominent banker, was born at Washington, Beaufort County (North Carolina). He wrote a family sketch which is valuable as far as his own life and that of his father, and that of his grandfather are concerned, but which illustrates the fallibility of family narratives, when the writer ventures on hearsay to go beyond this limit."

And again this article says, referring to the letter of Sydney Lanier printed as an appendix (to the second printing): "It is interesting to notice that one of these sons [of Thomas Lanier] *Sterling Lanier* had the same name as the grandfather of the Poet Sydney Lanier, born in Rockingham Co., N. C. But to observe what a charming mangle of facts can be made by a

---

[86]Not copyrighted, and bearing no publisher's or printer's name or imprint.
[87]III, 126-147.

poet, when he lets his imagination run rampant in genealogy, compare his letter in Mr. F. D. Lanier's interesting 'Sketch' with the account stated here taken from the records," etc.

LESTER.

Bryant Lester (sometimes spelled Bryan Lester) was a soldier of the French and Indian Wars,[88] or at least furnished supplies to the forces engaged in those wars. He was a vestryman of Cumberland Parish from 1786 to 1789, and died in Lunenburg County in 1796.

There is a genealogy of the descendants of Bryant Lester in *The Old Free State*,[89] based largely on an account in Volume I of *Southern Historical Association*,[90] together with supplemental matter collected by this writer. The account mentioned was prepared by Dr. Thomas McAdory Owen, of Alabama, who married Marie Susan Bankhead, a daughter of United States Senator John Hollis Bankhead, a descendant of Bryant Lester. In this account the name "Winbush" occurs. The present writer is of opinion that the name should be rendered "Wimbish."

MACFARLAND.

This name is frequently rendered McFarland; but the correct spelling of the Lunenburg family seems to be Macfarland.

One of the earliest notings of the name in Lunenburg County, Virginia, is the listing of Jno. Macfarling in 1749 for three tithes, upon the list taken by Lyddall Bacon. In 1750 he is also on Lyddall Bacon's list located at James Barnes Quarter. Thereafter he seems to disappear from the lists.

It is said that James Macfarland (evidently the Vestryman of Cumberland Parish 1812 to 1816), who was the father of the distinguished Virginian, William H. Macfarland, was a Scotsman, and the immigrant ancestor. This tradition of his being the immigrant seems to lack verification as the family tradition seems vague.

---

[88]*The Old Free State*, I, 196.
[89]Vol. II, 299-311.
[90]Pages 128-9.

There is a very brief note on the Macfarland Family in *The Old Free State*.[91]

From that brief account one of the children of Honorable William H. Macfarland is omitted. There should be added a fifth child, as follows:

"(5) Nannie Beirne[3] Macfarland (b. in Richmond, Va., 1857, living 1929, 52 Gramercy Park, New York City), m. in Baltimore, Md., in 1880, Frank Donaldson, Jr., of Baltimore, Md., and had:

  (a) Francis[4] Donaldson who married in 1906, Anne Harvey Talbot, only child of Bishop of the diocese of Bethlehem, Pa.

  (b) Wm. Hamilton Macfarland[4] Donaldson (d. 1914).

  (c) John Willcox[4] Donaldson, m. 1917, Rence de Pelleport du Pont, dau. Coleman du Pont of Wilmington, Delaware."[92]

MARRABLE.

On May 8, 1755, Matthew Marrable secured grants for many tracts of land in Lunenburg County, Virginia.[93] He became a sort of stormy petrel of Lunenburg politics, engaging in many political campaigns and was involved in several contested election cases. He was a member of the County Court of Lunenburg County in 1752 and from 1759 to 1762; in fact he was probably a Justice of the County for the period from 1752 to 1762.[93]

He was a Vestryman of Cumberland Parish from 1757 to 1759; and was a burgess of Lunenburg County from 1754 to 1761. His first appearance in the House of Burgesses was as the successor of William Byrd.[94]

He was, doubtless, a son of William Marrable, as seems to be indicated by the entry upon the list of tithes of Abraham Martin for 1750.

The will of Matthew Marable was probated in Mecklenburg

---

[91] Vol. II, 310-11.
[92] The data for this correction comes to the writer directly from Mrs. Frank Donaldson, Jr., herself.
[93] *The Old Free State*, I, 106.
[93] Id., 330.
[94] Id., II, 68.

County, Virginia, in 1786. In it he mentions his wife Mary Marable and the following children:

1. Matthew Marable,
2. Richard Marable,
3. Champion Marable,
4. John Marable,
5. Elizabeth Marable.

He also mentions his son-in-law David Stokes (this was David Stokes, Jr., who married Elizabeth Marable); and his brother John Marable.

The will of John Marable, dated March 13, 1804, and probated Sept. 13, 1804,[95] mentions his wife Tabitha Marable, and the following children:

> Hartwell Marable,
> Matthew Marable,
> John Marable,
> William Marable,
> Edward Travis Marable.

The executors were Hartwell Marable, Vallentine Brown and William Ellis.

MARTIN.

Abraham Martin was a soldier of the French and Indian Wars.[96]

He was a Vestryman of Cumberland Parish from 1747 to 1754, and was a Justice of the County Court of Lunenburg County, Virginia, from 1750 to 1754.[97] He lived at least as "high up" the County as Cub Creek, and his later history was doubtless associated with Bedford or Charlotte Counties.

There is no record of any will in Lunenburg County by a person named Martin from 1746 to 1825.

---

[95] Recorded in Lunenburg County, Virginia, in W. B. 6, p. 92-93.
[96] *The Old Free State*, I, 194.
[97] Id., 330.

NASH.

Thomas Nash, the Vestryman of Cumberland Parish, 1754 to 1757, was a Justice of the County Court of Lunenburg County in 1757,[98] and was a burgess in 1758.[99]

He was doubtless the Thomas Nash who married Mary Read, daughter of Colonel Clement Read, and was the progenitor of the well known family of the name in Charlotte County, Virginia, and elsewhere.

NEBLETT.

Sterling Neblett, the Vestryman of Cumberland Parish from 1781 to 1801, was a son of Francis Neblett, the progenitor of the Lunenburg family of the name. He was a member of the County Court of Lunenburg County, Virginia, from 1789 to 1793.

There is a genealogy of the family in *The Old Free State*.[100]

PARRISH.

John Parrish was Vestryman of Cumberland Parish from 1757 to 1762.

He was, it seems, a son of Charles Parrish whose will, dated Feb. 20, 1764, was probated in Lunenburg County, Virginia, October 11, 1764.[101]

No mention of a wife is made in the will but it does mention the following sons and daughters:

1. Charles Parrish,
2. David Parrish,
3. Robert Parrish,
4. Jowell (Joel?) Parrish,
5. Hannah Parrish,
6. Millippie Parrish,
7. Mary Parrish Patillo,
8. Lucy Parrish,
9. John Parrish.

---

[98]*The Old Free State*, I, 331.
[99]Id., II, 68.
[100]Vol. II, 319-327.
[101]It is recorded in W. B. 2, page 235.

John and Charles Parrish, sons, and Millippie Parrish, daughter, were named executors.

The Lunenburg County records also contain the will of Peters Parrish, dated September 10, 1777, and probated November 11, 1779.[102]

It mentions only two brothers, Samuel Parrish and William Parrish.

The will of James Parrish also is recorded in Lunenburg County, Virginia.[103] It was dated October 9, 1803, and probated December 8, 1803. It mentions his wife Martha Parrish,[104] and the following sons and daughters:

1. Sterling Parrish,
2. John Parrish,
3. James Parrish,
4. William Parrish,
5. Matthew Parrish,
6. Joel Parrish,
7. Elizabeth Parrish,
8. Lucy Parrish (and "Lucicy" Parrish—probably the same person),
9. Sarah Epperson,
10. Mary Ferguson.

Sarah Parrish married (M. B. in Lunenburg County, dated Dec. 28, 1789), Jonathan Epperson.[105]

Mary Parrish married James Farguson (Ferguson) (M. B. in Lunenburg County, dated Dec. 17, 1792),[106] who was doubtless the son, James Farguson, of Joel Farguson, of Lunenburg County, Virginia, whose will was dated January 29, 1788, and probated September 11, 1788.[107]

---

[102]It is recorded in W. B. 3, page 29.
[103]In W. B. 6, pages 68-69.
[104]The Lunenburg records contain a marriage bond dated March 27, 1791, for the marriage of James Parrish and Pattey Dixon—*The Old Free State*, II, 393; and the certificate of their marriage April 1, 1791, by Rev. Henry Ogburn—*The Old Free State*, II, 432.
[105]*The Old Free State*, II, 390.
[106]Id.
[107]It is of record in W. B. 3, page 322. Besides the son, James Ferguson, the will of Joel Ferguson mentions his wife Catharine and sons: William, Thomas, Joel, Horatio; and daughters, Catherine Ferguson, Sarah Wilson, Joicy Winn, Mary Hoskins, Elizabeth Webb, Jemima Dicks.

PETTUS.

The spelling of this name seems to have given the early clerks and scriveners considerable trouble. At the hands of different persons or at different times it is spelled, Pettis, Petties, Peaties, in addition to the correct way.

Thomas Pettus was Vestryman of Cumberland Parish from 1759 to 1779; he was a member of the House of Burgesses from 1769 to 1775, except for a time in 1772 when his election was contested by Henry Blagrave who was given the seat. Upon a new election, however, Pettus was again returned to the House.[108] He was also a member of the House of Delegates in 1777-1778, from Lunenburg County.[109] He was also a member of the County Court of Lunenburg County, Virginia, from 1770 to 1779.[110]

His will in Lunenburg County, Virginia, bears date January 14, 1779, and was probated April 19, 1780.[111]

His will does not mention his wife but he does mention the following sons and daughters:

1. Thomas Pettus,
2. Samuel Pettus,
3. Overton Pettus,
4. David Pettus,
5. Walker Pettus,
6. John Pettus,
7. Rebecca Pettus,
8. Mary Brown,
9. Anne Shelborne.

Other Pettus wills in Lunenburg County, Virginia, are those of John Pettus, Sr., dated June 11, 1781, and probated October 11, 1781.[112]

He mentions his wife, but not her name. It was, however, Sarah Pettus, as we know from her own will.

---

[108]*The Old Free State*, II, 69.
[109]Id., 70.
[110]Id., I, 331.
[111]It is recorded in W. B. 3, page 33.
[112]And recorded in W. B. 3, page 89.

He also mentions the following sons and daughters:
1. John Pettus,
2. Julian Pettus,
3. Ragland Pettus,
4. Elizabeth Pettus,
5. Mary Palmer,
6. Susanna Pettus,
7. Sarah Pettus.

Sarah Pettus, evidently the wife of the above mentioned John Pettus, Sr., made her will December 12, 1797, and it was probated Jan. 11, 1798.[113] In it she mentions the following persons:

John Pettus, a son,
Sarah Pettus, a daughter,
Fanny Bain, a granddaughter, and the following persons whose relationships are not indicated:
John Ragland,
Chilian Parmer,
Karon Bayne,
Mrs. Sarah Sammons,
Mrs. Martelia Jennings,
Elizabeth Pettus.

John Pettus and Edmund P. Bacon were named Executors.

David Pettus, doubtless the son of Thomas Pettus, the Vestryman, Burgess and Justice, made his will November 1, 1805; it was probated December 12, 1805.[114] In it he mentions his wife Elenor Pettus, and the following sons, daughters and son-in-law:
1. Thomas Pettus, son,
2. David Pettus, son,
3. Samuel Pettus, son,
4. Elizabeth Rowlett, daughter,
5. Nancy Pettus, daughter,
6. Matthew Rowlett, son-in-law.

William Stone, Matthew Rowlett and Thomas Pettus were named Executors.

David Pettus, Jr., married Elenor Willson, Sept. 25, 1802.[115]

---

[113]It is recorded in W. B. 4, p. 208-209.
[114]It is recorded in W. B. 6, pages 129-130.
[115]*The Old Free State*, II, 427.

Thomas Pettus married Susanna Gregory, Dec. 24, 1816.[116]

Elizabeth Pettus married Matthew J. Rowlett in 1794, according to a certificate returned to court, February 13, 1794, by Rev. William Creath. He does not give the month or the day of the marriage.[117]

John Pettus, who was Vestryman of Cumberland Parish in 1793, is not placed with confidence, as both John Pettus, Sr., and Thomas Pettus had sons by that name, both presumably of sufficient age to make it possible for either to have held the position.

This family was numerously represented on the County Court of Lunenburg County, Virginia:

In addition to Thomas Pettus, whose service on the court has already been noted, there were:

John Pettus, 1789-92, 1795, 1799,
John Pettus, 1804-1808,
Stephen Pettus, 1819, 1821-22, 1827, 1829, 1838.[118]

PHILLIPS.

On the list of tithes for 1748, which is the earliest year for which such lists have been found in Lunenburg County, there appear on the list taken by Hugh Lawson, George Philips and John Phillips, George charged with two tithes and John with one.

They seem not to be on his list for 1752.

Captain Jno. Philips, commissioned to command "a company of Rangers to be raised in Bedford County,"[119] in 1756, was probably this early John Phillips of Lunenburg County, before Bedford was cut off.

George Phillips married in Lunenburg County (M. B. dated Feb. 9, 1768), Ann Brown.[120]

This was the George Phillips who was the Vestryman of Cumberland Parish from 1761 to 1779, and again in 1783.

His will was dated December 14, 1785, and was probated in Lunenburg County, Virginia, June 8, 1786.[121] In it he mentions

---

[116]*The Old Free State*, II, 429.
[117]Id., 435.
[118]*The Old Free State*, I, 331.
[119]*The Old Free State*, I, 180.
[120]Id., II, 393.
[121]It is recorded in W. B. 3, page 248.

his wife Ann Phillips, a son Dyer Phillips and the following daughters:

    Betsy Phillips,
    Mary Elam, wife of Martin Elam, and
    Martha White.

The marriage bond of Martin Elam and Mary Philips is in Lunenburg County, Virginia, and is dated June 9, 1775.[122]

Dyer Phillips married Lotty Hart. The marriage bond is dated July 18, 1781.

The will of John Phillips is the earliest of the name to be found in Lunenburg County. It was dated November 29, 1760, and probated August 4, 1761.[123]

In it he mentions his wife Mary Phillips and the following sons and daughters:

    1. John Phillips,
    2. Anthony Phillips,
    3. Robert Phillips,
    4. Mary Ann Phillips,
    5. Nancy Phillips,
    6. Edith Phillips.

Edward Waller was named Executor.

Anthony Phillips married Lillian Buford; the marriage bond is in Lunenburg County, and is dated March 26, 1779.[124]

A Robert Phillips married Lucy Meanly in Lunenburg County. The marriage bond is dated Aug. 8, 1793.[125]

Priscilla Phillips made her will July 23, 1764, and it was probated in Lunenburg County, Virginia, March 14, 1765.[126] She mentions two sons and a daughter, as follows:

    1. John Phillips,
    2. Micaja Phillips,
    3. Suckey Barnes Phillips.

Robert Phillips, doubtless a son of John Philips (whose will

---

[122] *The Old Free State*, II, 390.
[123] It is of record in W. B. 2, page 14.
[124] *The Old Free State*, II, 392.
[125] *The Old Free State*, II, 392.
[126] It is recorded in W. B. 2, page 248.

was dated November 29, 1760), made his will April 13, 1823; it was probated Aug. 11, 1823.[127] The only person mentioned in it was his wife Ellen Philips.

RAGSDALE.

"Godfrey Ragsdale lived in Bristol Parish, Henrico County, on the north side of Appomattox River in the vicinity of the Falls."[128]

Godfrey Ragsdale, it seems a son of Godfrey Ragsdale, on Jan. 13, 1688, secured a grant for 450 acres of land on the North side of the Appomattox, a part of it being land sold by one John Buster on February 25, 1642, "to Godfrey Ragsdale father of the present possessor."[129]

The will of Godfrey Ragsdale, presumably this Godfrey[2] Ragsdale was dated April 20, 1697, and probated April 10, 1703, in Henrico County, Virginia.[130]

He lived in Bristol Parish.

His wife's name was Rachael and he had the following children:

1. Godfrey[3] Ragsdale,
2. Peter[3] Ragsdale,
3. Daniel[3] Ragsdale,
4. Rachael[3] Ragsdale.

These we understand from the note above referred to in the *Peter Jones and Richard Jones Genealogies,* were the children mentioned in the will.

It is suggested as a possibility that there might have been two more:

5. Joseph[3] Ragsdale,
6. Drury[3] Ragsdale,

and possibly also,

7. Benjamin[3] Ragsdale.

---

[127]And is of record in W. B. 8, page 297.
[128]Fothergill: *Peter Jones and Richard Jones Genealogies,* 251, note.
[129]Id.
[130]Id.

Godfrey³ Ragsdale, married "Eliz." (last name not learned), and had (at least):

1. Tab. (Tabitha)⁴ Ragsdale (b. March 13, 1722).[131]
2. Edward⁴ Ragsdale (bap. Jan. 12, 1723-4),[132]
3. Baxter⁴ Ragsdale (b. June 16, 1730).[133]

Peter³ Ragsdale married Alice (last name not ascertained), and had (at least):

1. Faith⁴ Ragsdale (b. Oct. 24, 1722),
2. Joseph⁴ Ragsdale (b. Jan. 17, 1725),
3. Ann⁴ Ragsdale (b. May 25, 1727),
4. Rachel⁴ Ragsdale (b. Feb. 27, 1732).[134]

Benja. Ragsdale, whose wife was Martha, and who may have been Benjamin³ Ragsdale (Godfrey,² Godfrey¹), had (at least):

1. Dan.⁴ Ragsdale (b. Oct. 10, 1724).[135]
2. Rachael⁴ Ragsdale (b. June 28, 1726).[136]
3. John⁴ Ragsdale (b. June 23, 1728).[136]
4. Winfred (Winifred?)⁴ Ragsdale (a daughter)[137] (b. Feb. 17, 1731).
5. Benjamin⁴ Rags*dail* (b. March 28, 1734).

It seems fairly certain, indeed very satisfactorily so, that the Benjamin³ Ragsdale above, the births of five of whose children were recorded in Bristol Parish Register, was the Benjamin Ragsdale who died in Mecklenburg County, Virginia, in 1772, whose will was dated December 9, 1770, and probated May 9, 1772.[138]

By the will it appears he had the following children:

1. Daniel⁴ Ragsdale,
2. Rachel⁴ Moor(e),
3. John⁴ Ragsdale,
4. Mary⁴ Rowland,

---

[131] *Bristol Parish Register*, 356.
[132] Id., 357.
[133] Id., 358.
[134] Id., 359.
[135] *Bristol Parish Register*, 357.
[136] Id., 358.
[137] Id., 359.
[138] And recorded in Mecklenburg County Will Book 1, page 123.

5. Richard⁴ Ragsdale,
6. Peter⁴ Ragsdale,
7. Thomas⁴ Ragsdale,
8. Winnefred⁴ Ragsdale,
9. Godfrey⁴ Ragsdale,
10. Jesse⁴ Ragsdale,
11. William⁴ Ragsdale,
12. Benjamin⁴ Ragsdale.

The son William Ragsdale was appointed executor.

From the circumstances of the case, it is a safe assumption that five of his children were born in Bristol Parish; that he moved to Lunenburg County—that part of it afterwards cut off into Mecklenburg County—and had seven other children, and died in Mecklenburg County, Virginia, in 1772.

William Ragsdale who was appointed executor of the will in Mecklenburg County, Virginia, at least kept up his contacts with the old home county of Prince George, for we find in Mecklenburg County a deed of trust conveying to Charles Duncan & Co., of Prince George County, Virginia, a tract of land on Middle Bluestone Creek, in Mecklenburg County, to secure the payment of a debt of 78 pounds sterling. It is dated April 7, 1773.[139]

This William Ragsdale was, in all probability, the Revolutionary soldier of that name.[140]

Some of the Ragsdales came to Lunenburg County, Virginia, certainly as early as 1750, for in that year we find John Ragsdale, Senr., charged with two tithes on the list of Richard Witton, and John Ragsdale, Junr., charged with three tithes on the same list.

In 1764, John Ragsdale, Richard Ragsdale and Joseph Ragsdale were on the list of Richard Witton for St. James Parish, Lunenburg County, Virginia,[141] while William Ragsdale was on the list of Edmund Taylor for three tithes and 300 acres of land, in the same parish.

The will of Godfrey Ragsdale is the earliest Ragsdale will found in Lunenburg County, Virginia.

---

[139]And is recorded in D. B. 4, page 8.
[140]*Report of the State Librarian,* 1910-1911, 364.
[141]This parish became Mecklenburg County, in 1765.

It is dated April 26, 1751, and was probated Oct. 3, 1751.[142] It mentions:

1. Brother, Joseph Ragsdale,
2. Brother (brother-in-law?), Richard Witton,
3. Nephew, Peter Ragsdale, son of Joseph Ragsdale,
4. Nephew, Drury Ragsdale, son of brother Drury Ragsdale,
5. Nephew, James Ragsdale, son of brother Drury Ragsdale.

The will named Joseph Ragsdale and Richard Witton, Executors.

This Godfrey Ragsdale was probably the son of Godfrey[2] Ragsdale and his wife Rachel above mentioned.

This writer is disposed to question the correctness of the descent of Captain Drury Ragsdale (1750-1804), of the Revolution as traced in *The Abridged Compendium of American Genealogy*.[143]

It seems to him, unless there is evidence of which he is not aware to the contrary, that it is more likely Captain Drury Ragsdale was a son of Drury Ragsdale, who was a son of Drury Ragsdale (brother of Godfrey Ragsdale, who made the will aforesaid), who was son of Godfrey[2] Ragsdale and his wife Rachel.

The next oldest Ragsdale will in Lunenburg County, Virginia, is that of Edward Ragsdale, doubtless

Edward[4] Ragsdale (bap. Jan. 12, 1723-4), son of Godfrey[3] Ragsdale.

The will, dated Dec. 17, 1779, was probated July 13, 1780.[144]

It mentions his wife Mollie Ragsdale, and the following children:

1. Edward[5] Ragsdale,
2. William[5] Ragsdale,
3. John[5] Ragsdale,
4. Baxter[5] Ragsdale,
5. Joshua[5] Ragsdale,
6. Martha[5] Petty Poole,
7. Ann[5] Neblett,

---

[142]It is recorded in W. B. 1, page 50.
[143]Vol. II, 113.
[144]It is of record in W. B. 3, page 46.

8. Elizabeth⁵ Ragsdale,
9. Tathy⁵ Ragsdale,
10. Jemima⁵ Ragsdale.

The sons Edward Ragsdale and William Ragsdale were named executors.

In Lunenburg County, Virginia, there are marriage bonds or certificates of ministers for the marriages of the following:

John Ragsdale and Sally Scarberry, Dec. 25, 1783,[145]
John Ragsdale and Martha Gee, Dec. 18, 1792,[145]
John Ragsdale and Mary Jones, Dec. 3, 1792.[145]
Baxter Ragsdale[146] married Sally Morgain, Feb. 13, 1799.
Joshua Ragsdale and Leniza Maddox, Dec. 2, 1789.[147]
Jemime Ragsdale married Woodson Jordan, July 12, 1792.[148]
John Ragsdale's will was made in 1787, and probated June 14, 1787, in Lunenburg County.[149]

In it he mentions the following sons and daughters:

1. Joshua Ragsdale,
2. Edward Ragsdale,
3. John Ragsdale,
4. William Ragsdale,
5. Annie Ragsdale,
6. Priscella Ragsdale,
7. Frances Ragsdale,
8. Elizabeth Ragsdale,
9. Mary Ragsdale,

and also two grandsons: John Hardy Ragsdale and Thomas Lowry.

The sons Joshua Ragsdale and John Ragsdale were named executors.

This testator was very probably John⁵ Ragsdale, son of Edward⁴ Ragsdale.

---

[145] *The Old Free State*, II, 392.
[146] He was an early Methodist preacher.
[147] *The Old Free State*, II, 392.
[148] Id., 436.
[149] It is recorded in W. B. 3, p. 277.

Joshua[5] Ragsdale made his will May 19, 1789, and it was probated in Lunenburg County, Virginia, February 11, 1790.[150]

He mentions his wife Letitia Ragsdale and the following children:

1. Peter[6] Ragsdale,
2. Henry[6] Ragsdale,
3. Edward[6] Ragsdale,
4. James[6] Ragsdale,
5. Priscilla[6] Ragsdale,
6. Catherine[6] Ragsdale.

He names his wife Letitia Ragsdale, William Buford, John Ragsdale and James Buford, executors.

John Ragsdale, doubtless John[5] Ragsdale, made his will March 27, 1790, and it was probated April 11, 1795.[151]

In it he mentions the following children:

1. Drury[6] Ragsdale,
2. Samuel[6] Ragsdale,
3. John[6] Ragsdale,
4. Lucy[6] Young,
5. Elizabeth[6] Ballard,
6. Mary[6] Gee.

The will named the son, John Ragsdale, executor.

The will of Joseph Ragsdale, of Lunenburg County, Virginia, was dated May 23, 1796, and was probated Jan. 9, 1800.[152]

This was likely Joseph[4] Ragsdale (b. Jan. 17, 1725), son of Peter[3] Ragsdale. He married Sarah Shelburne (M. B. dated Nov. 17, 1791),[153] but this was surely a second marriage.

In addition to mentioning his wife, Sarah Ragsdale, the will mentions:

1. Peter[5] Ragsdale,
2. Drury[5] Ragsdale,
3. John[5] Ragsdale,
4. Alse[5] Ragsdale (a daughter),

---

[150]It was recorded in W. B. 3, page 355.
[151]It is recorded in W. B. 4, page 35.
[152]It is recorded in W. B. 5, pages 5-6.
[153]*The Old Free State*, II, 393.

5. Ann⁵ Burchett,
6. Jane⁵ Hooper,
7. Mary⁵ Lester,
8. Frances⁵ Clarke,
9. Rebecca⁵ Ragsdale,
10. Sarah⁵ Williamson,
11. Elizabeth⁵ Beever,
12. Permelia⁵ Ragsdale,
13. Armenia⁵ Ragsdale.

William Stone, William Scott and George Clarke were named executors.

Edward Ragsdale, likely Edward⁵ Ragsdale, son of Edward⁴ Ragsdale, made his will October 10, 1797, and it was probated in Lunenburg County, Virginia, July 9, 1801.[154]

He mentions no children, only his wife, Ann Ragsdale; and names her and Peter Lamkin and Sterling Niblett, executors.

John⁶ Ragsdale made his will December 8, 1798, and it was probated in Lunenburg County, Virginia, December 9, 1813.[155]

He mentions his wife Mary Ragsdale (doubtless Mary Jones, of the marriage bond dated Dec. 3, 1792), and his nephew, Peter Ragsdale, son of his youngest brother Samuel Ragsdale.

John⁵ Ragsdale (Edward⁴ Ragsdale), made his will January 30, 1805, and it was probated in Lunenburg County, Virginia, May 10, 1810.[156]

He mentions his wife Elizabeth Ragsdale, and the following sons and daughters:

1. John Edwin⁶ Ragsdale,
2. Thomas Morgan⁶ Ragsdale,
3. Nancy Harrison⁶ Ragsdale,
4. Elizabeth⁶ Ragsdale,
5. Sally Baxter⁶ Ragsdale,
6. Patsy Gee⁶ Ragsdale.

The will also mentions Harriet Ragsdale Beadle, daughter of Elizabeth Beadle.

---
[154]It is recorded in W. B. 5, pages 65-66.
[155]It is recorded in W. B. 7, page 72.
[156]It is recorded in W. B. 7, page 7.

The will named his brother Baxter Ragsdale and Joshua Ragsdale executors.

Joshua[5] Ragsdale made his will April 15, 1817, and it was probated in Lunenburg County, Virginia, October 9, 1817.[157]

The will mentions the following children:

1. James[6] Ragsdale,
2. John L.[6] Ragsdale,
3. Harrison[6] Ragsdale,[158]
4. Edward[6] Ragsdale,[158]
5. Nancy[6] Ragsdale,
6. Elizabeth[6] Ragsdale,
7. Rebecca[6] Ragsdale.
8. Bedee Martha[6] Ragsdale.

The will names Washington Maddux and his brother Baxter Ragsdale, executors.

William[5] Ragsdale made his will July 9, 1819, and it was probated January 12, 1824, in Lunenburg County, Virginia.[159]

In it he mentions the following sons and daughters:

1. Joel M.[6] Ragsdale,
2. John B.[6] Ragsdale,
3. Frances[6] Maddux, married (M. B. Nov. 11, 1817),[160] Washington Maddux.
4. Elizabeth[6] Ragsdale,
5. Mary[6] Ragsdale,
6. Sicily[6] Ragsdale,
7. Jane[6] Ragsdale.

The son-in-law, Washington Maddux, was named executor.

This family has been numerously and prominently connected with the affairs of the section through a long period of time.

John Ragsdale, either John Senr. or John Junr., mentioned as being on the Lunenburg lists of tithes in 1750, was a soldier of the French and Indian Wars.[161]

---

[157]It is recorded in W. B. 7, page 341.
[158]The will does not specifically call Harrison and Edward children, but the context seems to imply that they were.
[159]It is recorded in W. B. 8, page 319.
[160]*The Old Free State*, II, 403.
[161]*The Old Free State*, I, 193.

GENEALOGICAL NOTES—CONTINUED 281

John Ragsdale, very probably John[4] Ragsdale, son of Benjamin[3] Ragsdale was a soldier of the Revolution.[162] He served first as a private and later as a corporal in the Company of Captain James Johnson; and is said to have attained and doubtless did attain a captaincy.

In 1757 John Ragsdale was an ensign in a company under Captain David Garland.[163]

In 1765 he was Captain of Militia, in Lunenburg County.[164]

A John Ragsdale was a Vestryman of Cumberland Parish from 1757 to 1814. It may be difficult now to separate this service and allocate it to the different parties entitled to it. It is probable that several of the same name, including

    John[4] Ragsdale (Benjamin[3] Ragsdale),
    John[5] Ragsdale (Edward[4] Ragsdale), and
    John[6] Ragsdale (John[5] Ragsdale),

shared that service.

Edward Ragsdale who was Vestryman from 1790 to 1793, was very likely Edward[5] Ragsdale, son of Edward[4] Ragsdale, and William Ragsdale who was Vestryman from 1812 to 1815, was William[5] Ragsdale, son of Edward[4] Ragsdale.

The following have been members of the County Court of Lunenburg County, Virginia:

    John Ragsdale, 1766-1786,[165]
    Edward Ragsdale, 1786-1797,[165]
    William Ragsdale, 1798, 1802-1823,[165]
    Joel M. Ragsdale, 1839-1850.[165]

Joel M. Ragsdale was also a Justice of the Court from 1852-1856, under the Constitution of Virginia of 1850.[166]

READ.

Clement Read, who was Vestryman of Cumberland Parish from 1747 to 1757, was the celebrated Colonel Clement Read:

---

[162] *The Old Free State*, 217, 219.
[163] O. B., October, 1757.
[164] O. B. July 11, 1765.
[165] *The Old Free State*, I, 331.
[166] *The Old Free State*, I, 341.

First Clerk of Lunenburg County; Colonel in the Colonial Wars; Burgess from Lunenburg County from 1748 to 1754, and from 1759 to 1763.[167]

This family resided in that part of Lunenburg County later cut off into Charlotte County, and its later history is more intimately connected with that county.

ROBERTSON.

Christopher[1] Robertson was a Captain in the Revolutionary War from Lunenburg County, Virginia.[168]

The order books of the County Court show his designation as such March 13, 1777. He was a member of the County Court of Lunenburg County from 1781 to 1797,[169] and was Sheriff of the County from 1800 to 1802.

He, or a person of that name, married (M. B. dated March 22, 1787), Constant Edmundson.[170]

SMITH.

Luke Smith was a Vestryman of Cumberland Parish in 1749. In 1748, 1749 and 1750, he was on the list of tithes taken by William Caldwell whose precinct was "from Cubb Creek to Falling River." He was charged with a single tithe each year. He disappears from this list in 1752.

It would be difficult, without considerable collateral research, to place the James Smith who was vestryman of Cumberland Parish from 1786 to 1806.

There are wills by the following Smiths in Lunenburg County, Virginia, from its formation up to 1825.

Charles Smith, probated April 17, 1815, W. B. 8, p. 6.
Elizabeth Smith, probated Jan. 13, 1825, W. B. 8, p. 428.
John Smith, probated Dec. 13, 1804, W. B. 6, p. 100.
Joseph Smith, probated Dec. 11, 1794, W. B. 4, p. 70-71.
Joseph M. Smith, probated March 10, 1823, W. B. 8, p. 268.

---

[167]*The Old Free State*, II, 68, 69 and passim.
[168]*The Old Free State*, I, 267.
[169]Id., 331.
[170]Id., II, 393.

Richard Smith, probated Feb. 5, 1760, W. B. 1, p. 286.
Robart Smith, probated July 10, 1820, W. B. 8, p. 118.
Thomas Smith, probated Aug. 10, 1780, W. B. 3, p. 58.
William Smith, probated April 2, 1751, W. B. 1, p. 502.
William Smith, probated April 10, 1806, W. B. 6, p. 149.

When a genealogist gets into a problem involving this name, it, of course, requires, usually, extensive and painstaking examination, because of the great number of names and wealth of material to be considered.

Doubtless William Smith and Richard Smith, those making the two earliest wills, were progenitors of many of those of the name found in the section at a later date. Brief abstracts of their wills are given.

William Smith:

Will dated May 16, 1750, probated April 2, 1751, and recorded in W. B. 1, p. 502.

It mentions only, wife Elizabeth Smith, and son, John Smith.

Richard Smith:

Will dated July 6, 1757, probated Feb. 5, 1760, and recorded in will book 1, page 286. It mentions wife Agnes Smith and the following sons and daughters:

1. Abraham Smith (mentioned in connection with lands in Dinwiddie County, Virginia).
2. Peter Smith,
3. Benjamin Smith,
4. Richard Smith,
5. Jane Cross,
6. Agnes Smith,
7. May Smith (May Booth),
8. Ann Smith Hightower,
9. Temperance Booth,
10. Sarah Mays,
11. Martha March,
12. Lucy Smith.

It names Abraham Cocke, and sons Abraham Smith and Peter Smith, executors.

SPEED.

John Speed settled in that part of Lunenburg County, Virginia, afterwards to be cut off into Mecklenburg County. He was a Vestryman of Cumberland Parish from 1755 to 1760, and was a Justice of the County Court of Lunenburg County from 1756 to 1765,[171] when Mecklenburg County was formed. He was a deputy sheriff in 1759 under Lyddall Bacon, and was a deputy sheriff under Thomas Bouldin from 1759 to 1761, and thereafter for several years under Richard Witton and Matthew Marable.

He was one of the first Justices of Mecklenburg County, both John Speed and John Speed, Jr., being of the bench of thirteen to whom the commission of the peace was directed for organizing the county.[172]

Joseph Speed, with Bennett Goode, represented Mecklenburg County, Virginia, in the famous convention of May 6, 1776, and helped to frame "the first written constitution of a free people in the annals of the world."[173]

James Speed was a burgess from Charlotte County, Virginia, from 1772 to 1775.[174]

He married (M. B. in Charlotte County, Virginia, dated Dec. 7, 1767), Mary Spencer, daughter of Thomas Spencer; and it was, probably, his brother Henry Speed who married Elizabeth Julia Spencer, another daughter of Thomas Spencer (M. B. in Charlotte County, Virginia, dated Sept. 8, 1772).

A part, at least, of the Speed family emigrated from the original Lunenburg section to Kentucky, and descendants are numerous in the west and southwest.

STEVENSON.

Thomas Stevenson was a Vestryman of Cumberland Parish from 1786 to 1788; and John Stevenson a Vestryman from 1791 to 1793.

These names are sometimes spelled (in some of the records met with), Stephenson.

---

[171]*The Old Free State*, I, 332.
[172]Opening order, Order Book 1, page 1, Mecklenburg County, Virginia.
[173]*The Old Free State*, I, 210-211.
[174]*Colonial Virginia Register*, 190-198.

Thomas Stevenson died in 1795. His will was dated July 14, and probated October 8, of that year.[175] He mentions no children, only his wife, Martha Anderson Stevenson, and named her executrix.

His wife was the daughter of Rev. James Craig, Minister of Cumberland Parish; and they were married before November 3, 1789, for that is the date of Rev. James Craig's will, and in it he mentions his daughter "Martha Anderson Stevenson."

John Stevenson, the Vestryman 1791 to 1793, was very probably the son of Francis Stevenson. On the list of tithes taken by John Glenn in 1783, there is an entry of "Francis Stephenson" and "John Stephenson" in such way as to indicate that John was (very probably), the son of Francis.

John Stevenson and Mary B. Craig (daughter of Reverend James Craig), were married in Lunenburg County, Virginia, on July 17, 1796, by Reverend John Cameron.[176]

STOKES.

There is some account of the Stokes family in *The Old Free State*.[177]

It is thought that all the Vestrymen of Cumberland Parish by that name are mentioned in that genealogy. These Vestrymen in the order of their service were:

    David Stokes, 1747-1769.
    David Stokes, Jr., 1780-1783.
    Henry Stokes, 1781-1802.
    William Stokes, 1796-1815.
    John Stokes, 1815-1816.

STREET.

Considerable data respecting the Street family are embodied in the Stokes-Street genealogy in *The Old Free State*.[178]

The Vestrymen of Cumberland Parish of the name were:

---

[175] It is recorded in Lunenburg County, Virginia.
[176] See his Register, printed in this volume, Chapter XIV.
[177] Vol. II, 328-362.
[178] Vol. II, 328-362.
    Id.

Anthony Street (the elder), 1780-1786.
John Street, 1793-1796.
David Street, 1796-1806.
Waddy Street, 1815-1816.

Anthony Street was the father of the other three vestrymen.

The Vestryman, Anthony Street, was a Captain in the Revolution.[179]

The Street Genealogy[180] says he volunteered a private in the Continental Army and continued in the service until the close of the war; "was in the bloody battle of Guilford Court House and King's Mountain and when the war ended he was Colonel commanding a regiment."[181]

Unfortunately, no authority is cited for the several statements. That he was a soldier of the Revolution is well established; but some of the details as given may be questioned.

The Street family had a notable line of service upon the County Court of Lunenburg County, Virginia, as follows:

Col. Anthony Street, 1777-1788,
Waddy Street, 1798-1818,
David Street, 1799-1819,
Anthony Street, 1802-1808,
James Street, 1818,
John T. Street, 1823-1846,
David Street, 1825-1848,
Waddy Street, 1847-1849.

TABB.

It is said that the first of the Tabb family in Virginia "was Humphrey Tabb, who appears from the Land-Books to have settled in Elizabeth City County about 1637, and was a Justice of that County in 1652. In 1662 there is a grant to Thos. Tabb, son and heir of Humphrey Tabb, deceased. From these descended the families of the name in Elizabeth City, York, Gloucester, Mathews, Amelia, Norfolk, Mecklenburg, etc."[182]

---

[179]*The Old Free State*, I, 267.
[180]Henry A. Street and Mary A. Street, Exeter, N. H., 1895.
[181]P. 271.
[182]*William and Mary Quarterly*, III, 120.

Thomas Tabb, the Vestryman 1759 to 1780, was a Justice of the County Court in Lunenburg County from 1757 to 1770; and probably until 1780; if he was not, then another of the same name was Justice from 1772 to 1780.[183]

He was Sheriff of the County from 1769 to 1771, and was a member of the Virginia Convention of 1775 from Lunenburg County, along with David Garland.[184]

There is a genealogy of the Tabb family in *William and Mary Quarterly*,[185] from which it appears that Thomas Tabb of Lunenburg County was fifth in descent from Humphrey Tabb, the emigrant.

The preceding generations are given in detail in this account.

Thomas[5] Tabb of Lunenburg, was the son of Thomas[4] Tabb, and his wife Mary Armistead, dau. of Anthony Armistead (son of Anthony Armistead and grandson of William Armistead, the emigrant).

Thomas[5] Tabb was "born December 18, 1730; emigrated to Lunenburg County, where he was living in 1767, when he made a deed to John Tabb, of Elizabeth City County for land left by his mother May Wills."[186]

TALBOTT.

Matthew[1] Talbott, on January 12, 1746, after the act creating Lunenburg County was passed, but before the County was organized, secured a patent for 600 acres of land, "being an Island in Staunton River below the mouth of Seneca Creek."[187] When the County was organized he was one of the members of the first County Court, the Court which organized the County, and set the machinery in motion.[188]

He was likewise a member of the first vestry of Cumberland Parish, and continued a vestryman from 1746 to 1750.

His son Matthew Talbott, Jr., on September 10, 1755, secured

---

[183] *The Old Free State*, I, 333.
[184] *Colonial Virginia Register*, 204; *The Old Free State*, I, 209.
[185] Vol. XIII, 121-128; 168-175; 270-278; Vol. XIV, 50-51; 150-154.
[186] *William and Mary College Quarterly*, XIII, 123. His mother was married three times.
[187] *The Old Free State*, I, 103.
[188] Id., 108.

a grant or patent for 400 acres of land on both sides of Johnson's Creek and south branch of Otter River.[189]

The first court appointed Mathew Talbot to take the lists of tithes from Falling River to the mouth of Otter River. These several facts indicate that this family lived in the part of Lunenburg County which was later to be created into Bedford County. When that county was created in 1754, Matthew Talbot, the elder, was designated by the act creating the county, as one of the persons to make settlement of accounts for taxes, etc., between the two counties.

When Bedford County was formed, Matthew Talbot was one of the first Justices of the County Court of that county; and the first court of the county was held at his house.[190]

He died in Bedford County, Virginia, in 1758, his will being dated January 4, and probated November 27, of that year.

He resided in Bristol Parish, Prince George County, doubtless, before coming to Lunenburg County, for there is the record that Matthew and Mary Tolbert had born to them there:

Matthew Tolbert, b. November 27, 1729,[191] and James Tolbert, b. Nov. 7, 1732.[192]

The elder Matthew Talbot was probably married twice, as the wife named in his will was Jane.

The will mentions the following children:

1. Charles[2] Talbot,
2. Matthew[2] Talbot,
3. James[2] Talbot,
4. John[2] Talbot,
5. Isham[2] Talbot,
6. Mary[2] Arthur.

Charles[2] Talbot married Drusilla (last name not learned), and died in Bedford County, Virginia, in 1779.

His will was dated July 4, 1779, and probated August 23, 1779. In it, in addition to his wife Drusilla, he mentions:

---

[189]*The Old Free State*, 106.
[190]*William and Mary Quarterly*, X, 61.
[191]*Bristol Parish Register*, 374.
[192]Id., 376.

1. Williston[3] Talbot,
2. Charles[3] Talbot,
3. Moile[3] Talbot,
4. Providence[3] Talbot,
5. George[3] Talbot,
6. Yaskey[3] Talbot,
7. David Given[3] Talbot,
8. Christianna[3] Talbot,
9. Mary[3] Thurston, wife of Plummer Thurston.

James[2] Talbot died in 1777, and his will was probated in Bedford County, March 27, 1777. From it, it appears his wife's name was Elizabeth. It mentions the following children:

1. Isham[3] Talbot,
2. James Smith[3] Talbot,
3. John[3] Talbot,
4. Williston[3] Talbot,
5. Nancy[3] Talbot,
6. Martha[3] Talbot,
7. Sarah[3] Talbot.

John[2] Talbot married, first Sarah Anthony of Bedford County, Virginia, and secondly, Phoebe Moseley, of Henrico County, Virginia. He moved to Wilkes County, Georgia, in 1784. His children were:

1. Phoebe[3] Talbot,
2. Thomas[3] Talbot,
3. Matthew[3] Talbot,
4. Mary[3] Talbot,
5. Elizabeth[3] Talbot.

Matthew[2] Talbot married twice: first, Mary Day, and second, Agnes (last name not learned). He moved to North Carolina in 1784.[193]

There is a memorandum on the Talbot family printed in *William and Mary College Quarterly*,[194] said to have been written by Edmund Talbot, son of Matthew[2] Talbot. There are patent

---
[193] *William and Mary College Quarterly*, X, 62.
[194] IX, 257-259.

errors in the statement such as that his grandfather "then moved to Bedford County, now Culpeper."[195]

According to this sketch Matthew[1] Talbot came from England and first settled in Maryland, "where he married a Miss Annie Williston, by whom he had a son named Charles. He then moved to Amelia County, Va., where he had three other sons born, viz., Matthew, James and John. His wife died; he then moved to Bedford County, now Culpeper, where he married a Miss Clayton, by whom he had a son and daughter, Isham and Martha. He then died, age unknown. I have often passed by his grave in my boyhood in the neighborhood where I was born."

This memorandum omits the residence of the grandfather in Prince George County, and his highly interesting connection with the early history of Lunenburg County, Virginia. It is undoubtedly accurate in its main features. Supplementing it by other authentic items, it seems that these facts may be regarded as fairly established:

That Matthew[1] Talbot was the immigrant, that he came from England to Maryland, and thence to Virginia; that he was married three times:

First, in Maryland, to Annie Williston, by whom he had:
    1. Charles[2] Talbot.

Second, in Virginia, to Mary (last name not known), by whom he had:

    2. Matthew[2] Talbot,
    3. James[2] Talbot,
    4. John[2] Talbot, and

Third, "a Miss Clayton"—doubtless Jane Clayton, as the wife mentioned in his will was named Jane, by whom he had:

    5. Isham[2] Talbot,
    6. Mary[2] (or Martha[2]) Arthur.

From the statement or sketch prepared by Edmund[3] Talbot, it is learned that

Charles[2] Talbot "became a Baptist before his death, which took

---

[195] Possibly Campbell was meant.

place during the Revolutionary War. He had several sons and two daughters."[196]

Matthew[2] Talbert, as stated above, married Mary Day. Of her Edmund Talbert in the memorandum says that his father married "a young widow (with one child, a daughter) by the name of Day, her maiden name being Hale."

Matthew[2] Talbot and Mary (Hale) Day (d. 1785), had:

1. Mary[3] Talbot,
2. Hale[3] Talbot,
3. Matthew[3] Talbot,
4. Thomas[3] Talbot,
5. Edmund[3] Talbot (who made the family sketch),
6. Clayton[3] Talbot.

Matthew[2] Talbot married a second time, but there were no children by that marriage.

"All his sons were engaged in the war (Revolutionary) except Edmund and Clayton, who were too young to enter the service. Mathew was commissary, and was at the retaking of Augusta; Thomas was wounded, a ball struck the top of his head and cut a furrow."

Matthew[2] Talbot moved "from Virginia to Tennessee .... in consequence of his business being stock raising." He went first "to East Tennessee, and finally settled in Wilkes County, Georgia."[197]

Of James[2] Talbot, whose children as given in the will are mentioned above, the memorandum has this to say:

"James died during the Revolutionary War. He had four sons and a daughter, viz.: Mary, Isham, James, John and Williston."[198] They all went west.

Of John[2] Talbot, Edmund Talbot says in his statement:

"John was a member of the Legislature of Virginia for twenty-

---

[196] His children as mentioned in the will are given above.
[197] *William and Mary College Quarterly*, IX, 257.
[198] The will names the sons mentioned, but gives the names of three daughters as follows: Nancy, Martha and Sarah. See above.

five years,[199] and after he moved to Wilkes County, Ga., was elected several years to the Legislature. He was a great Whig during the Revolutionary War. He was the pleasantest man I ever knew. . . . He died at sixty years of age."

The children as given in the memorandum are as given above. Of them the statement, which was written by Edmund[3] Talbot in 1858 says:

"Thomas is still living in Wilkes County, Georgia.

"Matthew was a senator of the Georgia Legislature for twenty years, and was candidate for governor, but died during the canvass in the year 1827."

Of Isham[2] Talbot the statement says:

"Isham moved to Kentucky from Virginia" and "became a great lawyer and statesman in Kentucky. He was generally called little Isham."

"He had as many as three sons:"

Isham[3] Talbot,
James[3] Talbot,
Edmund[3] Talbot.

Of these James was a doctor and married the eldest daughter of Hale[3] Talbot, son of Matthew[2] Talbot.

It is strange that this sketch omits the fact that Matthew Talbot was Governor of Georgia in 1819.[200]

Isham[2] Talbot was born in Bedford County, Virginia, in 1773, moved to Harrodsburg, Ky., studied law, practiced at Versailles, Ky.; moved to Frankfort, and continued to practice law. Member of the State Senate from 1812 to 1815; United States Senator from January 3, 1815, to March 3, 1819, and again from October 19, 1820, to March 3, 1825. Died near Frankfort, Kentucky, September 25, 1825.[201]

---

[199] The *Virginia Colonial Register* shows that John Talbot was a member of the House of Burgesses from Bedford County from 1761 to 1775 (pp. 154-198), and was a member of the Conventions of 1775 and 1776 (pp. 201, 208). John Talbot was also a member of the Legislature from Bedford County, Virginia, from 1776 to 1782. *Register of the General Assembly 1776-1918*, p. 434.

[200] *Virginia Historical Magazine* 11, page 80; *The Old Free State*, II, 101.

[201] *Congressional Directory*, 1774-1911, 1040.

Edmund³ Talbot (who wrote the sketch or memorandum so freely quoted), son of Matthew² Talbot and his wife Mary Hale (widow Day), was born in Bedford County, Virginia, March 28, 1767.[202] At about twenty years of age he joined the Baptist Church under the preaching of Sanders Walker. He married in 1787 Mary Harvey (d. 1807), daughter of John Harvey, of Washington County, Georgia.

They had (to arrive at maturity):

1. William⁴ Talbot,
2. Sally⁴ Talbot, who married a Mr. Davis of Georgia.
3. John⁴ Talbot,
4. Martha⁴ Talbot, who married a Mr. Ashburn.
5. Matthew⁴ Talbot (in 1804 of Matagorda, Texas),
6. Polly⁴ Talbot, who married a Mr. Bullard(?).
7. Elizabeth⁴ Talbot, who married a Mr. Walker.

Edmund³ Talbot married a second time, "a widow by the name of McCulloch, but whose maiden name was Cauthorn," and by her had, to grow to maturity:

8. Eliza⁴ Talbot, who married a Mr. Cason, and resided in Florida.
9. Amelia⁴ Talbot, who married a Mr. Porter, of Alabama.
10. Amanda⁴ Talbot, who married Dr. A. I. Robinson, of Columbus, Georgia.

TAYLOR.

The Taylor family is one of the distinguished families of old Lunenburg.

This family descended from Reverend Daniel Taylor, Minister of Blissland Parish in New Kent County, Virginia, who came to Virginia in 1703.

There is a sketch of the family in *The Old Free State*.[203]

---

[202] A sketch from *Georgia Baptist*, appended to Edmund Talbot's statement and printed in *William and Mary College Quarterly* (IX, 258), says he was "born in Campbell County, Va., 28th of March, 1767." This, of course, was an error. Campbell County was not created until 1781.
[203] Vol. II, 362-368.

All the Vestrymen of Cumberland Parish of this name, were of this family. They were:

    Edmund Taylor, 1759,
    William Taylor, 1768-1795,
    William H. Taylor, 1812-1815.

William Taylor was Clerk of Lunenburg County from 1763 to 1814, a period of fifty-one years; and his son William H. Taylor from 1814 to 1846.[204]

From this family was sprung United States Senator Waller Taylor, the first senator from Indiana; and Lieutenant William Taylor, of the United States Navy, who for deeds in the war of 1812 distinguished by valor was thanked by the legislature of Virginia, and presented a sword;[205] and Lieutenant Colonel Lewis Littlepage Taylor, who distinguished himself at the Battle of Lundy's Lane, and who died during the war of 1812, at Norfolk, Virginia, where he is buried in St. Paul's Churchyard.

TOMLINSON.

Benjamin[1] Tomlinson, who was a Vestryman of Cumberland Parish from 1772 to 1780, was during the Revolutionary War successively Lieutenant, Captain, Major and Colonel.[206]

His will in Lunenburg County, Virginia, was dated September 29, 1787, and probated December 10, 1789.[207] In it he mentions his wife Jane Tomlinson and the following children:

1. Harris[2] Tomlinson, who was a first lieutenant from Lunenburg County, in the Revolution.[208]
2. Phoebe[2] Cross, wife of Charles Cross. Their marriage bond in Lunenburg County, is dated November 8, 1770.[209]
3. Amye (Amey)[2] Williams, who married John Williams, whose will was dated December 9, 1796, and probated June 8, 1797.[210]

---

[204] *The Old Free State*, I, 345.
[205] The history and fate of the sword is mentioned in *The Old Free State*, II, 365-6.
[206] *The Old Free State*, I, 266, 267.
[207] It is recorded in W. B. 3, page 353.
[208] *The Old Free State*, I, 267.
[209] Id., II, 395.
[210] It is recorded in Lunenburg County, Virginia, in W. B. 4, pages 171-172.

Their sons and daughters named in the will were:

1. Benjamin[3] Williams,
2. William[3] Williams,
3. Sarah[3] Williams,
4. Jane[3] Williams,
5. Martha[3] Williams,
6. Mary[3] Williams,
7. Elizabeth[3] Williams,
8. Amey[3] Williams.

4. Sary[2] Wiatt,
5. Mary[2] Tomlinson,
6. Patty[2] Tomlinson.

It is possible that Benjamin[1] Tomlinson had a son Benjamin[2] Tomlinson, not mentioned in his will.

There is in Lunenburg County the marriage bond, dated Dec. 21, 1814, for the marriage of Benjamin Tomlinson to Nancy Gee.[211] This Benjamin Tomlinson made his will March 27, 1818, and it was probated May 14, 1818.[212] He mentions no children; only his wife Nancy Tomlinson; and Lucas and Reubin Gee Executors.

There is in Lunenburg County, Virginia, the marriage bond dated May 12, 1791, for the marriage of Benjamin Edmundson to Martha Tomlinson.[213]

This is thought to be the "Patty[2] Tomlinson," above, the daughter of Benjamin[1] Tomlinson.

TUCKER.

There were two William Tuckers on the list of tithes for Lunenburg County, Virginia, for the year 1774. Both were charged with two tithes each. They were doubtless father and son, the son being old enough to be charged separately from the father. In 1775 we find William Tucker, Senr., charged for himself, George Tucker and one other tithe. George was doubt-

---
[211] *The Old Free State*, II, 400.
[212] It is recorded in W. B. 7, page 380.
[213] *The Old Free State*, II, 395.

less the son, who had just arrived at sixteen, and became taxable.

On the list of tithes for the year 1783, there were at least nine Tuckers, two of whom were named William. It might be, therefore, a little difficult to positively identify the William Tucker who was Vestryman of Cumberland Parish from 1790 to 1792.

The only will of a Tucker recorded in Lunenburg County, Virginia, from 1746 to 1825, is that of

George Tucker.

It is dated September 25, 1780, and was probated March 11, 1784.[214] In it he mentions his wife Catherine Tucker, and the following sons and daughters:

1. Joel Tucker,
2. Lew (Lewellyn) Tucker,
3. Robert Tucker,
4. William Tucker,
5. Henry Tucker,
6. George Tucker,
7. Joseph Tucker,
8. Milley Clay,
9. Biddy Tucker,
10. Fanny Coleman.

The wife, Catharine Tucker, and sons, William and Joel Tucker, were named executors.

TWITTY.

Some member of the Twitty family was doubtless the first to settle the stream, a tributary of the Little Roanoke, and thereby gave it the name of Twitty's Creek.

On January 12, 1746, John Twitty (called Twetty in the grant) secured a patent for 1000 acres of land on Meherrin River.[215]

Aside from this item, and the service of John Twitty as Vestryman of Cumberland Parish from 1747 to 1749, but little if any trace of the family is noted in the Lunenburg section. No

---

[214] It is recorded in W. B. 3, page 153.
[215] *The Old Free State*, I, 103.

will by any person of the name is found in Lunenburg County from 1746 to 1825, nor is any marriage by any person of the name found:

In Lunenburg County from 1746 to 1853,
In Mecklenburg County from 1765 to 1810,
In Charlotte County from 1765 to 1815, nor
In Amelia County from 1735 to 1809.

WINN.

The name of this family in some of the records is spelled Wynn; but the accepted modern spelling of the name of the Lunenburg family is Winn.

Thomas[1] Winn was Vestryman of Cumberland Parish from 1766 to 1780. His will is of record in Lunenburg County, Virginia.[216] It was dated September 18, 1779, and probated April 12, 1781. He mentions his wife Sarah Winn and the following sons and daughters:

1. Bannister[2] Winn,
2. Edmund[2] Winn,
3. Washington[2] Winn,
4. Henrietta[2] Winn,
5. Maria[2] Winn.

He named his wife Sarah Winn, John Winn, of Amelia County, William Winn and Lyddal Bacon, Executors.

There are quite a number of early wills in Lunenburg County, Virginia, by persons of the name, but to establish their relationships would be difficult, and require investigation which this writer has not had opportunity to make.

Thomas[1] Winn the Vestryman, was a member of the County Court of Lunenburg County from 1766 to 1781.

And others of the name were also members of the Court, as follows:

Edmund Winn (doubtless son of Thomas[1] Winn), from 1799

---
[216]In W. B. 3, page 75.

to 1817, and probably later. A person of the name served up to 1847.

Alexander Winn, 1796 to 1822.
Joseph Winn, from 1779 to 1799.
Edmund C. Winn, from 1847 to 1851, and
Elder C. Winn, in 1851.[217]

[217] *The Old Free State*, I, 333.

CHAPTER XIV

Reverend John Cameron's Registers

Register of Marriages

Bristol Parish,	1784-1793,
Nottoway Parish,	1794-1795,
Cumberland Parish,	1796-1815.

Register of Baptisms and Funerals

Cumberland Parish,   1815.

THERE were ordinarily kept by parish ministers:
A record of births and baptisms in the parish,
A record of marriages, and
A record of deaths.

In the case of the Reverend John Cameron, no register of births kept by him has been found, nor has any register of marriages for the period, about ten years, when he was rector of St. James' Parish, been discovered, and the only record or register of deaths kept by him, so far discovered, is a brief page or two, entitled:

"A Register of baptisms & funerals for Cumberland Parish, By John Cameron, Rector," containing sixteen entries made in the year 1815.

It seems reasonable to suppose that he had theretofore kept such a record, probably in a book, whose space had been filled, and this was but the continuation, really, of a preceding register. This is, however, but a surmise, as no trace has been found of any such book or record, for prior years, kept by him.

The Register of Marriages kept by Rev. John Cameron, here presented, begins in 1784 and ends in 1815.

It is entitled "A Register of Marriages for Bristol Parish." The first entry in it is of the marriage, May 23, 1784, of Dudley Brown and Anne Todd, of Dinwiddie County. This Register of

Marriages continues through the time of his rectorship in Bristol Parish, in Nottoway Parish and in Cumberland Parish. Reference to his change of office to Nottoway is made by his writing on the page preceding that which carries the title "A Register of Marriages for Bristol Parish," the following entry: "John Cameron Nottoway County January 28th, 1794," and "Cumberland Parish" is written boldly across the page at the point where his service begins in that parish.

This Register evidently contains the complete record of marriages celebrated by him during the period of thirty-one years covered by it. The entries, while not very numerous, relatively, and in fact few indeed for some years, are consecutive, and the list has, in the original, all the appearance of completeness.

The Doctor, to make this register, evidently found an old ledger, of suitable size, but partly used, with sufficient pages left untouched for his purpose. This is indicated by what was apparently the first writing done in the volume, and which indicates that it was begun as a ledger in 1757. This entry is:

"Ledger 1757 Commenced, of Private Acco^{ts}; Inputs; Taylor; &c & what money I owe to Sundrie People."

Whose ledger it was originally does not appear.

The Marriage Register contains the record of four hundred and fifty-nine marriages. And while, as we have seen, Dr. Cameron during the period covered by it had official connection with but three parishes, Bristol, Nottoway and Cumberland, yet, it should be observed, these marriages are by no means confined to these three parishes. In fact the register is quite as important to other localities as it is to these particular parishes. This fact clearly appears from an analysis of data contained in it.

The marriages were celebrated in eleven counties—all Southside Counties—and in Petersburg. One hundred and fifty-six of them took place in Prince George County; seventy-three in Petersburg; fifty-seven in Lunenburg; fifty in Chesterfield; thirty-nine in Dinwiddie; thirty-eight in Sussex; twenty-five in Nottoway; while a very few occurred in Surry, Brunswick, Prince Edward and Amelia.

This distribution of the marriages is interesting and important and gives the Register a value, of a kind, and possibly a greater one than it would have, if confined to a more limited area.

An added value is to be attached to the Register because the marriages appearing therein were not returned to court in lists such as were required by dissenting ministers, under the Act of October, 1780.[1]

If that law contemplated that all persons performing marriage ceremonies should return such lists, Dr. Cameron did not so construe it. He resided in Lunenburg County and celebrated marriage ceremonies there from 1796 to 1815, but no list returned to court by him has been found, although there are many such lists returned during that period by ministers of the Presbyterian, Baptist and Methodist Churches.[2]

The gradual decline in the number of marriage ceremonies performed by Dr. Cameron, may indicate, not only the difficulty of his financial situation, but is suggestive also of the increasing strength of the "dissenting" denominations. From 1785 through 1788, the number of marriage ceremonies performed by him ranged from fifty to sixty per year; from 1789 to 1793 from twenty to forty; during the lean years in Nottoway, 1794 and 1795, he performed but twelve ceremonies, seven the first and five the second of those years; and the situation in this respect did not improve after his final removal to Cumberland Parish in 1796. From this time until his death there were only from one to ten couples per year who came his way for the marriage vows. In 1812 he performed a single ceremony, in 1813 none at all, and there were but two ceremonies in each of the years 1814 and 1815.

The records show that more and more people were resorting to ministers of other churches, the leaders of the groups known as the "dissenters," in the days of the Established Church, to marry them.

Thus in 1800, Reverend John Cameron married but two couples from Lunenburg County, while in that year, other ministers married in Lunenburg County, thirty-five couples, according to the

---
[1] X *Hening*, 361-2; *The Old Free State*, I, 387.
[2] These are compiled and printed in *The Old Free State*, II, 424-463.

returns now available made to court.[8] Some of the returns made by such ministers may not now be extant. During that year one Baptist minister married fourteen couples, another seven; while one Methodist preacher celebrated eleven marriages. The ratio did not improve, from the standpoint of the Episcopal Church, as the years went by, to the end of Dr. Cameron's earthly mission.

The Registers; first, the *Marriages*, and next, the *Baptisms and Funerals*, follow:

[8] *The Old Free State*, II, 425-463.

Ledger 1757 Commenced

of Private Acco^{ts}; Inputs; Taylors; &c & what money
I owe to Sundrie People

JOHN CAMERON
NOTTOWAY COUNTY
January 28th, 1794

A Register of Marriages for Bristol Parish

1784		County	L	S	D
May 23	Dudley Brown and Anne Todd	Dinwiddie	"	12	"
July 7	Duncan Young & Susannah Womack	Do.			
Aug. 1	Hezekiah Brown & Tabitha Irby	Do.	1	16	"
28	Peter Vaughan & Elizabeth Raines	Prince George	2	"	"
Dec. 9	Joshua Wynne & Mary Todd	Dinwiddie	"	12	"
23	Thomas Hanks & Margaret Clements	Do.	"	15	"
1785					
Jan. 8	William Gray & Maria Randolph	Prince George	2	8	"
13	William Wills & Mary Watkins	Dinwiddie	4	16	"
Feb. 10	Joel Cheaves & Sarah Sturdivant	Prince George	1	8	"
17	Sampson Grantham & Elizabeth Manull Simmons	Sussex	2	8	"
Mar. 17	Joseph Watkins & Polly Bushell	Dinwiddie	2	8	"
Apr. 2	Samuel Demovill & Elizabeth Taylor Eppes	P. George	2	8	"
17	Ephraim Vaughan & Parthena Ridout	Dinwiddie	"	9	"
May 17	John Carter & Ursella Pennington	Sussex	2	8	"
26	Martin Murphy & Rebeckah Russel	Petersburg	1	7	"
June 18	Francis Haddon & Becky Raines	P. George	1	8	"
July 28	Henry Moss & Keziah Freeman	Sussex	1	10	"
	David Allen & Mary Hair	P. George	"	12	"
30	William Hart & Anne Stainback	Dinwiddie	1	8	"
Aug. 6	Philip Jones & Martha Erskine	P. George	2	2	"
..	Thomas Carter & Anne Broadnax	Do.	4	4	"
7	Seth Foster & Anne King	Do.	7	"	"
25	James Williams & Patsey Fewqua	Do.	1	8	"
27	Nathaniel Nunnelly & Polly Andrews	Dinwiddie	"	6	8
27	Edmund Cooper & Elizabeth Hodges	Petersburg	1	4	"
Sept. 1	Thomas Hawkins & Courtney Irvin	Do.	1	10	"
7	William Cunningham & Obedience Hacker	Do.	1	8	"
20	Antonio Lu Park & Betty Cain	P. George	"	6	"
23	John Freeman & Milly Heath	Do.	2	2	"

Marriages (*Continued*)

1785		County	L	S	D
Sept. 29	Halcott Palmour & Effee Epes	Do.	1	10	"
..	James Peebles & Elizabeth Atkins Rives	Do.	1	4	"
Oct. 13	John Shore & Anne Bolling	Petersburg	4	4	"
Nov. 5	John Baugh & Anne West	P. George	1	16	"
10	Moses Andrews & Betsey McLeane	Dinwiddie	"	5	"
19	Shepherd Davis & Martha Williams	P. George	1	8	"
Dec. 8	Pleasant Hunnicutt & Mary Cocke	Sussex	3	10	"
10	Archibald Smith & Lucretia Rosser	Prince George	"	6	"
11	James Valentine & Anne Owens	Petersburg	"	6	"
12	Thomas Brockwell & Jemimah Williams	P. George	"	6	"
15	William Jackson & Sally Eckles	Sussex	"	9	"
..	William Major & Susanna Williams	Dinwiddie	"	6	"
22	Thomas Barnes & Elizabeth Anderson	Prince George	"	6	"
..	John Bonner & Mary Heth Bonner	Dinwiddie	1	9	"
..	Jesse Wrenie & Mary Hall	Sussex	1	10	"
..	William Burge & Rebecca Hall	Do.	1	10	"
24	James Thompson & Sarah Newall	P. George	"	6	"
..	Burwell Livesay & Frankey Grammer	Do.	"	6	"
30	Henry Nicholl & Francis Hackney	Do.	2	16	"
1786					
Jan. 5	George Ivy & Amelia Peterson	P. George	"	6	"
7	John Goody & Susanna Cain	Do.	"	6	8
11	Abram Allen & Mary Griffin	Do.	"	6	"
12	John Blick & Sarah Partrick	Dinwiddie	1	7	6
21	Buckner Ezell & Elizabeth Birchett	P. George	1	10	"
26	William Clements & Anne McCulloch	Dinwiddie	"	6	"
31	William Lanthrop & Susanna Davenport	P. George	"	6	"
Feb. 11	William Timberlake & Elizabeth Turnbull	Petersburg	1	10	"
20	John Crider & Mildred Hobbs	P. George	"	6	"
25	John Hase & Anne Burton	Chesterfield	1	8	"
26	John Anderson & Betsy Norton	Dinwiddie	"	6	"
Mar. 1	Noel Waddill & Eliza L. Watkins	Petersburg	1	8	"
4	Josiah Harrison & Mary Underhill	Sussex	"	12	"
5	John Gary & Sally Weaver	Do.	1	10	"
6	Smallwood Coghill Marlow & Mildred Flack	Petersburg	"	19	"
24	Christopher Slokam & Sally Ash	Do.	"	18	"

MARRIAGES (Continued)

1786		County	L	S	D
Mar. 25	James Scot & Nelly Norton	Dinwiddie	"	6	"
Apr. 6	William Ramsden & Mary Roberts	Petersburg	"	6	"
9	John Davis & Susanna Swepson	Mecklenburg	2	"	"
15	James Goodwyn & Frances Lowry Brown	Petersburg	1	4	"
22	Drury Allen & Salley Jeffries	Prince George	"	12	"
27	John McLeod & Isabella Hamilton	P. George	2	8	"
May 6	Joseph Badger & Nancy Shepherd	Petersburg	1	"	"
7	Austin Heath & Sarah Woodleif	Pr. George	1	8	"
May 18	Francis Thompson & Rebeckah Harvie	Petersburg	"	6	"
20	James Howle & Pamelia Tyus [?]	Sussex	"	6	"
June 1	James Tench & Sarah Williams	Pr. George	"	6	8
3	William Nichols & Nancy Park	Petersburg	1		
8	Erasmus Gill & Sarah Newsum	Dinwiddie	4	16	"
14	George Turner & Lurany Russell	Petersburg	1	4	"
15	William Skinner & Jenny Black	Do.			
..	Thomas Brooks Jones & Rebeccah Edwards Jones	Chesterfield	"	18	"
24	Maurice Moriarty & Judy Hammond	Petersburg	1	4	"
July 6	John Angus & Lucy Wortham	Petersburg	2	2	"
9	Joseph Westmore & Elizabeth Baird	Pr. George	5	10	"
13	Nathaniel Dunn & Betty Thweatt	Do.	1	16	"
Aug. 20	Hugh Tulloch & Elizabeth Thomas	Petersburg			
Sept. 7	John Jeffries & Anne Elizabeth Jones	Chesterfield	1	4	"
24	Jesse Herring & Anne Woodleif	Pr. George	1	6	"
Oct. 7	William Underhill & Mary Ann Caroline Meachum	Sussex	"	6	"
14	John Potts & Elizabeth Gee	Pr. George	1	10	"
15	Charles Morgan & Rebeccah Thompson	Do.	"	6	"
18	Henry Lynch & Eleanor McDonnell	Petersburg	1	10	"
18	Peter Vaughan & Mary Godwyn Boisseau	Dinwiddie	1	10	"
22	George Cameron & Elizabeth Hattaway	Petersburg	1	10	"
Nov. 4	Aaron Brandom & Silvia Lewis	Petersburg	"	6	"
Nov. 7	Edmund Holliday & Elizabeth Chapel	Petersburg	1	4	"
23	Joseph Lenox & Nelly Field	Do.	1	8	"
Dec. 9	Joseph Dougherty & Letty Machen	P. George	1	16	"
..	William Epes & Patience Morison	Do.	2	16	"

Marriages (Continued)

1786		County	L	S	D
Dec. 13	John Chapman & Margaret Hogan	Petersburg	"	6	"
23	Burwell Rosser & Ann Hobbs	Pr. George			
..	Stephen Goodwyn & Elizabeth Watkins	Dinwiddie	2	8	"
25	Henry Young & Winney Tucker Goodwyn	Do.	1	7	6
26	David Mosely & Amey Finn	Pr. George			
30	Joshua Hawthorn & Nancy Heth	Do.	2	"	"
..	William Cosby & Millender Holsey	Petersburg	1	4	"
1787					
Jan. 2	William Robertson & Margaret Duran	Petersburg	"	6	8
7	Abraham Johnston & Sukey Tench	Prince George	"	12	"
14	Edmund Harrison & Mary Murray	Do.	4	8	"
17	William Thompson & Frances Rives	Do.	1	11	4
20	Stephen Edwards & Elizabeth Watts	Do.	"	6	"
Feb. 1	John Cate & Winney Meachum	Sussex	2	2	"
8	Nicholas Ogburn & Mary Harrison	Do.	2	2	"
..	Augustine Ogburn & Elizabeth Massenburg	Do.	2	8	"
10	William Poythress & Elizabeth Blair Bland	Pr. George	4	16	"
12	Robert Dixon & Joannah Thrift	Do.	"	5	3
13	Robert Tucker & Sarah Parham	Do.	1	18	"
22	David W. Collier & Patty Williams	Dinwiddie	"	6	"
24	Clark Smith & Ann Campbell	Petersburg			
Feb. 28	Theophilus Field & Susan Thweatt	Pr. George	4	16	"
Mar. 24	John McFarquhar & Frances Vaughan	Dinwiddie	1	4	"
Apr. 3	Benjamin Smith & Ann Buckmire	Petersburg	1	8	"
11	Edward Murphey & Elizabeth Kerr	Do.	"	6	"
..	John Brownlow Knox & Elizabeth Jones	Do.	"	6	8
14	John Macfarlan & Frances Williamson	Do.	1	10	"
17	Thomas Dunn & Lucy Green	Pr. George	2	1	6
22	Francis Burwell Green & Mary Batte	Do.	1	10	"
May 31	John Cotton & Celia Lee	Pr. George	"	6	8
June 5	Joel Hall & Betsey Chambliss	Sussex	1	16	"
23	James Blakely & Jemima Hobbs	Petersburg	"	13	6
30	Joseph Bass & Mary Robertson	Chesterfield	1	11	4
July 3	Thomas Harris & Elizabeth Womack	Pr. George	"	6	"

Marriages (Continued)

1787		County	L	S	D
July 14	James Cattle & Martha Butler	Petersburg	1	1	6
17	Alexander Marshall & Anne Walthall	Chesterfield	1	10	"
19	Thomas Welch & Jane Edgar	Pr. George	—	7	6
25	Daniel McLaurin & Susannah Edwards	Chesterfield	"	6	8
28	Peter Thweatt & Lucretia Parish	Dinwiddie	"	18	"
Aug. 11	Alexr. Drayman & Mary Ann Murphy	P. George	"	6	"
21	Duncan Young & Mary Moore	Petersburg	"	"	"
Sept. 2	James Bromley & Margaret Falkner	Petersburg	1	16	"
Nov. 1	Daniel Dyson & Jinny Gill	Chesterfield	1	4	8
4	Michael Heathcote & Mary Wily	Petersburg	4	10	"
5	Charles Binford & Nancy Stephens	Prince George			"
8	John Ravenscroft Fisher & Elizabeth Wily	Pr. George	2	16	"
10	Jesse Smith & Martha Keys	Chesterfield	"	6	"
21	James Skelton Gilliam & Mary Field	Pr. George	3	—	"
24	James Moore & Martha Williams	Do.	"	5	"
Dec. 1	Hiles Andrews & Maxon Perkinson	Do.	"	6	"
4	John M. Clarren & Martha Berry	Chesterfield	"	6	"
8	Thomas B. Lacey & Frances Hopkins	Petersburg	1	4	"
9	Jacob Rollings & Mary Riley	Do.			
12	Charles Gee & Susannah Peebles	Sussex	1	16	"
..	Carter Seward & Rebecca Rives	Pr. George	1	6	"
13	Daniel Perkinson & Mary Mann	Chesterfield	"	6	"
15	David Williams & Mary Peebles	Sussex	1	10	"
18	Richard W. Cooper & Priscilla Inglish	Petersburg	"	12	"
22	Edmund Orin & Sarah Rives	Pr. George	1	10	"
..	Miles Hunter & Martha Pritchett	Petersburg	1	8	"
24	Richard Bland & Susanna Poythress	Pr. George	2	16	"
..	Joseph Davenport & Judith Richardson	Petersburg	"	18	"
26	James Newall & Jemimah Leath	Pr. George	"	6	"
..	William Burt & Patsey Daniel	Do.	"	7	"
27	William Heth & Rebeccah Young	Dinwiddie	"	6	"
1788					
Jan. 2	Francis Roberts & Liddy Richardson	Prince George	"	6	"
5	William Williams & Martha Reese	Do.	"	6	"
10	Thomas Gary & Elizabeth Proctor	Do.	1	10	"
15	David Ventris & Jenny Dixon	Do.	"	6	"
20	Thomas Tod Hunter & Alice Harrison	Do.	2	16	"

Marriages (Continued)

1788			County	L	S	D
Jan.	..	William Young & Eleanor Healy	Petersburg	1	2	6
	22	James Sturdivant & Patsey Burchett	Pr. George	1	8	"
	24	Cuthbert Harrison & Fanny Holt	Chesterfiled	2	8	"
	30	Nathan Heath & Elizabeth Dunn	Sussex	2	4	"
	31	Lewis Perkins & Leah Moody	Pr. George	"	6	"
Feb.	2	Edward Glover & Rebeccah Major	Do.	2	1	"
	5	Robert Baugh & Martha Cleveland	Sussex	2	8	"
	13	Jesse Stiles & Sarah Potter	Chesterfield	"	6	8
	21	Edward Lee & Polly Bonner	Pr. George	"	6	"
	23	Daniel Heath & Mary Levisay	Do.	"	6	"
Mar.	7	Joseph Weisiger & Anna Baird	Do.	3	18	"
	8	Mark Killingworth & Charlotte Caleb	Do.	"	6	"
	12	Alexander Franklyn & Anne Hoy	Chesterfield	"	6	"
	20	John Johnson & Alley Peterson	Pr. George	"	6	"
	26	Benjamin Totty & Mary Blankenship	Chesterfield	"	6	"
	27	Edward Newall & Lucy Lanier	Pr. George	1	16	"
Apr.	15	William Rives & Elizabeth Baugh	Do.	1	7	"
	26	David Bradley & Sally Lessinberry	Do.	"	6	"
May	1	John Grammer & Priscilla Withers	Dinwiddie	2	16	"
	17	Thomas Tenney & Elizabeth Temple	Pr. George	"	6	"
	29	David Buchanan & Elizabeth Gilliam	Do.	2	16	"
June	14	John Reaby & Mary Avery	Pr. George	"	6	"
	19	Patrick M. Shiffery & Patsy Johnson	Surry	"	12	"
	21	Jonathan Herbert & Nanny Wilkins	Pr. George	1	10	"
July	24	Benjamin Wycke & Elizabeth Mason	Sussex	2	8	"
	31	Eppes Temple & Nancy Temple	Pr. George	1	10	"
Aug.	3	John Baxter & Patsey Wilkinson	Do.	1	8	"
	14	John Pollard & Frances Swanson	Do.	1		
Sept.	10	William Thompson & Lucy Herbert Cocke	Sussex	4	4	"
	20	Roger Atkinson, Jr., & Agnes Poythress	Pr. George	2	8	"
Oct.	18	Abraham Womack & Joanna Levisay	Do.	"	6	"
	25	David Maitland & Susanna Poythress	Do.	4	4	"
Nov.	15	Joseph Gill & Mary Brown	Chesterfield	"	6	6
	..	George Godfrey & Mary Silvie	Pr. George	"	12	"
N.B.	11	Robert Lewis & Anne Bugg	Mecklenburg	"	6	"
	27	William Scoggin & Celia Cotton	Sussex	"	6	"
Dec.	4	Joseph Gill & Fanny Glassco	Chesterfield	"	6	"
	6	William Perry & Pheby Walthall	Do.	"	19	"
	..	William Harrison & Ann Morison	Pr. George	2	8	"

Marriages (Continued)

1788		County	L	S	D
Dec. 17	John Gee & Judith Rives	Do.	"	6	"
19	George Booth & Mary Eldridge	Surry	2	8	"
22	William McCarter & Elizabeth Weeks	Pr. George	"	6	"
23	Jesse Lee & Elizabeth Williams	Do.	"	6	"
25	Nader Gill & Elizabeth Granger	Chesterfield	"	5	"
..	William Ferguson & Rebecca Patterson	Pr. George	"	6	"
1789					
Jan. 2	William Oxley & Elizabeth McLaughlan	Prince George	1	8	"
7	John Lanier & Catharine Fallett	Do.	1	8	"
11	Daniel Jamison & Polly Watts	Do.	"	6	"
12	Buckner Traylor & Mary Handy	Chesterfield		3	9
22	Jeremiah Ford & Nancy Draper	Pr. George	"	6	"
..	Benjamin Gary and Mary Underhill	Sussex	"	6	"
..	John Brown & Elizabeth Harrison	Pr. George	4	4	"
29	Isham Hobbs & Elizabeth Clark	Sussex	"	6	"
..	John Rowlett & Mary Dance	Chesterfield	"	6	"
31	Robert Massenburg & Mary Jones	Dinwiddie	1	8	"
Feb. 7	William Royal & Sarah Singleton	Pr. George	"	6	"
12	George Hatch & Mary Shaw Thompson	Sussex	2	2	"
19	Shadrack Denhart & Lettie McDowell	Pr. George	"	12	"
Mar. 5	William Prentis & Mary Geddy	Petersburg	1	8	"
11	William Davis & Maxon Hardaway	Dinwiddie	1	10	"
14	Stephen Alley & Lucy Lee	Pr. George	"	6	"
19	George Wilson & Mary Ann Banister	Petersburg	4	4	"
Apr. 30	William Gilliam & Christian Eppes	Pr. George	4	2	"
..	James Geddy, Jr., & Euphan Armistead	Petersburg	2	1	"
June 1	Isham Belcher & Winifred Royall	Chesterfield	"	6	"
27	John Green & Jane Morison	Pr. George	1	16	"
July 21	John Kelly & Elizabeth Holden	Petersburg	"	6	"
25	Robert Stuart, Jr., & Sally Haldane	Do.	2	8	"
Aug. 12	Frederick Wilkinson & Patsey McDowell	Pr. George	"	6	"
Aug. 20	Hardy Cotton & Patty Saunders	Sussex	"	6	"
Sept. 10	William Williams & Betty Anderson	Pr. George	"	6	8
Oct. 13	Hardemar Poythress & Elizabeth Golder	Do.	"	6	"

MARRIAGES (*Continued*)

1789		County	L	S	D
Oct. 17	George Wilson & Dinny Browder	Do.	1	8	"
Dec. 6	Robert Marky & Ann Bradley	Petersburg	2	8	"
15	James Northington & Martha Chappell	Prince George	1	·4	"
17	John Holloway Daniel & Nancy Davenport	Pr. George	"	6	"
22	Ezekiel Jackson & Rhode Dance	Chesterfield	1	4	"
23	Briggs Rives & Ann Cureton	Pr. George	1	4	"
24	Jeremiah Meacham & Milly Cate	Do.	1	4	"
26	William Ragsdale & Ann Green Tucker	Do.	1	8	"
31	Leadbetter Lanthrupe & Lucretia Livesay	Do.	"	6	"
1790					
Jan. 6	Thomas Blunt & Judith Rives	Sussex	1	17	4
12	Bland Blankinship & Lucy Moore	Chesterfield	–	5	6
19	William Fawn & Elizabeth Stainback	Prince George	1	4	"
23	John Eanes & Margaret Dodd	Chesterfield	1	"	"
28	Jermiah Browder & Susanna Clements	Dinwiddie	–	6	"
..	John Sturdivant & Lucretia Sadler	Pr. George	1	"	"
Feb. 7	William Gill & Anne Andress	Chesterfield	–	6	"
15	George Greenhan & Margaret Granger	Petersburg	–	12	"
Mar. 12	John Kent & Elizabeth K. Halsey	Dinwiddie	–	12	"
27	James Grammer & Nancy Wells	Petersburg	–	6	"
Mar. ..	George Morrison & Mary Gracie	Petersburg	4	16	"
30	Alexander McKeever & Sally Jones	Chesterfield	1	7	9
31	Peter Harwell & Betsey Hawthorn	Sussex	–	6	"
Apr. 3	David Wells & Eliza Wamock	Petersburg	–	6	"
15	Aaron Gill & Jency Gill	Chesterfield	–	5	"
17	Benjamin Cook & Mary Blakely	Petersburg	–	14	"
May 20	John Kirkland & Agness Lee	Pr. George	–	6	"
June 24	Thomas Clayton & Mary Smith	Chesterfield	–	5	"
Sept. 16	Jesse Heth & Agnes Peebles	Pr. George	1	"	"
..	John Smith & Sally Dyson	Chesterfield			
Oct. 7	John Taylor Lee & Sarah Chappell Moore	Pr. George	"	18	"
30	John Hood & Elizabeth Osborne Downman	Chesterfield	1	4	"
Nov. 4	John West & Elizabeth Mitchell Jones	Pr. George	"	6	"
14	Richard Booker & Margaret McFarlane	Chesterfield	1	8	"

Marriages (Continued)

1790		County	L	S	D
Nov. 30	William Whitehead & Clarissa Lamb	Petersburg	1	"	"
Dec. 25	Edward Hall & Lucy Hardaway	Dinwiddie	1	8	"
..	William Clark & Mary Ann Hare	Chesterfield	2	8	"
31	Christopher Haskins & Elizabeth Booker	Petersburg	2	"	"
1791					
Jan. 1	John Blick & Rebecca White	Dinwiddie	"	6	–
6	William Cogbill & Elizabeth Covington	Chesterfield	1	8	–
20	Thomas Livesay & Ann Womack	Pr. George	–	6	–
Jan. 27	John Mason & Lucy Massinburg	Sussex	2	15	–
Feb. 3	Robert Mitchell & Celah Smith	Pr. George	–	6	–
5	James Dinton & Winefred Alley	Do.	–	6	–
10	Henry Harrison & Elizabeth Underhill	Sussex	–	6	–
Mar. 1	Obediah Read Harrison & Maxon Cain	Pr. George	–	6	–
12	James Todd & Franca Cotton	Do.	–	6	–
Apr. 23	John Rowlett & Locky Brown	Chesterfield	–	6	–
..	John Bland & Mary Lang	Prince George	2	–	–
May 12	George Swinbrod & Patsey Burrow	Do.	1	–	–
June 2	Lodowick Slater & Polly James	Petersburg	–	6	–
9	William Womack & Elizabeth Perkinson	Chesterfield	–	6	–
13	Gerreld Scott & Amey Dyer	Dinwiddie	–	6	–
16	Jacob Reese & Dyancy Meacham	Sussex	1	8	–
July 9	William Smith & Mary Adler	Petersburg	–	14	9
14	Bartley Tackett & Sarah Wren	Pr. George	–	6	–
30	John Bottom & Mary Hunnicutt	Sussex	3	–	–
Aug. 4	Thomas Hatton & Anne Redwood	Petersburg	1	1	–
6	Joseph Calvin & Elizabeth Wells	Chesterfield	1	8	–
18	George Mitchell & Rebecca Livesay	Pr. George	–	6	–
..	Nathaniel Colley & Martha Jones	Do.	2	6	8
20	William Sharp & Winefred Timberlake	Dinwiddie	2	8	–
Sept. 21	John Smith & Jane Walch	Petersburg	–	5	–
24	William Bingham & Mary Crammer	Pr. George	1	4	–
Oct. 10	Alexander S. Field & Jane Stewart	Do.	1	8	–
Nov. 19	James Baird & Frances Cogbill	Chesterfield	1	10	–
Dec. 17	Donald Cameron & Mary Anderson	Pr. George	1	8	–
21	Matthew M. Claiborne & Ann Carter Harrison	Sussex	1	10	–

Marriages (Continued)

1791		County	L	S	D
Dec. 24	John Perkinson & Elizabeth Anderson	Chesterfield	–	5	–
..	Joseph Nader & Sarah Ford	Dinwiddie	–	6	–
1792					
Jan. 7	John Mosley & Nancy Folks	Chesterfield	1	4	–
14	Benjamin Cook & Melinda Cosby	Petersburg	–	12	–
Feb. 11	Joshua Temple & Martha Williams	Pr. George	1	–	–
13	Daniel Hatcher & Mary Walthall	Chesterfield	1	8	–
28	George House & Ann Wells	Do.	1	8	–
Mar. 1	Eppes Temple & Elizabeth Peebles	Pr. George	1	4	–
10	John Perkinson & Lyncia Andrews	Chesterfield	–	6	–
Apr. 1	Richard Gary & Mary Bonner	Pr. George	–	12	–
7	William Rosser & Susanna Rives	Do.	–	6	–
May 3	Robert Stewart & Amey Goodwyn Raines	Dinwiddie	4	4	–
7	Simon Swail & Martha Browder	Petersburg	2	16	–
12	Lancelot Stone & Elizabeth Baugh	Do.	1	7	–
26	John Blackwell & Martha Vaughan	Pr. George	1	4	–
June 14	John Marks & Martha Lanier	Dinwiddie	1	8	–
16	Francis Osborne & Ann Turnbull	Prince George	4	4	–
21	Ashly Adams & Mary Riddlehurst	Dinwiddie	1	8	–
Aug. 1	John Bedingfield & Polly Cook	Sussex	1	16	–
Aug. 30	Matthew Lee & Elizabeth Crowder	Dinwiddie	–	6	–
Oct. 11	John Bobbitt & Frances Mitchell	Sussex	–	6	–
Nov. 15	Benjamin Thomas & Elizabeth Young	Petersburg			
17	Field Perkinson & Pricilla Perkinson	Chesterfield	–	6	–
Dec. 6	Thomas Daniel & Lucretia Denhart	Prince George	1	–	–
8	Bartley Kirkland & Lucy Grammer	Do.	–	6	–
..	William Thomson & Nancy Blakely	Petersburg	–	12	–
13	Cary Cotton & Nancy Harrison	Sussex	–	6	–
..	Herbert Lee & Lucy Daniel	Prince George	–	6	–
15	Michael Crasmuch & Elizabeth Barlow	Petersburg	–	12	–
1793					
Jan. 1	Nathan Grammer & Frances Russell	Petersburg	–	18	–
2	Benjamin Montgomery & Sarah Cook	Sussex	1	16	–
10	Robert Totty & Sandal Andrews	Chesterfield	–	6	–
19	Drury Disleman & Margaret Totty	Do.	–	6	–
Feb. 9	David McKittrick & Obedience Cunningham	Petersburg	–	12	–
Mar. 7	Frederick Heath & Judtih Rives	Prince George	1	4	–

MARRIAGES (*Continued*)

1793		County	L	S	D
Mar. 30	John Barber & Pricilla Evans	Chesterfield	–	6	–
Apr. 13	Francis Perkinson & Frances Andrews	Chesterfield	–	6	–
May 2	John Osborne & Jane Pleasant Harrison	Prince George	2	16	–
June 13	Hartwell Gary & Rebecca Butterworth	Do.	1	4	–
15	Richard Titmarsh & Sarah Braser	Do.	1	4	–
July 6	John Gibbs & Mary Gill	Chesterfield	1	4	–
11	Lemuel Noden & Winny Blankenship	Do.	–	5	–
18	Edmund Stone & Sarah Baugh	Petersburg	1	–	–
27	Burwell Sadler & Mary Sturdivant	Prince George	–	19	6
Nov. 2	Thomas Livesay & Sally Livesay	Do.	–	6	–
28	John LeMessurier & Frances Bolling	Petersburg	4	10	–
Dec. 14	Francis Woolfolk & Eliza Taylor	Sussex	2	16	–
21	Benjamin Harrison & Ann Osborne	Prince George	2	16	–
..	William Maitland & Elizabeth Eppes	Do.	7	–	–
25	Neil McLaren & Elizabeth Andrews	Petersburg	–	6	–
1794					
Jan. 9	George Marable & Rebeccah Williams	Prince George	2	2	–
11	Joseph Heath & Ede Williams	Do.	1	16	–
16	John McDowell & Mary Duran	Petersburg	–	12	–
..	George Cox and Mary Friend	Chesterfield	2	2	–
	[NOTTOWAY PARISH]		Dollars		
Jan. 30	Thomas Wilkes & Sally Gunn	Nottoway	5.		
Aug. 21	Francis FitzGerald & Catharine Ward	Do.	11.		
Nov. 27	Melcijah Spragins & Rebecca B. Bolling	Do.	7		
1795					
July 2	Richard Jones (L. D.) & Mary Ellis	Do.	8		
Nov. 19	John Archer Robertson & Elizabeth Royall	Do.	4		
Dec. 3	Richard Kenner Cralle & Sarah Jones	Lunenbg.	8.50		
Dec. 17	William Carter & Jane Crenshaw	Nottoway	4.50		
20	William Robertson & Elizabeth Jane Mason	Lunenbg.	6.		
1796	CUMBERLAND PARISH				
Jan. 12	Richard F. Burks & Betsey Perkerson	Pr. Edwd.	8.80		
Apr. 14	Green Coleman & Betsey Watkins	Nottoway	9.		
July 17	John Stevenson & Mary B. Craig	Lunenbg.	4.25		

MARRIAGES (*Continued*)

1796		County	Dollars
Aug. 21	Thomas Lowry & Martha A. Stevenson	Do.	8.
Oct. 6	Lewellyn Jones & Prudence Ward	Amelia	10.
Nov. 1	John Paterson & Susanna Irby Epes	Nottoway	14.
1797			
Feb. 22	Richard Cross & Sally Chambers	Lunenbg.	5.
Aug. 19	Daniel Anderson & Mary Read Cameron	Do.	
Sept. 12	David Harrison & Mary Moore	Do.	6.
Oct. 26	Daniel Robertson & Betsy Edmundson	Do.	8.
Dec. 21	Ewen Cameron & Frances Buford	Do.	
30	William H. Robertson & Susannah Winn	Nottoy.	13
1798			
Feb. 15	Peter Epes & Rebecca Cross	Lunenburg	8.
23	John Bowers & Betsy Bowers	Do.	5.
24	Matthew Turner & Mary Ingram	Do.	8.
June 14	John Morrison & Mary Chappel Bagley	Do.	8.
16	John Robertson & Polly Davis	Do.	5.
Sept. 1	Littlebury H. Jones & Elizabeth Fitzgerald	Nottoway	10.
Oct. 16	David Street & Sarah Stokes	Lunenbg.	5
Nov. 8	Allan Love & Mary Edmund	Brunswk.	12½
24	Waddy Street & Elizabeth Smith	Lunenbg.	5
Dec. 18	Henry S. Ellis & Sally D. Pettus	Do.	7
1799			
Mar. 20	John R. Mason & Sarah H. Cargill	Brunswk.	15
June 11	Francis Robertson & Mary Jones	Lunenbg.	4
July 19	Miles King & Frances Powell Burwell	Mecklenbg.	8
Sept. 26	Francis Epes & Sarah G. Williams	Nottoway	10
Nov. 22	Richard Boyd & Panthea Burwell	Mecklbg.	16
1800			
Jan. 16	Joseph Townes & Susanna Cralle	Lung.	5
July 10	Richard Epes & Martha G. Williams	Nottoway	10
Oct. 28	Thomas Taylor & Martha C. Hamblin	Meckg.	10
30	William White & Polly Voden Jackson	Lunenbg.	5

Marriages (*Continued*)

1801		County	Dollars
Jan. 29	Robert Clinton Masters & Rebecca Tarry	Lunenbg.	
Oct. 1	Thomas Tredway & Jean Lochead	Do.	
.... 3	Warning Peter Robertson & Lucy Mackie	Do.	
1802			
Jan. 20	Thomas T. Cocke & Lucy W. Nicholson	Nottoway	14
21	John Epes & Frances H. Campbell	Do.	8
May 12	Samuel Broadnax & Margaret B. Holmes	Do.	10
Oct. 7	William Pully, Jr., & Patsy Thompson	Lunenbg.	
Nov. 1	Samuel Jordan & Jean Scott	Do.	7
1803			
Apr. 21	Thomas Gordon & Elizabeth Westmore, widow	Petersburg	14½
May 2	John D. Hawkins & Jane A. Boyd	Mecklenburg	20
14	Robert Boyd & Tabitha Walker	Do.	20
16	James Smith & Ann Park Street	Lunenburg	9
Sept. 15	Ellyson Currie & Anne Gilliam	Petersburg	20
21	Robert Graham & Eliza Lochead	Lunenburg	10
Oct. 20	Alexander Boyd & Matilda Burrell	Mecklg.	16
Nov. 15	John Taylor & Elizabeth Jones	Lunenburg	8
Dec. 24	William Hawkins & Nancy Boyd	Mecklenbg.	20
1804			
Jan. 3	Baxter Jordan & Polly L. Pettus	Lunenburg	9
May 9	Isaac Oliver & Mary A. G. Bacon	Do.	10
Nov. 20	Miles Jordan & Harriott Pettus	Mecklenbg.	10
1805			
Jan. 30	Raleigh Carter & Susanna Stokes	Lunenbg.	5
Mar. 2	John Pettus & Martha Ragsdale	Do.	6
7	Nathan Fletcher & Mary Nicholson	Nottoway	20
Apr. 3	Charles Brydie & Jane F. Billups	Lunenburg	8
July 11	George Craig & Anne W. Chambers	Do.	8
Oct. 17	Richard C. Gregory & Frances Craig	Do.	8
Nov. 4	Francis Fitzgerald & Frances Jones	Nottoway	10

Marriages (*Continued*)

1806		County	Dollars
1806			
Jan. 2	Irby Baker & Dorothy Moor	Lunenbg.	6
May 13	Peter B. Jones & Martha Epes	Nottoway	9
Sept. 18	David G. Leigh & Mary B. Stevenson	Lunenburg	8
27	Rev^d. Andrew Syme & Jean Cameron	Do.	
Oct. 9	David G. Williams & Mary E. P. Doswell	Nottoway	8
1807			
May 4	John Somervill & Betsey Ann Degraffenreid	Lunenburg	12
June 2	Peter Jones, Jr., & Sally G. Bacon	Lunenburg	6
July 9	Samuel G. Williams & Gracie B. Cowan	Do.	8
Nov. 4	John Epes & Mary Ann Wells	Nottoway	20
20	Peter R. Bland & Susanna R. Bacon	Lunenburg	10
24	John Beggis & Sally M. Stokes	Do.	7
1808			
June 29	William Cralle & Sally Jones	Nottoway	12
..	Edward Bland & Rebecca Jones	Do.	20
Dec. 22	Thomas Buford & Martha Manson	Do.	6
1809			
Jan. 16	Archibald Hatchett & Mary Epes Jones Lamkin	Lunenbg.	10
Feb. 14	Edmund F. Taylor & Petronilla Lamkin	Do.	9
May 18	John Hamlin & Mary Williams	Do.	8
Aug. 14	William Stokes & Martha A. Lowry	Lunenbg.	4
Sept. 16	Boswell B. Degraffenreidt & Frances Garland	Do.	7
30	Peter Bland & Martha W. Nash	Prince Edward	20
Nov. 1	John Vaughan & Sally Thompson	Lunenbg.	
14	Stephen Pettus & Susanna Jordan	Do.	5
Dec. 21	Joseph G. Williams & Catharine Fitzgerald	Nottoway	10
1810			
July 12	William B. Cowan & Catharine G. Epes	Nottoway	14

Marriages (*Continued*)

1810		County	Dollars
Dec. 20	Thomas Fitzgerald & Ann R. Williams	Nottoway	20
1811			
Jan. 22	Samuel D. Davies & Mary Randolph Stout	Lunenburg	6
Feb. 21	Thomas Bolling & Eliza Williams	Do.	10
Apr. 9	Henry Newbill & Jane Moore	Do.	6
1812			
July 2	John C. Chappell & Milly T. Sandys	Lunenburg	10
1814			
May 24	John Stokes & Susanna R. Jones	Lunenburg	8
Dec. 6	William G. Pettus & Jane C. Lamkin	Lunenburg	8
1815			
Jan. 4	Charles Betts & Martha C. Chambers	Lunenburg	10
Oct. 14	Henry H. Burwell & Catharine Buford	Lunenburg	10

A Register of Baptisms & Funerals For Cumberland Parish

By JOHN CAMERON, *Rector*.

1815

Lucy Park Smith Dau. of James Smith & Ann Park his wife, was born May 25th, 1814, & baptized February 6th, 1815.

John Ragsdale died Nov. 30th, 1814 & was buried March 19th, 1815.

Martha Lenis Dau. of John Pettus & Martha his wife, was born Jan. 13, & baptized March 19th, 1815.

Charles Smith died the 27th & was buried the 29th of March, 1815.

Susanna H. Buford, wife of Abraham Buford, of Nottoway, died October the 5th, 1814, & was buried April 2, 1815.

George Ragsdale died Feb. 15th & was buried April 9th, 1815.

Milly Ragsdale, wife of William Ragsdale, died Feb. 6th & was buried April 9th, 1815.

Peter Jones Sen. died the 24th of January & was buried the 7th of April, 1815.

Elizabeth Turner, an adult, Dau. of James Turner of Warren County in N. Carolina, was baptized May 28th, 1815.

Sarah Williams, Dau. of Fran Epes & Sarah G. his wife was born Dec. 26th, 1808 & baptized May 31st, 1815.

Martha, Dau. of the above born May 17th, 1811 & baptized May

Eliza Ann, Dau. of the above, was born Sept. 2, 1813, & baptized May 31st, 1815.

James Henderson, Son of Isaac Oliver & Mary A. G. his wife, was born April 7th, 1814, & baptized May 31st, 1815.

Thomas Buford, Son of Thomas Buford & Martha his wife, was born

William Waller, Son of Edmund F. Taylor & Petronella his wife, was born April 9th, 1813, & baptized Aug. 6th, 1815.

George Griffin Lewis, Son of the above, was born February 13th, & baptized Augt. 6th, 1815.

CHAPTER XV

The Vestry Book, 1746-1816

HE Vestry Book of Cumberland Parish is presented in print for the first time in this chapter. The manuscript volume from which the copy here appearing was taken is, as already mentioned, in the library of the Theological Seminary at Alexandria, Virginia. This volume the Virginia State Library carefully copied by the photostat process. When the writer conceived the idea of printing the Vestry Book, and thus making its contents available to interested persons, he was unwilling to trust anyone to make a copy for printing, unless he, personally, had the opportunity to compare and verify it. This desire led him to secure for his own use a photostat copy of the entire volume as it is now preserved.

The difficulty of deciphering some of the writing in the volume furnished the principal reason why he desired to personally compare a typewritten copy, for printing, with the original text.

The writer, in preparing this material for printing, while endeavoring to present the text, entire and intact, errors of spelling and all, has indulged the liberty of transposing some (a very small part), of the material of the volume. This he has done for good reasons, which may now be explained.

It is evident that many of the pages of the volume became at some time wholly detached from the book; it is also highly probable that the pages of the book were originally not numbered at all, or that there was confusion in the numbering, and that at a time, after the pages had become detached (and a few lost), there was an effort by someone to arrange them in order and to number them. There are as many as three separate numberings on some of the pages, all of which can be accounted for, but which it would serve no particular purpose to discuss here.

There are a few marginal notations written by Rev. W. C. Phillips, which indicate that he had difficulty about the proper assembling of the pages of the book. Thus on page 212, opposite those figures at the top of the page, he has written: "or 202 See date of Vestry meeting."

Again on blank page 220 he has written: "See page 255. William C. Phillips, 1830," a reference which is not clearly understood unless he desired to direct attention to the fact that on that page began a record of minutes of the Vestry, which was at that point inserted among the Processioners' returns.

An examination of the volume shows that some pages are certainly, and others most probably not, in the order in which they first appeared in the original book. Thus two pages with Processioners' returns made in 1784 appear just ahead of returns made in 1760. Not only by the date, but by the numbers as well—the returns are those numbered 23 to 29—it appears that these pages belong to a later date in the volume. They have been transferred herein to their proper places.

Again a part of the proceedings of the Vestry on December 13, 1771, was the entry of a series of orders appointing processioners. This part of the proceedings of the Vestry appear in the volume, not among the minutes of the Vestry, but in the back of the book among the Processioners' returns. This part of the material of the volume has been transferred to its appropriate chronological place among the Vestry minutes.

A similar situation occurs respecting the appointment of Processioners at the meeting of the Vestry on February 26, 1776; and a similar transposition has been made.

In this last named instance there is a reference in the order as follows: "See page two hundred and fifty-five, fifty-six, fifty-seven and two hundred & fifty-eight," which were referred to for the descriptions of the precincts.

No change in the contents of the text has been made in any instance, but the material has been simply transferred to a different place, in the volume, for the reasons stated.

Vestry Book
of
Cumberland Parish
Lunenburg County, Virginia,
1746-1816

Vestry Book

of

Cumberland Parish

Lunenburg County, Virginia.

[The first two pages of the Vestry Book are missing and the existing record begins abruptly in the midst of the record of the minutes of what was evidently the first meeting of the vestry as follows:]

A. D.
1746

Matthew Talbot Gent. is made choice of as a Vestryman to serve in this parish in the room of John Cauldwell Gent. who has refused to take the oath of a Vestryman and resign'd.

Order'd that John Twitty inspect into the treatment that Howard Jackson and John Williams give two orphan children under their care and by what title they hold them and report the same.

Order'd that David Stokes John Twitty and Lyddal Bacon fix on some convenient place near Reedy creek to erect a Chappel 48 by 24 and when they have so done to treat with workmen or let the building to undertakers as they think fit.

Thomas Bouldin Abraham Martin Clement Read are appointed to fix on some convenient place near Little Roanoke to erect a Chappel and to make report to the next Vestry.

Lewis Delony William Howard and John Boyd are appointed to fix on some convenient place near the fork of Roanoke to erect a Chappel, and make report to the next Vestry.

Thomas Boulden Matthew Talbot and John Phelps are appointed to fix on some convenient place near Ottar river to build a house 20 feet square for the reader to read in and make report to the next Vestry.

Robert Allen and Josias Randal are appointed Readers in their Several Precincts.

Lewis Delony has leave given him to erect a Pew for his family in a vacant place in the Church near his house.

Clement Read
L. Delony   C Wardens

A. D.
1747

At a Vestry held for this Parish in the County of Lunenburg, the 8th day of Sep^t 1747.

Present   Lewis Delony   David Stokes
           Clement Read   Daniel Ferth
           Matthew Talbot   Thomas Boulden   Vestrymen
           Abraham Martin   John Twitty
           Lyddal Bacon

Henry Bates on his motion is exempted from paying Parish Levies for the future.

Abram Michaux is also exempted from pay Parish levies for the future.

1. Order'd that the precinct from flatt Creek to the extent of the County downwards and from the line to Maherin river be one, and that Daniel Nance and Drury Malone be processioners of the same.

2. Order'd that below Hounds Creek and Reedy Creek between Nottoway and Maherin be one precinct above and below the said Creeks and between the aforesaid Rivers to the extent of the County upward and downwards and that Samuel Jones and Reps Jones be appointed processioners of the same.

3. Order'd that from flatt Creek to Allens Creek between the Country line and Maherin be one precinct and that Frances Howard and John Speed be appointed processioners of the same.

4. Order'd that from Allens Creek to Bouchers Creek from Hogans Road to the Country line be one precinct and that

James Coleman and Bird Thomas Lanier be processioners of the same.

5. Order'd that from Bouchers Creek to Irbys Tract be one precinct, and John Cargill and Samuel Harris be processioners of the same.

6. Order'd that from Irbys Tract to Kings Road to South Maherin be one precinct and that William Harriss and Samuel Goode be processioners of the same.

7. Order'd that from Kings Road to roanoke as farr as Twittys path be one precinct and that Charles Allen and Joseph Perrin be processioners of the same.

8. Order'd that from Twittys path up Roanoke to the extent of the county on Kings road be one precinct and that Richard Womack & Philip Jones be processioners of the same.

9. Order'd that from the South fork of Maherin to the north Fork to Kings road be one precinct and that James Daniel and Jesse Brown be processioners of the same.

10. Order'd that from little Roanoke to Cub creek be one precinct and that John David and William Johnson be processioners of the same.

11. Order'd that between Cub creek and falling river to the extent of the County be one precinct and that Mattox Mays and William Fuqua be processioners of the same.

12. Order'd that from falling river to Otter River be one precinct and John Webster and W^m. Hunter be processioners of the same.

13. Order'd that from Otter to the extent of the County upwards be one precinct and that Richard and William Callaway be processioners of the same.

14. Order'd that in the fork from Stanton river to the Line as farr as Miry Creek to be one precinct and that Andrew Wade and Wm. Wynne be processioners of the same.

15. Order'd that from Miry Creek to Wilsons be one precinct and that Hugh Moor and Robert Wilky be processioners of the same.

16. Order'd that from the mouth of Grassy creek to the mouth of Hico be one precinct and that Richard Griffin and Luke Smith be processioners of the same.

17 Order'd that from the Mouth of Grassy creek downwards to the Country line be one precinct and James Mitchel and John Gillam be processioners of the same.

18 Order'd that from the mouth of Hico upwards to the extent of the County be one precinct, and Alexander Irwin and Francis Lawson be processioners of the same.

Order'd that Cornelius Cargill Gent be allow'd 700 lbs. Tobacco for attending and burying Darby Talen.

Thomas Boulden, Abraham Martin and Clement Read pursuant to an order of Vestry have view'd the most convenient place to erect and build a Church on little Roanoke and reported that at or near a Spring on Randolphs and Talbots road near the fork be the most convenient place.

The report of Thomas Boulden and Matthew Talbot in pursuance of an order of this Vestry for fixing a place to build a Church at, say that where the road goes from Irwins ford to Callaways mill is the most convenient place and that the reader continue at the school house till the same be built.

Clement Read
L. Delony } C Wardens.

At a Vestry held for this Parish in Lunenburg County the 7th day of December, 1747.

Present

Lewis Delony   Daniel Ferth
Clement Read   John Twitty and
Thomas Boulden   Abraham Martin
Matthew Talbot

Vestrymen

Clement Read and Lewis Delony chosen Church Wardens for the ensuing year.

To John Speed as Clerk and Sexton	1200
To Robert Allen a reader	750
To James Read Dº	750
To James Wood Dº	750

To John Speed as Clerk of the Vestry		500
To Dº for Extry Services		300
To Robert Jones att for prose 3 suits on behalf of the Parish Vs Dean Vs Parish Vs Doran	2 5 0	
To Clemt Read fees on Dº		400
To Thomas Boulden his account	2 0 0	
Lewis Delony's acct inspected and allow'd bal. to pish.	72 11 0	
To John Twittys list of insolvents		697
To Philip Jones		17
To Alexander Irwin		17
To Charles Talbot		476
To John Sifer		17
To John Watson for keeping his sister		1000
To Clement Read John Hungarfords acct.	1 13 1½	
To James Wood		500
To Cornelius Cargill for attends and Buriing Darby Talen		700
To Lawrence Wingfield		750
To Tobacco rais'd as a fund to be paid by the Collector to the C. Wardens to be by them sold and acc'ted for		15000
		23824
Cr in the Sheriff's hands		2030
		21794
6p Ct for collecting		1307
Depositum		1203
Parish Cr.		24304
By 1519 Tyths at 16p pole		24304

Lewis Delony Abraham Martin and Daniel Ferth are appointed to fix on some convenient place near the fork of Roanoke to erect a Chappel and make report to next Vestry.

Order'd that David Williams be exempted from paying parish levies for the future.

Order'd that Abraham Ardin and Samuel Harris are appointed readers the old readers are continued and their respective salaries are to be 1000 lbs. Tobacco for the future.

Order'd that Mr Talbot Mr Boulden Mr Martin Mr Read Mr Ferth and Mr Twitty view the most convenient place for a Church near little Roanoke & make report to the next Vestry.

Clement Read
L. Delony   C Wardens

A. D.
1748

At a Vestry held for this parish in the County of Lunenburg the Second day of August 1748.

Present

Lewis Delony	Thomas Boulden
Clement Read	Abraham Martin
William Howard	John Twitty
Lyddal Bacon	and Matthew Talbot
David Stokes	Vestrymen.

Letters recommendatory from Sir William Gooch Barronet, Lt Governour and Mr Commissary Dawson in favour of the Reverend Mr John Brunskill Clerk, together with his Deacons and Priests orders being presented to this Vestry are willing to pay all due respects and defference to the Governour and Mr Commissarys recommendation and are willing to receive the said Mr Brunskill into this parish as a Minister of the Gospel for one year and at the expiration thereof to cause to be paid to him the salary by law appointed. But for as much as they are not willing to be compelled to entertain and receive any Minister other than such as may answer the end of his Ministerial Function they only intend to entertain and receive him as a probationer for one year being fully minded and desirous that if they should in that time disapprove his conduct or behaviour they may have it in their power to receive another.

Order'd that the Reverend Mr Brunskill preach alternately at one of the four Churches in this County (viz) at the Church near Mr Delony's at the Church near Mr Bacons at the Church near little Roanoke and at the Church near the fork. And at the Chappel near Mr Phelps's four times in the year. Also at or near Hogans on the South river four times in the year. In the months of April, October June and December.

Order'd that a Chappel be built at the place appointed near Mr Phelps's 36 by 24 and that Mr Martin Mr Boulden and Mr Delony let the same to undertakers.

Order'd that the Church appointed to be built near Little Roanoke of 24 by 48 be lett to undertakers by L. Delony Abraham Martin and Clement Read as soon as they conveniently can.

Henry Isbell is appointed Clerk of the Church near little roanoke and to be paid the usual salary.

Order'd that L. Delony Abra. Martin and Clem. Read lett the Church at the fork to undertakers and fix on a convenient place to lett the same.

Order'd that Capt Howard Mr Delony Mr Bacon Mr Stokes and Mr Twitty are appointed to view the several lands offer'd to be sold for a Glebe and make report to the next Vestry.

Clemt Read
L. Delony

At a Vestry held for this parish the eighth day of Feb. 1748 [1749].

Present

Clemt Read	David Stokes
Matthew Talbot	Thos. Boulden
John Hall	John Twitty
Lyddal Bacon	Vestrymen

Order'd and 'tis the opinion of this vestry that the Reverend Mr John Brunskill be reciev'd Minister of the parish and be paid the salary by law appointed.

Dr.

To the Reverend Mr John Brunskill	16000
To 4 p Cent for cask thereon	640

To 6 p Ct for conveniency		960
To John Speed as Clerk and Sexton		1500
To D° as clerk of the Vestry		500
To John Watson for keeping his sister		1000
To John Blaxton for clearing Reedy Creek Church yard	00 10 0	
To James Read or his administrators		1000
To James Wood a reader		1000
To John Hix D°		1000
To Robert Allen D°		1000
To Abraham Arden D°		1000
To Samuel Harriss D°		1000
To the Reverend Mr Ormsby for 3 Sermons		1050
To the C. Wardens for maintaining Hungerfords child		1000
To John Twitty for money advanc'd for D°	1 00 0	
To John Gwinn for his list of insolvents		225
To Charles Talbots D°		594
To Mary Upton	1 00 0	
To the Church wardens for the support of Michael Charlesworth	———	1000
	2 10 0	
To John Williams		21
To the Collector 6 p C^t on 41548 lbs. Tob.		2492
		32982
Depositum		8566
Cr		41548
By 1598 Tyths at 26 p pole is		41548

Order'd that John Twitty and John Cox view the most convenient place to build a Chappel on and make report to the next Vestry.

Order'd that Matthew Talbot, John Phelps Thos Boulden and Clement Read or any two of them agree with workmen to build a Church on Otter River pursuant to a former order of Vestry.

Mr Hall and Mr Talbots chosen C. Wardens for the ensuing year.

Order'd that they recieve the depositum & acct with the next Vestry.

Order'd that Clemt Read Matthew Talbot John Hall Lyddal Bacon Hugh Lawson and Mr Stokes settle with the late church wardens

    John Brunskill   John Hall
            Matthew Talbot

At a Vestry held for this parish at Mr Bouldens on the eleventh day of November 1749

  Present

Thomas Boulden	John Cox
Field Jefferson	Francis Ellidge
John Edloe	Abraham Martin &
Matthew Talbot	Clement Read
Luke Smith	Vestrymen

John Speed is chosen Clerk of this Vestry & to have the usual salary.

Henry Isbell chosen Clk of Little roanoke Church the usual salary.

James Wood continued Reader at the usual salary.

Robert Allen the same order.

Abraham Ardin the same order.

Samuel Harriss the same only Daniel Barker to have 1 years salary.

John Hix continued Clerk of Reedy C Church the usual salary.

Mr Cox, Mr Martin and Mr Ellidge or any two of them to state and settle an Acc^t with the Church Wardens of the late Vestry and report a state thereof to this Vestry.

Order'd that the same persons settle with the late C. Wardens in the same manner.

Order'd that Mr Boulden Mr Edloe and Clem^t Read or any two of them state an acct of the demands this parish hath against the parish of St Andrews in the County of Brunswick settle the same with the members of that Parish with power to demand and receive of them what shall be found due and to render an acct of their proceeding to this Vestry.

Order'd that Mʳ Cox Mʳ Jefferson Mʳ Martin and Mʳ Ellidge treat with workmen to undertake and build a Church near the Court House of this Coty at such place as they shall think most convenient and that Mackness Good and Julius Nichols assist them in search of a convenient Spring the Church to be fourty by twenty four.

The petition of Wᵐ Hill and others for a Church rejected.

Ordered that Mʳ Jefferson Mʳ Martin and Mʳ Smith treat with workmen to build a Church 40 by 24 at or near the fork and search for the most convenient place to set it.

Order'd that 1000 lbs. Toba. be levied annually and paid to John Caldwell Gent. towards the payment of a reader on the Cub creek settlement.

Dr.

To the Reverend Mʳ John Brunskill	16000
To 4 p Cᵗ for cask	640
To John Speed as Clerk and Sexton	1500
To D° as Clerk of the Vestry	500
To John Watson for keeping his sister	1000
To John Blaxton Sexton of Reedy Creek Church	300
To Henry Isbell Clerk of little roanoke Church	1000
To James Wood another Clerk	1000
To John Hix D°	1000
To Robert Allen D°	1000
To Abraham Arding D°	1000
To Daniel Basket for Samuel Harriss D°	1000
To Wᵐ. Dobbyns for his insolvents	1650
To D°	150

To Drury Allen for Burying Wᵐ Dalton	£1	00	0
To John Bacon for burying Joseph Jeter	5	00	0
To John Hill for burying a poor Traveller	2	00	0
To John Boyd for burying Thoˢ Bryant	1.	10	0
To Wᵐ Dobyns for elements for the Sacrament	0	10	0

To D° for tending the Election of Vestry	2	10	0
To John Austin for a Coffin for John Hunks	0	10	0
To Henry Cockram for a Tub in Reedy C. Church Spring	0	10	0
To the C. Wardens for Register book for this parish	3	00	0
To John Wyborne			26
To a Depositum in the hands of the Collector			40721
To the Collector 6 p C^t			4109
			72596

Cr.

By 1851 Tyths at 39 p pole is	72189
By Wm Dobyns	364
By a fraction due to the Collector	43
	72596

Order'd that Thos Boulden & John Cox be C. wardens the ensuing year.

Order'd that Matthew Talbot provide for Isaac Watkins & bring his Acct to next Vestry.

Order'd that David Gwin have till the first of July next to Comply with his first agreement.

Order'd that Wm Dobyns have a Copy of his List of Insolvents referr'd to this Vestry this year in order to do his Endeavor to Collect the same of the Several persons and acct for them at the Laying the next Levy.

Order'd that Mr Clement Read be allow'd his Toba: on the producing his Acct, order'd out of the depositum in the hands of the Collector.

Order'd the Collector pay John Cauldwell 1000 lbs. Tobacco out of the Depositum.

          Thomas Boulden
          John Cox

At a Vestry held for this parish on the 12th day of Feb. 1749 [1750].
Present

	Thomas Boulden	C. Wardens
	John Cox	
Field Jefferson	Francis Ellidge	
John Edloe		Vestrymen
Clement Read	and Wm Embry	

The Reverend Mr George Purdie having presented to this Vestry Letters from the president of the Council of this Colony and Mr Commissary Dawson recommending him to succeed Mr Brunskill as Minister to this parish. This Vestry on consideration thereof think fitt to receive him the said Purdie as a probationer for Six months and that he be entituled to receive half the Salary Levied at the last Vestry as an Article in the said levies to the Reverend Mr John Brunskill & The Depositum of the other Moiety thereof to be referr'd to the Consideration of the next Vestry. And it is mutually agreed between the said Mr Purdie and this vestry that if either hath design or inclination to part with other that they respectively give each other Six months notice. 'Tis farther consider'd that Mr Purdies firs Six months Commence from the first day of January last.

George Purdie
Thos Boulden
John Cox

At a Vestry held for this parish the 1st of October, 1750.
Present

Thos Boulden	Fran^s Ellidge
Field Jefferson	Wm Embry
Peter Fontane	Abra: Martin
Matt Talbot	& Clem^t Read
John Cox	Vestrymen

Field Jefferson and John Edloe are chosen Church Wardens for the Ensuing year.

Order'd that 1000 lbs. Tob: be raised and deposited in the hands of Mʳ Edloe for the use of Eleanor Hungerford & her children.

Wᵐ Broomfield to be allow'd one parish levie at Laying the Levy on.

Order'd that the Collector pay Mʳ Matthew Talbot 35 £ Current money in part of payment for a Church.

Also that he pay the Dᵒ Talbot £ 3 13 for his Accᵗˢ.

Order'd that Wᵐ Redman he allow'd 1000 lbs. Tob: for Supporting Michael Charles [illegible].

Order'd that Robᵗ Allen be Sexton at Otter R. Church the usual salary.

Order'd that a Vestry be held the 22nd of next month.

Order'd that Wᵐ Hunt be Clerk at Blue Stone Church.

Order'd that Richard Hix be Sexton at L. Roanoke Church usual allowance. The Reverend Mʳ George Purdie having given this Vestry notice that his affairs calling him abroad and that he cannot officiate as Minister of this parish Longer than till the last of March next begs leave to resign.

Order'd that an allowance be made at the Laying the next levy to the Said Mʳ Purdie till the said last day of March in proportion as the law directs.

This Vestry recommends the Reverend Mʳ Geo. Purdie to the Reverend and Honourable Mʳ Commissary Dawson as a person who hath with diligence and Industry perform'd his Ministerial Function in the discharge of every duty Incumbent upon him to pform as a Minister of the Gospel in this parish In consideration of which the parish has made him an allowance of 2000 lbs. Tob: Extraordinary and having Signify'd to us that his necessary affairs call him abroad he has Resign'd.

Order'd the Collector pay Mʳ Gwyn the money due to him for building Church.

Order'd Cha Sullivant be allow'd 1000 lbs. Tob: for the trouble of his house.

George Purdie
Field Jefferson.

At a Vestry held for this parish the 22nd day of November, 1750.

Present

Mr Boulden	Mr Martin
Mr Cox	Mr Talbot
Mr Jefferson	Mr Phelps
Mr Fontane	& Colo Read
Mr Ellidge	Vestrymen

Dr.

To the Revd Mr John Brunskill for 18 weeks salary in this parish	6000
To Tob: Levied for the present Minister	16000
To Cask thereon	640
To the Revd Mr Purdie as p order	2000
To Mr Edloe for Hungerford and her children as p order	1000
To Wm Broomfield	39
To Wm Redman for supporting Michael Charlesworth	1000
To Charles Sullivant as p order	1000
To Philip Young for the Support of his Mother and Sister	1000
To John Speed as Clerk and Sexton	1700
To John Watson for keeping his sister	1000
To John Speed as Clerk of the Vestry	500
To John Blaxton as Sexton at Reedy C. Church	300
To Henry Isbell Clk L. Roanoke Church	1200
To James Wood a Reader	1200
To John Hix Clk Reedy creek Church	1200
To Robert Allen Clk O^r River Church	1200
To D^o as Sexton	300
To Abraham Arden a reader	1200
To Richard Hix as Sexton	300
To the Ex^{or} of John Sullivant 1 Tyth overlisted	39
To John Denny and John Denny juⁿ each 39	78
To Abra Martin 2 D^o	78
To Henry Embry 5 Levies twice listed	195
To Wm Embry 4 D^o	156

To Samuel Harris a Reader	1200
To Wm Cauldwell to imploy a reader	1000
To John Cox C: Warden for his Elements	400
To Wm Embry for Anne Barnes	350
To Field Jefferson for burying Henry Jolly a poorman	250
To Wm Redman	39
To John Este	39
To Thomas Harriss	39
To John Steward for John Wyborne	39
To Robert Weakly	39
To Clem^t Reads acct.	126..
To the Admi of Dobyns Insolv^ts	273..
To Saml Hariss D^o	105..
To the Collector 6 p C^t on 58548 lbs. Toba.	23...
[Part of record missing]	......

A. D.
1751

Order'd that the Collector pay Mr Fontaine 400 Tobacco to be by him apply'd to'rd the maintainance of Wm Brooks as he thinks fit.

Order'd that the Collector pay Wm Harris 52 lbs. Tobacco on his producing his receipt and the Clerks comparing that with the list of Tyths.

James Handly Exempted from payment of parish Levies for the future.

Owen Sullivant to be paid £3 for burying a poor man by the Collector.

Order'd that Wm Cook read upon blackwater at the houses of Joseph Rentfroe and Mark Cole and be allowd the Usual Salary.

Richard Jones to officiate for Sam Harriss the ensuing year.

To pay the Reverend Mr Purdie 14480 lbs. Tobacco out of the Tobacco levi'd last year to pay the present Minister.

Dr.

To the Reverend Mr William Kay Minister	16000
To Cask thereon	640

To Philip Young for the Support of his mother & sister		1000
To John Speed as Clerk and Sexton		1700
To D° for Extry Services		500
To D° as Clerk of the vestry		500
To John Watson for keeping his sister		1000
To John Blaxton as Sexton of Reedy C. Church		300
To Henry Isbel Clk of Little Roanok Church		1200
To James Wood a Reader		1200
To John Hix Clk Reedy creek Church		1200
To Robert Allen Clk and Sexton of Otter river Church		1500
To Abraham Ardin Clerk		1200
To Richard Hix Sexton		300
To Samuel Harriss a reader at the Fork Church		1200
To John Cox for providing the Elements		400
To William Caldwell for providing a reader		1200
To Mr Purdie for the Cask of 8000 lbs. Tobacco		320
To Margret Baker for burying a poor man	£5 0 0	
To Richard Witton for the negros	0 7 6	
To Owen Sullivant for burying a poor man	3 0 0	
To John Speed for benches at the Church		100
To Clement Reads Account		3575
To Cash levi'd to buy books	10 0 0	
To Mr Fontain p. Wm Brooks		800
To John Blackwell		28
	18 7 6	3586..

From the Mouths of Cane and Cherrystone creeks upwards to where the Cou[nty line?] crosses Irwin and the head of Banister be one precinct Peter Wilson & Abra. Little proces....

From thence all the land on Smiths river and all its branches from the place where the Co[unty line?] crosses it upwards be one precinct that Henry Lansford & Wm Blevin procession the same.

From thence all the lands on all the waters of Dan and Mayo rivers with their several branches as high as Augusta line be one precinct that Henry Short & Hamar Crites procession [same].

From the mouth of Allens creek to Mayo's ford and upwards to a cross line from the head of Banister to the mouth of Pig river be one precinct that Luke Smith and James Collins procession the same.

From thence all the lands on the waters of Pig river from the mouth upwards be one precinct and that Thomas Hall and Timothy Dalton procession the same.

From thence on all the waters between Smiths and Mayo's and the main Stanton as high as Augusta line be one precinct that James Standeford & Robert Jones procession the same.

That all the lands on Grassy creek the Country line Roanoke Dan and Hico rivers be one precinct that Luke Smith and Josiah Seat procession the same.

That all the lands between Hico and Dan rivers and the Country be one precinct and Francis Lawson and James Irwin do procession the same.

Whereas it was agreed at a Vestry held for this parish the 1st day of Octo^r 1750 with the Reverend Mr William Kay that the said Mr Kay should act as a minister of the gospel in this parish from the first day of April 1751 as a probationer for two years and at the same time it was also agreed that at the expiration of one year from the said first day of April the said Kay and the said Vestry that if either disliked other that there should be a years notice for each to provide the said agreement is hereby confirmd and accordly by mutual assent Entered.

Mr Lyddal Bacon Elected Vestry man in the room of Mr Edloe.

Mr Robert Wade the same in the room of Mr Ellidge.

Order'd that Margret Baker be paid £5 for taking care of and Burying Thomas Tucker.

Order'd that John Blackwell be allow'd 28 lbs. Tob: as Constable.

Order'd that Joseph Ray hath farther time till October next to finish his Church and that the present Collector pay him £42-17-6 out of the money in his hands.

Order'd that Mr Witton be allow'd 7/6 to be paid the negro's for Burying Byrds Doctor.

Order'd that Richard Brooks be allow'd 1000 lbs. Tobacco for maintaining Anne Barnes.

Order'd the Church wardens for Nathaniel Russell 2000 lbs. of Toba. for his care and cure.

... 58548 .. [illegible]

A. D.
1752

Mr Nash and Mr Walton are Elected Vestry men in the room of Capt Wade and Capt Smith.

It appears that the Collectors owe the Parish £ 12-9-11 on Settlement of their Acc^{ts} Order'd that they pay the same to the Church wardens of this Parish.

Lyddal Bacon
Abram Martin

A. D.
1753

At a Vestry held for this parish the 4th of April 1753

Present

The Revd Mr Wm Kay	William Embry
Abraham Martin	John Cox
Lyddal Bacon	Peter Fontaine
Field Jefferson	and Geo. Walton
Clement Read	Vestrymen

In pursuance of a former order of Vestry the persons appointed to view 302 acres of Land belonging to John Cox Gent. for a Glebe do vallue the said land to £ 75-10 to which this Vestry have farther agreed for the same and under Cox's conveyance accordingly it is thereupon order'd that the parish do pay the said Summ to the said Cox.

The Vestry do think it absurd and unreasonable there should be any Church or Chapel built between Reedy Creek Church and little roanoke Church.

Wm Kay
Lyddal Bacon
Abra: Martin

A. D.
1754

At a Vestry held for this parish the 2nd day of January 1754

Present

Thomas Boulden	Peter Fontaine
John Cox	Wm Kay
Abra: Martin	Lyddal Bacon
Clement Read	Geo: Walton

Vestry men

Dr.

To the Reverend Mr William Kay	16000
To Cask thereon	640
To Shrinkage	640
To Do for the 2 last years	1280
To Thos Boulden for the support of Mary Jones & her daughter	1500
To John Speed as Clk and Sexton of Roanoke Church	1700
To Do as Clk of the Vestry	500
To John Watson for keeping his sister	1000
To John Blaxton Sexton of reedy creek church	300
To Henry Isbell Clk of Little Roanoke Church	1200
To John Hix Clk of Reedy creek Church	1200
To Robert Allen as Clk & Sexton of Otter river Church	1500
To William Hunt Clk of Bluestone Church	1200
To John Speed for the support of Mary & Betty Hatsel	600
To Do for Agnes Dodd	600
To Wm Embry for the support of Elinour Hungerford	1000
To John Jennings for burying Wingfield Cobb 0 13 9	
To Thos Hawkins for supporting the son of Pat Frail	1000
To William Bacon for his Acct. 6 0 0	
To Paul Carrington his Account 4 17 9	
To Richard Jones Clk of a church	1200
To James Wood Do	1200
To Wm Boulden for Tarring the Church 7 0 0	
To Clement Read for copying the List of Tyths	196

To Abra: Martin paid Hanah Austin care of Agnes Jones	6	0	0	
To D° to Hugh Creighton for nursing a bastard child	5	0	0	
To Richard Brooks for Anne Barnes				1200
To John Cox his list insolvents				2147
To D° for the Elements one year				400
To D° for D°				133
To James Hunt to imploy a reader				1200
To Mr Garland for a reader	4	0	0	
To the Collector 6 p C^t for collecting				3249
To a Depositum				11679.
	33	11	6	54464

Cr.

By 2462 tiths at 22 lbs. Tob: p pole is 54164

Order'd that Mr Kay preach twice a year at Rich: Palmers to the grassy C. people.

Mr Walton and Mr Nash Chosen Church wardens.

Wm Kay
Geo: Walton.

At a Vestry held for this Parish the 6th day of August 1754

Present

Clement Read	Wm Embry
Thos Boulden	Lyddal Bacon
Peter Fontaine	Field Jefferson
John Cox	Abraham Martin
Geo: Walton	Vestrymen

Mr Fontaine intending shortly to leave the pish desires to be Exempted from the Vestry.

Thos Hawkins made choice of for a Vestryman in the room of Mr Fontaine.

absent Abra: Martin

Order'd that the Vestry be adjourn'd till tomorrow twelve of Clock.

Geo: Walton.

At a Vestry continued for this parish the 7th day of August 1754

Present

Clement Read
John Cox
Field Jefferson
George Walton
Tho⁸ Hawkins

Lyddal Bacon
Wᵐ Embry
Abra: Martin
Tho⁸ Nash

Vestrymen

absent Abra: Martin
Present Tho⁸ Boulden

Order'd that the Collector of the parish levy pay the Sherif of this County the Ballance of an Execution levi'd on the Estate of Abra: Martin to James Roberts Assignee of James Ray on a judgment obtained against him by the said Roberts in the General Court and that he settle the said Ballance with Geo: Walton one of the Church wardens who is to report the State of the Account to the next Vestry.

Absent John Cox

Order'd that the residue of the money in the Collectors hands after paying the above Execution be paid by them to Robert Wade assignee of William Moss for services done for the parish.

Order'd that the Collectors after payment of the above orders pay Colo Jefferson 400 lbs. Tob: for his Ferry.

Order'd that the present Collectors settle their parish Accᵗˢ with the Church wardens and pay them, and they to Accᵗ for the same at next Vestry and that they settle with the old Collectors and report the same & from the year 1749.

Tho⁸ Nash
Geo Walton.

At a Vestry held for this parish the 7th day of Novem 1754

Present

The Revd Mʳ Wᵐ Kay
Tho⁸ Boulden
John Cox
Tho⁸ Hawkins
Field Jefferson

Abraham Martin
Thomas Nash &
George Walton

Vestrymen

Dr.

To the Reverend Mr Wm Kay salary, cask and Shrinkage				17280
To Thos Boulden for Mary Young and her daughter				1500
To the Reverd Mr Kay for preaching twice at Palmers				600
To John Speed as Clk Sexton and Clk of the Vestry				2200
To John Watson for keeping his sister				1000
To John Blaxton Sexton Reedy Creek Church				300
To Henry Isbel Clk little roanoke Church				1200
To John Hix D^o Reedy Creek Church				1200
To Robert Allen D^o and Sexton at Otter river Church				1500
To Wm Hunt D^o at Bluestone Church				1500
To John Speed for Support of Mary & Betty Hatsel and Agnes Dodd				1200
To Richard Yancy for Patrick Frail				1000
To Wm Embry for Elinor Hungerford				1000
To Richard Brooks for Anne Barnes				1500
To Benjamin Clements for doctoring J and Mary Brown	£5	10	0	
To D^o for doctoring M. Young	4	0	0	
To John Chandler				1300
To M. Hunt for 17 Insolvents				374
To J Hobson for 59 D^o				1298
To J. McNess for 20 D^o				440
To W^m. Irwin for 80 D^o				1760
To John Cole for one Levy 1752				25
To Richard Booker 7 levies last year				154
To William Goode for Insolvents				84
To Lyddal Bacon for John Stone for Tarring R. C. Church	6	13	0	
To Robert Poe a Sexton				300
To Wm Hunt one years salary omitted if due to be pd by C: Wardens				1200
To D^o for Extry Services				300
To James Hunt Gent to imploy a reader				1200
To Ben: Howard his Account				98
To the Reverend Mr Kay for Elements &c				500
To Paul Carrington for Indentures	7	13	9	
To Thos Harvy to employ a reader				1200

To Thos Boulden for J. Adams				1000
To L: Claiborne his Acct.	8	1	3	
To Wm Lax to support his Child				1000
To 6 p Ct Collecting 59620 lbs. Tob:				3577
To a depositum in Collectors hands				10830
	31	18	—	59620

Cr.

By 2710 Tyths at 22 lbs. Tob: p pole is   59620

Ordered John Cox and Abra: Martin be first paid out of the Depositum.

John Speed and Wm Watkins are Elected Vestrymen in Lieu of Mr Talbott & Mr Phelps.

Thomas Hawkins and John Speed appointed Church Wardens the Ensuing year.

Ordered that the Church wardens do purchase books for the Several Churches and provide Elements for the Ensuing year and bring in their Accot at Laying next Levy.

Ordered that the Collectors pay Josiah Allen 22 lbs. Tobo and Daniel May 66 lbs. Tobacco out of the Depositum in their hands.

                                 Wm Kay
                                 Thomas Hawkins.

A. D. 1755

At a Vestry held for this Parish the 4th day of Novembr 1755

         Present
         John Cox   Wm Embry
         Lyddal Bacon   Field Jefferson
         Thomas Hawkins -   Thos Nash
         Geo: Walton   John Speed
         & Clemt Read

Ordered that Thomas Rogers and Wm Fuquay do on the last Monday in January next meet at the Bridge Over Cub Creek & do Procession all the Land about the said Creek between the Road from thence to Roger's Mill & Hallifix & Bedford Countys and make return thereof according to Law.

Ordered that John Smith Fran⁸ Grimes & John M°neess do meet on the Second Monday in December next at the Bridge over Cub Creek & do Procession all the Land above the said Creek on the North side of the said road from thence by Rogers's Mill to Bedford County & make return thereof According to Law.

Ordered that Robert Weakly: Thomas Wood and Thomas Harvey do meet on the first Monday in Decemb^r next at the Mouth of Rough Creek and do Procession all the Land between the said Creek & Cub Creek to Prince Edward and Bedford Countys and return thereof according to Law.

Ordered that And^w Martin: James Rutherford and Alex^r Joyce do meet on the first Monday in Feb^{ry} next at the Bridge over Cub Creek and do Procession all the Land below the . . . & Ruff Creek on the North side of the Old Road down to Little Roanoak Bridge & so up the said Little Roanoak & by Prince Edward County and make return thereof according to Law.

Ordered that Benjamin Farmer and David Logan do meet at the Bridge over Cub Creek on the third Monday in February next and do Procession all the Land between the said Creek, Stanton River, Little Roanoak and the Road that goes from the said Bridge to the Bridge at the Mossing Ford & make return thereof according to Law.

Ordered that John & Thomas Varnon do meet on the first Monday in December next at the Bridge over Little Roanoak at the Mossing Ford & do Procession all the Land between the said Roanoak and the upper Old Road and the Road from the said Bridge up into the said Old Road and make return thereof according to Law.

Ordered that George Foster Senr and James Easter do meet on the third Monday in January next at the Mouth of Ash Camp Creek and do Procession all the Land between the said Creek Little Roanoak Kings and Randolphs Roads and Prince Edward County and do make return thereof according to Law.

Ordered that Thomas Bedford, Thomas Jones & Abraham

Vaughan do meet at the Mouth of Ash Camp Creek on the first Monday in December Next & do Procession all the Land between Little Roanoak the Horse Pen Creek and Kings Road & do make return thereof according to Law.

Ordered that Henry May & Charles Allen do meet on the last Monday in January next at the Mouth of the Horse Pen Creek and do Procession all the Land between the said Creek, Blue Stone Creek & Stanton River, and make return thereof according to Law.

Ordered that James Arnold Reubin Vaughn James Thomson & Christop[r] Johnson meet at Mizes Ford the Second Monday in Decemb[r] next & do Procession all the Lands between Mizes Ford Old Road & Meherrin River up to Greeirs Road & make return thereof according to Law.

Ordered that W[m] Hill Thomas Lanier & Thomas Easland do meet at Allens Creek Bridge the first Monday in Decemb[r] next and do Procession all the Lands between Allens Creek, Butchers Creek Roanoak & Mizes Ford Road and make return thereof According to Law.

Ordered that W[m] Davies Richard Fox, Cap[t] Mitchell Saterwhite & Sharwood Bugg do meet at the Horse ford the Second Monday in Decemb[r] next and do Procession all the Lands on the South side of Roanoak River to the Country Line and do make return thereof according to Law.

Ordered that Francis Wray & Henry Childs do meet on the first Monday in February next at the Mouth of Stony Creek on Meherrin River and do Procession all the Lands Between the said Creek & River and the Road that goes from Hatchers Bridge by Jennings & the Dividing Ridge between Nottoway River & Maherrin & make return thereof according to Law.

Ordered that George Phillips and Reps Jones do on the last Monday in January Next Meet at Cocks Bridge on Nottoway & do Procession all the Land belowe the Road from thence by Jennings down to the County Line & make return thereof according to Law.

Ordered that John Howel, & John Parker do on the Second Monday in February Next Meet at the Mouth of Stony Creek on Meherrin River & do Procession all the Land on the North branch of the said River between the said Creek and Brunswick Line and make return thereof according to Law.

Ordered that Richard Palmer & Joseph Granger do on the first Monday in February Next Meet at the Mouth of Butchers Creek and do Procession all the Land between the said Creek and Roanoak & Andersons Road & Mizes Ford Road and do make return thereof according to Law.

Hutchins Burton agrees to take Margrett Bevil & her three children at two Thousand pounds of Tobacco p year and Support, Cloath, & Maintain them at that rate which is to be paid out of the Depositum &c in the Coll^{rs} hands.

Ordered that Step^h Evans (& Wm Harris down the Creek) do meet at Coxes Bridge over South Meherrin River on the Second Monday in February next & do Procession all the Land between the said South Meherrin River, Main Blue Stone Creek & the Road from Andersons to the said Bridge and make return thereof according to Law.

Ordered that James Cunningham & Joel Chandler do on the last Monday in January Meet at the Mouth of the Robertson fork of Meherrin River & do Procession all the Land between the said Robertson Fork & south Fork & Kings Road and make return thereof according to Law.

Ordered that John Doak and Thomas Pettis do meet at the Fork of Meherrin River on the Second Monday in February next and do Procession all the Land between the North South & Robertsons Forks up to Coxes Road & make return thereof according to Law.

Ordered that Henry Blagrove & Joseph Johnson do meet at Walkers Bridge on the forth Monday in January next and Procession all the Lands between the North Meherrin, Coxes Road Robertson Fork of Meherrin, Kings & Winninghams roads, and make return thereof according to Law.

Ordered that George Wells & Thomas Winningham do meet on the Second Monday in December next at the Mouth of Ledbetters C^k & do Procession all the Land between the said Creek, Winningham road, King's road, Randolph road, & Prince Edward County & make return thereof according to Law.

Ordered that Roger Madison & Joseph Billops do meet at the Mouth of Ledbetter Creek on the first Monday in February next

& do Procession all the Land between the said Creek Winninghams Road and Nottoway River & make return thereof according to Law.

Ordered that Daniel Claiborn Silvanes Walker & Robert Allen do on the third Monday in February meet at the Mouth of Ledbetters Creek & do Procession all the Land between North Meherrin River Winninghams Road and the Road from Winninghams Bridge to Stokes's Race Ground & make return thereof according to Law.

Ordered that Nathaniel Garland and Thomas Wynn do meet the first Monday in February at Reedy Creek Church and do Procession all the Land between the Road from thence to Wades Bridge & the Road from thence to Cocks Bridge & Nottoway River & make return thereof according to Law.

Ordered that John Williams & John Ragsdale do meet at Walkers Bridge on the third Monday in January & do Procession all the Land on the North side of Meherrin River between that Road & the Road from Hatchers Bridge to their Intersection by Pettys & make return according to Law.

Ordered that Julius Nickols, Drury Mallone, Joshua Mabry & Thomas Taylor do meet at the Horse Ford on Roanoak River on the first Monday in February and do Procession all the Land between Roanoak River & the Old Road, County line, & flatt Creek and make return thereof according to Law.

Ordered that John Ezell, John George Pedington and George Vaughan do meet at Mizes Ford on the Second Monday in December & do Procession all the Land between Mizes Ford Road & Pedingtons ford Road up to flatt Creek & make return thereof according to Law.

Ordered that Cap. William Pool & Sam[ll] Mannin do meet at John Taylor Dukes on the third Monday in February next & do Procession all the Lands between the Old Road, Roanoak River, flatt Creek, & Miles's Creek & do make return thereof accord to Law.

Ordered that John Watson & James Hamner do meet at the said Hamners on the first Monday in February next and do Procession all the Lands between the two Old Roads, Flatt Creek & Miles's Creek & make return thereof according to Law.

Ordered that Cap[t] George Baskervil, Hutchens Burton, John

Ballard & Stephen Mallet do meet at Allens Creek Bridge on the last Monday in Jan^{ry} & do Procession all the Lands between Allens Creek, Miles's Creek, Roanoak River & Mizes ford Old Road & do make return thereof according to Law.

The State of the Parish Levy for the Year 1755.

To the Executor or Adm^r. of the Revd Mr William Key Clerk late Deceased for 6 months Sal^{ry}				8600
To Thomas Bouldin for Mary Young & Daughter				1500
To Jo^n Speed Clk Vestry, Sexton & Clerk				2500
To John Watson for keeping his sister				1000
To John Blackson a Sexton				300
To Henry Isbell Clerk				1200
To John Hix Clk				1200
To William Hunt Clk & Sexton				1500
To Henry Isbell Sexton				300
To John Speed for the Support of Mary & Betty Hastrell				800
To D^o for Agness Dodd				600
To Richard Young for Patrick Frailes Son				1000
To Wm Embry for Elinor Hungerford				1000
To Richd Brookes for Ann Barns				1500
To James Hunt Gent to Imploy a Reader				1200
To Paul Carrington his accot for Indentures	7	13	9	
To Geo: Carrington for Ditto	2	12	6	
To Lyddall Bacon for his Acco^t Pd John Stone for taring Reedy Creek Church	6	13	0	
To Wm Lax for Support of his Child				0500
To James Mitchell for Support of Margret Bevil and three Children				1250
To Sarah Glass for Support of Margret Bevil & three Children				1000
To Lenonard Claiborn Gent: his acco^t	8	2	6	
To George Mosely for Support of Mary Hudson & three children				0200
To Lyddal Bacon Gent: for Support of Rich Wetherford				1000
Carried Over	25	01	9	28150
Bro^t Over	25	01	9	28150

352   Cumberland Parish

Ordered that Tho⁸ Boulden Gent Acco wth the Parish at the next Vestry for the Tobacco Levyed in his hands for the Support of Thomas Adams.	
To Valentine Mullins for Support of Wm Leake	450
To Field Jefferson Gent. for his Church Ferry	400
To D° for 2 other years a 200 each	400
To Capt. Mitchell for D°	200
To John Akin for his Wifes Support	400
To Memucan Hunt for his Acco^t of Insolvents	1680
Ordered that out of the Depositum to be raised the Coll. pay P. Hawkins his costs of Suit ad. Bacon & others	
To John Hobson his Acco^t	98
To D° for his Insolvants	974

                                       25   01   9   32682

                      Cr.

By Clem^t Read	3575	
By Memucan Hunt	800	4375
		28307
To Richard Tomson for a Levy Overcharged	22	
To the Collector for his Commissions on 52536 at 6 p C^t	3152	3174
		31481
To a Depositum in the Hands of the Collector		21055
		52536

                      Cr.

By 2388 Tiths at 22 p Poll   52536

    Joseph Morton is Elected a Vestry man in the room of Wm Watkins Field Jefferson & Thomas Hawkins are Elected Church Wardens. Thomas Hawkins appointed Collector & to give Bond &c.

                                           Field Jefferson
                                           Thomas Hawkins.

At a Vestry held for this Parish in the County of Lunenburg the 4th day of February 1756.

Present	Field Jefferson Thos. Hawkins	C: Wardens
	Lyddal Bacon W^m. Embry Thomas Nash George Walton Clem^t. Read	Vestry Men

The Reverend M^r. John Barclay being mentioned by one of the Members of the Vestry as a Person the people were desirous should be received as Minister of this Parish in the room of the late Rev^d. M^r. Key his motion was approved by the unanimous consent of the Vestry present.

Whereupon M^r. Barclay being also present was applyed to to fill up the Vacancy. Who declared his acceptance on the terms following (To Wit) that he would be at Liberty at any time when he thought fit to leave the Parish, and that the Vestry might also when they thought fit imploy anyone other, and that he should be paid in Proportion to the time he stayed among us, and that the Parish should pay for his Board till they mutualy agreed (To Wit) M^r. Barclay to be received & the Vestry to receive him; to which terms & Proposals the Vestry agreed.

Ordered that the present Collector of the Parish Levy & pay to Robt Wade the residue of his Debt and Costs for which a Suit is now depending in the General Court against Cox and Martin.

Ordered that the Present Collector pay to Lyddal Bacon the Debt and Costs due to Mathew Talbott for which a Suit is now depending in the County Court of Lunenburg, and that he pay both the afforesaid Debt and Costs as soon as he shall have so much in his hands.

M^r. Newsom being desired to provide four Surplaces for the four Churches in this Parish; agreed to do so, and for which he is to be paid out of the Money that will be in the hands of the Collector.

Field Jefferson
Thomas Hawkins.

CUMBERLAND PARISH

At a Vestry held for this Parish in Lunenburg County the 5th day of Novembr 1756.

Present Clemt Read
Thomas Nash
Lyddal Bacon
Thomas Boulden
John Cox
Thomas Hawkins
& John Speed

The State of the Parish Levy (to Wit)

To the Revd. Mr John Barclay			16000
To 6 p Ct thereon			960
To 4 Do for Shrinking			640
To Thos Boulden for Mary Young			1500
To John Speed Clk of the Vestry, Do of a Church & Sexton			2000
To John Wadson for keeping his Sister			1000
To John Blaxton a Sexton			300
To Henry Isbell Clk and Sexton	1500		
To Do for taking care of the Surplice	100		01600
To Do his Account	1	02 1½	
To John Speed for taking care of the Surplice			0100
To John Blaxton for Do			100
To Hutchins Burton for Support of Mary & Betty Hatswell			1550
To John Speed for Agness Dod			600
To Richard Yansey for Frails Son			1000
To Wm Embry for Enion Hungerford			1000
To Richard Brookes for Ann Barns			1500
To George Carringtons Acco for Indentures	7 10 0		
	8 12 1½		30050

The Reverd Mr Barclay, Mr Read, Mr Boulden & Mr Nash are appointed to view a place about little Roan Oak to Build a Church & report &c.

The Rever^d Mr Barclay, Mr Thomas Hawkins & Thomas
  Anderson are appointed to view a place to build a
  Church nigh Butchers Creek & report &c.

To Wm Lax for Support of his Child				500
Thomas Boulden returned his acco^t of Adams Tobacco in his hands.				
To Thomas Boulden his Acco^t		9	5	
To Richd Yancy his acco^t for goods found Joseph Owen	1	2	10	
To Elizabeth Green for care of Joseph Owen	2	2	0	
To Richard Yancy for Joseph Owen				600
To John Akin for Support of his Wife				600
To Hutchens Burton for Mary Bevil &c				2000
To Jo^n Speed his Acco^t	3	9	5	
To Thomas Smith Reader Butchers Cr^k				1200
To Pink Hawkins				28
To John Cox for Wm Cox for repairs Chu.	2	13	9	
To Wm Hunt for repairs of Chu				225
To John Camp his Acco^t for Ellem^{ts}		10	0	
To Isaac Hudson overcharg'd last Year				44
To John Speed for D^o				22
To Wm Hunt for D^o				22
To Fra^s Bracy for D^o				66
To Edwd Lewis for D^o				66
To John Cox for Attorneys fee	2	10	0	
To Richard Coalman		10	0	
To The Revd Mr Barclay his Board	25			
	46	17	6½	35423
To 6 p C^t for Collecting 64675 Sherrfs. Coms.				3880
Depositum raised				25572
				64875
By 2587 Tithables at 25 lbs. Tob p Poll				64675

Thomas Hawkins and Wm Embry Apt^d

Church Wardens for the Ensuing Year.
Wm. Traylor free from Parish Levys &c.

John Barclay Minister
Thomas Hawkins.

At a Vestry held for this Parish in Lunenb^g County the 7th day of June 1757.

  Present The Reverend Mr John Barclay
        Thomas Hawkins
        Lyddal Bacon
        John Speed
        Field Jefferson
        Thomas Boulden
        & Clem^t Read

Mr Barclay mentioning a mistake in his favour of 695 lbs. of Tobacco levyed at the last Vestry, thereupon Order a ratification thereof, and that the same be laid out by him if he pleases in purchasing Books for the use of the Churches in this Parish.

Memorand^m That the Present Wardens settle with the former for 695 lbs. Tobacco.

Ordered that the Collector pay Wm Hunt as Clk and Sexton &C^a 1600 lbs. Tobacco.

Ordered that the Collector pay Mr Embry is acc^t out of the Depositum C^{ta}.

Mr Barclay intimating to this Vestry that he intended soon to leave this Parish & at the same time requesting the favour of this Vestry to give a Title to Mr James Craig a Student in Divinity & to recommend him to the Rever^d & Honourable Mr Commissary Dawson as a person they are informed very well qualified to receive Holy Orders, into which he is desirous to enter; do unanimously agree to the above motion; and do hereby impower the Church Wardens to give a Title & recommendation to M^r Ja^s. Craig upon his entering into Bond wth proper securitys that he shall not by Virtue of the Title insist upon being Minister of this Parish if he shall not be found agreeable to the Gentlemen of the Vestry & Parishioners after Tryal.

Ordered that the Collector pay to the Rever^d Mr Proctor Two

Thousand pounds of Tobacco, if he please to accept it, for his fav[rs] done this Parish in Preaching in the Vacancy between the Death of M[r] Key and the coming of the Rev[d] M[r] Barclay into this Parish & that they pay the same to M[r] Lyddal Bacon for M[r] Proctors use; and M[r] Embry and we the Vestry on behalf of ourselves and the said Parish take this first opportunity to return our grateful thanks to M[r] Proctor for such his favours and Services to us and them done.

                              John Barclay Minist[r]
                              Thomas Hawkins.

At a Vestry held for this Parish in Lunenburg County the 5th of July 1757.

    Present   Field Jefferson
                       Thomas Boulden
                       Thomas Nash
                       John Speed
                       Thomas Hawkins
                       W[m] Embry
                       John Cox & Clem[t] Read
                                  Vestry Men

M[r] John Cox, M[r] Thomas Hawkins, M[r] Thomas Boulden & M[r] George Walton are Commissioners appointed to attend the Surveyor of this County in running the Parish Dividing line between this and the Parish of Cornwall and that they find Necessarys for the Surveyor and imploy Chain Carryers and Markers.

                              Thomas Hawkins
                              William Embry.

At a Vestry held for this Parish the 5th of Dec[r] 1757 at M[r] Joseph Boswells in Lunenbg County.

    Present   Field Jefferson
                       Henry Blagrove
                       John Jennings
                       Matt[w] Marrable
                       John Parish
                       John Ragsdale

John Speed &
Wm Embry
Vestrymen

Ordered that John Hix be appointed Clerk to the said Vestry. Upon a Motion of the Revd Mr Jacob Townsend to Serve this Parish as a Minister it is Ordered that he be rec^d into the Parish for the Space of three Months.

A State of the Parish Levy

To the Revd Mr John Barclay	8000		
To 4 p C^t thereon	320		8320
To D^o for Cash for his Board		12 10 0	
To John Speed Clk and Sexton	1500		
To D^o for the Surplice	100		1600
To John Watson for keeping his Sister			1000
To John Blackstone Sexton & for the Surplice			400
To John Speed for Agnis Dod			600
To Richard Yancy for Frail's Son			1000
To John Jennings for Elinor Hungerford			1000
To Richard Brookes for Ann Barns			1200
To William Hunt Clk and Sexton	1500		
To D^o for his care of the Surplice	100		1600
To Wm Lax for Support of his Child			500
To John Akins for Support of his Wife			600
To Henry Delony for Margret Bevil			1500
To Thomas Smith Reader on Butcher's Creek			1200
To Rubin Morgan for keeping Eliz. Hatchel one month and for burying her		3 00 0	
To Thomas Boulden his Proportion for Running the Parish line		7 14 8	
To John Cox for D^o 7 14 8 & 5/.		7 19 8	
To Geo. Walton Com^r for running the Parish line		2 3 11	
To Thos Hawkins D^o for D^o		2 3 11	
To John Hurl for keeping Richard Watts			1000
To Wm Allen for keeping Ann Nobles			500

THE VESTRY BOOK, 1746-1816   359

To John Hurl for keeping Richard Watts last year	500
To John Camp for Elim^{ts} found the Court House Church	100
To Stephen Caudle for Supporting his Daughter	500
To John Jennings for Sarah Rogers	500
To Clack Courtney for the Care of Thomas Gadis an Orphan	5 00 0
To David Garland for holding the Election of Vestry and other Services	535
To John Hobson	7

Ordered that a Church be Built 48 by 24 on the Branches of Flatt Rock Creek in the Lower End of this Parish & that Nath^{ll} Garland, John Jennings, John Parish & John Ragsdale do agree on the most proper place and let the same to be paid in the following manner (to Wit) one half upon Raising, & the other half upon Finishing the same.

Ordered that John Tomson Act as a Reader Every Sunday at the most proper place in the Settlement near Mr Richd Bookers on Bush Run & that he be allowed for the same   600

To Doctor Crawford for Medisons given Nancy Keney	1 12 0	
To Joseph Davies for keeping Ditto 6 weeks	15 0	
To Joseph Boswell for keeping Ditto the Ensuing year		1000
To John Hix Clk Reedy Creek Church		1200
To Ditto for Clk of the Vestry		500
	42 19 2	27462
Depositum Raised		10402
6 p C^t Com to the Collector		2416
		40280
By 2014 Tiths at 20 lbs. p Poll		40280
By the Amount of Mary Hatchells Estate in David Garlands hands	4 8 3	
	38 10 11	

John Jennings and Matt^w Marrable are appointed Church Wardens for the Ensuing year, and it is Ordered that they settle with the Church wardens of the upper Parish their Account and report the same at the Next Vestry.

Ordered that Mr John Speed settle and receive the money due from Mr George Baskervil and that he be accountable for the same at the next Vestry.

Ordered that the present Church Wardens, John Jennings & Matt^w Marrable settle with the Old Church wardens of this Parish for the preceeding Years, and receive the Ballances in their Hands and be accountable at the next Vestry held for the Parish. Otherwise Sue them.

Ordered that the Church Wardens of this Parish settle with Coll^o Clem^t Read his account against this Parish and allow the same out of the Depositum, by an Order on the Collector.

Ordered that John Speed and Thomas Hawkins settle with Coll^o Field Jefferson the Parish Depositums rais'd the two years he was Sherriff.

John Jennings
Ma Marrable

At a Vestry held for this Parish the 6th day of March 1758 at Mr Joseph Boswells in Lunenburg County.

Present	Matt Marrable	John Jennings
	Henry Blackgrove	Dan^{ll} Claiborne
	Thomas Hawkins	Jo^n Ragsdale &
	William Embry	Vestrymen

On the Motion of the Revd Mr Jacob Townsend it is Ordered that the present Collector pay him for three Months Sallary 4240 lbs. of Tobacco & Three pounds fifteen Shillings Curr^t money for his Board in that time & that the same be paid out of the Present Depositum in the Collectors hands.

Upon receipt of a Letter from the Revd Mr John Barclay Dated 22^d Decemb^r 1757 the above Vestry proceeded to take the purport of the said Letter into their Consideration & were of opinion that the said Letter was Unreasonable; But agree that in case he makes it appear that he has served the Parish a longer time than he has been paid for, that then the Collector Mr Thomas Hawkins pay him for two Months Sallary.

Upon a Motion made by the present Church Wardens that they have no opportunity of putting the Order of the last Vestry in Execution it is Ordered that the said Orders be continued and that they make report at the next Vestry.

Upon the Motion of the Rever^d Mr Townshend Whether he is to be continued Minister of this Parish any longer the Vestry were of Opinion that he shall be continued three Months longer provided he will agree to have his Sallary and Board Levyed for him at the next Levy. To which the said Mr Townsend agreed.

           John Jennings
           Matt Marrable.

At a Vestry held for this Parish the 29th day of Novr. 1758.

Present Messrs. John Jennings Wm Embry
      Dan^{ll} Claiborn Henry Blagrave
      John Speed John Ragsdale
      & Matthew Marrable

A State of the Parish Levy

Mr Edm^d Taylor is chose a Vestry Man in the room of Mr Thomas Hawkins Deceased.

Mr Thomas Pettis is chose a Vestry Man in the room of Mr Nath^{ll} Garland who is removed out of the Parish.

To John Speed Clk and Sexton of Roanoak Church	1500	
To D^o for care of the Surplice	100	1600
To John Wadson for Support of his Sister		1000
To John Blaxton Sexton of Reedy C^k Church & taking care of the Surplice		400
To John Speed is account as p Ballance	1 17 2	
To Mr Edmond Taylor for Patrick Frails Son		1000
To Capt John Jennings for Elinor Hungerford		1000

Cumberland Parish

To Richard Brooks for Ann Barns	1200
To Wm Hunt Clerk and Sexton of ye C^thouse Church & taking care of the Surplice	1600
To Wm Lax for the Support of his Child	500
To John Akin for Ditto of his Wife	600
To Noel Burton for the Support of Margret Bevil & Her youngest Child	700
To the Revd Mr Proctor to Imploy a Reader at two of the most convenient places over Roanoak	1200
To John Earl for Suport of Richard Watts	1000
To Mrs Agness Hobson for the Support of Nancy Kenny	600
To John Hicks Clerk Reedy Creek Church 1200	
To D^o as Clerk of the Vestry 500	1700

To Mr Edm^d Taylor for Support of Mary Mitchell   800

Ordered that Mrs Agness Hobson take immediately under her care the Youngest Daughter of Margrett Bevil & keep her till an Order of Court Issue for binding her out.

To Capt John Jennihgs for keeping John Consolvent last Year   7 00 0

To Mrs Sarah Gill for keeping the said John Consolver the Ensuing Year   5 00 0

Phillip Cockerham is Exempted from paying Parish Levies from this day forward

To John Price for the Support of John Rook	5	8	4			
D^r To Rookes Mare &C^t	4	4	0	1	4	4

To Francis Sanders for his Acco^t	3	1	0
To Joseph Dobson for his Acco^t for caring Elizabeth Taylor	5	0	0
To John Ballard for the Support of Ann Butler and her children	4	0	0
To Capt Joseph Freeman for the Support of Sarah Williams and her Children	4	-	-
To John Blaxton his Account		3	00

To the Revd Mr Jacob Townsend his Acco^t for Eight Sermons			2648
To Col^o Richard Witton for Ditto's board 2 Months	4	00	0
To John Ballard his Account	4		
To Wm Burgemy for removing the frame of the Lower Church	7	10	-
To the Rever^d Mr Garden for several Sermons Preached some time ago			1050
To the Revd Mr Purdie for his services in ye Parish			2100
To the Rever^d Mr Proctor for his Ditto in Ditto			7000

Ordered that the Present Church Wardens Employ the Rever^d Mr Proctor to supply the vacancy of a Minister in this Parish, and that they agree with him to Preach at such times and places as they shall agree, and that the said Church Wardens give proper notice of the same.

To Capt John Jennings the expense of moving Andrew Glasco to the Parish of Brunswick	1	- -
To Ditto for wine found the Church	10-10	

John Jennings and Matt^w Marrable former Church Wardens reported that they according to a former Order of the Vestry of the Parish have had under their Consideration the several Accounts between this Parish and the former Collectors—Mr Pinkethman Hawkins & Mr Thomas Hawkins and find that the said Collectors are indebted to this Parish the Ballance of One Hundred eighty three pounds two shillings and two pence, that the s^d Hawkins's Acknowledged the same to be due, but that they had not received of the said Hawkins's any part thereof.

Ordered that the present Church Wardens Messrs William Embry and John Speed, apply to the above mention'd, Thomas & Pinkithman Hawkins or their Agent's for the above Ballance of £ 183-2-2 and if they receive the same or .... part thereof that then they pay the Revd Mr John Barclay Two Thousand eight Hundr^d & Eighty pounds Nett Tobacco & the sum of four pounds three Shillings & four pence cash as a Ballance due to him for two Months Sallary & Board; It's further Ordered that in case the said Church Wardens do not receive money Enough of the said Hawkins's to pay the above said Barclay that they they shall discharge the same out of the present Depositum.

Ordered that Mr Wm Embry be allowed his Acco^t for an Execution of Elizabeth Coxes vs. him.

Mr Wm Embry & Mr John Speed appointed Church Wardens for the Present Year.

Mr David Garland is appointed Collector of the Parish Levy for this present year, and it is Ordered that he give Bond and Security for the same to the Present Church Wardens.

	£ s d	lbs. Tob^o
Bro Over	£ 48 5 6	27698
To a Depositum raised		9132
6 p C^t to the Collector		2350
Error of 10 lbs.		39170
By 1959 Tithables at 20 lbs. p Poll		39180

William Embry
John Speed

At a Vestry held for Cumberland Parish the 22nd of May 1759.

Present Messrs Daniel Claiborn, John Speed,
Henry Blagrove, John Jennings,
John Ragsdale, Thos Pettis, &
Matt Marrable,

Upon a Motion made by Matt: Marrable Gent: a Member of this Vestry that the Reverend Mr James Craig now offers and is willing to undertake for this Parish, the Office of a Minister, Recommending him in his Opinion to be highly deserving of the same, & further that he thinks the said Rever^d James Craig from an Order of the Old Vestry is Justly Entitled to the same, whereupon the said Vestry took the same into their Consideration, & came to the following Resolution.

Resolved that it is the unanimous Opinion of this Vestry that the said Rever^d James Craig, ought and is hereby chosen, Elected, Constituted, & appointed, Rector, and Minister of this Parish, and that his time shall begin and commence Immediately from and after the date hereof.

Resolved that it is the Opinion of this Vestry that Thomas Lanier ought and is hereby chose Elected, constituted, and appointed a Vestry man in the room of Wm Embry Dec^d.

Resolved that it is the Opinion of this Vestry that Daniel Claiborne Gent: shall Succeed Wm Embry Gent Dec^d in the Office of a Church Warden for the remainder of this Present Year.

Upon a Motion made by Joseph Williams Gent. that he— together with many others of his Neighbours live at a great distance from any place of Divine Service, Praying that this Vestry would take their case into consideration and give them such relief as to them shall seem reasonable.

Resolved that it is the Oppinion of this Vestry that the Said Neighbourwood ought to have a Reader & that Joseph Williams Gent: be imployed therein & to read at such places, and times, as he the said Williams shall think proper.

Resolved that it is the Opinion of this Vestry that the Revd Ja^s Craig ought and is hereby agreed to be allowed in the next Levy Twenty five pounds Current Money of Virginia as a Compensation for the Expence he may be at for his Board &C for the Ensuing Year.

Resolved that it is the Opinion of this Vestry that the Bonds given by Messrs John Jennings, Thos Pettis, John Speed, Dan^ll Claiborne, & Wm Embry, in favour of the Rever^d John Barclay, ought & are hereby agreed to be allowed out of the Money due from the Hawkins's to this Parish.

           John Speed
           Daniel Claiborne.

At a Vestry held for this Parish the 17th of Sept 1759

Present   The Revd Mr James Craig
    Messrs John Speed & Danll Claiborne Church Wardens
    Messrs Thomas Tabb, John Ragsdale
      Tho Pettis   Thom Lanier &
      John Jennings
              Vestry men

Thomas Lanier & Thomas Pettis Gent. two of the members of the Present Vestry having already taken the Oaths prescribed by Law & Subscribed the Test in the Court of Lunenburg, Now in Open Vestry Subscribe as follows:

We Thomas Lanier & Thomas Pettis do Promise to be conformable to the Doctrine & Discipline of the Church of England by Law Established.

           Thomas Lanier
           Thomas Pettis

It has been taken into consideration by this Vestry that John Hicks formerly chose to be Clerk of this Vestry is not capable of acting in the said office, they have therefore chose Richd Witton to Act for the future as Clerk.

1. Pursuant to an Order of the Court of this County Ordered that Drury Malloone Thomas Malloone Stepn Jones & Wm Riddle do meet at the Horse Ford on Monday the 12th day of Novembr & do Procession all the Land between the County Line, Roanoak River, Foxes Road & Penningtons Old Road & make return thereof According to Law.

2. Ordered that John Pennington, George Vaughan, John Ezell & Wm Pennel do meet at Mizes Ford on Monday the Twelfth day of Novembr & do Procession all the lands between the County Line, Penningtons Old Road, Taylor Dukes Old Road to Mizes Ford & Meherrin River & make return according to Law.

3. Ordered that Dennis Larke Joshua Mabry Amos Tims Junr do meet at Sherwood Buggs on Monday the Twelfth of Nvr & do Procession all the Lands between Roanoak River

Miles Creek, Penningtons Old Road, Foxes Road, & make return according to Law.

4   Ordered that David Dortch, Howel Collier, Wm Lucas & Robt Lark do meet at Sherwood Buggs on Monday the 12th of Nov^r & do Procession all the Lands between Mizes Ford Road, Dukes Old Road, & Penningtons Old Road & make return according to Law.

5   Ordered that James Hamner, Wm Holmes & James Lett, do meet at Sherwood Buggs on Monday the 12th of Novemb^r & do Procession all the Lands between Mizes Ford Road, Miles Creek & Mountains Creek Road & make return according to Law.

6   Ordered that Randolph Bracy John Speed, Jacob Bugg George Baskervill, John Ballard & Henry Dolony do meet at the Mouth of Miles Creek on Tuesday the Thirteenth of Nov. & do Procession all the Lands between Miles Creek, Roanoak River Cocks Creek & Mountains Creek Road & make return according to Law.

7   Ordered that John Humphreys, John Clerk, Thomas Farrar & Hugh Norwell, do meet at John Humphreys on Monday the 12th of November next & do Procession all the Lands between Cocks Creek, Allens Creek, & Mountains Creek Road & make return according to Law.

8   Ordered that Sam^{ll} Bugg, Sam^{ll} Young, Isaac Mitchell, Joseph Easland, James Coalman & Stephen Mallet do meet at the Mouth of Allens Creek on Wednesday the fourteenth day of Novemb^r & do Procession all the Lands between Allens Creek, Roanoak River & Taylors Ferry Road, leading to Humpreys Ordinary & make return according to Law.

9   Ordered that Robert Alexander, Richd Fox, & Wm Davies do meet on Monday the 12th of Novemb^r at the Horse Ford & do Procession all the Lands between the Country line Roanoak River & Cotten Creek & make return according to Law.

10   Ordered that George Farrar Peter Field Jefferson Edm^d Bugg and Anselm Bugg do meet at the Mouth of Cotten Creek on Monday the Twelfth of Novemb^r & do Procession all the Land between Cotten Creek the Country

Line, Nutbush Creek and Roanoak River & make return according to Law.

11 Ordered that James Arnold, Rubin Vaughan, & Ephraim Andrews do meet at Mizes Ford on Monday the Twelfth of Novemb^r & do Procession all the Lands between Meherrin River Mountains Creek Road & Buckhorn & make return according to Law.

12 Ordered that Joseph Gill, John Tomson & Edward Goode do meet at John Humpreys on Monday the Twelfth of Novr next & do Procession all the Lands between Buckhorn Mountains Creek Road, Boswells Road & Meherrin River & make return according to Law.

13 Ordered that Robert Dyer, Reps Jones, John Callaham do meet at Reps Jones's on the 12th of Novr next & Procession all the Lands between Flatrock Creek & Brunswick line & between Meherrin & Cocks Road & make return according to Law.

14 Ordered that Israel Brown, James Dawes & Henry Vindike do meet at Henry Vindikes on the 12th of Novr next & do Procession all the Lands between Flatrock Creek & Bears Eliment Creek & from Meherrin to Cocks Road & make return according to Law.

15 Ordered that George Phillips Wm Pollard Daniel Wynn, Jon. [Jos.] Stone & John Wynn do meet at Dan^{ll} Wynns on the 12th of Novr next & do Procession all the Lands between Cocks Road Nottoway River, to Hampton Wades Road & to the North side Reedy Creek Road, & make return according to Law.

16 Ordered that Richard Williams Lazeras Williams John Scott, Robert Brookes & John Rogers do meet at Lazeras Williams's on Monday the 12th of Novemb^r Next & Procession all the Lands from the Fork of Reedy Creek Road between that road & Cocks Road to Meherrin River & do make return according to Law.

17 Ordered that Wm Gee, John Hobson, & John Hawkins do meet on the 12th of Novemb^r next at Wm Gees & Procession all the Lands from Bears Eliment & between Meherrin & Cocks Road & make return according to Law.

18   Ordered that Wm Gordon Wm Love Wm Pool David Christopher & George Grimes do meet at Richard Coalmans on Monday the 12th of Novemb^r next & Procession all the Lands between Nottoway River & Meherrin River from Hampton Wades Road to Winninghams road & make returns according to Law.
19   Ordered that Joseph Miner Jarred Mackconnico, John Night Chris. Billaps, John Hoskinsson, do meet at the Fork of Winninghams Road & Roberts's road on the 12th of Novr next & Procession all the Lands from the North Side of Winninghams Road to the Parish line & from Nottoway River to Meherrin & make return according to Law.
20   Ordered that Capt Freeman Chris. Hudson & John Hide, do meet at John Hides on the 12th of Novemb^r next & Procession all the Lands from Mizes ford Old Road to Wittons Road & from Butcher Creek to Allens Creek and make return according to Law.
21   Ordered that Guy Smith John Cox Junr & Joseph Boswell do meet at Joseph Boswells on the 12th of Novemb^r next & Procession all the Lands Between Boswells Road Meherrin River Parish line Marrables Road to the Court House & Wittons Road to Boswells & make return according to Law.
22   Ordered that Richard Palmer, Thomas Anderson & Thomas Carlton do meet at the Mouth of Butchers Creek on the 12th of November Next & Procession all the Lands from the Mouth of Butchers Creek to Blue Stone Creek & to the Court House & to Wittons Road to the Head of Allens Creek & make return according to Law.
23   Ordered that Willm Harris Finniwood Wm Harris Peckerwood & Stephen Evans do meet at the Court House on the 12th of Novr next & Procession all the Lands between Blue Stone Creek and the Parish line & Roanoak River & make return according to Law.
24   Ordered that John Bracie, James Lewis & Nathaniel Robertson do meet at the Mouth of Nutbush on the 12th of Novemb^r Next & Procession all the Lands between Nutbush Creek the Country Line Grassy Creek & Roanoak River & make return according to Law.

25 Ordered that Richard Yansey Wm Coalbreath, Wm Royster, Thomas Wiles, Peter Overby, & Nicholas Overby, do meet at the Mouth or Grassey Creek on the 12th of Novemb^r next, & Procession all the Lands between Grassey Creek, County Line, Arons Creek & Roanoak River & make return according to Law.

26 Ordered that Wm Stone, Dan^ll Price, Volindine Brown do meet on the Fork of Meherrin River on the 12th of Novemb^r next & Procession all the Lands in the Fork of Meherrin up to Coxes Road & make return according to Law.

27 Ordered that Joseph Williams, Henry Blagrove, Jos. Johnson & Thomas Smithson & Wm Chandler do meet at the School House on Coxes Road on the 12th of Novemb^r next & Procession all the Lands above Coxes Road Above Coxes Road between the North & South Meherrins & the Parish line & make return according to Law.

28 Ordered that Tignal Jones, Frances Jones & Zack Baker do meet at Mitchells Ferry on the 12th of Novemb^r Next and Procession all the Lands between Taylors Ferry Road Roanoak River and Butchers Creek to Mizes Ford Old Road and make return according to Law.

Upon complaint made by the Inhabitants of Roanoak & Butchers Creek &C that a great number of Inhabitants in that part are at too great a distance for any place of Divine Worship to give their attendance, it's therefore considered and ordered that John Speed, Thomas Lanier, John Hide, Wm Harris Finniwood Matthew Marrable George Baskervil & John Humphreys be appointed to make Enquiry into the reasonableness of the complaint & to find out the most proper place for a Church to be fixed if it's found reasonable & make report to the next Vestry.

Ordered that John Earl, Lewis Delony, Thomas Tabb & John Speed View Miles's Creek Church & make report if it be worth repairing, or not, to the next Vestry.

James Craig
John Speed
Daniel Claiborne.

THE VESTRY BOOK, 1746-1816   371

At a Vestry held for the Parish of Cumberland November 12th 1759

Present the Reverend Mr Jas Craig
   John Speed & Danll Claiborn Gent Church Wardens

   John Parish   John Ragsdale   Gent.
   Thomas Pettis   John Jennings   Vestry men
   Henry Blagrove   Edmd Taylor

I, Edmund Taylor do promise to be conformable to the Doctrine & Discipline of the Church of England as by Law Established.

                                          Edmund Taylor.

A State of the Levy

To John Speed Clerk & Sexton at Roanoak Church	1500	
To Do for his care of the Surplis	100	
To John Watson for keeping his Sister	1000	
To John Blaxton Sexton & his care of the Surplis	600	
To Mr Edmund Taylor for Patrick Frails Son	1500	
To Elinor Hungerford to the care of Capt Jennings	1500	
To Richard Brooks for Ann Barns	1200	
To Wm Hunt Clerk & Sexton of the Court House Church & his care of the Surplis	1600	
To Wm Lax for Support of his Child	500	
To John Akin for Support of his Wife	600	
To John Hicks Clerk of Reedy Creek Church	1200	
To Mrs Hobson for the Support of Margret Bevil	500	
To John Earl for Do of Richard Watts	[Amount illegible]	
To Mrs Agness Hobson for the Support of Ann Kenny	"	
To Mr Edmund Taylor for the Support of Mrs Mary Mitchell	"	
To the Revd Mr James Craig his Salary	16000	
To Ditto for Cash and Srinkage	01200	17200

Cumberland Parish

To the Reverend Mr Proctor his Services in the Parish			[Amount illegible]

To the Reverend Mr Proctor his Services in the Parish [Amount illegible]

To Richard Witton for the Revd Mr Craig's Board   25 00 0

To D^o as Clerk of the Vestry for Ord^{ry} & Extraordinary Services   "

To the Rev M Proctor for Wine found for ye Sacrem^{ts}   10 0

To Wm Hunt for Supporting Old Rook   "

To Mr John Jones a Reader on the south side Roanoak for Reading once a fortnight   600

To Samuel Rudder reader at Flatrock Church from the first of May last   700

Ordered that Robert Hatcher take Burral Bevil the son of Margret Bevil who Obliges himself to Clear the Parish from any further charge for 1000 lbs. Tobacco   1000

       Present Matthew Marrable Gent.

To Wm Burgimy for putting up Horse Blocks & Benches & Grubbing 25 yds. square at Flatrock Church (The Revd Mr Craig absent)   2 10 0

To Stephen Codle for the Support of his Child   500

To Ditto for Burying Robert Nun & Maintaining him 31 days (Mr Craig Present)   500

To John Speed Gent. the Ballance of his Acco^t   5 14 6

To Dan^{ll} Claiborn Gent: his acco^t   3 15 0

To Mrs Eliz: Embry for 4 Bottles of Wine for the Church   15 0

To Doctor Joseph Dobson his Acc^t   6 10 0

To Doctor Clack Courtney his acc^t   5 10 6

To Stephen Hatchell for keeping Agness Dodd two months   1 0 0

To Lucias Tanner for removing Elizabeth Matthis to Meherrin Parish in Brunswick County   100

To Moses Street for making a coffin for Ephraim Best   10 0

To John Perant for Thomas Smith's Salary	1200	
To Mrs Sarah Gill for keeping John Consolvents child	600	
To Mrs Sarah Williams	300	
To Mr David Garland for 66 Tithes which belonged to the upper Parish and by mistake was given to him to collect at 20 lbs. p Poll 1320 at 23/ p Ct	15 3 7	

The said 15-3-7 he has Credit for in his Accot. for the Year 1758.

David Garland Collector of the Parish Levy for the Year 1757, rendered his Accot. and the ballance appearing in his favour of 6/10 is carried to his new account for 1758.

Mr. David Garland rendered his account for the Year 1758, and the ballance appearing to be due from him, to the Parish is £ 10-17-6½ which he is to settle for out of the Cash Accounts for the Ensuing Year.

Ordered that Pinkethman Hawkins pay Joseph Davies 15/ out of the cash due from him to the Parish the said 15/ being levyed for him in the year 1757 and not paid.

Ordered that the Revd. Mr. Pasture be paid for his services in this Parish   2000

Ordered that a Church be lett to be built at Tuslin Quarter Spring 60 foot by 30 foot and that Mr. Edmund Taylor and Mr. Thomas Lanier do lett the same to undertakers. Ordered that the Letters do agree with the Undertakers to build the gallery and do the inside work as they think proper, & that they take good Bond & Security, and agree to pay one half of the money upon covering and the other at compleating the same.

Ordered that the Church at Miles's Creek be repaired and an addition be made to the

Broad side of the same 28 foot by 20 foot, & that Mr. Jon. Speed and Mr. Edmund Taylor lett the same to undertakers & take good Bond & Security.

To a Depositum rais'd			30000
	66	18 7	84380
To the Sherriff for Collecting			5365
To a further Depositum of			255
			90000
By 2000 Tithables supposed at 45 lbs. p Pole			90000

Ordered that David Garland be appointed Collector & that he receive from each Tith 45 lbs. Tobacco.
Ordered that the old Church Wardens be continued (to wit) Mr. Daniel Claiborne & Mr. Jon. Speed.

James Craig
John Speed
Daniel Claiborne.

At a Vestry held for Cumberland Parish the 9th day of January, 1760.

Present
The Reverd. Mr. James Craig

John Speed, Danll. Claiborne Gent. Church Wardens

Thomas Tabb	Henry Blagrove
John Ragsdale	Thos. Pettus
& John Jennings	Gt VMen

Whereas it is represented to this Vestry by Sundry Inhabitants of this Parish that Tuslin Quarter & Miles's Creek Churches are uncentrical & inconvenient; in order to give satisfaction to all parties by ascertaining the proper center

It is ordered that that part of the Parish bounded on the North by South Meherrin, on the East by Brunswick Line; on the South by the County Line, from Brunswick Line as high as

Taylors Ferry, & by Roanoak from thence to the upper Parish Line and on the West by the upper Parish, shall be surveyed so as to find the exact centers, in or near which the said churches should be built, and that the said survey may be faithfully performed. It is further ordered that John Speed Gent. agree with a proper surveyor upon the easiest terms he can who shall have an oath of fidelity administered to him; that Mr. Speed attend him during the survey & shall for his trouble have five shillings p day. And lastly it is ordered that the building a Church at Tuslin Quarter Spring be suspended till the said survey is compleated, and that the repairing the Church at Miles Creek be suspended till the laying of the next Levy.

          James Craig
          John Speed
          Daniel Claiborne.

At a Vestry held for this Parish the 3rd day of Novembr. 1760.

  Present

    The Reverend Mr. James Craig

John Speed, Danll. Claiborne Gent. Church Wardens

John Jennings	Thomas Tabb	
Thomas Pettus	Henry Blagrove	Gent.
John Ragsdale	John Parish	Vestry Men.

    A State of the Levy

To John Speed Clerk and Sexton of Roanoak Church & his care of the Surplis	1600
To John Wadson for keeping his Sister	1000
To John Blaxton Sexton & his care of the Surplis	600
To Mr. Edmund Taylor for Patrick Frails Son	1500
To Elinor Hungerford to the care of Capt. Jennings	1500
To Ann Barns to the care of Richard Brooks	1200
To Wm. Hunt Clerk & Sexton of the Court House Church & his care of the Surplis	1600
To Wm. Lax for his child	700

To John Hix Clerk of Reedy Creek Church		1200
To Margret Bevil to the care of Jerimiah Hatcher		400
To Richard Watts, to the care of John Earl		500
To Nancy Kelly to the care of Mrs. Agness Gilliam		600
To Mary Mitchell to the care of Mr. Edmund Taylor		800
To Stephen Codell for supporting his child		500
To Samll. Rudder Reader at Flatrock		1200
To John Jones Reader at Grassy Creek		1200
To Abram. Whitimore for Old Rook		790
To George Hungerford as Sexton of Flatrock Church 300 & for Extra Services 100		400
To the Reverd. Mr. James Craig his salary	16000	
To Do for Cask & Shrinkage	1280	17280

To Richard Witton Clerk of the Vestry for his services		800
To Do. for the Revd. Mr. Craig's Board	25　0　0	

Present The Revd. Mr. James Craig &
    Mr. Thomas Lanier, Gent.

To Mrs. Sarah Gill for keeping John Consolvents child		500
To Mrs. Sarah Williams		300
To Fras. Amos for his son Nicholas		500
To Doctr. Joseph Dobson for curing Agatha Dodd	3	
To Ditto for means given Mary Matthis as p accot.	7　14　10½	
To Thomas Easland for keeping Do. in her sickness		500
To John Glass for keeping Do. two months which will expire the last of this month		400
To Mrs. Hatcher for keeping two poor children a year & curing them of sore heads		500
To Field Jefferson Gent. for sundry ferryages		400
To Thomas Tabb Gent. his accot.	2　11　9	
To Stephen Willis for himself & child to the care of Thomas Anderson Gent.		500
To Mr. Edmund Taylor what he paid a poor man by order of the Church Wardens	1　02　0	

To Brice Miller for undertaking to maintain one Samll. Wheelers son & keep him from being any further charge to the Parish	1000
The Gentlemen who were appointed to lett Bethel Church, having reported to this Vestry that the said church is finished in a workmanlike manner as according to the articles of agreement; we are unanimously of opinion that the said Church ought to be received, and it is by us received accordingly.	
To Wm. Burgimy for work done to Flatrock Church call'd Bethel more than he was obliged to do by agreement	2000
To Joseph Williams Gent. for reading as Clerk 6 mo.	600
To Robt. Chandler for keeping Edward Parham 8 mo.	600
To Joseph Chandler for Levys given in more than he had the years 1757 & 1758	40
To Samuel Phelps 3 Levys given in twice last yr.	135
Ordered that Matt Marrable & Edmund Taylor Gent. settle Colo. Reads accounts agst. the Parish & that they draw upon the Collector for what shall appear to be due which is ordered to be paid out of the Depositum.	
To Wm. Lax for keeping Edward Parham one year	500
To Richard Witton for a quire of paper for a record book for the returns of processioning	1-3
To John Speed Gent. for to attend the Churches one year with the Plate &c & finding bread & wine which yr. will expire in Novembr. next	5 0 0
Ordered that Richard Witton do coppy all the old Vestry Book into the New Record Book & bring his account for the same to this Vestry.	

David Garland Collector of the Parish Levys for the year 1759 rendered his account and the ballance appearing to be due *for* him to the said Parish is £ 105-01-2

Ordered that a Chappel of Ease be built on the South Side of Roanoak River at or near Edward Goalbreaths of 40 foot by 24 foot and that Edmund Taylor Gent. Mr. Thomas Anderson & Mr. Jacob Royster lett the same to undertakers in such manner as they think proper and that they agree to pay one half of the money at raising & the other at finishing the same which money the late Collector is ordered to pay.

To Edward Coalbreath for making benches & harbors	250
To The Collector	3470
To a Depositum to be paid to the Church Wardens	7010
	44 9 10½ 54575

	£ s d	
By 2183 Tithabes at 25 p Pole		54575
By Mr. David Garland	120 4 9	
By John Speed Gent. the Balla. his accot.	2 17 1½	
By Danll. Claiborne Gent. the Balla. his accot.	8 3 9	
	131 5 7½	

Mr. Edmund Taylor & Mr. John Ragsdale are chose Church Wardens for the Ensuing Year.

Mr. David Garland is appointed Collector of the Parish Levy for the present year & it is ordered that he give Bond and Security for the same to the present Church Wardens.

Ordered that Mr. David Garland do pay the Reverend
Mr. John Barclay or his attorney the ballance of
his judgment against the Parish.
James Craig
Edmond Taylor
John Ragsdale.

The Preceding Orders were made before the Division of Cumberland Parish.

At a Vestry held for this Parish July the 13th 1761.

Present The Revrd. Mr. Jas. Craige Minister &

The following Members of the Vestry who having already taken the Oaths prescribed by Law & Subscribed the Test in the Court of Lunenburg; Now in Open Vestry subscribe as follows:

We Danll. Claiborne, Lyddal Bacon, Henry Blagrove, David Garland, David Stokes, John Ragsdale, George Phillips, John Jennings, John Hobson, Thomas Pettus & Wm. Gee, do promise to be conformable to the Doctrine & Discipline of the Church of England by Law Established.

David Garland, Lyddal Bacon, George Phillips, Henry Blagrave, Thos. Pettus, John Ragsdale, John Hobson, David Stokes, Daniel Claiborne, William Gee, John Jenings, John Parrish.

[These are autograph signatures on the Vestry Book.]

Richard Witton is continued Clerk till his year is expired.

Messrs. Lyddal Bacon & David Garland are appointed Church Wardens for the ensuing year.

John Inloe is appointed Sexton of Reedy Creek Church & it is agreed he shall have the usual salary for the same.

John Inloe is also appointed to keep the Surplis for which he's to have 100 £ of Tobacco as usual.

Present John Jenings Gent.

Messrs. David Garland, John Jenings & John Ragsdale are appointed to look out for a tract of land proper for a Gleeb & make report to this Vestry at the next meeting.

James Craige
David Garland
Lyddal Bacon.

At a Vestry held for this Parish August 10th, 1761.

Present

The Reverd. Mr. James Craige, Minister

David Garland, George Phillips, Henry Blagrave,
Thos. Pettus, John Parish, John Ragsdale,
John Hobson, Daniel Claiborne & Willm. Gee, Gent.

Mr. David Garland, one of the gentlemen appointed to view a tract of land proper for a gleeb, reports that they have view'd all the lands that are centrical & he reports that they can't find any so suitable to Mr. Craig, & so much for the convenientcy of the Parish as Mr. John Ragsdales Plantation, for which he asks Two Hundred & fifty Pounds which this Vestry have agreed to give & to pay him that sum at such times as will suit him after the 1st of June next & Mr. Craig agrees to accept of the buildings that are there when properly finished with the addition of a Gleeb House, & a Garden, & Yard made compleat.

Ordered that a Gleed House & a Garden & a Yard be lett to be built & that Messrs. David Garland & Lyddal Bacon lett the same. The Dimentions of the Mention House to be fifty by eighteen foot with with inside chimneys to be four foot deep, the Hall 18 foot square, the passage 10 foot wide, the Chamber 18 foot by 14 with a Dutch Roof, & two rooms & passage above. The dimentions of the Garden & Yard to be known at the time of letting.

The said buildings are ordered to be lett on Thursday the 1st of October.

James Craig
David Garland.

At a Vestry held for this Parish Octobr. 30th, 1761.

Present

Messrs. David Garland, Lyddal Bacon, Thomas Pettus, John Parish, John Ragsdale, John Hobson, Danll. Claiborne, Wm. Gee.

A State of the Levy

To the Reverd. Mr. James Craig his salary	16000
To Do. for Cask and Shrinkage	1280

To Do. for his Board	25 00 0		
To Richard Witton Clerk of the Vestry			800
To John Hicks Clerk of Reedy Creek Church			1200
To John Inloe, Sexton of Do.	300		
To Do. for his care of the Surplis	100		400

To Samll. Rudder Clk. of Bethel Church   1200
To Geo. Hungerford Sexton   300
To Do. for other services   10 00
To Ann Barns, to the care of Richard Gilliam   [Amount illegible—page torn]
To Wm. Lax[?] for his child   "
To Margrett Bevil to the care of Jeri Hatcher   "
To Nancy Kelly to the care of Richard Gilliam   "
To Mrs. Sarah Gill for keeping Jon. Consolvents Child   . . .
To John Inloe for services about the Church   200
To Edward Parham to the care of Jeremiah Hatcher   500
To Francis Amos for his son Nicholas   500
To Stephen Cadel for his child   600
To Elliner Hungerford to the care of Capt. Garland   1200
To Richard Witton for coppying the records as p accot.   1 10 00
To John Blaxton his accot.   7 6
To Mr. John Ragsdales Accot.   0 5 0
    he at the same time give credit for a fine   0 5 0
To Allen Gentry for keeping Ann Nobles 3 months   [Amount illegible]
To William Allen for keeping Ditto 2 months   "
To Matthew Lines to the care of George Phillips Gent.   "

                                                          27 10 6   "
To a Depositum   39000
To a further Depositum   "
To Commissions for Collecting at 6 p C^t "

                                                                           "

By 1030 Tithables at 68½ lbs. p Pole   70555
By Capt. David Garlands Accot.   £   s   d
   the Balla. of Depositum for 1760   11 16 10½

Ordered that if the number of Tithables be more than 1030 the Sherriff shall settle for the same & if less that he shall be [page torn].

Ordered that Messrs. David Garland & Lyddal Bacon be Church Wardens for the Ensuing Year.

Mr. David Garland is appointed Collector of the Parish Levy for the present year.

Ordered that David Garland Gent. be allowed in proportion to the Tiths in Cumberland Parish the Insolvent Levies in the said Parish for the years 1757, 58, 59 & 60, & that he at the same time shall account for all supernumeraries.

David Garland
Lyddal Bacon.
C. W.

At a Vestry held for this Parish Jany. 23rd, 1762.

Present

Messrs. David Garland, Lyddal Bacon, Thomas Pettus, John Ragsdale, John Hobson, David Stokes, Danll. Claiborne

Ordered the Collector pay Colo. Read his account of **493 lbs.** Neat Tobacco dated in the year 1761.

Upon a motion made by Mr. John Ragsdale to this Vestry to be released from the bargain he had made to sell his land for a gleebe, it as been taken under consideration by them & they have hereby agreed to release him from the same.

It is ordered that the whole body of the Vestry meet as soon as convenient and fix upon another place for a Gleebe.

David Garland
Lyddal Bacon

At a Vestry held for this Parish May 20, 1762.
Present   Major Lyddal Bacon   Church Warden
Messrs. David Stokes
Thomas Pettus
John Ragsdale
Daniel Claiborne   Vestry men.
John Jennings
John Hopson

Whereas Mr. Deverix Jarratte, a Candidate for Holy Orders, applied to Vestry for a Title to this Parish; and whereas our present incumbent intends to leave us, and we are of opinion that, he the said Mr. Deverix Jarratte qualified in point of Virtue and Piety for that sacred Office; it is therefore

Ordered that the Church Wardens give a Title and recommendation to Mr. Deverix Jarratte, upon his giving Bond and Security he shall not by virtue of the Title insist upon being Minister of this Parish [if he] shall not be found agreeable to the Church Wardens & Vestry and Parishioners after trial.

David Garland
Lyddal Bacon

[Pages 66 and 67 of the Vestry Book, at this point, are missing, and page 68 is blank.]

At a Vestry held for this Parish June 4th, 1762
Present Messrs. David Garland, Lyddal Bacon,
Thomas Pettus, John Ragsdale, John Hobson,
David Stokes, John Jennings, Henry Blagrove,
Daniel Claiborne.

The Reverd. Mr. James Craig by his consent & the unanimous consent of this Vestry is received into this Parish as Rector of the same.

Ordered that the Revd. Mr. James Craig be allowed forty pounds p An. for his Board till the Gleebe is compleated.

Ordered the Gleebe Buildings be lett according to an order of Vestry made August 10th, 1761.

James Craig, Minister
David Garland
Lyddal Bacon

At a Vestry held for this Parish August 21st, 1762
  Present   The Revd. Mr. Jas. Craig &
    Messrs. David Garland, Lyddal Bacon, Thomas Pettus, John Ragsdale, David Stoakes, John Jennings, John Parish, Geo. Phillips, Wm. Gee, Henry Blagrove & Jon. Hobson.

Whereas it is found by the consultation with workmen of good judgment that the former plan of 50 foot by 18 is defective, it is therefore judged more advantageous to the Parish upon the whole to adopt the following, viz: one 48 by 22, 3 rooms on a floor, with a passage 10 foot wide & 11 foot from the floor to the ceiling &C which said house together with the kitchen & Landry 28 by 16 & 9 foot Pitch & a Dairy 12 foot square & 9 foot Pitch & Garden 124 by 176 according to the plan thereof lodged with the Vestry by which it is lett this day. Upon the Vestrys consent to this alteration the Revd. Mr. Craig consents to drop £ 15 p an. of his Board from this day & the said Buildings are accordingly lett with the necessary house 8 by 8 by 10 with a sash window containing 4 pains 10 by [missing].

David Garland
Lyddal Bacon

At a Vestry held for this Parish Novr. 1st, 1762.
Present
The Revd. Mr. James Craig

Lyddal Bacon
David Garland   Gent. Church Wardens

  Messrs. Thomas Pettus, John Ragsdale, Wm. Gee, John Jenings, David Stokes, John Hobson, Danll. Claiborne.

A State of the Levy

To the Revd. Mr. James Craig his salary	16000
To Do. for Cask and Shrinkage	1280
To Do. for his board 1 year 25 00 0	
To Richard Witton Clk of the Vestry	800
To John Hix Clk of Reedy Creek Church	1200

THE VESTRY BOOK, 1746-1816 385

To John Inloe Sexton		300			
& for his care of the Surplis		100			
		———			
					400
To Samll Rudder Clk of Bethell Church					1200
To George Hungerford Sexton					300
To Ann Barnes to the care of Richd. Brookes					900
To Margrett Bevil to the care of Jon. Pettis					350
To Nancy Kelly to the care of Wm. Lax					400
To Edward Parham to the care of Oby Hooper					800
To Fras. Amos for his son Nicholas					500
To Stephen Cadel for his child					600
To John Inloe for services about the Church Spring		0	12	0	
To Geo. Hungerford for his care of the plate &C & Surplis					150
To Wm. Allen for keeping Ann Nobles two years 61-62					1600
To Eliner Hungerford to the care of Jonathan Patison					1200
To Mr. Hampton Wade his accot.			16	6	
To Edwd. Cuttillo for his child					200
To Lyddal Bacon Gent. for the Eliments		1	3	0	
To Colo. Read his Accot.			1	3	91
To John Hobson Gent. his accot.		8	2	4½	
To the Accot. from St. James's Parish due from this		95	4	½	
St. James's Parish Dr.					
To a proportion of Jon. Hobson Gent. Accot.	3	2	9		
Cornwell Parish Dr.					
To a proportion of Jon. Hobson's Accot.	2	11	11½		
To a Depositum of					[Amount illegible]
					"
					"
To the Collector 6 p C^t					
					66805

To a further Depositum	[Amount illegible]
By 1061 Tithes at 62 Each	65782
Due to the Collector	1023

Messrs. David Garland & Lyddal Bacon are continued Church Wardens.

Mr. David Garland is appointed Collector of the Parish Levy & is ordered to receive from each tithe 62 lbs. Tobo.

         James Craig, Minr.
         David Garland
         Lyddal Bacon
            C. W.

At a Vestry held for this Parish Septembr. 30th, 1763

       Present

The Revernd. Mr. James Craig, Minister

Messrs. David Garland, Lyddal Bacon, Church Wardens.

Messrs. Geo. Phillips	Thos. Pettus
Jon. Jennings	David Stokes
	Danll. Claiborne

           Vestry Men

Pursuant to an Order of the Court of the County dated the 14th of July, 1763

Ordered that John Callaham, James Dicks & Francis Nibblet do meet at Jon. Callahams the 1st of Novembr. next & possession all the lands from where Brunswick Line crosses Meherrin River up the river as far as Flat Rock Creek thence up the said Creek to the road that crosses from Capt. John Jenings to Flat Rock Church thence down the said road to Brunswick line thence along the said line to the first station.

Ordered that Reps Jones, Thomas Chambers & Chas. Hamlin do meet at Charles Hamlins on the 1st of Novr. next & possession all the lands (to wit) beginning at Brunswick Line where it crosses Flatt Rock Road near Wm. Matthews thence as the said line runns to Nottoway River thence up the said river to the mouth of Hounds Creek thence up the said Creek to Hugh Lawsons Path thence as the Path goes by Danll. Hayes into the main road that leads to Flatt Rock Creek near Capt. John Jennings thence down the said Creek to the road that leads to Flatt Rock Church thence down the said road to the first station.

Ordered that Mathew Burt, Everd. Dowsing & Thos. Edwards do meet at Everd. Dowsings on the 1st Novembr. next & possession all the lands (to wit) beginning on Hounds Creek where the Path call'd Lawsons crosses it, thence up the sd Creek to Jon. Strawans to where it crosses the Little Road that leads to Reedy Creek Church, thence up the said road to the Fork that leads to Jonathan Pattisons & the bridge over Meherrin River at John Hawkins, thence down the River to the mouth of Flatt Rock Creek, thence up the said creek to where the main road crosses, thence down the road to Hugh Lawsons path by Danll. Hayes, thence as the path goes to the first station.

Ordered that Danll. Wynn, Elisha Eastis & Joel Farguson do meet at Daniel Wynns on Novembr. the 1st & possession from the Mouth of Hounds Creek to where the road crosses at Nottoway at Hampton Wades thence along the road to Reedy Creek Church thence down Reedy Creek Road opposite to the head of Hounds Creek.

Ordered that Jarrott Mcconico, Sill [Sylvanus?] Stokes & Lodwk. Farmer do meet at Jarrott Macconicoes on the 1st of Novembr. next & procession all the land from Jarrott Maconicos between Wininghams Road & the road that leads to Reedy Creek Church to the bridge at Jon. Scotts.

Ordered that Jon. Night, Joseph Miner & Covie Christopher do meet at Joseph Miners on the 1st of Novembr. next & possession all the lands from where the road crosses at H. Wades between Wininghams road & Great Nottoway to Cornwell line.

Ordered that Wm. Stone Vol. Brown, & Cleveres Coalman do meet at Wm. Stones on the 1st of Novembr. next & possession all the land between the North & South Meherrin below the road that leads from Reedy Crk Church to Jon. Coxes.

Ordered that Wm. Chandler, Joseph Ship & Stephen Wood do meet at Joseph Ships on the 1st of Novembr. next & Procession all the land that lies between Coxes Road & Cornwell Line & between North & South Meherrin.

Ordered that Wm. Jeter, Robt. Scott & Jon. Scott, do meet at Robert Scotts on the 1st of Novembr. next & procession all the land bounded by the Road that leads from Jon. Scott's Bridge towards Reedy Creek by the new road that leads towards Jona. Pattisons by the Main Road that leads to Hawkins's Bridge & by the North Branch of Meherrin to Jon. Scotts Bridge.

Ordered the above Processioners make their returns of processioning of the several precincts according to Law.

Ordered that there be a Corn Crib built on the Gleeb of Cumberland Parish of 20 foot long & 12 foot wide & that Messrs. David Garland & Jon. Jenings lett the same to undertakers.

David Garland
Lyddal Bacon

At a Vestry held for this Parish Novembr. 8th, 1763
Present
The Revd. Mr. James Craig, Minister
David Garland & Lyddal Bacon, Gent. Church Wardens

Messrs. Henry Blagrove, Thos. Pettus, Jon. Jenings
Jon. Ragsdale, Wm. Gee,   Vestry Men.

A State of the Levy				Dr.
To the Revd. Mr. James Craig his salary				16000
To Do. for Cask & Shrinkage				1280
To Do. for his Board	25	00	0	
To Richd. Witton Clk. of the Vestry				0800
To Do. for Extraordinary Services				200
To John Hix Clk of Reedy Creek Church				1200
To John Blaxton Sexton & for his care of the Surplis				0400
To Samll. Rudder Clk of Bethell Church				1200
To George Hungerford Sexton of Do.				300

To Do. for his care of the Surplis & Plate			150
To Ann Barns to the care of Rd. Brooks			700
To Margrett Bevil			175
To Nancy Kelly to Richd. Gilliam			400
To Edwd. Parham to Richd. Gilliam			590
To Fras. Amos for his son Nicholas			...
To Stephen Cadel for his child			600
To Ann Nobles to Allen Gentry			600
To Elinor Hungerford			...
To Edwd. Cuttillo for his child			...
To George Hungerford for some services at Reedy Creek Church	0	15	0

Present Geo. Phillips Gent.

To Jon. Trustie to Mr. Phillips			300
To Joseph Gentry for keeping Stephen Crump 10 months to this date			800
To Stephen Crump to the care of Thos. Garrett			750
To Capt. Jenings for Colo. Read his Tickett for prosecuting a suit agst. Pin. Hawkins &C part			89½
To Richd. Haggard for maintaining Jo. Traylor			400
To Majr. Lyddal Bacon his accot.	6	00	0
To Wm. Justice for support of his father & mother			800
To Joel Farguson for a levy overcharge in 1761			68½
To Mr. Taylor Clk. for his Tickett			10½
	31	15	0 27813½
To a Depositum			24967½
To Commission to the Collector			3369
			56150

Cr.

By 1123 Tithables at 50 lbs. p Pole   56150

Capt. Geo. Phillips & Mr. Henry Blagrove are appointed Church Wardens for the ensuing year.

Col. Witton is appointed Collector for Do. and is ordered to receive 50 lbs. from each Titheable.

By Capt. David Garland's accot. due from him being the Balla. of the depositum in his hands for
1761 & 1762   1 6 8

         James Craig
         George Phillips
         Henry Blagrave

At a Vestry held for this Parish May 26, 1764
Present
Mr. Henry Blagrove & Mr. George Phillips, Church Wardens

Messrs. David Garland, Lyddal Bacon, Thos. Pettus, John Jennings, Wm. Gee,   Vestrymen
Mr. John Ragsdale, Colo. David Stokes & Mr. Jon. Hobson.

We of the Vestry mett this day to receive the returns of the Processioners which returns are committed to record in this book following the former entrys begining at page 221.

Mr. John Parish being removed from this Parish has resigned his place as Vestryman & by the vote of the Vestry Mr. Thos. Tabb is chose in his place.

I, Thomas Tabb do promise to be conformable to the Doctrine & Discipline of the Church of England as by Law established.
            Thomas Tabb.[1]

Ordered that the Church Wardens imploy a workman to put one window in each of the upper pews in the Church at Reedy Creek.

         Henry Blagrave[1]
         George Phillips.[1]

At a Vestry held for this Parish Novbr. 23rd, 1764
Present
Messrs. John Jennings, John Ragsdale, Thos. Pettus John Hobson, George Phillips & Thos. Tabb & Wm. Gee.

---
[1]Autograph signature on the record, page 76.

A State of the Parish Levy

To the Revd. Mr. James Craig his salary		16000
To Do. for Cask & Shrinkage		1280
To Do. for his Board	25 0 0	
To Richard Witton Clk of Vestry		800
To John Hix Clk of Reedy Creek Church		1200
To Edwd. Self Sexton & for the Surplis		400
To Samll. Rudder Clk of Bethell Church		1200
To Geo. Hungerford Sexton of Do.		0300
To Do. for his care of the Surplis & Plate		150
To Ann Barns in the hands of John Calvin		650
To Margrett Bevil to Richd. Witton		200
To Nancy Kelly to Richd. Gilliam		650
To Edwd. Parham to Wm. Lax		550
To Fras. Amos for his son Nicholas		500
To Stephen Caudel for his child		...
To Ann Nobles to Wm. Allen		800
To John Trustie in Mr. Geo. Phillips's hands		500
To Stephen Crump to Thos. Garrott		800
To Richd. Haggard for Joseph Trayler		...
To Edward Cotillo for his child		250
To Thomas Pound for present relief		600
The above Thos. Pound is discharged from paying levies.		
To Thomas Riddle		200
To Jon. Braughton in the hands of the Revd. Mr. James Craig		600
To Mr. Wm. Taylor Clk of the Court *is* accot.		97
To Richd. Wyatt for attending to prove a deed from Fras. Williams for ye Gleeb land		25
To Mr. Jon. Hobson to convey Jas. Shelbon to Jas. City County to Samll. Duffeys	2 00 0	
To Thomas Shelbon for his Bror. James		0700
To Capt. Geo. Phillips for Eliments	2 00 0	
To Do. his Accot.	0 11 6	
To the Revd. Mr. James Craig his Accot. wch. is ordered the Collector shall pay out of the Depositum	6-6	

To Mr. Robt. Eastis for putting up horse blocks & seats at Reedy Creek Church				0500
To Edwd. Self for cleaning the spring &c	0	02	6	
To Drury Moore for Jon. Inloes Coffin		15	0	
To Mr. Geo. Phillips to pay Isaac Brown for benches &c at Bethel Church out of the Depositum wch. the Collector is ordered to pay £ 3-00-0				
	30	9	0	29752

Ordered that the Collector pay Mr. Jon. Powel what money is now in his hands & to make up the same as soon as it can be collected One Hundred Pounds provided his present securitys assent to the said payment. Capt. Jon. Jennings one of the Suritys assigns his assent.

        Jno. Jenings

Ordered the Collector settle for the Depositum at 15/ p lb. & that he return a list of insolvents at the next laying the levy.

To a Depositum raised to pay the cash debts	17032
To the Collector 6 p Ct for Collecting	2986
	49770
The Parish has credit for 1185 Tithes at 42 P Pole	49770

 Messrs. Thomas Pettus & Jon. Ragsdale are appointed Church Wardens for the ensuing year.

 Mr. George Jefferson is appointed Collector of the Parish Levy & is ordered to collect 42 lbs. Tobo. for each tithe & to give bond & security to the Church Wardens for the same.

 Ordered that the Kitchens at the Gleeb be finished off in the following manner, viz. The walls of the kitchen proper be lined wth. ¾ Plank the Floor to be layed wth. tile a dresser & 4 shelves to be fixed up on each side extending from the fire place to each door, the floor of the Landry to be layed with plank, the walls to be lath'd & plastered, a floor to be lay'd up stares & the upper room lathed & plastered, 2 windows at each end of 4 paynes each, a step lather with a rail to it, & it is ordered the Church Wardens lett the same to the lowest bidder as soon as convenient some time in 3 weeks from the date.

NB the steps to be eased at the bottom & risers of 7 inches.

Memorandm. that the Tobacco is overcast 800 wch. is to be added to the Depositum & accounted for by the Collector.

James Craig
John Ragsdale
Thos. Pettus

Accots. coppy'd as followes which have been allowed by this Vestry.

Nov. 1st, 1762, at the Vestry held that day.

Mr. Hampton Wades Accot.

Nov. 23, 1761, To a large stock[?] Lock	0	07	6	
Jan. 7, 1762 To 1/4 Wine		3		
Oct. 2, To 3/4 Do.		6	0	
		—0	16	6

Nov. 23rd, 1764, at a Vestry

Mr. Andw. Johnsons Accot. allow'd to Capt. Phillips

Nov. 2, 1764, to 8 Bottles of Wine for the Church	2	00	0

At the same Vestry

Capt. Geo. Phillips's Accot.

To 1/2 a barrel of Corn to Thos. Riddle	0	05	0	
To 1 Ell Ozbo. for a wallet for the church plate		1	6	
To George Hungerford for putting up blocks at the church		5	0	
		—0	11	6

At a Vestry held for this Parish, Novr. 12th, 1765.

Present The Revd. Mr. James Craig

Messrs. John Ragsdale & Thos. Pettus, Gent. Church Wardens Messrs. Lyddal Bacon, Henry Blagrove, David Stokes, John Hobson, Thos. Tabb, & John Jennings, Wm. Gee, Gent. Vestrymen, & also Geo. Phillips, Gent.

Cumberland Parish

A State of the Parish Levy

To the Revd. Mr. James Craig his salary	16000	
To Do. for Cask & Shrinkage	1280	17280
To Do. 2 months Board 4 2 4		
To Richard Witton Clk of the Vestry		800
To John Hix Clk of Reedy Creek Church		1200
To Edwd. Self Sexton of Do.	300	
his care of the Surplis	100	
		400
To Samll. Rudder Clk. of Bethel Church		1200
To Geo. Hungerford Sexton of Do.	300	
& for his care of the Surplis & Plate	150	
		450

(NB that this Tobo. is to be divided between Colulias Priest)

To Ann Barns	...
To Margrett Bevil 200	200
To Nancy Kelly to Joseph Davies	500
To Edwd. Parham 550 to Thomas Tureman	700
To Nicholas Amos 500 to Fras. Amos	500
To Ann Nobles 800 to Wm. Allen	800
To John Trustie 500 to Capt. Phillips	500
To Stephen Crump to Obedia Hooper	900
To Edwd. Catillo for his child 250	250
To Thos. Riddle	200
To Jon. Broughton	

To Jas. Shelborn 96 lbs. Tob. & 4/ to be paid to Thos. Shelborn	0	4	0	96
To Wm. Lax for keeping Jas. Shelborn 7 months & a half				656
To Richd. Gilliam for sundrys for James Shelborn	0	15	0	

1765
Nov. 12

To Mr. Jon. Ragsdale his Accot.	2	10

1764
Mar. 27

To Mr. Hampton Wade his Accot.	17	7½	
To Wm. Grissam his levy being twice listed			042
To Jacob Davies for the same			042
To Drury Moore for his attending the Court for an evidence to a deed for the Gleeb land			025
To Edwd. Self for services done to the Chh. Spring	0	2 6	
Mr. Daniel Claiborne having declined serving as a Vestryman this Vestry have made choyce of Mr. Thomas Wynn to serve in his stead.			
To a Depositum raised			12213
To 6 p Ct. to the Collector			2486
	8	12 5½	41440
The Parish hath credit by 1184 Tithables at 35 lbs. Tobo. p Pole			41440
Ordered that has Mr. John Hobson has given up his right to forty Shillings levyed for him at the laying of the last Levy that the same be pd. by the Collector to Wm. Allen for keeping Ann Nobles.			
By Mr. Thomas Petties's Accot. a Balla. due to the Parish	0	7 6	
Mr. Daniel Claiborne Cr. By Cash pd. Mr. Henry Blagrove	3	2 0	

Ordered that Mr. John Jennings, Mr. Thomas Tabb & Mr. David Garland settle with St. James's Parish the Accot. unsettled between this Parish & that.

Ordered that the Church Wardens imploy a Person to dig a well at Reedy Creek Church.

Colo. David Stokes & Mr. William Gee are appointed Church Wardens for the insuing year.

Ordered that the present Church Wardens settle with David Hopkins & Daniel Claiborne & all other persons in debt to the said Parish.

Ordered that John Ballard be appointed Collector for this Parish Levy & that he give the Church Wardens satisfactory security.

Ordered that the Collector pay Mr. John Powel fifty pounds if so much in hands.

> James Craig
> David Stokes
> William Gee

At a Vestry held for this Parish the 15 Janry. 1766.

Present

The Reverd. Mr. James Craig

Messrs. David Stokes & Wm. Gee, Gent. Church Wardens

David Garland, Lyddel Bacon, Jon. Jennings
Thos. Petties, Thos. Wynn, Jon. Ragsdale,
Vestrymen.

Ordered that the 500 lbs. of Tobo. levyed for Jos. Davies for keeping Nancy Kelly should not be paid by the Collector till further orders.

Ordered that Robert Wilson take James Shelborne & keep him twelve months from this day & that he shall have 700 lbs. Tobo. for the same.

Pursuant to a former order of Vestry that Jon. Ballard, Junr. collect the Parish Levy for 1765 provided he give satisfactory security to the Church Wardens whereupon Jon. Ballard, Senr. & David Garland, Gentn. undertakes to be his security untill further orders are made by this Vestry.

Ordered that Mr. George Jefferson settle for the Depositum in his hands at 15/ p lb. & that he pay Mr. John Powel Thirteen Pounds five Shillings & 3d in part of the last order for 50 £.

Ordered that the Church Wardens sell the former Gleebe land & give credit as they think proper.

> James Craig
> David Stokes
> William Gee

Mr. George Jefferson Cr. in part of
the Depositum (to wit)

By wt. pd. Capt. Phillips	2	11	6
By pd. Mr. Jas. Craig	25	00	0
By pd. Drury Moore	0	15	0
By pd. Mr. Powel by Capt. Garland	20		
By pd. Do. £ 30 & £ 12	42	00	0
By pd. Do. by Mr. Ragsdale	2	08	10
By pd. the Qt. Rents of the Gleebe Land 827 acres	1	17	6½
	94	12	10
By the above sum pd. this day	13	5	3
	107	18	1

At a Vestry held for this Parish Novr. 25th, 1766.

Present

The Reverend Mr. James Craig

Messrs. Lyddel Bacon, David Stokes, John Jennings, Thos. Tabb, John Ragsdale, Thomas Petties & George Phillips.

A State of the Parish Levy

To the Reverd. Mr. James Craig	16000	
To Do. for Cask & Shrinkage	1280	
		17280
To Richard Witton Clerk of the Vestry		500
To John Hix Clk of Reedy Creek Church		1200
To Edward Self Sexton of Do.	300	
his care of the Surplis	100	
		400
To Samuel Rudder Clerk of Bethel Church		1200
To George Hungerford Sexton of Do.	300	
& for his care of the Surplis & Plate	150	
		450
To Margrett Bevil		
To Nancy Kelly to the Church Wardens or Mrs. Gillam		500

To Edward Parham to the Church Wardens or Thos. Garrot	700
To Nicholas Amos to Do. or Fras. Amos	500
To Ann Nobles	800
To John Trustie in the hands of Capt. Phillips	500
To Edward Cottillo for his child to the Ch. Wardens	250
To Thomas Riddle to the Ch. Wardens	500
To James Shelborne to Do. or Obediah Hooper	1350

Present Wm. Gee, Gent.

To Philp. Cockerham for keeping Jas. Shelborne 20 days	62
To John Price for keeping Ann Barnes last year & to take her out of the Parish & clear the Parish of her for the future	2000

Robt. Wilson enters himself security for John Price that he shall clear the Parish of the charge of Ann Barns.

To Robt. Eastis for making the steps at Reedy Ck. Church	5	00	
To the Ch. Wardens for Jon. Hazlewoods child			500
To Mr. Wm. Gee for wine for the church (this is paid)	1	05	00
To Cash to purchase Wine for the use of the Churches	3	12	00

Present David Garland, Gent.

Mr. Taylor is chose Vestryman in the place of Jon. Hobson.

Richd. Witton Collector for this Parish in the year 1763 has delivered his Accot. & paid the ballance of 0-14-8½ to Mr. Thomas Tabb.

To Mr. Andw. Johnsons Accot.	3	10	2
To Mr. Jos. Williams for the Qt. Rents of the former Gleebe land 302 acres being for 5 years	3	8	4

The above is ordered to be converted to the use of ye Parish.

Memorandm.

That this day we settled with Mr. John Powell & he agrees he has recd. £ 445-16-1 wch. is £ 17-16-1 more than was agreed to give him at the letting of the Gleebe.

Mr. Jon. Ballard has delivered his accot. as Collector of the Parish Levys for the last year, by which he makes himself debtor to this Parish £ 27-5-6 errors excepted.

Ordered that a stable be built for the Gleeb of sawed loggs of 20 foot by 16 with a shed of 8 foot the length of the stable, & to be shingled, to have 8 stalls with a passage between; the side of the shed to be clapboarded the whole length; but open at the ends, & be lett by the Church Wardens & to [be] lofted with Inch Plank join'd, but not plan'd.

Ordered that a Closett be made in the Gleebe house to be lett at the discreation of the Ch. Wardens.

Thos. Tabb & John Jenings Gent. are appointed Church Wardens for the insuing year.

Ordered that the present Ch. Wardens sell the old Gleebe land & give two years credit.

To a Depositum	9066
To the Collector	2282
	38040
By 1268 Tithables at 30 Each	38040

Ordered that Collector Richd. Wittons list of insolvents & John Ballards be put into the next Collectors hands to collect,

Richd. Witton being	3450
John Ballards	2520
	5970

Ordered that Mr. John Ballard the late Collector pay Mr. Thos. Tabb the present Ch. Warden the Balla. due from him.

Ordered that the present Ch. Wardens settle with Daniel Claiborne, David Hopkins & all other persons indebted to the Parish.

>James Craig
>Thos. Tabb
>Jno. Jenings

Memorandum

That there is a mistake in casting the Tobo. on the other side it is 28692.

Mr. John Powel   Dr.

To cash paid by Colo. David Garland	200	00	0
To Ditto by Richard Witton	118	02	0
To Ditto by George Jefferson	77	14	1½
To Ditto by John Ballard	50		
To Shingles by David Hopkins	445	16	1½
Ditto Cr.	428	..	..
By the Gleebe undertaking when done 428 00 0			
Carryed forward	17	16	1½

A Coppy of Richard Wittons Accot. for the Parish Collection in the Year 1763.

Dr.   Richard Witton   Cr.

To a Depositum 24968 lbs. Tobo. at 15/ £ 187 5 2½	By paid the Rev. Mr. James Craig	25	00	00
	By Ditto to Ditto by ordr. of Vestry	6	01	6
	By Geo. Hungerford		15	00
	By Colo. Bacon	6		
	By David Hopkins	4	14	6
	By Mr. John Powell	118	2	00
	By 69 Insolvents 50 lbs. each at 15/ p lb.	25	17	6
		186	10	6
	Balla. paid Mr. Thos. Tabb		14	8½
		187	04	2½

A Coppy of John Ballards Accot. Collector for the Year 1766
Dr.   John Ballard   Cr.

To a Depositum 12213 lbs. Tobo.				By paid the			
at 16/2½	£ 98	19	6½	Revd. Mr. Craig	4	03	04
To Supernumerarys				By pd. Jas. Shelborne	0	04	00
1190 at 16/2½	9	11	10½	By pd. Richd. Gilliam	0	15	
				By pd. John Ragsdale	2	10	
	108	11	5	By pd. Hampton Wade		17	7½
				By pd. Edwd. Self		2	6
				By pd. Wm. Allen	2	5	
				By pd. Jon. Powell by ordr. of the Ch. Wardens	50	-	
				By Insolvents 2520 at 16/2½	20	8	5½
					81	5	11
				By Balla. pd. Mr. Thos. Tabb Ch. Warden	27	5	6
					108	11	5

At a Vestry held for this Parish the 14th March, 1767.
      Present   The Revd. Mr. James Craig

Thomas Tabb & Jon. Jenings, Gent. Church Wardens

Messrs. David Garland, Lyddal Bacon, John Ragsdale, Geo. Phillips, Thomas Wynn, Gent. Vestrymen.

Mr. John Powell   Dr.

To cash paid by Sundrys brot. from the other side	445	16	01½
To Shingles by David Hopkins (to wit)			
4214 at 10/ 4000 at 12/6	4	12	00
	450	08	01½
Ballance due to John Powell	66	00	04½
	516	8	6

    Contra   Cr.

By the sum allowed him by agreemt.	428	00	00
By sundry additions & alterations	88	08	06
	516	08	6

Ordered that the Collector pay Robt. Wilson 700 lbs. of Tobacco out of the Depositum in his hands.

Ordered that the Gleebe Buildings of this Parish be received, being viewed by this Vestry & judged to be compleated according to the contract made with John Powel, the undertaker of the same; & it is further ordered that the said John Powell be paid for additions & alterations agreed upon by this Vestry to be made to the said buildings after the first contract; the sum of Eighty Eight Pounds Eight Shillings & Six pence, & it is ordered that Mr. Thos. Tabb Church Warden pay Mr. Powell what he has in his hands.

James Craig
Thomas Tabb
Jno. Jenings.

At a Vestry held for this Parish the 23rd of Septembr., 1767.

Present

Messrs. Lyddal Bacon, Henry Blagrove, Thomas Tabb, John Ragsdale, David Stoakes, Thomas Petties & Thomas Wynn.

Joshua Ragsdale is appointed Clerk of the Vestry in the room of Richd. Witton.

Present Wm. Gee, Gent.

1 Ordered that Frans. Niblitt & Thomas Moody possession all the land between Brunswick line & Stony Creek up to Flatt Rock Road & Meherrin & between that road & Meherrin River.

2 Ordered that Alexr. Rudder & John Hight possession all the land from between Stony Creek & Flatt Rock & from Flatt Rock Road to Meherrin River.

3 Ordered that Henry Vandyck & French Haggard possession all the land between Flatt Rock Creek & Crockett Creek up to Flatt Rock road that goes to Capt. Jenings, & from thence along the great road that leads to Crockett Creek & all the land between the two creeks & Meherrin.

4 Ordered that Henry Gee & Nevel Gee possession all the land between Crockett Creek & Bears Elimint up to the great road & all the land between that & Meherrin.

5 Ordered that Benjn. Tomlinson & John Lucas possession all the land between Bears Eliment & the great road that goes to Mr. Pattisons & from thence to Meherrin River.

6 Ordered that Robt. Baylie & John Smithson possession all the land between the North & Middle Meherrin frm. Coxes Road to the forks of the river.

7 Ordered that Robt. Dixon & Benj. Clerk possession all the land between the South & Middle Meherrin from Coxes Road to the fork of Meherrin.

8 Ordered that John Williams attorney & David Johnson possession all the land between the South & Middle Meherrin from Coxes Road to Charlotte line.

9 Ordered that Nathaniel Mason & Fredrick Brown possession all the land between the Middle & North Meherrin from Coxes Road to Charlotte line.

10 Ordered that Jonathan Davis & Daniel Mallone possession all the land between Winingham Road & Charlotte line from the North Meherrin to Tusakia Creek to Degraffenreidts rowling road from thence to ledbetter Creek & up the said creek to Charlotte line.

11 Ordered that Joseph Billips & Ben Collier possession all the land between Winingham Road & Nottoway River to Tusakia Creek to Degraffenreidts Rowling Road from thence to Ledbetter Creek & up the same to Charlotte line.

12 Ordered that Leonard Dosyer & Giddion Moon possession all the land between Wininghams Road Couches Creek and Nottoway River.

13 Ordered that Zack. Eastis & Colonel Petti Poole possession all the land between Couches Creek the North Meherrin & the Court house road, to the head of Couches Creek.

14 Ordered that Wm. Cureton & Allen Stokes possession all the land between Murrels rowling road & Wininghams Road & Allen Stokes Mill Creek & the Court house road to the Mouth of this Creek.

15 Ordered that Joseph Wynn & Nicholas Brown procession all the land between Nottoway River, Allen Stokes Mill Creek, the Cot. house road to the Mouth of great *Ounds* [Hounds] Creek to Wards Rowlg. Road.

16 Ordered that John Hazlewood & Bartlett Eastis procession all the land between the Cot. House Road, Rowland Wards Rowling Road & Reedy Creek Old Road.

17 Ordered that Wm. Hardie & John Hardie procession all the land from Rowld. Wards Road between Great Hounds Creek, Reedy Crk. Old Road & Nottoway River to Crosses Bridge.

18 Ordered that Robt. Chappell, Jon. Heighour,[1] Robt. Liverett & Edwd. Thweat procession all the land between Nottoway River & Flatt Rock Road, Brunswk. line & Jenings Road.

19 Ordered that Richard Williams & Lazers. Williams procession all the land between Jenings Road & Reedy Creek Old Road from the fork of the said roads belowe Reedy Creek.

20 Ordered that Jeremiah Glenn & Tschr. Degraffenreidt procession all the land between Reedy Creek & Reedy Creek Old Road, Coxes Road & the North Meherrin River.

Thomas Tabb.

At a Vestry held for this Parish November the 25th, 1767

Present   The Revd. Mr. James Craig
                Messrs. Thomas Tabb, Thomas Winn,
                Henry Blackgrave, David Stokes,
                Thomas Peaties, John Ragsdale,
                George Phillups, Gent. Vestrymen.

A State of the Parish Levy

To the Revd. Mr. James Craig	16000	
To Do. for Cask and Shrinkage	1280	
	17280	17280
To John Hix Clerk of Reedy Creek Church		1200
To Edward Self Sexton of Do. 300 lbs. Tobo.		
To his care of the Surplis 100		400
To Samuel Rudder Clerk of Bethel Church		1200
To George Hungerford Sexton of Do.	300	
To his care of the Surplis & Plate	200	
		500

---

[1] Probably "Hightower" is here intended.

To Joshua Ragsdale Clerk of the Vestry	800
For Nany Kelley to the Ch. Wardens or Obediah Hooper	500
For Nicholas Amos to Do. or Frans. Amos	750
For Ann Nobles to Wm. Allan	800
For John Trustie to Capt. Phillups	500
To Edward Cutillo for his child	250
For James Shelborne to Wm. Lax	900
To the Church Wardens for Jno. Hazlewoods child Present Jno. Jenings Gent.	500
For Martha Justice to the Ch. Wardens	500
To Elisha Eastis one levy overpaid	30
To Samuel Harris one levy overpaid	25
	26135
To a Depositum	11261
Six p Ct. to the Collector	2280
	39676
The Parish hath credit by 1417 Tithes at 28 lbs. Each	39676

	£	s	d
Dr. John Jenings to Cumberland Parish			
To cash recd. of Capt. Billups for a fine	1	0	
Cr. Cumberland Parish to Jno. Jenings Dr.			
By 1/2 Barrel Corn 5/ to Nancy Marsh			
By Finding Bread for Bethel Church 5/			
By four pair of Indenters 5/		15	
The Balla. due the Parish		5	
Cumberland Parish Dr. to Thos. Tabb C. W.			
To 17 pair of Indenters and 2 Acts of Assembly	1	2	
To Thos. Garrot for burying Edward Parham	0	10	00
To George Hungerford as p acct.	0	5	
	1	17	
To John Powell the Ballance of his acct.	25	11	
	27	9	

Colo. Thos. Winn Dr.
   To Cash received as Ch. Warden   2   5
   The Balla. due by the Collector as
      appears by his acct.   1   18   0¼
      Cr. by cash paid   1   15   0
                                              ─────────────
      The Balla. due   0   3   0¼

A List of Insolvents returned by Antony Street and
   received by this Vestry
   37 Insolvents at 30 lbs. each 1110 lbs. Tobo.
Messrs. Thos. Winn and Wm. Taylor are appointed
   Ch. Wardens for the ensuing year.
Ordered that Antony Street collect the Parish Levy
   the ensuing year and that he receive 28 lbs. Tobo.
   from each tithe.
Recd. Mr. Thos. Tabbs Acct. whereby it appears
   he is indebted to the Parish   0   10   0
By the Balla. Paid   10

                  James Craig   Thos. Winn

1767   A Copy of Mr. Thos. Tabbs Accompt.

   Dr. Cumberland Parish   £   s   d
   To Cash to Capt. Joseph Williams   5   0   0
   To Cash to Wm. Gee 25/   1   5   0
   To Cash to Mr. Andrew Johnston   3   10   2
   To Cash pd. the Sheriff for Qtr. &
      taxes of the Glebe land   1   17   0¼
   To 18 bottles Port wine from Petersburg
      with the expences & troubles
      proceeding therefrom   3   0   0
   To cash paid Mr. Powel on acct.
      of the Glebe   11   10   0
   To Pd. on old Mrs. Journeys acct. 13/3   0   13   3
   To cash now in hand   0   10   0¾
                                              ─────────────
                                             27   5   6

THE VESTRY BOOK, 1746-1816 407

Contra	Cr.			
1766 November 26th By cash received for Cumberland Parish of Jno. Ballard		27	5	6

A Copy of George Hungerfords Acct.
Cumberland Parish Dr.

Septr.
1767 To putting new feet to a bench & fastening sundry pews & benches that were loose in Bethel Church — 5

A Copy of Anthony Streets Acct.
Dr. Cumberland Parish

	£	s	d
1767 To a Depositum levy'd 9066 lbs. Tobo.			
To Cash paid Mr. Jno. Powel	30	7	0
To Cash paid for Capt. Daniel Claiborne	10	15	3
To Cash pd. Edward Self for mending the Surplice	0	2	6
To Expences for Toddy to Anthony Street for trouble of selling the Glebe land & for trouble of selling	0	8	9
To the undertaker of the Glebe Closet	2	17	0
To the Balls. now in the Collectors hands	1	18	0¼
	46	08	6¼

	lbs. Tobo.
Contra Cr.	
By a mistake made in the Depositum	2000
By paying Robert Wilson	700
By 37 Insolvents Retd. at 30 lbs. Tobo. p Poll	1110
	3810
By a Ballance due the Depositum	5256
lbs. Tobo.	9066

By the sale of 5256 lbs. Tobo. at 17/8 p Ct.   46   8   6¼

At a Vestry held at the Courthouse for Cumberland Parish in Lunenburg County the 10th day of December, 1767.

Present

  Thomas Winn & William Taylor Church Wardens
   William Gee   John Ragsdale
   Thomas Tabb Lyddal Bacon
   John Jenings Gent. Vestrymen

Everard Dowsing appointed Clerk of the present Vestry and no longer. Test Everard Dowsing C. W.

On the motion of David Garland late Collector of this Parish and agreeable to a former order of Vestry, his list of Insolvents of Supernumeraries for the years 1757-58-59 and 1760 being examined, it is ordered that the present Collector pay him 1449 pounds of Tobo. out of the depositum for this year if so much remaining after paying what was levyed in the last levy for the several persons therein mentioned.

On the motion of David Garland late Collector for the years 1761 and 1762 its ordered that the Collector pay him 6296 pounds of Tobo. out of the present Depositum if so much remaining after paying what was levied for the several persons therein mentioned, the same being allowed for his Insolvents for the years above mentioned.

           Thos. Winn
           Wm. Taylor

At a Vestry held for Cumberland Parish the 22nd of November, 1768
Present
  The Revd. James Craig
  Messrs. Thomas Winn and William Taylor Ch. Wardens
  Lyddal Bacon and David Garland, John Ragsdale
  Henry Blagrave and Thomas Peatis Gent. Vestrymen.

A State of the Parish Levy		Tobacco
To the Revd. James Craig	16000	
To Do. for Cask and Shrinkage	1280	
	———	17280
To John Hix Clerk of Reedy Creek Church		1200

THE VESTRY BOOK, 1746-1816   409

To Edward Self Sexton of Do.	300	
For his care of the Surplis	100	
		400
To Samuel Rudder Clerk of Bethel Church		1200
To George Hungerford Sexton of Do.	300	
To his care of the Surplis & Plate	200	
		500
To the Clerk of the Vestry		600
For Nancey Kelley to the Ch. Wardens		500
For Nichs. Amos to Do. or Frs. Amos		500
For Ann Nobles to Do. or William Allen		800
To Edward Cutillo or Do. for his Child		250
For James Shelborne to Do. or William Lax		900
To the Ch. Wardens for Jno. Hazlewoods child		500
For Martha Justice to the Ch. Wardens		500
To Edward Jordon Senr. one Levy overpaid last year		28
To John Lucas Do. Do.		28
For Jno. Self to the C. Wardens		500
Present Jno. Jenings, Gent.		
For John Askew to the Church Wardens		300
To David Garland for the ballance of his account (For Insolvents ordered to be paid by the Collector last year) which was paid short		1145
To a Depositum raised		7344
To the Collector 6 per Cent		2200
		36675
The Parish has credit by 1467 Tithes at 25 lbs. pr Tithe		36675

	£	s	d
To Colo. Thos. Winn the ballance of his account	0	2	3
To Thos. Tabb the ballance of his account	1	18	-
To the Ch. Wardens for the Eliments for this present year (supposed)	6	0	-
To George Hungerford for his Acct.	-	15	-
To Edward Self for putting a barrel in the spring & other services	-	10	-
To Henry Granger for services done in 1765	-	10	-
	9	15	3

Ordered that the Ch. Wardens do let to the lowest bidder the building of a Barn (or Granary) on the Glebe 32 by 20 as pr the plan.

Thos. Chambers Gent. is chosen a Vestryman in the room of William Gee, Gent. who has removed into Brunswick.

Ordered that Lyddal Bacon and Thos. Chambers Gent. be Ch. Wardens for the ensuing year.

Ordered that Anthony Street collect the present Parish Levy.

James Craig
Lyddal Bacon

The Depositum of Cumberland Parish To A. Street

Dr.				Cr.			
1768				By a Depositm. Levy'd			
Nov. 22				1126 lbs. Tobo.	£	s	d
To 43 Insolvents at 28 lbs.		1204		By ball. due the Depo.			
To Paid Colo. Garland		6600		Sold at 17/6 p Ct.	30	4	11
By Ballance due		3457		To Ball due the Coll.		5	1
		11261			30	10	-
	£	s	d	By a fine of Peter Jones			
To Cash Paid Colo. Winn	2	0	0	for prophane swear-			
To Qts. of 823 acres				ing one oath		5	
Land for 1767	1	1	0	By ballance due from my			
To Paid Mr. Jno. Powell	25	11	6	acct. last year		3	0¼
To Paid Mr. Tabb	1	2	6				
To Pd. Mr. Geo. Hungerford		5					
To Pd. Mr. Thos. Garrett		10	0				
	30	10	0				
To Ballance due							
as p Contra		5	1				
Anthony Street							

George Hungerford Acct. against Cumberland Parish

1768
To bracing and nailing the
gates and putting latches
to them.

To glewing and mending
the lid of the Chest.
To nailing buttons to the
window shutters.
To nailing on 12 banisters
in the gallery and 4 in
the communion table.
To mending a bench in the
gallery.
To mending the pew doors
and nailing buttons to
them.   0 15 0
                         _____

           Cumberland Parish to Thos. Tabb.

       Dr.
To building a closet to
   the Glebe house   4 15 0

       Cr.
By cash Recd. of the Parish
   Collector   2 17 0
                         _____
                         1 18 0
                         _____

           Cumberland Parish to Ths. Winn

1767   Dr.   P Contra.
Feb. 10   By Thos. Tabb   0 10 0
To mending the Surplis 0 2 6   By Anthony Street   1 15 0
Nov. 22   By Anthony Street   2   0 0
To bread and wine for   To ballance due T. W. 0   2 3
   the churches   2 6 0   _____
To 7 setts of Indentures - 8 9   4   7 3
To 3 barrels corn for
   Jno. Self   1 10 0
                        _____
                        4   7 3
                        _____

At a Vestry held for Cumberland Parish at the Glebe the Twentieth Day of February, 1769.
           Present   The Reverend James Craig
   Messrs. Thos. Chambers and Lyddal Bacon, Ch. Wardens,
           David Garland, Thos. Winn and David Stokes,
   .   Jno. Ragsdale and Jno. Jenings and Thos. Tabb,
           Gent. Vestrymen.
Ordered that the present Church Wardens, to wit, Lyddal

Bacon and Thomas Chambers, Gent. do as soon as may be, give notice to David Hopkins that he meet at a certain time within one month at least and settle his accounts with the Vestry for this Parish, and also that he finish the crib on the Glebe according to contract.

Ordered that the present Church Wardens (to wit) Lyddal Bacon and Thos. Chambers Gent. do as soon as may be, give notice to Jno. Powell that by the last day of May next, he amend the plaistering and brickwork on the Mansion house at the Glebe in this Parish, according to his promise;, or if he should not, to let the said work to the lowest bidder.

Ordered that the present Ch. Wardens do as soon as may be give notice to Daniel Claiborne that he meet at a certain time within one month at least and finish the stable on the Glebe according to contract.

Ordered that a glass window (with four lights eight by ten inches) be made to the closet in the mansion house at the Glebe and that the same be so contrived as to slip up and down.

James Craig, Minister
Lyddal Bacon
Thomas Chambers.

At a Vestry held for Cumberland Parish the 28th of November, 1769.

Present

The Reverend James Craig
Messrs. Lyddal Bacon & Thos. Chambers Ch. Wardens

Thomas Tabb, David Stokes, Thos. Winn, William Taylor and John Ragsdale, Vestrymen.

A State of the Parish Levy

To the Reverend James Craig	16000	
To do. for Cask and Shrinkage	1280	
	———	17280
To John Hix Clerk of Reedy Creek Church		1200
To Edward Self Sexton of do.	300	
For his care of the Surplis	100	
	———	400

THE VESTRY BOOK, 1746-1816   413

To Samuel Rudder Clerk of Bethel Church		1200
To Geo. Hungerford Sexton of do.	300	
To his care of the Surplis & Plate	200	
	—	500
To the Clerk of the Vestry		600
For Nancy Kelley to the Ch. Wardens, or Mrs. Gillum		500
For Nicholas Amos to do. or Frs. Amos		500
For James Shelborne to do. or William Lax		500
For Jno. Hazlewoods child to do.		400
For Martha Justice to do.		500
For John Self to the Ch. Wardens		500
For John Askew to do.		300
For Jno. Gosee to do.		250
For William Owen and his mother to Jacobus Christopher		800
To Cunningams Estate one levy overpaid		25
To a Depositum Raisd		1364
To the Collector 6 per cent		1711
		28530

The Parish has credit by 1585 Tithes at 18 lbs. Tobo. per Tithe		28530	
		£	s
Thomas Chambers Acct. allowed			15
To the Ch. Wardens for Geo. Hungerford			5
Allowed Mrs. Mourning Hix for cureing of Joel Gunter		4	
			5

Mr. Richard Claiborne Gent. is chosen a Vestryman in the room of Mr. Henry Blagrave who has resigned.

Thomas Tabb and Jno. Ragsdale appointed Ch. Wardens for the ensuing year.

Ordered that Anthony Street collect the Parish Levy the ensuing year and that he give bond and security to the Ch. Wardens.

      James Craig
      Thomas Tabb
      John Ragsdale
        C. W.

At a Vestry held for Cumberland Parish the 20th July, 1770
Present

    The Revd. Mr. James Craig, John Ragsdale Ch. Warden,
Lyddal Bacon, Thos. Winn, Thos. Pettus, Thos. Chambers, Richard Claiborne and George Phillips, Gent. Vestrymen.

It is ordered that the Church Wardens do let the repairing of the brickwork and whitewashing on the mansion house at the Glebe, to the lowest bidder, as soon as may be.

                            James Craig
                            John Ragsdale.

At a Vestry held for Cumberland Parish at the Courthouse, 26th November, 1770.

Present

    Lyddal Bacon, David Garland, Thos. Winn, John Ragsdale, Thos. Tabb, Church Wardens.

    Thomas Pettus, George Phillips, William Taylor, Thomas Chambers, Richard Claiborne, Gent. Vestrymen.

Whereas Colo. David Stokes has resigned his place as a Vestryman, this Vestry has made choice of Capt. Christopher Billups to act in his stead.

Present The Revd. James Craig and John Jenings.

                A State of the Parish Levy.

To the Revd. James Craig	16000	
To do. for Cask & Shrinkage	1280	
		17280
To John Hix Clerk Reedy Creek Church		1200
To Edwd. Self Sexton of do.	300	
For his care of the Surplis	100	
		400
To Saml. Rudder Clerk Bethel Church		1200
To Geo. Hungerford Sexton of do.	300	
For his care of the Surplis & Plate	200	
		500
To the Clerk Vestry		600

For Nanny Kelly to the Ch. Wardens or Mrs. Gillum	500
For Nicholas Amos to do. or Frans. Amos	750
For James Shelborne to do. or Willm. Lax	500
For John Hazelwoods child to do.	400
For John Self to do.	500
For John Askew to do.	400
For Jno. Gosee to do.	300
For Willm. Owen to do. or Barnett Owen	750
For Willm. Cuttillo to do.	250
To Mattw. Laffoon one levy overpd.	18
To Sylvanus Walker do.	18
To a Depositum raised	6075
To the Collector for his Comsn. at 6 p Ct.	2019
	33660
Cr. by 1683 Tithes at 20 lbs. Tobo. pr. Tithe	33660

Ordered that there be an addition to the Reedy Creek Church twenty eight feet by twenty four, with five pews to each side, and three windows, also, with eighteen lights in each, and a gallorey with two windows and eight lights to each window, and that the old church be repaired.

George Phillips and Richard Claiborne appointed to act as Ch. Wardens the ensuing year.

Ordered that George Phillips and Richd. Claiborne settle with Thos. Moody for the ballance he owes the Parish & acct. with the Vestry for the same.

Ordered that the present Ch. Wardens receive of Lyddal Bacon Fifty Three Pounds Ten Shills. as pr. acct.

Ordered that the present Church Wardens, Lyddal Bacon, John Ragsdale, Thos. Tabb and Thos. Winn, do let the addition and the repairs to Reedy Creek Church to the lowest bidder as soon as is convenient.

Ordered that Anthony Street collect the Parish Levy and that he give bond and security to the present Ch. Wardens.

	Accts. against the Parish	Dr.		
		£	s	d
Willm. Herrings acct. allowed for burying Jno. Hopkins		2	0	0
Edward Self acct. allowed			5	
George Hungerford acct. allowed for services done the Church			5	
To Jno. Ragsdale his acct. as Ch. Warden			9	9½
To John Ragsdale by order of Baxter Ragsdale for work done on the Glebe		8	19	
Ordered that the Church Wardens do pay Ann Mitchel		1	10	
		13	8	9½

James Craig
George Phillips
Richd. Claiborne.

	Cr.		
	£	s	d
By the Ballance in Major Thos. Tabbs hands being the ballance of his acct. to the Parish	8	8	0
By Capt. Jno. Jenings his service the last year not listed	1	13	6
By do. for an old ballance		5	0
	1	18	6
By Anthony Street Collector the Ballance of his acct. for 1769	0	19	10
	13	4	10

The Depositum for C. Parish in acct. with the Collector

Dr.				Cr.			
1770				1769			
To 43 Insolvents at 18 lbs. Tobo.	774			By a Depositum raised	1364		
To Ballance due the Depositum in Tobo.	590			Nov. 15th, 1770	£	s	d
	1364			By Ballance due the Depositum in Tobo. 590 lbs. at 16/9	4	18	10
	£	s	d				
To the quitrents of 832 acres land	1	1	0	By ballance due the Depositum in cash as pr. debit	1	18	10
To the Clk. Lunenbg.	75	12	6			19	
To Do.	39	6	6				
To Pd. Willm. White	1	0	8	due		19	10
	3	0	0				
Nov. 15 To Ball due the Depom. in Cash	1	18	10	Cr. By charged above		19	10
	4	18	10				
To Cash I am to pay Mr. Taylor		19					

At a Vestry held for Cumberland Parish in the County of Lunenburg the first day of May, 1771.

Present   The Revd. James Craig

Lyddal Bacon, David Garland, John Ragsdale, Thos. Tabb, George Phillips, Richard Claiborne, Ch. Wardens.

William Taylor & Thos. Chambers, Gent. Vestrymen.

It is the opinion of this Vestry that the addition and repairs to Reedy Creek Church was not let according to the order or sence of the last Vestry and as no bonds have been exicuted from the undertakers to the Ch. Wardens nor from the Church Wardens to the undertakers, this Vestry takeing it into consideration are of opinion that it will be more to the advantage of the Parish to set aside the old order and to make a new one, and it is accordingly ordered that an entire new Church be erected at or near the old Reedy Creek Church Sixty feet long Twenty Eight feet wide, and Eighteen feet pitch in the clear, & agreeable to a certain plan and bill of scantling lodged in the hands of the Clerk, and it is further ordered that the said building be advertised in the Virginia Gazette, to be let at August court next and to be finished by the last day of October, 1773, and that the payments be in manner following, The first payment of about One Hundred Pounds to be made the last day of October next, and half the ballance to be paid at the end of October, 1772, and the other half at the time of delivering and receiving the building.

Ordered that the Depositum for the Sheriffs hands be paid to the Church Wardens, and by them to be disposed of to the best advantage for the Parish.

Ordered that George Phillips and Richard Claiborne Church Wardens together with Lyddal Bacon, John Ragsdale, Thomas Tabb and Thomas Winn or the majority of them do let the above mentioned building to the lowest bidder on August Court day of Lunenburg County or the next fair day.

Ordered that Five hundred pounds of Tobo. part of the Depositum be paid to William Justice for his mother Martha Justice.

James Craig
George Phillips
Richd. Claiborne.

At a Vestry held for Cumberland Parish the 8th day of August, 1771

Present

  The Revd. James Craig & Richard Claiborne, C. W.
  Lyddal Bacon, David Garland, Thos. Pettus,
  John Ragsdale, Thos. Tabb, Thos. Winn,
  William Taylor & Christopher Billips, Gent. Vestr.

It is the opinion of this Vestry that the alterations in the plan and bill of scantling of the Church to be built near the old Reedy Creek Church for this Parish will be an advantage and therefore it is ordered that a Church be built agreeable thereto.

James Craig
Richard Claiborne.

At a Vestry held for Cumberland Parish at the Courthouse on Friday, the Thirteenth of Decr. 1771.

Present-

    The Rev. James Craig and Richard Claiborne C. Warden Lyddal Bacon, David Garland, Thos. Pettus, John Ragsdale, Thos. Winn, Christopher Billups, Gent. Vestrymen.

A State of the Parish Levy.

To the Rev. James Craig	16000	
To Do. for Cask and Shrinkage	1120	
		17120
To Saml. Rudder Clerk of Bethel Church		1200
To John Hix Clerk of Reedy Creek Church		1200
To Edward Self Sexton of do.	300	
For his care of the Surplis	100	
		400
To Geo. Hungerford Sexton of Bethel Church	300	
For his care of the Surplis & Plate	200	
		500
To the Clerk of the Vestry		800
For Nancey Kelley to the Ch. Wardens or Mrs. Gilliam		500
For Nicholas Amos to Do. or Frans. Amos		750
For James Shelborne to Do. or William Lax		600
For John Hazlewoods child to do.		400
For John Self to do.		500
For John Askew to do.		400
For John Gosee to do.		300
For William Owen to do. or Barnett Owen		750
For William Cuttillo to do.		250
To Robert Scott two levies overpaid 1770		40
To Geo. Hungerford one do.		20
To Matthew Laffoon do.		20
To William Wallace do.		20
To William Herring do.		20
To William Justice for his mother		500
To William White for Ann Dingles		200

To Thos. Deuprey for Laneford Walker	500
To Geo. Hungerford for services last year to Flatrock Church	50
Present Geo. Phillips Ch. Wd. & Thos. Chambers, Gent.	
To a Depositum raised	16614
To the Sheriffs Commissions for collecting	2786
	46440
The Parish has credit by 1720 Tithes at 27 lbs. Tobo. per Tithe is	46440

	£	s	d
Dr. Cumberland Parish to George Phillips Ch. Wd. as p acct.	1	12	10
Cr. Dr. Anthony Street to Cumberland Parish			
To Ballance due the Depositum as p acct. settled		18	9
The Parish has credit by Richard Claiborne late Church Warden for the ballance in his hands as p acct. delivered in	89	2	4
By the Revd. James Craig		8	0
By Major Thos. Tabb	8		
	98	9	1

Ordered that David Garland collect the Parish Levy the ensuing year and that he receive 27 lbs. Tobo. from each Tithe.

David Garland and Christopher Billups appointed Ch. Wardens for the ensuing year.

Ordered that the present Church Wardens collect the ballances due the Parish, and pay the same to Pines Ingram, undertaker of the Church.

         James Craig
         David Garland
         Christopher Billups.

At a Vestry held for Cumberland Parish in the County of Lunenburg, at the Courthouse on Friday the 13th of Decr., 1771.
Present

> The Revd. James Craig, Minister, Lyddal Bacon, David Garland, Thomas Pettus, John Ragsdale, Thomas Winn (Richard Claiborne, George Phillups, Ch. Wardens), Thomas Chambers and Christopher Billups, Gent., Vestrymen.

No. 1 Ordered that James Calais and Joseph Dunman procession all the land between Brunswick line, Stony Creek, Flattrock road and Meherrin River.

2. Ordered that Henry Freeman and Henry Haies procession all the land between Stony Creek and Flattrock, Flattrock road and Meherrin River.

3. Ordered that Phillip Reeks and Henry Gill procession all the land between Flattrock Creek and Crooked Creek & from Flattrock road and Jeningses road to Meherrin River.

4. Ordered that Abraham Andrews and John Granger procession all the land between Crooked Creek and Bears element Creek, Pools old path and Meherrin River.

5. Ordered that John Ragsdale and Benjamin Gee procession all the land between Crooked Creek and Bears Element, Pools old path & Jeningses road.

6. Ordered that Richard Booker and James Gee procession all the land between Bears Element Creek, the Great road that goes by Mr. Pattesons & Meherrin River.

7. Ordered that Micajah Smithson & John Brown, Junr. procession all the land between the North and Middle Meherrin, from Coxes road to the fork of the river.

8. Ordered that John and William Cunninghams procession all the land between the South and Middle Meherrin, from Coxes road to the fork of the river.

9. Ordered that Ellison Ellis and Jessee Saunders procession all the land between the South and Middle Meherrin, from Coxes road to Charlotte line.

10. Ordered that Bryan Lester and Robert Estes, Junr. proces-

sion all the land between the Middle and North Meherrin, Coxes road and Johnsons road.

11. Ordered that Stephen Wood and Joseph Johnson procession all the land between the middle and North Meherrin & from Johnsons road to Charlotte line.

12. Ordered that Robert Beasly and William Herring procession all the land between Winninghams road and Charlotte line from the North Meherrin to Tursakia Creek, to DeGraffenriedts rolling road, from thence to Ledbetter Creek and up the said creek to Charlotte line.

13. Ordered that John Ingram and Matthew Gale procession all the land between Winninghams road and Nottoway river, to Tursakia Creek, to DeGrafenriedts rolling road, from thence to Ledbetter Creek and up the same to Charlotte line.

14. Ordered that William Crymes and Arthur Herring procession all the land between Robertses rolling road, Tursakia Creek, Meherrin River and Winninghams road.

15. Ordered that James Easthem and John Glenn procession all the land from Robertses rolling road to the head of Couches Creek (west fork) down the said creek to Meherrin river.

16. Ordered that Edward Jordan, Jr. and Benjamin Walker procession all the land from the head of Couches Creek (west fork) the North Meherrin and the Courthouse road.

17. Ordered that Henry Stokes and John Winn, Junr. procession all the land between Murrells rolling road, Winninghams road, Allen Stokes Mill Creek, and the Courthouse road to the mouth of the said creek.

18. Ordered that Robert Crenshaw and John Winn (son of Daniel Winn) procession all the land between Nottoway River, Allen Stokes Mill Creek, the Courthouse road and Wards rolling road, to the mouth of great hounds creek.

19. Ordered that James Johnson and John White, Senr. procession all the land between the Courthouse road, Rowland Wards rolling road & Reedy Creek old road.

20. Ordered that Everard Dowsing and Michael Johnson procession all the land between Reedy Creek, the Courthouse road, Hixes road & Reedy Creek old road.

21. Ordered that Covington Hardy and James Buford procession all the land between Great Hounds Creek, Wards rolling road, Reedy Creek old road and the path as goes from Daniel Winns to the old road.
22. Ordered that Stith Hardiway and Thomas Cocke procession all the land between Great Hounds Creek, [mutilated] road, and the path as goes from Daniel Winns to the old road, [mutilated] road as goes by John Hightowers to Crosses bridge and Nottoway river.
23. Ordered that Samuel Garland and Abraham Cocke procession all the land between Jeningses road, Flattrock road and Reps Joneses road.
24. Ordered that Robert Blackwell and Charles Parish procession all the land from the Great road to Crosses bridge down the river to Brunswick line, thence along the line to Robert Mores, thence along the path as goes by Marshes house to Reps Joneses road, thence to the first station.
25. Ordered that Edward Ragsdale & Nathl. Laffoon procession all the land between the path as goes from Robert Mores by Marshes house, Reps Joneses road, Flattrock road & Brunswick line.
26. Ordered that William Loury and Thomas Hardy procession all the land between Reedy Creek old road, Jeningses road, Wards rolling road and the path as goes from Wards road to Jeningses road, near Mrs. Loury.
27. Ordered that Thomas Edwards and Nicholas Williams procession all the land between Reedy Creek, Reedy Creek old road, [illegible] and the horse pen branch.
28. Ordered that Michael Mackie, Samuel Jeeter and John Hix procession all the land between the horse pen branch, Reedy Creek, Hixes road and Jeningses road to the path as goes by Mrs. Lourys to the horse pen branch near Tho. Edw[ards].
29. Ordered that Anthony Street and Robert Willson procession all the land between Reedy Creek, Meherrin river, Jeningses road and Hixes road.
30. Ordered that William Shepherd and Craddock Vaughn procession all the land between Reedy Creek, Coxes road, Hixes road and the North Meherrin river.

31. Ordered that Joseph Minor and Richard Stokes Senr. procession all the land between Winninghams road, Nottoway River and Ledbetter Creek.

Ordered that the returns of processioning be made by the last Thursday in March next.

      Signed James Craig
           David Garland
           Christopher Billups.

[These orders of December 13, 1771, appointing processioners are transferred to the chronological order of entry among the Vestry Minutes. No change is made in the text of the material.]

At a Vestry held for Cumberland Parish at the Courthouse, on Friday the tenth day of July, 1772.

Present
  David Garland and Christopher Billups, C. W.
  Lyddal Bacon, Thomas Pettus, John Ragsdale,
  Thomas Tabb, William Taylor, Thomas Winn
  and Thomas Chambers, Gent. Vestrymen.

It is ordered that Lyddal Bacon, Thomas Winn, Thomas Tabb, Gent. or any one of them agree with Mr. Peter Jones of Amelia County for three acres of land to set the Church on to be built near the Reedy Creek old Church and take a deed from him for the same. And it is further ordered that the said gentlemen or any one of them treat with Mr. Richard Haies of the said county for three acres of land where Flatrock Church now stands and make him a generous offer for the land and take a deed from him for the same.

Mary Read and Thomas Read, Excrs. of Clement Read, Deceas'd offered an account to this Vestry against the Parish of £13-16-8, which is rejected, except paying the costs of two suits against Moody and Brown which is Thirty two Shillings and Sixpence, and is ordered to be paid.

On the removeall of Capt. John Jenings to Carolina this Vestry has chose Capt. Benjamin Tomlinson to act in his stead.

           David Garland
           Christopher Billups
             C. Wardens.

At a Vestry held for Cumberland Parish at the Courthouse on Monday the Fifteenth of November, 1772.

Present
>   The Revd. James Craig, David Garland
>   & Chrsr. Billups, C. W.
>
>   Lyddal Bacon, John Ragsdale, Thos. Tabb,
>   William Taylor, Thomas Winn, Richard
>   Claiborne, Thomas Chambers & Benjn.
>   Tomlinson, Gent. Vestrymen.

A Proportion of the Parish Levy.		lbs. Tobo.
To the Revd. James Craig his salary	16000	
To do. for Cask and Shrinkage	1120	
		17120
To John Hix Clerk of Reedy Creek Church		1200
To Edward Self, Sexton of do.	300	
For his care of the Surplis	100	
		400
To Samuel Rudder Clerk of Bethel Church		1200
To Geo. Hungerford Sexton of do.	300	
For his care of the Surplis & Plate	200	
		500
To the Clerk of the Vestry		600
For Nancey Kelley to the Ch. Wardens or Mrs. Gilliam		500
For James Shelborne to do. or William Lax		600
For Nicholas Amos to do. or Francis Amos		750
For John Hazlewoods child to do.		400
For John Self to do.		500
For John Askew to do.		400
For John Gosee to do.		300
For William Owen to do. or Barnett Owen		750
For William Cuttillo to do.		250
For Martha Justice to do. or William Justice		500
		25970
To a Depositum raised		18492

To the Sheriffs Commissions for collecting			2838
			47300

The Parish has credit by 1892 Tythes at 25 lbs. per Poll is   47300

Dr. Cumberland Parish
   In acct. with Sundry Persons

	£		
To the Revd. James Craig as pr. acct.	4	19	7¼
To Capt. Christopher Billups his acct. as Ch. Warden	3	11	6
	8	11	1¼
To Jane Pounds for burying Mary Mitchell	3	0	0
To James Johnson for takeing care of and maintaining William Brooks	2	0	0
To Mr. Richard Haies for three acres of land at Bethel Church	10	0	0
To Mr. Peter Jones for three acres of land at Reedy Creek Church	3	0	0
	18	0	0

Ordered that David Garland late Collector pay to the Church Wardens and the Revd. James Craig their accounts if so much in his hands of the last years depositum.

David Garland and Thomas Winn are appointed Church Wardens the ensuing year.

Ordered that David Garland Collect the Parish Levy the ensuing year and that he receive Twenty Five Pounds of Tobacco from each tythe.

David Garland
Thomas Winn
James Craig
C. Wardens.

At a Vestry held for Cumberland Parish the 9th day of Decr. One Thousand Seven Hundred and Seventy Three.
Present
>   The Revd. James Craig, Lyddal Bacon, Thomas Pettus, John Ragsdale, Thomas Tabb, Thomas Winn, Richard Claiborne & Christopher Billups Gent. Vestrymen.

The Reverend James Craig and this Vestry have entered into an agrement that his salary should be paid in money at Fifteen Shillings pr. Hundred.

A Proportion of the Parish Levy

To the Revd. James Craig his salary	16000				
For Cask and Shrinkage	1120	17120	128	8	0
To John Hix Clerk of Reedy Creek Church		1200			
To Edward Self Sexton of Do.	300				
For his care of the Surplis	100	400			
To Samuel Rudder Clerk of Bethel Church		1200			
To Geo. Hungerford Sexton of Ditto	300				
For his care of the Surplis and Plate	300	600			
To the Clerk of the Vestry		600			
For Nancey Kelley to the Ch. Wardens or Mrs. Gilliam		800			
For James Shelborne to Do. or William Lax		700			
For Nicholas Amos to Do. or Francis Amos		750			
For John Hazlewoods child to do.		400			
For John Self to do.		600			
For John Askew to do.		500			
For John Gosee to do.		400			
For William Owen to do.		750			
For William Cuttillo to Do.		250			
For Martha Justice to do.		750			
For Ann Dingles to do.		400			
For Sarah Hobson to do.		200			
		27620			

Ford.	27620		
To a Depositum raised	8852		
To the Collectors Commissions at 6 p Ct. is	2328		
	38800		
The remainder after deducting the Ministers salary is 21680 calculated at 12/6 p Ct. is		135	10
		263	18
By 1940 Tythes at 20 lbs. each is	38800		
Ordered that the Collector receive of each Tythe 20 lbs. Tobo. or Two Shills. and Eight Pence Half Penny, which is		263	18

Ordered that Anthony Street collect the Parish Levy the ensuing year and that he give bond and security to the Church Wardens.

Thomas Winn and John Ragsdale are appointed Church Wardens the ensuing year.

Thos. Winn
John Ragsdale
C. Wardens

At a Vestry held for Cumberland Parish at the Courthouse on Tuesday the 24th of May, 1774.

Present

> The Revd. James Craig, John Ragsdale and Thomas Winn, Ch. Wardens. David Garland, Lyddal Bacon, Thomas Tabb, Richard Claiborne and Benjamin Tomlinson, Gent., Vestrymen.

Ordered that David Garland late Ch. Warden and Collector pay to the present Church Wardens the ballance in his hands due the Parish.

Ordered that the Revd. James Craig pay to Mr. John Warran the amount of the order he shall present to him from Pines Ingram undertaker of the Church, not exceeding Twenty Five

Pounds (from which interest is to be deducted for six months from the time of payment) out of the sum of Fifty Nine Pounds and five pence three Farthings due from him to the Parish for a part of the Depositum for one Thousand Seven hundred and seventy two.

      Signed by
       Thomas Winn
       John Ragsdale
          C. W.

At a Vestry held for Cumberland Parish at the Courthouse on Tuesday the fifteenth of November one thousand seven hundred and seventy four.
Present
  The Revd. James Craig, Lyddal Bacon, Thomas Pettus, John Ragsdale, Thos. Winn, Ch. Wardens; Thomas Tabb, William Taylor, Richard Claiborne, Thomas Chambers, Christopher Billups, Benjamin Tomlinson, Gent., Vestrymen.

    A Proportion of the Parish Levy

The Revd. James Craig makes choice of his Tobacco which if not collected is ordered to be bought for him as the law directs; at any of the warehouses the notes of which passes in payment of levies in this Parish by Law		16000	Settled at 2d pr Pound
Cash and Shrinkage		1120	£ s
		17120	142 13
To John Hix Clerk of Reedy Creek Church		1200	
To Edward Self Sexton of Do.	300		
For his care of the Surplis	100		
		400	
To Samuel Rudder Clerk of Bethel Church		1200	
To George Hungerford Sexton of Ditto	300		
For his care of the Surplis and Plate	300		
		600	

To the Clk of the Vestry	600
For Nancey Kelley to the Ch. Wardens or Mrs. Gilliam	966
For James Shelborne to do. or William Lax	700
For Nicholas Amos to do. or Francis Amos	750
For John Self to do.	600
For John Askew to do.	500
For John Gosee to do.	400
For William Owen to do. or Barnet Owen	750
For William Cutillo to do.	250
For Martha Justice to do.	750
For Ann Dingles to do. or James Anderson	290
For Sarah Hobson to the Ch. Wardens	350
George Simmons to the Ch. Wardens	600
For Mary Cockerham to do.	300
For the sundry accounts against the Parish	6461
Depositum raised	9276
Commissions for collecting	2812
	46875
By 1875 Tythes at 25 lbs. Tobo. pr Tythe	46875

Ordered that the Collector receive 25 lbs. Tobo. or 4s-2 from each Tythe.

After deducting the Ministers salary there remains 29755 lbs. calculated at 2d pr Pound makes [247 19 2][1]

Total Amt. £[390 12 6][1]

The amount of the several accounts for the discharge of which is levied six thousand four hundred and sixty one pounds of Tobacco.

To John Pattesons Acct. against the Parish for George Simmons	4	7	1
To Doctor Walter Bennet for attending Geo. Simmons	20	0	0

---

[1]Figures supplied; page torn.

To Allen Stokes for provision attendance upon Geo. Simmons	22	9	6
To John Callaham, his acct.	1	3	6
To Lodowick Farmer, his acct.	1	6	10
To Henry Stokes, his acct.	1	10	0
To Jno. Ragsdale, his acct. as Church Warden	3	0	0
	53	16	11
	£	s	d
By 6461 lbs. Tobo. levied at 2d pr. Pound	53	16	10

Ordered that according to an agreement with Daniel DeGernett there be a gallory built in the new church at Reedy Creek 30 feet by 10½ feet to be finished in a workman like manner and agreeable to the plan of the other building and to be delivered with the other building, for which he is to receive £16 and the old church at the delivery of the new church.   16 0 0

Ordered that there be paid to Doctor Walter Bennet a further sum of £2 10/ out of the depositum   2 10 0

William Taylor and Benjamin Tomlinson are chose Church Wardens the ensuing year.

Ordered that Anthony Street collect the Parish Levy the ensuing year and that he give bond and security to the Church Wardens.

Ordered that the present Church Wardens do view the houses &c on the Glebe Plantation and make the repairs necessary thereto.

Anthony Street presented an acct. of Insolvents and supernumeraries to this Vestry which were received, as also his other acct as Collector last year.

Signed by

Thomas Winn
John Ragsdale.

432 CUMBERLAND PARISH

A copy of Anthony Streets Account for 1773 Returned 1773.

The Depositum of Cumberland Parish

Dr.

1773	£	s	d	£	s	d
To the quit rents of 832 acres of land	1	1	3			
To 58 insolvents agreeable to list delivered in, at 20 lbs. Tobacco per Tithe is 1160 lbs. at 12/6	7	10	0			
To the difference in the sale of 17120 lbs. Tobo. between 12/6 and 15/8 hundred is	21	8	0			
Nov. 15, 1774						
To paid the Ch. Warden this day	4	16	9	34	16	0
Contra. Cr.						
By a Depositum raised 8852 lbs. Tobo. at 12/6				55	6	6
Due the Parish				20	10	6

At a Vestry held for Cumberland Parish at the Courthouse on Thursday the eighth of June, 1775.

Present

   The Revd. James Craig, David Garland, Lyddal Bacon, Geo. Phillups, John Ragsdale, Thos. Tabb, Thos. Winn, Christopher Billups, Gent., Vestrymen.

Ordered that the Collector pay to the Revd. James Craig one hundred and ninety six pounds seventeen shillings and seven pence for his salary for the year one thousand seven hundred and seventy four, deducting out of the same four pounds and two pence.

Ordered that the Revd. James Craig pay to Henry Robertson thirty pounds five shillings (out of fifty nine pounds five shillings and two pence, due from him to the Parish) by the order of

Pines Ingram when the Church the said Ingram has undertaken in this Parish shall be finished.

> James Craig
> Lyddal Bacon
> Thos. Tabb
> John Ragsdale
> Thos. Winn
> George Phillups
> Christopher Billups
> David Garland

At a Vestry held for Cumberland Parish at Reedy Creek Church on Saturday the 8th of July, 1775.
Present

> The Revd. James Craig, Benjamin Tomlinson, Ch. Warden David Garland, Lyddal Bacon, Thomas Pettus, John Ragsdale, Thos. Tabb, Thos. Winn and Thos. Chambers, Gent. Vtymen.

Resolved that the Gallory is not finished agreeable to the plan, and that it be finished agreeable thereto.

Ordered that the new gallory be finished agreeable to the plan of the other.

Ordered that the Collector pay to Pines Ingram undertaker of the church Thirty Six Pounds.

Ordered that the Collector pay Daniel DeGernett undertaker of the new gallory twelve pounds.

Ordered that at the request of Pines Ingram the Collector pay Daniel DeGernett twenty pounds, out of the thirty six pounds above mentioned.

Ordered that the Church Wardens let to the lowest bidder the clearing of the yard around the new Church, as far as the trees are blazed, with sufficient benches, and one horse block agreeable to the plan of the other new ones.

Ordered that the Church Wardens repair the horse blocks, benches and steps to the doors of Flatrock Church, and replace the banisters in the said Church.

This Vestry haveing reserved in their hands money enough

for sufficient security for the finishing of the Church do agree to receive the same of the undertakers.

Signed by James Craig Rector
Benjamin Tomlinson, C. Warden.

At a Vestry held for Cumberland Parish at the Courthouse the Twenty Sixth day of February one thousand seven hundred and seventy six.

Present

>Benjamin Tomlinson, Ch. Warden, David Garland, Thomas Pettus, John Ragsdale, George Phillups, Thomas Tabb, Thomas Winn, Thomas Chambers and Christopher Billups, Gent., Vestrymen.

A Proportion of the Parish Levy.

To the Reverend James Craig his salary	16000	
For Cask and Shrinkage	1280	
		17280
To the Clk of Reedy Creek Church		1200
To the Sexton of Do.	500	
For his care of the Surplis	100	
		600
To the Clk of Bethel Church		1200
To the Sexton of Ditto	300	
For his care of the Surplis & Plate	300	
		600
To the Clk. of the Vestry		800
For Nancy Kelly to the Church Wardens or Mr. Gilliam		966
For James Shelborne to do. or William Lax		700
For Nicholas Amos to do. or Francis Amos		750
For John Self to the Ch. Wardens		600
For John Askew to the Ch. Wardens		500
For John Gosee to do.		400
For William Owen to do.		750
For William Cuttillo to do.		250
For Martha Justice to do.		750

For Ann Dingles to Mrs. Hooper	300
For Sary Hobson to the Ch. Wardens	600
For Mary Cockerham	300
For John Forest and wife	500
To Covington Hardy for a bed for John Foust [or Forest]	400
The Revd. James Craig present	
For priseing and carrying down Tobacco	8686
For the several cash accts.	5600
The Revd. James Craig absent.	
To Benjamin Estes one levy overpaid last year	40
To Samuel Ward twice listed this year	28
To a Depositum raised	1359
To the Collector 12 p cent	5437
	50596

The Parish has credit by 1807 Tythes at 28 lbs. Tobo. each 50596

Anthony Street presented his acct. as Collector last year which was received by this Vestry.

William More set levy free from this time forward.

Pines Ingram undertaker of the Church presented a petition to this Vestry praying that a bad five pound bill which he received of the Collector in part of pay for the said Church might be made good, which was thought reasonable and accordingly levied the same in Tobo. with the cash debts.

Ordered that if the Collector should have so much money in his hands after paying the several accts. before mentioned, that he then pay Daniel Dejernett four pounds due for the new gallory and five pounds for the horse blocks and benches to the Church when finished.

Samuel Garland Gent. is chose a vestryman in the room of Lyddal Bacon, Gent. dec'd. and Elisha Betts Gent. is chose a vestryman in the room of Ricd. Claiborne Gent. dec'd.

John Ragsdale and Thomas Chambers are chose Church Wardens the ensuing year.

Ordered that John Ragsdale collect the Parish Levy and that he receive Twenty Eight Pounds of Tobo. from each tythe.

Signed by   James Craig Minister

Benjamin Tomlinson, C. Warden.

A copy of Anthony Streets Accompt.

The Depositum of Cumberland Parish to the Collector.

Dr.

	£	s	d
1774			
To cash paid Daniel Dejernett	12	0	0
To cash paid do. on account of Pines Ingram	20	0	0
To cash paid Pines Ingram	4	12	11½
To quitrents of 832 acres of land	1	1	3
To paid the Clk. Lunenburg Tickett 100 lbs. Tobo.		12	6
To paid the Clk. Charlottes Tickett against the Parish		6	3
	38	12	11½
To the difference paid Mr. Craig on on 17120 lbs. Tobo. of 16/8 and 23/ p Hundred	54	4	3
	92	17	2½
To cash paid Doctor Bennett	2	10	0
	95	7	2½

Cr.

	£	s	d
By a Depositum raised at 2d per lb. 9276 lbs. Tobo.	77	6	-
To William Hardy on acct. of John Forest		10	
To Jno. Pattison his acct.	6	6	0
To Hugh Wallace his acct.	17	3	11
	23	19	11

Cr.

	£	s	d
By 3839 lbs. Tobo. levied at 12/6	23	19	11

At a Vestry held for Cumberland Parish the 26th day of February, 1776, the following Gent. were appointed processioners for their precincts, see page two hundred and fifty five, fifty six, fifty seven and two hundred & fifty eight.[1]

No. 1 Thomas Moody and James Sturdivant
2 William Fisher and John Ussery
3 Stephen Edward Brodnax & William Taylor
(Henry VanDyke appointed at a Vestry after this date in room of William Taylor.) J. R. C. C. V.
4 Loury Booker and Thomas Jones
5 Henry Gee and Matthew Mills
6 John Booker and John Hawkins
7 William Stone and Francis Robertson
8 William Stone, Junr. and John Scott, Senr.
9 Ellison Ellis and Jessee Saunders
10 David Johnson and Isaac Johnson
11 John Brown and Richard Hudson
12 Thomas Harding and Gideon Moon
13 William DeGraffenriedt and John Ingram
14 Thomas Crymes and Edward Hatchett
15 Richard Ingram and Ward Hudson
16 William Love and William Gordon
17 William Matthew Cralle and Allin Stokes
18 Richard Stone and William Hatchett
19 Thomas Walker and John Hazlewood
20 William Stokes and William Dozer
21 John Hardy and Theophilus Eddings
22 George Hightower and John Cross
23 Thomas Liveret and William Eddings
24 Joel Pewet and Thomas Williams
25 David More and William Haies
26 James Buford and Thomas Buford
27 William Wrenn and David Abernathy
28 Micl. Mackie, Saml. Jeeter and John Hix
29 Anthony Street and Robert Wilson

---

[1]The reference to these pages is to the designation of precincts, in the order of Vestry of Dec. 13, 1771.

30 Tscharner DeGraffenriedt and Robt. Scott
31 Joseph Billups and James Hamlet,
    Josiah Crews and William Evans.

Ordered that the returns of processioning be made on or before the last day of March.

                    Signed
                        James Craig Minister
                        Benja. Tomlinson, Ch. Warden

[NOTE: This order of Feb. 26, 1776, found among the processioning returns is transferred to its chronological place among the Vestry Minutes, as preserving the material in better order. No change is made in the material itself.]

At a Vestry held for Cumberland Parish at the Courthouse on Thursday the 12th day of Septr. 1776.

Present

    The Revd. James Craig, Thomas Winn, Thomas Pettus, John Ragsdale, Benjamin Tomlinson, Thomas Tabb, Christopher Billups, and William Taylor, Gent., Vestrymen.

Application being made to several members of this Vestry by sundry inhabitants of the lower end of this Parish for liberty to erect a gallory in Flattrock Church, who being convened in Vestry are unanimously agree that the building the said gallory would be of great publick utility. It is therefore ordered that if the said petitioners will agree that the same shall be for the use of the congregation in general that leave be given to erect a gallory agreeable to a plan to be drawn up by the Revd. James Craig, and this Vestry will hereafter refund to them the expence of building. Ordered that the workmanship of the new gallory correspond with that of the Church. The length to be from the front door to the old gallory, and the width from the wall to the alley.

                    Signed James Craig
                               John Ragsdale.

At a Vestry held for Cumberland Parish at the Courthouse the Twenty Second day of April, 1777.
Present

The Revd. James Craig, John Ragsdale and Thomas Chambers, Ch. Wardens. Thomas Pettus, Thomas Tabb, Thomas Winn, William Taylor, Benjamin Tomlinson and Elisha Betts, Gent. Vestrymen.

A Proportion of the Parish Levy

		Tobacco
To the Revd. James Craig his salary		16000
For Cask and Shrinkage		1280
To the Clerk of Reedy Creek Church		1200
To the Sexton of Ditto	500	
For his care of the Surplis	100	
		600
To the Clerk of Bethel Church		1200
To the Sexton of Ditto	300	
For his care of the surplis and plate	300	
		600
To the Clerk of the Vestry		600
		21480

	£	s	d
For Nancy Kelly to the Church Wardens or Mrs. Gilliam	8		
For Nicholas Amos to do. or Frs. Amos	7		
For John Askew to the Ch. Wardens	5		
For John Gosee [or Gosse] to do.	4		
For William Owen to do.	7		
For William Cuttillo to do.	2	10	
For Martha Justice to do.	7		
Mary Cockerham to do.	3		
For ...... Dizmang to do.	4		
	47	10	
To Thomas Chambers his acct. as Ch. Warden	4	5	
To John Ragsdale his acct. as do.	2		
To the Revd. James Craig his acct.	5	19	7¼

To William Willson for the relief of his daughter	5	
For a Depositum		712
To the Collector 6 per cent		1412
		23604
Cr. by 1686 Tythes at 14 lbs. Tobo. pr Tythe		23604

Ordered that Jeremiah Glenn collect the Parish Levy and that he receive 14 lbs. Tobo. from each Tythe.

Elisha Betts and Samuel Garland Gent. are chose Church Wardens the ensuing year.

£64 14 7¼

Ordered that the last years Collector employ proper persons to carry down the Tobo. in hand, of his collection, and that he sell the same for the best price to be got, and settle with the present Church Wardens for the same, and that he be allowed a reasonable price for his trouble and expence of carrying down.

Ordered that after the sale of the above mentioned Tobo. and settlement with the Collector, the present Church Wardens pay the cash away to the Parishoners and creditors as levied.

Ordered that Edward Self deliver to John Hix the Parish bible in his hands.

      Signed James Craig, Minister
          Thomas Chambers
          John Ragsdale, C. W.

At a Vestry held for Cumberland Parish in Lunenburg County at the Courthouse the 28th day of Jany. 1778.

Present

  Elisha Betts, Ch. Warden, Thos. Tabb, Thos. Pettus, John Ragsdale, George Phillups, Thos. Winn, Benjamin Tomlinson, G. Vestrymen.

  The Revd. James Craig also present.

A Proportion of the Parish Levy

	£	s	d
For Nancey Kelley to the Ch. Wardens or Mrs. Gilliam	10	0	0
For Nicholas Amos to do. or Francis Amos	10	0	0
For John Askew	10	0	0
For John Gosee	10	0	0
For William Owen	20	0	0
For William Cuttillo	5	0	0
For Martha Justice	10	0	0
For Mary Cockerham	3	0	0
For the Clerk of the Vestry	6	0	0
To Tho. Winn, Jr. for provisions found Margaret Mitchell	2	10	0
	86	10	0

George Phillups and John Ragsdale are chose Church Wardens the ensuing year.

Ordered that the above mentioned Ch. Wardens pay the money as levied above out of the Tobo. in hand.

                        Signed   Elisha Betts, C. W.

At a Vestry held for Cumberland Parish at the Courthouse the 8th day of April, 1779

Present

    The Revd. James Craig, John Ragsdale & Geo. Phillups, C. W. Thomas Pettus, William Taylor, Thomas Chambers, Christopher Billups, Benjamin Tomlinson and Thomas Winn, Gent. Vestrymen.

A Proportion of the Parish Levy.

	£	s	d
For Nancy Kelly to the Ch. Wardens or Mrs. Gilliam	50	0	0
For Nicholas Amos to ditto or Henry Stokes	50	0	0
For John Askew and wife to the Ch. Wardens	50	0	0
For John Gosee to do.	50	0	0
For William Owen to do. or Barnett Owen	100	0	0
For William Cuttillo to do. or Edward Cuttillo	25	0	0
For Martha Justice to the Ch. Wardens	50	0	0

To John Bevil for his expences with Ruben Mitchel	10	0	0
For Ruben Mitchel to the Ch. Wardens	40	0	0
To the Clk of the Vestry	30	0	0
To Ann Strange for keeping a young child	60	0	0
To Samuel Harris for two barrels of Corn	20	0	0
To Robert Dixon a Lawyer fee pd. as Exr. for Lyddal Bacon		15	0
To William Taylor a Clerks fee		18	9
To the Collector his Commissions	38	1	9
To a Depositum raised	60	0	6
	634	16	0
Cr. by 2116 Tythes at 6/ Each	634	16	0

Ordered that Nicholas Hobson collect the parish levy and that he give bond with security for performance of the same and that he receive 6/ from each tythe.

Christopher Billups and Benjamin Tomlinson Gent. chose Ch. Wardens for this year.

Ordered that the present Ch. Wardens settle with John Ragsdale and Jeremiah Glenn the last collectors for this Parish, and acct. with the next Vestry for the ballances due the Parish.

Sign'd James Craig
John Ragsdale
George Phillups

At a Vestry held for Cumberland Parish at the Courthouse the Tenth day of February, 1780

Present

The Revd. James Craig and Christopher Billups & Benjamin Tomlinson, C. W. William Taylor, Thomas Winn, John Ragsdale, Thomas Tabb, Thomas Chambers and Elisha Betts, Gent. Vestrymen.

A Proportion of the Parish Levy

	£	s	d
For Nancy Kelly to the Ch. Wardens or Mrs. Gilliam	150	0	0

For Nicholas Amos to do. or Francis Amos	150	0	0
For William Cuttillo to do. or Edwd. Cuttillo	75	0	0
For Martha Justice to do.	150	0	0
For Ruben Mitchell to do.	120	0	0
For Ann Stranges for keeping of a young child	138	0	0
For Samuel Harris	60	0	0
For Daniel Taylor	60	0	0
To Obadiah Hooper for keeping Anna Dingles the last and present year	200	0	0
For Joseph Taylor to the C. Wardens	80	0	0
To Robert Blackwell for keeping Ruben Mitchell three months and finding him a shirt and boots	60	0	0
For Catherine Boaz to the Ch. Wardens Tho. Chambers absent	210	0	0
To Thomas Winn for finding provision for Catherine Boaz	204	10	0
To Elisha Betts for one bushell corn for do.	6	0	0
To Saunders Ray for keeping Joseph Taylor	20	0	0
To the Clk of the Vestry	120	0	0
To Joseph Billups by order of John Ragsdale Parish Collector	60	2	0
To a Depositum raised	312	13	8½
To the Collector his commissions	138	19	3½
	2315	5	0
The Parish has credit by 2205 Tythes at 21/per Tythe	2315	5	0

Lodowick Farmer Gent. appointed a Vestryman in the place of Colo. David Garland resigned.

Anthony Street Gent. appointed a Vestryman in place of Capt. Saml Garland resigned.

Tho. Chambers and Lodowick Farmer Gent. chose Ch. Wardens the ensuing year.

Ordered that Tho. Chambers Gent. collect the Parish Levy this year and that he receive 21/ from each tythe.

Signd. Christopher Billups
Benja. Tomlinson

At a Vestry held for Cumberland Parish at the Courthouse the 13th of July, 1780.

Present

    Tho. Chambers, Gent. Ch. Warden. Tho. Winn, William Taylor, John Ragsdale, Tho. Tabb, Anthony Street and Tho. Buford, G. Vestrymen.

Agreeable to a former resolution of Vestry Thos. Buford Gent. was chose a Vestryman for this Parish in the room of Colo. Tomlinson, resigned, and having taken the oath prescribed by law take place accordingly.

William Hardy Gent. chose a Vestryman in room of Elisha Betts G. resigned.

David Stokes Gent. chose a Vestryman in the place of Tho. Pettus, G. deceased.

John Ballard Gent. chose a Vestryman in the place of Lodowick Farmer Gent. deceased.

Robert Dixon Gent. chose a Vestryman in the room of Colo. Billups resigned.

Tho. Buford Gent. chose Ch. Warden for this year in the room of Lodowick Farmer Gent. deceased.

                Signed   Tho. Chambers
                            Tho. Buford   Ch. Wardens

At a Vestry held for Cumberland Parish the 10th day of August, 1780.

Present

    Tho. Chambers and Tho. Buford Ch. Wardens.
    John Ragsdale, Wm. Taylor, Anthony Street, William Hardy and David Stokes, Gent. Vestrymen.

Edward Jordan Gent. chose a Vestryman in the place of Tho. Tabb Gent. resign'd.

Ordered that Tho. Chambers furnish Joseph Taylor and wife with wheat or corn to the amount of five bushels including in the price of the said wheat or corn the cash before levied and 23 £ cash.

Robert Dixon and John Ballard present

Ordered that the present Ch. Wardens provide a place for Reuben Mitch__[1] to live at on the most reasonable terms it can be got.

      Signed Tho. Chambers
          Tho. Buford C. W.

At a Vestry held for Cumberland Parish at the Courthouse the 16th day of November, 1780.

Present

  Thomas Buford Ch. Warden, Thomas Winn, William Hardy, David Stokes, Robert Dixon, Edward Jordan and John Ballard Gent. Vestrymen.

    A Proportion of the Parish Levy

For Nancy Kelly to the Ch. Wardens or Mrs. Gilliam	200	
For Nicholas Amos to Ditto. or Frs. Amos	250	
For William Cuttillo to do.	100	
For Martha Justice to do.	250	
For a young child, to Ann Strange or the Ch. Ward.	140	
For Joseph Taylor to the Ch. W. or Jno. Callaham	250	
For Saml. Harris	100	
For Daniel Taylor	100	
To John Hazlewood for his son	150	
To John Calaham for boarding Joseph Taylors children till bound out and three weeks past	30	
To Tho. Buford his acct. as Ch. Warden	221	
To the Clerk of the Vestry	200	
To the Collector his commissions at 6 pr cent	278	
To a Depositum raised	2372	12
	4641	12
Cr. by 1934 Tythes at 48/ pr Tythe	4641	12

Ordered that Nicholas Hobson Gent. collect the above levy

---

[1] Part of word gone.

of 48/ pr Tythe, and that he give bond with security to the Church Wardens.

Nicholas Hobson Gent. chose a Vestryman in the place of Thomas Chambers Gent. resigned.

Tho. Buford and John Ballard Gent. chose Church Wardens the ensuing year.

Signed Tho. Buford
Jno. Ballard, Jr.

At a Vestry held for Cumberland Parish at the Courthouse the 13th day of December, 1781.

Present

    Thomas Buford and John Ballard, Ch. Wardens.
    John Ragsdale, William Hardy, Robert Dixon, Edward Jordan and David Stokes Jr. Gent. Vestrymen.

A Proportion of the Parish Levy	lbs. Tobo.
For Nancy Kelly to the Ch. Wardens or Mrs. Gilliam	750
For Nichs. Amos to Do. or Frs. Amos	500
For William Cuttillo to do. or Edwd. Cuttillo	300
For Martha Justice to do.	750
For Joseph Taylor to Do. or John Ussery	750
For Samuel Harris	250
To John Hazlewood for his son	750
For Ruben Mitchel to the Ch. Wardens or Ellick More	750
To the Clk. of the Vestry	300
To the Collector 6 pr Centum	480
To a Depositum raised	2420
	8000
Cr. By. by 2000 Tythes at 4 lbs. Tobo. pr. Tythe	8000

Henry Stokes Gent. chose a Vestryman in the place of Tho. Winn, Gent. dec'd.

Sterling Niblett Gent. chose a Vestryman in the place of Wm. Taylor Gent. resigned.

    Sterling Niblett and Henry Stokes Gent. present.

·John Ragsdale Gent. appointed to collect the above levy of 4 lbs. Tobo. per Tythe.

Ordered that the above levy be collected in Tobacco or money at the price setled for the time being by the Grand Jury at the respective General Courts.

Ordered that Thomas Buford and John Ballard settle with all former Collectors for this Parish.

Ordered that the Collector pay Colo. Tomlinson 45 lbs. Tobo. out of the above Depositum.

Ordered that the Collector pay William Hardy 70 lbs. Tobo. out of the above depositum.

John Ragsdale and Anthony Street chose Ch. Wardens the ensuing year.

Ordered that the money in the last Ch. Wardens hands be paid to Jno. Callaham and Richd. Gilliam equally.

     Signed Tho. Buford
         Jno. Ballard Jr. Ch. Wardens

At a Vestry held for Cumberland Parish at the Courthouse the 10th day of May, 1782

Present

  John Ragsdale and Anthony Street Ch. Wardens.
  Tho. Buford, John Ballard, Jnr., Henry Stokes,
  Sterling Niblet & Edwd. Jordan Gent. Vestrymen.

Ordered that the Collector settle with the inhabitants of this County for the Parish Levy at Eighteen Shillings pr Hundred and pay of the several parishoners at the same price.

     Signed John Ragsdale
         Anthy. Street Ch. Wardens

At a Vestry held for Cumberland Parish at Micl. Johnsons the 21st of Novr. One Thousand Seven Hundred and Eighty Two.

Present

  John Ragsdale and Anthony Street Ch. Wardens.
  Thomas Buford, David Stokes, Jr., William Hardy,
  Nicholas Hobson & Sterling Niblett, Gent. Vestrymen.

Cumberland Parish

A Proportion of the Parish Levy

	lbs. Tobacco
For Nancy Kelly to the Ch. Wardens or Richd. Gilliam	750
For Nicholas Amos to ditto or Francis Amos	1000
For William Cuttillo to do. or Abrm. Cuttillo	750
George Phillips Gent. present	
For Joseph Taylor to do.	750
For Samuel Harris	500
To John Hazlewood for his son	1000
For Ruben Mitchell to the Ch. Wardens	750
For Jemima Lax to ditto or John Hawkins Senr.	1000
To the Clerk of the Vestry	500
To the Collector 6 pr Centum	569
To a Depositum raised	1919
	9488
Cr. by 2372 Tythes at 4 lbs. Tobo. pr Tythe	9488

Ordered that there be paid to John Ussery of the last year's allowance for Joseph Taylor £ 5-13, the ballance of £ 1-11 to be applyed to the payment of Edward Ragsdales account.

Ordered that the Collector pay William Hardy 500 lbs. Tobacco out of the last years depositum for keeping Ruben Mitchell the year before.

Ordered that John Ragsdale collect the parish levy of 4 lbs. Tobo. pr tythe after giveing bond with security as usual.

Ordered that the Collector settle with the inhabitants of this County for the parish levy at 20/ pr hundred and pay of the parishoners &c at the same rate.

John Ragsdale and Anthony Street are chose Church Wardens the ensuing year.

Ordered that Nicholas Hobson and Edward Ragsdale meet this Vestry at Reedy Creek Church the 13th day of December to settle their accts. for the Parish collection.

Signed   John Ragsdale
         Anthy. Street Ch. Wardens.

At a Vestry held for Cumberland Parish at Mr. Joseph Smiths the 17th day of May, 1783.

Present

    The Revd. James Craig.
    John Ragsdale and Anthony Street Church Wardens.
    Tho. Buford, William Hardy, David Stokes, Edward Jordan, Robert Dixon and Nicholas Hobson Gent. Vestrymen.

It appearing to this Vestry that Edward Hambleton and Richard Sansom, Senr. are men who need assistance from the Parish, it is therefore ordered that the Church Wardens give to the said Edward Hambleton the sum of £3, and furnish the said Richard Samsom with necessaries to the same amount.

John Ragsdale and Anthony Street Ch. Wardens having settled with Nicholas Hobson Gent. for his collection for the years 1779 and 1780 and 1781 and find the ballance due the Parish to be £2085-1-2½ paper money, the said collector engages to pay the sum of £800 Continental money. It is ordered that the Ch. Wardens receive the same and that the ballance be lodged in the Treasury, by the said Collector for the use of the Parish.

                                James Craig
                                John Ragsdale
                                Anthy. Street.

At a Vestry appointed and held for Cumberland Parish the 11th day of December, 1783.

Present

    John Ragsdale and Anthony Street, Ch. Wardens.
    David Stokes, Edward Jordan, Thomas Buford, George Phillups, John Ballard, William Hardy and Nicholas Hobson, Gent. Vestrymen.

John Cureton is appointed a Vestryman in the room of Nicholas Hobson who resigns.

Lyddal Bacon is appointed a Vestryman in the room of Robert Dixon who resigns.

Christopher Robertson is appointed a Vestryman in the room of George Phillups who resigns.

      Signed John Ragsdale
          Anthy. Street Ch. W.

At a Vestry held for Cumberland Parish at the Courthouse the 8th day of January, 1784

Present

  The Revd. James Craig & John Ragsdale, Ch. Warden. Henry Stokes, Thomas Buford, William Hardy, Edward Jordan, Sterling Niblett & John Cureton, Gent. Vestrymen. John Cureton, Gent. having taken the oath of a vestryman took place accordingly.

A Proportion of the Parish Levy	lbs. Tobo.
For Nancy Kelly to the Ch. Wardens or Mrs. Gilliam	750
For Nicholas Amos to do. or Frs. Amos	1000
For William Cuttillo & Elizabeth Cuttillo to the Ch. Ward. or A. Cuttillo	1000
For Joseph Taylor to the Ch. W. or Henry Haies	1000
For Samuel Harris	750
To John Hazlewood for his son	1000
For Ruben Mitchell to the Ch. Wardens or Saml. Snead	1200
For Jemima Lax to do. or John Hawkins, Jr.	1000
John Ballard Gent. present	
For Mary Cockerham to the Ch. Wardens	600
For Edward Hambleton	400
For Richard Sansom to the Ch. Wardens	400
To Catharine Boaz	400
To the Clerk of the Vestry for ordinary and extraordinary services to this day	1000
To the Sheriffs commissions at 6 pr. cent for collecting	1334
To a Depositum to discharge the parish accts.	10408
	22242
By 2022 Tythes at 11 lbs. Tobacco per tythe	22242

THE VESTRY BOOK, 1746-1816 451

Ordered that Jonathan Patteson Gent. collect the Parish levy and that he receive 11 lbs. Tobacco pr tythe, and that he give bond with security to the Ch. Wardens for the performance of the same.

Ordered that the Collector settle with the inhabitants of this Parish for their parish levys at 25/ per Ct. and acct. for it at the same price.

Edward Jordan and Tho. Buford Gent. are chose Ch. Wardens for the present year.

Ordered that the Church Wardens now appointed settle with all persons in arrears with the Parish and discharge the parish accts. as far as money or tobacco sufficient and produce their accts. at the laying of the next levy.

1 Ordered that John Niblet and William Hutson procession all the land between Brunswick line and Stony Creek, Flattrock road and Meherrin river.
2 Ordered that William Fisher and John Ussery procession all the land between Stony Creek and Flattrock Creek, Flattrock road and Meherrin river.
3 Ordered that John Ragsdale and John Moody, procession all the land between Flattrock Creek & Crooked Creek and from Flattrock road and Jenings road to Meherrin river.
4 Ordered that Thomas Ingram and John Granger procession all the land between Crooked Creek and Bears Element creek, Pools old path and Meherrin river.
5 Ordered that John Ragsdale and John Dixon procession all the land between Crooked Creek and Bears Element, Pools old path and Jenings's road.
6 Ordered that John Booker Junr. and Thomas Walker procession all the land between bears clement creek, the great road that goes by John Hawkins's and Meherrin River.
7 Ordered that David Pettus and John Barry procession all the land between the North and Middle Meherrin from Coxes road to the fork of the river.
8 Ordered that John Overton and James Jones procession all the land between the South and Middle Meherrin, and from Coxes road to the fork of the river.

9 Ordered that Robert Willson and John Marrable procession all the land between the South and Middle Meherrin, and from Coxes road to Charlotte line.

10 Ordered that Christopher Robertson and Martin Elliott procession all the land between the Middle and North Meherrin Coxes road and Johnsons road.

11 Ordered that John Pettus and Henry Cook procession all the land between the middle and North Meherrin and from Johnsons Road to Charlotte line.

12 Ordered that William DeGraffenriedt and Obed Clay procession all the land between Winninhams road and Charlotte old line from the North Meherrin to Tursakia Creek to DeGraffenriedts rolling road and from thence to Ledbetter Creek and up the same to Charlotte old line.

13 Ordered that Abner Wells and Frederick Nance procession all the land between the old County Line Spring Creek and Charlotte line.

14 Ordered that John Chappell and Seth Farley procession all the land between Spring Creek, Prince Edward line and Ledbetter Creek.

15 Ordered that John Billups and Woodson Knight procession all the land between Winninghams road and Nottoway river to Tursakia Creek to DeGraffenreidts rolling road from thence to ledbetter creek and up the same to Charlotte old line.

16 Ordered that Lodowick Farmer and William Herring procession all the land between Robertses rolling road Tursakia Creek Meherrin River and Winninghams road.

17 Ordered that Field Clarke and Richard Ingram procession all the land from Robertses rolling road to the head of Couches Creek (Keatts's fork) and down the said creek to Meherrin River.

18 Ordered that Jeremiah Glenn and William Tucker procession all the land from the head of Couches Creek (Keatts fork) to the North Meherrin, thence to Loves Ford, thence along the road by the old Courthouse to Murrell rolling road, thence along that road to Robertses rolling road thence to the first station at Keattses.

19   Ordered that John Cureton Jun. & William Betts procession all the land between Murrells rolling road, Winninghams road, Allen Stokes Mill Creek and the Courthouse road to the mouth of the said Creek.

20   Ordered that Alexander Winn and Daniel Gunn procession all the land between Nottoway river Allen Stokes Mill Creek the Courthouse road and Wards rolling road to the head of Great hounds creek, thence to the mouth of the creek.

21   Ordered that Joseph Smith and Peter Jones procession all the land between the Courthouse road, Rowland Wards rolling road and Reedy Creek old road.

22   Ordered that William Dowsing and Henry Embry procession all the land between Reedy Creek, the Courthouse road, Hixes road, & Reedy Creek old road.

23   Ordered that James Buford and Covington Hardy procession all the land between Great hounds creek, Wards rolling road Reedy Creek old road and the path as goes from Daniel Winns to the old road.

24   Ordered that John Cross and Edward Chambers procession all the land between Great Hounds Creek, Reedy Creek old road, and the path as goes from Daniel Winns to the old road, and the great road that goes by Ben Edmondsons to Crosses bridge and Nottoway river.

25   Ordered that John Ussery and George Marrable procession all the land between Jeningses road, Flattrock road and Reps Jones's road.

26   Ordered that Charles Hamlin and David Parrish procession all the land from the Great road at Crosses Bridge, down the river to the County line, thence along the line to Robert Mores, thence along the line as goes by Marshes house to Reps Jones road, thence to the first station.

27   Ordered that Edward Ragsdale and David More procession all the land between the path as goes from Robert Mores by Marshes house to Reps Jones Road; Reps Jones road, Flattrock road and Brunswick line.

28   Ordered that Thomas Buford and Thomas Hardy procession all the land between Reedy Creek old road, Jeningses road,

Wards rolling road and the path as goes from Wards road to Jenings road near Mrs. Gregorys.

29 Ordered that Nicholas Williams and Daniel Williams procession all the land between Reedy Creek, Reedy Creek old road, Wards road and the horse pen branch.

30 Ordered that William Parrott and Benjamin Estes, Junr. procession all the land between Meherrin River & Reedy Creek, the horsepen branch and the path that goes from Wards road to Jeningses road near Mrs. Gregorys, and Jenings road.

31 Ordered that William Cockerham and Tscharner DeGraffenreidt procession all the land between Reedy Creek, Coxes road, Hixes road and the north Meherrin river.

32 Ordered that Thomas Cralle and William Hamlett procession all the land between Winninghams road Nottoway river and Ledbetter creek.

Ordered that the returns of processioning be made the last Saturday in March next.

Signed   John Ragsdale C. W.

At a Vestry held for Cumberland Parish the 31st day of July, 1784.

Present

    The Revd. James Craig, Edward Jordan and Thomas Buford, Ch. Wardens. John Ragsdale, William Hardy, Henry Stokes, Lyddal Bacon and John Cureton, Gent. Vestrymen.

It being represented to this Vestry that the Glebe house in this Parish is in a decaying condition and that it will be a great advantage to the Parish to make the repairs necessary thereto, this Vestry takeing it into consideration find it will be to the advantage of the Parish to make the necessary repairs as far as the Law permits, it is therefore ordered that the Revd. James Craig apply the £ 15 due from him to the Parish (for damages done the Glebe land by the building of his mill) towards makeing the said repairs.

Signed   Edwd. Jordan
Thos. Buford, Ch. Wardens.

At a Vestry held for Cumberland Parish the Ninth day of Sept., 1784.
Present
Edward Jordan and Thomas Buford, Ch. Wardens. John Ragsdale, Henry Stokes, William Hardy, John Ballard and Christopher Robertson, Gent. Vestrymen. David Stokes, Gent. present.

Jeremiah Glenn Parish Collector for the year 1777, being called upon to settle with the Vestry for the depositum for the above mentioned year, and it appearing to this Vestry that the said Glenn made his collection in paper money at the rate Thirty three Shillings and four pence pr. hundred weight of Tobacco which money being of no value, they have discharged the said Glenn for the same.

Edw'd. Jordan
Thos. Buford.

A Copy of Jonathan Pattesons Acct. for the Depositum Raised the 8th day of January, 1784.
Cumberland Parish To Jona. Patteson Collector

Dr.				Cr.			
1784				By depositum			
To paid Langston Bacon	18	1	0	10408 lbs. Tobo. 25/	130	2	0
To do. on replevy bond Read ag. Stokes	76	18	4	By ballance due on setmt.	35	2	8
	94	19	4	By allows. for R. Sansom never pd. he died	5	0	0
Ballance due the p.	35	2	8	By mistake in adding Tythes 58 at 2/9	7	16	6
	130	2	0		47	19	2
				J. Patteson			

At a Vestry held for Cumberland Parish at the Courthouse the 11th day of November, 1784.
Present
Thomas Buford and Edward Jordan, Ch. Wardens. John Ragsdale, Henry Stokes, John Ballard, Jr., Sterling Niblet, John Cureton and Christopher Robertson, G., Vestrymen.

A State of the Parish Levy.

	lbs. Tobo.
For Nancy Kelly to the Church Wardens, or Mrs. Gilliam	750
To Francis Amos for removing his son Nicholas and keeping him from being further chargeable to the Parish	2000
For William Cuttillo to the Ch. Wardens or Abrm. Cuttillo	1000
For Joseph Taylor to ditto	1000
William Hardy, Gt. present	
To John Hazlewood for his son	1000
For Jemima Lax to the Ch. Wardens	1000
For Mary Cockerham	600
For Samuel Harris	750
For Catherine Boaz to the Ch. Wardens	400
For Ruben Mitchel to the Ch. Wardens	1000
To the Clk. of the Vestry	500
For a Foundling Child to Nevil Gee	556
To a depositum raised	1100
To the Collectors Commissions at 6 pr Ct.	744
	12400
Cr. by 2480 Tythes at 5 lbs. Tobo. pr Tythe is	12400

Ordered that the Church Wardens collect the above levy and settle with the vestry at laying the next levy.

By a settlement with the Church Wardens, Thomas Buford and Edwd. Jordan, for their settlement with the Collectors for this Parish for the year 1782, and for the levy laid the 8th day of Jany. 1784, by which there appears to be due (after paying the judgment of Clement Reads Admrs. against David Stokes Junr. Gt. one of this vestry, and the judgement of Mary Read Extr. and Tho. Read, Executor of Clement Read, against Lyddal Bacon Gt. dec'd, formerly a vestryman in this parish) the sum of £ 48-18-1,* which is at present in the hands of the Collector, and is ordered to be paid to the Ch. Wardens next appointed who

*N. B.—£ 47-19-2 is the sum in the Collectors hands, 18/11 being in the Ch. Wardens hands, which makes the above sum of £ 48-18-1.

is hereby empowered to pay of the accts. hereafter levied, and are ordered to account for the ballance at laying the next levy.

	£	s	d
To Thomas Buford his acct.	3	18	6
To William Burchit for his trouble and expences with Jean Johnson	1	10	0
To the widow Sansom for her part of £5 levied for Rd. Sansom	1	0	0
To Daniel DeGernatt the ballance of his acct. for the gallory and horseblocks	6	10	0
To ditto for interest thereon	2	18	6
To John Snead for keeping Jean Johnsons child	1	4	0
To the Ch. Wardens for the use of Sylvanus Stokes	3		
	20	1	0
Cr. by cash in the Collectors hands	48	18	1
due the Parish	28	17	1

Henry Stokes and Wm. Hardy Gent. are chose Ch. Wardens for the ensuing year.

Ordered that the Ch. Wardens settle with the people of this Parish for the Parish levys at 25/ pr Ct. and settle with the parishoners at the same price.

Ordered that the next Ch. Wardens settle with Major Anthony Street for the money which appears to be due from him to the parish and in case he refuses settlement that they then bring suit against him for the ballances due, and acct. for the same at laying the next levy.

Ordered that Joshua Ragsdale settle with Cornwall and St. James Parishes for their proportions of the judgement obtained by Clement Reads Admrs. in Charlotte County Court, against this Vestry, and in case they refuse payment, that he bring suit against the respective vestrys, and lay an acct. of his proceeding from time to time before this Vestry; and that he be paid liberally for his trouble and expences.

                    Signed   Edwd. Jordan
                                  Thos. Buford, Ch. W.

At a Vestry held for Cumberland Parish at the Courthouse the Twenty first day of February One Thousand Seven Hundred and Eighty five.

Present

    Henry Stokes & William Hardy, Ch. Wardens.
    John Ragsdale, Anthony Street, Thomas Buford, Edward Jordan, Sterling Niblet, John Cureton, Christopher Robertson and Lyddal Bacon, Gent., Vestrymen.

By a state of Edward Ragsdales acct. Collector for John Ragsdale Parish Collector, for the levy laid the 13th of Decr. 1781, there appears to be due the Parish £ 3-17-1. It is ordered that the Ch. Wardens collect the same and in case the said Ragsdale has a list of insolvents that they be allowed him, on his producing a list of supernumeraries.

Major Anthony Street presented his acct. as Church Warden for the year 1783, by which there appears to be due the Parish £ 16-18-3, which is ordered to be paid the Church Wardens.

On a settlement with Major Anthony Street for all former accounts there appears to be due £ 2-9-3½ which is ordered to be paid to the Church Wardens as a final settlement of all accounts to this time beside the above £ 16-18-3.

Ordered that if in case Edmund Johnson does not perform a contract which he has entered into with Capt. Edward Jordan in pay for the support of his wife that then the Church Wardens pay the said Jordan £ 2-10 for supporting the said woman.

This Vestry having setled with Pines Ingram for the money due for his building Reedy Creek Church, find there is due the said Ingram the sum of £ 52-18 of which sum £ 32-18 is ordered to be paid immediately; and the ballance of Twenty Pounds is ordered to be paid on his compleating his Church agreeable to bargain, except the leading the windows, which he is to finish in such a manner that they may slip up and down with ease, and put buttons so as to hold them up when required.

                        Signed Henry Stokes
                                    Wm. Hardy.

At a Vestry held for Cumberland Parish at the Courthouse on Thursday the 11th day of May, 1786.
Present
Thomas Buford, Anthony Street, Henry Stokes, Edward Jordan, William Hardy, Christopher Robertson, Lyddal Bacon & John Cureton, Gt. Vestrymen.

Resolved that Reedy Creek Church be received of Pines Ingram as compleated agreeable to his bargain, and it is ordered that the Church Wardens collect the monies due the Parish and pay to the said Ingram the money due him, for the said Church, which is Twenty Pounds, and take the said Ingrams receipt in full, which receipt shall be lodged with the Clerk of the Vestry among the parish papers & also entered on record.

Teste   Joshua Ragsdale Clk.

      Henry Stokes
      Wm. Hardy Ch. Wardens.

A Copy of Jonathan Pattesons acct. for the depositum levied Nov. . . .

Cumberland Parish to Jonathan Patteson

Dr.				Cr.			
1786				By a depositum			
To Pd. Edw. Hambleton	3	0	0	1100 at 25/	13	15	0
To ballance of Insolvents & Sup. 53 at 1/3	3	6	3	Cr. by ballance due	7	8	9
Ballance due	7	8	9	J. Patteson			
	13	15	0				

May 12, 1786
Cash paid H. Stokes 7 8 9

      May 12, 1786,
       Received the above
        Henry Stokes.

N. B. This money for the above acct. was paid by Henry Stokes to the overseers of the poor May the 20th, 1786, on a settlement with them as Ch. Warden, which with other money to the amt. of £ 13-7-4 may be seen on the overseers list.

Agreeable to order of Vestry of the 11th of May, 1786, the then acting Church Wardens paid to Pines Ingram the ballance of his acct. in full for the building of Reedy Creek Church for which the Sd. Ingram gave the following receipt which was ordered to be recorded.

May the 11th, 1786.

Received of Henry Stokes and Wm. Hardy, Church Wardens for Cumberland Parish, the sum of Twenty Pounds, in full for the money due for the building of Reedy Creek Church received by me.

Pines Ingram.

Teste
 Joshua Ragsdale
 Covington Hardy

A true copy
Teste   Joshua Ragsdale C. C. V.

At a meeting of the Vestry of the Protestant Episcopal Church In the Parish of Cumberland

Present

    The Revd. James Craig
 Thomas Buford, Christopher Robertson, Henry Stokes, Lyddal Bacon, Samuel Garland, James Buford, Covington Hardy, William Buford and Ellison Ellis, who previous to entering on their office agreeable to law subscribe as followeth:

We, Thomas Buford, Christopher Robertson, Henry Stokes, Lyddal Bacon, Samuel Garland, James Buford, Covington Hardy, William Buford and Ellison Ellis, do promise to be conformable to the doctrine dicipline and worship of the Protestant Episcopal Church in Virginia.

Thos. Buford
Ch. Robertson
Henry Stokes
Lyddal Bacon
Sam Garland
James Buford
Covington Hardy
William Buford
Ellison Ellis.

Joshua Ragsdale is chose Clerk to this Vestry, and Thomas Buford and Christopher Robertson are chose Church Wardens for the present year.

Stephen E. Brodnax present

I, Stephen Edward Brodnax do promise to be conformable to the doctrine decipline and worship of the Protestant Episcopal Church in Virginia.

Edwd. Brodnax.

Thomas Buford is chose to represent the Episcopal Church of this Parish in convention agreeable to act of assembly.

James Craig Minr.
Thos. Buford   C. W.
Ch. Robertson.

At a Vestry held for the Protestant Episcopal Church in Cumberland Parish at Reedy Creek Church the Eleventh day of August, 1785[6].

Present

The Revd. James Craig, Thomas Buford, Church Warden. Henry Stokes, Lyddal Bacon, Edward Broadnax, William Buford and James Buford, Gent. Vestrymen, also Anthony Street Gent. who previous to entering on business subscribe agreeable to law as followeth: I, Anthony Street, do promise to be conformable to the doctrine, decipline and worship of the Protestant Episcopal Church in Virginia.

Anthy Street.

Samuel Garland Gent. present.

This Vestry haveing taken into consideration the resolve of the convention of the twentieth of May, have agreeable thereto come to the following resolution. Resolved that the sum of Five Pounds be raised by the whole body of the Vestry the Minister & Clerk to this Vestry, upon which the members present paid down the sum of four pounds and four pence; which sum was paid to the Revd. Mr. Craig, who is also requested to apply to the absent members for their proportions and transmit the same to the Revd. Mr. Buchanan by the earliest opportunity.

This Vestry takeing into consideration the motion of the convention of the twenty third of May, have come to the following resolution thereon.

Resolved that the Parish be laid of into eleven districts by the Clerk; who shall also give to each Vestryman in writeing a district properly bounded, who shall immediately apply to the inhabitants of his district, to know who are members of the Protestant Episcopal Church and take a list of the same. Each Vestryman to have transcripts of such parts of the proceedings of the late convention as are requisite for the present occasion.

Christopher Robertson Gent. present

Resolved that the Church Wardens be requested to restrain and check disorderly behaviour during the time of divine service, and that they particularly superintend the behaviour of the youth in each Church.

Resolved that the Revd. James Craig and Thomas Buford Gent. be continued as representatives of the Protestant Episcopal Church in this parish till the end of next convention.

Resolved that our present incumbent have leave to officiate in other Parishes as he has done for some time past till the end of the present year.

Teste	Signed James Craig
Joshua Ragsdale C. C. V.	Thos. Buford

At a meeting of the Vestry of the Protestant Episcopal Church in the Parish of Cumberland and County of Lunenburg at the Glebe on Tuesday the 15th day of August, 1786.

Present

  The Revd. James Craig and Thomas Buford, Ch. Warden & Sterling Niblett, Lyddal Bacon & Henry Stokes, Edward Brodnax, James Buford, Covington Hardy and William Buford, Gent. Vestrymen.

 I, Sterling Niblett, do promise to be conformable to the doctrine, decipline and worship of the Protestant Episcopal Church in Virginia.

Sterling Niblett.

Agreeable to a resolve of the convention of clergy and laity of the 25th of May, 1786, a petition to the next assembly was prepared and read, and being unanimously approved of and subscribed by this Vestry they do recommend to the members of the Protestant Episcopal Church to assign the same.

This Vestry takeing into consideration the second resolve of the above mentioned convention have come to the following resolution: Resolved that the members of this Vestry for the use of the Minister of this Parish for his services for the present year will subscribe and pay Ten pounds of Tobacco pr. Tythe and do recommend it to the members of the Episcopal Church to subscribe and pay the like quantity of Tobacco pr. Tythe.

Resolved that this Vestry accede to the fourth resolution of the before mentioned convention and that a subscription be raised for the said purpose, upon which the members present subscribed the sum of Seven Pounds one shilling and eight pence of which sum five pounds three shillings and eight pence was paid down.

Resolved that this Vestry duly sensible of the faithfullness and zeal with which Mr. Thomas Buford has discharged his duty as a representative of this Church in convention do for themselves and the members of the Church return him their sincere thanks for the faithful discharge of the trust reposed in him.

Resolved that the Revd. James Craig and Henry Stokes Gent. do represent the Protestant Episcopal Church in this parish till the end of the convention to be held in May next.

In consequence of a former Order of Vestry which empowered the Revd. James Craig to make the necessary repairs to the mansion house on the Glebe, this Vestry do receive the repairs made to the chimnies, the glazeing of the windows & the plastering and white washing, and discount with him in payment for the said repairs the fifteen pounds due from him to the Parish for the damages done the Glebe land by the overflowing of his mill pond.

Ordered that Thomas Buford and Sterling Niblett Gent. be Church Wardens the ensuing year, and that they particularly carry into execution the former order of Vestry concerning the restraining disorderly behaviour of people dureing divine service.

This Vestry takeing into consideration the smallness of Flattrock Church do resolve that Sterling Niblett, Edward Brodnax, Samuel Garland & James Buford Gent. be appointed to raise by subscription a sum of money sufficient to build an addition to the said Church, which money so raised shall be paid by the subscribers to the Church Wardens on or before the twenty fifth day of December next, and it is further ordered that the before mentioned Gent. as soon as they shall have got a sufficient sum subscribed shall call a Vestry to consider on a proper plan for building the said addition.

Teste   Joshua Ragsdale Clk.
James Craig, Minr.
Thos. Buford
Sterling Niblett, Ch. Wardens.

Agreeable to an Ordinance of the Convention of the Protestant Episcopal Church held in the City of Richmond on the 16 day of May, 1787, for the election of Vestrymen to serve as such till Easter Monday in the year One Thousand Seven Hundred and Ninety notice for such election being publickly given such of the members of said church as met at the Courthouse on Monday the 4th day of June, proceeded to elect the following Gent. to serve as Vestrymen for the above mentioned time (Viz) Thomas Buford, Lyddal Bacon, Thomas Garland, Christopher Robertson, Sterling Niblet, Henry Stokes, William Buford, John Ragsdale, James Smith, James Buford, Thomas Stevenson and Bryan Lester, Gent. who being met in Vestry at Reedy Creek Church on the 14th day of June in the said year, agreeable to the said Ordinance do subscribe as follows:

We, Thomas Buford, Lyddal Bacon, Thomas Garland, Christopher Robertson, Sterling Niblet, Henry Stokes, William Buford, John Ragsdale, James Smith, James Buford, Thomas Stevenson & Bryan Lester do promise to be conformable to the doctrine discipline and worship of the Protestant Episcopal Church.

>Thos. Buford
>Lyddal Bacon
>Thos. Garland
>Ch. Robertson
>Sterling Neblett
>Henry Stokes
>Wm. Buford
>John Ragsdale
>James Smith
>James Buford
>Thos. Stevenson
>Bryan Lester.

Joshua Ragsdale is chose Clerk to this Vestry, during pleasure. Lyddal Bacon & Thomas Garland, Gent. are chose Church Wardens for the ensuing year.

>Lyddal Bacon
>Thos. Garland

At a Vestry held for Cumberland Parish at Reedy Creek Church the 11th day of October, 1787.

Present

>Thomas Buford, Lyddal Bacon & Thos. Garland, Ch. Wardens, Henry Stokes, William Buford, John Ragsdale, James Buford, Thomas Stevenson and Bryant Lester, Gent. Vestrymen.

This Vestry considering the present state of the Episcopal Church in this Parish have come to the following resolution. Resolved that it is the opinion of this Vestry that the Parish be laid of into eleven districts to correspond with those formerly made out that the Vestry men most convenient be appointed to apply to the people in their respective districts so laid of, and to raise by subscription a sum sufficient for paying the Minister Clerk & Sextons of the Church in this parish, and that it be recommended to the people to subscribe and pay the sum of ten pounds of Tobacco per tythe, and that each Vestryman be at liberty to pursue the plan he thinks proper for collecting the said subscriptions and that the Clerk make out subscriptions for that purpose.

Teste   Joshua Ragsdale, Clk.

      Signed Lyddal Bacon
          Thos. Garland, Ch. W.

At a Vestry held at Reedy Creek Church for the Parish of Cumberland in the County of Lunenburg, on Thursday the 12th day of June, 1788.

Present

  Messrs. Thomas Buford, Henry Stokes, William Buford, John Ragsdale, James Buford, Thomas Stevenson and Bryan Lester, Gt. Vestrymen.

Resolved that the Clerk of this Vestry do settle the ballances due upon the several subscriptions to James Craig for his services in this Parish, that he give a state of the said ballances due in each district to each Vestryman according to the last division and allotment; and that the said Vestrymen doe use their utmost endeavours to collect the ballances in their respective districts, as soon as they can, & pay the same to the said James Craig when collected.

Teste   Joshua Ragsdale, Clk.

      Thos. Buford
      Henry Stokes
      William Buford
      Jno. Ragsdale
      James Buford
      Thos. Stevenson
      Bryant Lester

At a meeting of the Vestry for the Episcopal Church in

The Vestry Book, 1746-1816   467

Cumberland Parish at Reedy Creek Church the 11th day of September, 1788.

Present

> The Revd. James Craig, Thomas Buford, Sterling Niblet, Chr. Robertson, Henry Stokes, William Buford, John Ragsdale, James Buford, Tho. Stevenson and Bryan Lester, Gent., Vestrymen.

The year being expired for which Capt. Lyddal Bacon and Capt. Thos. Garland were chose Church Wardens, it is therefore ordered that Mr. Sterling Niblet and Capt. Christopher Robertson be appointed Church Wardens for the ensuing year.

Teste   Joshua Ragsdale, Clk.

> James Craig
> Sterling Niblett
> Ch. Robertson

At a Vestry held at Reedy Creek Church the 13 of August, 1789, for Cumberland Parish.

Present

> Christopher Roberts, Sterling Niblet, Thos. Bufor, William Buforde, Thos. Garland, James Beuford, James Smith, John Ragsdale and Briant Lester, Gent. Vestrymen.

Edwd. Jordan is appoint Clarke to the Vestry.

John Ragsdale Execr. of Joshua Ragsdale Dec'd. produced Joshua Ragsdales acct. for his trouble and expences for defending a sute against this parrish and was received and pass'd and there was a ballance due to the Parrish of £ 10-5-3 with interest from 1st October 1787 till paid.

> Present Thos. Stevenson.

Edwd. Jordan is appointed to conduct the sute of this Parris agains St. James's Parris in the room of Joshua Ragsdale dec'd. and upon the same principals.

John Billups is appointed a Vesteryman in the room of Liddal Bacon who is mooved away.

The year being expired which Capt. Christopher Roberts and Sterling Niblet was Church Wardens, and Henry Stokes & William Beuford is appointed for the ensuing year.

Ch. Robertson
Sterling Neblett.

At a Vestery held for Cumberland Parish at Lunenburg Courthouse the 8th day of Octr. 1789.

Present

> Sterling Niblet, James Smith, Wm. Beuforde, James Beuford, Briant Lester, Thos. Beuford, John Ragsdale and Thos. Garland, Gent. Vestn.

It is resolved by this vestery a sum of money that was in the hands of Joshua Ragsdale decd. be deposited in the hands of Edwd. Jordan by John Ragsdale Executor of Joshua Ragsdale Decd. to prosicute a sute against St. James's Parrish and to defend one against Cumberland parris. It is further the oppinions of this Vestery that the Execr. of Joshua Ragsdale pay no interest on the sum of £ 10-5-3.

Test   Edw. Jordan, Clk.

Signed   Henry Stokes
Wm. Beuford   Ch. W.

Agreeable to an order of convention of the Protestant Episcopal Church held in the City of Richmond on the   day of 17   for the election of Vestrymen to sarve as such till   notis of such election being duly given such of the members of the said Church as met at the Court House the 5th day of April, 1799, and proceeded to elect the following Gent. to serve as Vestrymen the aforementioned time (Viz) Thomas Buford, Henry Stokes, Wm. Buford, James Buford, Edwd. Ragsdale, Covington Hardy, William Glenn, Obediah Clay, Wm. Tucker, Chrsr. Robertson, Edmd. P. Bacon and Thos. Garland, Gent.

At a Vestry held at Lunenburg Courthouse for the Parrish of Cumberland on Thursday the 8th of April, 1790.
Present

> Thomas Buford, Henry Stokes, Wm. Glenn, James Buford, William Tucker, Christopher Robertson, William Buford, Gent., Vestrymen.

We do promise to be conformible to the doctrin diciplin and worship of the Prodistant Espicopal Church.

> Thos. Buford
> Henry Stokes
> Wm. Glenn
> James Buford
> Wm. Tucker
> Chr. Robertson
> Wm. Buford

Edwd. Jordan is chose clarke to the Vestery.

Resolved that Edwd. Ragsdale be appointed as lay deputy to represent the Prodistant Episcopal Church in this parrish till the end of the next Convention with the Revd. James Craig.

Edwd. Ragsdale and Wm. Tucker is appointed Church Wardins.

John Ragsdale is chose a Vesteryman in the room of Obey Clay who has resignd.
Test Edwd. Jordan, Clk.

> Wm. Tucker
> Edwd. Ragsdale, Ch. W.

At a Vestry held at Lunenburg Courthouse the 8th day of July, 1790.
Present

> John Ragsdale, Covanton Hrdy, Wm. Tucker, James Buford, Henry Stokes, William Buford, Edwd. Ragsdale, William Glen, Thos. Buford, Christopher Robertson, & Thos. Garland.

We Thos. Garland, John Ragsdale, Edwd. Ragsdale, Covington

Hardy, we do promise to be conformitable to the doctrin disciplin of the prodistant Espicopal Church.

        Thos. Garland
        Edwd. Ragsdale
        John Ragsdale
        Covington Hardy

This Vestry do agree to pay to the Reverend James Crag, sixty pounds for one year service provided he returns to his Parrish & preaches every Sunday.

Test Edwd. Jordan Clk.

        Edwd. Ragsdale
        Wm. Tucker Ch. W.

At a Vestry held for the Parish of Cumberland in the County of Lunenburg, the 27th of April, 1791.

Present

  The Revd. James Craig, Thomas Buford, Edward Ragsdale, James Buford, William Tucker, Covington Hardy, William Buford, John Ragsdale, Edmund P. Bacon, Henry Stokes.

Resolved that an inventory of the property of the Protestant Episcopal Church in this Parish be sent to the next convention agreeable to a Resolution to the last Convention. Consisting of a Glebe containing 825 acres of land with a mansion house and necessary out houses in need of repairs judged to be worth £412-10/.

One wooden Church 60 feet by 30 in good repair
One Do. 48 by 24 in need of repairs
One Surplice
A large silver flagon or tankerd, a Chalice & patten which cost about twenty pound Sterling.
Two large Folio Bibles
Four Do prayer books.

Resolved that agreeable to a Resolution of the last Convention the Church Wardens do certify to the Reverd. W. Buchanon of the City of Richmond that the Revrd. James Craig holds this parish as Rector thereof.

Resolved that agreeable to a Resolution of last Convention the sum of twelve dollars be raised by the Minister of this Vestry and be sent to the Revrd. Mr. John Buchanon by the Debuty who are to represent this parish in the next Convention to be applied to the general purposes of the Protestant Episcopal Church in this State.

Resolved that whereas Captain William Glenn hath sold his land in this County intending to remove from it and we are informed that he wishes to resign his place in Vestry therefore we do make choice of and appoint Mr. John Stevenson in his as a Vestry man in his room.

Resolved that Mr. John Stevenson be appointed a Lay Deputy to represent this parish in the next Convention with the Reverd. James Craig.

In consequence of my being elected a Vestryman I do subscribe to be conformable to the doctrine and dicippline and worship of the Prodistant Episcopal Church agreeable to the ordinance of Convention.

Present John Stevenson   Jno. Stevenson.

Resolved that agreeable to an order of Vestry held at Lunenburg Courthouse 8th day of July, 1790, this Vestry do bind and oblige themselves to pay or cause to be paid to James Craig on or before Easter Monday 1792 on his order the sum of Sixty Pounds certain for officiating in his churches as usual before the Revolution from Easter day 1791 to Easter day 1792 If more money can be raised by contribution a sum not exceeding ten pounds shall be paid to the Clerk and Sextons If more than £70 shall be raisd. the over plus shall be paid to the said James Craig.

Resolved that Covington Hardy and James Buford are appointed Church Wardens the ensuing year.

Edward Ragsdale
William Tucker.

At a Vestry held at Reedy Creek Church for the Parish of

Cumberland in the County of Lunenburg on Thursday the 14th day of July, 1791.

Present

> The Revd. James Craig, John Ragsdale, Edward Ragsdale, James Buford, John Stevenson, Henry Stokes, Christopher Roberson, Covington Hardy, William Tucker, Edmund P. Bacon.

Orderd. that this parish be laid of in eleven districts and that one member of Vestry be appointed to each district in order to take the number of professors of the Protestant Episcopal Church and to make the best collection he can in his district for the support of the said Church.

1 Orderd. that from Brunswick line up Flatrock road to Flatrock Creek down the said creek to Meherin River down the said river to Brunswick line along the said line to the beginning be one district and that John Ragsdale apply to the inhabitants thereof for subscribers to raise a sufficient support for the Episcopal Church in this parish.

2 Orderd. that from Flatrock Creek Flatrock road to Cock road up the said road to bares Ellyment [Bears Element] Creek down the said Creek to Meherrin down Meherrin to Flatrock Creek up the said Creek to the beginning be one district and that Captain Thomas Garland apply to the inhabitants for subscribers to raise a sufficient support for the Episcopal Church in this parish.

3 Orderd. that from Brunswick line Flatrock road Chappells road and Nottoway River be one district and that Capt. Edward Ragsdale apply to the inhabitants for subscribers to raise a sufficient support for the Episcopal Church in this Parish.

4 Orderd. that between Chappells road Nottoway River Hounds Creek Wards Road and Cocks road be one district and that James Buford apply to the inhabitants for subscribers to raise a sufficient support for the Episcopal Church in this parish.

5 Orderd. that between Wards road the road by Hungrytown

Nottoway river and Great Hounds Creek be one district and that Covington Hardy apply to the inhabitants for subscribers to raise a sufficient support for the Episcopal Church in this Parish.

6 Ordered that from Couches Creek down Meherrin to Bears Ellyment thence up the Creek to Ward Road, thence along that to the road that goes by Hungrytown, thence up Murrells road near Samuel Sneads to the middle fork of Couches Creek and so to the river be one district and that William Buford apply to the inhabitants for subscribers to raise a sufficient support for the Episcopal Church in this Parish.

7 Orderd. that from Wades Bridge up to Murrells Road, thence along Murrells Road to James Smiths thence down Couches Creek to the mouth thence up Meherrin River to the Bridges thence down Winninghams Road to where it crosses the Prince Edward Road thence along the Prince Edward Road to Georges thence down Nottoway to the beginning be one district and that Henry Stokes apply to the inhabitants for subscribers to raise a sufficient support for the Episcopal Church in this Parish.

8 Orderd. that from William Georges along Prince Edward line to Meherin thence down Meherrin to the bridges thence down Winninghams Road to where Prince Edward crosses thence along Prince Edward Road to the beginning be one district and that Edmund Parkes Bacon apply to the inhabitants for subscribers to raise a sufficient support for the Episcopal Church in this Parish.

9 Orderd. that from Coxes Road between North & South Meherrin to the fork be one district and that John Stevenson apply to the inhabitants for subscribers to raise a sufficient support for the Episcopal Church in this Parish.

10 Orderd. that from Loves bridge up the road to Johnsons Road thence up Johnsons Road to Nances Road thence up Nances road to the County Line thence along County line to the North Meherrin down that to the beginning be one district and that William Tucker apply to the inhabitants for subscribers to raise a sufficient support for Episcopal Church this Parish.

11 Orderd. that from Coxes bridge up the South Meherrin to the County line thence along the said line to Nance road down said road to Johnsons road thence down Johnson Road to Coxes thence up Coxes to the beginning and that Christopher Robertson apply to the inhabitants for subscribers to raise sufficient support for Episcopal Church this Parish.

Test Edwd. Jordon C. C. V.

      Signd. James Buford
         Covington Hardy C. W.

At a Vestry held at Reedy Creek Church for the Parish of Cumberland in the County of Lunenburg on Monday the twenty third day of April, 1792.

Present

  Henry Stokes, Thomas Buford, James Buford, Covington Hardy, John Ragsdale, William Buford, William Tucker, Thomas Garland, John Stevenson, Edmd. P. Bacon.

Resolved that Mr. John Stevenson be appointed a lay deputy to represent this Parish in the next Convention with the Reverd. James Craig.

Paid by Henry Stokes to Mr. John Ragsdale for the Revd. James Craig £ 5-15-6 in part of his last year sallery.

			£	s	d
Do.	Do.	By Thomas Buford	1	19	4
Do.	Do.	By Thomas Garland	2	-	-
Do.	Do.	By William Tucker	1	10	-
Do.	Do.	By William Buford	5	16	-

      Signd. James Buford
         Covington Hardy C. W.

Carried up & Continued

£	s	d
5	15	6
1	19	4
2	0	0
1	10	
5	16	0
17	-	10

Resolved that the Minister raise Sixteen Dollars to be sent to the Revd. John Buchannan by the deputy who is to represent this Parish in the ensuing Convention to be applyed to the general purposes of the Protestant Episcopal Church—paid by the following person for the above purpose (To wit)

Henry Stokes	£0	6	0
Wm. Buford	0	6	0
John Ragsdale	0	6	0
James Buford	0	6	0
Wm. Tucker	0	6	0
Thos. Garland	0	6	0
Thos. Buford	0	6	0
Covington Hardy	0	6	0
John Stevenson	0	6	0
Edmd. P. Bacon	0	6	0
	£3	0	0

Signed   James Buford
         Covington Hardy, C. W.

Richmond 4 May, 1792. Recd. of Cumberland Parish in the County of Lunenburg, by the hands of James Craig the sum of Sixteen Dollars to be applied by the Convention in such proportions as they shall judge necessary to enable the Bishop to make his visitations & to perform the other duties of his office, & for the other purposes of the Protestant Episcopal Church in this State.

John Buchanan, Treasurer.

At a Vestry held at Reedy Creek Church for the Parish of Cumberland and County of Lunenburg, on Monday the twenty first day of May, 1792.
Present
Reverend James Craig, Thomas Buford, Henry Stokes, Christopher Robertson, James Buford, Covington Hardy, William Buford, John Ragsdale, John Stevenson, William Tucker and Edmund P. Bacon, Vestrymen.

Resolved that the ballance from ten to sixteen dollars be paid to the Revd. James Craig.

Orderd. that the ballance from ten to sixteen dollars be paid to the Reverend James Craig. (to wit)

			£	s	
Do.	Do.	By Colo. Christopher Roberson	0	8	0
Do.	Do.	By Covington Hardy	0	2	0
Do.	Do.	By William Buford	0	2	0
Do.	Do.	By Henry Stokes	0	2	0
Do.	Do.	By John Stevenson	0	2	0
Do.	Do.	By Thomas Buford	0	2	0
Do.	Do.	By William Tucker	0	2	0
Do.	Do.	By John Ragsdale	0	2	0
Do.	Do.	By Edmd. P. Bacon	0	2	0

Paid by Colo. Christopher Roberson to the Revd. Jas. Craig for his last year sallary			1	0	0
Do.	Do.	By Edmd. P. Bacon	1	10	0
Do.	Do.	By William Tucker	0	12	0
Do.	Do.	By Covington Hardy	5	0	0
Do.	Do.	By Thomas Buford	3	0	8
Do.	Do.	By John Ragsdale	5	0	0
Do.	Do.	By James Buford	1	6	8

Signd. James Buford
Covington Hardy C. W.

At a Vestry held at Reedy Creek Church the 18th day June 1792 in the Parish of Cumberland and County of Lunenburg.

Present

The Reverd. James Craig, Henry Stokes, James Buford, Covington Hardy, John Ragsdale, Thomas Garland, John Stevenson, William Tucker, Edward Ragsdale and Edmd. P. Bacon, Vestrymen.

Cash collected by the Vestry and paid to the Revrd. James Craig in part of Sixty Pounds which was his last year sallary.

By Thomas Buford	£5	0	0
By William Buford	6	7	0

By James Buford	5	2	1
By Henry Stokes	6	12	2
By Thomas Garland	3	10	0
By John Ragsdale	2	6	6
By William Tucker	2	2	0
By Edmund P. Bacon	1	10	0
By Christopher Roberson	1	0	0
By Covington Hardy	0	12	0
Do. Do. by Thomas Garland	0	14	8
Do. Do. by William Buford	0	10	0
	35	6	5

```
            60  0  0
            35  6  5
```

Proportioned 11) 24 13 7   Ballance due Revd. Jas. Craig
                 ─────────   due by each Vestrymen to
             2   4 10¼   Revd. James Craig.

By cash paid by Henry Stokes in full of his part of the above mentioned sixty pounds,   £2 4 10¼

Do.	Do.	By Edmd. P. Bacon	2 4 10¼
Do.	Do.	By William Tucker	2 4 10¼
Do.	Do.	By Edward Ragsdale	2 4 10¼
Do.	Do.	By William Buford	2 4 10¼
Do.	Do.	By John Ragsdale	2 4 10¼
Do.	Do.	By Covington Hardy	2 4 10¼

July 27,
1793
    Do. Do. By James Buford   2 4 10¼

       Colo. Christopher Roberson present

Cash paid by Colo. Christopher Roberson to the Revd. James Craig,   £1 1/

Henry Stokes and William Buford are chose Church Wardens the ensuing year.

           Signd.   James Buford
                  Covington Hardy   C. W.

Resolved that each Vestry man make application to the Episcopum in his district between this and the next meeting to subscribe two shillings per tythe for the services of the Revd. Jas. Craig from Easter Day 1792 to 1793 and make a return thereof to the meeting of the next Vestry on August Court day by 10 o'clock.

      Signed James Buford
          Covington Hardy C. W.

At a Vestry held at Reedy Creek Church for the Parish of Cumberland and County of Lunenburg the 14th day of March, 1793.

Present

  Reverand James Craig, Henry Stokes, Edward Ragsdale, William Buford, James Buford, Covington Hardy, John Ragsdale, John Stevenson & Edmund P. Bacon, Vestrymen.

Ordered that each Vestryman make a return of the amount of the last years subscription.

		£	s	d
The amount of Edwd. Ragsdales subscription		5	18	0
Do. Do.	Henry Stokes	8	7	0
	William Buford	2	5	0
	John Ragsdale	8	14	0
	Covington Hardy	0	18	0
	James Buford	10	0	0
	Edmd. P. Bacon	3	11	0
	Christopher Roberson	3	6	0
Cr. By John Ragsdale for the above mentioned subscription		0	12	0
Do. Do. By William Buford		0	6	0

Resolved that those Vestrymen who have not made their returns as above do it the next meeting Vestry.

Ordered that the members of the present vestry meet on Easter Monday in order to make their returns for the last years subscription at Lunenburg Courthouse by 10 o'clock in the forenoon.

      Signd. Henry Stokes C. W.
         Wm. Buford

At a Vestry held at Lunenburg Courthouse for the Parish of Cumberland and County of Lunenburg the first day of April one thousand seven hundred and ninety three.

Present

  Reverd. James Craig, Henry Stokes, James Buford, Covington Hardy, William Buford, John Ragsdale, Christo. Roberson and Edmd. P. Bacon, Vestrymen.

Orderd. that each Vestryman pay to the Reverand James Craig the money they collected from Easter 1792 to 1793

By Henry Stokes	£ 5	10	0
By Christ. Roberson	1	12	0
By William Buford	1	7	0
By John Ragsdale	0	16	0
By Edmd. P. Bacon	0	12	0

      Signd. Henry Stokes
         William Buford.

At an Election Vestry held at Lunenburg Courthouse on Easter Monday 1793, a majority votes were found in favour of

    Henry Stokes
    John Ragsdale
    Christo, Roberson
    James Buford
    Wm. Buford
    Edmd. P. Bacon
    John Street
    Peter Lamkin
    Philip W. Jackson
    William Taylor
    Thos. Garland
    John Pettus

At a Vestry held at Reedy Creek Church the 11th day of April, 1793, for the Parish of Cumberland and County of Lunenburg.
Present

  Henry Stokes, Wm. Taylor, Philip W. Jackson, James Buford, Christopher Roberson, Thos. Garland, John Street, William Buford and Edmd. P. Bacon, who previous to entering on business do subscribe to be conformable to the doctrine and discipline of the Protestant Episcopal Church.

  Henry Stokes
  Ch. Robertson
  James Buford
  William Buford
  Edmd. P. Bacon
  John Street
  Philip W. Jackson
  Wm. Taylor
  Thos. Garland

  Peter Lamkin, Jr. present

I, Peter Lamkin, Jr. do subscribe to be conformable to the doctrine and discipline of the Prodestant Episcopal Church.

I, John Ragsdale, do subscribe as above.

Resolved that Capt. Peter Lamkin make application to the Episcopalians to raise a sufficient sum of money to repair Flat Rock Church and Mr. Henry Stokes for Ready Creek Church and Philip W. Jackson is appointed collector in Covington Hardys district, Capt. Peter Lamkin in James Buford district, Wm. Taylor in Edward Ragsdale district, Colo. Roberson in John Stevensons district, John Billups in Colo. Robersons old district, John Street in William Tuckers old district.

Orderd. that each Vestryman make a return on the 27th of April the number of the Episcopalians and tythes in his district at Reedy Church.

Orderd. that the sum of fifteen dollars be raised to be sent to the Reverand Mr. Buchannon for the general purposes of the Protestant Episcopal Church.

	Paid by Henry Stokes	£0	8	3	0
	by Philip W. Jackson		8	3	0
	William Buford	0	8	1	½
James Buford	John Ragsdale	0	8	1½	
	John Street	0	8	8	0
	John Ragsdale	0	8	1½	
d	Peter Lamkin	0	8	3	-
6/8	Thos. Garland	0	8	3	
	William Taylor	0	8	3	
	Christo Roberson				

Resolved that Philip W. Jackson be appointed a lay deputy to represent this Parish in the next with the Reverand James Craig.

Resolved that Captain Peter Lamkin make application to the Episcopalians to raise a sufficient sum of money to repair flatt Rock Church & Henry Stokes for Ready Creek Church.

Orderd. that Philip W. Jackson are appointed a Church Warden with Wm. Taylor for the ensuing year.

    Signd. Wm. Taylor
       Philip W. Jackson C. W.

At a Vestry held at Reedy Creek Church for the Parish of Cumberland and County of Lunenburg, the 27th day July, 1793.

Present

 Reverand James Craig, Henry Stokes, Wm. Buford, James Buford, John Street, John Ragsdale, Peter Lamkin, Tho. Garland & Edmd. P. Bacon, Vestrymen.

Orderd. that each Vestry man pay to the Revard. James Craig the money collected by them for the year 1792.

By Wm. Buford	£1	12
By Peter Lamkin		6 9
By John Ragsdale	1	14
Do. John Ragsdale		16
Do. Edward Ragsdale		9

    Signd. James Craig
       Henry Stokes

At a Vestry held at Reedy Creek Church the second day of April, 1794, for the Parish of Cumberland and County of Lunenburg.

Present Henry Stokes, James Buford, William Buford, John Ragsdale, Thomas Garland, Peter Lamkin, Edmd. P. Bacon, Vestry men.

Ordered that John Billups be appointed a Vestry man in the room of Capt. John Pettus who refuses to serve.

Ordered that the subscriptions be made out from Easter day 1793 to Easter 1794, for each Vestry man to raise a sufficient sum of money for the support of the Protestant Episcopal Church.

Orderd. that Philip W. Jackson be appointed a lay deputy to represent this parish in the next convention with the Reverand James Craig.

Orderd. that each Vestry man pay the sum of money they have collected to James Buford for the Reverand James Craig.

	£	s	d
By Capt. Thomas Garland	0	6	0
By John Ragsdale	0	1	6
By James Buford	5	0	0
By Captain Peter Lamkin	0	5	0
	£5	12	6

Orderd. that Edmd. P. Bacon be appointed a Clerk to the Vestry of Cumberland Parish and County of Lunenburg.

Signed Henry Stokes
William Buford.

At a Vestry held at Lunenburg Courthouse the 15th May, 1795, for the Parish of Cumberland and County of Lunenburg.

Present William Taylor, Henry Stokes, James Buford, William Buford, John Ragsdale, John Billiups, Edmd. P. Bacon, John Billups, John Street, Vestry Men.

Orderd. that the Church Wardens of this Parish do advertise for a Minister to supply the vacancy in this parish occasioned by the death of the Reverd. James Craig.

Signed Wm. Taylor
Philip W. Jackson.

At a Vestry held at Reedy Creek Church the 6th July day of July for the purpose of choosing a Minister for the Parish of Cumberland and County of Lunenburg to supply a vacancy in the said Parish occasioned by the death of the late Reverand James Craig.

At a Vestry held at Lunenburg Courthouse on Wednesday the 23d of December, 1795, for the Parish of Cumberland and County of Lunenburg.

Present: Christopher Roberson, John Billups, James Buford, William Buford, John Ragsdale, Philip W. Jackson, John Street, Edmd. P. Bacon, Vestry men.

Orderd. that this Vestry do appoint Vestry men in the room of William Taylor & Thomas Garland Gent. who has resignd.

Henry Buford is chosen a Vestry man in the room of William Taylor and James Smith in the room of Thos. Garland.

We Henry Buford and James Smith do subscribe to be conformable to the doctrine & discipline and worship of the Protestant Episcopal Church.

Henry Buford
James Smith

On a motion made by Philip W. Jackson Gentleman a member of this Vestry that the Revrd. Dr. John Cammeron now offers and is willing to undertake for this Parish the office of a Minister recommending him in his opinion to be highly deserving of the same whereupon the said Vestry took the same into their consideration and came to the following resolution:

Resolved that it is the unanimous opinion of this Vestry that the said Reverand Dr. John Cammeron is hereby chosen elected constitued and appointed Rector and Minister of this Parish and that his time shall commence from the first day of January one thousand seven hundred and ninety six.

Orderd. that Edmd. P. Bacon issue subscriptions to each Vestry man in order to raise a sufficient [fund] to repair the Glebe & Churches in this Parish.

Henry Stokes is appointed Church Warden in the room of William Taylor who has resignd.

Signed   Philip W. Jackson
Church Warden.

At a Vestry held at Lunenburg Courthouse on the 11th March, 1796, for the Parish of Cumberland and County of Lunenburg.

Present: The Rev. Dr. John Cammeron, Henry Stokes, Philip W. Jackson, Christ Roberson, William Buford, James Buford, Peter Lamkin, John Ragsdale, John Street, James Smith, John Billups, Edmd. P. Bacon, Vestry men.

Orderd. that this Vestry do deliver all subscription papers in their possession due the Revd. James Craig Decd. for his services in this Parish, to Mary Craig his Exetrix.

Orderd. that the Church Wardens make application to Mary Craig for fifteen dollars recevd. by the Revd. James Craig Decd. for the general purposes for the 1794 and transmitt the same to Mr. Buchannon treasurer.

Orderd. that this Vestry do raise the sum of 15 dollars for the 1795 to be sent to the Revrd. Mr. Buchannon for the general purposes of the Church.

Paid by James Buford	£0	8	1½
By Henry Buford	0	8	1½
By Christopher Roberson	0	8	1½
By John Street	0	8	1½
By William Taylor	0	8	1½
By William Buford	0	8	1½
By Philip W. Jackson	0	8	1½
By Henry Stokes	0	8	1½
By James Smith	0	8	1½
By John Billups	0	8	1½
By Peter Lamkin	0	8	1½
By John Ragsdale	0	8	1½
	4	17	8

Signd.   by Henry Stokes
Philip W. Jackson C. W.

THE VESTRY BOOK, 1746-1816   485

At an Election of Vestrymen and Trustees held for Cumberland Parish at Lunenburg Courthouse on Monday the 28th day of March, 1796, being Easter Monday under the superintendance of the Reverd. John Cammeron D. D., Rector of the Parish and William Buford and John Ragsdale Gentlemen members of the former Vestry, the following Gentlemen were duly elected Vestry men and Trustees for the said Parish for three succeeding years, viz., Henry Stokes, Edmund P. Bacon, James Buford, William Buford, John Ragsdale, Christopher Roberson, John Billups, Philip W. Jackson, David Street, William Stokes, James Smith and Sterling Niblett certifyd. by

        John Cammeron Rector
        William Buford
        John Ragsdale.

We the above mentioned Vestrymen and Trustee for said Parish do subscribe to [be] conformable to the doctrine discipline and worship of the Protestant Episcopal Church in the United States of America and to the Cannons and orders of the said Church in this State.

        Henry Stokes
        Edmd. P. Bacon
        James Buford
        William Buford
        John Ragsdale
        Christopher Roberson
        Philip W. Jackson
        John Billups
        David Street
        William Stokes
        James Smith
        Sterling Niblett

At a Vestry held at for Cumberland Parish at the Glebe on Saturday the 16th of April, 1796.

Present: The Reverand John Cammeron, Rector, Henry Stokes, James Buford, William Buford, John Ragsdale, Christopher Roberson, Philip W. Jackson, David Street and William Stokes, Gent. Vestrymen.

Henry Stokes and William Buford Gent. are appointed Church Wardens. Christopher Roberson is appointed a lay deputy to attend the next state convention of the Protestant Episcopal Church to be holden in the City of Richmond on the first Tuesday in May next.

Orderd. and Resolved that the Revrd. John Cammeron D. D. do find elements for administring the sacrament in the parish for the present year and that he be paid by the Vestry.

Orderd. and resolved that the Church Wardens prepare a petition to be preferd. to the next Convention requesting parmission to sell that part of the land lying on the north side of Reedy Creek road in order to enable the Vestry to repair the buildings on the Glebe and present the same as early as possible for subscription.

Orderd. and resolved that the sum of 15 dollars be raised by the Vestry and sent by the Revrd. John Cammeron to the Treasurer of the Convention to answer the genaral purposes of the Church, and is accordingly done.

       Signd. Henry Stokes
          Wm. Buford C. W.

At a Vestry held at Reedy Creek Church the 28th day of May, 1796, for the Parish of Cumberland and County of Lunenburg.

Present: Reverand Dr. John Cammeron, Henry Stokes, William Buford, James Buford, John Ragsdale, Philip W. Jackson, David Street, William Stokes and Edmd. P. Bacon, Vestrymen.

Orderd. that Henry Stokes, William Buford, John Ragsdale and William Stokes or any 3 of them do sell that part of the Glebe land which lies on the North side of Reedy Creek road for the best price that can be obtained and lay out the same on the repairs of the Glebe and that they also let the said repairs as early as possible to the lowest bidder.

(Present James Smith)

Orderd. that the same gentlemen sell that part of the glebe land which lies between Reedy Creek road and the land belonging to James Craig Decd. if they think it will conduce to the interest of the Parish and lay out the proceeds as above directed.

Orderd. that Edmund Parkes Bacon furnish each Vestryman with subscription papers in order to raise a sufficient sum of money for the support of the Reverand John Cammeron.

Orderd. that John Ragsdale *that John Ragsdale* apply to Peter Lamkin for the amount of the money subscribed to repair Flatrock Church and collect the same as early as possible.

Orderd. that James Smith and John Billups receve the subscription paper from H. Stokes and collect the money due thereon in order to repair Reedy Creek Church.

At a Vestry held at Reedy Creek Church the first day of April, 1797, for the Parish of Cumberland & County of Lunenburg.

Present Revrd. John Cammeron, Henry Stokes, James Buford, William Buford, Christopher Roberson, John Ragsdale, Edmd. P. Bacon, James Smith, William Stokes, David Street, Vestrymen.

Sterling Niblett present.

I, Sterling Niblett do subscribe to be conformable discipline doctrine and worship of the Protestant Episcopal Church.

Sterling Niblett.

Orderd. that John Billups be appointed a lay deputy to serve in the next convention with the Reverand John Cammeron on the first Tuesday in May next.

Orderd. that the sum of fifteen dollars be raised by the Vestry & sent by the Reverand John Cammeron to the Reverand John Buchannon Treasurer of the Convention of the Protestant Episcopal Church.

Test Edmd. P. Bacon   Signd. Wm. Buford
      Clk of C C Vestry   Henry Stokes C. W.

At a Vestry held at Reedy Creek Church the 27th day of May [1797] for the Parish of Cumberland and County of Lunenburg.

Present — The Reverand John Cammeron, James Buford, William Buford, John Billups, Covington Hardy, John Ragsdale, James Smith, Edmd. P. Bacon, Vestrymen.

Covington Hardy present.

I, Covington Hardy do subscribe to be conformable to the doctrine discipline & worship of the Protestant Episcopal Church.

           Covingto Hardy.

Orderd. that John Billups and Edmd. P. Bacon apply to Edward Jordon & receve from him such monies as may appear to be due to the Parish of Cumberland and deliver the same to the Commissioners appointed by a former order to lett the repairs of the Glebe who are hereby authorized to lay out same in such further repairs as they judge most necessary.

Test Edmd. P. Bacon, C. C. V.
      Signd. John Cammeron, Rector
          William Buford, C. W.

At a Vestry held at Lunenburg Courthouse the Ninth day of November, 1797, for the Parish of Cumberland and County of Lunenburg.

Present — Revrd. John Cammeron, Henry Stokes, John Billups, William Buford, Christopher Roberson, William Stokes, Covington Hardy, James Smith, Edmd. P. Bacon, Vestrymen.

Orderd. that William Buford, John Ragsdale and Sterling Niblett or any two of them be appointed to renew the lines round land upon which Flatrock Church stands upon.

Test Edmd. P. Bacon, C. C. V.
      Signd. Henry Stokes
         William Buford C. W.

We do hereby certify that an election of Vestry men for Cumberland Parish in the County of Lunenburg held at Lunenburg Courthouse on Monday the 25th day of March, 1799, being Easter Monday, the following gentlemen was duly elected Vestrymen & Trustees & Trustees for the said Parish agreable to the Cannons of the Protestant Episcopal Church (viz) William Buford, Henry Stokes, Edmd. P. Bacon, John Ragsdale, Christopher Roberson, John Billups, James Smith, William Stokes, David Street, Sterling Niblett, Covington Hardy and Peter Epps.

        John Cammeron, Rector.
        Henry Stokes, C. W.

At a meeting of the Vestry this 24th April, 1799, at Lunenburg Courthouse, the following Gentlemen mett and qualifyd. agreable to the Cannons of the Protestant Episcopal Church.

      William Buford
      Henry Stokes
      Edmd. P. Bacon
      John Ragsdale
      Chrir. Roberson
      John Billups
      James Smith
      William Stokes
      David Street
      Sterling Niblett
      Covington Hardy
      Peter Epps

At a Vestry held at Lunenburg Courthouse the 22d day of April, 1800, for the Parish of Cumberland, County of Lunenburg.

Present — Reverand John Cammeron, Henry Stokes, Wm. Buford, John Ragsdale, Peter Epes, William Stokes, Covington Hardy, Edmd. P. Bacon & Sterling Niblett, Vestrymen.

Orderd. that Peter Epes Gent. be appointed a lay deputy to represent this Parish in the next convention to be held in Richmond the first Tuesday in May next.

Orderd. that 15-$ collected as the requisition for the general purposes of the Protestant Episcopal Church shall be sent to the Revd. Dr. Buchannon by the Reverand Dr. John Cammeron.
Test Edmd. P. Bacon   Signd. Henry Stokes
      Clerk C. C. Vestry   Wm. Buford C. W.

At an Election Vestry for the Parish of Cumberland & County of Lunenburg the 13th day of May, 1802, the following Gent. was duly elected: Henry Stokes, Willm. Buford, Peter Epes, Edmund P. Bacon, John Ragsdale, W. Stokes, John Billups, James Smith, Chrs. Robertson, David Street, Covington Hardy & Danl. Robertson.

We being duly elected Vestrymen for this Parish do subscribe to be conformable to the doctrine, discipline & worship of the Protestant Episcopal in the United States of America and to the orders and cannons of the said Church in this State.

> Henry Stokes
> William Buford
> Peter Epes, Jr.
> John Ragsdale
> J. Billups
> Wm. Stokes
> Danl. Robertson
> Edmd. P. Bacon
> James Smith
> D. Street
> Chrs. Robertson
> Covington Hardy.

At a Vestry held at Lunenburg Courthouse for the Parish of Cumberland and County of Lunenburg on Saturday the third day of May, 1806.

Present Reverand John Cammeron, William Buford, Edmund P. Bacon, John Ragsdale, Peter Epes, James Smith, David Street, Lodwick Farmer, Vestry Men.

We the subscribers do hereby subscribe to be conformable to

the doctrine and worship of the Protestant Episcopal Church in the United States of America and to the orders & Cannons of the said Church in this State.

William Buford
Edmd. P. Bacon
John Ragsdale
Peter Epes
James Smith
David Street
Lodwick Farmer.

Orderd. that the Reverand John Cammeron find elements for the churches as heretofore & that the Vestry provide payments for the same.

Orderd. that the sum of fifteen dollars be raised and sent to the Reverand Doctor Buchannon for the genaral purposes of the Protestant Episcopal Church, in this Parish.

Orderd. that Peter Epes & David Street be appointed Church Wardens.

Test Edmd. P. Bacon   Signd. Peter Epes
      C. C. Vestry   David Street C. W.
                      April 30th, 1807.

Recd. of Peter Epes, John Ragsdale, William Buford, William Ragsdale & Edmd. P. Bacon, five dollars for furnishings elements for the Church in this parish.

At an election of Vestry for the Parish of Cumberland & County of Lunenburg at Reedy Creek Church the 5th day September 1812, under the superintendence of the Reverd. Doctor John Cammeron Rector of the Parish aforesaid & William Buford, Senr. a member of the former Vestry. Agreable to a cannon concerning Vestries & Trusties, the following gentlemen was duly elected Vestrymen (viz) William Buford, John Ragsdale, Emd. P. Bacon, Lodwick Farmer, James Mcfarland, William Stokes, William Ragsdale, William Buford, jr., William H. Taylor, Thomas Cammeron, Thomas Buford & John Buford.

We certify that the above election was duly conducted and the above persons elected Vestrymen and Trustees agreeable to Cannon.

Test Edmd. P. Bacon, C. C. V.

John Cammeron, Rector.
William Buford.

At a meeting of the Vestry for the Parish of Cumberland and County of Lunenburg the 5th September, 1812.

Present — Revrd. Dr. John Cammeron, William Buford, Senr., John Ragsdale, Edmd. P. Bacon, James Mcfarland, Lodwick Farmer, William Buford, jr. & John Buford, Vestrymen.

We the subscribers duly elected Vestrymen for the Parish of Cumberland, County of Lunenburg, do subscribe to the doctrine, disceepline and worship of the Protestant Episcopal Church in the United States of America & to the orders & Cannons of the said Church in this State.

William Buford, Senr.
John Ragsdale
Edmd. P. Bacon
James Mcfarland
Lodwick Farmer
William Buford, jr.
John Buford.

Orderd. that James Mcfarland & Lodwick Farmer be appointed Church Wardens.

Orderd. that the Reverand John Cammeron find elements for the Churches as heretofore and that the Vestry provide payment for the same.

Orderd. that the Reverand John Cammeron and the Church Wardens be authorized by the Vestry to have the doors and windows of both Churches repaired & secured.

Test   Edmd. P. Bacon, C. C. V.

John Cammeron, Rector
James Mcfarland
Lodwick Farmer   C. W.

At a meeting of the Vestry & Trustees of Cumberland Parish held at Lunenburg Ct. House the 12th of November, 1812.

Present The Reverand John Cammeron, James Mcfarland, C. W. William Ragsdale, William Stokes, William Buford, jr., Thomas Buford and Thomas Cammeron, Vestrymen.

We whose names are under written do subscribe to be conformable to the doctrine & worship of the Protestant Episcopal Church in the United States of America.

Attest Edmd. P. Bacon
    Clk. Cumberland Vestry.

                William Ragsdale,
                William Stokes
                Thomas Buford
                Thomas N. Cameron

Orderd. that the Reverand Doctor John Cammeron contract with some proper person for repairing Reedy Creek Church as to underpinning.

Attest Edmd. P. Bacon, C. C. V.
                      John Cameron, Rector.

At a meeting of the Vestry and Trustees of Cumberland Parish at Reedy Creek Church the 13th of May, 1813.

Present Reverd. John Cameron, John Ragsdale, Edmd. P. Bacon, James Mcfarland, William Ragsdale, Lodwick Farmer, Thomas Buford, William Buford, John Buford and William Buford, jr. Vestrymen.

Orderd. that James Mcfarland be appointed a lay deputy to represent this Parish with the Reverd. John Cammeron for the ensuing convention of the Protestant Episcopal Church in Virginia to be holden in the City of Richmond on the fourth Tuesday of this month.

Orderd. that William Buford jr. be appointed Clerk of this Vestry in room of Edmd. P. Bacon, resignd., also Collector & Treasurer of the subscriptions of the contingent funds of the Protestant Episcopal Church in this Parish.

Orderd. that the sum of fifteen dollars be sent the Reverand Dr. Buchannon for the genaral purposes of the Protestant Episcopal Church in this Parish.

Attest   Edmd. P. Bacon, C. C. V.

                                              John Cameron, Rector.

At a meeting of the Vestry of Cumberland Parish & County of Lunenburg held at Reedy Creek Church 18th of April, 1814.

Present   The Revd. Doct. John Cameron, Rector, Lodewick Farmer & James Macfarland C. W., John Ragsdale, William Ragsdale, Thomas Buford, John Buford & Wm. H. Taylor, Vestrymen.

Ordered that John Buford be appointed a lay deputy to represent this Parish in the ensuing annual convention of the Protestant Episcopal Church to be held in the City of Richmond on the first Wednesday in May next.

Ordered that John Buford be appointed Clerk and Treasurer to the Vestry, in the room of William Buford, jr. removed.

William Buford, jr., the late Treasurer, has presented his accounts by which it appears there is a balance in favour of the Vestry of thirteen dollars which was paid into the hands of the Treasurer.

Mr. Wm. H. Taylor for the first time, have taken his seat in the Vestry, subscribes to be conformable to the doctrine & worship of the Protestant Episcopal Church.

Test
John Buford, C. C. V.

                        Wm. H. Taylor
                        John Cameron Rector
                        James Macfarland
                        Lodowick Farmer   C. W.

Ordered that the sum of fifteen dollars be sent the Revd. Doct. Buckanan for the general purposes of the Protestant Episcopal Church in this Parish.

Test   John Buford, C. C. Vestry.

                                              John Cameron, Rector.

At an election of Vestry for the Parish of Cumberland & County of Lunenburg at Reedy Creek Church the 1st day of May, 1815, under the superintendance of the Revd. John Cameron, Rector of the Parish aforesaid, and James Macfarland, William H. Taylor, Thomas Buford and John Buford Members of the former Vestry, agreeable to the cannons concerning Vestrys, the following gentlemen were duly elected, (viz) William Buford, Sr., James Macfarland, Edmond P. Bacon, Lodowick Farmer, William Stokes, William Ragsdale, William H. Taylor, Thomas Buford, Waddy Streete, John Stokes, Robert Cappell and John Buford.

We certify that the above election was duly conducted and the above gentlemen elected Vestrymen agreeable to cannon.

        John Cameron, Rector.
        James Macfarland, C. W.
John Buford, C. C. V.
William H. Taylor
Thos. Buford

[At this point, page 212 of the Vestry Book is this marginal notation opposite the figures 212, "or 202 see date of Vestry meeting, W. C. Phillips." He evidently thought the loose pages might have been gathered and incorrectly numbered. The meetings are here given in their chronological order.]

At a meeting of the Vestry of Cumberland Parish in the County of Lunenburg held at Reedy Creek Church the 11th day of May, 1815.

Present The Revd. Doct. John Cameron, Rector, James Macfarland, Waddy Street, John Stokes, Thomas Buford, John Buford, William Stokes, and Lodowick Farmer, Vestrymen.

We whose names are underwritten do subscribe to be conformable to the doctrine discipline and worship of the Protestant Episcopal Church in the United States of America.

       James Macfarland
       Waddy Street
       John Stokes
       Thomas Buford
       John Buford
       William Stokes
       Lodowick Farmer.

Ordered that James Macfarland and Waddy Street be appointed Church Wardens.

Ordered that John Buford be appointed a lay deputy to represent this Parish in the ensuing convention to be held in the City of Richmond on the fourth Tuesday in this month.

Test John Buford, C. C. V.

       John Cameron, Rector
       Waddy Street
       James Macfarland C. W.

Ordered that the sum of fifteen dollars be sent to the Treasurer at Richmond for the general purposes of the Church.

Test
John Buford, C. C. V.

       John Cameron, Rector
       James Macfarland
       Waddy Street C. Wardens.

Ordered that a coppy of a letter from the Revd. Doct. John Cameron, together with a letter from the Church Wardens to the Right Revd. Richard Channing Moore D. D., with the resolutions of this Vestry thereon be inserted in this book.

Coppy of a letter from The Revd. Doct. John Cameron to the Vestry of Cumberland Parish.

Gentlemen

Finding from my advanced time of life and increasing infirmities that I am becomeing daily less able to discharge the duties of my clerical office, I take this method of notifying to you my intention of resigning the charge of this parish, in the course of the present year. My design in giving you this early notice is, that you may take the necessary steps to provide a successor, who may be ready to take upon him the care of the parish, as soon as I shall relinquish it. And as the Church in this Diocese is now blessed with an able, vigilant, zealous & pious Bishop at its head, I would recommend as early an application as possible to him, requesting him to look out and provide a suitable pastor for this parish.

That the Supreme head of the Church may direct you, and grant you success in this important business & in all other measures that you may undertake for the welfare of our Zion, is the fervent prayer of   Gentlemen
       your truly sincere friend & very humb. Ser.
                               John Cameron.

Cumberland Glebe
April 29th, 1815.

The Revd. Doctor Cameron, Rector of this Parish, having notified to the Vestry, his intention of resigning his charge of the Parish in the course of the present year, the Vestry have unanimously resolved & ordered that the Church Wardens do immediately apply, by letter, to the Right Reverend Richard Channing Moore, D. D. Bishop of the Protestant Episcopal Church in Virginia informing that a vacancy is about to take place in this parish, and earnestly to request him to use his best endeavours to procure a suitable character to fill the same.

It is also resolved & ordered that the Church Wardens do inform the Bishop of the prospect there is of supporting a Clergyman in this Parish.

Right Reverend Sir

    We beg leave to lay before you a letter from The Revd. Dr. John Cameron to the Vestry of this parish, which gave occasion to the Resolutions now accompanying it, and as we consider them both sufficiently expressive of the sentiments of the Vestry on the subject to which they refer, we deem it unnecessary to add any argument of ours to induce our Diocesan to comply with so reasonable a request.

Deeply impressed with a sense of the unspeakable advantages of Religion to our present and future Felicity, and fully convinced, from experience, that the publick profession of it cannot be maintained without the assistance and co-operation of learned, virtuous, exemplery, and pious Pastors, we earnestly beg you Sir, to use your best endeavours to procure one of this discription for our Parish. The salary may be considered as equal to an hundread pounds p annum, which arises from a small estate consisting of *Land* and *Negroes,* left, about twenty years ago, to the Protestant Episcopal Church in this parish, by a very pious and zealous member of the Church, whose name was Thomas Buford. The Revd. Doctor John Cameron and Mr. John Buford our lay-deputy to the approaching Convention, are authorised to confer with you on the subject of this letter, and when you can make it convenient to address us on the same, be pleased to direct your letter to the P. Office at Macfarlands. It will give the members of this Vestry and many well wishers to the Church in this parish, sincere pleasure by your visiting us in the course of this Summer or Fall, and we shall be pleased by your informing us when it will be convenient, that we may give notice thereof. With sentiments of the most perfect respect and esteem we inscribe ourselves,

   Right Revd. Sir, your most obdt. humble srvts.

          James Macfarland
          Waddy Street C. W.

May 13th, 1815.

At a meeting of the Vestry for the Parish of Cumberland in the County of Lunenburg, held at Lunenburg Courthouse the 14 day of March, 1816.

Present Waddy Street, James Macfarland, Church Wardens. Edmond P. Bacon, Lodowick Farmer, Thomas Buford, John Buford and John Stokes, Vestrymen.

James Macfarland and Waddy Street having present a letter

from the Revrd. Doct. Moore Bishop of the Protestant Episcopal Church in Virginia recommending to this Vestry as lay reader Mr. John S. Ravenscroft and he having made known his desire to perform the same in this parish, the Vestry now present have unanimously elected him to the said office of Reader.

Test

 John Buford, C. C. V.

      Waddy Street,
      James Macfarland,   C. Wardens.

      Richmond, Febr. 17th, 1816.

Brothering,

 Mr. John S. Ravenscroft having expressed to me his intention of entering into holy orders, and his desire of rendering every assistance to the Church in his power, I have thought it my duty to recommend him to you and to the members of our communion as a lay reader until the period [ma]rked out by the canons of the Church shall arrive in which he may be regularly ordained.

 In several Parishes in this diocese, the friends of our establishment have willingly accepted the labour of those who are candidates for the ministry; and as Mr. Ravenscroft appears to possess those pious and literary qualifications which bid fair to render him very useful in the Church, I have no doubt that the interest of our communion in your district, will be sensibly promoted by his zealous and active exertions.

 Should my life be spared until the latter end of March, I hope to have the pleasure of seeing you, at which time we can converse at large upon the subject.

 Believe me brethren with great affection
   your friend & Pastor,   Richard Channing Moore.

 At a meeting of the Vestry of Cumberland Parish in the County of Lunenburg at the Courthouse on 15 day of April, 1816.

    James Macfarland, Waddy Street, C. Wardens.
Present John Stokes, Robert Chappell, Thomas Buford and John Buford, Vestrymen.

An election of Vestry men was held under the superintendence of the above gentlemen, and James Macfarland, Waddy Street, John Stokes, Robert Chappell, Thomas Buford, John Buford, Edmund P. Bacon and Peter Epes were elected for the ensuing year, and qualified as the canon directs by subscribing the following form.

[Form missing.]

Returns of Processioning
in obedience to an Order of Vestry of the 17th Septembr, 1759.
Before the Division of Cumberland Parish
(to-wit)

Returns by Drury Malloone & Thomas Malloone

No. 1   1760

The land of Daniel Nance	Present Joel Winfield, Thomas Malloone
of Wm. Parham	Do. Robt. Hudson & Ephm. Hudson
of Thomas Dixson	Do. the same
of John Boseman	Do. John & George Lankford
of Francis Rainey	Do. the same
of Wm. Cleaton	Do. John Lankford & Jon. Cleaton
of Edward Epps	Do. Do. & Wm. Cleaton
of Old Ward	Do. Thoms. Taylor & Isham Malloone
of Thomas Malloone	Do. Joel Winfield & Thos. Nance
of Isham Malloone	
of Drury Malloone	Do. Isham Malloone
of Wm. Nance	Do. himself
of Wm. Bartlet	Do. John Lankford Jon. Boseman
of John Langford	Do. George Langford
of George Langford	Do. Fras. Rainey & Jon. Boseman

1760

Returns by Joshua Mabry, Dennis Larke, Amos Timms, Junr.

No. 3

The land of Rubin Morgan	Present himself & Labin Wright
of Charles Evans	Present himself, Labin Wright, Majr. Evans.
of Robt. Jones Junr.	Do. Wm. Head & Rubin Morgan
of Capt. Wm. Davis	Do. himself, Wm. Rottonbery, Hump. Hewy.
of John Hendrick	Do. Wm. Davies & Ditto.
of Robt. Brox	Do. John & Samll Rottonbery
of Humphry Hewey	Do. himself, John Rottonbery, Wm. Blanton.
Part of Wm. Blantons & part of Dinis Larks	Do. Wm. Blanton & Hump. Hewey

Part of the land of Labin Wright Present Philp. & Rubin Morgan, Amos Timms, Junr. & Thos. Roberts, Senr.
The land of John Wadson, Junr. present himself, Wm. Pool, Senr. Thos. Tay [lor]

of Thomas Taylor Senr.,	Do. himself, Wm. Pool, Senr., Jon. Watson.
of Thomas Taylor, Junr.,	Do. himself, Thos. Taylor, Senr., Doct. Cortney.
of Clack Cortney	Do. himself & Thos. Taylor, Senr.
of Wm. Pool, Senr.	Do. himself, Clack Cortney, Adam Pool & Thomas Taylor, Senr.
of John Robertson,	Do. Jon. Sarjant, Adam Pool.
of John McLin,	Do. Wm. Pool & Son Adam, John Watson.
of John Patrick,	Do. himself & Sherwd. Bugg.
of Sharwood Bugg,	Present himself & Jon. Patrick.
of Samll. Manning,	Do. John Manning.
of Thomas Mclin,	Do. himself.
of Lucias Tanner	Do. himself & Thos. Tanner.

Part of Labin Wrights   Do.   Thomas Roberts, Senr.
    of Thomas Tanner   Do.   himself & Lucias Tanner.
Part of Robt. Langleys &
Part of Dick Evans   Do.   Do.
    of Joseph Bennit   Do.   himself.

Part of Dennis Larke
    of Wm. Blantons
    of Joshua Mabrys   Present Wm. Blanton.
    of Wm. Bells
    of Amos Timms

1760   David Dortch
No. 4   Febry. 9th,   Returns by   Howel Collier
                                          Wm. Lucas
                                          Robt. Larke

The land of Nathll. Collier
    of Howell Collier
    of David Dortch   Present James Hamner.
    of Charles Cozens

    of Robt. Larke
    of Dinnis Larke   Present Dinnis Larke
    of Robt. Campbell

    of Wade Ward   Do.   himself

    of Wm. Lucas
    of Saml. Lucas   Do.   Denis Larke

The lands of Clack Cortney & Taylor Duke not processioned for want of attendance.

1760   James Hamner
No. 5   March   Returns by   Wm. Thomas &
                                          James Lett

The land of Wm. Whitemore   Present Fras. Lett
    of Fras. Lett   Do.   John Watson Senr.

of Hannah Butler	Do.	Do.
of John Watson Senr.	Do.	himself
of John Lett	Do.	Himself, Fras. Lett, Jon. Watson.
of James Lett, Junr.	Do.	John Lett
of Abram. Whitemore	Do.	John Whitemore.
of James Lett, Senr.	Do.	Jacob Matthis, Isham Lett.
of James Harnel, Senr.	Do.	Jas. Harnel, Junr.
of Samll. Homes	Do.	Isaac Homes.
One line of Colo. Ruffins land		Present the same.
One line of Nathll. Cooks.		
One line of Benjn. Bairds		Prest. Nathll. Cook
One line of Henry Delonys	Do.	Wm. & Isaac Homes.
One Do. of James Hammer	Do.	the same
One Do. of David Dortches	Do.	the same
One Do of Chas. Cozens's	Do.	the same

1760
No. 6   Febry. 11th   Returns by   John Speed
Henry Delony
Geo. Baskervil
Jacob Bugg
John Ballard

The land of Field Jefferson		Present George Jefferson.
of George Baskervil	Do.	Bennit Holloway.
of Bennit Holloway	Do.	Geo. Jefferson & himself.
of James Ferril	Do.	himself & John Earl.
of John Earl	Do.	himself.
of Jacob Bugg	Do.	John Earl.
of Hutchens Burton	Do.	John Jefferson.
of John Ruffen	Do.	Jos. Gray, Spittle Pulley.
of George Baskervil	Do.	Huchens Burton.
of Rubin Morgan	Do.	himself.
John Speed	Do.	Bennit Holloway.
of John Speed	Do.	James Ferril & John Earl.

of John Ballard	Do.	Bennit Holloway, Wm. Williams.
Wm. Williams	Do.	himself & Bennett Holloway.
Robert Cozens	Do.	James Ferrel & Joseph Gray.
Henry Delony	Do.	Ditto.
Richard Newman	Do.	Henry Tally, Spittle Pully.
Wm. Linsey	Do.	Thomas Adams & Hen. Tally.
John Mclin	Do.	Henry Tally & Jas. Ferrel.
Thomas Adams	Do.	himself & Joseph Gray.
Bryan Coadle	Do.	Thos. Adams &
Peter Parish		Jas. Ferrel.

The land of Randolph Bracy
    Robt. Ruffen   Present Thomas Adams, Petr. Parish.
    John Heightour

    Samll. Homes
    Benjn. Baird   Jas. Ferrel & Joseph Gray.

Thomas Edmundson gave no attendance.

1760
No. 10   Febry. 12.   Returns by   George Farrar
    Anselm Bugg
    & Edmund Bugg

The land of Joseph Burchett	Present	himself.
James Cock	Do.	Samll. Hopkins.
Samll. Hopkins	Do.	himself.
Anselm Bugg	Do.	Samll. Hopkins.
Edmund Bugg		
Wm. Howard		
Fras. Howard		
Danll. Johnson	Do.	Thos. Adams.
Mary Stephens	Do.	Ditto.
James Cunningham	Do.	Ditto.

THE VESTRY BOOK, 1746-1816   505

1760   Edward Goode
No. 12   Febry. 20.   Returns by   John Thompson
                                        Joseph Gill
The land of John Pleasant
          Joseph Gill   Present John Childress,
          Edward Goode   Petr. Gill.

          Isaac Young Husband   Do.   Ditto.
          Cleuviers Coalman   Do.   himself & Wm. Mcdow.
          John Weatherford   Do.   Wm. Weatherford.
          Henry Tally   Do.   Abram. Tally.
          Richard Booker   Do.   John Thompson.
          Joseph Grier   Do.   himself.
          John Humphreys   Do.   himself & Abram. Coalson.

1760
No. 14 March 1st.   Returns by   James Dawes
                                    Henry Vendike

The land of David Garland   Present himself.
          Henry Jackson   Do.   himself.
          French Haggard   Do.   Wm. Jackson,
                                        Wm. Parker.
          Allen Gentry   Do.   Wm. & David Gentry.
          John Brookes   Do.   Wm. & Alen Gentry.
          John Granger   Do.   John Brookes,
                                        Thos. Andrews.
          Peter Andrews   Do.   Ditto.
          John Cooper   Do.   John Brookes,
                                        Jon. Granger.
          Crowder   Do.   Jon. Andrews,
                                        Jon. Cooper.
          Jos. Blanks Orphants Do.   Henry Gill.
          Henry Gill   Do.   himself.
          Israel Browns Orpts. Do.   Cornelius Priest.
          John Sandford   Do.   himself.
          Baxter Ragsdale   Do.   himself.
          Wm. Wallice   Do.   himself.

John Ragsdale	Do. himself.
James Dawes	Do. David Garland.
Richd. Haggard	Do. John Brookes.
John Jennings	Do. Cornelius Priest.

The following not processioned for want of attendance (to wit) Wm. Bookers Orphants, Wm. Butler, Wm. Craws, Jonathan Pattison, John Edloes Orphants, Colo. Cox, Henry Gee, Nevel Gee & Leonard Cheatom.

1760
No. 16   March 4th   Returns by   Robert Brookes
                                                                             John Scott
                                                                             Richard Williams
                                                                             Lazs. Williams

The land of Lazs. & Richard Williams   Present Robt. Brooks, John Scott, John Rogers, Thos. Edwards & John Williams.

Wm. Newsom   Present Hugh Whiley, Jno. Williams, & James Barclay.

John Williams	Do. himself.
Part of Thos. Edwards	Do. Wm. Hawkins & Son Wm.
Mattw. Burt	Do. himself, John Blaxton, Wm. Getse, Wm. Hawkins & son Wm.

The line Wm. Hawkins & John Blaxton & the line between Blaxton & Mrs. Embry Present John Blaxton. & the line between Mrs. Embry & Drury Hawkins, Present himself, Wm. Getse & Joseph Gentry at all the three lines.

The line between Drury Hawkins & Edward Dowsings. Prest. Mattw. Burt, Wm. Getse, Jon. Blaxton, Jos. Gentry & themselves.

The line between John Hannah & Moses Cockerham. Present Joseph Gentry.

The line between Moses Cockerham & Edward Dowsing. Present himself, Jos. Gentry & Richard Brooks.

The line between John Hannah & Joshua Hawkins. Presant

Drury Hawkins, Joseph Gentry & Richd. Brookes. NB Hannahs line was run to Hobsons Corner.

The line between Wm. Shelton & Jon. Hix, & the line between the said Shelton & Wm. Brookes; the line between the said Brookes & John Hix, likewise Hix's back line, the line between Joshua Hawkins and the said Shelton. The line between Joshua Hawkins & Joseph Gentry, the line between Drury Hawkins & Rowland Ward done in presents of Wards overseer.

No other persons attended to have their lands processioned.

The land of Lazeras Williams, John Blaxton, Wm. Embrys Decd., the widw. Brookes or orphans land Elisha Brookes, Widw. Cockerhams, John Prices, Richd. Brookes, Nick. Gentrys, Robt. Scotts, Wm. Loves, Wm. Getoes, James Berrys, Willm. Hawkins, Senr., Richard Coalman, present the owners or some one instrusted by them to show the lines.

1760
No. 19   March 31st   Returns by   John Hoskinson
                                             & Chris. Billups

The lands of Jonathan Davies   Present Danll Malloone,
                                       Wm. Davies.
            Roger Madison   Do. Thos. Staples
            Thomas Staples   Do. Roger Madison,
                                       Wm. Nance.
            Richard Nance   Do. himself.
            Robert Beasley   Do. himself.
            Danll Meloone   Do. Jonathan Davies.
            John Beasley   Do. Edwd. Hatchett.
            Joseph Billups   Do. himself.
            Samll. Ingram   Do. John Midleton.
            Thomas Pound   Do. himself.

            Tscharner Degraffenreidt, Present Roger Madison.
            John Hoskinson   none present.
            Chris. Billups   Do. James Coal, Jon. Middleton.
            Martin Wilkinson   Do. Thomas Staples &C.

Danll. Ealbank
Ralph Shelton
John Camp
Wm. Gregg
John Ellis   Not processioned for want
Wm. Getoe   of attendance.
Richd. Burks
Lewis Dupree
John Nance, Senr.
Benjn. Hawkins
John Stone

1760   Returns by   Chris. Hudson
No. 20   May 4th   Joseph Freeman
                                     John Hide

The land of John White   Present himself & Edwd. Bevil.
      Edward Bevil   Do.   himself & John White.
      Joseph Freeman   Do.   himself & Chris. Hudson.
      Wm. Edwards   Do.   Joseph Freeman.
      Joseph Greer   Do.   himself.
      James Tucker   Do.   himself.
      Pirmenas Palmer   Do.   himself.
      Chris. Hudson   Do.   James Tucker.
      John Hide   Do.   Do.
      Sarah Royal   Do.   John Royal.
      Colo. Lewis Burwell   Do.   Thomas Carlton.
      John Hubbard   Do.   himself & Do.
      Anthony Hughs   Do.   himself.
      Soloman Drapier   Do.   himself.
      Colo. Lewis Burwell   Do.   John Jeffris,
                                          Richd. Swepson.
      Abraham Crowder   Do.   himself.
      Capt. Peter Jones   Do.   Hugh Franklin but the
                                   lines could not be made out.

      Richard Stith   Not processioned for
      Wm. Jones & Joseph Boswell   want of attendance.

1760			Thos. Anderson
No. 22	March 31st.	Returns by	Richard Palmer
			Thos. Carlton

Processioned the line between Thomas Saterwhite & Peter Purcer & between Robert Munford & Purcer, & between Munford & David Bullock. Between Bullock & Rachell Taber. Between James Wilkins & Edward Lewis, & between William Lidderdales orphans, & between Thomas Saterwhite and Richard Palmer to Roanoak River. Present Jas. Wilkins. Then began at Palmers corner and processioned the line between Richd. Palmer & Wm. Lidderdales orphans & between Palmer & Bassill Wagstaff to Roanoak & between Wm. Donithon & George Bruce, beween Bruce and Saterwhite & between Edward Lewis & Wm. Lidderdales orphan. Present Willm. Donithon. Between Richd. Palmer & Fras. Bracie to Butchers Creek, between Bracie and Edwd. Lewis, Robt. Easter & Wm. Taber orphans, & Thomas Hawkins orphans to Butchers Creek. Present George Bruce, Richard Long, Benjn. Pulliam, Between Mattw. Tanner and Wm. Tates orphan, Henry Ward & Thomas Hawkins orphans to Butchers Creek. Present Mattw. Tanner & Wm. Tate. Between Henry Ward & Thos. Avorys orphans & John Mays orphans, between Robert Easter & Henry Ward & James Avory & Volintine Mullins & Tates orphans. Pres. Mattw. Tanner, Edwd. Hogan. Between Rachel Taber and Robt. Munford and Volentine Mullins & Mary Ann Wilkins & John Wilkins's line. Present Vol. Mullins & Riah Taber. Then began at Wilkins's corner & from thence to Luke Folios and on Avorys line to Armsteads & John Mays's orphans & to Avorys & to Robt. Easters line & the lines between Thos. Avorys orphans & John Purcer & to Butchers Creek & beginning at Wilkins's corner run to Robt. Easters line. Present Vol. Mullins & Riah Taber. The line between James Wilkins and David Bullock & the line between Wm. Lidderdales orphan & Edward Lewis to Thomas Saterwhites lines and James Wilkins's & Edward Lewis & Mary Ann Wilkins's to the end. Present James Wilkins & Edward Lewis. The line between Colo. Lewis Burwell & Colo. Wm. Jones & the line between the said Jones & Peter Jones & between Wm. Hill & Colo. Wm. Jones &

Colo. Burwell. Present John Jeffris & Rd. Russell. The lines between Colo. Burwell & James Murray, a line between James Murray & Wm. Harris & between Wm. Harris & Colo. Burwell, a line between Wm. Harris & Stephen Evans, a line between Colo. Burwell & David Alliburton. Present Stepn. Evans, John Camp, John Jeffris, Richard Swepson.

1760
No. 26   March 31st.   Returns by   Danll. Price
                                     Volintine Brown
                                     & Wm. Stone

The land of Wm. Love   Present John Scott.
    John Scott   Do. Wm. Love,
                                     Benja. Burchett.
    Robt. Scott   Do. the same.
    Robt. Brookes   Do. himself & Benja.
                                     Burchett.
    Auther Brookes   Do. the same.
    Wm. Roberts   Do. the same.
    Fras. Smithson   Do. Jesse Brown &
                                     Jon. Smithson.
    Abram. Cock   Do. Do. & John Smith.
    Jesse Brown   Do. John Smithson,
                                     Benja. Burchett.
    Jon. Colwell Brown Do. Jon. Smith &
                                     Jesse Brown.
    Volintine Brown   Do. Robt. Brookes,
                                     B. Burchett.
    Joseph Asher   Do. Ditto.
    Wm. Lax   Do. the same.
    Obediah Hooper   Do. the same.

Danll. Prices land where he lives & the land bot of John Doake. Present Robt. Brookes, Thos. Green.

    Thomas Petties   Do. Wm. Lax,
                                     Philp. Cockerham.
    Philp. Cockerham   Do. Thos. Petties.

Miner Cockerham	Do.	Do.
John Hobson	Do.	Do.
Wm. Stone	Do.	Do.
John Pleasant	Do.	Jerimiah Hatcher
Wm. Mackadon	Do.	Do.
Jerimiah Bowles	Do.	Obediah Hooper

1763/64. RETURNS OF PROCESSIONING in obedience to an Order of Vestry of the 30th of Septembr., 1763, of Cumberland Parish.

No. 1 By John Callaham, James Dicks & Fras. Niblett, viz.

Jeremiah Mises land, Thos. Rights, John Rights, Wm. Turners, John Parkers, Thomas Moores, Matt. Williams's, Wm. Johnsons, Thomas Moodys, Matt. Organs, Honor Buckenhams, Fras. Nibletts, Richard Wyatts, James Masons, living in Sussex County whereon Joseph Hix now lives. Daniel Taylors, William Haymores, James Dicks's, Edwd. Cowingtons, James Garrots, John Callahams, Eliz. Richs's, living in Surry County, Eliz. Parnalls living in Isle White County, Edwd. Petaways, Hamlin Freemans living in Sussex County, Thos. Whites, David Callahams, John Hights, Wm. Parkers, Michael Vaunes, James Fishers, living in Brunswick County. Robt. Campbells, Wm. Baileys, James Mises, Matt Turners, David Moses, Stephen Mises, Thos. Garriots, John Greens, Freemans land whereon William Burgamy lives. Chiles's land where Alexr. Rudd lives, Broadnaxes land where Phil. Russell lives, Henry Hazes part of Edloes lying on Kettlestick Branch, there was nobody to show Edloes land on Flatrock but the people that lived on it & they were present at processioning.

No. 2 The persons appointed to procession say their order miscarried.

No. 3 Processioned by Everd. Dowsing, Mattw. Burt & Thomas Edwards, viz.

The line between Mattw. Burt and Richard Williams and between Lazeras Williams & Mattw. Burt & between Lazeras Williams & Kings land part of the line & between Do. & Richard Williams. The other part they refused to procession by reason of a dispute in the presents of both parties. The line between Jon. Blaxton & Mattw. Burt & the line between Jon. Blaxton & Lazeras Williams & between John Blaxton & Peter Jones & between Jno. Blaxton & the land of Wm. Embrys estate & between Mattw. Burt & Blaxton & between Mattw. Burt & Mattw. Wells, between Matt Burt & Thomas Edwards. Present Jon. Blaxton & Richd. Williams, and by the order of Peter Jones the line between Rowland Ward & Matt Wells & between Matt Wells & Thomas Edwards & between Thos. Edwards & Roland Ward & between Wm. Tisdel & Rowland Ward & the line between Wm. Tisdel & Matt Wells, between Matt. Wells & Wm. Embrys Estate. The line between Everard Dowsing & Wm. Tisdel & the line between Everard Dowsing & Wm. Embrys estate. Present Mattw. Wells, Wm. Tisdel, Thomas Murrey for Ward. The line between John Hix & Jonathan Pattison & John Bacon in presents of John Hix, Jonathan Pattison, Joseph Gentry & John Hawkins. John Hawkins & Jonathan Pattison refuseth to show their lines. The lines between Joseph Gentry & Richd. Hanson & between Joseph Gentry & Everard Dowsing in the presence of Joseph Gentry & Henry Finch for Rd. Hanson. The line between Willm. Wallis & John Kirby & between Wm. Wallis & Jon. Rogers in the presence of Wm. Wallis, Jon. Jenings & Jon. Rogers. The line between Jon. Jenings & Thos. Tabb & between John Jennings & Abram. Cock & the line between Jon. Jenings & Cornelias Priest in presence of Jon. Jenings & Jon. Epps for Thos. Tabb. The line between Thomas Tabb & Samll. Devol & between the Gleeb land & Mr. Cross & the line between the gleebe land & Jon. Rogers, part of the line not found, in presence of the Revd. Jas. Craig, Mr. Cross & John Epps, & the line between Jon. Rogers & Mr. Cross & between Cross & Wm. Wallis & between Cross & Peter Cock & between Cross & Chisolm & between Cross & Ruffen, between Cross & Samll. Devoll, in presence of Mr. Cross. The line between Lazeras Williams & Mr. Jones (by order of Jones) & the line between Rowland Ward & the other unknown, the line between Rowland Ward & Thos. Lowery, between Rowland Ward, Thos. Edwards, between Thos.

Lowery & Thos. Edwards, the line between Lowery & Matt Burt & between Burt & Jon. Cuttilla & between Jon. Epps & Burt & between Burt & Thos. Biddy in the presence of Rowland Ward & Crab Voan for Lowery. All the remaining lines are not processioned the owners not attending.

No. 4 Processioned by Daniel Wynn, Elisha Estis & Joel Farguson, (to wit) Joel Fargusons land, Evan Evans, Elisha Estis's, Richd. Ellis's & Nicholas Browns & Richard Ellis present.

Jerrott McConnicos land, Robt. Boultons & Nicholas Browns, Jerrott McConnico, Robt. Boulton & Nicholas Brown presant.

John Wynn, Thomas Stones orphans & Samll. Sneads land, John Wynn present.

John Stone, Senr., Allen Stokes, Senr. & Thomas Wynns lands, present Thomas Wynn, John Stone & Assebyas Stone.

John Whites land, John Hazlewoods, John Ellis's, Lazeras Williams & Peter Jones, present John White, John Hazlewood, Lazeras Williams & Joseph Townsend.

Richard Stones land, Geo. McClaughlins, Mary Stones, Elizabeth Stones & John Stones, Junr., all the men were present.

Robt. Estis's line in presence of himself.

Daniel Wynn's land, Benjn. Bridgfords & Jon. Knights, the last & Samll. Snead being present.

Processioned Fras. Epps land, John Strawans, Jeffrey Murrells, in presence of John Strawan, Jeffrey Murrell, Jon. White & John Hardy & Stephen Evans's & David Hopkins's in presence of Robt. Evans. Thomas Williams's & Jonas Vassers in presence of Thomas Walker & Jonas Vasser & John Hardys in presence of himself.

Lands not processioned, viz: Isaac Winstons, Richard Evans's, Hugh Lawsons, Abram Cocks & Mary Cockerhams, as no attendance was given.

No. 5 Processioned by Lodwk. Farmer & Silvanus Stokes (to wit)

The lines between Richard Claiborne & Michael Johnson & between the said Claiborne & Lodwk. Farmer & between the said Farmer & Daniel Malloon & between the said Melloon & Jarrald Winningham & between Arther Herrin & Lodwk. Farmer & between the said Farmer & Mark Thornton & between the said Farmer & Edmd. Belcher & between the said Belcher & Thos. Stunks & between the said Stunks & Gidion Moon & between the said Moon & Geo. Grimes & between the said Moon & Leonard Dayer & between the said Grimes & Stunks & between Edmund Belcher & Thos. Hardin. David & Silvanus Stokes's Present Colo. David Stokes, Young Stokes, Lyddal Bacons Present Lyddal Bacon & Wm. Stokes. Thomas Wynns, Allen Stokes, John Stones, Wm. & Chas. Stokes's, part of Garrard McConnicoes, Curtis Cates, Richd. & Evans Stokes's & John Parkers, Present Capt. Thos. Wynn, Allen & Wm. Stokes. Colo. Peter Fountains [Fontaine], Danll. Claiborns, Geo. Grymes's, Giddion Moons, Wm. Braggs & Arthor Herrins, present Colo. David Stokes & Daniel Claiborne. Henry Wimpys, Joseph Pulliams, James Pulliams, Peter Jones's, Wm. Briggs's, Wm. Murrils, Danll. Browns, Mr. Stephensons, & Jon. Johnsons, presant Jas. Pulliam, Jno. Johnson & Wm. Murril. Leonard Doziers, Thos. Duprees, Chas. Graviats, Wm. Pettipools, Nicholas Edmonds's, Robert Estis's & Willm. Gordons, presant Thos. Dupree, Wm. Pettypool, Robt. Estis & Bartilot Estis. A considerable quantity of land Silvanus Stokes says was not processioned within the bounds mentioned in the order by reason that Lodwick Farmer & Jarrard McConnicoe fail'd to meet & assist according to order.

No. 6 Processioned by Joseph Minor, Jacobus Christopher & John Knight the lands (to wit) belonging to the following persons. Jarrard McConnicoes, Richd. Stokes's Junr. & Richd. Stokes's Senr., John Barns & Evan Stokes, presant Richd. Stokes.

Colo. John Nash's, John Knights, Joseph Minors, Wm. Monroes, Fras. Amos's, presant Jon. Whitworth, Wm. Monroe, Anthony Puckett, Fras. Amos, Jos. Smith.

Thomas Hudsons, Jos. Smiths & Jacobus Christophers, in presence of Fras. Amos, Jos. Smith & Thos. Hudson.

Josiah Gates's, Richd. Crews, Waltho Owens, Wm. Owens, James Hamletts, Charles Stokes's, David Owens, Benjn. Colliers, in presence of Josiah Gale, Richd. Crews, Chas. Stokes, David Owen & Benjn. Collier.

Joseph Billips's, himself & Wm. Pamplet present.

THE VESTRY BOOK, 1746-1816   515

Henry Stokes's, present Mark Thornton, Henry Stokes & Eli Fennil.
Christopher Billips's, himself & Jos. Owen present.
Richd. Ealbanks, presant Chris. Billips, Wm. Pamplett & Joseph Owen.
Lands not processioned (to wit) as no one attended to show the lines, Winstons, Dicksons, Harrisons & Robert Evans.

No. 7 The following peoples lands were processioned by Vol. Brown, Cleveris Coalman & Wm. Stone (towit)
Geo. Elliotts, Wm. Chandlers, Jane Cunninghams & John Scotts, presant Geo. Elliott & Wm. Chandler. John Scotts & Thomas Taylors line & themselves presant. Robt. Scotts & Jas. Calhorns line, John Scotts & Benjn. Burchetts line, John Scott & Wm. Loves line, Wm. Love & Fras. Smithsons line, John Smithson & Love presant. Fras. Smithson & Cocks line, Nathll. Mason & Frances Smithsons line, Val. Brown & Masons line, Mason & John Colwell Brownes line, Mason & Brown presant. Benj. Burchetts & Cocks line, Burchett & Val. Browns line, Auther Brookes & Val. Browns line, Val. Browns & Ben. Cockerhams line, Val. Brown & Robt. Brookes line, Val. Brown & Danll. Prices line, Benjn. Burchett & Brown present. Amos Hix & John Cox Junr. line, John Cox & Danll. Gory presant. Thomas Taylors line between him & the Gleeb land, Taylor presant. Taylors & Elliotts line, Taylor presant. Joseph Davies's & Elliott line, Davies & Taylor presant. Jos. Davies's & Richd. Elliotts line, Richd. Elliotts & Wm. Stones line, Geo. Elliotts & Wm. Stones lines, Wm. Stones & Danll. Prices line, Danll Price & Elliotts line, Danll. Price & John Scotts line, Scott & Val. Brown presant. Thos. Garrot & Wm. Stones line, Garrot & John Petties's line, Wm. Lax & John Petties's line, Lax & Thos. Petties line, Lax & John Chandlers line, Garrot & Robt. Brooks line, Garrot & John Chandler presant. Price & Stones line, Robt. Brookes's & Stones line, John Petties's & Wm. Stones line, Petties & Stone presant. Abram. Maury & Oebdiah Hoopers line, Maury & Chandlers line, Maury & Edins line, Maury & Wm. Roberts's, Maury & Auther Brooks, Maury Nicholas Gentrys line, presant Abra. Maury, Philp. Poindexter, Obediah Hooper, Wm. Roberts

and Auther Brooks. Nicholas Gentry, Tscharner Degraffenreidt line, Degraffenreidts & Robt. Scotts line, Scott & Degraffenreidt presant. Auther Brooks & Scotts line, Degraffenreidt & Robert Scott presant. Auther Brooks & James Calhoons line, Auther Brookes & Benj. Cockerhams line, Wm. Roberts & Wm. Eddins line, Wm. Eddins & Robt. Brookes line, presant Roberts & Brooks. Robt. Brookes & John Chandlers line, Auther Brookes presant. Robt. Brookes & Danll. Prices line, Auther Brookes presant. John Chanders &. Obediah Hoopers line, Obediah Hooper's & Jerimiah Bowles's line, Hooper & Chandler present. Jerimiah Bowles's & Robt. Wilsons line, Bowles's & Thos. Turemans line, Turemans & Wilsons line, Turemans & Phil. Cockerhams line, Cockerhams & Jon. Hobsons line, Hobsons & Thos. Petties's line, presant Thos. Petties, John Hobsons & John Pleasants line, John Pleasants & Cleveris Coalmans line, Jerimiah Hatcher presant. Cleveris Coalman & Mattw. Hayes line, Nicholas Hobsons orphants & Cleveris Coalman line by consent of John Hobson gardian.

Thomas Lowrys lines not processioned nor Joseph Chandlers Decd. as nobody attended.

No. 8 The following peoples lands were processioned by William Chandler, Joseph Ship & Stephen Wood (to wit):

A line between Henry Roberson & Edward Slaughter, Henry Robertson presant, between Henry Robertson & David Johnson, presant Henry Robertson, a line between Charles Sullivant & Henry Robertson, David Johnson presant. Between Henry Robertson & Stephen Wood, Robertson presant. Between Joseph Johnson & Stephen Wood, J. Johnson presant. Between Chas. Sullivant & Step. Wood, J. Johnson presant. Between Elson Ellis & Colo. Fleming, Richd. Ellis presant. Between Ship & Elson Ellis, Rd. Ellis presant. Between Wm. Chandler & Elson Ellis, Rd. Ellis presant. Between Jos. Ship & Henry Robertson, Robertson presant. Between Wm. Maples & David Johnson, Maples presant. Between Joseph Ship & Wm. Maples, Maples presant. Between Chas. Sullivant & John Cox, Sullivant presant. Between Isaac Johnson & John Cox, Chas. Sullivant presant. Between John Cox & Joseph Williams, Williams presant. Between Colo. Fleming & Williams Evans, between Jos. Hunt & Evans & between Evans & Colo. Jon. Fleming, Wm. Brown presant. Between John Cox & Fleming, Nash presant. Between Wm. Chanler & Fleming, Chandler presant. Between Lowry & the Gleeb land, Chandler presant. Between Wm. Chandler & Comer, Chandler presant. A line between Henry Robertson & Comer, Robertson presant. Ditto between Henry Blagrove & Mary Glenn & others to Lesters line then between Lester & Blagrove, presant Blagrave & John Cook. A line between Henry Blagrave & Lester, both parties presant. A line between Lester & Hundly, Lester & Henry Blagrave present. Ditto between Wm. Journey & Lester, Blagrave present. A line between Lester & John Smith, both parties present. A line between Smith & Wm. Journey, Smith & Henry Blagrave presant. A line between John Journey & Robt. Hutchens, John Journey presant. A line between John Journey & Andrew Johnson, Journey presant. A line between Wm. Journey & Handly, John Journey presant. A line between Henry Blagrave & Hundly, Lester presant. A line between Henry Blagrave & Richard Claiborne & between H. Blagrave & James Williams, John Cook presant. A line between James Williams & Hundly Williams presant. A line between Richard Claiborn & Jas. Williams, both parties presant. A line between Richd. Claiborn and Jas. Coal, Claiborne presant. A line between James Williams & Andrew Johnson, Williams presant. A line between Andrew Johnson & Hundly, Williams presant. A line between Thos. Smith & Cornelias Crinshaw, both parties presant. A line between Andw. Johnson & Hutchens, Jas. Williams presant. A line between Thomas Smith & Jas. Williams, Smith presant. A line between Robt. Beasley & Jas. Williams. A line between Robt. Beasley & Fredk. Nance, Beasley presant. A line between John Ward & Robt. Beasley, the latter presant. A line between John Ward & Catholick Man, Benjn. Wilk presant. A line between Jon. Owen & Catholick Man, Ben. Wilks presant. A line between Catholick Man & Jas. Coal, Ben. Wilks presant. A line between Irvin & Covington & between Jon. Ward & Covington & Beasley & Covington, Beasley presant. A line between Jas. Williams & Covington & between James Williams & Jon. Irvin & between Jas. Williams & Wm. Fullylove & between Jas. Williams & Jas. Coal, Jas. Williams presant. A line between Jon. Irvin & Wm. Fullylove & between Jon. Irvin & Jas. Coal, Wm. Fullylove presant. John Browns land & Chas. Sullivants, Brown presant. A line between Chas. Sullivant & Isaac Johnson, Johnson presant, then round Johnsons lines & Slaughters, Johnson presant. Round Richd. Hudsons lines & a line between Val. Brown & Hudson, then round Thos. Warrens, Jon. Lucas's & Samll. Comers lines, Thos. Warren & Wm. Sammons presant. Then round Sammons's lines & a line between John Smith & Sammons & a line between Hutchens & Smith & a line between Garland & Sammons, Edwd. Slaughter and Sammons, then round Edwd. Coates's lines & Robt. Estis's, also Jos. Chandlers lines & a line between Glenn & James Williams & between Jesse Brown & Estis, also Henry Coats's, Robt. Estis presant., then round Fras. Smithsons lines & a line between Wm. Love & Smithson & a line between Glenn & Smithson, Jon. Love, Wm. Smithson.

No. 9. Processioned by Jon. Scott, Robt. Scott & Wm. Jeter (to wit) Beginning at Robt. Wilsons line between him & Wm. Wilsons, Tscharner Degraffenreidt & Wm. Wilson in company. Hix's, Tirsdels & Glenns lines, Wm. Wilson, Jon. Hix & Tirsdel presant. John Prices, Daniel Prices, Nicholas Gentrys, Wm. Cockerhams, Tscharner Degraffenreidts lines, the last named three in company. Wm. Loves lines, himself presant. John Scotts, Robt. Scotts, Wm. Jeters & Combs's lines all the processioners in company.

Returns of Processioning in obedience to an order of the Vestry of Cumberland Parish, the 23d day of September, 1767.

No. 1 Returns by Francis Neblett and Thomas Moody, processioners.

All the lands processioned according to order of Vestry between Stony Creek and Brunswick line, Flattrock Road and Meherrin River, being present the owners thereof, Philemon Russell, Humphrey Garrett, Richard Wyatt, Robert Garrett, Duncan Hammons, Joseph Hicks, James Dicks, Edmond Covington, James Garrett, William Harnour, Daniel Taylor, Matthew Williams, [illegible] Jackson, James Killis, Joseph Dunmans, William Johnson, Thomas Mores, Jeremy Mize, Stegalls and Matthew [illegible].

2 Returns by Alexander Rudder and Jno. Hight, Processioners.

In obedience to the worshipfull Vestry of Cumberland Parish we the processioners between Flattrock Creek and Stone Creek, did possession all the lands in our boundry only Mr. Petteways and Mr. Reekses and Mr. Freemans, and the reason their lands was not processioned they never appeared to shew the lines.

3. Returns by Henry VanDyck and Franch [or Franck] Haggard, processioners.

In obedience to an order of the worshipfull Vestry of Cumberland Parish, we the subscribers have processioned the following lands (to wit) the lines between Henry Gill and David Garland, present the said Gill and Garland and Peter Garland. The lines between Augustine Claiborne and David Garland, present the same persons as above said. The lines between Leonard Cheatham & David Garland, present the said Garland and Peter Garland. The lines between Peter Garland and Leonard Cheatham, present the said Garland and David Garland. A line between Peter Garland and other persons unknown to us, present the same persons as last. The lines between the Revd. Mr. James Craig and David Garland, present William Ballard and the said Craig. The lines between the Revd. Mr. Jas. Craig and William Taylor, present the same persons as last. The lines between Stephen Edward Brodnax and Edward Jackson, present the said Jackson and John Robertson. The lines between John Davis and Stephen Brown, present Isaac Brown & Robt. Brown. The lines between Isaac Brown and Cornelius Priest, present the said Brown & Priest, and Robert Brown and Stephen Brown. The lines between Robert Brown & Curtis, present the said Curtis and Isaac Brown. The lines between Joseph Blanks & Roger Atkinson, present Benjamin Farguson and Henry Gill. The lines between Augustin Claiborne and Roger Atkinson, present the same persons as last. The lines between William Cross and Augustine Claiborne, present Richd. Cross, Joseph Blanks and Jessie King. The lines between Augustine Claiborne and Roger Atkinson, present Henry Gill, Joseph Blanks, Benjamin Farguson & Jessie King.

4. Returns by Henry Gee and Nevil Gee, Processioners.

Thomas Smiths, John Ragsdale present. Capt. John Ragsdale, his son John present. John Ragsdales, his son John present. Benjamin Tomlinson and Colo. Richard Cockes, present Robert Bruce. Abraham Andrews, John Grangers, Peter Andrews and John Williamses, present Abraham Andrews. John Coopers, present John Williams. Richard Haggards, present Harbert Hite. Roger Atkinsons, present Thomas Young, William Allen. John Brooks and Frank Coopers, present John Brooks. Henry Gees, Nevil Gees and John Baileys, Bookers and a piece called Tarrys, lines not found. No body to shew the lines.

5. Returns by Benjamin Tomlinson and John Lucas, Processioners.

The lines between James Gee and Mason, between James Gee and Sarah Hobson, between William Gee and Mason, the line between William Gee and Richard Cocke, the line between Mason and Booker shown by James Gee, the line between Benjamin Tomlinson and Booker shown by John Lucas, the line between Benjamin Tomlinson and William Gee shown by James Gee, the line between James Gee and Mrs. Loury shown by James Gee & Capt. John Ragsdale, the line between Mrs. Loury and Hobson shown by Capt. John Ragsdale & James Gee, the line between Mrs. Loury and Geo. Walton shown by Capt. John Ragsdale & James Gee, the line between Capt. John Ragsdale and William Loury, shown by Capt. John Ragsdale & James Gee, the line between Capt. John Ragsdale and Geo. Walton and Richard Cocke shown by Capt. John Ragsdale and James Gee. The line between Isaac Reeves and Hobson shown by Isaac Reeves and James Gee. The line between Moses Cockerham and John Hawkins shown by John Hawkins. The line between Isaac Reeves and Hobson shown by Isaac Reeves. The line between Jonathan

Patteson and Moses Cockerham shown by Patteson and Phil Cockerham. The line between Patteson and Phill Cockerham, by Phil Cockerham and Patteson. The line between Phil Cockerham and Hobson shown by Patteson and Phil Cockerham. The line between Richard Booker and Hobson shown by Abrm. Talley. The line between Richard and William Booker deceast, shown by Abram Talley. The line between John Lucas and Booker shown by Benjamin Tomlinson. A line between Patteson & John Hawkins shown by Isaac Reeves and John Hawkins. A line between Patteson and Hobson shown by Isaac Reeves and John Hawkins. Land not processioned John Burnetts and a line between Richard Cocke and Daniel Mason, a line between Benjamin Tomlinson and John 'Booker, a line between William Gee and John Booker.

6. Returns by Robert Bailie and John Smithson, Processioners, March the 10th, 1768.

Between Thomas Stuman & Phillip Cockerham, present Thomas Stewman. Also between J. Botts & Stewman, present Stuman. Also between Pettus & Pettus, also between Lax and Pettus, also between Pettus and Henson, also between Pettus and Stone; also between Cockerham and Bilbo; also between Botts and Hooper; also between Bragg and Hooper, present Thomas Pettus, Senr. Also between Freeman and Hooper; also between Freeman and Patteson; also between Freeman and Garrett; present Henry Freeman. Also between Bailie & Stone; also between Bailie and Patteson; also between Patteson and White; also between White and Brown; also between Bailie and White; present William White, Cluverious Coleman and Jno. Tounsin. Robert Wilsons lines not processioned for want of attendance. The line between William Glenn and William Love, in the presence of Love. Between Francis Smithson and Love, in the presence of Love. Between John Scott and Ben. Burchit, in the presence of Love. Between Richard Coleman and John Scott, in the presence of William Smithson. Between Richard Coleman and Robert Scott, in the presence of Ben Burchit. Between Tscharner DeGraffenriedt and Robert Scott, in the presence of Richd. Coleman. Between Richard Coleman and Matthew Brooks in presence of Ben Burchit. Between Richard Coleman and Henry Pollard in presence of William Smithson. Between Ben Burchit and Jonas Sikes, in presence of Henry Pollard. Between Ben. Burchit and Henry Pollard in presence of Jonas Sikes. Between Jonas Sikes and Henry Pollard, in presence of William Smithson. Between Jonas Sikes and Valentine Brown, in presence of Henry Pollard. Between Ben Cockerham and William White, in presence of William Smithson. Between Ben Cockerham and Jonathan Patteson, between Ben Cockerham and The Eddings, between the Eddings and Patteson, between Colo. Maury and The Eddings, between William Roberts and The. Eddings in presence of William Smithson, between Nathaniel Mason and John Brown, in presence of Robert Mason, between Francis Smithson and Nat. Mason, in presence of John Brown, between Valentine Brown and Nathaniel Mason in presence of John Brown, between Valentine Brown and John Brown, in presence of William Smithson. Between Maury and Hooper in presence of Abraham Maury, between Matthe . . . . and Colo. Maury in presence of Maury. Between Tscharner DeGraffenreidt and Matt Brooks, in presence of William DeGraffenreidt, between DeGraffenreidt and Aaron Drummon, in presence of William DeGraffenreidt. Matt Brooks and Aaron Drummon was not at home to show part of their lines.

7. Return by Benjamin Clark, Processioner, 24th March, 1768.

In obedience to an order of the Vestry of Cumberland Parish in the County of Lunenburg, we have possessioned all the land between the road and the south branch of Meherrin River from Coxes bridge to the fork of the said river, except part of the land belonging to the estates of John Fleming and Thomas Loury, which was omitted for want of proper attendance. Also part of Thomas Taylors land for the same reason. The proprietors of the other lands was present on their lines, all except Joseph Boswell and his lines was shewed by Joseph Davis.

8 [Space blank.]

9 Returns by Nathaniel Mason and Frederick Brown, Processioners, March the 10th, 1768.

We the processioners have processioned Thomas Warrens land in presence of Valentine Brown, also Richard Hudsons in presence of William Smithson & Thomas Warren, also Francis Smithsons & Robt. Esteses in presence of John Glenn & Charles Smithson. Nathanl. Masons in presence of Valentine Brown. Richard Hudsons in presence of Valentine Brown & Henry Crenshaw. William Glenns in presence of Henry Blagrave & Wm. Smithson. William Fishers in presence of John Cook. Manoah Smithsons also Henry Blagraves in presence of John Cook and John Glenn. Likewise Bryan Lesters in presence of John Smith and Henry Blagrave. Likewise John Hawkinses in presence of James Eastham and Richard Claiborne. Likewise John Scotts in presence of Richard Claiborne & James Eastham. Likewise Richard Claibornes in presence of James Easthem and Henry Blagrave. Likewise Henry Crenshaws in presence of Valentine Brown and Richd. Hudson. Likewise Anthony Hundleys in presence of Wm. Bush and Anthony Fullilove. Likewise Anthony Fulliloves in presence of William Bush and Benja. Tatum, also Catlett Manns in presence of Benjamin Wilkes and Zadock Ward, also John Wards in presence of Benjamin Wilks and Zadock Ward. Likewise Benjamin Tatums in presence of Anthony Fullilove and Zadock Ward, also James Shelbornes & Thomas Shelbornes in presence of Benjamin Tatum. Also Isaac Johnsons in presence of John Hailey and David Stokes, also John Blankinships in presence of Isaac Johnson & Edward Slaughter. Also David Stokeses in presence of John Blankinship & Edward Slaughter. Also John Cuninghams in the presence of Isaac Johnson and David Stokes. Likewise Isaac Johnsons in presence of Edwd. Slaughter and Thomas Bruce. Also Thomas Smiths in presence of Isaac Johnson and Edward Slaughter. Also Joshua Irbys in presence of Thomas Smith & Edwd. Slaughter. Also Edward Slaughters in presence of Joshua Irby and Thomas Smith. Also John Stembridge and Andrew Gregreys in presence of I. Irby & Thomas Smith. John Smiths line & John Sammons & William Sammons Senr. in presence of

Joshua Irby and Edward Slaughter. Henry Robinsons line in presence of John Brown and William Parrott, also John Browns in presence of William Parrott. Also Stephen Woods in presence of David Johnson and John Wood. Also Joseph Johnsons in presence of Thomas Smith and Edward Slaughter. Also William Bushes in presence of James Lawson. Also John Levears in presence of Wm. Bush & James Lawson. Also Charles Sullivants in presence of Isaac Johnson and John Hailey. James Williams's land not processioned for want of attendance. Benedick Alderson refused to shew his lines.

11. Return by Benjamin Collier, Processioner.

In obedience to the order of Vestry, I have processioned these lands (to wit) Henry Stokes land, Warren Buford and himself present. Elisha Bettses land, Andrew Johnston and Richard Stokes. Andrew Johnstons land, Richard Stokes and himself. Then Richd. Stokes, Senr., Richard Stokes, Jun., Evans Stokeses, the old man and Shadrick present. Richard Crews land, William Munroes land, Barnett Owens land, themselves present. Joseph Minor deny'd going. William Owens, James Hamblet and Charles Stokes land, James Hamblet, William Owen & Peter Crews present. William Handley denyed. Jacobus Christopher denyed.

13. Returns by Zachary Estes and Coldwell P[etty] P[oole], Processioners, 30th of March, 1768.

Agreeable to order of Vestry we the subscribers have processioned all the land mentioned in the said order.

14. Returns by Allin Stokes and William Cureton, processioners.

In obedience to an order of Vestry to us directed, we have processioned the lines between Richard Stokes and William Wade, William Wade and Allen Stokes, William Stokes and Richard Stokes, Evans Stokes and William Stokes, Evans Stokes and Booker, William Stokes and Booker, Young Stokes and Booker, Young Stokes and David Stokes, in presence of William Stokes. Also the line between Colo. Bacon and Young Stokes, Bacon and Henry Wimpe, Wimpe and Hannah Williams, Williams and John Baugh, Williams and William Murrell, Williams and James Pulliam, Pulliam and Peter Jones, Murrell and Jones, in presence of Colo. Bacon. Also the lines between David Stokes and William Cureton, David Stokes and Booker, David Stokes and Charles Stokes, Charles Stokes and Robert Evans, Charles Stokes and Curtis Keatts, in presence of David Stokes. Also the lines between John Baugh and William Murrell, Baugh and **Isaac Brisindine, Baugh and Curtis Keatts, Baugh and Cureton,** Cureton & Keatts, in presence of Daniel Baugh. Also the lines between William Murrell and Isaac Brisindine, Keatts and Brizindine, Cureton and Brisindine, John Stone and Peter Jones, in presence of Isaac Brisindine. Also the lines between Colo. Tho. Winn and Allen Stokes, Colo. Winn and Richard Stone, Colo. Winn and Peter Jones, in presence of Colo. Winn. Also the lines between John Winn, Senr. and Allen Stokes, John Winn and Andrew Johnston, Allen Stokes and Andrew Johnston, Richard Stokes and Andrew Johnston, William Wade and Andrew Johnston, John Ellis and Winston Ellis and Elisha Betts, Betts and Winston, Betts and John Winn. Also the lines of Barnett Owen & William Owen, Barnett Owen and Booker, Barnet Owen and Evans Stokes (also between Allin Stokes & Richard Stone in presence of Colo. Winn).

16. Returns by John Hazlewood and Bartlet Estes, processioners 30th of March, 1768.

We, John Hazlewood and Bartlett Estes, Senr. have processioned all the lands according to our order and have here made returns of the same (viz) Processioned the lines between John Ellis and Lazarus Williams, the line between Peter Jones and Lazarus Williams, the said Williams present. The line between John Hazlewood and Peter Jones, the said Jones present. The line between Peter Jones and John White, Senr., the said Jones and White present. The line between John White, Senr. and Mary Cockerham, the said John White, Senr. present. The line between John White, Senr. and Peter Jones, the said Jones and White present. The line between John Hazlewood and Peter Jones, the sd. Jones present. The line between John Hazlewood & John Ellis, John White, Senr. present. The line between John Hazlewood & Peter Jones, the sd. Jones present. The line between Peter Jones and Mary Cockerham, Jno. White, Senr. present. The line between Peter Jones and Robert Estes, Senr., the said Robert Estes, Senr. present.

No. 17. Returns by William Hardy and John Hardy, Processioners.

In obedience to an order of Vestry in Cumberland Parish of Sept. the 23d, 1767, we the subscribers have processioned the following lands.

Jany. 2nd The land of Mr. Francis Epps, Mr. Daniel Winn and Joseph Winn present.
    30th The land of Mr. William Puryear, himself present
    1784 and part of Mr. Edward Thweatts, himself present.
Feb. 1st The land of Mr. Thomas Chambers, Mr. Daniel Hay present.
    18th The land of Mr. Henry Buford, himself present.
    19th The land of Mr. Joseph Winn, himself present.
Mar. 12th The land of Mr. Joseph Hightower, Colo. Banister & Wm. Jenings, Mr. Joseph Hightower and John Beasly present.
    21st Part of the lands of Mr. Jeffry Murrel, himself present.
    28 Part of the land of Mr. Daniel Winn, himself present.

18. Returns by Robert Chappell & John Hightower, processioners.

Agreeable to order of Vestry, we have processioned the lines between George Phillups and James Amos, Samuel Meanly and Phillups, Phillups and Robt. Dyer Estate, Phillups and Charles Hamlin, Dyers Estate and Charles Hamlin. In presence of George Phillups, James Amos, Samuel Meanly & Robt. Phillups. Between Thomas Chambers and Charles Hamlin, Thomas Chambers, Charles Hamlin & Reps Jones present. Between Charles Hamlin & Reps Jones, William Cross and Thomas Chambers and Jones, Robert Chappell and William Cross, Jones, and Chappell, Chappell and William Eddings, Chappell and Agness May, Chappell and Chambers, Chambers and Thomas Williams, Williams and John Cross, Chambers and Agness May, William Roads and

THE VESTRY BOOK, 1746-1816   527

Reps Jones, in presence of Thomas Chambers, Reps Jones and Robert Jones. Between Thomas Williams and Robert Blackwell, Williams and John Cross, Thomas Williams & Robert Blackwell present. The lines of John Cross, Robert Blackwell & Joel Pewit, in presence of John Cross, Robert Blackwell & Joel Pewit. The lines of Henry More & Atha Elmore, in presence of Henry More & Atha Elmore. The lines of John Hammock, Lewis Lambert, James Kirk, Thomas Jones, Benjamin Strange, Abraham Cocke, Charles Parrish, Matthew Hubbard, James Turner & Claptons, in presence of Ralph Hubbard and William Hammock. The line of William Butler, Nathaniel Owen, John Weaver, James More, Robert More, Cary Wells Daniel, John More, John Usry, John Forrest, Henry More, Matthew Laffoon, James Waller, James Buckner, Jarrel Burrow, in presence of John Hammock. No attendance given to procession any more.

18. Returns by Edward Thweatt, processioner, 29th of Mar., 1768.

Who processioned between Mr. Liverets path from Hardiways quarter, Mr. Cross's Church Road to Flatt Rock Church, Flattrock Creek & Capt. Jeningses road, and every persons land in that bounds is done as well as I could do it. There was about a quarter of a mile between Colo. Garland and Capt. Jenings we could find no line & I made none. A hundred yards between the Colo. & Mr. Dick Haies we could find none, and none was made. Ben Franklin & Mr. Hall. Hayes was present but could show no further. The line between Colo. Hardiway and Mr. Liveret some part could not be found.

No. 19. Returns by Richard Williams & Lazarus Williams, Process.

Pursuant to an order of Vestry of Cumberland Parish directed to us the subscribers bearing date the 23d day of September, 1767, for processioning lands in our precinct we make return as
Feb. followeth, (viz). Processioned two lines between the
7th, King and Lazarus Williams, one line between the King
1768 and Richard Williams, two lines between Lazarus Williams and Richard Williams, all the lines between Charles Hamlin, Gent. and Richard Williams, Zachariah Davis present.

22d. The lines between Charles Hamlin, Gent. and Thomas Edwards, one line between Charles Hamlin Gent. and Charles Cook, one line between Embry and Charly Cook, five lines between Thomas Edwards and Rowland Ward, present Zachariah Davis, Thomas Edwards, Charles Cook, William Wren & Samuel Harwell.

24th. One line between Thomas Smith and Edward Cuttillo, two lines between Thomas Smith and John Ragsdale, Gent., two lines between the King and Edward Cuttillo, one line between Edward Cuttillo and John Evans, the land of John Evans and Thomas Biddie intirely. Thomas Hardys land intirely, and part of the Glebe land. Present the Revd. Mr. James Craig, John Ragsdale, Gent., John Evans, Abraham Cuttillo & Thomas Biddie.

25th. Processioned the rest of the Glebe land, also three lines of James Daws, one line of John Kirbys and two lines of Henry Bufords. Present the Revd. Mr. James Craig, George Tarry and James Daws.

March 1st. Two lines between the King and Thomas Edwards, three lines between the King and Charles Hamlin, Gent. Present Thomas Edwards and Zachariah Davis.

2d. One line between Charles Hamlin, Gent. and Charles Cook. Two lines between Charles Hamlin, Gent. and John Blackstone, present Charles Hamlin, Charles Cook, Zachariah Davis and John Blackstone.

March 29th. The land of Everard Dowsing Gent. processioned, Jeremiah Glen present. One line between Joseph Gentry and Jeremiah Glen, a line between Jeremiah Glenn and Richard Henson, a line between Jeremiah Glenn and John Hix, a line between Jeremiah Glenn and Anthony Street, present Jeremiah Glenn, Everard Dowsing Gent. and Allen Gentry. Other lands not processioned for want of attendance according to publick notice.

No. 20. Returns by Jeremiah Glenn & Tscharner DeGraffenreidt, process., 30th of March, 1768.

In obedience to an order of Vestry we, Jeremiah Glenn & TsCharner DeGraffenreidt have processioned the following lands lying between Reedy Creek, Reedy Creek old road, Coxes road and the North Meherrin River (to wit) The line between David Hopkins and William Cockerham, between David Hopkins and Abraham Maury, between William Cockerham and Allen Gentry, between William Cockerham and TsCharner DeGraffenreidt. Between William Cockerham and Edward Self, between Wm. Cockerham & Wm. Embry, between Wm. Cockerham and Everard Dowsing. Present David Hopkins, Wm. Cockerham, Everard Dowsing & Zacy. Estes. The line between TsCharner DeGraffenreidt and Edward Self, between TsCherner DeGraffenriedt and William Overby, between William Overby and Craddock Vaughn, between Craddock Vaughn and Wm. Jeter, between Craddock Vaughn and Batt Baker. Present John Wood & Edward Self. The line between Craddock Vaughn & TsCharner DeGraffenreidt, between Robert Scott & Tscharner DeGraffenriedt, between Robert Scott & Craddock Vaughn, between Robert Scott and John Scott, between Craddock Vaughn and John Scott, Between John Scott and Batt Baker, between John Scott and William Love, between William Love and Batt Baker, between Wm. Love and Moses Estes, between Moses Estes and Wm. Jeter, between Batt Baker and Wm. Jeter, between Batt Baker and Moses Estes, the parties all present. The line between John Wood and William Overby, between Wm. Overby and Wm. Jeter, between John Wood and Clardy, present John Wood & Edward Self. The line between John Blaxtone and Charles Hamlin, between John Blaxton and Lazarus Williams, between John Blaxton and Peter Jones, between John Blaxton and Wm. Embry, between William Embry and Peter Jones, between William Embry and John Berry, between William Embry and Colo. Bacon, between Lyddal Bacon and Wm. Mills, between Wm. Mills and John Berry, between Michael Johnson and John Berry, between Michael Johnson & Peter Jones. Present Samuel Harwell, John Blaxton, Wm. Holland and Michael Johnson. The line between William Embry and Jonathan Patteson, between Wm. Embry & Clardy, between William Embry and John Wood, between William Embry & Edward Self, between Wm. Embry and Everard Dowsing. Present Everard Dowsing, Samuel Har-

'well and Edward Self. The line between Allen Gentry and TsCharner DeGraffenriedt, between Allen Gentry & Abraham Maury, Allen Gentry present to show the lines. Wm. Jeter & Jona. Pattesons land partly undone, they refusing to attend to show their lines.

Returns by John Ragsdale and Benjamin Gee, processioners, 24th of March, 1772.

In obedience to an order of Vestry to us directed we have processioned the land in our precinct in presence of the several owners or their overseers.

Returns by James Gee and Richard Booker, Processioners, 25th of March, 1772.

In obedience to an order of Vestry to us directed we have processioned all the land in our precinct in presence of the several owners, except Edward Bookers, John Bookers and William Kellys, no attendance given.

Returns by Micajah Smithson and John Calwell Brown, Processrs. February, 1772.

In obedience to an order of Vestry held for Cumberland Parish we the subscribers have processioned the lines of the following gentlemens lands (viz) Messrs. Burnet and Coleman, both present, Atkinsons and Smithsons, in presence of Willson and William Barry, Robert Willsons, Jeremiah Boles & Frank Robertsons, in presence of John Brown & Obadiah Hooper. Obadiah Hoopers, James Lawrances, Henry Freemans and William Brags, in presence of Brown and Smithson. John Thorntons, Wm. Lax, Sr., Thos. Garot & Job Hanson, in presence of Mr. Lax, Brown and Smithson. Thomas Turemans, William Barrys, Phil Cockerhams Senr., in presence of Wilson and Smithson. A small part of Mr. Atkinsons line not to be found. William Loves line in presence of Brown and Smithson. Fras. Smithson in presence of Brown and Smithson. Nat. Masons in presence of Brown, Smithson & Sikes. Jonas Sikes in presence of Brown & William Smithson. Benjamin Burchits in presence of Brown

& Smithson and Robert Scott. Robert Scotts line in presence of Brown and Smithson. William Stones line in presence of James Anderson & Smithson. Valentine Browns lines, Andersons & Stones, Wm. line in presence of Stone and Anderson. Benjamin Cockerhams line in presence of Anderson and Smithson. Richard Colemans line in presence of Scott and Burchit. John Calwell Browns in presence of Brown and Mason. Luke Thorntons line, Matt Brookses line not processioned no attendance given to show the lines.

No. 8 Returns by John Cunningham and William Cunningham, Process.

In obedience to the Vestry of Cumberland Parish agreeable to order we have processioned the following lines (viz) John Cunninghams line in presence of John Scott, Senr., also John Scotts line in presence of said Scott. Also William Stones line in presence of said Stone. James Andersons line in presence of the said Anderson, also Joseph Boswells line in presence of William Stone, Joseph Davis & William Cureton. Also Joseph Davis's line in presence of the said Davis and Cureton. William Curetons line in presence of said Davis & Cureton. Benjamin Clarks line in presence of Benjamin Clark & Wm. Cureton. Also John Freemans line in presence of Jas. Freeman and Benjamin Clark. Mrs. Lourys line not processioned for want of attendance, also Benjamin Whiteheads & Flemmings.

9. Returns by Ellison Ellis and Jesse Saunders, Processioners March the 21st, 1772.

Pursuant to an order of Vestry held for Cumberland Parish 13th of Decr., 1771, we, Ellison Ellis and Jesse Saunders have possessioned the lands within our bounds as followeth, beginning at Coxes road near Crupper run, between Thomas Moody & John Flemming deceast, unprocessioned, no person to show the lines. Between William Chandler and Thomas Moody, Chandler present. Between Thomas Moody & Thomas Neal. Between William Chandler and Thomas Neal. Between Field Archer & Thos. Neal. Neal present. Between Field Archer & Wm. Chandler, between Field Archer & Henry Robertson, between

Wm. Maples & Henry Robertson, Wm. Parrot present. Between Josiah Ship and Henry Robertson, Ship present. Between David Johnson and Henry Robertson, Johnson present. Between Josiah Ship and John Cox, both present. Between David Johnson and John Cox, Ship & Johnson present. Between Stephen Wood and John Cox, Wood & Ship present. Between Isaac Johnson and Cox, Ship, Michael Johnson & Stephen Wood present. Between Joseph Williams & John Cox, Williams present. Between Gustavus Hendrick and Williams, both present. Between John Hunt & Cox, both present, & Wm. Brown & Josiah Ship. Between John Hunt & Wm. Brown, Hunt, Brown, Cox & Ship present. Between William Evans and Jesse Saunders, Ben Evans present. Between Jesse Saunders & John Flemming, Ben Evans present. Between Josiah Ship and Flemming, Ship present. Between Flemming and Bartlett Cox, Bartlett Cox present. Between Josiah Ship and Ellison Ellis, both present. Between Ellis and Flemming, between Chandler & Flemming, Josiah Ship prest. Between Chandler & Ellis, between Ellis and Robertson, between John Cox and William Maples, Josiah Ship present. The lines between John Cox and Thomas Erskine unprocessioned, also between John Cox & John Flemming, also between John Flemming and Thomas Erskine, no person as we could find that could show these lines.

10. Returns by Bryan Lester and Robert Estes, Jr., Process. 24th of March, 1772.

We have processioned the lands in the bounds appointed us as followeth.

John Glenns	Present John Cook
Elijah Bakers	Do. William Smithson
Francis Smithson	Do. Manoah Smithson
James Shelbornes	Do. Thomas Shelborne
Thomas Smiths	Do. John Stembridge
Joshua Irbys	Do. John Slaughter
Edward Slaughters	Do. John Stembridge
John Stembridge	Do. James Gregory
Andrew Gregorys	Do. John Stembridge

John Halys	Do. John Sammons
John Sammons	Do. Wm. Sammon
Thomas Shelbornes	Do. John Sammons
William Bardit	Do. Tho. Shelborne
Everard Dowsing	Do. Saml. Jordan
William Fishers	Do. John Cook
Robert Estes's	Do. Charles Smithson
John Lesters	Do. John Glenn
Capt. Blagraves	Do. John Cook
Bryan Lesters	Do. Capt. Blagrave
John Hankins	Do. Nathaniel Dacus
John Dacuses	Do. John Hankins
David Holts	Do. Thomas Ladd
Anthony Fullilove	Do. Wm. Fullilove
John Locks	Do. John Cook
William Jordan	Do. John Lock
William Bushes	Do. James Gregory
James Gregorys	Do. Wm. Bush
Henry Blagraves, Jr.	Do. Wm. Bush, Tho. Crenshaw
John Arvins	Do. Wm. Fullilove
John Wards	Do. Benjamin Tatoms
Benj. Tatoms	Do. Richd. Ward

Capt. Richard Claibornes land in presence of Richard Ward. Some small lines no parties appeared.

No. 11 Returns by Stephen Wood and Joseph Johnson, Process.

With submission to an order of Vestry, we the subscribers have possessioned the lands following.

A line between James Sammon and Joseph Johnson, James Sammon present.

A line between Edward Slaughter and James Sammons, James Sammon present.

A line between John Blankinship & Edward Slaughter, James Sammons and John Blankinship present.

A line between Isaac Johnson and John Blankinship, James Sammon pres.

A line between John Blankinship and William Cunningham &

John Cunningham, James Sammon & John Blankinship present.

A line between Henry Robertson and John Brown, Frederick Brown pres.

A line between Frederick Brown and William Burdit, John Brown present.

A line between Frederick Brown and Benjamin Tatom, John Brown present.

A line between William Parrot and Frederick Brown, John Brown present.

A line between John Brown and Frederick Brown, John Brown present.

A line between Henry Robertson & Andrew Gregory, William Parrot pres.

A line between Henry Robertson & Stephen Wood, William Parrot present.

A line between David Johnson and Stephen Wood, David Johnson present.

A line between David Johnson and Henry Robertson, David Johnson pres.

A line between Richard Hudson and Henry Crenshaw, the sd. Hudson & Crenshaw present.

A line between Benjamin Tatom & Henry Crenshaw, Henry Crenshaw pres.

A line between William Parrot and Henry Crenshaw, William Parrot pres.

A line between Henry Crenshaw & Samuel Comer, Henry Crenshaw present.

A line between William Parrot & Samuel Comer, William Parrot present.

A line between Henry Robertson & William Parrot, William Parrot pres.

A line between Benjamin Tatom & William Parrot, Wm. Parrot present.

A line between Nathaniel Mason & Francis Smithson, Nathaniel Mason present.

A line between Valentine Brown & Nathaniel Mason, said Mason present.

A line between Thomas Warrin & Valentine Brown, Valentine Brown pres.
A line between Thomas Warrin & Richd. Hudson, Thomas Warrin present.
A line between Francis Smithson & Richd. Hudson, Richard Hudson pres.
A line between Samuel Comer & Richard Hudson, Richard Hudson present.
A line between Valentine Brown & Richard Hudson, Richard Hudson pres.
A line between Stephen Wood & Joseph Johnson, Joseph Johnson present.
A line between Stephen Wood & James Sammons, James Sammon present.
A line between Stephen Wood & Isaac Johnson, James Sammon present.
A line between Isaac Johnson & James Sammon, Isaac Johnson present.
A line between Isaac Johnson & John Blankinship, Isaac Johnson pres.
A line between Isaac Johnson & John Cunningham.
A line between Edward Slaughter & Isaac Johnson, Isaac Johnson pres.
A line between Thomas Bruce & Edward Slaughter, Thomas Bruce present.

No. 12. Returns by Robert Beasly and William Herring, Processrs.

The line between Daniel Malloone & Jonathan Davis, both present.
Between Robert Beasly & Jonathan Davis, both present.
Between Thompson Staples & Robert Beasly, Jonathan Davis present.
The line between Thompson Staples and Lodowick Farmer, Wm. Staples & Thompson Staples present.
Between William Wilkerson & Thompson Staples,
Between TsCharner DeGraffenriedt & Thompson Staples, William Staples and Thompson Staples present.
Between Henry Farley and William Staples, both present.

Between Richard Crafton and William Staples, Henry Farley & William Staples present.
Between Robert Beasly and John Patterson, Robert Beasly and Henry Farley present.
Between William Gordon and Robert Beasly, William Herring & Robert Beasly present.
Between Jared McConico and Richard Sansom, both present.
Between Joseph Townsend & Richard Sansom, both present.
Between Joseph Townsend & Robert Beasly, both present.
Between Richard Burks & Robert Beasly, both present.
Between Frederick Nance & Richard Burks, both present.
Between Edward Clay & William Wilkerson, John Huskerson and Edward Clay present.
Between John Huskerson and Jean Pounds, John Huskerson and Edward Clay present.
Between Lodowick Farmer & Wm. Wilkerson, John Huskerson and Joseph Holt present.
Between Lodowick Farmer & Shelton, Jno. Huskerson & Joseph Holt pres.
Between Thomas Harding & William Herring, both present.
Between Jonathan Davis & William Herring, both present.
Between Jonathan Davis & Shelton, Jonathan Davis & Thomas Harding present.
Between Lodowick Farmer & Jonathan Davis, Jonathan Davis and Thomas Harding present.
Between Henry Stokes & William Jeeter, Jonathan Davis & William Herring present.
Between William Jeeter and William Herring, both present.
Between Thomas Harding & Daniel Mallone, Thomas Harding & Jonathan Davis present.
Capt. DeGraffenreidt, notice given but no attendance.

Returns by William Crymes and Arthur Herring, Processioners 27th of March, 1772.

We have processioned all the land between Robertes old road from Meherrin to the fork at Winninghams road up to Tursakia creek bridge and goes as the Creek runs into Meherrin. A quiet procession we have made which may be manifested by each owner of the said land.

No. 15. Returns by James Easthem and John Glenn, Processioners.

The line between Walker and Jordan, between Jordan and Eastham, between Jordan & Tucker, between Jordan and Jordan, Clarke & Jordan present. Between Clarke and Tucker, and Clarke and Hudson, between Clarke & Harris, between Clarke & Gafford, between Clarke and Eastham, John Clarke present. Between Hudson & Edmonds, and Hudson and Ingram, Hudson present. Between Jordan and Ingram & Ingram and Pool, Ingram present. Between Dupree and Pool, between Dupree and Brisindine, between Dupree and Edmonds, Js. Dupree present. Between Ingram and Edmonds, between Ingram and Tucker, between Jordan and Tucker, between Brisindine and Edmonds, between Dozier and Edmonds, between Tucker and Edmonds, William Jeeter, Senr. present. Between Gafford and Eastham, between Claiborne and Eastham, between Claiborne and Gafford, between Harris and Gafford, Tho. Gafford present. Between Keatts & Tucker, Keatts present, between Pool and Jordan, William Pool present. Between Walker & Glenn between Walker and Easthem, between Eastham & Glenn, Silvanus Walker present. Between Tucker and Dozier and Dozer & Brisindine no attendance.

16. Returns by Edward Jordan, Jr. and Ben Walker, Processioners.

We have peaceably processioned all the land in our bounds, except one line between Billups and Evans, that no attendance.

No. 17. Returns by Henry Stokes and John Winn, Junr., Processrs.

In obedience to order of Vestry held for Cumberland Parish, 13th Decr., 1771, we the subscribers have processioned all Peter Jones lines thats in our bounds in presence of Colo. L. Bacon and Js. Pulliam, also Samuel Sneads lines in presence of the same.

All William Murrels lines, also all James Pulliams lines, in presence of Colo. Lyddal Bacon. Also Lyddal Bacons lines in presence of James Pulliam and himself. All Hannah Williams lines, also James Baughs lines, all James Boisseaus lines, in presence of Lyddal Bacon & James Pulliam.
All Robert Dixons lines, all Curtis Keatts lines, in presence of Robert Dixon.
All David Stokes lines in presence of Colo. L. Bacon and David Stokes, Junr.
All Bookers lines in presence of David Stokes.
All Elizabeth Stokes lines, all Henry Stokes lines, in presence of David Stokes & Allin Stokes.
All Allin Stokes lines in presence of David Stokes.
All Richard Stokes lines in presence of David Stokes and Shadrack Stokes.
All Peter Crews lines, All Barnett Owens lines, in presence of Peter Crews.
All Evan Stokes lines in presence of Shadrack Stokes.
Likewise Richard Stokes, Junr. lines in presence of David Stokes and Shadrack Stokes.
John Pattersons lines in presence of David Stokes & John Winn, Senr.
All John Winns lines, All Richard Stones lines, in presence of John Winn.
All Colo. Thomas Winns lines in presence of John Winn, except one line between him and Peter Jones, no one to show the line.
John Curetons not done, no one to show the lines.
Elisha Betts and Wm. Cralle's not done, both present and both refused showing their lines.

No. 18. Returns by Robert Crenshaw and John Winn,
             Processioners.

In obedience to a Vestry held for Cumberland Parish, 13th of Decr., 1771, we the subscribers have processioned all Daniel Winns lines, present Daniel Winn and Alexr. Howard.

All Thos. Winns lines,	Present George McLaughlain & Thos. Winn.
All George McLaughlains lines	Do. Geo. McLaughlain, Tho. Winn & Richd. Stone.
All James McLaughlains lines	Do. Geo. McLaughlain and Richard Stone.
All Phillip Combs lines	Do. Tho. Winn, Junr. & Richard Stone.
All John Winns lines	Do. Thomas Winn.
All Richard Stones lines	Do. Richard Stone
All William Stones lines	Do. Richd. Stone, Colo. T. Winn & Alexr. Howard.
All William Crosses lines	Do. Daniel Winn
All Carter Whites lines	Do.
All Samuel Sneads lines	Do. Samuel Snead
All Alexr. Howards lines	Do.
All Richd. Stone, Junr. lines	Do. Alexr. Howard & Samuel Snead
All Peter Jones lines	Do. Samuel Snead & Peter Jones
All Joel Fargusons lines	Do. Joel Farguson, Nicholas Brown & Belcher.
All John Winn, Junr. lines	Do. Richard Stone
Nicholas Browns line	Do. Nicholas Brown
All John Winn, Senr. lines	Do. Richard Stone
All Colo. Tho. Winns lines	Do. himself, Richd. Stone and Richard Estes.
All Robert Crenshaws lines	Do. Wm. Buford, Daniel Winn & Richard Estes.
Daniel Gunns lines	Do. Joel Farguson and Belcher

Varsaws lines	Do. William Buford
Thomas Williams lines	Do. William Buford & Richard Estes
William Hatchetts lines	Do. Belcher and Richard Stone
John Sneads lines	Do. John Winn and R. Estes
Benja. Bridgeforths lines	Do. Daniel Winn
Allen Stokes lines and Robert Elliotts lines	Do. Richard Stone

Other lines not processioned for want of attendance.

No. 19. Returns by James Johnson and John White, Processioners. 4th of March, 1772.

By an order of the Vestry held for Cumberland Parish the 13th of Decr., 1771, we, James Johnson and John White, have processioned the line between John White, Senr. and Peter Jones, the line between John Hazlewood & Peter Jones, also between John White, Senr. and Theophilus Eddings, also between Peter Jones & Theophilus Eddings, also between Peter Jones and Mary Cockerham, also Carter White and Peter Jones, also between Carter White and Mary Cockerham, also between John Hazlewood & John White, Jr., also between John. Hazlewood and Peter Jones, also between Thos. Winn & Jno. Hazlewood, also between Thos. Walker & John Hazelwood, also between Thos. Walker and Lazarus Williams, also between Lazarus Williams and Peter Jones, present John Hazlewood.

No. 20. Returns by Everard Dowsing and Michael Johnson, Processrs.

In obedience to an order of Vestry dated 13th of Decr., 1771, we the subscribers met at Michael Johnsons the 2d day of March, 1772, in order to procession the lands in the said order mentioned and began as follows (viz): The line between Peter Jones and Zac. Davis, the line between Zach. Davis and Lazarus Williams, the line between Lazarus Williams and David Abernathy, the line between Lazarus Williams and Charles Hamlin, the line between Charles Hamlin and David Abernathy, the line between

David Abernathy and Zach. Davis, the line between Peter Jones and David Abernathy, the line between Embrys and David Abernathy, Present David Abernathy and Zach. Davis, the line between Everard Dowsing and Henry Embry, Benj. Cobb pressent. The line between Michael Johnson and James Berry. All other lines in the precinct not done for want of the parties.

No. 21. Returns by James Buford and Covington Hardy, Processrs.

We, James Buford and Covington Hardy, pursuant to an order of Vestry dated December the 13th, 1771, have processioned all the lines of the land between Wards rolling road, Great hounds creek, the path as goes from Daniel Winns to Reedy Creek old road, and the old road, the owners of the said land being present.

No. 23. Returns by Abraham Cocke and Saml. Garland, Processioners.

In obedience to an order of Vestry to us directed, we have caused the lands in our precinct to be processioned, the line between William Cross and Robert Chappel, Robt. Chappell pres. The line between Robert Chappell and William Eddings, line between Robert Chappell and Abraham Cocke, Robert Chappell & Wm. Eddings present.

Line between William Eddings and Abraham Cocks, present Eddings.
Line between Stith Hardiway & William Eddings, present Robt. Liveret, Wm. Eddings & Jno. Coal.
Line between Abraham Cocke and Robert Liveret. Present Liveret.
Line between Stith Hardiway & Robert Liveret, present Liveret & Wm. Chisolm.
Line between Edward Thweatt & Robt. Liveret, present Liveret & Wm. Chisolm and Peter Cousins.
Line between Peter Cousins & Robert Liveret, present Wm. Chisolm, Peter Cousins & Robert Liveret.
Line between Wm. Landrum and Peter Cousins, present Cousins and Landrum.

Line between Frans. Landrum & Peter Cousins, present Cousins.
Line between William Landrum and David Garland, present Landrum.
Line between William Landrum & James Gunn)
Line between Wm. Landrum & Frans. Landrum)
William Landrum present.
Line between Robert Liveret and Frans. Landrum, present William Chisolm, William Landrum, Landrum and Liveret.
Line between Robt. Liveret and James Gunn, present the men last mentioned.
Line between Reps Jones and Robert Chappell)
Line between Reps Jones and Abrm. Cocke)
Robert Jones present.
Line between Richard Haies and David Garland, Pres. Richd. Haies & Wm. Haies.
Line between Peter Cousins & David Garland, present Peter Cousins.
Line between Peter Cousins and Edward Thweatt, present Cousins & Thweatt.
Line between Cousins and Kirby, present Cousins.
Line between Daniel Thweatt and Stith Hardiway, present Daniel Thweatt.
Line between Newsum and Daniel Thweatt, present Thweatt.
Line between Drury More & Newsum, pres. Daniel Thweatt & D. More.
Line between Edward Thweatt and Drury More, present Daniel Thweatt.
Line between Drury More & Kirby)
Line between Edward Thweatt & Kirby)
Present Daniel Thweatt.
Line between Peter Cousins & Tho. Tabb, Peter Cousins present.
Lines of Francis Epps, Theo. Tabb & Peter Garland not processioned for want of attendance.

No. 24. Returns by Robert Blackwell and Charles Parrish, Processioners, 11th of March, 1772.

Agreeable to an order of the Vestry of Cumberland Parish, dated 13th of Decr., 1771. We have processioned the lands contained in the said order in presence of the owners.

No. 25. Returns by Edward Ragsdale and Nathaniel Laffoon, Process., 14th of March, 1772.

Who processioned the lands under mentioned.

John Coopers land	Present	John Coopers Senr. & Christopher Hinton
David Thomas's land	Do.	The same persons
Robert Mores land	Do.	Frederick Pool & Charles Parish
Frederick Pools land	Do.	Samuel Peace & Frederick Pool
Samuel Peaces land	Do.	James Waller and James Gallimore
George Phillups land	Do.	James Waller, Jas. Gallimore and Samuel Peace.
James Wallers land	Do.	The same as above
Edward Wallers land	Do.	The same
James Thompsons land	Do.	John Matthews Senr., Jno. Matthews, Jr., Daniel Apperson & Jas. Thompson.
John Matthews Jr. land	Do.	The four last men-
James Parishs land	Do.	tioned men.
Nathl. Laffoons land	Do.	Daniel Apperson, James Thompson & John Matthews, Junr.
Daniel Appersons land	Do.	James Thompson and John Matthews, Jr.
Wm. Gallimores land	Do.	Danl. Apperson, Jas. Thompson, John Matthews Jr. and Wm. Gallimore.

Tho. Hardings land	Do.	Danl. Apperson, Wm. Gallimore, John Matthews Jr. & Tho. Harding.
George Stiles land		Danl. Apperson, Wm. Gallimore, Jas. Thompson & Tho. Harding.
Wm. Samfords land	Do.	John Matthews, Sr., Keen, Samford, Matthew Bishop & Wm. Samford.
Wm. Davis land	Do.	John Matthews, Jr., Wm. Samford, Matthew Bishop & Wm. Davis.
Matthew Bishops land	Do.	John Matthews, Jr., William Lamford & Matthew Bishop.
Charles Bishops land	Do.	The three last mentioned men.
Matthew Laffoons land	Do.	Daniel Apperson, James Thompson & Wm. Gallimore.
James Buckners land	Do.	John Cooper, Christopher Hinton & Edmond Buckner.
Part of Phillip Reeks land Part of John Callahams & Jere. Morgans land	Do.	James Bishop & Jere. Morgan
Henry Haies and Richard Haies land	Do.	Samuel Rudder, Alexr. Rudder, Wm. Haies & Henry Haies.
Thomas Greens Richard Dennis's Ben Franklins John Martyns Edward Ragsdales & Henry Gees	Do.	Henry Gee, Thomas Green, Charles Buckner, Joseph Hix, James Gallimore & Edward Ragsdale.

No. 26   Returns by William Loury and Thomas Hardy,
Processrs.

Pursuant to an order of the Vestry of Cumberland Parish, dated the 13th of Decr., 1771.

We the subscribers have processioned all the lands according to the said order, the owners of the lands being present only one line between Major Tabb and Robert Chappell could not be found.

No. 27.   Returns by Thomas Edwards and Nicholas Williams,
Process.

In obedience to an order of Vestry we have processioned all the lands within our precinct (viz) two lines between Mr. Dowsing and Mr. Mackie, one line between the said Mackie & William Tisdale, one line between the said Dowsing and Tisdale, one between Dowsing & Embrys estate, one between R. Ward and Tisdale, between Tisdale and Wells, between Wells and Embry. Present Mr. Dowsing, Zachariah Davis and William Wrenn. Between Charles Cook and Embry, between Cook and Charles Hamlin, between Tho. Edwards and P. Hamlin, between said Edwards and Wells, between said Edwards and Ward, one line between Hamlin & Wells, one between Edwards and Wm. Loury, Wm. Wrenn and Zachariah Davis present. A line between Mr. Hamlin & the estate of Richard Williams, a line between said Hamlin and James Loman, between Nicholas Williams & Aaron Drummon. Also between Lazarus Williams and said Drummon, a line between Lazarus Williams and Nicholas and Daniel Williams, a line between Lazarus Williams and William Evans (or the King). Lazarus Williams, Aaron Drummon and Zachariah Davis present.

No. 28.   Returns by Michael Mackie and John Hix,
Processioners, 24th of March, 1772.

Agreeable to an order of Vestry bearing date the 13th of Decr., 1771, we Michael Mackie and John Hix have processioned the following lines.

Between Jona. Patteson and John Hix, between Jonathan Patteson & Ben Vaughn, between John Hix and Ben Vaughn, between

John Hix and Bilbo, between John Hix and John Milner, between Michael Mackie and Bilbo, between Michael Mackie & John Milner, between Michael Mackie & Samuel Jeeter, between John Milner and Samuel Jeeter, between John Milner and Jeremiah Glenn. Present John Milner & Jeremiah Glenn. The line between Rowland Ward and Mrs. Loury and between Mrs. Loury and William Loury. Present William Loury.

No. 29. Returns by Anthony Street and Robert Willson, Process., 26th of March, 1772.

In obedience to an order of Vestry held the 13th of Decr., 1771, we the subscribers appointed hath processioned the lands of William Wilson, John Hawkins, Jeremiah Glenn, John Hix, Jonathan Patteson, Robert Wilson & Anthony Streets. Present William Wilson, Henry Blagrave, Senr., Jere. Glenn, Jonathan Patteson, John Hix & John Hawkins, Senr.

No. 30. Returns by Wm. Shepherd, Craddock Vaughn, Process.

We have processioned all the lines of Wm. Cockerham and all the lines of Edward Self. Present Cockerham and Self. The line between Mason and Maury not shown. All the lines of T. DeGraffenriedt, Present Robert Scott and DeGraffenriedt, all Robert Scotts lines, Wm. Shepherds, Craddock Vaughns and William Loves, the parties all present. Isaac Webbs, John Woods & John Pattersons lines not shown.

No. 3 No returns.

No. 4 Returns by Loury Booker and Thomas Jones, Processioners, 18th of March, 1776.

The line between Atkinson and Reeks, the line between Atkinson and Ingram, between Atkinson and Moody, between Francis Cooper and Ingram, between Atkinson and Fras. Cooper, Thomas Young present.
The line between John Granger and Ingram, both present.
The line between Tho. Jones and Granger, both present.
The line between Abraham Andrews and Granger, Tho. Ingram present.

The line between Francis Cooper and Moody, between Henry Gee and Cooper, Francis Cooper present.

The line between Thomas Jones and Cooper, both present.

The line between Abraham Andrews and Thomas Jones, both present.

The line between Thomas Jones and Peter Andrews, the lines between Peter Andrews, Atkinson and Williams, Abraham Andrews present.

The line between Atkinson and Williams, Peter Andrews present.

The line between Atkinson, Williams and Floyd, the line between Williams and Tho. Jones, the line between Loury Booker and Robert Floyd, the line between Floyd and Jones, Abraham Andrews present.

The line between Nevil Gee and Tho. Jones, both parties present.

The lines between Thomas Jones and David VanDyck, between David VanDyck and Joel Traylor, Nevil Gee present.

The line between Loury Booker and Nevil Gee, Capt. Tomlinson present.

The line between Loury Booker and David VanDyck, Nevil Gee present.

The line between Capt. Tomlinson and Loury Booker, both parties pres.

The line between Loury Booker and Abraham Davis, Capt. Tomlinson pres.

The line between Capt. Tomlinson and John Booker, Loury Booker and Abrm. Davis, all present.

The line between Capt. Tomlinson and Henry Gee, the line between Capt. Tomlinson, Fras. Cooper and Wm. Barrett, the line between Loury Booker and Wm. Barrott, Capt. Tomlinson present.

No. 5 No return.

No. 6 Returns by John Hawkins and John Booker, Processioners, 8th of April, 1776.

The line between William Hobson and Tho. Foster, the line between John Hawkins and Jonathan Patteson, the line between Moses Foster and Richard Milner, between Milner and Churchhill Gibson, the line of James Gee, Thomas Loury, Daniel Mason, Winfield Mason and Richard Gilliam present James Gee, Richard Gilliam and William Turbyfill. The line between Benjamin Tomlinson and John Booker, between John Booker and John Williams, the line between Richard Booker and John Booker, the line between Richard Booker and John Williams, and the line between Daniel Mason and John Williams, between Jessee Gee and Jno. Williams, the line between Benjamin Tomlinson and Jessee Gee, Benja. Tomlinson present. The line between Jessee Gee and John Cocke, the line between Cock and Joshua Ragsdale, present Benjamin Tomlinson and James Gee. Between John Ragsdale and Wm. Loury, not processioned, no attendance. Between Richard Booker and Richard Booker, Richard Booker present.

No. 7 No return.

No. 8 Returns by John Scott and Wm. Stone, Jr., Process.

In obedience to the Vestry of Cumberland Parish agreeable to order we have processioned the following lines (viz) the line between John Scott and John Cunningham, between Scott and Taylor, in presence of Cunningham. Line between Scott and Anderson, Stone and Anderson present. Line between Anderson and Winn, between Anderson and Stone, in presence of Stone and Anderson. Between Stone and Wm. Stone, between Stone and Davis, Between Stone and Boswell, in presence of Stone. Line between Cox and Whitehead, between Cox and Freeman, between Burwell and Freeman, between Clarke and Freeman, between Cunningham Company and Stone, between Stone and Winn, between Stone and Taylor, lines between Taylor and Loury, between Winn and Taylor, between Bo [illegible] and is not processioned for want of attendance.

No. 9 Returns by Ellison Ellis and Jessee Saunders, Proc., 30th of March, 1776.

In compliance with an order of Vestry held for Cumberland Parish the 26th day of Feb., 1776, we Ellison Ellis and Jessee Saunders processioned the land within our order as follows (viz): The line between William Chandler and Thomas Neal, Chandler present. The line between Thomas Neal and Field

Archer, processioned, no attendance. The line between Archer and Ellison Ellis, between Ellison Ellis and Henry Robertson, Robt. Ingram present. The line between Timothy Chandler and Henry Robertson, Chandler attended. The line between Samuel Estes and Timothy Chandler, David Johnson and Estes attended. The line between Timothy Chandler and John McCutchin, Chandler attended. The line between John Cox and David Johnson, Johnson attended. The line between Cox and Stephen Wood, the line between Michael Johnson and Cox, Michael Johnson attended, the line between John Hunt and John Marrable, both attended. The line between Marrable and Benja. Evans, both attended. All the rest of the lines within our order not processioned by reason of no attendance. We advertised at Church and Meeting House, besides verbal notice for the people to meet us on Monday the 25th of March in order to show their lines and not one person appeared.

No. 10. Returns by David Johnson and Isaac Johnson, Processrs., 30th of March, 1776.

In obedience to an order of Vestry we the subscribers have processioned the line of Stephen Wood, Christopher Robertson, Joseph Johnson, John Brown and Isaac Johnson, they being present. The lines of John White, Isaac Johnson, John Blankinship, Robert Harden and Edward Slaughter, John White, John Blankinship and Joseph Johnson present. Samuel Estes lines, he present. The lines between John Blankinship, Edward Slaughter and Joseph Johnson, they present. The lines of John Brown, Wm. Parrot, John Lester and Tho. Reese, John Brown and Lockey Brown present, and the lines of Tho. Reese, Edward Slaughter, John Stembridge, Tho. Smith, Isaac Johnson and James Breedlove, Cornelius Crenshaw and David Holt, Edward Slaughter and Thomas Smith present.

No. 11. No return.

No. 12. Returns by Thomas Harding and Gideon Moon, Processioners.

We have processioned all the land in our bounds with peace and quietness.

No. 13. Returns by William DeGraffenriedt and John Ingram, Processioners, 14th of March, 1776.

Agreeable to order we have processioned the lines of the following persons within our bounds (to wit) the lines of John Ingram, the lines of John Elliott, also the lines of Matthew Gayle, in presence of Major Billups, also the lines of Major Billups in presence of Matthew Gayle, also the lines of William DeGraffenriedt, in presence of Francis Robertson. Several parcels of land within our bounds unknown to us, not processioned for want of attendance.

No. 14. Returns by Thomas Crymes and Edward Hatchett, 14th March, 1776.

Agreeable to order we have processioned all the said land in our precinct which may be manifest by each owner.

No. 15. Returns by Richard Ingram and Ward Hudson, Processioners.

We have processioned all the lands in our bounds, only Capt. Glenns, Mr. Easthems and Mr. Dozers, who said their lines is plain enough.

No. 16. Returns by William Love and William Gordon, Process.

In obedience to an order of Vestry held for Cumberland Parish the 26th day of Feby., 1776, we the subscribers have processioned the lands of John Love, William Love, Wm. Glenn, Henry Blagrave, Capt. Edward Jordan, Daniel Dejernatt, Joseph Billups, Theo. Evins (the dividing line between Billups and Evins could not be found as there was no attendance). James Johnsons (raleigh), Matt Mills, Colo. Thomas Tabb, Wm. Dozer, Michl. Johnson, Wm. Gordon, the estate of Robert Estes, Wm. Stevensons, Leonard Dozer, Wm. Tucker, Curtis Keatt, Wm. Murrell, Capt. James Boisseau and Peter Jones.

No. 17. Returns by William M. Cralle and Allin Stokes, Processioners, 28th of March, 1776.

In obedience to the within order we have processioned the lands therein mentioned except two or three short lines no attendance.

No. 18. Returns by Richard Stone and Wm. Hatchitt.

We the subscribers have processioned all that we were attended on.

No. 19. No return.

No. 20. Returns by William Stokes and William Dozer, Processrs., 19th of March, 1776.

Agreeable to the within order we have processioned all the land within the bounds mentioned in the within order.

No. 21. Returns by John Hardy, Theo. Eddings, Process. 9th of May, 1776.

Agreeable to order of Vestry to us directed, we have processioned all the lines of the lands in our precinct, the owners of the land being present except Daniel Winn, for whom Saml. Winn appeared,

No. 22. Returns by John Cross and George Hightower, Proc.

We have processioned the lines of William Jenings, James Scott and John Cross, in presence of Saml. Sparks. The lines of William Eddings, Thomas Cocke, James Scott, John Cross, Robt. Chappell, James Scott, in presence of Thomas Cocke. The lines of William Eddings, George Hightower, Thomas Cocke, Wm. Hardy, in presence of Wm. Chambers and Thomas Cocke. The lines of Wm. Chambers, Tho. Cocke, John Hightower, Wm. Chambers, Wm. Hardy, in presence of William Chambers. The lines of William Hardy, Leroy Buford, in presence of Wm. Hardy. The lines of Joseph Winn, Wm. Hardy, LeRoy Buford, Glebe land, Joseph Winn and Wm. Hardy, in presence of William Hardy.

No. 23. Returns by Thomas Liveret and William Eddings, Process.

In obedience to an order of Vestry to us directed, dated Feby. 26th, 1776, we have processioned the within land.

March 13th, processioned the line between Robert Chappell and John Cross, in presence of John Graham and John Cross.

March 14th, processioned the line between Abraham Cocke and William Eddings, Abrm. Cocke prest. The line between P. Cocke and George Pike, the line between Stith Hardiway and George Pike, the line between Stith Hardiway and Wm. Eddings, the line between William Eddings and George Pike, in presence of Abrm. Cocke and George Pike. The line between Tho. Liverett and Stith Hardiway, the line between Stith Hardiway and Wm. Chisolm, the line between Daniel Thweatts estate and Wm. Chambers, Abra. Cocke present.

March 15th. Processioned the line between Drury More and Newsoms estate, the line between Drury More and Kirby, in presence of Abra. Cocke and Drury More, the line between Colo. Tho. Tabb and Kirby, in presence of Abra. Cocke and Wm. Brintle, the line between Cousins's estate and Colo. Thomas Tabb, the line between Colo. Tho. Tabb and Peter Garland, in presence of Abraham Cocke, Wm. Brintle and John Hastings. The line between Fras. Epps and Natha. Booth, the line between Fras. Epps and Samuel Garland, in presence of Abra. Cocke, Nathl. Booth and Chas. Cabiness.

March 16th. Processioned the line between Robert Chappell and Wm. Eddings, the line between Robert Chappell and Abra. Cocke, in presence of John Graham, Robert Chappell and Abra. Cocke. The line between Reps Jones and Robert Chappell, in presence of John Graham and Robert Chappell. The line between Reps Jones and Abraham Cocke, present Abra. Cocke.

March 18th. Processioned the line between Francis Landrum and the estate of Peter Cousins, in presence of Fras. Landrum and Wm. Chisolm, Jr., the line between Fras. Landrum and James Gunn, the line between James Gunn and the estate of Wm. Landrum, the line between Colo. Garland and the estate of Wm. Landrum, the line between Saml. Garland and the estate of Peter Cousins, the line between the estate of Peter Cousins and Kirby, the line between Edward Thweatt and Kirby, in presence of Wm. Chisolm, Junr. Fras. Landrum and Jno. Hastings. The line between Edward Thweatt and the estate of Peter Cousins in presence of John Hastings and George Hightower, the line between Tho. Liverett and Abra. Cocke, the line between Wm.

Chisolm and Tho. Liverett, the line between Wm. Chisolm and the estate of Peter Cousins, in presence of Willm. Chisolm, Junr.

No. 24. Returns by Joel Pewet and Thomas Williams, Processioners.

In obedience to the within order we make this return, a peaceable and quiet procession of all the lands in this order, only Saunders Ray and Benjamin Taylor stopt us and their lands is not processioned.

No. 25. No return.

No. 26. [Space blank.]

No. 27. Returns by William Wrenn and David Abernathy, Processioners.

We in obedience have processioned all the lines within our bounds, and no objection made by no body.

No. 28. Returns by Michael Mackie, Samuel Jeeter and John Hix, Processioners.

Pursuant to order of Vestry bearing date Feby. 26th, 1776, we have processioned the following lines (to wit) A line between the estate of Thomas Loury and Rowland Ward, also between the said estate and Wm. Loury, a line between Michael Mackie and Rowland Ward, a line between Michael Mackie and Bilbo, a line between Mackie and Saml. Jeeter, Drury McDaniel present. A line between Mackie and Jeeter, also between Hix and Mackie, a line between Hix and Jeeter, a line between Patteson and Hix, a line between Patteson and Milner, a line between Hix and Milner, the same between Hix and Bilbo.

No. 30. Returns by Robert Scott and TsChr. DeGraffenriedt, Processioners, 11th of April, 1776.

Processioned the lands of Wm. Longmire, Wm. Love, John Love, Danl. Dejernatt, Craddock Vaughn, Robert Scott, Tschr. DeGraffenriedt, Thos. Wood, Edward Self, Wm. Cockerham, Abrm. Maury & Daniel Mason, being the whole of our bounds, the owners of each line being present, John Webb and Daniel Mason excepted.

No. 31. No return.

At a Vestry held for Cumberland Parish at the Courthouse the 10th day of Feby., 1780, the following processioners were appointed, (viz) for

No. 1 Sterling Niblett and William Niblett
    2 Henry Haies and Alexander Rudder
    3 John Ragsdale and John Moody
    4 Thomas Jones and Abraham Andrews
    5 William Buford and Benjamin Gee
    6 John Booker, Junr. and Thomas Walker
    7 Micajah Smithson and John C. Brown
    8 John Powel and John Overton
    9 Christopher Robertson and John Hightower
   10 Valentine Brown and Henry Hailey
   11 Stephen Wood and John Pettus, Senr.
   12 Colwell P. Pool and Robert Harding
   13 Christopher Billups and Francis DeGraffenriedt

Ordered that Phillip Rowlett and Robert Walton procession all the land between the Old County line, Spring Creek & Charlotte line.

Ordered that Thomas Chappell and Henry Farley procession all the land between Spring Creek, Prince Edward line and Ledbetter Creek.

No. 14 Arthur Herring and Edward Hatchett
   15 Richard Ingram and Ward Hudson
   16 Edward Jordan and William Gordon
   17 Henry Stokes and Allin Stokes
   18 Richard Stone, Jr. and Peter Winn.
   19 James Johnson and John Hazlewood
   20 Henry Embry and Zachariah Davis
   21 Minor Wilks and Covington Hardy
   22 William Chambers and Benjamin Edmondson
   23 Samuel Garland and Robert Chappell

24 John Jordan and Charles Hamlin
25 Edward Ragsdale and David More
26 Abraham Cocke and Drury More
27 Thomas Edwards and Daniel Williams
28 Robert Estes and Michael Mackie
29 Anthony Street and Robert Willson
30 Craddock Vaughn and TsCharner DeGraffenriedt
31 Cyrus Minor and William Evans

Ordered that the returns of processioning be made the last Thursday in March next.

Signed
Christopher Billups
Benja. Tomlinson

Mem. for the Processioners precincts see page two hundred and fifty five, fifty six, fifty seven and fifty eight.

No. 5. Returns by William Buford and Benjamin Gee, Processrs.

Agreeable to an order of Vestry held for Cumberland Parish, Feby. the 10th, 1780, we have processioned all the lands in our district with the owners of the said land present, except those that gave no attendance and such as did not choose to go round their lines.

No. 8. Returns by John Powel and John Overton, Processioners, 30th of March, 1780.

Pursuant to an order of Vestry bearing date the 10th day of Feby., 1780, we have processioned the following lines in our precinct (viz) a line between Joseph Davies heir and Joseph Boswell, a line between the said Davis and William Stone, a line between James Anderson and John West, a line between the said Anderson and William Stone, a line between said Anderson and Ransom Foster. Present at the above lines Clement Whitamore, William Stone and James Anderson. Also a line between William Stone, Junr. and said Davis's heir, also a line between sd. Stone and Ransom Foster, a line between sd. Stone and Thomas

Taylor, a line between sd. Stone and Richard Winn, and a line between sd. Stone and William Cureton. Present William Stone, Junr. Also a line between Richard Winn and William Cureton, and part of a line between Benjamin Clark and Cureton, begining at the river to a corner hiccory, and the remainder of the lines between Clark and others not shown. Prest. Benjamin Clark. Also a line between John Overton and Benjamin Clark, a line between sd. Overton and Colo. Burwell, a line between sd. Overton and Bartlet Cox, a line between sd. Overton and Benj. Whitehead. Also a line between John West and Ransom Foster, a line between said West and Thomas Taylor, and a line between sd. West and John Powel. Present John West. The lines between Foster and Taylor, line between Burwell and Cox, line between Whitehead and Cox, line between Loury and Burwell unprocessioned not being shown.

No. 13. Returns by Christopher Billups and Frans. DeGraffenriedt, Processioners, March the 30th, 1780.

In obedience to order of Vestry we the processioners have advertised to procession all the land in the bounds and not one person met us.

No. 15. Returns by Richard Ingram and Ward Hudson, Processioners.

We the processioners make the following return. Processioned the line between Burton and Ingram, the line between Burton and Jordan, the line between Jordan and Ingram, the line between Jordan and the Widow Tucker, the line between Jordan, Junr. and Jordan, Senr., the line between Jordan, Senr. and Blagrave, Senr., the line between the Widow Tucker and Jordan, Senr., the line between Jordan, Senr. and Easthem, the line between Clark and Easthem, the line between Gafford and Easthem, the line between Glenn and Easthem, the line between Gafford and Clark, the line between Eastham and Moon, the line between Gafford and Harris, the line between Clark and Harris, the line between Clark and the Widow Tucker, between Clark and Ward Hudson, the line between Hudson and Ingram, the line between Ingram and the Widow Tucker, the line between Ingram and Tucker, the line between Tucker and Hudson, the line between Tucker and Edmunds, the line between Tucker and Brisley, the line between Tucker and Dupree, the line between Edmunds and Tucker, Junr., the line between Edmunds and Dozer, the line between Keatts and Tucker, the line between Dozer and Brisley, the line between Brisley and Dupree, the line between Brisley and Pool, the line between Pool and Crenshaw, the line between Dupree and Crenshaw, the line between Burton and the Widow Pool.

No. 22. Returns by William Chambers and Benj. Edmondson, Processrs.

In obedience to an order of Vestry of Cumberland Parish dated the 10th of Feby., 1780, we the subscribers have processioned all the lines in our district (to wit), beginning between Tho. Chambers and George Hightower, between Tho. Chambers and William Eddings, between sd. Chambers and James Scott and between James Scott and Robert Chappell, and between Robert Chappell and Jacob Wray, and between Jacob Wray and James Scott, between Robert Chappell and John Cross, between John Cross and Jacob Wray, between George Hightower and William Eddings, between George Hightower and Benjamin Edmonson. Present George Hightower, Tho. Chambers and John Cross. Also between Tho. Chambers and William Chambers, between Tho. Chambers and William Hardy, between Tho. Chambers and Benjamin Bridgeforth, between William Hardy and Danl. Winn, between Wm. Hardy and Wm. Chambers, between Wm. Chambers and Benjamin Edmonson. Present Tho. Chambers and Wm. Hardy. Between William Hardy and Joseph Winn, between Wm. Hardy and LeRoy Buford. William Hardy present.

No. 24. Returns by John Jordan and Cha. Hamlin, Process.

In obedience to an order of Vestry we the subscribers have processioned all the land in our district in presence of the several owners.

No. 28. Returns by Robert Estes and Micl. Mackey, Processrs., 16th of March, 1780.

In compliance with an order of Vestry in 1780, appointing Robert Estes and Micl. Mackie processioners, have in compliance with said appointment processioned the following lines (to wit) John Hixes and Robert Esteses, no more attendance.

Returns of Processioning agreeable to order of Vestry held for Cumberland Parish the 8th day of January, 1784.

Nos. 1, 2, 3 and 4, space blank.

No. 5. Returns by John Ragsdale and John Dixon, Processioners, 8th of May, 1784.

In obedience to order of Vestry, we have processioned the lines between William Buford and Benjamin Gee, between the said Buford and John Ragsdale, Joshua Ragsdale and Wm. Buford present. One other line between the said Ragsdale and Buford, both present. Between Henry Gee and John Ragsdale, between the said Ragsdale and Benjamin Gee, between the said Ragsdale and John Dixon, said Ragsdale present. The lines of Jessee Gee, Junr. and John Ragsdale Senr., Jessee Gee, Junr. and Drury Ragsdale, present. Also one line between John Tabb and John Dixon, only ourselves present. The other part of Tabbs land, Alexander Rudders and William Barrotts lands not processioned. No attendance given to show the lines.

No. 6. [Space blank.]

No. 7. Returns by David Pettus and John Barry, Processioners.

In obedience to an order of the Vestry of Cumberland Parish in Lunenburg County, we have proceeded to procession the dividing lines contained in our district (viz) between David Pettus, William Stone and John Barry, William Stone, Junr. present. Between David Pettus, Thomas Garrott and William Bragg, present Wm. Bragg and Garrott. Between Stephen Johnson, John Barry and Edward Wilson, present Wilson and Johnson. Between Micajah Smithson, Edward Wilson and Roger Atkinson, present Smithson and Wilson. Between Andrew

Barry and Roger Atkinson, present Andrew Barry; between David Pettus and William Barry, present Richard Barry. Part of Roger Atkinsons and Clus. Colemans lines not processioned, no one to show the lines. Between John Barry, William Bragg and Thomas Wood, present William Bragg. Between Wm. Bragg, Thomas Garrott and John Barry, present Bragg and Garrott. Between Jas. Anderson, William Stone and Robert Wilson, present James Anderson. Between John Hankins and James Anderson, Anderson present. Between John Brown, Nathl. Mason and William Mason and John Hankins, present I. Brown and Wm. Mason. Between William Mason, Robert Wilson and John Burchit, present William Mason. Between John Hightower, William Mason and William Smithson and John Smithson decd. Present Wm. Smithson and William Mason. Between Benjamin Burchit, John Smithson and Samuel Estes. Present Benjamin Burchit, Between Benjamin Burchit, Thomas Scott and Samuel Estes, present Thomas Scott. Between Joseph Ragsdale, Bartlett Smithson and William Love and William Glenn, present Jos. Ragsdale and William Love. Between William Love, Bartlet Smithson and Samuel Estes, present Wm. Love and Sm. Estes. Between Thomas Scott, Wm. Burchit and Robert Scott and Wm. Scott and William Burchit, present Tho. Scott and William Burchit. Between Henry Pollard, Benjamin Burchit and John Hightower, present B. Burchit and H. Pollard. Between Henry Pollard, John Hightower and John Burchit, present Henry Pollard and John Burchit. Between Robert Wilson and Henry Pollard and Barnabas Owen, present Henry Pollard. Between Henry Pollard and William Scott and James Laurance and Thos. Wood, present William Scott and James Laurance. Between John Barry and the est. of Francis Robertson, decd., present William Scott. Between Barnabas Owen, John Hightower and Thomas Hoopper, present Barnabas Owen. Between Thomas Wood and B. Owen, present Barnabas Owen. Between Thomas Hoopper and the estate of Francis Robertson, decd., not processioned, no one to show the line.

No. 8. Returns by John Overton and James Jones, processioners.
March, 1784.

[Space blank.]

No. 9. [Space blank.]

No. 10. Order returned Capt. Robertson as a Justice of peace refused to serve.

No. 11. [Space blank.]

No. 12. Returns by Wm. DeGraffenriedt and Obediah Clay, Processioners, 25th of March, 1784.

We appointed by the Vestry of Cumberland Parish to procession in the district laid of for us, for that purpose advertised according to law our intentions, and no person or persons attended in our boundaries to show us our [over] their lines.

No. 13. Returns by Abner Wells and Frederick Nance, Processrs., 27th of March, 1784.

Gentlemen

According to the order received of you we have advertised our willingness to execute the same . . . [illigible] one wishes to have their lands processioned but no [ne]. . . Meeting or desireing it of us we did not think it our . . . to do it without their consent.

No. 14. Returns by John Chappell and Seth Farley, processioners, 20th of March, 1784.

In obedience to an order of the Vestry of Cumberland Parish, bearing date the 8th day of January, 1784, we the subscribers have assembled such of the freeholders as would attend between Springfield Creek, Prince Edward line and Ledbetter Creek (viz) William Nance, William Smith, Thomas Chappell and George Moor, and in presence of the above mentioned persons have processioned the land marks of William Nance, William Smith, William Chappell, Thomas Chappell, George Moor, John Chappell and Seth Farley, and as Doctor Anderson, Edward Branch, William George, John Mohorne, John Newby, William Ell . . ., Henry Farley, James Crafton, Richard Puckett and Thomas H. Puckett did not attend on the day appointed, therefore their land marks are not renewed.

No. 15. [Space blank.]

No. 16. Returns by Lodwk. Farmer and William Herring, Processrs.

[Space blank.]

No. 17. Field Clarke and Richard Ingram, Processrs., 15th of April, 1784.

Processioned a line between Field Clarke and Jeremiah Glenn, Glenn present, a line between John Glenn and Jere. Glenn, between Jere. Glenn and James Easthem, Easthem present. A line between Edward Jordan and Joseph Smith, between Jordan and Richard Ingram, between Jordan and the widow Tucker, between [mutilated] and Field Clark, Edward Jordan present. A line between Gid. Moon and [page torn] Harris, a line between Moon and John Clark, between Moon and Jas. Easthem, [page torn] Moon and John Clark present. A line between John Glenn and James Easthem, between Easthem and John Clark, between Clark and Martha Tucker, between Clark and Ward Hutson, between Field Clark and Tucker. These five lines are not processioned. Lines are plain and no one to show them. A line between George Crymes and William Tucker, also between Thomas Crymes and Tucker, Col. Edmunds and William Tucker, Wm. Tucker prest. A line between George Tuckers widow and Edmunds, Lewelling Tucker present. A line between Richard Ingram and the widow Tucker, Lewelling Tucker present. A line between Leonard Dozer and Brisindine, between Dupree and Brisindine, and Tucker and Brisindine, Edmunds and Brisindine, also between Stephen Cheatham and Brisindine, Brisindine present. A line between Joseph Smith and Thomas Dupree, Dupree present. A line between Tucker and Keatts. A line between Edmunds and Ward Hutson. A line between Joseph Smith and the widow Pool. These three last lines are not processioned, the lines are plain and no one to show them.

No. 18. Jeremiah Glenn and William Tuckers returns.

Agreeable to an order of Vestry the 8th of January, 1784, Jeremiah Glenn and William Tucker processioned the following lines. Between Craghead and Dozer, between ditto and Micl.

Johnson, between ditto and William Gordon, between ditto and Edward Jordan, between ditto and Field Clark, between ditto and Jeremiah Glenn, between ditto and Wm. Glenn, between ditto and Craddk. Vaughn, between ditto and Nathl. Newbell, between ditto and Nathl. Boothe, between ditto and James Johnson, between ditto and John Neal, present Saml. Garland, Mr. Craghead, George Craghead and William Craghead.

Between Nathl. Newbell and Nathl. Boothe, between James Johnson and John Neal, between Nathl. Newbell and Cradk. Vaughn, between William Love and Cradk. Vaughn, between Wm. Love and Wm. Glenn, present Wm. Love, Nathl. Newbell and James Johnson. Between Wm. Gordon and Edwd. Jordan, present Edwd. Jordan, between Michl. Johnson and Peter Jones, present Michl. Johnson, between Curtis Keatts and William Hearingue, between John Cureton and Wm. Hearingue, between Wm. Tucker and John Cureton, present Curtis Keatts and John Cureton.

Between James Keatts and Wm. Tucker, Curtis Keatts present. Between John Boisseau and Wm. Tucker, between John Stevenson and John Boissau, between Peter Jones and John Boisseau, between Peter Jones and the widow Murrell, between John Boisseau and the widow Murrell, present John Boisseau and Drury Murrell. Between Ben Estes and John Stevenson, between Ben Estes and Jos. Smith, between Ben and Elisha Estes, present Ben Estes. Between Jos. Smith and Elisha Estes, between Wm. Gordon and Elisha Estes. Elisha Estes present. Between Michl. Johnson and Wm. Gordon, present Wm. Gordon. Between Michl. Johnson and Peter Jones, between Michl. Johnson and Wm. Gordon, between Wm. Gordon and Peter Jones, between Gordon and Smith, present Wm. Gordon. Between Peter Jones and Joseph Smith, Jones and Snead, Stevenson and Jones, Stevenson and Brisindine, Dozer and Brisindine, Stevenson and Dozer, Dozer and Tucker, and John Stevenson and Wm. Tucker has refused to attend when called upon.

No. 19. [Space blank.]

No. 20. [Space blank.]

No. 21.   Returns by Joseph Smith and Peter Jones, Processrs.
March, 1784.

Lands processioned by Joseph Smith and Peter Jones. Beginning at Reedy Creek road, processioned the lines between the said Jones and Lazarus Williams, pres. Williams and ourselves, thence along a line between said Williams and John Hazlewood by the said Hazlewoods consent, then along the lines between the said Williams and Jos. Smith, then between the said Smith and John Hazlewood, then between the said Smith and Peter Jones, then between Jones and John Hazlewood, then between Jones and John White, then between P. Jones and Mrs. Winn, then between Mrs. Winn and Peter Jones, then between Mrs. Winn and Carter White, then between John White and Peter Jones, then between Carter White and Peter Jones, the parties present.

No. 23.   Returns by Covington Hardy & James Buford,
Processioners.

Pursuant to an order of Vestry dated the 8th of Jany., 1784, we the subscribers have processioned the lands of John Cross, Jeremiah Blankenship present, of John Hardy himself present, of Covington Hardy, Joseph Winn present, of Minor Wilks, Jeremiah Blankenship present, of James Buford, Thomas Hardy present, Sarah Winns land not shewn.

No. 24.   Returns by John Cross and Edward Chambers,
processrs. 1784.

In obedience to an order of the Vestry of Cumberland Parish we have processioned the lines of Jacob Wray and James Scott, the line between James Scott & Robert Chappell, also the line between Anny Eddings & said Scott. Between Thomas Chambers and said Scott, also the line between the said Scott and John Tucker in presence of the said Scott, also the line between Thomas Chambers and George Hightower, between the above mentioned Chambers and Tucker, and Eddings and Hightower, in presence of the said Chambers & Hightower. And the line between George Hightower & Benja. Edmondson in presence of the same. Also the lines of Jacob Wray and John Cross, and the line between Robert Chappell and John Cross, in presence of Robert Chappell, the line between William Hardy and William Chambers, said Chambers present, also the line between Wm. Hardy and LeRoy Buford. Present LeRoy Buford. Between Wm. Hardy and Jos. Winn, in presence of Jos. Winn, also the line between Wm. Chambers & Ed Chambers in presence of Wm. Chambers.

No. 25. One of the Processioners appointed died.

No. 26. Charle Hamlin as a Justice of Peace refused to serve & return his order.

28. Returns by Thomas Buford & Thomas Hardy, Processioners.

Pursuant to an order of Vestry dated Jany. the 8th, 1784, we the subscribers have processioned, Thomas Hardys land, James Buford, Junr. present. Part of James Bufords land the owner present. The Revd. James Craigs land on the North side of Flattrock Creek, the land of Joel Daws, Dec., Henry Bufords land, the Revd. James Craig present. William Hardys land, the owner present. Ellick Mores land himself present. Newsoms Orphans land, Ellick More present. Aaron Drummonds land, William Ellis's land, James Buford present. James Lomans Land, the owner present. John Epps's land, himself present. Processioned Abraham Cuttillos land, the owner present. Thomas Bufords land, Joseph Tuckers land, Robert Chappells land, the Revd. James Craigs land on the south side of Flattrock Creek, Joseph Tucker present.

No. 29. Returns by Nicholas and Daniel Williams, Processrs, March 27th, 1784.

In obedience to the within order we the subscribers have processioned all the land therein directed and no objection made.

May 9th, 1831. James Macfarland, David Street & Edward R. Chambers being all the surviving Trustees—at present they then made choice of Wm. Bagley and Roger B. Atkinson to supply the vacancy occationed by the removal of Colo. Edmd. L.

Taylor and Edmd. P. Bacon deceased, leaving the other vacancy occationed by the death of the Revd. John Philips, to be filled with his successor who shall be chosen as the Minister of this Parish.

May 9th, 1831. Roger B. Atkinson was elected lay deputy to represent (this parish say Cumberland Parish Lbg. County) in the General Convention to be held in the Borough of Norfolk the third Thursday, in this month (May), by the Vestry this day, and it is ordered that he be furnished with his certificate signed by the Vestry (by David Street) one of the Church Wardens. Also that each of the other seven vestry men pay him two dollars each and himself one dollar, making fifteen dollars which the said Roger B. Atkinson is to pay into the Treasurer of the General Convention for this Parish's contribution for the present year.

NOTE

It is important for those using the index to search for variant spelling of many names.

The different spellings may not refer to different families or persons, but in fact, usually, are intended to refer to the same person or family.

No attempt will be made here to list the variants which may be intended to have the same significance, but a few may be given as illustrative. Some of them are: Allan, Allen; Anders, Andress, Andrews, Andrus; Billaps, Billips, Billops, Billups; Blackgrove, Blagrave, Blagrove; Blackstone, Blaxton, Blaxtone; Boulden, Bouldin; Burrell, Burwell; Coalman, Coleman; Cock, Cocke, Cox; Cousins, Cozen, Cozens; and many others of like import will be readily observed from even a casual examination of the index. An extreme case is that of Knight and Night; most of the illustrations, however, have the same initial letter.

INDEX

A

Aarons Creek, 370.
Abernathy, David, 107, 437, 540, 541, 553.
Abridged Compendium of American Genealogy, 149, 276.
Adam, Eliza, 160.
Adams,
  Ashley, 313.
  J., 346.
  J. R., 123.
  Mary Jacqueline, 123.
  Thomas, 352, 504.
  Thomas (Rev.), 192.
Adler, Mary, 312.
Akin, John, 352, 355, 358, 362, 371.
Alberta, Va., 123.
Alderson, Benedict, 524.
Alexander, Robert, 367.
Allan, Wm., 405.
Allegany Mts., 213.
Allen,
  Abram, 305.
  Ad., 230.
  Charles, 169, 212, 326, 348.
  David, 304.
  Drury, 306, 333.
  John, 107.
  Josiah, 346.
  Mary, 169, 355, 356.
  Robert, 33, 73, 324, 327, 331, 332, 333, 337, 339, 342, 345, 350.
  Wm., 358, 381, 385, 391, 394, 395, 401, 409, 520.
Allen Creek, 201, 252.
Allen's Creek, 261, 262, 325, 340, 348, 351, 367, 369.
Allen Stokes Mill Creek, 403.
Allen and Jefferson, Marriage Articles, 255.
Alley,
  Stephen, 310.
  Winefred, 312.
Alliburton, David, 510.
Amelia County, 41, 65, 113, 114, 424.
Amherst College, 119.
Ammons,
  Ashley D., 222.

Ammons—Continued
  Emery, 222.
  Fletcher W., 221.
Amon, Fras, 389.
Amos,
  Francis, 381, 425, 427, 430, 434, 441, 443, 448, 456.
  Frans., 405, 415, 419.
  Fras., 376, 385, 391, 394, 398, 514.
  Frs., 409, 413, 439, 445, 446,, 450.
  James, 526.
  Nicholas, 376, 381, 385, 389, 391, 394, 398, 405, 409, 413, 415, 419, 425, 427, 430, 434, 439, 441, 443, 445, 446, 448, 450, 456.
Amoss, James, 107.
Anders, Abraham, 107.
Anderson, 548.
  Bettie, 155.
  Betty, 310.
  Daniel, 151, 315.
  Doctor, 560.
  Duncan Cameron, 153.
  Edith Harvey, 152.
  Edward, 153, 164.
  Edward Cameron, 153.
  Elizabeth, 305, 313.
  Elizabeth Cameron, 153.
  Emily, 152.
  George Burgwyn (Gen.), 154.
  Grace Fontaine, 152.
  Halcott Cameron, 153.
  Helen Cameron, 153.
  James, 131, 430, 531, 555, 559.
  Jane Maury, 152.
  John, 305.
  John H., 154.
  Julia, 153.
  Malcolm, 152.
  Malcolm Cameron, 152.
  Mary, 155, 312.
  Mary Lightfoot, 232.
  May, 153.
  Mildred, 154.
  Mildred Devereux, 153.
  Phebe, 154.
  Ravenscroft, 153.

Anderson—Continued
  Rosa, 152.
  Thomas, 39, 355, 369, 376, 378, 509.
  Walker, 131, 152, 153, 156, 165.
  Walker (Capt.), 155.
  Walter, 153.
  William, 154.
  William E., 151, 154, 155, 159.
  William Edward, 131, 152.
Andress, Anne, 311.
Andrew, Moses, 305.
Andrews,
  Abraham, 421, 520, 546, 547, 554.
  Amey, 243.
  Elizabeth, 244, 247, 314.
  Ephraim, 368.
  Frances, 314.
  George, 244, 247.
  Hiles, 308.
  John, 505.
  Lyncia, 313.
  Patsey, 246.
  Peter, 505, 520, 545.
  Polly, 304.
  Sandal, 313.
  Thos., 505.
Andrus,
  Peter, 107.
  Thos., 107.
Anglican Church,
  decline of, 80 et seq.
  disestablishment of, 89.
Angus, John, 306.
  Anthony, Sarah, 289.
Antietam, 155.
Antrim Parish, 22.
Apperson, Daniel, 543, 544.
Appomattox C. H., 162.

Archer,
  Field, 531, 549.
  Judith, 113, 115.
Archives,
  Department of, in Virginia, 18.
Arden, Abraham, 73, 331, 337.
Ardin, Abraham, 73, 329, 332, 339.
Arding, Abraham, 333.
Armstead, 509.
Armistead,
  Anthony, 287.
  Euphan, 310.
  Mary, 287.
  William, 287.
Army of Northern Virginia, 155.
Army of Tennessee, 155.
Arnold, James, 348, 368.
Arthur, Mary, 288, 290.
Arvin, John, 533.
Asheville, N. C., 160.
Ash Camp Creek, 347, 348.
Ash, Sally, 305.
Ashburn, 293.
Asher, Joseph, 510.
Askew, John, 409, 413, 415, 419, 425, 427, 430, 434, 439, 441.
Assessment Bill, 92.
Athens, Ga., 180.
Atkinson, 530, 546, 547.
  Robert, Jr., 309.
  Roger, 519, 520, 558, 559.
  Roger B., 71, 564, 565.
  Thomas (Bishop), 164.
Augusta County line, 79.
Austin,
  Hanah, 343.
  John, 334.
Avery, Mary, 309.
Avory, Thos., 509.

B

Bacon Family, 167.
Bacon, 331.
  Addie, 117.
  Alex., 172.
  Alice, 168.
  Anne, 168, 169.
  Colonel, 400, 524, 525, 529.
  Drury Allen, 169.
  Edmund, 167, 168, 170.
  Edmd. P., 489.
  Edmund P., 26, 58, 71, 270, 468, 470, 472, 474, 475, 476, 478, 479, 480, 481, 482, 483, 484, 485, 486,

Bacon—Continued
  487, 488, 489, 490, 491, 492, 493, 494, 495, 498, 500.
  Edmund Parkes, 168, 169, 170, 172, 173.
  Elizabeth, 168, 169, 170.
  Fanny, 168.
  Frances, 168.
  George, 172.
  Gillie E., 170.
  Gillie Marion, 171.
  Gillie Marion, Sr., 172.
  James Parish, 171.

Bacon—Continued
  John, 168, 170, 333, 512.
  John Barrett, 172.
  L., 195.
  Langston, 169, 455.
  Lucy, 169.
  Lyddal, 26, 29, 30, 33, 40, 43, 52, 53, 98, 101, 168, 169, 170, 242, 297, 324, 325, 329, 331, 340, 341, 342, 343, 344, 345, 346, 351, 353, 354, 356, 357, 379, 380, 382, 383, 384, 385, 386, 388, 389, 390, 393, 396, 397, 401, 402, 408, 410, 411, 412, 414, 415, 417, 418, 419, 421, 424, 425, 427, 428, 429, 432, 433, 435, 442, 449, 454, 456, 458, 459, 460, 461, 462, 464, 465, 466, 467, 514, 529.
  Lyddal (Col.), 538.
  L. (Col.), 537.
  Lyddall, 170, 172, 178, 183, 202, 203, 248, 250, 264, 284.
  Martha, 172.
  Mary, 168, 169.
  Mary A. G., 170, 316.
  Mary Gillie, 171.
  Mary Jane, 172.
  Montfort S., 171.
  Mr., 48.
  Narcissa, 170.
  Nathaniel, "the Rebel," 167.
  Nathaniel, 168, 169.
  Parke, 172.
  Parke Street, 172.
  Polly, 170.
  Richard, 169.
  Richard C., 170.
  Sally, 170.
  Sally G., 317.
  Sarah, 168, 169, 170, 248.
  Susanna, 168, 169.
  Susanna R., 170, 317.
  Sydney Montfort, 172.
  "The Rebel," 173.
  Thomas, 167, 172.
  Waddy Lee, 172.
  William, 168, 342.
  Young H., 171.
Badger, Joseph, 306.
Bagley,
  Anderson, 192, 226.
  Mary Chappel, 315.
  Polly Chappell, 192.
  Robert S .(Dr.), 116, 190.
  Sarah C., 211.

Bagley—Continued
  Wm., 71, 564.
Bagley's Mill, 104.
Bailey,
  John, 107, 520.
  Wm., 511.
Bailie, Robert, 521.
Bain,
  Fanny, 270.
  Margaret, 149.
Baird,
  Anna, 309.
  Benj., 503, 504.
  Elizabeth, 306.
  James, 312.
Baker,
  Batt, 529.
  Elijah, 532.
  Elijah (Rev.), 88.
  Irby, 317.
  Lowry, 107.
  Margret, 339, 340.
  Zach, 370.
Ballard Family, 174.
Ballard,
  Anne, 173, 174.
  Ann Eliza, 174.
  Becky, 176.
  Betty, 176.
  Catherine, 174.
  Elizabeth, 173, 174, 176, 177, 278.
  Faitha, 175, 176.
  Frances, 174.
  Francis, 173, 174, 176.
  Francis (Maj.), 175.
  Francis Dancy, 174.
  John, 30, 173, 175, 176, 177, 219, 351, 362, 363, 367, 396, 399, 400, 401, 407, 444, 445, 447, 449, 450, 455, 503, 504.
  John (Capt.), 174.
  John, Jr., 26, 107, 396, 446.
  Katharine, 173.
  Lucy, 174, 175, 176.
  Mary, 173, 174, 176.
  Matthew, 173.
  Rebecca, 176.
  Robert, 173, 174, 176, 177.
  Servant, 174.
  Thomas, 172, 173, 174, 177.
  Thomas (Maj.), 13.
  William, 173, 174, 176, 177, 519.
  William Talbot, 174.
Banister,
  Col., 526.
  Mary Ann, 310.

Bankhead,
  Marie Susan, 264.
  John Hollis, Senator, 264.
Banks, Moses E., 161.
Banns, Marriage,
  Substitute for license, 7.
Banns, publication of, 8.
Baptist General Association, 92.
Baptist,
  oppose general assessment, 92.
Barber, John, 314.
Barclay, 357, 364.
Barclay,
  James, 67, 506.
  John, 356, 379.
  John (Rev.), 66, 67, 72, 98, 353, 354, 358, 360, 363, 365.
  Rev. Mr., 354, 355.
Bardit, William, 533.
Barker, Daniel, 332.
Barlow, Elizabeth, 313.
Barnes,
  Anne (or Ann), 338, 340, 343, 345, 351, 354, 358, 362, 371, 375, 381, 385, 389, 391, 394, 398.
  Thomas, 305.
Barnes, James, Quarter, 264.
Barns, John, 514.
Barn, on Glebe, 410.
Barrett, Wm., 547.
Barrott, William, 558.
Barry,
  Andrew, 558, 559.
  John, 451, 558, 559.
  Richard, 559.
  Sarah, 243.
  William, 530, 559.
Bartlet, Wm., 500.
Baskervil,
  George, 360, 367, 370, 503.
  George (Capt.), 350.
Baskerville,
  George, 38, 256.
  Samuel, 115.
Basket, Daniel, 333.
Baskett, Martha Ermin, 117.
Bass, Joseph, 307.
Bates, Henry, 325.
Bath County, Va., 132.
Batte, Mary, 307.
Baugh,
  Daniel, 525.
  Elizabeth, 309, 313.
  James, 538.
  John, 305, 524, 525.
  Robert, 309.

Baugh—Continued
  Sarah, 314.
Baxter,
  Ellen Taylor, 237.
  John, 309.
Baxter,
  Lowry, 107.
Baylie, Robt., 403.
Baylor,
  Ann George, 123.
  Julia, 123.
  Robert, 123.
Bayne, Karon, 270.
Beadle,
  Elizabeth, 279.
  Harriet Ragsdale, 279.
Bears Element Creek, Little, 229.
Bears Eliment Creek, 368, 402.
Bears Ellyment Creek, 473.
Beasley,
  Mary F., 220.
  John, 507.
  Robert, 507, 517.
Beasly,
  John, 526.
  Robert, 422, 535, 536.
Beaverpond Branches, 203.
Beck, Anna Buxton, 161.
Bedford County, 22, 104, 249.
Bedford,
  Frances, 179.
  Robert, 179.
  Thomas, 212, 347.
Bedingfield, John, 313.
Beever, Elizabeth, 279.
Beggis, John, 317.
Belcher, 540.
Belcher,
  Edmd, 514.
  Isham, 310.
Bell,
  Isaac Bonaparte, 229.
  Wm., 502.
Belo, Agnes, 161.
Bennehan,
  Margaret, 156.
  Rebecca, 156.
  Richard, 156.
Bennet, Walter (Dr.), 430, 431.
Bennett, Dr., 436.
Bennit, Joseph, 502.
Berry,
  James, 507, 541.
  John, 529.
  Martha, 308.
Best, Ephraim, 372.

INDEX

Bethel Church, 39, 377, 381, 392, 394, 397, 405, 407, 413, 414, 419, 425, 426, 429.
Bethel Church, 385, 388, 391.
Betts Family, 177.
Betts,
  Charles, 190, 318.
  Elisha, 26, 30, 177, 435, 439, 440, 441, 442, 443, 444, 524, 525, 538.
  William, 453.
Beuford,
  Henry, 187.
  James, 468.
  Jas., Senr., 107.
  Thos., 468.
  William, 30, 468.
Beuforde, Wm., 468.
Bevil,
  Burral, 372, 508.
  John, 442.
  Margrett, 349, 381, 385, 389, 391, 394, 397.
  Mary, 355.
Biddie, Thos., 528.
Biddy, Thos., 513.
Biggers, Edward, 154.
Bilbo, 521, 546.
Bilbo, Nicholas, 252.
Billaps, Chris, 369.
Billips,
  Christopher, 418, 515.
  Joseph, 403, 514.
Billops, Joseph, 349.
Billups Family, 178.
Billups, 537.
Billups,
  Ann, 178.
  Capt., 208, 405.
  Christopher (Capt.), 414, 426.
  Chris, 507.
  Chrsr., 425.
  Col., 444.
  Jane F., 316.
  Jane Flippen, 179, 181.
  John, 27, 58, 178, 179, 180, 452, 468, 480, 482, 483, 484, 485, 487, 488, 489, 490.
  Joseph, 178, 438, 443, 507, 550.
  Major, 550.
  Mariah, 180.
  Mary, 179.
  Nancy, 180.
  Richard, 178.
  Robert, 178, 180.
  Robert Bedford, 179.

Billups—Continued
  Ruth, 179.
  Susanna, 179.
  Susannah J., 180.
  Virginia, 180, 181.
Binford, Charles, 308.
Bingham, William, 312.
Birchett,
  Edward H. (Dr.), 260.
  Elizabeth, 305.
Births, Register of, 9.
Bishop,
  Charles, 544.
  James, 544.
  Matthew, 544.
Bishop of Chester, 132, 145.
Bishop of London, 59.
Black, Jenny, 306.
Blackgrove, 183.
Blackgrave, Henry, 404.
Blackstone, John, 358, 528.
Blackwell,
  Joel, 254.
  John, 313, 339, 340.
  Louise, 129.
  Robert, 423, 443, 427, 543.
Blackwell's Neck, 215.
Blagrave,
  Capt., 533.
  Henry, 27, 30, 99, 269, 361, 380, 390, 408, 413, 523.
  Henry, Jr., 533.
  Henry, Senr., 546.
  Mary Newsteys, 184.
  Nancy, 184.
Blagrove, 183, 556.
Blagrove,
  Anne, 184.
  Benjamin (Rev.), 183.
  Henry, 183, 349, 357, 360, 364, 370, 371, 374, 375, 379, 383, 384, 388, 389, 393, 395, 402, 517, 550.
  Henry, Jr., 184.
  John, 183.
Blakely,
  James, 307.
  Mary, 311.
  Nancy, 313.
Bland,
  Edward, 317.
  Elizabeth Blair, 307.
  John, 312.
  Peter R., 170, 317.
  Richard, 308.
Blandford Cemetery, 129.

Blandford Church, 149.
Blandford Church, Old, 132.
  Memorial to Rev. John Cameron, in, 144.
Blank, Jos., 505.
Blankenship,
  Jeremiah, 563.
  Mary, 309.
  Winny, 314.
Blankinship,
  Bland, 311.
  John, 523, 533, 534, 535, 549.
Blanks, Joseph, 519, 520.
Blanton,
  Elizabeth, 121.
  John Ellyson, 121.
  Lucy, 121.
  M. Linwood, 121.
  Rebecca, 121.
  R. Walter, 121.
  Wm., 501, 502.
Blaxton, John, 34, 331, 333, 337, 339, 342, 345, 354, 361, 362, 371, 375, 381, 388, 506, 507, 512, 529.
Blaxtone, John, 529.
Blevin, Wm., 339.
Blick, John, 305, 312.
Blissland Parish, 293.
Bluestone Church, 336, 342, 345.
Blue Stone Creek, 348, 349, 369.
Blunt, Thomas, 311.
Boaz, Catherine, 443, 450, 456.
Bobbitt, John, 313.
Boissau, John, 562.
Boisseau,
  James, 538, 550.
  John, 562.
  Mary, 123.
  Mary Godwyn, 306.
Boldin, Thomas, 212.
Boles, Jeremiah, 530.
Bolling,
  Anne, 305.
  Anne, 305.
  Capt., 120.
  Frances, 314.
  Rebecca B., 314.
  Thomas, 318.
Bond,
  Annie, 128.
  Thomas (Maj.), 128.
Bonner,
  John, 305.
  Mary, 313.
  Mary Heth, 305.
  Polly, 309.

Booker, 520, 524, 525.
Booker,
  Ann, 113.
  Edmund, 112.
  Edward, 113, 115, 530.
  Edward (Col.), 113.
  Elizabeth, 113, 312.
  Frances, 113.
  George, 113.
  Henrica, 113.
  James, 114.
  John, 107, 113, 114, 437, 521, 530, 547, 548.
  John, Jr., 451, 554.
  Judith, 112, 115.
  Kitty, 115.
  Loury, 437, 546, 547.
  Mary, 112, 113, 114.
  Mary Marshall Parham, 115.
  Parham, 113.
  Rebecca, 113, 114, 115.
  Richd., 74.
  Richard, 112, 113, 114, 115, 311, 345, 359, 505, 521, 530, 548.
  Richard Morot, 113.
  Statira, 115.
  Susannah, 113.
  Wm., 506, 521.
  Wm. Marshall, 113.
Booth,
  George, 310.
  May, 283.
  Natha., 552.
  Temperance, 283.
Boothe,
  Eliza, 181.
  Nathl., 562.
Boseman, John, 500.
Boswell, 369, 548.
Boswell,
  Claire, 229.
  Edmund, 229.
  Garland, 229.
  Joseph, 357, 359, 360, 369, 508, 522, 531, 555.
  William W., 229.
Bottom, John, 312.
Botts, 521.
Botts, J., 521.
Bouchers Creek, 325, 326.
Boulden, 34, 329, 331, 332, 337, 354.
  Thomas, 26, 27, 29, 35, 36, 98, 324, 325, 327, 328, 329, 331, 332, 334, 335, 342, 343, 344, 345, 346, 352, 354, 355, 356, 357, 358.
  William, 342.

Bouldin,
  Francinia, 197.
  Thomas, 34, 182, 197, 284, 324, 327, 351.
Boulton, Robt., 513.
Bowers,
  Betsy, 315.
  John, 106, 315.
  Nanny, 243.
  Sanford, 107.
  Young, 107.
Bowles, Jeremiah, 511, 516.
Bowman, Mary Belle, 125.
Boyd,
  Alexander, 316.
  Christian Blair, 228.
  Jane A., 316.
  John, 35, 324, 333.
  Nancy, 316.
  Panthea, 228.
  Richard, 228, 315.
  Robert, 316.
Bracie,
  Fras., 509.
  John, 369.
Bracy,
  Fras., 355.
  Randolph, 367, 504.
Bradley,
  Ann, 311.
  David, 309.
Brag, Wm., 530.
Bragg, 521.
Bragg,
  Blanche, 159.
  Thomas, 159.
  Wm., 514.
  William, 558, 559.
Branch, Edward, 560.
Brandom, Aaron, 306.
Brandy Station, 120.
Braser, Sarah, 314.
Braughton, John, 391.
Breedlove, James, 549.
Brent, Meade S. (Dr.), 238.
Brickland, 128.
Bridgeforth, Benja., 540.
Bridges, Charles H., 122.
Bridgforth,
  Benj., 513.
  George Baskerville, 122.
  Mary Collier, 122.
Briggs, Wm., 514.
Brintle, Wm., 552.
Brisindine, 537, 562.
  Isaac, 525.

Brisley, 557.
Bristol Parish, 19, 20, 135, 144, 145.
  Cameron, Rev. John resigns, 137.
  History of, 193.
  Register, 151, 258, 274.
  Slaughter's Hist. of, 138.
  Vestry Book, 132.
Bristol Parish Register, 258.
Broadnack's Quarter, Edward, 186.
Broadnax, 511.
  Anne, 304.
  Edward, 186, 461.
  Martha, 225.
  Samuel, 316.
  Stephen Edward, 186.
Brockenbrough, John (Dr.), 158.
Brockwell, Thomas, 305.
Brodnax Family, 184.
Brodnax,
  Edward, 44, 106, 185, 243, 461, 462, 464.
  Edward (Capt.), 186.
  John, 185.
  Martha, 225.
  Robert, 185.
  Stephen E., 461.
  Stephen Edward, 27, 185, 186, 437, 519.
  William, 185.
Bromley, James, 308.
Brookes,
  Auther, 510, 515.
  Elisha, 507.
  John, 505, 506.
  Richard, 351, 354, 358, 385, 507.
  Robert, 368, 506, 510, 515, 516.
  Widow, 507.
  Wm., 507.
Brooking,
  Robert Edward, 202.
  Vivian, 202.
Brooks,
  Auther, 516.
  Eliza Embry, 206.
  Frances, 208.
  John, 520.
  Matthew, 521, 522.
  Matt, 522, 531.
  Richard, 340, 343, 345, 362, 371, 375, 389, 506.
  William, 426.
Broomfield, 337.
Broomfield, Wm., 336.
Broughton, John, 394.
Browder,
  Dinny, 311.

Browder—Continued
  Isham, 199.
  Jermiah, 311.
  Martha, 313.
Brown,
  Alexander, 150.
  Ann, 271.
  Arthur Aylett, 153.
  Danll., 514.
  Dudley, 299, 304.
  Elizabeth, 158.
  Frances Lowry, 306.
  Frederick, 403, 523, 534.
  Halcott Cameron, 153.
  Hezekiah, 304.
  I., 559.
  Isaac, 392, 519.
  Israel, 368, 505.
  Jesse, 326, 510, 518.
  John, 310, 437, 518, 522, 524, 534, 549, 559.
  John C., 554.
  John Calwell, 530, 531.
  John Colwell, 510.
  John, Jr., 421.
  John W., 158.
  Lawrence, 153.
  Locky, 312.
  Mary, 269, 309, 345.
  Malcolm Cameron, 153.
  Margaret, 153.
  Matilda Gault, 153.
  Mildred Cameron, 153.
  Nicholas, 403, 513, 539.
  Norborne, 153.
  Rob, 107.
  Robt., 519.
  Stephen, 519.
  Val., 515, 518.
  Vallentine, 266.
  Vol., 387, 515.
  Volindine, 370.
  Volintine, 510.
  Wm., 517, 532.
  William Edward, 153.
  Zell, 122.
Browne, John Colwell, 515.
Brox, Robt., 501.
Bruce,
  George, 509.
  Richard, 236.
  Robt., 520.
  Thos., 523.
  Thomas, 535.
Brunskill, 333.

Brunskill,
  John, 61, 332.
  John (Rev.), 48, 59, 60, 62, 72, 329, 331, 335, 337.
  John, Jr. (Rev.), 60.
  John, Sr. (Rev.), 60.
  Richard, 61.
Brunswick County, 21, 25, 32, 116, 182, 185.
Brunswick line, 38.
Bryan,
  Annie S., 159.
  Carter Braxton, D. D., 145.
Bryant, Thos., 333.
Brydie,
  Alexander F., 181.
  Charles, 179, 181, 194, 316.
  Frances Ann, 181.
  George Canning, 181.
  James Lawrence, 181.
  Martha Jane, 181.
  Mary Emily, 181.
  Robert Bedford, 181.
Brydon, G. MacLaren (Rev.), 84.
Buchanan,
  David, 309.
  John, 475.
  John (Rev.), 471, 487.
  Mr. (Revd.), 462, 480, 490, 491, 494.
  W. (Rev.), 470.
Buckanan, Mr. (Rev.), 494.
Buckenham, Honor, 511.
Buckmire, Ann, 307.
Buckner,
  Charles, 544.
  Edmond, 544.
  Ezell, 305.
  James, 527, 544.
Buford Family, 187.
Buford,
  Abraham, 320.
  Catherine, 318.
  Frances, 133, 315.
  George Washington, 187.
  Henry, 187, 483, 484, 526, 528, 564.
  James, 27, 30, 44, 107, 278, 423, 437, 453, 460, 461, 462, 464, 465, 466, 467, 469, 470, 472, 473, 474, 475, 476, 477, 478, 479, 480, 481, 482, 483, 484, 485, 486, 487, 488, 541, 563, 564.
  John, 27, 187, 491, 492, 493, 494, 495, 496, 498, 499, 500.
  Joseph, 133.

Buford—Continued
  LeRoy, 107, 551, 557, 564.
  Lillian, 272.
  Marcus B., 187.
  Martha, 320.
  Sally, 254.
  Susanna H., 320.
  Thomas, 27, 30, 143, 317, 320, 437, 444, 445, 446, 447, 449, 450, 451, 453, 454, 455, 456, 457, 458, 459, 460, 461, 462, 463, 464, 465, 466, 467, 469, 470, 474, 475, 476, 491, 493, 494, 495, 496, 498, 499, 500, 564.
  Warren, 524.
  William, 27, 30, 31, 58, 187, 278, 460, 461, 462, 464, 465, 466, 467, 469, 470, 474, 475, 476, 477, 478, 479, 480, 481, 482, 483, 484, 485, 486, 487, 488, 489, 490, 491, 492, 493, 539, 540, 554, 555, 558.
  William, Jr., 27, 187, 491, 492, 493, 494.
  Wm., Sen'r., 491, 492, 495.
Bugg,
  Anne, 309.
  Anselm, 367, 504.
  Edmund, 367, 504.
  Elizabeth, 252.
  Jacob, 367, 503.
  Lucy, 244.
  Saml., 367.
  Sharwood, 348, 501.
  Sherwd., 501.
Buggs, Sherwood, 366, 367.
Bullard, 293.
Bullock,
  David, 509.
  Edward, 104.
Burch, Eliza, 262.
Burchett,
  Ann, 279.
  Benj., 510, 515.
  Joseph, 504.
  Patsey, 309.
Burchit,
  Ben, 521, 522, 530, 559.
  John, 559.
  Thomas, 457.
Burdit, William, 534.
Burgamy, Wm., 511.
Burge, William, 305.
Burgemy, Wm., 363, 372, 377.
Burgimy, Mr., 39.
Burgwyn, Eliza, 154.

Burks,
  Richd., 508.
  Richard, 536.
  Richard F., 314.
Burnet, 530.
Burnett,
  Jeremiah, 107.
  John, 521.
Burnsall, 64.
Burnside, 114.
Burrell, Matilda, 316.
Burrow,
  Jarrel, 527.
  Patsey, 312.
Burt,
  Matthew, 387, 506, 511, 512, 513.
  William, 308.
Burton, 556.
Burton,
  Anne, 305.
  Hutchins, 256, 349, 350, 354, 503.
  Noel, 362.
Burwell, 548.
Burwell,
  Ann Powell, 235.
  Col., 510, 556.
  Frances Powell, 315.
  Henry H., 318.
  Lewis (Col.), 228, 508, 509.
  Panthea, 228, 315.
Busbee, Margaret, 161.
Bush Run, 74, 359.
Bush,
  Wm., 523, 524, 533.
Bushell, Polly, 304.
Bushy Forest, 150.
Buster, John, 273.
Butcher Creek, 369.
Butcher's Creek, 36, 37, 74, 252, 262, 348, 349, 355, 358, 370, 509.
Butler,
  Ann, 362.
  Benj. F. (Gen.), 109.
  Hannah, 503.
  Martha, 308.
  Wm., 506, 527.
Butterworth, Rebecca, 314.
Buxton,
  Anna Nash, 161.
  Cameron, 161.
  Caro, 161.
  Eliza McQueen, 161.
  Frances Ellen, 161.
  Jarvis, 161.
  Jarvis (Rev.), 160.
  Jarvis Barry, 161.

Buxton—Continued
  John Cameron, 161.
  Katherine Cameron, 160.
  Margaret Halliday, 161.
  Mary R., 161.
Buzendine, J., 107.

Byng, John, 104.
Bynum, Curtis, 197, 198, 256.
Byrd, 340.
Byrd,
  William, 162, 213, 265.
  William (Col.), 65.

C

Cabell,
  Ed. A. (Col.), 238.
  George C., 221.
  George K., 238.
  Pauline, 150.
  Sallie, 221.
  William (Col.), 150.
Cabells and Their Kin, The, 150.
Cabiness, Chas., 552.
Cadel, Stephen, 381, 385.
Cadle, Stephen, 389.
Cain,
  Betty, 304.
  Maxon, 312.
  Susanna, 305.
Calais, James, 421.
Caldwell,
  John, 333.
  William, 282, 339.
Caleb, Charlotte, 309.
Calhoon, James, 516.
Calhorn, Jas., 515.
Call,
  Anna, 161.
  Daniel, 161.
Caldwell,
  John, 25, 27, 73, 187.
  William, 73.
Calendar, Va. St. Papers, 108.
Callaham,
  David, 511.
  John, 368, 386, 431, 445, 447, 511, 544.
Callaway,
  Richard, 326.
  William, 326.
Callaway's Mill, 36, 327.
Calnel, John, 108.
Calvin,
  John, 391.
  Joseph, 312.
Camden Parish, 22, 23.
Cameron,
  Alan, 164.
  Anna, 164.
  Anna Nash, 160.

Cameron—Continued
  Anne, 157, 161.
  Anne M., 141.
  Anne Ruffin, 156.
  Ann Owen, 141.
  Ann Owen Nash, 151.
  Belle Mayo, 145.
  Bennehan, 144, 146, 148, 157.
    Memorial to Rev. John, 144.
  Bennehan (Mrs.), 131.
  Catherine, 161.
  Donald, 132, 164, 312.
  Duncan, 145, 149, 155, 157, 160, 164.
  Duncan (Judge), 146.
  Edward of Lochiel (Sir), 149.
  Elizabeth, 164.
  Emma, 164.
  Evelyn, 163.
  Evelyn Byrd, 163.
  Ewen, 132, 133, 315.
  Fanny, 163.
  Francis, 163.
  Frank (Capt.), 164.
  Frank (Prof.), 164.
  George, 306.
  George W., 163.
  Helen, 153, 164.
  Isabella Mayo, 157.
  Jean, 158, 317.
  Jeannie, 164.
  John, 163, 494, 496.
  John (Dr.), 188.
  John (Rev.), 20, 45, 84, 90, 97, 104, 132, 133, 134, 135, 136, 137, 138, 139, 140, 141, 142, 144, 145, 148, 149, 150, 151, 155, 198, 285, 299, 495, 498.
    Death of, 141.
    Elected Minister Cumberland Parish, 70.
    Marriage bond, 133.
    Memorial tablet to, 144.
    Miniature of, 131.
    Proposes to resign, 71.

Cameron—Continued
    Register of, 124, 170.
    Resigns, 140, 496-7.
    John Adams, 159.
    John D. (Col.), 151.
    John Donald, 160.
    Kate, 153, 155, 165.
    Katherine, 160.
    Margaret, 157.
    Margaret Bain, 145.
    Marshall, 164.
    Mary, 160, 164, 165.
    Mary Read, 131, 151, 315.
    Mary Warren, 157.
    Mildred Coles, 157.
    Paul, 155.
    Paul Carrington, 146, 156, 157
    Pauline Carrington, 157.
    Rebecca, 132, 155, 164.
    Rebecca Bennehan, 157.
    Robert Walker, 163.
    Sallie Talliaferro, 145, 157.
    Susie C., 163.
    Thomas, 27, 151, 164, 188.
    Thomas N., 141, 493.
    Walker Anderson, 162.
    William, 132, 141, 161.
    William (Dr.), 164.
    William (Rev.), 149.
    William E.,
        Editor, 162.
        Governor, 144, 145, 163.
        Mayor of Petersburg, 163.
    William Evelyn, 162.
    William Walker, 163.
Cameron Clan, 149.
Cameron, Genealogy, 149 et seq.
Cammeron,
    John, 489, 492.
    John (Rev.), 483, 484, 485, 486, 487, 488, 490, 491, 493.
    Thos., 491, 493.
Camp, John, 355, 359, 508, 510.
Campbell,
    Ann, 307.
    Frances H., 316.
    Robt., 502, 511.
Campbell Chronicles, 233, 239.
Campbell County, 22.
Cane Creek, 339.
Cappell, Robert, 495.
Cargill,
    Cornelius, 36, 49, 327, 328.
    John, 326.
    Sarah H., 315.
Carleton, Susannah, 199.

Carleton, Thomas, 369, 508, 509.
Caroline County, 60.
Carrington,
    George, 351, 354.
    Paul, 155, 256, 342, 345, 351.
Carter,
    Ann Hill, 229.
    Charles, 229.
    Francis, 211.
    Isabella, 127.
    John, 304.
    Josephine, 127.
    Landon (Col.), 64.
    Raleigh, 127, 316.
    Sharpe, 127.
    Thomas, 304.
    William, 127, 314.
    William R., 127.
Cason, 293.
Cate,
    John, 307.
    Milly, 311.
Cates,
    Curtis, 107, 514.
    Curtis, 107, 514.
    Jas., 107.
Cattillo, Edward, 394.
Cattle, James, 308.
Caudel, Stephen, 391.
Caudle, Stephen, 359.
Cauldwell,
    John, 324, 334.
    Wm., 338.
Cauthorn, 293.
Chamberlayne, C. G. (Dr.), 19.
Chambers Family, 188.
Chambers,
    Ann W., 190.
    Anne W., 316.
    Ann Walthall, 108, 116.
    Cincy, 189.
    Edward, 116, 188, 189, 453, 563, 564.
    Edward R., 71, 116, 190, 564.
    Eliza, 116, 189.
    Elizabeth, 189.
    Henry, 190,
        Senator from Ala., 190.
        Monument to, 116.
    Jennie, 189.
    John, 188.
    Judge, 190.
    Lucy, 189.
    Martha, 116, 190.
    Martha C., 318.
    Moses, 188.

Chambers—Continued
  Nancy, 189.
  Polly, 189.
  Robert, 116.
  Sally, 315.
  Tempie, 189.
  Thomas, 27, 30, 53, 116, 188, 386, 410, 411, 412, 413, 414, 417, 420, 421, 424, 425, 429, 433, 434, 435, 439, 440, 441, 442, 443, 444, 445, 446, 526, 527, 557, 563.
  William, 188, 551, 552, 554, 557, 564.
Chambers, Old place, 116.
Chambliss, Betsey, 307.
Chandler,
  Joel, 349.
  John, 345, 515, 516.
  Joseph, 377, 516, 518.
  Keziah, 198.
  Rebecca, 198.
  Robert, 377.
  Timothy, 549.
  William, 198, 370, 388, 515, 516, 517, 531, 548.
Chapel, Elizabeth, 306.
Chapman, John, 307.
Chappel,
  Robert, 541.
  Thomas, 560.
Chappell,
  Anna, 191.
  Betsy, 192.
  James, 191.
  John, 191, 192, 452, 560.
  John C., 318.
  Martha, 192, 311.
  Mary, 191.
  Molly, 192.
  Phil E., 191.
  Robert, 27, 106, 190, 192, 404, 499, 500, 526, 542, 545, 551, 552, 554, 557, 563, 564.
  Thomas, 191, 554.
  William, 191, 560.
Chappell, Dickie and Kindred Families, 191.
Chappells Road, 472.
Chapel, ordered, 36.
Charles[worth], Michael, 336.
Charlesworth, Michael, 331, 337.
Charlotte County, 22, 86, 134, 155.
Chase City, 37.
Chase, Melvin Dietz, 152.
Chase, Melvin D. (Mrs.), 131.

Cheatham,
  Leonard, 519.
  Stephen, 561.
  Thomas, 259.
Cheatom, Leonard, 506.
Cheaves, Joel, 304.
Cherrystone Creek, 339.
Chester, Bishop of, 132.
Chestney, Mary Courtney, 156.
Chesterfield County, 109, 115.
Childress, John, 505.
Childs, Henry, 348.
Chiles, 511.
Chipley, Clara, 154.
Chisolm, 512.
Chisolm,
  William, 541, 542, 552.
  Wm., Jr., 552.
Christ Church, Middlesex Co., 18.
Christanna, Fort, 213.
Christian County, Ky., 171.
Christian, Mrs. Aurelius, 233.
Christopher,
  Covie, 387.
  David, 369.
  Jacobus, 413, 514, 524.
Christ's Church, Pensacola, 159.
Church, dis-establishment of, 147.
Cinque Ports, 214.
City Point, 110.
Claiborn,
  Daniel, 99, 257, 350, 361, 364, 372.
  Leonard, 351.
Claiborne Family, 192.
Claiborne, 537.
Claiborne,
  Augustine, 519, 520.
  Daniel, 27, 29, 54, 192, 193, 360, 365, 366, 370, 371, 374, 375, 378, 379, 380, 382, 383, 384, 386, 395, 400, 412, 514.
  Daniel (Capt.), 407.
  Henry, 193.
  John, 193.
  John Herbert (Dr.), 193.
  Leonard, 193.
  L., 346.
  Mary, 193.
  Matthew M., 312.
  Richard, 27, 30, 41, 192, 413, 414, 415, 416, 417, 418, 419, 420, 421, 425, 427, 428, 429, 435, 513, 517, 523.
  Richard (Capt.), 533.
  Richard Henry, 193.
Claiborne County, Miss., 244.

INDEX

Clan, Cameron, 149.
Clapton, 527.
Clardy, 529.
Clark, 556.
Clark,
  Alice, 123.
  Benj., 522.
  Benjamin, 531.
  Elizabeth, 310.
  Field, 561, 562.
  John, 561.
  Richard, 113, 556.
  William, 312.
Clarke, 537.
Clarke,
  Field, 452, 561.
  Frances, 279.
  George, 278.
  John, 537.
Clarren, John M., 308.
Clay Family, 194.
Clay,
  Betsy, 194.
  Charles Carlus, 194.
  Edward, 536.
  Eliza, 194, 195.
  John, 194.
  Levi, 194, 195.
  Martha, 194.
  Milley, 296.
  Mitchell, 194.
  Obed, 194, 195, 452.
  Obediah, 27, 468, 560.
  Obey, 469.
  Olin, 194.
  Orbin, 194.
  Polly W., 194.
  Thomas, 194.
  Thomas Chappell, 191.
  Woodson, 194.
Clayton,
  Jane, 290.
  Miss, 290.
  Thomas, 311.
Cleaton,
  John, 500.
  Wm., 500.
Clements,
  Benjamin, 345.
  Margaret, 304.
  Susanna, 311.
  William, 305.
Clergy, Colonial,
  Character of, 84.
  Migratory course of, 142.
  Poorly supported, 142.

Clerk,
  Benj., 403.
  John, 367.
Cleveland,
  Kate, 125.
  Martha, 309.
Clopton, John, 170.
Coadle, Bryan, 504.
Coal, James, 507, 517, 518.
Coalbreath,
  Edward, 378.
  Wm., 370.
Coalman,
  Cleuviers, 505.
  Cleveres, 387.
  Cleveris, 515, 516.
  James, 367.
  Richard, 355, 369, 507.
Coalson, Abram, 505.
Coates, Edwd., 518.
Coats, Henry, 518.
Cobb,
  Benj., 541.
  Wingfield, 342.
Cobbs,
  Anne, 115.
  John P. (Dr.), 238.
Cobham, 104.
Cock,
  Abram, 510, 512, 513.
  James, 504.
  Peter, 512.
Cocke,
  Abraham, 107, 283, 423, 527, 541, 542, 552, 555.
  John, 548.
  Lucy Herbert, 309.
  Mary, 305.
  P., 552.
  Richard, 520, 521.
  Richd. (Col.), 520.
  Thomas, 423, 551.
  Thomas T., 316.
Cockerham,
  Ben, 515, 516, 522.
  Benjamin, 531.
  Mary, 430, 435, 441, 540, 456, 513, 525, 526, 540.
  Miner, 511.
  Moses, 506, 520, 521.
  Philip, 398.
  Phillip, 362.
  Phil, 516, 521.
  Phil, Sr., 530.
  Philp, 510.

Cockerham—Continued
  Widow, 507.
  William, 454, 518, 529, 545, 553.
Cockram, Henry, 334.
Cock Road, 472.
Cocks, Abraham, 541.
Cocks Creek, 367.
Codell, Stephen, 376.
Codle, Stephen, 372.
Cogbill,
  Frances, 312.
  William, 312.
Cole,
  Johanna, 189.
  John, 345.
  Mark, 74, 338.
Coleman, 530.
Coleman,
  Clus, 559.
  Cluverius, 521.
  Fanny, 296.
  Frances Rebecca, 121.
  Green, 314.
  James, 326.
  John, 205.
  L. Ashton, 121.
  Mary Embry, 205.
  Richard, 521, 522, 531.
  Walter Emerson, 121.
College Plantation, 203.
Colonial Church,
  Corrupt state of, 85.
Colonial Church in Va., The, 136, 138.
Colonial Dames, 18.
Colonial Governors,
  Controversy with vestries, 59.
Colonial Virginia Register, 150, 284.
Colonial Wars, 187.
Columbia Institute, 160.
Colley, Nathaniel, 312.
Collier,
  Ben, 403, 514, 524.
  David W., 307.
  Howel, 367, 502.
  Nathll., 502.
Collins,
  Annie Cameron, 156.
  Alice Ruffin, 157.
  George Pumpelly (Maj.), 156.
  George William Kent, 157.
  Henrietta Page, 157.
  James, 340.
  Mary Arthur, 157.

Collins—Continued
  Paul Cameron, 157.
  Rebecca Anderson, 157.
Combs, 518.
Combs, Phillip, 539.
Comer, 517.
Comer, Samuel, 518, 534.
Confederate States, 108.
Connell, John, 107.
Connolly, Reps (Capt.), 119, 120.
Conquest, E. H., 128.
Consolvent, John, 362, 373, 376, 381.
Consolver, John, 362.
Convention of 1776, 207.
Convention of May 20, 1786, 461.
Cook,
  Benjamin, 311, 313.
  Betty, 176.
  Charles, 528, 545.
  Henry, 452.
  John, 517, 523, 532, 533.
  Nathll., 503.
  Polly, 313.
  Sarah, 313.
  William, 74, 338.
Cooper,
  Edmund, 304.
  Francis, 546, 547.
  Frank, 520.
  John, 543, 544, 505, 520.
  John, Senr., 543.
  Richard W., 308.
Corbin, Frances, 150.
Cornett, Mary, 119.
Cornwall Parish, 22, 134, 457, 385.
Cortney,
  Clack, 501, 502.
  Doct., 501.
Cosby,
  John, 218.
  Melinda, 313.
  William, 307.
Cotten Creek, 367.
Cotton,
  Cary, 313.
  Celia, 309.
  Franca, 312.
  Hardy, 310.
  John, 307.
Cotillo, Edward, 391, 398.
Couche's Creek, 205, 403, 422, 452, 473.
Council, Betty, 158.
County Courts, 25.
Court House, 37.

INDEX 583

Courthouse Church, 362, 371.
Court House Road, 403, 422, 453.
Courtney, Clack, 359, 372.
Cousins,
  Martha, 108, 116, 189.
  Peter, 541, 542, 552.
Covington, 517.
Covington,
  Edmond, 519.
  Elizabeth, 312.
Cowan,
  Gracie B., 317.
  Grizel Bowie, 180.
  Peggy, 180.
  Peggy Baker, 207.
  William, 179, 207.
  William B., 317.
  William Bowie, 180.
Cowington, Edwd., 511.
Cox Family, 195.
Cox, 333, 337, 353, 548.
Cox,
  Anne, 197.
  Barclay, 199.
  Bartlet, 556.
  Bartlett, 532.
  Bartley, 195, 196, 199.
  Col., 506.
  Delitia, 198.
  Edith, 199.
  Elizabeth, 364.
  Franky Coleman, 199.
  Frederick, 196, 199.
  George, 314.
  John, 27, 29, 36, 48, 49, 63, 195, 196, 197, 199, 331, 332, 334, 335, 338, 339, 341, 342, 343, 344, 346, 354, 355, 357, 358, 387, 516, 517, 532, 549.
  John, Jr., 369, 515.
  Mary, 196, 197, 199.
  Mr., 37.
  Nancy, 197.
  Richard, 197.
  Tabitha, 199.
  Talitha, 196.
  Tallitha, 199.
  Wm., 355.
Coxes Bridge, 474.
Coxes Road, 403, 404, 421, 423, 473, 451, 452, 454, 531.
Cozen, Chas., 503.
Cozens,
  Charles, 502.
  Robert, 504.

Crafton,
  James, 560.
  Richard, 536.
Craghead,
  George, 562.
  George (Maj.), 261.
  Mr., 562.
  William, 562.
Craig, 401.
Craig,
  Ann Mary, 117.
  Ann Walthall, 119.
  Catherine, 117.
  Edward Chambers, 116.
  Edward Chambers (Maj.), 108.
  Edward Orgain, 117.
  Elizabeth, 119.
  Elizabeth Montfort, 117.
  Ella Archer, 117.
  Florence Overton, 118.
  Frances, 124.
  Francis, 316.
  George, 108, 116, 190, 316.
  George Edward, 109, 116.
  Gladys, 121.
  Hal Chambers, 117.
  Henrietta Chambers, 119.
  James, 356, 370, 374, 375, 379, 386, 390, 393, 396, 397, 400, 402, 406, 410, 412, 413, 416, 418, 424, 433, 434, 436, 438, 440, 442, 461, 464.
  James (Dr.), 119.
  James (Rev.), 20, 41, 44, 49, 51, 52, 53, 56, 57, 66, 67, 68, 69, 70, 72, 83, 84, 91, 95, 96, 98, 99, 100, 101, 102, 103, 104, 105, 108, 111, 112, 114, 115, 124, 139, 142, 177, 190, 285, 364, 365, 366, 371, 376, 383, 384, 388, 391, 394, 404, 408, 411, 414, 417, 419, 420, 421, 425, 426, 427, 428, 429, 432, 435, 439, 441, 449, 450, 454, 460, 462, 463, 467, 470, 471, 472, 474, 475, 476, 477, 478, 479, 481, 482, 483, 484, 487, 519, 528, 564.
    death of, 70,
    Mill of, 102.
  James W., Jr., 117.
  James White, 117.
  Jayne Stokes, 118.
  Jesse Basket, 117.
  John Anthony, 109, 112, 116.
  John Tyre, 117.
  Katherine Daisy, 117.

Craig—Continued
  Martha Anderson, 124.
  Martha Cousins, 116.
  Mary, 484.
  Mary Ann, 117.
  Mary Booker, 124.
  Mary B., 285, 314.
  Mary Tarry, 116.
  Minnie, 117.
  Philip, 98.
  Robert Lee, 119.
  Samuel Bacon, 117.
  St. George Tucker, 118.
  Sue, 117.
  Thomas, 117, 119.
  Virginia, 117.
  Waddy Street, 109, 110, 111, 117.
  William Stone, 117.
Craige, James (Rev.), 380.
Cralle,
  Richard Kenner, 314.
  Susanna, 315.
  Thomas, 454.
  William, 317, 538.
  William M., 550.
  William Matthew, 437.
Crammer, Mary, 312.
Crasmuch, Michael, 313.
Crawford, Dr., 359.
Craws, Wm., 506.
Creath, William (Rev.), 271.
Crenshaw, 557.
Crenshaw,
  Cornelius, 549.
  Daniel, 257.
  Henry, 523, 534.
  Jane, 314.
  Robert, 422, 539.
  Tho., 533.
Creighton, Hugh, 343.
Crews,
  Josiah, 438.
  Peter, 524, 538.
  Richd., 514, 524.
Crider, John, 305.
Crenshaw, Cornelius, 517.
Crites, Hamar, 339.
Crockett Creek, 402.
Crooked Creek, 203, 421, 451.
Cross, 512.
Cross,
  Chas., 107, 294.
  Jane, 283.
  John, 107, 223, 437, 453, 526, 527, 551, 557, 563, 564.

Cross—Continued
  Mary, 223.
  Phoebe, 294.
  Rebecca, 315.
  Richard, 315, 520.
  William, 520, 526, 539, 451.
Crosses Bridge, 404, 423, 453.
Crouse, Prue, 161.
Crowder, 505.
Crowder,
  Abraham, 508.
  Bartholomew, 246.
  Elizabeth, 313.
  Martha J., 246.
Cruickshank, Mrs. Ernest, 160.
Crump, Stephen, 389, 391, 394.
Crupper Run, 531.
Crymes,
  George, 561.
  Nancey, 208.
  Thomas, 437, 550, 561.
  William, 422, 536.
Cub Creek, 326, 333, 346, 347.
Cubb Creek, 212, 282.
Cumberland Parish, 19, 20, 21, 25, 32, 33, 39, 48, 51, 61, 64, 66, 73, 80, 91, 98, 139, 142, 143, 145, 182, 242, 314.
  Cameron, Rev. John, resigns, 140.
  Decline of, 95 et seq.
  Map of, facing, 23.
  Trustees elected 1831, 565.
Cunningham,
  James, 349, 504.
  Jane, 515.
  John, 421, 531, 534, 535, 548.
  Martha, 222.
  Obedience, 313.
  William, 304, 531, 533.
Cunninghams, William, 421.
Cureton Family, 200.
Cureton,
  Ann, 311.
  Charles, 200.
  Edward, 528.
  Frances, 200.
  John, 27, 106, 200, 449, 450, 454, 455, 458, 459, 538, 562.
  John, Jr., 453.
  Louisey, 200.
  Nathaniel, 200.
  Wm., 403, 524, 525.
  William, 531, 556.
Currie, Ellyson, 316.
Curtis, 519.

Currytuck, 213.
Cushman,
  Rebecca, 160.
  Walter, 160.
Cuttilla, John, 513.
Cuttillo,
  A., 450.
  Abrm., 448, 456.
Cuttillo—Continued
  Abraham, 528, 564.
  Edward, 385, 389, 405, 509, 443, 446.
  Elizabeth, 450.
  Willm., 415.
  William, 419, 425, 427, 430, 434, 441, 443, 445, 446, 448, 450, 456.

D

Dacus,
  John, 533.
  Nathaniel, 533.
Daily News, 162.
Dalton,
  Timothy, 340.
  Wm., 333.
Dance,
  Mary, 310.
  Rhode, 311.
Dandridge, Mary, 228.
Daniel,
  Cary Wells, 527.
  James, 326.
  John Holloway, 311.
  John W., 163.
  Lucy, 313.
  Patsey, 308.
  Thomas, 313.
Dan River, 36, 79, 339, 340.
Dante, Va., 123.
Davenport,
  Joseph, 308.
  Nancy, 311.
  Susanna, 305.
David, John, 326.
Davies,
  Jacob, 395.
  Jonathan, 507.
  Joseph, 359, 373, 394, 396, 515, 555.
  Samuel (Rev.), 86.
  Samuel D., 318.
  Wm., 367, 501, 507.
Davis, 293.
Davis,
  Abraham, 547.
  Amanda Eliza, 222.
  Ashley, 223, 224.
  Ashley L., 221.
  Copeland, 220, 223, 225.
  Eliza, 220, 222, 223, 225.
  Elizabeth, 223.
  Hannah, 200.

Davis—Continued
  Jane, 223, 224, 225.
  John, 306, 519.
  John, Jr., 176.
  Jonathan, 403, 535, 536.
  Joseph, 522, 531.
  Joseph Cabell, 221.
  Lucy, 221.
  Lucy Garland, 221, 223.
  Maria, 220, 225.
  Mary, 220, 224, 225.
  Mary C., 224.
  Mary Jane, 220.
  Jefferson (President), 128, 154.
  Mary Pocahontas, 221.
  Nicholas, 225.
  Nicholas E., 222.
  Nicholas Edmunds, 220, 221.
  Polly, 315.
  Shepherd, 305.
  William, 310, 348, 544.
  Wm. (Capt.), 501.
  Zachariah, 527, 528, 540, 541, 545, 554.
Dawes, James, 368, 505, 506.
Daws,
  James, 528.
  Joel, 564.
Dawson, Commissary, 59, 62, 99, 329, 335, 336, 356.
Day,
  John F., 211.
  Mary, 289, 291, 293.
  W. H., 164.
Dayer, Leonard, 514.
Dean, 328.
Declaration of Independence, 141.
DeGerrett, Daniel, 41, 42, 431, 433, 457.
DeGraffenreid,
  Betsey Ann, 317.
  Boswell B., 227, 317.
DeGraffenreidt,
  Capt., 536.

DeGraffenreidt—Continued
 Francis, 554.
 Frans., 556.
 T., 546.
 Tschr., 404.
 Tscharner, 438, 454, 507, 516, 518, 521, 522, 528, 529, 530, 535, 553, 555.
 William, 437, 452, 522, 550, 560.
Degraffenreidt's road, 403.
DeGraffenreidt's rolling road, 422, 452.
Degraffenreidt's Rowling Road, 403.
Dejarnott, Danl., 106.
Dejernatt, Daniel, 550, 553.
Dejernett, Daniel, 435, 436.
Delony Family, 201.
Delony, 331.
Delony,
 Edward, 202.
 Fanny, 202.
 Henry, 201, 202, 358, 503, 504.
 L., 26, 29, 35, 327, 329, 331.
 Lewis, 26, 27, 32, 33, 38, 201, 202, 262, 324, 325, 328, 329, 370.
 Lucy, 202.
 Mary, 202.
 Mr., 48.
 William, 202.
Demovill, Samuel, 304.
Denhart,
 Lucretia, 313.
 Shadrach, 310.
Denning, Vera, 221.
Dennis, Richard, 544.
Denny, John, 337.
Department of Archives, of Virginia, 18.
Derr. John S., 235.
Deuprey, Thos., 420.
Devoll, Samll., 512.
Devol, Samuel, 512.
Dick, James, 511.
Dickinson, William E., 215.
Dicks,
 James, 386, 511, 519.
 Jemima, 268.
Dickson, 515.
Dingles,
 Ann, 419, 427, 430, 435.
 Anna, 443.
Dinton, James, 312.
Diocesan School, 145.
Dis-establishment, of Episcopal Church, 7.

Disleman, Drury, 313.
Dissent,
 basis of movement of, 83,
 movement economic, 88.
Dissenters,
 Baptists, 86,
 Methodists, 86,
 Presbyterians, 86,
 Rise of, 11.
Dixon Family, 202.
Dixon,
 Jenny, 308.
 John, 451, 558.
 Pattey, 268.
 Robert, 27, 169, 202, 203, 307, 403, 442, 444, 445, 446, 449, 538.
 Robert (Capt.), 202.
Dixson, Thos., 500.
Doak, John, 349.
Doake, John, 510.
Dobbyns, Wm., 333.
Dobson,
 Joseph, 362, 372.
 Joseph (Dr.), 376.
Dobyns, 338.
Dobyns, Wm., 333, 334.
Dod,
 Agness, 354.
 Agnis, 358.
Dodd,
 Agatha, 376.
 Agnes, 342, 345.
 Agness, 351, 372.
 Margaret, 311.
Dolony, Henry, 367.
Donaldson,
 Francis, 265.
 Frank, Jr., 265.
 John Willcox, 265.
 Wm. Hamilton Macfarland, 265.
Donithon, Wm., 509.
Doran, 328.
Dortch, David, 367, 502, 503.
Doswell, Mary E. P., 317.
Dosyer, Lenonard, 403.
Dougherty, Joseph, 306.
Douglas Register, 19.
Dover Castle, 214.
Downman, Elizabeth Osborne, 311.
Downshire, Marquis of, 150.
Dowsing,
 Everd, 387.
 Everard, 408, 422, 511, 512, 528, 533, 540, 541.
 Mr., 545.
 William, 453.

INDEX 587

Dowsings, Edward, 506.
Dozer, 557, 562.
Dozer,
  Leonard, 550, 561.
  Mr., 550.
  William, 437, 550, 551.
Dozier,
  Leonard, 514.
  Thos., 107.
  William, 107.
Draper, Nancy, 310.
Drapier, Soloman, 508.
Drayman, Alexr., 308.
Dresser, Mr. (Rev.), 103.
Drummon, Aaron, 522, 545, 564.
Drumright, William, Jr., 244.
Drury's Bluff, 109.
Dudley,
  Ann, 193.
  Edward, 193.
Duffeys, Samuel, 391.
Duke,
  Taylor, 502.
  John Taylor, 350.
Duncan & Co., Chas., 275.
Dunman, Joseph, 421.
Dunmans, Joseph, 519.

Dunn,
  Archer (Capt.), 109.
  David, 224.
  Eliza, 224.
  Elizabeth, 224, 309.
  Fannie Gray, 222.
  Gray, 222.
  Nathaniel, 306.
  Thomas, 307.
du Pont,
  Coleman, 265.
  Rence de Pelleport, 265.
Dupree, 557.
Dupree,
  Lewis, 508.
  Thos., 514, 561.
Duran,
  Margaret, 307.
  Mary, 314.
Dyer,
  Amey, 312.
  Edward Ryan, 235.
  Robert, 368, 526.
Dyson,
  Daniel, 308.
  Sally, 311.

E

Ealbank, Daniel, 508.
Ealbanks, Richd., 515.
Eanes,
  E. Chambers, 124.
  John, 311.
  John E., 123.
  John Orgain, 124.
  Marie Harrison, 124.
  Virginia Craig, 124.
Earl, John, 38, 362, 370, 371, 376, 503.
Early, R. H., 233.
Early Virginia Immigrants, 215.
Easland,
  Joseph, 367.
  Thomas, 348, 376.
Easter,
  James, 347.
  John (Rev.), 88.
  Robert, 509.
Eastham, 537.
Eastham,
  Ann, 209.
  James, 523.
  Julany Ann, 208.

Easthem, 556.
Easthem,
  James, 422, 537, 561.
  Mr., 550.
Eastis,
  Bartlett, 404.
  Elisha, 387, 405.
  Robt., 392, 398.
  Zack., 403.
Eastmen, Julany Ann, 208.
Eccles, Olive, 160.
Eckles, Sally, 305.
Edin, 515.
Eddings, 522.
Eddings,
  Anny, 563.
  Theophilus, 437, 540, 551.
  William, 437, 526, 541, 551, 552, 557.
Eddins, Wm., 516.
Edgar, Jane, 308.
Edloe Family, 203.
Edloe, 336, 337, 340, 511.
Edloe,
  Ann, 217.

Edloe—Continued
  Henry L., 203.
  John, 27, 29, 203, 217, 332, 335, 506.
  Matthew, 203.
  William, 217.
Edmonds,
  Nicholas, 514.
  Thomas, 206.
Edmondson,
  Ben, 453.
  Benjamin, 554, 557, 563.
Edmund, Mary, 315.
Edmunds, 557.
Edmunds,
  Benj., 164.
  Col., 561.
  Elizabeth, 219.
  Lucy Gray, 220.
  Mary, 164.
  Nicholas, 219.
  Sterling, 219.
Edmundson,
  Benj., 106.
  Benjamin, 295.
  Betsy, 315.
  Constant, 282.
  Thos., 504.
Edwards,
  Caro Buxton, 161.
  Stephen, 307.
  Susannah, 308.
  Thos., 387, 423, 506, 511, 512, 513, 528, 545, 555.
  Walter, 164.
  William, 164, 508.
Egerton, Louisa C., 163.
Elam,
  Martin, 272.
  Mary, 272.
Eldridge, Mary, 310.
Ellidge Family, 203.
Ellidge, 332, 333, 337, 340.
Ellidge,
  Elizabeth, 204.
  Francis, 27, 203, 332, 335.
  Mary, 204.
  Mr., 37.
  William, 204.
Elliott,
  Geo., 515.
  John, 550.
  Martin, 107, 452.
  Richard, 515.
  Robert, 540.
Ellis Family, 204.

Ellis,
  Abraham, 204.
  Ann, 205.
  Daniel, 204.
  Ellison, 27, 421, 437, 460, 531, 532, 548, 549.
  Ellison (Capt.), 204.
  Ellyson, 204.
  Elson, 516.
  Henry S., 315.
  James, 204.
  Jeremiah, 204.
  Joanna, 205.
  John, 508, 513, 525.
  John (Col.), 237.
  Lucy, 237.
  Lydia, 204.
  Mary, 205, 314.
  Nathaniel, 204.
  Priscilla, 204.
  Richard, 513, 516.
  William, 266, 564.
  Winston, 525.
  W. M. (Rev.), 210.
Elizabeth City Parish, 183.
Elmore, Atha, 527.
Embry Family, 205.
Embry, 356, 357, 506, 528, 545.
Embry,
  Eliza, 206.
  Elizabeth, 372.
  Ermine, 206.
  Henry, 206, 337, 453, 541, 554.
  Henry (Col.), 205.
  Henry, Jr., 205, 206.
  Martha, 205.
  Mary, 205.
  Sarah, 205.
  William, 27, 29, 205, 206, 335, 337, 338, 341, 342, 343, 344, 345, 346, 351, 353, 354, 355, 357, 358, 360, 361, 363, 364, 365, 507, 512, 529.
Emmanuel College, 64.
Emporia, Va., 229.
Enquirer, The, 162.
Epes,
  Anne, 223.
  Archer Jones, 223.
  Bettie Garland, 222.
  Catherine G., 317.
  Copeland Davis, 222.
  Dudley Dunn, 223.
  Effee, 305.
  Edward Dromgoole, 223.
  Fannie, 222.

Epes—Continued
  Fannie Ashley, 223.
  Fletcher, 223.
  Fran, 320.
  Francis, 206, 315.
  John, 316, 317.
  John C., 206.
  Junius, 221.
  Martha, 317.
  Martha C., 222.
  Mary H., 222.
  Peter, 31, 206, 207, 315, 489, 490, 491, 500.
  Peter, Jr., 490.
  Richard, 222, 223, 315.
  Richard J., 222.
  Roberta L., 221, 223.
  Sarah G., 320.
  Susanna Irby, 315.
  Thomas, 222.
  Victor, 222.
  William, 306.
  William P., 206.
Episcopal Church,
  Convention of 1787, 464.
  Property of, 57, 470.
Episcopal Clergy,
  Failure to comply with law respecting marriages, 16.
Episcopal Ministers,
  Number of, in Colonial Era, 18.
Epperson,
  Jonathan, 268.
  Sarah, 268.
Epps Family, 206.
Eppes,
  Christian, 310.
  Elizabeth, 314.
  Elizabeth Taylor, 304.
  Francis (Col.), 207.
  Lewellin, 207.
  Littleberry (Col.), 207.
  Peter, 174, 175.
Epps,
  Edward, 500.
  Fras., 513.
  Francis, 526, 542, 552.
  John, 512, 513, 564.

Epps—Continued
  Peter, 27, 489.
Erskine,
  Martha, 304.
  Thomas, 532.
Essex Co., Eng., 218.
Established Church,
  Burden of taxes, 82.
  Davies, Rev. Samuel on, 86.
Este, John, 338.
Estes,
  Benjamin, 168, 435, 562.
  Benjamin, Jr., 454.
  Edmund, 247.
  Elisha, 107, 562.
  Martha, 247.
  Milly, 199.
  Moses, 529.
  Richard, 539, 540.
  Robert, 199, 523, 533, 550, 555, 558.
  Robert, Junr., 421, 532.
  Robert, Sr., 526.
  Samuel, 549, 559.
  Zachary, 524.
Esthem, Elizabeth, 200.
Estis,
  Bartilot, 514.
  Bartlett, Sr., 525.
  Elisha, 513.
  Robert, 513, 514, 518.
Evans, 537.
Evans,
  Ben, 532, 549.
  Charles, 501.
  Dick, 502.
  Evan, 513.
  John, 528.
  Major, 501.
  Pricilla, 314.
  Richard, 513.
  Robert, 513, 515, 525.
  Stephen, 349, 369, 510, 513.
  William, 438, 517, 532, 545, 555.
Evins, Theo., 550.
Evening Shade, Ark., 117.
Ewing, Mildred, 155.
Ezell, John, 350, 366.

F

Falkner, Margaret, 308.
Fallett, Catherine, 310.
Falling River, 249, 282, 288, 326.
Farguson,
  Benj., 519, 520.

Farguson—Continued
  James, 268.
  Joel, 268, 387, 389, 513, 539.
Farintosh, 151.

Farley,
  Henry, 535, 536, 554, 560.
  Seth, 452, 560.
Farmer Family, 207.
Farmer,
  America, 211.
  Benjamin, 208, 209, 211, 212, 347.
  Betsy W., 210.
  Bettie, 210.
  Dicey, 211.
  Dycie, 208.
  Edward Lambert, 117.
  Elijah, 208, 209.
  Elizabeth, 209.
  Grief, 211.
  Henry, 208, 210, 211.
  Isham, 212,
  James, 208, 209.
  James Hatchett, 117.
  Jeremiah, 208, 209.
  John, 208, 209, 210, 212.
  John Herrin, 211.
  Joseph, 210.
  Julany Ann, 208.
  "Lod," Jr., 208.
  Lodewick, 494.
  Lodowick, 27, 30, 31, 207, 208, 209, 211, 212, 431, 443, 444, 452, 495, 496, 498, 535, 536.
  Lodwk., 387.
  Lodwick, 490, 491, 492, 493, 513, 514, 561.
  Lucinda, 211.
  Mark, 212.
  Martha, 211.
  Mary, 211.
  Mary Anne, 211.
  Polly, 210.
  Sally Cheatham, 208.
  Sarah, 209, 212.
  Sarah C., 211.
  Stephen, 212.
  Thomas, 208.
  William A., 209, 210, 211.
Farrar,
  George, 367, 504.
  Thos., 367.
Fawn, William, 311.
Fayetteville, N. C., 160.
Fennil, Eli, 515.
Ferguson,
  Catherine, 268.
  Horatio, 268.
  James, 268.
  Joel, 268.
  Mary, 268.

Ferguson—Continued
  Thomas, 268.
  William, 268, 310.
Ferintosh, Scotland, 145.
Ferrel, James, 504.
Ferril, James, 503.
Ferth Family, 212.
Ferth, 329.
Ferth,
  Daniel, 26, 27, 35, 212, 325, 327, 328.
  Mr., 34.
Fertintosh, Scotland, 149.
Fewqua, Patsey, 304.
Field,
  Alexander S., 312.
  Mary, 308.
  Nelly, 306.
  Theophilus, 307.
Finch, Henry, 512.
Finn, Amey, 307.
Fisher,
  James, 511.
  John Ravenscroft, 308.
  William, 437, 451, 523, 533.
Fitzgerald,
  Catherine, 317.
  Elizabeth, 315.
  Francis, 314, 316.
  Thomas, 318.
Finneywood Creek, 195.
Firth,
  Danl., 212.
  Betty, 212.
Fitzpatrick, Eliz., 164.
Flack, Mildred, 305.
Flat Rock Church, 43, 44, 372, 376, 377, 386, 420, 424, 433, 480, 487, 488.
Flat Rock Creek, 37, 39, 102, 104, 185, 186, 203, 225, 368, 386, 472, 511.
Flatrock Road, 472.
Flatt Creek, 325, 350.
Flatt Rock Church, 387, 464, 527,
  Gallery in, 438.
  Repairs, 481.
Flatt Rock Creek, 359, 387, 451, 519, 527, 564.
Flatt Rock Road, 402, 404, 421, 423, 451.
Fleming,
  Col., 516, 517.
  John, 522, 531, 532.
  Jon. (Col.), 517.
Fletcher, Nathan, 316.

Flournoy, Gideon, 115.
Floyd, 547.
Floyd, Robt., 107, 547.
Folio, Luke, 509.
Folks, Nancy, 313.
Fontaine Family, 212.
Fontaine, 338.
Fontaine,
  Abraham, 174.
  Moses, 174.
  John, 213.
  Peter, 27, 212, 249, 341, 342, 343.
  Peter (Col.), 514.
  Peter (Rev.), 213.
  Peter, Jr., 213.
  Fontain, 339.
  Fontane, 337.
  Fontane, Peter, 335.
Foote, William Henry (Rev.), on condition of churches, 94.
Ford,
  Jeremiah, 310.
  Sarah, 313.
Forest, John, 435, 436.
Fork Church, 74, 339.
Forrest, John, 527.
Fort Christanna, 213.
Fortress Monroe, 109.
Foster,
  George, 347.
  Moses, 547.
  Ransom, 555, 556.
  Seth, 304.
  Tho., 547.
Fountains, Peter (Col.), 514.
Foust, John, 435.
Fowler,
  Mary Briggs, 192.
  Sarah, 192.
  Wilmouth, 192.

Fowlkes,
  Asa, 211.
  Sterling, 257.
Fox, Richard, 237, 348, 367.
Frail,
  Pat, 342, 375.
  Patrick, 345, 371.
Frailes, Patrick, 351.
Franklin,
  Ben, 527, 544.
  Hugh, 508.
Franklin County, 22, 23.
Franklyn, Alexander, 309.
Fray,
  A. G., 123.
  Audrey Lee, 123.
  Gaines, Jr., 123.
Freeman, 511.
Freeman,
  Benjamin, 531.
  Capt., 369.
  Hamlin, 511.
  Henry, 421, 521, 530.
  John, 304, 531.
  Joseph, 508.
  Joseph (Capt.), 362.
  Keziah, 304.
Freemans, 519.
French and Indian Wars, 187, 280.
Friend,
  Joseph B., 127, 130.
  Mary, 314.
Fullilove,
  Anthony, 523, 533.
  Wm., 533.
Fullylove, Wm., 518.
Fulton, Robert (Prof.), 235.
Fuqua, William, 326.
Fuquay, Wm., 346.

G

Gadis, Thos., 359.
Gafford, 537, 556.
Gafford, Tho., 537.
Gaines, Henry P., 198.
Gaines' Mill, 120.
Gale, Josiah, 514.
Gales, Seaton (Maj.), 165.
Gallimore,
  James, 543, 544.
  Wm., 543, 544.
Galt, Lucy, 235.

Garden,
  James (Rev.), 68, 72.
  Rev. Mr., 67, 363.
Garland Family, 214.
  Goochland Branch, 231,
  Louisa Branch, 231,
  New Kent Branch, 217,
  Sussex Branch, 215, 217.
Garland, 343, 518.
Garland,
  Addison, 234.
  Alexander Spotswood, 234.

Garland—Continued
  Althea C., 234.
  Anderson, 236.
  Ann, 218, 241.
  Annie, 235.
  Annie S., 238.
  Augustus H., 239, 240,
    Atty. Gen. U. S.
  Benami Stone, 234.
  Betsy Ann, 233.
  Bettie, 234.
  Burr, 233.
  Capt., 381, 397.
  Caroline, 235.
  Caroline A., 238.
  Catherine Malvina, 234.
  Charles, 231.
  Clifton, 235.
  Col., 410, 527, 552.
  David, 27, 30, 51, 101, 107, 176,
    203, 206, 217, 218, 219, 225, 226,
    227, 228, 230, 239, 240, 241, 287,
    359, 364, 373, 374, 378, 380, 383,
    386, 388, 395, 396, 398, 400, 401,
    408, 409, 411, 417, 418, 419, 420,
    421, 424, 425, 426, 428, 432, 433,
    434, 505, 506, 519, 542.
  David (Capt.), 281, 282, 390.
  David (Col.), 230, 443.
  David S., 227, 228.
  David Shepherd, 236.
  Edward, 215, 216, 217, 218, 220,
    224, 231, 236, 238, 239.
  Edward (Capt.), 225.
  Edward, Jr., 216, 218.
  Elizabeth, 219, 220, 224, 231, 232,
    236.
  Eliza Virginia, 238.
  Ella Rose, 237.
  Fanny, 226, 227, 228.
  Fleming, 232.
  Frances, 236, 317.
  Francis, 215.
  Garland, 225, 241.
  Goodrich, 236.
  Henrietta, 233, 234.
  Hudson Martin, 233.
  Hudson Martin, Jr., 233.
  Hugh A., M. C., 235.
  J., 106.
  James, 216, 218, 231, 232, 236,
    238.
  James, Jr., 233.
  James, M. C., 233.
  James Parker, 234.

Garland—Continued
  Jane, 217, 236.
  Jane Henry, 238.
  Jane Meredith, 237.
  Jennie, 235.
  John, 215, 216, 218, 225, 227, 228,
    230, 236, 239, 241.
  John (Gen.), 233.
  John Garland, 238.
  John Richard, 229.
  John T., 227, 228.
  Landon C., 238.
  Landon Cabell, 234,
    Chancellor, Vanderbilt Univ.,
      234,
    President Randolph-Macon
      College, 234.
  Louise, 234.
  Louise Ellis, 237.
  Louise Frances, 234, 238.
  Lucie, 230.
  Lucie Edley, 230.
  Lucy, 220, 224, 236.
  Lula, 230.
  Maggie, 235.
  Margaret, 216, 218.
  Maria, 232, 233.
  Marion, 230.
  Martha, 216, 218, 219, 241.
  Martha Elizabeth, 226, 241.
  Martha Henry, 238.
  Mary, 176, 216, 218, 219, 220,
    224, 225, 226, 228, 231, 232, 235,
    236, 241.
  Mary Rice, 233, 238.
  Maurice, 233, 235.
  May, 230.
  Mildred Irving, 237.
  Minnie, 235.
  Monitia Henry, 237.
  Nancy, 226, 241.
  Nannie R., 235.
  Nathaniel, 218, 232, 236, 238, 240,
    241, 350, 359, 361.
  Nathll., 37.
  Nelson, 236.
  Nicholas, 233.
  Panthea, 229.
  Patrick Henry, 238.
  Patty, 219.
  Paulus P., 237.
  Peter, 215, 216, 218, 219, 236, 238,
    241, 519, 542, 552.
  Peter (Capt.), 225, 226.
  Petty Powell, 237.
  Polly, 220.

INDEX 593

Garland—Continued
Rice, 232, 235.
Richard, 230.
Robert, 215, 218, 226, 230, 231, 235, 238.
Robert (Col.), 234.
Rosa, 230.
Rose, 234.
Salley, 192, 230, 237.
Sallie Macon, 230.
Sally Armistead, 238.
Samuel, 27, 30, 44, 219, 220, 226, 227, 228, 230, 232, 423, 435, 440, 460, 461, 464, 541, 552, 554, 562.
Samuel (Capt.), 224, 443.
Samuel (Gen.), 235.
Samuel Meredith, 236, 237.
Sarah, 220, 224, 232.
Spotswood, 235.
Susanna, 241.
Susanna T., 225.
Thomas, 27, 230, 231, 465, 466, 467, 468, 469, 470, 472, 474, 475, 476, 477, 479, 480, 481, 482, 483.
Thomas (Capt.), 226, 227, 228, 482.
Thomas L., 228.
Thomas Lowry, 226, 227, 228.
Victoria, 222.
Waller, 237.
William, 232, 236.
William Henry, 238.
William Terrell, 225.
Garland-Addison duel, 230.
Garland, Ex parte, 240.
Garland Homestead, 229.
Garland's Neck, 215, 218, 230, 239.
Garrard County, Ky., 235.
Garot, Thos., 530.
Garrett, 521.
Garrett,
Humphrey, 518.
James, 519.
Robert, 518.
Thos., 389, 410.
Garriot, Thos., 511.
Garrot,
James, 511.
Thos., 515.
Garrott, Thos., 391, 398, 559.
Gary,
Benjamin, 310.
Hartwell, 314.
John, 305.
Richard, 313.
Thomas, 308.

Gates, Josiah, 514.
Gayle, Matthew, 550.
Geddy,
James, Jr., 310.
Mary, 310.
Gee Family, 242.
Gee,
Alfred, 247.
Amy, 245.
Beckey, 245.
Benjamin, 242, 243, 245, 246, 530, 554, 555, 558.
Bridgett N., 246.
Catherine, 244.
Chappell, 244.
Charles, 242, 243, 245, 246, 247, 308.
Claiborne, 247.
David, 243.
Dolly, 244.
Drury, 245.
Elizabeth, 244, 245, 246, 247, 306.
Fanny, 245.
Francis, 245.
George, 243, 245.
George L., 247.
Henry, 107, 242, 243, 244, 245, 402, 437, 506, 520, 544, 547, 558.
James, 242, 243, 244, 520, 530, 548.
James I., 246.
James, Jr., 243.
James S., 246.
Jane, 246.
Jeremiah, 245, 246.
Jesse, 243, 244, 245, 246, 247, 548.
Jessee, Junr., 558.
John, 310.
Jones, 243, 244, 246.
Letty, 243.
Lucas, 244, 246, 247, 295.
Lucy, 244.
Luke, 244.
Martha, 277.
Mary, 278.
Matthew, 245.
Matthews, 247.
Nancy, 244, 245, 295.
Neavil, 243, 244, 246, 247.
Nevel, 247, 402, 506.
Nevil, 242, 243, 456, 520, 547.
Rebecca, 247.
Reubin, 295.
Sack, 246.
Salley, 244.
Thomas, 245.

Gee—Continued
    William, 27, 30, 242, 244, 247, 368, 379, 380, 384, 388, 390, 393, 395, 396, 398, 402, 406, 408, 410, 520, 521.
    William B., 247.
    William L., 246.
Genealogical Notes, 166 et seq.
General Assembly,
    Petition to approved, 463.
General Assessment, 91.
General Episcopal Seminary, 146.
Gentry,
    Allen, 381, 389, 505, 528, 529, 530.
    David, 505.
    Joseph, 389, 506, 507, 512, 528.
    Nicholas, 515, 516, 518.
    Nick, 507.
    Wm., 505.
George,
    Phebe Anderson, 154.
    William, 473, 560.
Getoe, Wm., 507, 508.
Getse, Wm., 506, 507.
Gettysburg, 116.
Gibbs,
    Caroline, 181.
    John, 314.
Gibson, Churchill, 548.
Gill,
    Aaron, 311.
    Erasmus, 306.
    Henry, 107, 421, 505, 519.
    Jency, 311.
    Jinny, 308.
    Joseph, 309, 368, 505.
    Mary, 314.
    Nader, 310.
    Peter, 505.
    Sarah, 362, 373, 376, 381.
    William, 107, 311.
Gillam, 397.
Gillam, John, 327.
Gilliam,
    Agnes, 376.
    Anne, 316.
    Charles M., 159.
    Charles M., Jr., 159.
    Charlotte, 159.
    Elizabeth, 309.
    James Skelton, 308.
    Mary Anderson, 159.
    Mrs., 419, 425, 427, 430, 434, 439, 441, 442, 446, 450, 456.

Gilliam—Continued
    Richard, 381, 389, 391, 394, 401, 447, 448, 548.
    William, 310.
Gillum, Mrs., 413, 415.
Glasco, Andrew, 363.
Glass,
    John, 376.
    Sarah, 351.
Glassco, Fanny, 309.
Glebe, of Cumberland Parish, 51, 52,
    Area of estate, 57,
    Buildings on, etc., 47, 52, 53, 54, 101, 402,
    How equipped, 47,
    Repairs, 454, 463, 483, 486,
    Sale of part, 486.
Glebes,
    Provided ministers, 46,
    What they were, 147.
Glen,
    Tyra, 248.
    William, 469.
Glenn Family, 247.
Glenn, 518.
Glenn,
    Anne, 248.
    Capt., 550.
    James, 249.
    Jeremiah, 184, 248, 404, 440, 442, 452, 455, 528, 546, 561, 562.
    John (Col.), 248.
    Mary, 193, 248, 517.
    Sally, 170.
    Sarah, 248.
    Sary, 248.
    Tyree, 247, 248, 249.
    W., 106.
    William, 27, 248, 468, 469, 521, 523, 550, 562.
    William (Capt.), 471.
Glenns, John, 532.
Gloucester County, 112, 150.
Glover, Edward, 309.
Goalbreath, Edward, 39, 378.
Godfrey,
    Benj. Ragsdale, 274.
    George, 309.
Godmersham, Eng., 185.
Golden Horse Shoe, Knights of, 213.
Golder, Elizabeth, 310.
Gooch,
    Governor, 25.
    William (Sir-Bart.), 59, 329.

INDEX 595

Goochland County, 19.
Good (Goode), Mackness, 37, 333.
Goode,
  Bennett, 201, 284.
  Edward, 252, 368, 505.
  William, 345.
Goodwin,
  E. L. (Dr.), 99.
  Rev. Dr., 133, 136.
  Virginia Randolph, 159.
Goodwyn,
  Edward L. (Rev.), 61, 63, 68.
  James, 306.
  Stephen, 307.
  Winney Tucker, 307.
Goody, John, 305.
Gordon,
  John B. (Gen.), 109, 116.
  Thomas, 316.
  William, 107, 169, 369, 437, 514, 536, 550, 554, 562.
Gory, Daniel, 515.
Gosee, Jno., 413, 415, 419, 425, 427, 430, 434, 439, 441.
Gracie, Mary, 311.
Graham,
  Anne Cameron, 156.
  George Mordecai, 156.
  Isabella Davidson, 156.
  John, 551, 552.
  John (Maj.), 165.
  John W. (Maj.), 156.
  Joseph, 156.
  Paul Cameron, 156.
  Robert, 316.
  William Alexander, 156, 157.
Grammer,
  Frankey, 305.
  James, 311.
  John, 309.
  Lucy, 313.
  Nathan, 313.
Granary, on Glebe, 410.
Granger,
  Elizabeth, 310.
  Henry, 409.
  John, 421, 451, 505, 520, 546.
  Joseph, 349.
  Margaret, 311.
Grantham,
  Marjorie, 125.
  Sampson, 304.
Granville County, N. C., 114.
Grassy Creek, 74, 326, 327, 340, 343, 369, 370.
Grassy Creek Church, 376.

Graviat, Chas., 514.
Gray,
  Faitha, 176.
  Joseph, 503, 504.
  William, 304.
Great Hounds Creek, 241, 403, 404, 422, 423, 453, 473, 541.
Great Road, 421, 423.
Great Toby's Creek, 205.
Green,
  Elizabeth, 355.
  Francis Burwell, 307.
  John, 310, 511.
  Lucy, 307.
  Thomas, 510, 544.
Greenhan, George, 311.
Greene's Army, 104.
Greer, Joseph, 508.
Gregg, Wm., 508.
Gregory,
  Agnes Lee, 126.
  Andrew, 532, 534.
  Annie, 129, 130.
  Charles Allen, 125.
  Edgar Price, 129.
  Edward W., 125.
  Esther Ellen, 126.
  Flavius J. (Dr.), 125.
  Frank Hancock, 129.
  Henry Chamberlain, 122.
  Henry Claiborne (Rev.), 129.
  Herbert Bailey, 129.
  Hugh Wingfield, 129.
  Hunter Lee, 125.
  James, 532, 533.
  James Craig, 124, 126.
  James Edward, 125.
  James F., 125.
  Lucius (Col.), 125, 126.
  Lucy, 129.
  Mamie Agnes, 125.
  Marjorie, 126.
  Martha Anderson Craig, 127.
  Myrtis Lestelle, 126.
  Pattie W., 125.
  Paul Whitehead, 129.
  Richard C., 124, 125.
  Richard Claiborne, 124.
  Richard F., 316.
  Richard Flavius, 126.
  Roger, 129.
  Rosa Lee, 125.
  Sallie E., 125.
  Sarena, 125.
  Stanhope R., 122.
  Sue A., 125.

Gregory—Continued
  Susan Ann, 125.
  Susanna, 271.
  Walter V., 125.
  Werter, 129.
  West, 129.
  William H., 125.
  William Payne, 129.
  W. V. & L., 126.
Gregory's, Mrs., 454.
Gregrey, Andrew, 523.
Grier, Joseph, 505.
Griffin,
  Mary, 305.
  Richard, 326.
Grimes,
  Francis, 347.

Grimes—Continued
  George, 369, 514.
  Grissam, Wm., 395.
  Grymes, Geo., 514.
  Guilliam, Richard, 251.
  Guinea Farm, 230.
Gunn,
  Daniel, 453, 539.
  James, 542, 552.
  Sally, 314.
Gunter, Joel, 413.
Gwin, David, 334.
Gwinn, John, 331.
Gwyn, 336.
Gwynne,
  Edward, 150.
  Lucy, 150.

H

Hacker, Obedience, 304.
Hackney, Francis, 305.
Haddon, Francis, 304.
Haggard,
  Franch, 519.
  French, 402, 505.
  Richard, 389, 391, 506, 520.
Haies,
  Dick, 527.
  Henry, 421, 450, 544, 554.
  Richard, 43, 424, 426, 542, 544.
  William, 437, 542, 544.
Hailey,
  Henry, 554.
  John, 523, 524.
Hair, Mary, 304.
Haldane, Sally, 310.
Hale, Mary, 291, 293.
Halifax County, 22, 103.
Hall Family, 249.
Hall, 332, 527.
Hall,
  Edward, 312.
  Elliball, 250.
  Joel, 307.
  John, 27, 331, 332.
  Mary, 305.
  Moses, 249, 250.
  Rebecca, 305.
  Thomas, 249, 340.
  William, 249, 250.
Halliday, Catherine McQueen, 160.
Halsey, Elizabeth K., 311.
Haly, John, 533.
Hamblet, James, 524.

Hambleton, Edward, 449, 450, 459.
Hamblin, Martha C., 315.
Hamilton,
  Isabella, 306.
  Mary E., 114.
  Patrick, 114.
Hamilton Parish, 61.
Hamlet, James, 438.
Hamlett, William, 454.
Hamletts, James, 514.
Hamlin,
  Charles, 193, 386, 453, 526, 527,
    528, 529, 540, 545, 555, 557, 564.
  John, 317.
  Mary, 193.
  Martha A., 124, 189.
  P., 545.
  Thomas, 223.
Hammock,
  John, 106, 527.
  Wm., 527.
Hammond, Judy, 306.
Hammons, Duncan, 519.
Hamner,
  Bessie, 232.
  Elizabeth, 232, 235.
  Edward C., Jr., 232.
  Edward C., Sr., 232.
  Henry Rowlings, 232.
  James, 350, 367, 502, 503.
  Nicholas, 232.
  Sallie Cole, 232.
  Samuel, 232.
  Samuel G., 232.
  Thomas, 232.

Hampden-Sidney College, 127.
Hand, Hannah, 113.
Handley, Wm., 524.
Handly, 517.
Handly, James, 338.
Handy, Mary, 310.
Hankins, John, 533, 559.
Hanks, Thomas, 304.
Hannah, John, 506.
Hanover County, 216.
Hanson,
    Job, 530.
    Richard, 512.
Hardaway,
    Lucy, 312.
    Maxon, 310.
Harden, Robert, 549.
Hardie, John, Senr., 107.
Hardin, Thos., 514.
Harding,
    Elizabeth, 208.
    Robert, 554.
    Thomas, 437, 536, 544, 549.
Hardison, Sarah, 164.
Hardiway,
    Col., 527.
    Stith, 423, 541, 552.
Hardy Family, 250.
Hardy,
    Covanton, 469.
    Covington, 27, 30, 108, 250, 423, 435, 453, 460, 462, 468, 469, 470, 472, 473, 474, 475, 476, 477, 478, 479, 480, 488, 489, 490, 541, 554, 563.
    John, 437, 513, 526, 551, 563.
    Thomas, 423, 453, 528, 545, 563, 564.
    William, 28, 30, 241, 250, 436, 444, 445, 446, 447, 448, 449, 450, 454, 455, 456, 457, 458, 459, 460, 526, 551, 557, 564.
Hare, Mary Ann, 312.
Hariss, Sam, 338.
Harlan, Ky., 119.
Harnel,
    James, Jr., 503.
    James, Senr., 503.
Harnour, Wm., 519.
Harris, 537.
Harris,
    Augustine, 181.
    Caroline, 181.
    Catherine, 181.
    Charles H., 182.
    Christie May, 178, 182.

Harris—Continued
    Edwin H., 182.
    Eliza, 181.
    Jeptha, 181.
    Junius, 182.
    Laura Frances, 182.
    Mary Ann, 181.
    Milton, 181.
    Robert Hiram, 182.
    Sam, 107.
    Samuel, 326, 329, 338, 405, 442, 443, 445, 446, 448, 450, 456.
    Thomas, 307.
    Thomas D., 226.
    Walton, 180, 181.
    William (Peckerwood), 369.
    Willis, 181.
    Wm. (Finniwood), 38, 369, 370.
    Wm., 338, 349, 510.
    Young L. G., 181.
Harrison, 515.
Harrison,
    Alice, 308.
    Ann Carter, 312.
    Benjamin of *Berkeley*, 162.
    Benjamin, 314.
    Cuthbert, 309.
    David, 315.
    Edmund, 307.
    Elizabeth, 310.
    Henry, 312.
    Jane Pleasant, 314.
    Josiah, 305.
    Mary, 222, 307.
    Matthew Myrick, 222.
    Mr. (Rev.), 135.
    Nancy, 313.
    Obediah Read, 312.
    Richard, 122.
    Richard M., 122.
    Sarah, 232.
    William, 309.
    William (Rev.), 135.
Harriss,
    Samuel (Rev.), 88.
    Samuel, 74, 331, 332, 333, 339.
    Thomas, 338.
Hart,
    Lottie, 272.
    William, 304.
Harvie, Rebecah, 306.
Harvey,
    John, 293.
    Mary, 293.
    Thomas, 347.
Harvy, Thos., 345.

Harwell,
  Peter, 311.
  Samuel, 528, 529.
Hase, John, 305.
Haskins, Christopher, 312.
Hastings, John, 552.
Hastrell,
  Betty, 351.
  Mary, 351.
Hatch, George, 310.
Hatchel, Eliz., 358.
Hatchell,
  Mary, 359.
  Stephen, 372.
  Hatcher, 376.
Hatcher,
  Daniel, 313.
  Elizabeth, 129.
  Jeremiah, 381, 516.
  Jerimiah, 376, 511.
  John, 130.
  John H., 129.
  Louise, 129.
  Lucy, 130.
  M. L., 129.
  Robert, 372.
  Samuel C. (Dr.), 129.
  Viola, 129.
  W. Gregory, 130.
Hatchers Bridge, 350.
Hatchett,
  Archibald, 317.
  Archibald (Dr.), 261.
  Edward, 184, 437, 507, 550, 554.
  Elizabeth, 209.
  Elizabeth E., 209, 211.
  William, 437, 540.
  William H., 209.
Hatchitt, Wm., 551.
Hatsel,
  Betsy, 342, 345.
  Mary, 342, 345.
Hatswell,
  Betty, 354.
  Mary, 354.
Hattaway, Elizabeth, 306.
Hatton, Thomas, 312.
Hawkins Family, 250.
Hawkins, 364, 365.
Hawkins,
  Benj., 508.
  Drury, 506, 507.
  Isaiah, 210.
  John, 250, 368, 387, 437, 451, 512, 520, 521, 523, 546, 547.
  John D., 316.

Hawkins—Continued
  John, Jr., 450.
  John, Sr., 448.
  Joshua, 506, 507.
  Mary, 250.
  Matthew, 250.
  P., 352.
  Pin., 389.
  Pink, 355.
  Pinkethman, 250, 363, 373.
  Sarah, 250.
  Thomas, 28, 29, 66, 98, 250, 304, 342, 343, 344, 346, 352, 353, 354, 355, 356, 357, 358, 360, 361, 363, 509.
  William, 316, 506.
  Willm., Sr., 507.
Hawks,
  Anna, 152.
  Frances, 163.
  John (Maj.), 152.
  Phebe Rice, 152.
Hawthorn,
  Betsey, 311.
  Joshua, 307.
Hay, Daniel, 526.
Hayes, 527.
Hayes,
  Daniel, 387.
  Henery, 107.
  Mattw., 516.
  R., 106.
  W., 106.
Haymore, Wm., 511.
Haywood,
  Harriet, 159.
  Margaret, 163.
Haze, Henry, 511.
Hazlewood, John, 398, 404, 405, 409, 413, 415, 419, 425, 427, 437, 445, 446, 448, 450, 456, 513, 525, 540, 554, 563.
Head, Wm., 501.
Healy, Eleanor, 309.
Hearingue, William, 562.
Heartt, Henrietta, 156.
Heath,
  Austin, 306.
  Daniel, 309.
  Frederick, 313.
  Joseph, 314.
  Milly, 304.
  Nathan, 309.
Heathcote, Michael, 308.
Heighour, Jon., 404.
Heightour, John, 504.

Henderson,
  Isaac Oliver, 320.
  James, 115, 320.
  Mary A. G., 320.
Henderson, Ky., 112.
Hendrick, John, 501.
Hendricks, Gustavus, 532.
Hendrickson, Dean W., 235.
Henrico Parish, 19.
Henry County, 22, 23.
Henry,
  Jane, 236.
  Patrick, 91, 236.
Henson, 521.
Henson, Richard, 528.
Herbert, Jonathan, 309.
Herrin, Arther, 513.
Herrin, Arthor, 514.
Herring,
  Arthur, 422, 536, 554.
  Elizabeth, 208.
  Jesse, 306.
  William, 416, 419, 422, 453, 535, 536, 561.
Heth,
  Jesse, 311.
  Nancy, 307.
  William, 308.
Hewey, Humphry, 501.
Hewy, Hump, 501.
Hico Creek, 326, 327.
Hico River, 340.
Hickory Hill, 127.
Hicks,
  Daniel, 202.
  John, 362, 366, 371, 381, 519.
Hide, John, 38, 369, 370, 508.
Higgins, Elizabeth, 153.
Hight, John, 402, 511, 519.
Hightower,
  Ann Smith, 283.
  Frances, 260.
  George, 107, 437, 551, 552, 557, 563.
  John, 404, 526, 551, 554, 559.
  Joseph, 526.
  Presley, 260.
Hightowers, John, 423.
Hill,
  D. H. (Gen.), 154.
  Isaac (Col.), 150.
  John, 333.
  Mary, 150.
  William, 37, 150, 333, 348, 509.
  William (Dr.), 93.

Hillsboro, N. C., 155, 160.
Hinton, Christopher, 543, 544.
Historical Col. Joseph Habersham Chap., 251.
History of Albemarle, 231, 239.
History of Bristol Parish, 193.
History of Henrico Parish, 218.
Hite, Harbert, 520.
Hix,
  Amos, 515.
  John, 34, 74, 107, 331, 332, 333, 337, 339, 342, 345, 351, 358, 359, 376, 384, 388, 391, 394, 397, 404, 408, 412, 414, 419, 423, 425, 427, 429, 437, 440, 507, 512, 518, 528, 545, 546, 553, 558.
  Joseph, 511, 544.
  Mourning, 413.
  Richard, 336, 337, 339.
Hixes Road, 422, 423, 453, 454.
Hobbs,
  Ann, 307.
  Isham, 310.
  Jemima, 307.
  Mildred, 305.
Hobson Family, 251.
Hobson, 371, 507, 521.
Hobson,
  Agnes, 170, 251, 252, 262.
  Agnes G., 252.
  Agness, 371.
  Allen, 252.
  Baker, 251.
  Christopher, 251.
  Elizabeth, 252.
  Francis, 251.
  John, 28, 82, 251, 345, 352, 359, 368, 379, 380, 382, 383, 384, 385, 390, 391, 393, 395, 398, 511, 515, 516.
  Margrata, 252.
  Matthew, 170, 251.
  Nicholas, 28, 170, 251, 442, 445, 446, 447, 448, 449, 516.
  Nicholas (Capt.), 251.
  Obedience, 252.
  Patsy, 252.
  Polly B., 252.
  Sarah, 252, 427, 430, 520.
  Sary, 435.
  William, 251, 252, 547.
Hodges, Elizabeth, 304.
Hogan, 331.
Hogan,
  Edwd., 509.
  Margaret, 307.

Hogans Road, 325.
Hoge, Mary, 118.
Holden, Elizabeth, 310.
Holland, Wm., 529.
Holliday, Edmund, 306.
Holloway,
  Becky, 176.
  Bennit, 503, 504.
  Martha, 176.
Holmes,
  Lucy, 176.
  Margaret B., 316.
  Wm., 367.
Holsey, Millender, 307.
Holt,
  David, 533, 549.
  Fanny, 309.
  Joseph, 536.
Homes,
  Isaac, 503.
  Samuel, 503, 504.
  Wm., 503.
Hood, John, 311.
Hooper, 521, 522.
Hooper,
  Jane, 279.
  Obadiah, 443.
  Obediah, 394, 398, 405, 510, 511, 515, 516, 530.
  Oby, 385.
Hoopper, Thomas, 559.
Hopkins,
  David, 53, 395, 400, 401, 412, 513, 529.
  Frances, 308.
  Jno., 416.
  Samuel, 504.
Hopson, John, 28, 383.
Horse Ford, 21.
Horse Pen Branch, 423, 454.
Horse Pen Creek, 348.
Horsley, Mary Cabell, 233.
Hoskins,
  Mary, 268.
  Robert, 235.
Hoskinson, John, 507.
Hoskinsson, John, 369.
Hounds Creek, 242, 325, 387, 472.
House, George, 313.
Houston, Tex., 119.
Howard & Sands, 127.
Howard Family, 252.
Howard,
  Alexr., 539.
  Ben, 345.
  Capt., 48, 331.

Howard—Continued
  Dianna, 253.
  Eleanor, 253.
  Elizabeth, 253.
  Frances, 325.
  Francis, 252, 253.
  Fras., 504.
  Hannah, 253.
  Mary, 253.
  William, 28, 35, 252, 253, 324, 329, 504.
Howe, Henry, *Hist. of Va.*, 105.
Howel, John, 348.
Howle, James, 306.
Howlett, Mary, 231.
Hoy, Anne, 309.
Huberd,
  John, 173.
  Katharine, 173.
Hubbard,
  John, 508.
  Matthew, 527.
  Ralph, 527.
  Rosa, 230.
Hudson,
  Chris., 369, 508.
  Ephm., 500.
  Isaac, 355.
  Mary, 233, 351.
  Richard, 437, 518, 523, 534, 535.
  Robt., 500.
  Thos., 514.
  Ward, 437, 550, 554, 556.
Hughes, Robert W., 163.
Hughs, Anthony, 508.
Humphreys,
  Annie Fulton, 235.
  Jeannette Rose, 235.
  John, 38, 367, 370, 505.
  Louise Garland, 234.
  Mary Meredith, 235.
  Milton Wylie, 234.
  John, 368.
Hundley, Anthony, 523.
Hundly, 517.
Hungarford, John, 328.
Hungars Parish, 158.
Hungerford, 337.
Hungerford child, 331.
Hungerford,
  Eleanor, 336.
  Eliner, 385.
  Elinor, 345, 351, 358, 361, 371, 378, 389.
  Elinour, 342.

INDEX 601

Hungerford—Continued
  Elliner, 381.
  Enion, 354.
  George, 376, 381, 385, 388, 389, 391, 393, 394, 397, 400, 404, 407, 409, 410, 413, 414, 416, 419, 420, 425, 427, 429.
Hungrytown, 472, 473.
Hunks, John, 334.
Hunnicutt,
  Mary, 312.
  Pleasant, 305.
Hunt,
  James, 72, 343, 345, 351.
  John, 532, 549.
  Jos., 517.
  M., 345.
  Memucan, 352.
  William, 336, 342, 345, 351, 355, 356, 358, 362, 371, 372, 375.

Hunter,
  Miles, 308.
  Thomas Tod, 308.
  Wm., 326.
Hurl, John, 358, 359.
Hurt,
  Merriweather, 211.
  Moses, 106.
Huskerson, John, 536.
Hutchens, 518.
Hutchens,
  Burton, 355.
  Robt., 517.
Hutcheson,
  Aaron, 184.
  Berta M., 125.
Hutchins, 517.
Hutson,
  Ward, 561.
  William, 451.

I

Index, 162.
Index and Appeal, 162.
Inglish, Priscilla, 308.
Ingram,
  John, 437, 550.
  Mary, 158, 315.
  Pines, 41, 42, 43, 428, 433, 435, 436, 458, 459, 460.
  Richard, 437, 452, 550, 554, 556, 561.
  Robt., 549.
  Saml., 507.
  Thomas, 451, 546.
Inloe, John, 379, 381, 385, 392.
Irby,
  I., 523.
  Joshua, 523, 524, 532.

Irby—Continued
  Tabitha, 304.
Irvin, 517.
Irvin, Courtney, 304.
Irwin,
  Alexander, 327, 328.
  James, 340.
  Jon., 518.
  Wm., 345.
Irwin's ford, 36, 327.
Isbel, Henry, 339, 345.
Isbell, Henry, 35, 331, 332, 333, 337, 342, 351, 354.
Isle of Man, 114.
Ivy Depot, 232.
Ivy, George, 305.
Ivy Hill, 114.

J

Jackson Family, 253.
Jackson (illegible), 519.
Jackson,
  Amy, 254.
  Andrew (Gen.), 233.
  Benjamin, 253, 254.
  Betsey Levington, 254.
  Carter, 253.
  Edward, 519.
  Elizabeth, 253, 254.
  Ezekiel, 311.

Jackson—Continued
  Frances, 254.
  Francis, 254.
  Francis Thompson, 254.
  Henry, 505.
  Howard, 324.
  Joel, 254.
  John, 254.
  Josiah, 253.
  Katy, 254.
  Lucy, 254.

Jackson—Continued
  Martha, 253.
  Patsy Noden, 254.
  Peter, 254.
  Philip W., 28, 30, 31, 139, 253, 479, 480, 481, 482, 483, 484, 485, 486.
  Polly Noden, 254.
  Polly Voden, 315.
  Sally, 254.
  Steward, 254.
  Stewart, 254.
  "Stonewall," 109.
  William, 305, 505.
  Willis, 254.
  Zatha, 254.
Jackson, Miss., 119.
James, Polly, 312.
Jamestown Island, 185.
Jamison, Daniel, 310.
Jarratt,
  Devereux, 69, 70, 100, 102.
  Devereux (Rev.), 72, 142.
Jarratte, Deverix, 69, 100, 191, 383.
Jeeter,
  Samuel, 423, 437, 546, 553.
  William, 536.
Jefferson Family, 255.
Jefferson, 333, 337.
Jefferson,
  Colo., 344.
  Field, 28, 29, 98, 219, 255, 256, 332, 335, 336, 338, 341, 343, 344, 346, 352, 353, 356, 357, 360, 376, 503.
  George, 219, 392, 396, 397, 400, 503.
  John, 503.
  John Garland, 219.
  Julia A., 192.
  Mr. (Field), 35, 37.
  Patsey, 243.
  Peter, 219.
  Peter Field, 367.
  Samuel, 192, 226.
  Thomas, 90, 145, 148, 149, 219, Charge of infidelity, 148.
Jefferson and Allen,
  Marriage Articles, 255.
Jeffress, Mary, 258, 259.
Jeffries,
  John, 306.
  Salley, 306.
Jeffris, John, 508, 510.
Jenings Family, 256.

Jenings,
  Capt., 389, 402, 527.
  Edmund (Gov.), 150.
  Frances, 150.
  John, 28, 30, 51, 399, 400, 402, 405, 408, 411, 414, 512.
  John (Capt.), 54, 257, 416, 424, Removed "to Carolina," 424.
  Margaret, 150.
  Priscilla, 150.
  Wm., 526, 551.
"Jening's Fortune," 256.
Jenings Road, 404, 421, 423, 451, 453.
Jenkins, Mary, 235.
Jennings, 348.
Jennings,
  Capt., 371, 375, 387, 392.
  Elizabeth, 257.
  James, 257.
  John, 28, 29, 37, 99, 342, 357, 358, 359, 360, 361, 364, 365, 366, 371, 374, 375, 379, 383, 384, 386, 390, 393, 395, 396, 397, 401, 506.
  John (Capt.), 361, 362, 363.
  Lemuel, 257.
  Mrs. Martelia, 270.
  Nancy, 257.
Jeter,
  Joseph, 333.
  Wm., 388, 518, 529, 530.
John, Isaac, 532.
Johnson,
  Andrew, 393, 398, 517.
  Christopher, 348.
  David, 403, 437, 504, 516, 524, 532, 534, 549.
  Edmund, 458.
  Isaac, 437, 518, 523, 524, 533, 535, 549.
  James, 106, 422, 426, 540, 550, 554, 562.
  James (Capt.), 187, 252, 281.
  Jean, 457.
  John, 309, 514.
  Joseph, 349, 370, 421, 516, 524, 533, 549.
  Joseph E. (Gen.), 154.
  Michael, 422, 513, 529, 532, 540, 541, 549, 550, 562.
  Michail, 107.
  Patsy, 309.
  Stephen, 558.
  Susannah, 254.
  William, 107, 326, 511, 519.

Johnson's Creek, 288.
Johnson's Road, 422, 452, 473, 474.
Johnston,
  Abraham, 307.
  Andrew, 406, 524, 525.
  Joseph E. (Gen.), 154.
Jolly, Henry, 338.
Jones, 512.
Jones,
  Agnes, 343.
  Anne Elizabeth, 306.
  Ann Park, 108, 116.
  Caty, 247.
  Claiborne, 122.
  Edward Montfort, 108, 116.
  Eliza, 160.
  Elizabeth, 307, 316.
  Elizabeth Mitchell, 311.
  Frances, 316, 370.
  Halcott, 160.
  Harris, 124.
  Hunter, 122.
  James, 451, 559.
  John, 74, 372, 376.
  John James, 109, 111.
  Joseph, 122.
  Julia, 170.
  Lewellyn, 315.
  Littlebury H., 315.
  Llewellyn C., 121.
  Marjorie, 122.
  Martha, 312.
  Mary, 160, 277, 279, 310, 315, 342.
  Mary Epes, 261.
  Peter, 41, 170, 410, 424, 426, 453, 509, 512, 513, 514, 525, 526, 529, 537, 538, 539, 540, 550, 562, 563.
  Peter (Capt.), 508.
  Peter, Jr., 317.
  Peter, Sen., 320.
  Peter B., 317.
  Philip, 304, 326, 328.
  Pride (Dr.), 160.
  R. Dan., 126.
  Rebecca, 317.
  Rebeccah Edwards, 306.
  Reps, 325, 348, 368, 386, 526, 527, 542, 552.
  Richard, 122, 261, 314, 338, 342.
  Robert, 328, 340, 527, 542.
  Robt., Jr., 501.
  Sally, 311, 317.
  Sallie G., 170.
  Samuel, 325.

Jones—Continued
  Sarah, 314.
  Semmie, 230.
  Stanhope, 121.
  Stephen, 366.
  Susanna R., 318.
  Thomas, 107, 347, 437, 527, 546, 547, 554.
  Thos. Brooks, 306.
  Tignal, 370.
  William, 508.
  William (Col.), 509.
  W. Mac, genealogist, 19.
Jones, Peter and Richard Genealogies, 273.
Jordan Family, 257.
Jordan, 537, 556.
Jordan,
  Baxter, 258, 260, 316.
  Benjamin, 258, 260.
  Caroline, 234.
  Edward, 28, 30, 58, 259, 260, 445, 446, 447, 449, 450, 451, 545, 455, 456, 457, 459, 467, 468, 469, 474, 488, 554, 561, 562.
  Edward (Capt.), 200, 257, 258, 550.
  Edward, Jr., 257, 259, 422, 537.
  Edward, Senr., 409.
  Elizabeth, 258, 259, 260.
  Elizabeth B., 259.
  Elizabeth T., 259.
  Francis, 258.
  Freeman, 259.
  Freeman, Jr., 259.
  James, 258, 259.
  John, 258, 555, 557.
  Laban, 258, 259.
  Martha Francis, 258.
  Mary Anne, 259.
  Mary E., 170.
  Mary L., 260.
  Miles, 258, 259, 316.
  Nancy, 258.
  Polly, 258, 259.
  Polly E., 259.
  Samuel, 260, 316, 533.
  Susannah, 258, 259, 317.
  Thomas, 259, 260.
  Thomas E., 259.
  Thomas, Jr., 259.
  Thomas W. J., 259.
  William, 258, 260, 533.
  Woodson, 277.

Jordans,
  Edward, 258.
  Milson, 258.
  Samuel, 258.
Joseph Habersham Hist. Col., 180.
Jourdan, Elijah, 226.
Journey,
  John, 517.
  "Old Mrs.," 406.
  Wm., 517.

Joyce,
  Alex., 347.
  Hannah, 197.
Justice,
  Martha, 405, 409, 413, 418, 425, 427, 430, 434, 439, 441, 443, 445, 446.
  William, 389, 418, 419, 425.

K

Kain, Charles, 161.
Kansas City, Mo., 118.
Kay, 343.
Kay, William (Rev.), 63, 64, 72, 338, 340, 341, 342, 343, 344, 345, 346.
Keatt, Curtis, 550.
Keatts, 537, 557.
Keatts, Curtis, 525, 538, 562.
Keatt's Fork, 452.
Keiley, Anthony M., 162.
Kelley,
  Nancey, 409, 413, 419, 425, 427, 430, 441.
  Nany, 405.
Kelly,
  John, 310.
  Nancy, 376, 381, 385, 389, 391, 394, 396, 397, 434, 439, 442, 445, 446, 448, 450, 456.
  Nanny, 415.
  Wm., 530.
Kenbridge, Va., 104.
Kenedy, Thomas (Rev.), 135, 136.
Keney, Nancy, 359.
Kenmore, 236.
Kenny,
  Ann, 371.
  Nancy, 362.
Kent, John, 311.
Kentish Genealogies, 184.
Kerr, Elizabeth, 307.
Kershaw, Minnie, 118.
Kettle Stick Branch, 511.
Key, 357.

Key,
  Mr. (Rev.), 353.
  William, 65.
  William (Rev.), 63, 72, 351.
Keys, Martha, 308.
Killingworth, Mark, 309.
Killis, James, 519.
King,
  Anne, 304.
  Edward, 128.
  Jessie, 520.
  John (Rev.), 88.
  Miles, 315.
King William Parish, 19.
King's Bounty, 98.
King's College, Aberdeen, 132, 145.
King's Road, 326.
Kirby, 542.
Kirby, John, 512, 528.
Kirk, James, 527.
Kirkland,
  Alex., 164.
  Bartley, 313.
  John, 311.
  William, 164.
Knight,
  Betsy, 208.
  Jo., 107.
  John, 514.
  Jon., 513.
  Polly, 208.
  Tarleton W., 210.
  Woodson, 452.
Knights of the Golden Horse Shoe, 213.
Knox, John Brownlow, 307.

L

Labonisse, John W., 157.
Lacey, Thomas B., 308.
Ladd, Thomas, 533.
Ladies' Memorial Association, 144.

Laggoon,
  Matthew, 415, 419, 527, 544.
  Nathaniel, 108, 423, 543.
Lamb, Clarissa, 312.

Lambert, Lewis, 527.
Lamford, William, 544.
Lamkin Family, 260.
Lamkin,
  Jane C., 318.
  Mary Epes Jones, 261, 317.
  Peter, 260, 261, 279, 479, 481, 482, 484, 487.
  Peter (Capt.), 480.
  Peter, Jr., 28, 260, 480.
  Petronella Sharp, 261.
  Petronilla, 317.
  Polly, 261.
  Sharp, 260, 261.
  Susanna L., 261.
  Susanna Lewis, 261.
Lampkin Family, 260.
Lampkin, Eliza Lewis P., 220.
Lancaster County, 187.
Land, Ellidge, 204.
Landrum,
  Frans., 542.
  Francis, 552.
  Wm., 541, 542, 552.
Lanear, Thomas, 201.
Lang, Mary, 312.
Langford,
  George, 500.
  John, 500.
Langley, Robt., 502.
Langston, Sarah, 167.
Lanier Family, 261.
Lanier,
  Benjamin, 261.
  Bird Thomas, 326.
  Elizabeth, 263.
  F. D., 264.
  James, 261, 262, 263.
  J. F. D., 263.
    Sketch of the Life of, 263.
  John, 310.
  Lemuel, 261.
  Lucy, 309.
  Martha, 313.
  Nicholas S., 262.
  Rebecca, 180.
  Richard, 262, 263.
  Sampson, 262, 263.
  Samuel, 262.
  Sidney, 262.
  Sterling, 263.
  Sydney, 263.
  Thomas, 20, 38, 201, 261, 262, 263, 348, 365, 366, 370, 373, 376.
  Thomas Byrd, 261.

Lankford,
  George, 500.
  John, 500.
Lanockshire, Scotland, 158.
Lansford, Henry, 339.
Lanthrop, William, 305.
Lanthrupe, Leadbetter, 311.
Lark,
  Dinis, 501.
  Robert, 367.
Larke,
  Denis, 502.
  Dennis, 366, 501, 502.
  Dinnis, 502.
  Robt., 502.
Laurance, James, 559.
Lawrance, James, 530.
Lawson,
  Francis, 327, 340.
  Hugh, 242, 271, 387, 513.
  James, 524.
Lax, 521.
Lax,
  Jemima, 448, 450, 456.
  Wm., 346, 351, 355, 358, 362, 371, 375, 377, 381, 385, 392, 394, 405, 409, 413, 415, 419, 425, 427, 430, 434, 510, 515.
  Wm., Sr., 530.
Leake,
  John, 112.
  Rebecca, 112.
  Wm., 352.
Leath, Jemimah, 308.
Ledbetter Creek, 403, 422, 424, 452, 454, 560.
Ledbetters Creek, 349, 350.
Lee,
  Agness, 311.
  Celia, 307.
  Edward, 309.
  Henderson (Rev.), 129.
  Henry (Gen.), 229.
  Herbert, 313.
  Jesse, 310.
  John A., 128.
  John Taylor, 311.
  "Light Horse Harry," 229.
  Lillie A., 128.
  Lucy, 310.
  Matthew, 313.
  Robert E. (Gen.), 150, 214, 228, 229.
Lee of Virginia, 150.
Leigh, David G., 317.

LeMessurier, John, 314.
Lenox, Joseph, 306.
Lessinberry, Sally, 309.
Lester Family, 264.
Lester, 517.
Lester,
  Briant, 468.
  Bryan, 28, 264, 421, 464, 465, 466, 467, 532, 533.
  Bryant, 28, 264.
  John, 533, 549.
  Mary, 279.
  Mary Jane, 172.
Lett,
  Fras., 502, 503.
  Isham, 503.
  James, 367, 502.
  James, Jr., 503.
  James, Senr., 503.
  John, 503.
Levears, John, 524.
Leveritt, Thomas, 107.
Levisay,
  Joanna, 309.
  Mary, 309.
Lewis,
  Amanda, 220.
  Benjamin, 220.
  Burwell B. (Prof.), 234.
  Edward, 355, 509.
  George Griffin, 320.
  James, 369.
  John Flood, 220.
  Nicholas Edmunds, 220.
  Robert, 309.
  Silvia, 306.
  Thos., 107.
Lewis County, W. Va., 232.
Lexington, Ky., 118.
Lidderdale, Wm., 509.
Ligon, Sally Ann, 118.
Lincoln's War, 127.
Lincolnton, N. C., 155.
Lines, Matthew, 381.
Linsey, Wm., 504.
Lisk, Dorothy, 232.
Little,
  Abra., 339.
  Lucy Davis, 114.
Littleberry, Elizabeth, 207.
Little Roanoke, 32, 34, 36, 296, 324, 327, 329, 331.
Little Roanoke Church, 35, 37, 332, 336, 337, 339, 341, 342, 345.
Little Roanoak river, 347, 348.

Liveret, 527.
Liveret,
  Robt., 541, 542.
  Thomas, 437, 551.
Liverett,
  Robt., 404.
  Tho., 552.
Livesay,
  Burwell, 305.
  Lucretia, 311.
  Rebecca, 312.
  Sally, 314.
  Thomas, 312, 314.
Lochead,
  Eliza, 316.
  Jean, 316.
Lock, John, 533.
Logan,
  David, 347.
  Petronella, 116.
Loman, James, 364, 545.
Long, Richard, 509.
Longmire, Wm., 553.
Longstreet, Gen., 233.
Lottery, to build Church, 137.
Louisville, Ky., 117.
Loury,
  Mrs., 423, 520, 531.
  Thos., 522, 548, 553.
  William, 423, 545, 546, 548, 553.
Love,
  Allan, 315.
  John, 550, 553.
  Jon., 518.
  Will, 107.
  William, 369, 437, 507, 510, 515, 518, 521, 529, 530, 546, 550, 553, 559, 562.
Loves Bridge, 473.
Loves Ford, 452.
Lowery, Thos., 512, 513.
Lowry, 517.
Lowry,
  Frances, 227.
  Martha A., 317.
  Mary, 226, 227.
  Polley, 226.
  Thomas, 227, 277, 315, 516.
Lucas,
  Elizabeth, 202.
  John, 403, 409, 518, 520, 521.
  Rebecca, 244.
  Saml., 502.
  William, 202, 244, 367, 502.

Lunenburg County, 20, 21, 22, 25, 32, 39, 41, 61.
Lunenburg Court House, 34, 489, 493.
Lunenburg parish, 64.
LuPark, Antonio, 304.

Luterloh, Herbert, 161.
Lyddall Family, 167.
Lyddall,
  Ann, 167.
  George (Capt.), 167.
Lynch, Henry, 306.

M

Mabry, Joshua, 350, 366, 501, 502.
Macfarlan, John, 307.
MacFarland Family, 264, 265.
Macfarland, 499.
Macfarland,
  James, 28, 31, 140, 264, 495, 496, 498, 500, 564.
  Nannie Beirne, 265.
  William H., 264, 265.
  William J., 128.
Macfarlands, post office, 498.
Macfarling, John, 264.
McBee, Sumner (Dr.), 161.
McCabe, Peyton C., 128.
McCarter, William, 310.
McClaughlin, Geo., 513.
McConico,
  Jared, 536.
  Jarrott, 387.
McConnico,
  Garrard, 514.
  Jerrott, 513.
McConnicoe, Jarrard, 514.
McCulloch, Anne, 305.
McCulloch, widow, 293.
McCutchin, John, 549.
McDaniel, Drury, 553.
McDonnell, Eleanor, 306.
Mcdow, Wm., 505.
McDowell,
  John, 314.
  Lettie, 310.
  Patsey, 310.
McDuffy, Roy, 157.
McFarland Family, 264.
Mcfarland, James, 28, 31, 491, 492, 493, 494.
McFarlane, Margaret, 311.
McFarquhar, John, 307.
McIntosh,
  Enoch Broyles, 153.
  Mildred, 153.
McKeever, Alexander, 311.
McKittrick, David, 313.
McLaren, Neil, 314.
McLaughlin, Elizabeth, 310.

McLaughlin,
  George, 539.
  James, 539.
McLaurin, Daniel, 308.
McLeane, Betsey, 305.
McLeod, John, 306.
McLin,
  John, 501, 504.
  Thos., 501.
McNeess, John, 347.
McNeill, Mary Hyman, 157.
McNess, J., 345.
McQuiston, Katherine Gertrude, 152.
McRee,
  Anna C., 161.
  Joseph, 160.
McWillie, Beatrice, 119.
Machen, Letty, 306.
Mackadon, Wm., 511.
Mackconnico, Jarred, 369.
Mackey, Micl., 558.
Mackie,
  Mr., 545.
  Lucy, 316.
  Michael, 423, 437, 545, 546, 553, 555.
Maddin,
  M., 158.
  Mary Cowan, 158.
Maddox, Leniza, 277.
Maddux,
  Frances, 280.
  Washington, 280.
Madison,
  Bishop, 132, 137, 145.
  James, 92,
    Author, *Memorial and Remonstrance*, 92.
  Roger, 349, 507.
Madisonville, Ky., 118.
Maharin river, 325, 326.
Mahood, Dr. Hugh B., 229.
Maitland,
  David, 309.
  William, 314.

Major,
  John, 173.
  Rebeccah, 309.
  William, 305.
Mallet, Stephen, 351, 367.
Malloon, Daniel, 513.
Mallone,
  Daniel, 403, 536.
  Drury, 350.
Malloone,
  Daniel, 507, 535.
  Drury, 366, 500.
  Isham, 500.
  Thos., 366, 500.
Mallory, Jno., 107.
Malone,
  Daniel, 191.
  Drury, 325.
  Mary, 191.
  Rebecka, 191.
  Thomas, 191.
  William, 191.
Manassas, battle of, 154.
Manchester Parish, 132.
Mann,
  Catlett, 523.
  Charles Benjamin, 122.
  Frances Harrison, 122.
  Margaret Gordon, 122.
  Mary, 308.
  Mary Orgain, 122.
  Richard H., 122.
  Wm. Hodges (Gov.), 126.
Mannin, Samll., 350.
Manning,
  John, 501.
  Samuel, 501.
Mansion House, on Glebe, 412.
Manson, Martha, 317.
Map of Cumberland Parish,
  following page, 23.
Maples, William, 516, 532.
Marable,
  Champion, 266.
  Edward Travis, 266.
  Elizabeth, 266.
  George, 314.
  Hartwell, 266.
  John, 266.
  Mary, 266.
  Matthew, 265, 266, 284.
  Richard, 266.
  Tabitha, 266.
  William, 266.
March, Martha, 283.

Marks, John, 313.
Marky, Robert, 311.
Marlow, Smallwood Coghill, 305.
Marquis of Downshire, 150.
Marrable Family, 265.
Marrable,
  George, 453.
  John, 452, 549.
  Matthew, 28, 29, 38, 69, 82, 99,
    100, 184, 265, 351, 360, 361, 363,
    364, 370, 372, 377.
  William, 265.
Marriages,
  Ceremonies by dissenting
    ministers, 12,
  Certificates of to be returned, 13,
  How celebrated in Colonial Era,
    10,
  Laxity of ministers, 16,
  Licenses or banns, 10,
  Statutes respecting, 7, 8, 9, 10,
    12, 13, 14.
Marsh, Nancy, 405.
Marshall,
  Alexander, 308.
  John (C. J.), 161.
  Mary Elizabeth, 189.
  Theodora, 164.
  William (Capt.), 113.
Martin Family, 266.
Martin, 329, 331, 333, 337, 353.
Martin,
  Abraham, 26, 28, 29, 34, 35, 49,
    265, 266, 324, 325, 327, 328, 329,
    331, 332, 335, 337, 341, 342, 343,
    344, 346.
  Andrew, 347.
  Benjamin, 236.
  Elizabeth, 150, 236.
  Frances, 113.
  John, 198.
  Mr., 34, 37.
  Thomas, 236.
Martins-Brandon, 183.
Martyn, John, 544.
Mason, 520, 546.
Mason,
  Daniel, 521, 548, 553, 554.
  Elizabeth, 309.
  Elizabeth Jane, 314.
  George, 92,
    opposes general assessment, 92.
  James, 511.
  John, 312.
  John R., 315.

Mason—Continued
  Nathaniel, 403, 515, 522, 523, 530, 534, 559.
  Robert, 522.
  Winfield, 548.
Mason's Creek, 229.
Massenburg,
  Elizabeth, 307.
  Lucy, 312.
  Robert, 310.
Masters,
  Chilton, 114.
  Robert Clinton, 316.
Mathews County, 178.
Matthews,
  John, Jr., 543, 544.
  John, Senr., 543.
  Wm., 387.
Matthis,
  Elizabeth, 372.
  Jacob, 503.
  Mary, 376.
Maury, 546.
Maury,
  Abram, 515.
  Abraham, 522, 529, 530, 553.
  Ann, 213.
  Col., 522.
  Elizabeth, 152.
  Lillie, 152.
Maxwell,
  Evelyn Croom, 153.
  John, 154.
  Judge, 153.
  Julia, 154.
  Julia Anderson, 153.
  Walker, 154.
May Family, 170.
May,
  Agness, 526.
  Anne, 120.
  Daniel, 346.
  David, 120.
  Emma, 120.
  Henry, 348.
  Henry (Dr.), 170.
  Henry Clay, 120.
  John, 509.
  John Orgain, 120.
  John Randolph (Dr.), 120.
  Odessa Baskett, 117.
  Richard, 120.
Mayo River, 79, 339.
Mayo, Sallie Taliaferro, 157.
Mayo's ford, 340.
Mays,
  Mattox, 326.
  Sarah, 283.
Meacham,
  Jeremiah, 311.
  Dyancy, 312.
Meachum,
  Mary Ann Caroline, 306.
  Winney, 307.
Meade, William (Bishop), 17, 23, 24, 32, 34, 63, 64, 66, 84, 85, 99, 105, 132, 134, 138, 139, 143, 147.
Meanly,
  Lucy, 272.
  Samuel, 526.
Mebane, Frank Carter, 157.
Mecklenburg County, 22, 33, 37, 90.
Meem,
  Eliza, 235.
  Gilbert (Gen.), 235.
  John, 235.
Meherrin Parish, 372.
Meherrin River, 242, 296, 348, 366, 369, 386, 387, 388, 402, 421, 451, 472, 473, 518, 522, 529.
Meloone, Danll., 507.
Memoirs of a Huguenot Family, 213.
Memorial and Remonstrance, 92.
Menonists, 12, 13, 15.
Meredith,
  Jane, 236.
  Samuel (Col.), 236.
Mexican War, 154.
Michaux, Abram, 325.
Middle Meherrin River, 421, 451, 452.
Middlesex County, 18.
Midleton, John, 507.
Miles Creek, 185, 350, 367, 373.
Miles's Creek Church, 38, 39, 370, 374, 375.
Milford Haven, 178.
Miller,
  Ashley, 222.
  Brice, 377.
  Copeland Davis, 221, 222.
  E. W., 222.
  Eliza Lewis, 222.
  Julia, 222.
  Lucy Garland, 221.
  Mary Shepard, 221.
  Nicholas E., 221.

Miller—Continued
  Nicholas Edmunds, 223.
  William H., 221, 223.
Mills,
  Matthew, 437, 550.
  Wm., 529.
Milner,
  John, 546.
  Richard, 547.
Miner, Joseph, 369, 387.
Miniature, of Rev. John Cameron, 131.
Minister's salary fixed by law, 46.
Ministers, Cumberland Parish, list of, 72.
Minister,
  Voluntary subscription for, 463.
Minor,
  Cyrus, 555.
  Edith, 196.
  Joseph, 199, 424, 514, 524.
  Letitia, 199.
Minter, Mildred Buford, 187.
Miry Creek, 326.
Mise,
  James, 511.
  Jeremiah, 511.
  Stephen, 511.
Mitchel,
  Ann, 416.
  James, 327.
  Ruben, 442, 446, 456.
Mitchell,
  Capt., 352.
  Frances, 313.
  George, 312.
  Isaac, 367.
  James, 351.
  Margaret, 441.
  Mary, 362, 371, 376, 426.
  Reuben, 445, 448.
  Robert, 312.
  Ruben, 443, 450.
Mitchell's Creek, 261, 262.
Mize, Jeremy, 519.
Mizes Ford, 348.
Mohorne, John, 560.
Monroe, Wm., 514.
Montgomery, Benjamin, 313.
Moody,
  Jno., 107, 451, 554.
  Leah, 309.
  Martha, 244.
  Thomas, 185, 402, 437, 511, 518, 531.
Moon,
  Gid., 561.
  Giddion, 403, 514.
  Gideon, 200, 249, 437, 514, 549.
  Julaney, 209.
  Rachel, 249.
  Sarah, 200.
Moor,
  David, 107.
  Dorothy, 317.
  George, 560.
  Hugh, 326.
  Rachael, 274.
Moore,
  Anne, 113, 120.
  Ann Butler, 229.
  Bernard (Col.), 229.
  Betsy Jennings, 245.
  Bishop, 143, 144, 499.
  Drury, 392, 395, 397.
  Ellick, 106.
  Emma, 164.
  James, 308.
  Jane, 318.
  Jincy, 244.
  Lucy, 311.
  Mary, 308, 315.
  Richard Channing (Bishop), 71, 140, 141, 496, 497.
  Sarah Chappell, 311.
  Thos., 511.
Mordecai, George, 156.
More,
  David, 437, 453, 555.
  Drury, 542, 552, 555.
  Ellick, 364, 446.
  Henry, 527.
  James, 527.
  John, 527.
  Robt., 527, 543.
  William, 435.
Mores,
  Robert, 423, 453.
  Thos., 519.
Morgain, Sally, 277.
Morgan,
  Charles, 306.
  Jennie F., 182.
  Jere., 544.
  Jeremiah, 107.
  Philip, 501.
  Rubin, 358, 501, 503.
  Sakamus, 107.
  Samuel T., 181, 182.
Morgin, Rubin, 256.

Moriarty, Maurice, 306.
Morison,
　Ann, 309.
　Jane, 310.
　Patience, 306.
Morris,
　Annie, 121.
　Henrietta, 121.
　John, 121.
　Mason Cabell, 121.
Morrison,
　George, 311.
　John, 315.
Morton,
　Claude Ambrose, 118.
　Harry E. Thixton, 118.
　Jayne Stokes, 118.
　Joseph, 352.
Moseley, Phoebe, 289.
Mosely,
　David, 307.
　George, 351.
Moses, David, 511.
Mosley, John, 313.
Moss,
　Henry, 304.
　William, 344.
Mossing Ford, 347.
Mowat, Oliver, 130.
Mt. Holly, 128.
Mulkey, Ann, 205.

Mullins, Valentine, 352, 509.
Muncaster,
　Charles Ashley, 221.
　George, 221.
　Maggie D., 221.
Munford, Robert, 509.
Munroe, Wm., 524.
Murfrey, Mary, 205.
Murphey, Edward, 307.
Murphy,
　Joseph (Rev.), 88.
　Martin, 304.
　Mary Ann, 308.
　William (Rev.), 88.
Murray,
　James, 510.
　Mary, 307.
Murrel,
　Jeffry, 526.
　William, 538.
Murrell,
　Drury, 562.
　Jas., 107.
　Jeffrey, 513.
　Widow, 562.
　Wm., 524, 525, 550.
Murrells Road, 473.
Murrells Rolling Road, 403, 452, 453.
Murrey, Thos., 512.
Murril, Wm., 514.

N

Nader, Joseph, 313.
Nance,
　Daniel, 325, 500.
　Frederick, 452, 517, 536, 560.
　John, Senr., 508.
　Richard, 507.
　Thos., 500.
　Wm., 500, 507, 560.
Nances Road, 473.
Nash Family, 267.
Nash, 341, 343, 354, 517.
Nash,
　Abner (Gov.), 149, 151.
　Ann Owen, 133, 145, 149, 150, 151.
　Clement Read (Maj.), 151.
　Elizabeth, 150.
　Francis (Gen.), 149, 151.
　John (Col.), 514.
　Martha W., 317.
　Mary, 150.

Nash—Continued
　Thomas, 28, 29, 150, 267, 344, 346, 353, 354, 357.
　Thomas (Col.), 149.
Neal,
　John, 562.
　Louisa Stokes, 181.
　Mary E., 181.
　Thomas, 531, 548.
　William H., 181.
　William Y., 181.
Neblett Family, 267.
Neblett,
　Ann, 276.
　Colin, 222.
　Frances Rebecca, 122.
　Francis, 267, 518.
　Isabella, 222.
　John (Rev.), 259.
　N. Macfarland, 122.
　Sterling, 28, 30, 267.

Neblett—Continued
  Virginia Macfarland, 122.
  William J., 128,
    In secession convention, 129.
Nelson,
  Edward, 218.
  James, 218.
  Thomas (Gov.), 105.
Nesbett, Nat., 248.
Newall,
  Edward, 309.
  James, 308.
  Sarah, 305.
Newbell, Nathl., 562.
Newbill, Henry, 318.
Newby, John, 560.
New Kent County, 18, 167, 215, 218.
New London, 104.
Newman, Richard, 504.
New Record Book, 79.
Newsom, 353.
Newsom, Wm., 506.
Newsom's orphans, 564.
Newsum, Sarah, 306.
New Vestry Book, 78.
Nibblet, Francis, 386.
Niblet,
  John, 451.
  Sterling, 30, 447, 455, 458.
Niblett,
  Fras., 511.
  Sterling, 28, 44, 279, 446, 450, 462, 464, 465, 467, 468, 485, 487, 488, 489, 554.
  William, 554.
Niblitt, Frans., 402.
Nicholas, George,
  Opposes general assessment, 92.
Nicholl, Henry, 305.
Nichols,
  Julius, 37, 333, 350.
  William, 306.
Nicholson,
  Lucy W., 316.
  Mary, 316.

Night, John, 369, 387.
Nipper, Priscilla, 204.
Nobles, Ann, 358, 381, 385, 389, 391, 394, 395, 398, 405, 409.
Noden, Lemuel, 314.
Norfolk Virginian, 162.
Norman, Lee, 117.
North Carolina,
  University opened after "Reconstruction," 156,
  University magazine, 151.
Northington, James, 311.
North Meherrin River, 350, 403, 404, 421, 422, 451, 473.
Norton,
  Betsy, 305.
  Nellie, 306.
Norvell, Lucie, 229.
Norwell, Hugh, 367.
Norwood,
  Charles (Prof.), 118.
  Mary Louise, 118.
Nottoway Blues, 119.
Nottoway Cavalry, 127.
Nottoway County, 119, 138.
Nottoway Grays, 119.
Nottoway Parish, 65, 138, 142, 143, 145, 187, 314.
Nottoway River, 21, 242, 325, 348, 350, 368, 369, 387, 403, 422, 423, 424, 452, 454.
Nuckolls,
  Asa, 231.
  David, 231.
  Ezra, 231.
  John, 231.
  Nathaniel, 231.
  Patsy, 231.
  Peter, 231.
  Rhodes, 231.
  Robert G., 231.
  Samuel, 231.
Nun, Robert, 372.
Nunnelly, Nathaniel, 304.
Nutbush Creek, 368, 369.

O

Ogburn,
  Augustine, 307.
  Henry (Rev.), 88, 268.
  Nicholas, 307.
Ogler,
  J. E., 222.
  Lucy, 222.

Ogler—Continued
  Mabel, 222.
  William, 222.
Old,
  John (Col.), 232.
  Sarah, 232.
Old Blandford Church, 158.

INDEX

Old Churches, Ministers and Families of Virginia, 17.
Old Courthouse, 452.
Old Free State, The, 108, 187, 225, 264, 265, 267, 285.
Oliver, Isaac, 170, 316.
Orange Co., N. C., 156.
Ordinances,
  controversy over, 11.
Orgain,
  Ann Craig, 123.
  Anne Collier, 123.
  Clarence, 123.
  Dean, 123.
  Edward, 119.
  Edward B., 120.
  Edward C., 119.
  Edward Stewart (Dr.), 121.
  Edward Thomas, 121.
  Elizabeth Field, 121.
  Eva Chambers, 123.
  George C., 121.
  George C. (Capt.), 108, 120, 121.
  George C. (Judge), 108.
  Henrietta Chambers, 123.
  Henrietta Craig, 122.
  James R., 120.
  James Robert, 123.
  James Robert, Jr., 123.
  Jessamine, 123.
  John, Jr., 119.
  John, Sr., 119.
  John Barbour, 121.
  John Barbour, Jr., 121.
  Josephine Addison, 122.
  J. Tarry, 123.
  Lucie Lee, 122.
  Lucy Marshall, 120.
  Mary, 123.
  Mary Collier, 123.
  Mary Jackson, 121.
  Rebecca, 121.
  Rebecca Lucas, 121.
  Robert, 123.
  Robert Sturdivant, 123.
  Rosa Chambers, 122.
  Sallie Lucas, 121.
  Sterling, 123.
  Sue E., 122.
  Theodore, 122.
  Theodore, Mrs., 119.

Orgain—Continued
  Thomas Adams, 120.
  Virginia, 122, 123.
  William, 123.
  William (Maj.), 119.
Organ, Matt., 511.
Orin, Edmund, 308.
Ormsby, Rev. Mr., 331.
Osborne,
  Ann, 314.
  Francis, 313.
  John, 314.
Otter River, 32, 35, 36, 288, 324, 326, 331.
Otter River Church, 337, 339, 342, 345.
Overby,
  Nicholas, 370.
  Peter, 370.
  Wm., 529.
Overstreet,
  Ann Parke, 118.
  Ralph M., 118.
  Ralph M., Jr., 118.
Overwharton Parish, 19.
Overton,
  Fathy Ballard, 176.
  John, 176, 177, 451, 554, 555, 556, 559.
  William, 218.
  William, Jr., 218.
  William B., 176.
Owen,
  Barnabas, 559.
  Barnett, 415, 419, 425, 430, 525.
  Jon., 517.
  Jos., 515.
  Joseph, 355.
  Nathaniel, 527.
  Thomas McAdory (Dr.), 264.
  William, 413, 415, 419, 425, 427, 430, 434, 439, 441.
Owens,
  Anne, 305.
  Barnett, 524, 538.
  David, 514.
  Waltho, 514.
  Wm., 514, 524.
Oxford, 98.
Oxley, William, 310.

P

Palmer, 345.
Palmer,
  Elizabeth, 113.
  John, 113.
  Mary, 270.
  Pirmenas, 508.
  Rich., 64, 346, 349, 369, 509.
Palmour, Halcott, 305.
Pamplet, Wm., 514.
Pamplett, Wm., 515.
Pamunkey River, 167.
Parham,
  Edward, 377, 381, 385, 389, 391, 394, 398.
  Sarah, 307.
  Wm., 500.
Parish of Cornwall, 357.
Parish,
  Charles, 423, 543.
  Elizabeth, 125.
  James, 543.
  John, 28, 37, 357, 359, 371, 375, 380, 384, 390.
  Lucretia, 308.
  Peter, 504.
Park,
  Ann, 320.
  Nancy, 306.
Parke,
  John, 167.
  Susannah, 167.
Parker,
  John, 348, 511, 514.
  Wm., 505, 511.
Parmer, Chilian, 270.
Parnall, Eliz., 511.
Parrish Family, 267.
Parrish,
  Charles, 267, 268, 527, 543.
  David, 267, 453.
  Elizabeth, 268.
  Hannah, 267.
  James, 268.
  James S., 171.
  Joel, 268.
  John, 267, 268, 379.
  Jowell, 267.
  Lucicy, 268.
  Lucy, 267, 268.
  Martha, 268.
  Mary, 268.
  Matthew, 268.
  Millippi, 267, 268.
  Peters, 268.

Parrish—Continued
  Robert, 267.
  Samuel, 268.
  Sarah, 268.
  Sterling, 268.
  William, 268.
Parrot, William, 534, 549.
Parrott, William, 454, 524.
Partrick, Sarah, 305.
Pasture, Rev. Mr., 373.
Paterson, John, 315.
Patillo, Mary Parrish, 267.
Patison, Jonathan, 385.
Patrick County, 22, 23.
Patrick, John, 501.
Patrick Parish, 22, 23.
Patterson,
  John, 536, 538.
  Rebecca, 310.
Patteson, 522.
Patteson,
  John, 430.
  Jonathan, 451, 455, 459, 521, 522, 529, 530, 545, 546, 547.
  Julia Meade, 237.
  Mr., 421.
  Robert Baskerville, 122.
Pattison,
  Jno., 436.
  Jonathan, 387, 388, 506, 512.
Payne, Sallie J., 129.
Peace, Samuel, 543.
Pearson, Thomas, 202.
Peaties Family, 269.
Peaties, Thomas, 404.
Peatis, Thomas, 408.
Pedington, John George, 350.
Peebles,
  Agnes, 311.
  Anne Ruffin, 157.
  Elizabeth, 313.
  Eva, 161.
  James, 305.
  Mary, 308.
  Robert B. (Judge), 157.
  Susannah, 308.
Pembroke College, 61.
Pendleton,
  Edmund, 233.
  Judge, 148.
  Letitia B., 233.
  Micajah, 233.
  Philip, 233.
  Reuben, 236.

INDEX 615

Penick,
  Bishop Clifton, 118.
  Mary Clifton, 118.
  Mary Hoge, 118.
Penn, William, 233.
Pennel, Wm., 366.
Pennington,
  John, 366.
  Ursella, 304.
Pensacola, 155.
Perant, John, 373.
Perkerson, Betsey, 314.
Perkins, Lewis, 309.
Perkinson,
  Daniel, 308.
  Elizabeth, 312.
  Field, 313.
  Francis, 314.
  John, 313.
  Maxon, 308.
  Pricilla, 313.
Perrin, Joseph, 326.
Perry, William, 309.
Persons, Mary, 202.
Pescud, Isabella Willis, 158.
Petaway, Edwd., 511.
Petersburg, 20, 109, 110, 111, 406.
  Lottery to build church in, 137.
Peter Jones & Richard Jones Genealogies, 273.
Petersburg Intelligencer, 138.
Peterson,
  Alley, 309.
  Amelia, 305.
Petteways, 519.
Petties Family, 269.
Petties,
  John, 515.
  Thos., 395, 396, 397, 402, 510, 515.
Pettipool, Wm., 514.
Petti Poole, Colonel, 403.
Pettis Family, 269.
Pettis,
  John, 385.
  Thos., 99, 240, 349, 361, 364, 365, 366, 371.
Pettus Family, 269.
Pettus,
  David, 269, 270, 451, 558.
  David, Jr., 270.
  Elenor, 270.
  Elizabeth, 270, 271.
  Harriott, 258, 316.

Pettus—Continued
  John, 28, 258, 269, 270, 271, 316, 320, 452, 479, 482.
  John, Sr., 269, 270, 554.
  Julian, 270.
  Martha, 320.
  Martha Lenis, 320.
  Nancy, 270.
  Overton, 269.
  Polly L., 316.
  Polly Lipscomb, 258, 260.
  Ragland, 270.
  Rebecca, 269.
  Sally D., 315.
  Samuel, 269, 270.
  Sarah, 269, 270.
  Stephen, 271, 317.
  Susanna, 270.
  Susannah, 258, 259.
  Thomas, 28, 30, 207, 240, 269, 270, 271, 274, 375, 379, 380, 382, 383, 384, 386, 388, 390, 392, 393, 414, 418, 419, 421, 424, 427, 429, 433, 434, 438, 439, 440, 441, 444.
  Thos., Senr., 521.
  W., 258.
  Walker, 269.
  William G., 318.
Pettypool,
  Martha, 170, 276.
  Coldwell (?), 324.
Pewet, Joel, 437, 553.
Pewit, Joel, 527.
Phelps, 331, 337, 346.
Phelps,
  John, 35, 36, 249, 324, 331.
  Samuel, 377.
Philips,
  Ellen, 273.
  George, 271.
  John (Capt.), 271.
  John (Rev.), 565,
    Death of, 565.
  Mary, 272.
Phillips Family, 271.
Phillips,
  Ann, 272.
  Anthony, 272.
  Betsy, 272.
  Capt., 394, 397, 398.
  Dyer, 272.
  Edith, 272.
  Elizabeth Penn, 233.
  George, 28, 30, 41, 271, 348, 368, 379, 380, 381, 384, 386, 389, 390,

Phillips, George—Continued
391, 392, 397, 401, 414, 415, 416,
417, 418, 420, 433, 448.
George (Capt.), 389, 391, 393.
John, 271, 272.
John (Rev.), 71.
Mary Ann, 272.
Micaja, 272.
Nancy, 272.
Priscilla, 272.
Robert, 272.
Suckey Barnes, 272.
W. C., 322, 495.
W. C. (Rev.), 321.
Phillups,
Capt., 405.
George, 404, 421, 432, 434, 440,
441, 442, 449, 450, 526, 543.
Robt., 526.
Pig River, 340.
Pike, George, 552.
*Pioneer Settlers of Grayson County,
Virginia*, 231, 239.
Pippen,
Lucie Garland, 230.
Sallie Garland, 228.
Sallie Macon, 230.
Walter Woodfin (Rev.), 230.
Pittman,
John, 209.
Sarah C., 209.
Pittsylvania County, 22, 23.
Pleasant, John, 505, 511, 515.
Poe, Robert, 345.
Poindexter, Philp, 515.
Pollard,
Henry, 522, 559.
John, 309.
Wm., 368.
Pond, William H., 163.
Pool, 557.
Pool,
Adam, 501.
Colwell P., 554.
Frederick, 543.
John, 107.
Widow, 557.
Wm., 369, 501.
Wm. (Capt.), 350.
Wm., Senr., 501.
Poole,
Baxter, 107.
Martha Petty, 276.
Pools Old Path, 421, 451.
Porter, 293.

Porter, Ovid, 159.
Pothyress,
Susanna, 308.
William, 307.
Potter, Sarah, 309.
Potts,
Eppa Hunton, 125.
John, 306.
N. Derrick, 125.
Pound, Thos., 391, 507.
Pounds,
Jane, 426.
Jean, 536.
Powel, 397.
Powel,
John, 392, 396, 400, 402, 407, 554,
555, 556.
Powell,
James (Dr.), 236.
John, 53, 55, 398, 401, 405, 410,
412.
Mildred Jordan, 236.
Poythress,
Agnes, 309.
Hardemar, 310.
Susanna, 309.
Prentis, William, 310.
Presbyterians,
Oppose general assessment, 92.
Price,
Daniel, 370, 510, 515, 516, 518.
John, 362, 398, 507, 518.
Priest,
Colulias, 394.
Cornelias, 512.
Cornelius, 505, 506, 519.
Prince Edward, 452.
Prince Edward C. H., 104.
Prince Edward County, 68, 86, 155,
554.
Prince Edward line, 560.
Prince Edward Road, 473.
Prince George Co., 200.
Prince of Wales, 128.
Prince William County, 61.
Prior, Lucy, 119.
Pritchett, Martha, 308.
Processioning lands, 75 et seq.,
Laws respecting, 75 et seq.
Proctor, 357.
Proctor,
Elizabeth, 308.
Rev. Mr., 67, 356, 362, 372.
William (Rev.), 65, 72.

Puckett,
  Richard, 560.
  Thomas H., 560.
Pugh, Mary T., 220.
Pulaski, ship, 160.
Pulley, Spittle, 503.
Pulliam,
  Benj., 509.
  James, 514, 525, 537, 538.
  Js., 537.
  Joseph, 514.
Pully,
  Spittle, 504.

Pully—Continued
  William, Jr., 316.
Purcer,
  John, 509.
  Peter, 509.
Purdie, 339.
Purdie,
  George (Rev.), 62, 72, 335, 336.
  Rev. Mr., 67, 337, 338, 363.
Puryear,
  Eva Marshall, 123.
  John, 123.
  Wm., 526.

Q

Quakers, 12, 13, 15.

R

Ragland, John, 270.
Ragsdail, Benjamin, 274.
Ragsdale Family, 273.
Ragsdale, 397.
Ragsdale,
  Alice, 274.
  Alse, 278.
  Ann, 274, 279.
  Annie, 277.
  Armenia, 279.
  Baxter, 274, 276, 277, 280, 416, 505.
  Bedee Martha, 280.
  Benjamin, 245, 273, 274, 275, 281.
  Catherine, 278.
  Daniel, 273, 274.
  Drury, 273, 276, 278, 558.
  Drury (Capt.), 276.
  Edward, 28, 30, 274, 276, 277, 278, 279, 280, 281, 423, 448, 453, 458, 468, 469, 470, 471, 472, 476, 477, 478, 480, 481, 543, 544, 555.
  Elizabeth, 245, 274, 277, 279, 280.
  Faith, 274.
  Frances, 245, 277.
  George, 320.
  Godfrey, 273, 274, 275, 276.
  Harrison, 280.
  Henry, 278.
  James, 276, 278, 280.
  Jane, 245, 280.
  Jemima, 277.
  Jemime, 277.
  Jesse, 275.

Ragsdale—Continued
  Joel M., 245, 280, 281.
  John, 28, 30, 37, 40, 51, 52, 69, 99, 107, 186, 206, 226, 242, 274, 276, 277, 278, 279, 280, 281, 320, 350, 357, 359, 360, 361, 364, 366, 371, 374, 375, 378, 379, 380, 381, 382, 383, 384, 388, 390, 392, 393, 394, 396, 397, 401, 402, 404, 408, 411, 412, 413, 414, 415, 416, 417, 418, 419, 421, 424, 425, 427, 428, 429, 431, 432, 433, 434, 435, 436, 438, 439, 440, 441, 442, 443, 444, 446, 447, 448, 449, 450, 451, 454, 455, 458, 464, 465, 466, 467, 468, 469, 470, 472, 474, 475, 476, 477, 478, 479, 480, 481, 482, 484, 485, 486, 487, 488, 489, 490, 491, 492, 493, 494, 506, 520, 528, 530, 548, 554, 558.
  John (Capt.), 187.
  John B., 280.
  John Edwin, 279.
  John Hardy, 277.
  John, Jr., 275.
  John, Sr., 275.
  John L., 280.
  Joseph, 273, 274, 275, 276, 278, 559.
  Joshua, 106, 276, 277, 278, 280, 402, 405, 457, 459, 460, 461, 462, 464, 466, 467, 468, 548, 558.
  Letitia, 278.
  Martha, 245, 274, 316.

Ragsdale—Continued
  Martha Gee, 247.
  Mary, 187, 245, 277, 279, 280.
  Milly, 320.
  Mollie, 276.
  Nancy, 280.
  Nancy Harrison, 279.
  Patsy Gee, 279.
  Permelia, 279.
  Peter, 273, 274, 275, 276, 278, 279.
  Priscella, 277, 278.
  Rachael, 273, 274, 276, 279.
  Rebecca, 280.
  Richard, 275.
  Sally Baxter, 279.
  Samuel, 278, 279.
  Sarah, 278.
  Sicily, 280.
  Tab., 274.
  Tabitha, 274.
  Tathy, 277.
  Thomas, 275.
  Thomas Morgan, 279.
  William, 28, 108, 244, 245, 275, 276, 277, 280, 281, 311, 320, 491, 493, 494, 495.
  Winfred, 274.
  Winnefred, 275.
  Will, 275.
Raines,
  Amey Goodwyn, 313.
  Becky, 304.
  Elizabeth, 304.
Raincy,
  Francis, 500.
  Fras., 500.
Raleigh, N. C., 146.
Raleigh Parish, 61.
Ramsden, William, 306.
Randal, Josias, 33, 74, 324.
Randolph-Macon College, 129.
Randolph,
  John, of Roanoke, 235.
  Maria, 304.
Randolphs Road, 327.
Randolph's and Talbot's road, 34.
Raney,
  Evelyn Cameron, 163.
  Judge, 163.
Ravenscroft,
  John S., 71, 97, 141, 499.
  John S. (Rev.), 72.
Ray,
  James, 344.
  Joseph, 340.

Ray—Continued
  Saunders, 443, 553.
  Reaby, John, 309.
  Read Family, 281.
  Read, 329, 354.
Read,
  Clement, 26, 28, 29, 34, 35, 36, 98, 184, 256, 324, 325, 327, 328, 329, 331, 332, 334, 335, 338, 339, 341, 342, 343, 344, 346, 352, 353, 354, 356, 357, 424, 456, 457.
  Clement (Col.), 150, 267, 281, 360.
  Clement, Jr. (Col.), 150.
  Col.; 337, 377, 382, 385, 389.
  Edmund (Maj.), 150.
  Isaac, 150, 205.
  James, 74, 327, 331.
  Mary, 149, 150, 267, 424, 456.
  Mr., 34.
  Tho., 456.
Reade,
  George, 150.
  Thomas, 150.
Readers, Cumberland Parish, 72 et seq.
Ready, Isham, 236.
Redman, Wm., 336, 337, 338.
Redwood, Anne, 312.
Reeds Creek, 205.
Reedy Creek, 32, 40, 205, 324, 325, 331, 388, 422, 423, 454, 529.
Reedy Creek Church, 33, 34, 37, 40, 41, 42, 43, 70, 103, 337, 339, 341, 342, 345, 350, 351, 359, 361, 362, 371, 376, 381, 384, 387, 388, 389, 391, 392, 394, 395, 397, 398, 412, 414, 415, 417, 419, 425, 429, 433, 448, 460, 464, 475, 476, 478, 480, 483, 488, 491, 493, 494, 495.
  Additions to, 415, 417.
  Alterations, 418.
  Completed, received, 459.
  Gallery in new, 431.
  New Church, 418.
  Repairs needed, 481.
  Settlement for work on, 458.
Reedy Creek Old Church, 424.
Reedy Creek Old Road, 404, 423, 453.
Reedy Creek Road, 58, 486, 541, 563.
Reeks, 546.
Reeks, Phillip, 421, 544.
Reekses, 519.

Reese,
  Jacob, 312.
  Martha, 308.
  Tho., 549.
Reeves, Isaac, 520, 521.
Religious Freedom, 92,
  Act for, 92,
  Jefferson's bill, 92, 93,
  Statute of, 146, 148.
Religious tax,
  Abolished, 89, 90,
  General assessment, 91,
  Petition respecting, 91.
Rentfroe, Joseph, 74, 338.
Reps Joneses Road, 423, 453.
Resaca, Battle of, 155.
Revely,
  Leslie, 230.
  Nowlin, 230.
  Panthea, 230.
Revolutionary War, 102,
  Churches after, 45, 93, 94.
Rice,
  David, 231.
  Mary, 231.
  Sarah, 152.
Rich, Eliz., 511.
Richardson,
  Judith, 308.
  Liddy, 308.
Richmond County, 64.
Richmond Enquirer, 229.
Richmond *Whig*, 162.
Riddle,
  Thos., 391, 393, 394, 398.
  Wm., 366.
Riddlehurst, Mary, 313.
Ridout, Parthena, 304.
Right,
  John, 511.
  Thos., 511.
Riley, Mary, 308.
Rives,
  Briggs, 311.
  Elizabeth Atkins, 305.
  Frances, 307.
  Judith, 310, 311, 313.
  Rebecca, 308.
  Sarah, 308.
  Susanna, 313.
  William, 309.
Roads, Wm., 526.
Roanoak Church, 361.
Roanoak River, 369, 370, 375, 378.
Roanoke Church, 342.

Roanoke River, 37, 201, 328, 340, 350, 351, 366, 368, 509.
Roberson, Christo., 481, 484.
Roberts,
  Christopher (Capt.), 468.
  Francis, 308.
  James, 344.
  Mary, 306.
  Thos., 502.
  Thos., Senr., 501.
  Wm., 510, 515, 516, 522.
Roberts Old Road, 536.
Robertses Rolling Road, 422, 452.
Robertson Family, 282.
Robertson, 28.
Robertson,
  Anna, 191.
  Capt., 560.
  Christopher, 30, 282, 450, 452, 455, 458, 459, 460, 461, 462, 464, 465, 467, 468, 472, 473, 475, 476, 477, 478, 479, 480, 484, 485, 486, 487, 488, 490, 549, 554.
  Daniel, 28, 315, 490.
  Francis, 315, 437, 550, 559.
  Frank, 530.
  Henry, 432, 516, 517, 531, 532, 534, 549.
  John, 315, 501, 519.
  John Archer, 314.
  Mary, 307.
  Nathaniel, 369.
  Warning Peter, 316.
  William, 307, 314.
  William H., 315.
Robertson fork, 349.
Rockhouse, N. C., 198.
Roe, Mary, 248.
Rogers,
  John, 368, 506, 512.
  Martha, 192.
  Sarah, 359.
  Thomas, 346.
Roger's Mill, 347.
Robinson,
  A. I. (Dr.), 293.
  Henry, 524.
  John, 107.
Robunson, John, 107.
Rollings, Jacob, 308.
Rook, John, 362.
Rose,
  C. A. (Dr.), 238.
  Hugh (Col.), 234.
  Lucinda, 234

Rosewood, 109.
Ross, Joseph Russell, 157.
Rosser,
  Burwell, 307.
  Lucretia, 305.
  William, 313.
Rottonberry,
  John, 501.
  Samuel, 501.
  Wm., 501.
Rough Creek, 347.
Rowland, Mary, 274.
Rowlett,
  Elizabeth, 270.
  John, 310, 312.
  Matthew, 270.
  Matthew J., 271.
  Phillip, 554.
  William B., 195.
Royal,
  John, 508.
  Sarah, 508.
  William, 310.
Royall,
  Elizabeth, 314.
  Winifred, 310.
Royster,
  Jacob, 39, 378.
  Wm., 370.
Rudd, Alexr., 511.
Rudder,
  Alexander, 402, 519, 544, 554, 558.

Rudder—Continued
  Alexander, Jr., 107.
  Edward, 189.
  Samuel, 74, 107, 372, 376, 381, 385, 388, 391, 394, 397, 404, 409, 413, 414, 419, 427, 429, 544.
Ruddy, Jon., 108.
Ruffen, 512.
Ruffen,
  John, 503.
  Robt., 504.
Ruffin,
  Anne, 156.
  Col., 503.
  Thomas (C. J.), 156.
Russel,
  Phillamon, 186.
  Rebeckah, 304.
Russell,
  Frances, 313.
  Lurany, 306.
  Martha, 219.
  Nathaniel, 341.
  Phil, 511.
  Philemon, 518.
  Rd., 510.
Rutherford, James, 347.
Rutledge, Polly, 194.
Ryan,
  Donald Hillsdon, 122.
  Richard Hillsdon, 122.

S

Sadler,
  Burwell, 314.
  Lucretia, 311.
Saint Peter's Parish, 19.
Samford, Wm., 544.
Sammon,
  James, 533, 534.
  Wm., 533.
Sammons,
  James, 535.
  John, 523, 533.
  Sarah (Mrs.), 270.
  Wm., 518.
  Wm., Senr., 523.
Sanders, Francis, 362.
Sandford, John, 505.
Sandys, Milly T., 318.
San Juan Hill, 161.
Sansom,
  R., 455.
  Richard, 449, 450, 457, 536.

Santa Rosa Island, 155.
Sarjant, John, 501.
Saterwhite,
  Mitchell (Capt.), 348.
  Thos., 509.
Saunders,
  Jesse, 531, 532.
  Jessee, 421, 437, 548.
  Patty, 310.
Scarberry, Sally, 277.
School house, mentioned, 36.
Scoggin, William, 309.
Scot, James, 306.
Scott, 548.
Scott,
  Abraham Glenn, 119.
  Annie Douglas, 119.
  Edward Chambers, 189.
  Edward Glenn, 119.
  Eliza Jane, 189.
  Frances Epes, 119.

Scott—Continued
  George Anna, 190.
  Gerreld, 312.
  James, 223, 224, 551, 557, 563.
  James Archer, 189.
  Jane, 223.
  Jean, 316.
  John, 211, 368, 387, 388, 506, 510, 515, 521, 523, 529, 531, 548.
  John, Senr., 437, 531.
  Jon., 518.
  Martha Ann, 189.
  Mary Elizabeth, 190.
  Michael Branch, 189.
  Milicent Chambers, 189.
  Robert, 116, 189, 388, 419, 438, 507, 510, 515, 516, 518, 529, 531, 546, 553.
  Robert Craig, 119.
  Robert, Jr., 189.
  Thomas, 205, 559.
  Thomas Chambers, 190.
  William, 279.
  William Henry, 189.
Seat, Josiah, 340.
Seay, Sallie, 122.
Secession Convention, 128, 237.
Selden v. *Overseers of the Poor*, 149.
Self,
  Edward, 391, 392, 394, 395, 397, 401, 404, 407, 409, 412, 414, 416, 419, 427, 429, 440, 529, 530, 546, 553.
  Jno., 409, 411, 413, 415, 419, 425, 427, 430, 434.
Seneca Creek, 287.
Servant,
  Bertrand, 174.
  Mary, 174.
Seventy-five Years in Old Virginia, 193.
Seward, Carter, 308.
Sharp, William, 312.
Sharpsburg, battle of, 154.
Shawneetown, Ill., 118.
Shelbon,
  Jas., 391.
  Joseph, 391.
  Thos., 391.
Shelborn,
  James, 394.
  Thomas, 394.
Shelborne,
  Anne, 269.

Shelborne—Continued
  James, 396, 398, 401, 405, 409, 413, 415, 419, 425, 427, 430, 434, 523, 532.
  Thomas, 523, 532, 533.
Shelburn, Elizabeth, 210.
Shelburne, Sarah, 278.
Shelton,
  Ralph, 508.
  Wm., 507.
Shepard,
  Anne Cameron, 156, 157.
  William Blount, 157.
Shepherd,
  Ann, 236.
  Christopher, 236.
  Nancy, 306.
  William, 423, 545.
Shiffery, Patrick M., 309.
Ship,
  Delitia, 196.
  Joseph, 388, 516.
  Josiah, 532.
  Anna, 161.
  Bartlett, 161, 198.
  John, 198.
  Josiah, 197.
  Kate C., 155.
  Kate Cameron, 145.
  Katherine Cameron, 131, 132, 150, 161, 198.
  Nancy, 198.
  Thomas, 197, 198.
  William, 198.
  William E. (Maj.), 161.
  William Ewen, 161.
  William M. (Judge), 161.
Shirley, 229.
Shore, John, 305.
Short,
  Henry, 339.
  Mary Bagby, 157.
Sifer, John, 328.
Sikes, Jonas, 522, 530.
Silvie, Mary, 309.
Simcoe, Etta, 125.
Simmons,
  Elizabeth Manull, 304.
  George, 430, 431.
  James W., 125.
Sims, Ellen, 163.
Singleton, Sarah, 310.
Skinner, William, 306.
Slater, Lodowick, 312.
Slaughter, 518.

Slaughter,
  Charles Rice, 234.
  Edward, 516, 518, 523, 524, 532, 533, 535, 549.
  John, 532.
  Philip (Rev. Dr.), 136.
  Philip (Dr.), 193, 206.
  Robert (Dr.), 234.
  Robert H., 233.
Slokam, Christopher, 305.
Smallwood, Robert F., 156.
Smith Family, 282.
Smith, 333.
Smith,
  Abraham, 283.
  Agnes, 283.
  Anne C., 163.
  Archibald, 305.
  Benjamin, 283, 307.
  Capt., 341.
  Celah, 312.
  Charles, 282, 320.
  Clark, 307.
  Elizabeth, 282, 283, 315.
  Guy, 369.
  James, 28, 282, 316, 320, 464, 465, 468, 473, 483, 484, 485, 487, 488, 489, 490, 491.
  Jennie Garland, 235.
  Jenny, 251.
  Jesse, 308.
  John, 282, 283, 311, 312, 347, 517, 518, 523.
  Joseph, 282, 449, 453, 514, 561, 562, 563.
  Joseph M., 282.
  Lucy, 283.
  Lucy Park, 320.
  Luke, 28, 282, 326, 332, 340.
  Mary, 311.
  May, 283.
  Peter, 283.
  Richard, 283.
  Robart, 283.
  Thomas, 74, 283, 355, 358, 373, 517, 520, 523, 524, 528, 532.
  William, 283, 312, 560.
Smiths Creek, 340.
Smiths River, 339.
Smithson,
  Bartlett, 559.
  Charles, 523, 533.
  Frances, 515.
  Francis, 521, 522, 523, 532, 534, 535.

Smithson—Continued
  Fras., 510, 515, 518, 530.
  John, 403, 510, 515, 521.
  Keziah, 199.
  Manoah, 523, 532.
  Mary, 196, 199.
  Micajah, 199, 421, 530, 554, 558.
  Thos., 370.
  Wm., 518, 522, 523, 530, 532, 559.
Snead,
  John, 457, 540.
  Saml., 450, 473, 513, 537, 539.
Somervill, John, 317.
Southampton County, 138, 142.
Southern Historical Association, 264.
South Hill, Va., 178.
South Meherrin River, 38, 349, 403, 421, 452, 474.
Southside Counties, 20.
Southwark Parish, 183.
Sowell, Pleasant, 232.
Sparks, Saml., 551.
Speed Family, 284.
Speed,
  Henry, 284.
  James, 284.
  John, 28, 29, 38, 98, 99, 284, 325, 327, 328, 331, 332, 333, 337, 339, 342, 345, 346, 351, 354, 355, 356, 357, 358, 360, 361, 363, 364, 365, 366, 367, 370, 371, 372, 374, 375, 377, 378, 503.
  Joseph, 284.
Spencer,
  Elizabeth Julia, 284.
  Mary, 284.
  Thomas, 284.
Spotswood,
  Alexander (Gov.), 213, 214, 228, 229.
  Ann, 228.
  Ann Catherine, 229.
  John, 228.
Spragins, Melcijah, 314.
Spring Creek, 452, 554.
Springfield Creek, 560.
Stainback,
  Anne, 304.
  Elizabeth, 311.
  Mary C., 223.
  Peter, 223, 224.
Standeford, James, 340.
Stanton River, 326, 347, 348.

INDEX 623

Staples,
 Thos., 507.
 Thompson, 535.
 Wm., 535, 536.
Statute of Religious Freedom, 146, 148.
Statutes, respecting marriages, 7, 8, 9, 10, 12, 13, 14.
Staunton River, 287.
Stegalls, 519.
Stembridge, John, 523, 532.
Stephens,
 Mary, 504.
 Nancy, 308.
Stephenson Family, 284.
Stephenson, 514.
Stevenson Family, 284.
Stevenson,
 Francis, 285.
 John, 28, 124, 284, 285, 314, 471, 472, 473, 474, 475, 476, 478, 480, 562.
 Martha A., 315.
 Martha Anderson, 124, 285.
 Mary B., 317.
 Thomas, 28, 124, 284, 285, 464, 465, 466, 467.
 Wm., 550.
Steward, John, 338.
Stewart,
 Jane, 312.
 Josephine, 121.
 Robert, 313.
Stewman, Thos., 521.
Stiles,
 George, 544.
 Jesse, 309.
Stith, Richard, 508.
Stoakes, David, 384, 402.
Stokes Family, 285.
Stokes, 331.
Stokes,
 Allen, 403, 431, 514, 525, 540.
 Allen, Sr., 513.
 Allin, 437, 524, 538, 550, 554.
 Anne Bond, 128.
 Charles, 514, 524, 525.
 David, 26, 28, 30, 33, 266, 285, 324, 325, 329, 331, 379, 382, 383, 386, 393, 396, 397, 411, 412, 444, 445, 449, 450, 514, 523, 524, 525, 538.
 David (Col.), 390, 395, 414, 514.
 D. Jr. (Col.), 106.

Stokes—Continued
 David, Jr., 29, 266, 285, 446, 456, 538.
 David R. (Capt.), 127.
 David R. Jr., 128.
 Elizabeth, 184, 538.
 Evan, 514, 525, 538.
 Evans, 514, 524.
 Henry, 29, 30, 31, 58, 285, 404, 431, 441, 446, 447, 450, 454, 455, 457, 458, 459, 460, 461, 462, 463, 464, 465, 466, 467, 469, 470, 472, 473, 474, 475, 476, 477, 478, 479, 480, 481, 482, 484, 485, 486, 487, 489, 490, 515, 524, 536, 537, 538, 554.
 Irby, 128.
 Isabella Overton, 128.
 John, 29, 285, 318, 495, 496, 498, 499, 500.
 John (Capt.), 169.
 Martha Craig, 128.
 Mr., 48.
 Richard, 514, 525, 538.
 Richard, Jr., 514, 529.
 Richard, Senr., 424, 514, 524.
 Richard Carter, 128.
 Richard Carter, Jr., 128.
 Richard H., 211.
 Sally M., 317.
 Sarah, 315.
 Shadrack, 538.
 Sill, 387.
 Silvanus, 513, 514.
 Susan Jones, 128.
 Susanna, 316.
 Sylvanus, 457.
 Terry, 128.
 W., 490.
 William, 29, 58, 285, 317, 437, 485, 486, 487, 488, 489, 491, 493, 495, 496, 514, 524, 551.
 Young, 184, 514.
Stokes Mill Creek, 403, 422, 453.
Stokes Race Ground, 350.
Stone, 521.
Stone,
 Assebyas, 513.
 Edmund, 314.
 Elizabeth, 513.
 John, 345, 351, 368, 508, 514, 525.
 John, Jr., 513.
 John, Sr., 513.
 Katura, 234.
 Lancelot, 313.
 Mary, 513.

Stone—Continued
  Richard, 437, 513, 525, 539, 540, 551.
  Richd. Junr., 539, 554.
  Thos., 513.
  Will, 107.
  William, 270, 279, 370, 387, 437, 510, 511, 515, 531, 539, 555, 556, 558, 559.
  William, Junr., 437, 548, 558.
Stone Creek, 519.
Stoneland, 228.
"Stonewall" Jackson's Brigade, 126.
Stony Creek, 348, 402, 421, 451, 518.
Stout, Mary Randolph, 318.
Stovall, Annie, 230.
Strange,
  Ann, 442, 445.
  Benjamin, 527.
Stranges, Ann, 443.
Strawan, John, 387, 513.
Street Family, 285.
Street,
  Ann Park, 316.
  Anthony, 29, 30, 49, 91, 286, 406, 407, 410, 411, 413, 415, 416, 420, 423, 428, 431, 432, 435, 436, 437, 443, 444, 447, 448, 449, 450, 458, 459, 461, 528, 546, 555,
    Poetry of, 50.
  Anthony (Col.), 286.
  Anthony (Maj.), 457, 458.
  D., 490.
  David, 29, 31, 71, 286, 315, 485, 486, 487, 489, 490, 491, 564, 565.
  James, 286.
  John, 29, 286, 479, 480, 481, 482, 483, 484.
  John T., 286.
  Mary Ann, 108, 116.
  Moses, 372.
  Waddy, 29, 31, 140, 286, 315, 495, 496, 498, 499, 500.
  Waddy (Col.), 108.
Street Genealogy, 286.
Streete, Wady, 495.
Stuart, Robert, 310.
Stuart's Cavalry, 120.
Stuman, Thos., 521.
Stunks, Thos., 514.
Sturdivant,
  Ann, 123.
  James, 309, 437.
  John, 311.
  Mary, 314.
  Sarah, 304.

St. Andrew Parish, 21, 22, 32, 33, 332.
St. Andrews, Scotland, 179, 181.
St. James Northam Parish, 19.
St. James's Parish, 39, 133, 134, 141, 145, 275, 385, 395, 457, 468.
  Created, 51.
St. John's Cemetery, Pensacola, 155.
St. John's Church, 19.
St. Margaret's Parish, 60.
St. Mary's School, 146.
St. Patrick's Parish, 68.
St. Paul's Parish, 216.
St. Peter's Parish, 167, 183.
St. Peter's Parish Register, 216, 247.
Suffolk, 104.
Suiter,
  Florence Carter, 128.
  John A., 128.
  Overton Stokes, 128.
Sullivan,
  Bernard J., 153.
  Kathleen, 152.
Sullivant,
  Charles, 336, 337, 516, 518, 524.
  John, 337.
  Owen, 338, 339.
Surry County, N. C., 197.
Sutherland, Joseph, 232.
Sutton, Emily, 164.
Swail, Simon, 313.
Swanson, Frances, 309.
Swepson,
  Richd., 508, 510.
  Susanna, 306.
Swift, Mary Ann, 181.
Swift's Creek, 111.
Swinbrod, George, 312.
Syme,
  Andrew, 159.
  Andrew (Rev.), 141, 158, 317.
  Blanche Bragg, 159.
  Duncan Cameron, 159.
  Elizabeth Batte, 158.
  George F., 159.
  Jean Cameron, 158.
  Jean M., 141.
  John Bryan, 159.
  John Cameron, 159.
  John W., 158.
  Mildred Cameron, 159.
  Mary, 154.
  Mary Louisa, 159.
  William Anderson, 159.

T

Tabb Family, 286.
Tabb,
  Humphrey, 286, 287.
  John, 287, 558.
  Major, 545.
  Thomas, 29, 30, 38, 40, 41, 43, 55, 104, 114, 188, 242, 286, 287, 366, 370, 374, 375, 376, 390, 393, 395, 397, 398, 399, 400, 401, 402, 404, 405, 406, 408, 409, 411, 412, 413, 414, 415, 417, 418, 424, 425, 427, 428, 429, 432, 433, 434, 438, 439, 440, 442, 444, 512, 542, 552.
  Thomas (Col.), 550, 552.
  Thos. (Maj.), 416, 420.
Taber,
  Rachell, 509.
  Riah, 509.
  Wm., 509.
Tackett, Bartley, 312.
Talbert,
  Edmund, 291.
  Matthew, 291.
Talbot, 329, 337.
Talbot,
  Agnes, 289.
  Amanda, 293.
  Amelia, 293.
  Anne Harvey, 265.
  Charles, 288, 289, 290, 328.
  Christianna, 289.
  Clayton, 291.
  David Given, 289.
  Drusilla, 288.
  Edmund, 289, 290, 291, 292, 293.
  Eliza, 293.
  Elizabeth, 289, 293.
  George, 289.
  Hale, 291, 292.
  Isham, 288, 289, 290, 291, 292.
  James, 288, 289, 290, 291, 292.
  James Smith, 289.
  Jane, 288.
  John, 288, 289, 290, 291, 293.
  Martha, 289, 290, 293.
  Mary, 289, 290, 291.
  Matthew, 25, 35, 36, 212, 249, 288, 289, 290, 291, 292, 293, 324, 325, 327, 331, 332, 334, 335, 336.
  Moile, 289.
  Mr., 34.
  Nancy, 289.
  Phoebe, 289.
  Polly, 293.

Talbot—Continued
  Providence, 289.
  Sally, 293.
  Sarah, 289.
  Thomas, 289, 291, 292.
  William, 293.
  Williston, 289, 291.
  Yaskey, 289.
Talbots, 332.
Talbots, Charles, 331.
Talbot's (and Randolph's) road, 34.
Talbott Family, 287.
Talbott, 346.
Talbott,
  Matthew, 29, 287, 353.
  Matthew, Jr., 287.
Tales of a Grandfather, 151, 155.
Talen, Darby, 327.
Talley, Abrm., 521.
Tally,
  Abram, 505.
  Henry, 504, 505.
Talman, Henry, 174.
Tanner,
  Lucias, 372, 501, 502.
  Mattw., 509.
  Thos., 501, 502.
Tappahannock, Va., 158.
Tarleton, Col. Banestre, 104.
Tarleton's Legion, 105.
Tarry, 520.
Tarry,
  Edward, 114.
  George, 114, 528.
  Gracy, 115.
  Mary Booker, 112, 114, 115.
  Rebecca, 114, 316.
  Samuel, 112, 113, 114.
  Thomas, 115.
  Virginia, 115.
  William Taylor, 114.
Tate, Wm., 509.
Tatom, Benj., 533, 534.
Tatum, Benj., 523.
Taxes, to support Church, 83.
Taylor Family, 293.
Taylor, 389, 398, 548.
Taylor,
  Benjamin, 553.
  Daniel, 443, 445, 511, 519.
  Daniel (Rev.), 293.
  Edmond, 379.
  Edmund, 29, 30, 38, 39, 275, 294,

Taylor, Edmund—Continued
361, 362, 371, 373, 374, 375, 376, 377, 378.
Edmund F., 261, 317, 320.
Edmund L. (Col.), 71, 564-5.
Eliza, 314.
Elizabeth, 362.
George Griffin Lewis, 320.
James Preston, 126.
John, 225, 316.
Joseph, 443, 444, 445, 446, 448, 450, 456.
Lewis Littlepage (Lt. Col.), 294.
Louis L. (Capt.), 108.
Mary H., 222.
Petronella, 320.
Sarah, 114.
Thomas, 315, 350, 500, 501(?), 515, 522, 556.
Thos., Jr., 501.
Thos., Senr., 501.
Waller, 226.
Waller (Senator), 294.
William, 29, 30, 106, 294, 391, 406, 408, 412, 414, 417, 418, 424, 425, 429, 431, 437, 438, 439, 441, 442, 444, 446, 479, 480, 481, 482, 483, 484, 519.
William H., 29, 294, 491, 494, 495.
William Henry, 171.
William K., 126.
William (Lieut.), 294.
William Waller, 320.
Taylor's Ferry, 38.
Temple,
Elizabeth, 309.
Eppes, 309, 313.
Joshua, 313.
Nancy, 309.
Tench,
James, 306.
Sukey, 307.
Tenney, Thomas, 309.
Terry, Frances, 121.
Thixton,
Harry Ellyn, 118.
Mrs. Lillian W., 98.
Thomas,
Anne, 173.
Benjamin, 313.
David, 543.
Elizabeth, 306.
Lillie Beatrice, 129.
Wm., 502.

Thompson,
Bettie Anderson, 155.
David, 257.
Francis, 306.
James, 305, 543.
John, 74, 505.
Mary Shaw, 310.
Patsy, 316.
Rebeccah, 306.
Sally, 317.
William, 307, 309.
Thomson,
David, 108.
James, 348.
William, 313.
Thornton,
Evelyn, 154.
John, 530.
Judith, 154.
Luke, 531.
Mark, 514, 515.
Willie, 153.
Three Creek, 261.
Thrift, Joannah, 307.
Thurston,
Mary, 289.
Plummer, 289.
Thweat, Edwd., 404, 541.
Thweatt,
Betty, 306.
Daniel, 542, 552.
Edward, 527, 542, 552.
Peter, 308.
Susan, 307.
William, 208.
Thweatts, Edward, 526.
Timberlake,
William, 305.
Winefred, 312.
Times-Dispatch, The, 214, 215, 239.
Timms,
Amos, 502.
Amos, Jr., 501.
Tims, Amos, Jr., 366.
Tirsdel, 518.
Tisdale,
Richard T., 125.
Wm., 107, 545.
Tisdel, Wm., 512.
Titmarsh, Richard, 314.
Todd,
Anne, 299, 304.
James, 312.
Mary, 304.

Tolbert,
  James, 288.
  Mary, 288.
  Matthew, 288.
Tolen, Darby, 328.
Toleration Act, 73.
Tomlinson Family, 294.
Tomlinson, 548.
Tomlinson,
  Benjamin, 29, 30, 107, 294, 295, 403, 425, 428, 429, 431, 433, 434, 436, 438, 439, 440, 441, 442, 443, 520, 521, 548, 555.
  Benjamin (Capt.), 257, 424.
  Capt., 547.
  Col., 444.
  Harris, 107, 294.
  Jane, 294.
  Martha, 295.
  Mary, 295.
  Nancy, 295.
  Patty, 295.
Tomson,
  John, 74, 359, 368.
  Richard, 352.
Totty,
  Benjamin, 309.
  Margaret, 313.
  Robert, 313.
Tounsin, Jno., 521.
Townes,
  Edmund W., 122.
  Edward Taylor, 122.
  Joseph, 315.
  Rosa Orgain, 122.
  Stuart, 122.
Townsend,
  Jacob, 358.
  Jacob (Rev.), 67, 68, 72, 99, 360, 363.
  Joseph, 513, 536.
Townshend, Rev. Mr., 361.
Trayler, Joseph, 391.
Traylor,
  Buckner, 310.
  Jo, 389.
  Wm., 356.
Tredway, Thomas, 316.
Trevillians, 127.
Trinity Church, Asheville, N. C., 160.
Trinity College, 64.
Trinity Parish, 241.
Trustie, John, 389, 391, 394, 398, 405.

Tryon, William (Gov.), 152.
Tucker Family, 295.
Tucker, 537.
Tucker,
  Ann Green, 311.
  Biddy, 296.
  Catherine, 296.
  Charles S., 259.
  Elizabeth, 260.
  Elizabeth B., 259.
  George, 295, 296, 561.
  Henry, 296.
  James, 508.
  Joel, 296.
  John, 190, 563.
  Joseph, 259, 296, 564.
  Lew, 296.
  Lewelling, 561.
  Lucy Goode, 116, 190.
  Martha, 561.
  Robert, 296, 307.
  Thomas, 340.
  Widow, 556, 561.
  William, 29, 30, 107, 295, 296, 452, 468, 469, 470, 471, 472, 473, 474, 475, 476, 477, 480, 550, 561, 562.
  William, Jr., 107.
Tulloch, Hugh, 306.
Turbyfill, William, 548.
Tureman, Thomas, 394, 516, 530.
Turnbull,
  Ann, 313.
  Elizabeth, 305.
Turner,
  Elizabeth, 320.
  George, 306.
  James, 320, 527.
  Matthew, 315, 511.
  Wm., 511.
Turpin et al. v. Locket, 147, 149.
Tursakia Creek, 422, 452, 536.
Tusakia Creek, 403.
Tuslin Quarter Church, 38, 373, 374, 375.
Tuslin Quarter Spring,
  Church at, 38.
Twitty Family, 296.
Twitty, 329, 331.
Twitty,
  John, 26, 29, 33, 36, 296, 324, 325, 327, 328, 329, 331.
  Mr., 34, 48.
Twitty's Creek, 296.

Tyler, Lyon G. (Dr.), 167, 174.
Tyler's Quarterly Magazine, 263.

Tyree Family, 247.
Tyus, Pamelia, 306.

U

Underhill,
  Elizabeth, 312.
  Mary, 305, 310.
  William, 306.
Upmanhall, 61.

Upton, Mary, 331.
Usry, John, 527.
Ussery, John, 107, 437, 446, 448, 451, 453.

V

Valentine, James, 305.
VanDyck,
  David, 547.
  Henry, 107, 402, 519.
Vandyke,
  David, 107.
  Henry, 437.
Varnon,
  John, 347.
  Thomas, 347.
Varsaw, 540.
Vasser, Jonas, 513.
Vaughan,
  Abraham, 348.
  Ephraim, 304.
  Frances, 307.
  George, 350, 366.
  John, 317.
  Martha, 313.
  Peter, 304, 306.
  Reuben, 227.
  Reuben, Jr., 226.
  Rubin, 368.
Vaughn,
  Ben, 545.
  Craddock, 423, 546, 553, 555, 562.
Vaugn,
  Craddock, 529.

Vaugn—Continued
  Reubin, 348.
Vaune, Michael, 511.
Venable,
  A. B., 221.
  Alexander B., 221.
  Charles M., 221.
Vendike, Henry, 505.
Ventris, David, 308.
Vera Cruz, 160.
Vestries,
  Controversy with Colonial Governors, 59,
  Powers, importance, 24.
Vestry Book, Cumberland Parish, copied, 78.
Vestry Books,
  Public records, 17.
Vestrymen,
  personnel, 81.
Vindike, Henry, 368.
Virginia Gazette, 40, 138.
Virginia Historical Magazine, 183, 192, 193.
Virginia Soldiers of 1776, 225, 251.
Virginia State Papers, 108.
Virginia and Virginians, 162.
Voan, Crat, 513.

W

Wade,
  Andrew, 326.
  Captain, 29, 341.
  Hampton, 385, 387, 393, 395, 401.
  Robert, 340, 344, 353.
  Wm., 524, 525.
Wades Bridge, 473.
Waddell,
  Edward, 121.
  Rebecca, 160.

Waddill, Noel, 305.
Wadson,
  John, 354, 361, 375.
  John, Jr., 501.
Wagstaff, Bassill, 509.
Walch, Jane, 312.
Walker, 293, 537.
Walker,
  Allen, 125.
  Benjamin, 422.

Walker—Continued
  Ben, 537.
  David, 107.
  Edward Craig, 118.
  Elizabeth Ann, 124.
  Elizabeth Harrison, 162.
  Florence Georgia, 118.
  Frank Hart K., 118.
  Jane Craig, 118.
  Laneford, 420.
  Lillian, 118.
  Louise Norwood, 118.
  Mary Hoge, 118.
  Rebecca, 202.
  Richard Mathew, 118.
  Robert, 152.
  Sally Ann, 118.
  Sanders, 293.
  Sarah Clarence, 118.
  Sarah Norwood, 118.
  Silvanes, 350.
  Silvanus, 537.
  Sylvanus, 415.
  Tabitha, 316.
  Thomas, 437, 451, 513, 540, 554.
  William Alonzo, 118.
  William Herbert, 118.
Walkers Bridge, 350.
Wall,
  Laura Green, 182.
  William Lewis, 156.
Wallace,
  Hugh, 436.
  Robert Lucius, 126.
  Rose Ellen, 126.
  William, 419.
Waller,
  Edward, 272, 543.
  James, 527, 543.
Wallice, Wm., 505.
Wallis, William, 238, 512.
Walthall,
  Anne, 308.
  Mary, 313.
  Pheby, 309.
Walthall Junction, 109.
Walton, 341, 343.
Walton,
  George, 29, 341, 342, 343, 344, 346, 353, 357, 358, 520.
  Martha A., 211.
  Robert, 554.
Wamock, Eliza, 311.
Ward,
  Catherine, 314.

Ward—Continued
  Henry, 509.
  John, 517, 523, 533.
  Old, 500.
  Prudence, 315.
  R., 545.
  Richd., 533.
  Rowland, 404, 422, 453, 507, 512, 513, 528, 546, 553.
  Samuel, 435.
  Wade, 502.
  Zadoch, 523.
Wards Road, 454, 472.
Wards Rolling Road, 422, 423, 453, 541.
Wards Rowling Road, 403, 404.
War of 1812, 108.
War Talks of Confederate Veterans, 110.
Warm Springs Mountain, 132.
Warran, John, 428.
Warren, Thos., 518, 523.
Warrin, Thomas, 535.
Warwick,
  Mollie, 193.
  Mrs., 229.
  William, 193.
Waters, Elizabeth, 218.
Watkins,
  Betsey, 314.
  Betsy, 192.
  Elizabeth, 307.
  Eliza L., 305.
  Isaac, 334.
  Joseph, 304.
  Mary, 304.
  Samuel, 192.
  Wm., 346, 352.
Watson,
  John, 328, 331, 333, 337, 339, 342, 345, 350, 351, 358, 371, 501, 503.
  John, Senr., 502, 503.
Watts,
  Elizabeth, 307.
  Polly, 310.
  Richard, 358, 359, 362, 371, 376.
Weakly, Robert, 338, 347.
Weatherford,
  John, 505.
  Wm., 505.
Weaver,
  Jeannie, 163.
  John, 527.
  Sally, 305.

Webb,
  Elizabeth, 268.
  Isaac, 546.
  John, 554.
  Thomas, 156.
  Thomas Norfleet, 157.
Webster, John, 326.
Weisiger, Joseph, 309.
Welch, Thomas, 308.
Weeks, Elizabeth, 310.
Wells,
  Abner, 452, 560.
  Ann, 313.
  David, 311.
  Elizabeth, 312.
  George, 349.
  Mary Ann, 317.
  Matt, 512.
  Nancy, 311.
Wesson, Mrs. James, 172.
West,
  Anne, 305.
  Cara A., 171.
  John, 311, 555, 556.
Westmore,
  Elizabeth, 316.
  Joseph, 306.
Westover, 65, 162.
Westover Parish, 183, 213.
Wetherford, Rich, 351.
Wheeler, Samuel, 377.
Whig, The Richmond, 162.
Whiley, Hugh, 506.
White,
  Carter, 539, 540, 563.
  Daniel, 236.
  Elizabeth, 232.
  H. J. Dean, Christ's Church Oxford, 98.
  Henry, 232.
  John, 508, 513, 540, 549, 563.
  John, Jr., 540.
  John, Sr., 422, 525, 526, 540.
  Jon, 513.
  Mary Ann, 236.
  Polly, 254.
  Rebecca, 312.
  Thos., 511.
  William, 315, 417, 419, 521, 522.
Whitehead, 548.
Whitehead,
  Benjamin, 531, 556.
  Thomas (Col.), 237.
  William, 312.

Whitemore,
  Abram, 503.
  John, 503.
  Wm., 502.
Whitfield,
  Byron C., 163.
  Evelyn Cameron, 163.
  Lou Egerton, 163.
Whitimore, Abram, 376.
Whitney,
  Betty, 153.
  Claire, 153.
  Hobart, 153.
Whorley, Joshua, 226.
Wiatt, Sary, 295.
Wilder,
  Jane, 164.
  Josepha, 164.
Wildwood, 114.
Wiles, Thos., 370.
Wilk, Benj., 517.
Wilkerson, William, 535, 536.
Wilkes,
  Benj., 523.
  Thomas, 314.
Wilkins,
  Ashley, 220.
  Edmonia Cabell, 221.
  Edmund W. (Dr.), 220.
  Elizabeth Garland, 221.
  Isabella, 164.
  James, 509.
  John, 509.
  Mary, 221, 222.
  Mary Ann, 509.
  Nanny, 309.
  Nicholas Davis, 221.
  William Webb (Dr.), 220.
Wilkinson,
  Frederick, 310.
  Martin, 507.
  Patsey, 309.
  Priscilla, 205.
Wilks, Minor, 554, 563.
Wilky, Robert, 326.
William and Mary College, 145, 150.
William and Mary Quarterly, 167, 168, 174, 203, 244, 287, 289.
Williams, 547.
Williams,
  Amey, 295.
  Amye, 294.
  Ann R., 318.
  Benjamin, 295.

INDEX

Williams—Continued
  Buckner Davis, 158.
  Daniel, 107, 454, 545, 555, 564.
  David, 308, 328.
  David G., 317.
  Ede, 314.
  Eliza, 318.
  Eliza Ann, 320.
  Elizabeth, 295, 310.
  Elizabeth Winthrow, 158.
  Emma Buckner, 159.
  Ewan Cameron, 158.
  Fras., 391.
  Hannah, 524, 538.
  Hugh Davis, 158.
  James, 304, 517, 518, 524.
  Jane, 295.
  Jemimah, 305.
  John, 294, 324, 331, 350, 403, 506, 520, 548.
  John Syme, 158.
  John (Rev.), 88.
  Joseph, 74, 365, 370, 377, 398, 516, 532.
  Joseph G., 317.
  Joseph (Capt.), 406.
  Lazarus, 529, 540, 545, 563.
  Lazeras, 368, 507, 511, 512, 513, 525, 527.
  Lazers, 404.
  Lazs., 506.
  Martha, 295, 305, 308, 313, 320.
  Martha G., 315.
  Mary, 295, 317.
  Mary Louisa, 158.
  Matt., 511.
  Matthew, 519.
  Nicholas, 423, 454, 545, 564.
  Patty, 307.
  Peter Pescud, 158.
  Rebecca Davis, 158.
  Rebeccah, 314.
  Richard, 368, 404, 506, 511, 512, 527, 545.
  Samuel G., 317.
  Sarah, 295, 306, 320, 362, 373, 376.
  Sarah G., 315.
  Susannah, 305.
  Thos., 107, 437, 513, 526, 527, 540, 553.
  Walker Anderson, 158.
  William, 295, 308, 310, 504.
Williamson,
  Frances, 307.
  Sarah, 279.

Willis, Stephen, 376.
Williston, Annie, 290.
Wills,
  May, 287.
  N. W., 237.
  William, 304.
  Willis H., 237.
Willson,
  Elenor, 270.
  Robert, 423, 452, 530, 546, 555.
  Wilson, 440.
Wilson,
  Bessie Garland, 237.
  Caleb, 176, 177.
  Charles Garland, 237.
  Daisy Powell, 238.
  Edward, 558.
  George, 310, 311.
  Helen Garland, 237.
  Helen Irving, 238.
  John, 259.
  Landon Pierce, 238.
  Louise Ellis, 237.
  Mildred Leigh, 238.
  Peter, 339.
  Richard T. (Rev.), 237.
  Robert, 396, 398, 407, 437, 516, 518, 521, 559.
  Rosary, 259.
  Samuel M. G., 237.
  Sarah, 268.
  Wm., 518, 546.
Wilson's, 326.
Wilson's Raid, 126.
Wily,
  Elizabeth, 308.
  Mary, 308.
Wimbish, 264.
Wimbish, John, 261.
Wimpe, Henry, 524.
Wimpy, Henry, 514.
Winbush, 264.
Winchester,
  Mary, 232.
  W. R. (Dr.), 232.
Windsor, Canon of, 67.
Winfield, Joel, 500.
Wingfield,
  Anne, 233.
  John, 233.
  Lawrence, 328.
Winningham Road, 403, 422, 424, 452, 453, 454, 473, 536.
Winn Family, 297.

Winn, 548.
Winn,
  Alexander, 298, 453.
  Bannister, 297.
  Col., 410.
  Edmund, 297.
  Edmund C., 298.
  Elder C., 298.
  Daniel, 422, 423, 453, 526, 539, 540, 541, 551, 557.
  Henrietta, 297.
  John, 297, 422, 539, 540.
  John, Junr., 537.
  John, Sr., 525, 538.
  Joicy, 268.
  Joseph, 298, 526, 551, 557, 563, 564.
  Maria, 297.
  Mourning, 249.
  Mrs., 563.
  Peter, 554.
  Richard, 556.
  Robert, 259.
  Saml., 551.
  Sarah, 297, 563.
  Susannah, 315.
  Thomas, 29, 30, 40, 41, 43, 297, 404, 408, 411, 412, 414, 415, 418, 419, 421, 424, 425, 426, 427, 428, 429, 431, 432, 433, 434, 438, 439, 440, 441, 442, 443, 444, 445, 446, 539, 540.
  Thos. (Col.), 406, 409, 525, 538, 539.
  Tho., Jr., 441.
  Washington, 297.
  William, 297.
Winningham,
  Jarrald, 513.
  Thomas, 349.
Winston, 515.
Winston, Isaac, 513.
Withers, Priscilla, 309.
Witherspoon, Henry, 164.
Witton, 340.
Witton,
  Col., 390.
  Richard, 175, 242, 275, 276, 284, 339, 366, 372, 376, 377, 379, 381, 384, 388, 391, 394, 397, 398, 399, 400, 402.
    Copied Vestry Book, 78.
  Richard (Col.), 363.
Wolfe, Elizabeth, 234.
Womack,
  Abraham, 309.

Womack—Continued
  Ann, 312.
  Elizabeth, 307.
  Richard, 326.
  Susannah, 304.
  William, 312.
Wood,
  Edwin LaFayette, 182.
  Edwin L. (Mrs.), 178, 179, 180.
  Frank, 157.
  James, 74, 327, 328, 331, 332, 333, 337, 339, 342.
  John, 524, 529, 546.
  Pattie May, 182.
  Samuel C., 182.
  Stephen, 107, 388, 422, 516, 532, 533, 534, 535, 549, 554.
  Thomas, 347, 553, 559.
Wooding, Robert, 256.
Woodleif,
  Anne, 306.
  Sarah, 306.
Woods,
  Edgar (Rev.), 239.
  James, 235.
  Stephen, 524.
Woodson, John, 236.
Woolfolk, Francis, 314.
Wootton, John Taylor, 181.
Worsham, John, 113.
Wortham, Lucy, 306.
Wray,
  Francis, 348.
  Jacob, 557, 563.
  Martha J., 181.
Wren,
  Sarah, 312.
  Wm., 528.
Wrenle, Jesse, 305.
Wrenn, William, 437, 545, 553.
Wright, Labin, 501, 502.
Wyatt, Richard, 391, 511, 518.
Wyborne, John, 334, 338.
Wycke, Benjamin, 309.
Wynn Family, 297.
Wynn,
  Daniel, 368, 387, 513.
  John, 368, 513.
  Joseph, 403.
  Thomas, 29, 350, 395, 396, 401, 402, 513, 514.
  Thos. (Capt.), 514.
Wynne,
  Joshua, 304.
  Wm., 326.
Wythe, Chancellor, 147.

Y

Yancey,
  Mrs. Elizabeth Field, 121.
  Sallie, 121.
Yancy, Richard, 345, 355, 358.
Yansey, Richard, 354, 370.
Yoder,
  William, 158.
  William, Jr., 158.
York County, 150, 215, 217.
Yorktown, 151.
Young,
  Duncan, 304, 308.
  Elizabeth, 313.

Young—Continued
  Henry, 107, 307.
  Lucy, 278.
  M., 345.
  Mary, 345, 351, 354.
  Philip, 337, 339.
  Rebeccah, 308.
  Richard, 351.
  Saml., 367.
  Thos., 520, 546.
  William, 309.
Young Husband, Isaac, 505.

Z

Zachary, Mary, 204.

www.ingramcontent.com/pod-product-compliance
Lightning Source LLC
Chambersburg PA
CBHW021223300426
44111CB00007B/410